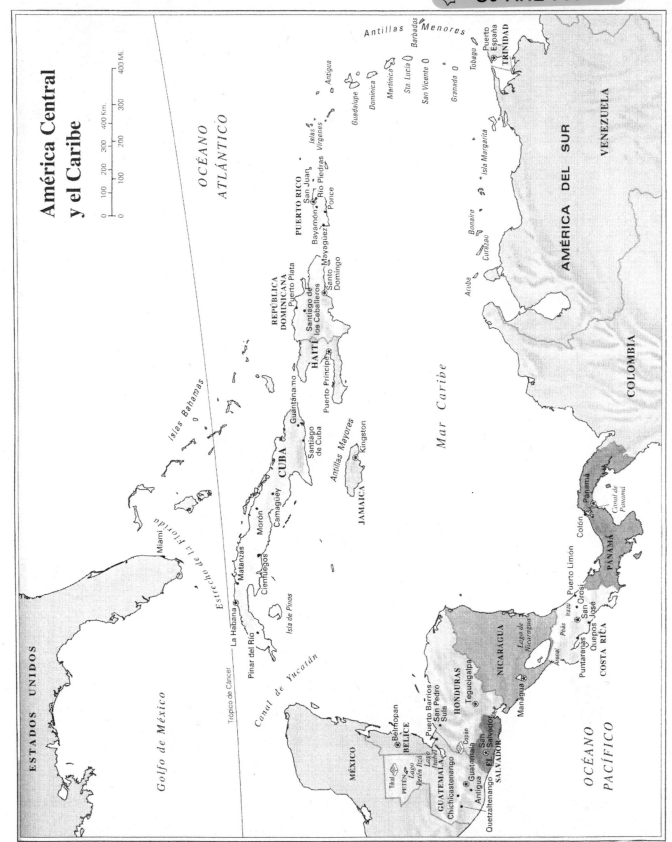

América Central y el Caribe

400 Km.
0 100 200 300 400
0 100 200 300 400 Mi.

OCÉANO ATLÁNTICO

ESTADOS UNIDOS

Golfo de México

Miami

Estrecho de la Florida

Trópico de Cáncer

Islas Bahamas

La Habana
Pinar del Río
Isla de Pinos
Matanzas
Cienfuegos
Morón
Camagüey
CUBA
Santiago de Cuba
Guantánamo

Canal de Yucatán

JAMAICA
Antillas Mayores
Kingston

Mar Caribe

HAITÍ
Puerto Príncipe

REPÚBLICA DOMINICANA
Puerto Plata
Santiago de los Caballeros
Santo Domingo

PUERTO RICO
San Juan
Bayamón
Río Piedras
Mayagüez
Ponce

Islas Vírgenes

Antillas Menores

Antigua
Guadalupe
Dominica
Martinica
Sta. Lucía
San Vicente
Barbados
Granada
Tobago
Puerto España
TRINIDAD

Isla Margarita
Bonaire
Curazao
Aruba

AMÉRICA DEL SUR

VENEZUELA

COLOMBIA

MÉXICO

Belmopán
BELICE
Tikal
PETÉN
Lago Petén Itzá
Lago Izabal
Puerto Barrios
San Pedro Sula
Copán
GUATEMALA
Guatemala
Antigua
Chichicastenango
Quetzaltenango
EL SALVADOR
San Salvador

HONDURAS
Tegucigalpa

NICARAGUA
Managua
Lago de Nicaragua

COSTA RICA
Puntarenas
Arenal
Poás
San José
Orosi
Irazú
Quepos
Puerto Limón
Colón

PANAMÁ
Canal de Panamá
Panamá

OCÉANO PACÍFICO

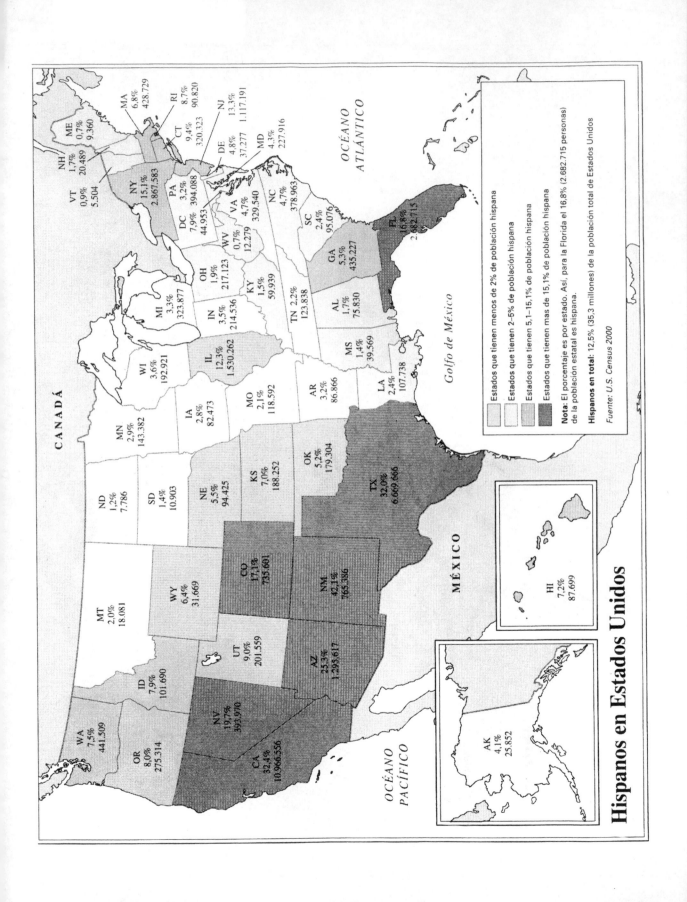

Hispanos en Estados Unidos

CANADÁ

OCÉANO ATLÁNTICO

OCÉANO PACÍFICO

MÉXICO

Golfo de México

WA 7,5% 441.509
OR 8,0% 275.314
ID 7,9% 101.690
MT 2,0% 18.081
ND 1,2% 7.786
MN 2,9% 143.382
WI 3,6% 192.921
MI 3,3% 323.877
NY 15,1% 2.867.583
VT 0,9% 5.504
NH 1,7% 20.489
ME 0,7% 9.360
MA 6,8% 428.729
RI 8,7% 90.820
CT 9,4% 320.323
NJ 13,3% 1.117.191
PA 3,2% 394.088
DC 7,9% 44.953
DE 4,8% 37.277
MD 4,3% 227.916
VA 4,7% 329.540
WV 0,7% 12.279
OH 1,9% 217.123
IN 3,5% 214.536
IL 12,3% 1.530.262
IA 2,8% 82.473
SD 1,4% 10.903
NE 5,5% 94.425
WY 6,4% 31.669
UT 9,0% 201.559
NV 19,7% 393.970
CA 32,4% 10.966.556
AZ 25,3% 1.295.617
NM 42,1% 765.386
CO 17,1% 735.601
KS 7,0% 188.252
MO 2,1% 118.592
KY 1,5% 59.939
TN 2,2% 123.838
NC 4,7% 378.963
SC 2,4% 95.076
GA 5,3% 435.227
AL 1,7% 75.830
MS 1,4% 39.569
AR 3,2% 86.866
LA 2,4% 107.738
OK 5,2% 179.304
TX 32,0% 6.669.666
FL 16,8% 2.682.715

HI 7,2% 87.699

AK 4,1% 25.852

Nota: El porcentaje es por estado. Así, para la Florida el 16,8% (2.682.715 personas) de la población estatal es hispana.

Hispanos en total: 12,5% (35,3 millones) de la población total de Estados Unidos

Fuente: U.S. Census 2000

Estados que tienen menos de 2% de población hispana

Estados que tienen 2–5% de población hispana

Estados que tienen 5,1–15,1% de población hispana

Estados que tienen mas de 15,1% de población hispana

SEVENTH EDITION
with Student Activities Manual

¡HOLA, AMIGOS!

Ana C. Jarvis
CHANDLER-GILBERT COMMUNITY COLLEGE

Raquel Lebredo
CALIFORNIA BAPTIST UNIVERSITY, EMERITA

Francisco Mena-Ayllón
UNIVERSITY OF REDLANDS, EMERITUS

with

STUDENT ACTIVITIES MANUAL
by

Ana C. Jarvis
CHANDLER-GILBERT COMMUNITY COLLEGE

Raquel Lebredo
CALIFORNIA BAPTIST UNIVERSITY, EMERITA

Houghton Mifflin Company
BOSTON   NEW YORK

¡HOLA AMIGOS!, SEVENTH EDITION
By Ana C. Jarvis, Raquel Lebredo, and Francisco Mena-Ayllón
Copyright © 2008 by Houghton Mifflin Company. All rights reserved.

Publisher: Rolando Hernández
Senior Sponsoring Editor: Glenn A. Wilson
Executive Marketing Director: Eileen Bernadette Moran
Marketing Assistant: Lorreen Ruth Pelletier
Senior Development Editor: Judith Bach
Editorial Assistant: Erin Beasley
Project Editor: Amy Johnson
Art and Design Manager: Gary Crespo
Cover Design Manager: Anne S. Katzeff
Senior Photo Editor: Jennifer Meyer Dare
Composition Buyer: Chuck Dutton

Photo credits are listed on page 397, which is hereby considered an extension of the copyright page.

!HOLA AMIGOS! STUDENT ACTIVITIES MANUAL, SEVENTH EDITION
By Ana C. Jarvis and Raquel Lebredo
Copyright © 2008 by Houghton Mifflin Company. All rights reserved.

Publisher: Rolando Hernández
Senior Sponsoring Editor: Glenn A. Wilson
Senior Sponsoring Editor: Judith Bach
Editorial Assistant: Erin Beasley
Project Editor: Amy Johnson
Executive Marketing Director: Eileen Bernadette Moran
Marketing Assistant: Lorreen Ruth Pelletier

Custom Publishing Editor: Dan Luciano
Custom Publishing Production Manager: Christina Battista
Project Coordinator: Jen Feltri

Cover Designer: Brian Moore
Cover Image: PhotoDisc

This book contains select works from existing Houghton Mifflin Company resources and was produced by Houghton Mifflin Custom Publishing for collegiate use. As such, those adopting and/or contributing to this work are responsible for editorial content, accuracy, continuity and completeness.

Printed in the United States of America.

ISBN-13: 978-0-618-95297-7
ISBN-10: 0-618-95297-7
1020850

1 2 3 4 5 6 7 8 9 – WP – 09 08 07

Houghton Mifflin
Custom Publishing

222 Berkeley Street • Boston, MA 02116

Address all correspondence and order information to the above address.

Scope and Sequence

1 Los estudiantes universitarios (pp. 2–51)

2 En familia (pp. 52–97)

3 ¿Qué comemos hoy? (pp. 98–147)

5 ¿Qué hacemos hoy? (pp. 200–245)

	Lección 9 No tengo nada que ponerme	Lección 10 Diligencias
Para hablar del tema	*(pp. 204–205)* La ropa El tiempo **De país a país**	*(pp. 224–225)* En el banco En la oficina de correos Un poco de tecnología **De país a país**
Para practicar el vocabulario	*(pp. 206–207)* *Online Study Center* A. En la tienda y en la zapatería B. ¿Qué se ponen? C. Hablando del tiempo D. Haciendo compras **Pronunciación** Pronunciation in context	*(pp. 226–227)* *Online Study Center* A. Preguntas y respuestas B. Rubén y Eva hacen diligencias C. ¿Qué necesito o qué tengo que hacer? D. ¿Qué necesita hacer? **Pronunciación** Pronunciation in context
Puntos para recordar	*(pp. 208–219)* *Online Study Center* 1. Some uses of *por* and *para* (p. 208) 2. Weather expressions *(p. 211)* 3. The preterit contrasted with the imperfect *(p. 213)* 4. *Hace...* meaning *ago* (p. 216) 5. Possessive pronouns *(p. 218)*	*(pp. 228–235)* *Online Study Center* 1. Past participles *(p. 228)* 2. Present perfect tense *(p. 230)* 3. Past perfect (pluperfect) tense *(p. 232)* 4. Formal commands: *Ud.* and *Uds.* (p. 233)
Entre nosotros	*(pp. 220–221)* **¡Conversemos!** **Para escribir** ¿Cómo era Ud.? **Un dicho**	*(pp. 236–237)* **¡Conversemos!** **Para escribir** En el banco **Un dicho**

Lectura *(pp. 238–239)*	*Lecciones de inglés* (Adaptado) (Germán Arciniegas)	**Video** *Online Study Center*
El mundo hispánico *(pp. 240–241)*	Ecuador Perú Bolivia Paraguay	**Video** *Online Study Center*
Tome este examen *(pp. 242–245)*	Lección 9	Lección 10

6 De vacaciones (pp. 246–291)

7 ¿Cómo te sientes? (pp. 292–339)

	Lección 13 En la sala de emergencia	Lección 14 Hablando con el médico
Para hablar del tema	*(pp. 296–297)* En el hospital El cuerpo Otras partes del cuerpo **De país a país**	*(pp. 314–315)* Medicinas Algunos especialistas El botiquín **De país a país**
Para practicar el vocabulario	*(pp. 298–299)* *Online Study Center* A. Preguntas y respuestas B. En la sala de emergencia C. ¿Qué sabes de anatomía? D. En el hospital **Pronunciación** Pronunciation in context	*(pp. 316–317)* *Online Study Center* A. Preguntas y respuestas B. ¿Qué debo tomar? C. ¿Qué especialista debo ver? D. En nuestro botiquín **Pronunciación** Pronunciation in context

Puntos para recordar	*(pp. 300–309)* *Online Study Center*
	
	1. Subjunctive to express doubt, denial, and disbelief *(p. 300)*
	2. Subjunctive with certain conjunctions *(p. 304)*
	3. First-person plural commands *(p. 306)*
	   RODEO: Summary of the Command Forms *(p. 307)*
	4. ¿Qué? and ¿cuál? used with ser *(p. 309)*
		(pp. 318–329) *Online Study Center*
		
		1. Future tense *(p. 318)*
		2. Conditional tense *(p. 320)*
		   RODEO: Summary of the Tenses of the Indicative *(p. 322)*
		3. The imperfect subjunctive *(p. 323)*
		4. If-clauses *(p. 325)*
		   RODEO: Summary of the Uses of the Subjunctive *(p. 328)*

Entre nosotros	*(pp. 310–311)* **¡Conversemos!** **Para escribir** Un accidente **Un dicho**	*(pp. 330–331)* **¡Conversemos!** **Para escribir** Con el doctor **Un dicho**
Lectura *(pp. 332–333)*	*Rimas* (Gustavo Adolfo Bécquer)	**Video** *Online Study Center*
El mundo hispánico *(pp. 334–335)*	España	**Video** *Online Study Center*
Tome este examen *(pp. 336–339)*	Lección 13	Lección 14

Un poco más (pp. 340–345)

1. Compound tenses of the indicative (*p. 340*)
   - Future perfect (*p. 340*)
   - Conditional perfect (*p. 341*)
2. Compound tenses of the subjunctive (*p. 342*)
   - Present perfect subjunctive (*p. 342*)
   - Pluperfect subjunctive (*p. 344*)

Appendices

Vocabularies

Brief Contents

An Overview of Your Textbook's Main Features

¡Hola, amigos!, Seventh Edition, consists of fourteen lessons thematically organized into seven units

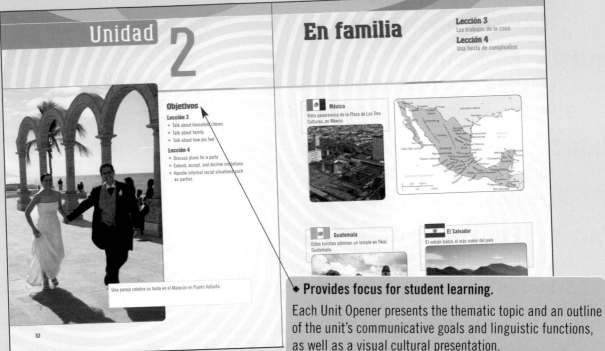

Provides focus for student learning.

Each Unit Opener presents the thematic topic and an outline of the unit's communicative goals and linguistic functions, as well as a visual cultural presentation.

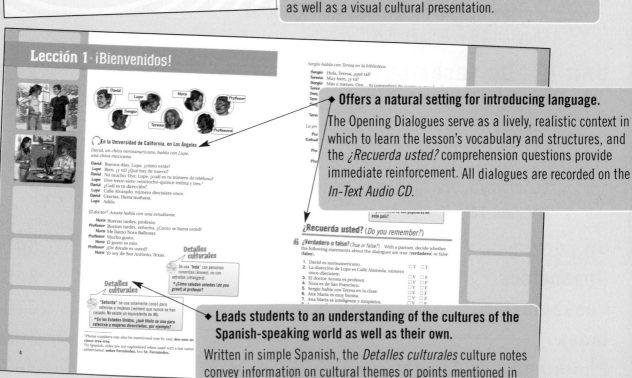

Offers a natural setting for introducing language.

The Opening Dialogues serve as a lively, realistic context in which to learn the lesson's vocabulary and structures, and the *¿Recuerda usted?* comprehension questions provide immediate reinforcement. All dialogues are recorded on the *In-Text Audio CD*.

Leads students to an understanding of the cultures of the Spanish-speaking world as well as their own.

Written in simple Spanish, the *Detalles culturales* culture notes convey information on cultural themes or points mentioned in the lesson's opening passage. To promote classroom discussion, cross-cultural reflection questions follow each note.

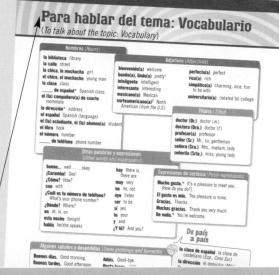

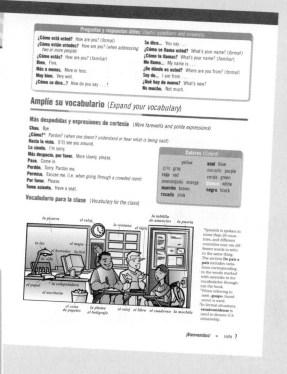

◆ Provides a solid foundation for building students' communication skills.

The *Vocabulario* section lists all active vocabulary, new words, and expressions introduced in the opening dialogue, as well as other words and phrases related to the lesson theme in the *Amplíe su vocabulario* section.

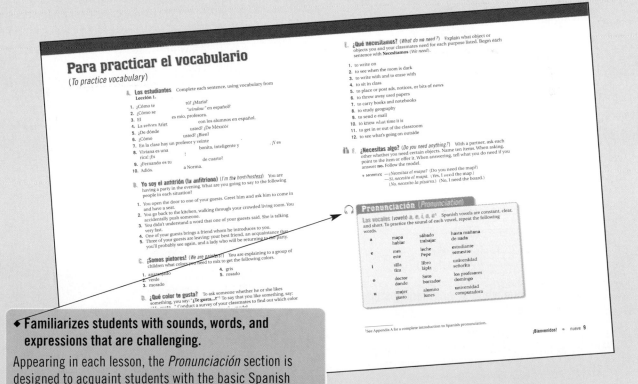

◆ Familiarizes students with sounds, words, and expressions that are challenging.

Appearing in each lesson, the *Pronunciación* section is designed to acquaint students with the basic Spanish sounds. This section is recorded on the *In-Text Audio CD*.

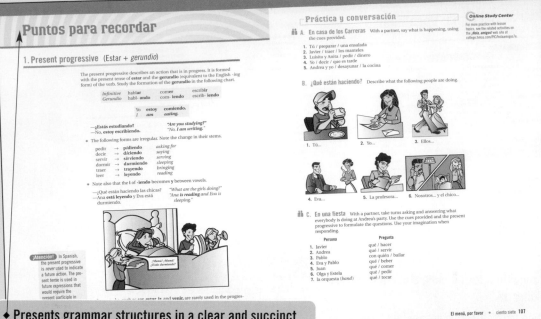

Puntos para recordar

1. Present progressive (Estar + *gerundio*)

The present progressive describes an action that is in progress. It is formed with the present tense of **estar** and the **gerundio** (equivalent to the English *-ing* form) of the verb. Study the formation of the **gerundio** in the following chart.

Infinitive	hablar	comer	escribir
Gerundio	habl- **ando**	com- **iendo**	escrib- **iendo**

	Yo	estoy	comiendo.
	I	*am*	*eating.*

—¿Estás estudiando? "*Are you studying?*"
—No, estoy escribiendo. "*No, I am writing.*"

- The following forms are irregular. Note the change in their stems.

pedir	→	pídiendo	*asking for*
decir	→	díciendo	*saying*
servir	→	sírviendo	*serving*
dormir	→	durmiendo	*sleeping*
traer	→	trayendo	*bringing*
leer	→	leyendo	*reading*

- Note also that the **i** of **-iendo** becomes **y** between vowels.

—¿Qué están haciendo las chicas? "*What are the girls doing?*"
—Ana está leyendo y Eva está durmiendo. "*Ana is reading and Eva is sleeping.*"

¡Atención! In Spanish, the present progressive is *never* used to indicate a future action. The present tense is used in future expressions that would require the present participle in...

Práctica y conversación

A. En casa de los Carreras With a partner, say what is happening, using the cues provided.

1. Tú / preparar / una ensalada
2. Javier / traer / los manteles
3. Luisito y Anita / pedir / dinero
4. Yo / decir / que es tarde
5. Andrea y yo / desayunar / la cocina

B. ¿Qué están haciendo? Describe what the following people are doing.

1. Tú... 2. Yo... 3. Ellos...
4. Eva... 5. La profesora... 6. Nosotros... y el chico...

C. En una fiesta With a partner, take turns asking and answering what everybody is doing at Andrea's party. Use the cues provided and the present progressive to formulate the questions. Use your imagination when responding.

Persona	Pregunta
1. Javier	qué / hacer
2. Andrea	qué / servir
3. Pablo	con quién / bailar
4. Eva y Pablo	qué / beber
5. Juan	qué / comer
6. Olga y Estela	qué / pedir
7. la orquesta (*band*)	qué / tocar

El menú, por favor • ciento siete **107**

Online Study Center
For more practice with lesson topics, see the related activities on the *¡Hola, amigos!* web site at college.hmco.com/PIC/holaamigos7e.

◆ **Presents grammar structures in a clear and succinct manner.**

The *Puntos para recordar* section presents an average of four or five grammar points in English. Each structure is immediately followed by a *Práctica* or *Práctica y conversación* section that ranges from controlled drills to open-ended activities, including illustration-based activities.

◆ **Presents opportunities to actively use the language in the classroom.**

¡Conversemos! consists of a series open-ended activities, including personalized pair activities, activities for vocabulary review, and pair and small group activities. The *Entre nosotros* section ends with *Para escribir*, a writing activity on a topic related to the thematic goals of the lesson.

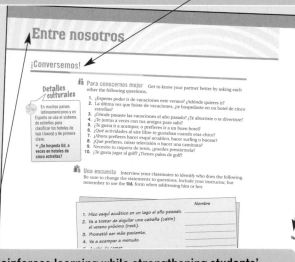

Entre nosotros

¡Conversemos!

Detalles culturales

En muchos países latinoamericanos y en España se usa el sistema de estrellas para clasificar los hoteles de lujo (*luxury*) y de primera clase.

◆ ¿Se hospeda Ud. a veces en hoteles de cinco estrellas?

Para conocernos mejor Get to know your partner better by asking each other the following questions.

1. ¿Esperas poder ir de vacaciones este verano? ¿Adónde quieres ir?
2. La última vez que fuiste de vacaciones, ¿te hospedaste en un hotel de cinco estrellas?
3. ¿Dónde pasaste las vacaciones el año pasado? ¿Te aburriste o te divertiste?
4. ¿Te juntas a veces con tus amigos para salir?
5. ¿Te gusta ir a acampar, o prefieres ir a un buen hotel?
6. ¿Qué actividades al aire libre te gustaban cuando eras chico?
7. ¿Ahora prefieres hacer esquí acuático, hacer surfing o bucear?
8. ¿Qué prefieres, mirar televisión o hacer una caminata?
9. Necesito tu raqueta de tenis, ¿puedes prestármela?
10. ¿Te gusta jugar al golf? ¿Tienes palos de golf?

Una encuesta Interview your classmates to identify who does the following. Be sure to change the statements to questions. Include your instructor, but remember to use the **Ud.** form when addressing him or her.

	Nombre
1. Hizo esquí acuático en un lago el año pasado.	
2. Va a tratar de alquilar una cabaña (*cabin*) el verano próximo (*next*).	
3. Prometió ser más paciente.	
4. Va a acampar a menudo.	

¿Cóm... ...might...

1. You ask a friend if he or she prefers to go to the beach, to go hiking, or to go camping near a lake or a river (**río**) for a couple of days.
2. You are going on a camping trip for the first time. Tell a friend what items you need and what you need to learn to do.
3. Tell someone what your favorite outdoor activities are. Mention at least four.

¿Qué pasa aquí? In groups of three or four, create a story about the people in the illustration. Say who they are and what their relationships are to one another. Also say what activities they are doing and what they will do later.

Para escribir

De vacaciones Write a conversation between you and a friend, in which you are deciding what you are going to do when you have a couple of days off. One of you loves outdoor activities and the other doesn't. Try to compromise.

Un dicho

El que ríe último, ríe mejor.

Undoubtedly, you know the English version of this saying. Memorize it in Spanish, and use it at appropriate times.

Las actividades al aire libre • ciento noventa y uno **191**

◆ **Reinforces learning while strengthening students' communication skills.**

The activities in *Entre nosotros* ask students to synthesize what they've learned in order to communicate in real-life situations.

xvi

◆ **Promotes the development of students' reading skills.**

Appearing at the end of each unit, the *Lectura* section develops reading comprehension while reinforcing the structures and vocabulary introduced in the preceding lessons. Pre-reading questions focus students' attention on detail and open-ended post-reading questions, and allow students to personalize topics related to the reading.

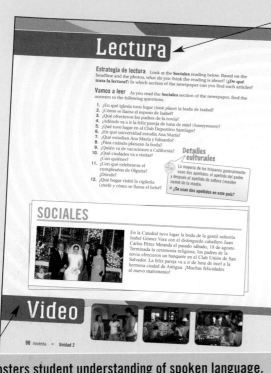

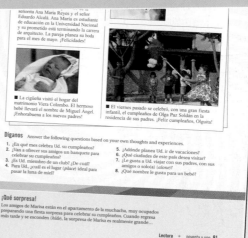

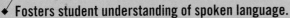

◆ **Fosters student understanding of spoken language.**

The situational video clips on the Video DVD and VHS, shot on location in Costa Rica, relate in theme and language level to each unit. Activities relating to each clip can be found at the *Online Study Center.*

◆ **Reinforces understanding of the cultures of the Spanish-speaking world.**

A longer cultural section, *El mundo hispánico,* provides unit-level cultural information with detailed visual presentations for many Hispanic countries. This section, found at the end of each unit, presents in more detail the Hispanic cultures introduced throughout the unit.

Tome este examen

Lección 11

A. Subjunctive with verbs of volition Write sentences in the present tense, using the elements given below. Use the present subjunctive or the infinitive, as appropriate, and add any necessary words.

1. Yo / querer / ella / ir / Viña del Mar
2. Nosotros / desear / viajar / avión
3. Ella / sugerirme / ir / Buenos Aires
4. El agente / querer / venderme / el pasaje
5. Ellos / aconsejarnos / comprar / seguro (insurance)
6. Yo / no querer / llevar / muchas maletas
7. Ellos / no querer / ella / llevarlos / en su coche
8. Nosotros / no querer / ir / contigo
9. ¿Tú / sugerirme / venir / luego?
10. Ella / necesitar / Uds. / darle / la maleta

B. Subjunctive with verbs of emotion Rewrite the following sentences, beginning each with the phrase in parentheses and using the subjunctive or the infinitive, as appropriate.

1. Ella se va pronto. (Espero...)
2. Los pasajes son muy caros. (Elsa teme...)
3. Yo estoy aquí. (Me alegro de...)
4. Ella se va de vacaciones. (Ella espera...)
5. Mamá se siente bien hoy. (Esperamos...)
6. Ellos no pueden ir a la fiesta. (Siento...)

C. Some uses of the prepositions _a, de,_ and _en_ Complete with **a, de,** or **en,** as necessary.

1. Anoche llamé _____ mi hermano por teléfono y hablamos _____ nuestros planes para el fin de semana. Pensamos ir _____ Chile. Él quiere viajar _____ tren pero yo prefiero ir _____ coche. Mi hermana no quiere ir con nosotros; prefiere quedarse _____ casa porque no tiene con quién dejar _____ su perro.
2. Ayer Marta llegó _____ la agencia _____ las ocho y media _____ la mañana, pero no empezó _____ trabajar hasta las diez.
3. Mi hija es muy bonita: es morena, _____ ojos verdes y yo pienso que es la más inteligente _____ todos mis hijos.

D. Vocabulary Complete the following sentences, using vocabulary from Lección 11.

1. No quiero un _____ de pasillo; quiero uno de _____
2. Voy a poner el bolso de _____ en el _____ de equipaje.
3. Voy a la _____ de viajes para comprar los pasajes.
4. Tiene que darle la tarjeta de _____ a la _____ de vuelo.
5. Tengo que pagar _____ de equipaje porque tengo cuatro maletas.
6. Quiero sentarme cerca de la _____ de emergencia.
7. Los paquetes _____ el pasaje, el hotel y algunas _____
8. ¿A cuánto está el _____ de moneda?
9. No podemos viajar hoy. Tenemos que _____ la reservación.
10. Cuando viajo siempre llevo cheques de _____
11. Este verano vamos a hacer un _____ por el Caribe.
12. Necesito una lista de los _____ de interés de la _____ de Chile.

E. Culture Complete the following sentences, based on the cultural notes you have read.

1. En Argentina se usa la forma _____ en lugar de **tú.**
2. La música típica de Argentina es el _____
3. En los países hispanos no existe tanta _____ entre las generaciones como en este país.

◆ **Encourages self-assessment of learning objectives.**

Following each unit, the *Tome este examen* section contains exercises designed to review the vocabulary and structures of the two lessons in the previous unit. The Answer Key is available in Appendix D.

Preface

¡Hola, amigos!, Seventh Edition, continues to be the complete, flexible program that has made it a successful introduction to Spanish for beginning college and university students throughout six editions. It presents the basics of Spanish grammar using a balanced, eclectic approach that stresses all four skills—listening, speaking, reading, and writing. The program has always emphasized the active, practical use of Spanish for communication in high-frequency situations. The completely redesigned seventh edition features all new art and a streamlined, color-coded layout. A special effort has been made to enhance the cultural presentation and integration by focusing on culture on a unit level, and giving more substance to the smaller culture notes throughout each lesson. The program's goal is to help you achieve linguistic proficiency and cultural awareness, and to motivate you to continue your study of the Spanish language and the many cultures in which it is spoken.

The Student Text

¡Hola, amigos!, Seventh Edition has been reorganized into seven units, each containing two thematically-related lessons. Each of the seven units contains the following features:

Unit-Opener Spread

Each unit begins with a list of communicative objectives for the two lessons included in that unit. This list serves to focus your attention on important linguistic functions and vocabulary you will encounter and to help you gain a sense of accomplishment when you finish a unit. Captioned photos and maps give you a first impression of the countries presented in each unit.

Diálogos

New vocabulary and grammatical structures are first presented in the context of several brief conversations in idiomatic Spanish dealing with high-frequency situations that reflect the lesson's central themes. Each conversation is illustrated in the text and recorded on the *In-Text Audio CD* that accompanies your book. A headphone icon will remind you of recorded text. You can listen to the recordings and check your comprehension by doing the *¿Recuerda usted?* activities that follow the dialogues. The dialogues are also recorded on the *SAM Audio Program* where additional practice is available.

- *Detalles culturales* These short culture notes written in easy-to-read Spanish promote cultural awareness in the language-learning process. They can be found throughout the entire unit and will give you important and interesting cultural information that helps integrate the learning of language with the learning of culture.

Para hablar del tema: Vocabulario

All new words and expressions introduced in the conversations are listed by parts of speech or under the general headings *Cognados* and *Otras palabras y expresiones*. You should learn the entries in these lists for active use. The *Amplíe su vocabulario* section that follows expands on the thematic vocabulary introduced in the dialogues.

Para practicar el vocabulario

This practice section immediately follows the vocabulary presentation and encourages you to use the expressions you have just learned in a meaningful way.

◆ *Pronunciación* The section ends with a pronunciation feature to present and practice the sounds of the Spanish language with special attention to features that pose difficulty for most English speakers. A headphone icon indicates that the section is recorded on the *In-Text Audio CD*.

Puntos para recordar

Each new grammatical structure featured in the lesson-opening dialogue is explained clearly and concisely in English so that the explanations may be used independently as an out-of-class reference. All explanations include examples of practical use in natural Spanish and some explanations are illustrated by a cartoon.

◆ *Práctica* and *Práctica y conversación*   After each grammar explanation, the activities in *Práctica* and *Práctica y conversación* offer immediate reinforcement through a variety of structured and communicative exercises. These activities are flexible in format so that you can do them in class or your instructor can assign them as written practice outside of class. Answers to these exercises are available at your instructor's discretion.

◆ *Rodeo*   The Rodeo boxed sections in Lessons 7, 13, and 14 summarize and practice major grammatical topics such as pronouns, commands, and the indicative and subjunctive moods.

Entre nosotros

This final section provides for the recombination and synthesis of each lesson's new vocabulary and grammatical structures in a series of communicative activities. Because language is best learned through interpersonal communication, most of these exercises are designed to be done orally and require interactions with your classmates.

◆ *¡Conversemos!* features personalized activities such as pair interviews and class surveys that ask you to interact with your peers. Also included in this end-of-lesson cumulative section are activities that involve photos, realia, or illustrations, providing additional communicative practice based on authentic materials. This section has been expanded in the Seventh Edition to provide more interactive, communicative practice.

◆ *Para escribir* guides you to express yourself in writing in a variety of formats, such as e-mails, lists, and descriptions.

◆ *Un dicho* or *Un proverbio*, a thematically-related popular saying or proverb, provides cultural enrichment and concludes each lesson.

Lectura

A reading section at the end of each unit contains authentic, theme-related material from newspapers or magazines from the Spanish-speaking world, and in Units 4, 5, 6 and 7 you will find literary selections. One or two pre-reading activities emphasize the development of reading strategies and the selections are followed by comprehension and personalized questions for writing practice or discussion.

El mundo hispánico

This section, written in easy-to-read Spanish, provides an integrated cultural presentation of the countries and regions presented on the unit opener and throughout the lessons. It offers an overview of the locale in which the introductory dialogues were set, with attention to such details as climate, points of interest, customs, politics, economy, and inhabitants. It will also inform you about prevailing customs in the Spanish-speaking world that relate to the lesson themes. A map highlighting important geographic locations can be found on the unit opener spread. Color photos visually depict the country or custom(s) discussed.

Tome este examen

After each unit, these self-tests review and synthesize important vocabulary and grammatical structures you have learned in that unit. Because cultural awareness is as important as linguistic competence, the self-tests will also check your knowledge of cultural concepts. Organized by lesson, the self-tests quickly enable you to determine what material you have already mastered and which concepts you need to target for further review. An answer key for immediate verification is provided in Appendix D of the student textbook.

Reference Materials

The following sections provide you with useful reference tools throughout the course.

◆ **Maps.** Up-to-date maps of the Hispanic world appear on the inside front and back covers of the textbook for quick reference.
◆ **Appendices.** Appendix A summarizes the sounds and key pronunciation features of the Spanish language, with abundant examples. Conjugations of high-frequency regular, stem-changing, and irregular Spanish verbs constitute Appendix B. Appendix C is a glossary of all grammatical terms used in the text, with examples. Appendix D is the answer key to the *Tome este examen* self-tests.
◆ **Vocabularies.** Spanish-English and English-Spanish glossaries list all active, core vocabulary introduced in the dialogues and the *Amplíe su vocabulario* and grammar sections, as well as the passive vocabulary employed in the readings and the *El mundo hispánico* section. The number following each entry indicates the lesson in which it first appears.
◆ **Index.** An index provides ready access to all grammatical structures presented in the text.

Supplementary Materials for the Student

In-Text Audio CD

A free 90-minute In-Text *Audio CD* containing recordings of all the lesson opener-dialogues and pronunciation sections is packaged with each copy of the *Student Edition*. This *In-Text Audio CD* is designed to maximize your exposure to the sounds of natural spoken Spanish and to help improve pronunciation. It is designed so you can use it outside of class or in the Language Laboratory.

Student Activities Manual (SAM)

Each lesson of the *Student Edition* is correlated to the corresponding lesson in the *Student Activities Manual (SAM)*. The *Workbook* section offers a variety of writing activities—sentence completion, matching, sentence transformation, and illustration-based exercises—that provide further practice and reinforcement of concepts presented in the textbook. Each lesson includes a crossword puzzle for vocabulary review and a reading comprehension passage. Writing strategies and topics appear in each lesson to further writing skills. In the Seventh Edition extra activities have been added to the workbook sections and new attention has been given to the cultural targets of each lesson. An answer key for all written exercises is available at your instructor's discretion. The *Laboratory Manual* section opens with an Introduction to Spanish Sounds designed to make learners aware of the differences between Spanish and English pronunciation. Each regular lesson of the *Laboratory Manual* includes pronunciation, structure, listening- and speaking practice, illustration-based listening comprehension, and dictation exercises to be used in conjunction with the audio program.

SAM Audio Program

Pronunciation exercises at the beginning of each lesson feature practice of isolated sounds; global pronunciation practice is also provided. The textbook dialogues then appear as listening and pronunciation exercises in each lesson. They are followed by comprehension questions on the dialogues, structured grammar exercises (one for each point in the lesson), a listening comprehension activity, and a dictation. Answers to all exercises, except the dictation, are provided on the SAM Audio CDs.

 ## Video

The video features footage of locations presented in the *El mundo hispánico* section. The footage in each lesson consists of two parts, each part being approximately two to four minutes long. In the first part you will view a situational dialogue featuring recurring characters demonstrating everyday life. In the second part you will be able to see and hear country-specific footage for selected countries, ethnic groups, and regions presented in the units. Both parts are designed to develop your listening skills and cultural awareness as you view diverse images of the Hispanic world and Hispanic life and lifestyles. Pre-viewing, post-viewing, and expansion activities along with active vocabulary lists are correlated to each video segment and are located at the *Online Study Center.*

Online Multimedia eBook

   The *Online Multimedia eBook* provides students with the entire text online, integrated with links to a wide variety of resources—from audio pronunciations to video clips to Web expansion activities and interactive practice—for a completely interactive experience. By clicking on a link at the relevant point in the text, you can immediately practice and reinforce what you have learned. A real-time voice chat feature allows you to complete pair and group activities with other students. The *Online Multimedia eBook* is available on Eduspace, Blackboard, and WebCT platforms.

eSAM

   The electronic version of the *SAM* includes a comprehensive grade book and offers your instructor the ability to make assignments and track your performance. The audio associated with the Lab section of the *SAM* is also included.

Online Study Center *Online Study Center* (college.hmco.com/PIC/holaamigos7e)

The *Online Study Center* includes the following components:

- ◆ *Audio Flashcards:* Flashcards with integrated audio help students learn the chapter's new vocabulary.
- ◆ *Web Search Activites:* These activities are designed to give you further practice with lesson vocabulary and grammar while exploring existing Spanish-language websites.

- *In-Text Audio:* Audio files from the *In-Text Audio CD*, provided in .mp3 format.
- *ACE Practice Tests:* Practice activities covering vocabulary, grammar, and video material. Additional language skills practice is also available.

Acknowledgments

As always, we wish to express appreciation to the users of *¡Hola, amigos!* who have provided feedback on their experience with the program and to the following colleagues for the many valuable suggestions they offered in their reviews of this and previous editions of *¡Hola, amigos!*

Amparo Font, Saddleback College
Pilar Hernández, Arizona Western College
Channing Horner, Northeast Missouri State University
Harriet Hutchinson, Bunker Hill Community College
Stephen Richman, Mercer County College
Dr. Tomás Ruiz-Fábrega, Albuquerque Technical Vocational Institute
Dr. Kristin Shoaf, Bridgewater State College
Vincent Spina, Clarion University of Pennsylvania
Susanna Williams, Macomb Community College
Lydia Bernstein, Bridgewater State College
Linda Burk, Manchester Community Technical College
Dimitrios Karayiannis, Southern Illinois University
David Korn, Anderson College
Barbar Kruger, Finger Lakes Community College
Ping Mei Law, McMaster University
Denis Mohan, University of Guelph
Stephen Richman, Mercer County Community College
Mercedes Rowinsky, Wilfred Laurier University
Virginia Vigil, Austin Community College at Rio Grande
Clementina Adams, Clemson University
Peter Alfieri, Salve Regina College
Jane Harrington Bethune, Salve Regina College
Joseph DiPaola, Macomb Community College
Rosita Marcella, Manhattan College
Joel B. Pouwels, University of Central Arkansas
Barbara Ross, Eastern Kentucky University

We also extend our sincere appreciation to the World Language Staff of Houghton Mifflin Company, College Division: Rolando Hernández, Publisher; Glenn A. Wilson, Senior Sponsoring Editor; Eileen Bernadette Moran, Executive Marketing Director; Judith Bach, Senior Development Editor; Amy Johnson, Project Editor; Erin Beasley, Editorial Assistant; and Lorreen Ruth Pelletier, Marketing Assistant.

Ana C. Jarvis
Raquel Lebredo
Francisco Mena-Ayllón

We would like to hear your comments on and reactions to *¡Hola, amigos!*, Seventh Edition. Reports on your experiences using this program would be of great interest and value to us. Please write us care of Houghton Mifflin Company, College Division, 222 Berkeley Street, Boston, MA 02116-3764, or e-mail us at college_mod_lang@hmco.com.

¡Hola, amigos!

Unidad

Objetivos

Lección 1

- ◆ Introduce yourself
- ◆ Greet and say good-bye to others
- ◆ Name colors
- ◆ Describe your classroom
- ◆ Describe people
- ◆ Request and give telephone numbers
- ◆ Express possession
- ◆ Give and request information regarding nationality and place of residence

Lección 2

- ◆ Discuss the courses you and your classmates are taking
- ◆ Order beverages
- ◆ Request and give the correct time
- ◆ Name the day of the week, months, and seasons
- ◆ Talk about your activities and what you have to do

Tres estudiantes universitarios se reúnen después de (*after*) las clases para ir *(to go)* a un café.

Los estudiantes universitarios

Lección 1
¡Bienvenidos!

Lección 2
Nuestras clases

Los mexicoamericanos

Una celebración del Cinco de Mayo con bailes folclóricos de México.

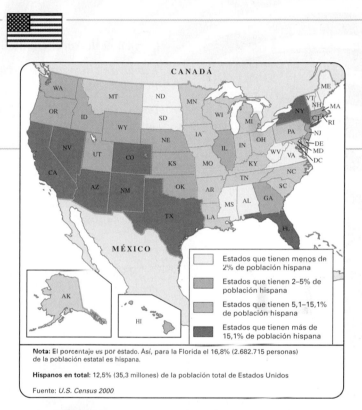

Estados que tienen menos de 2% de población hispana

Estados que tienen 2–5% de población hispana

Estados que tienen 5,1–15,1% de población hispana

Estados que tienen más de 15,1% de población hispana

Nota: El porcentaje es por estado. Así, para la Florida el 16,8% (2.682.715 personas) de la población estatal es hispana.

Hispanos en total: 12,5% (35,3 millones) de la población total de Estados Unidos

Fuente: *U.S. Census 2000*

Los cubanoamericanos

Bebiendo jugo en una cafetería cubana en Miami.

Los puertorriqueños

Celebrando el Día de Puerto Rico con un desfile en la ciudad de Chicago.

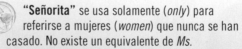

En la Universidad de California, en Los Ángeles

David, un chico norteamericano, habla con Lupe,
una chica mexicana.

David   Buenos días, Lupe, ¿cómo estás?
Lupe   Bien, ¿y tú? ¿Qué hay de nuevo?
David   No mucho. Oye, Lupe, ¿cuál es tu número de teléfono?
Lupe   Dos-trece-siete-veintiocho-quince-treinta y tres.[1]
David   ¿Cuál es tu dirección?
Lupe   Calle Alvarado, número diecisiete-once.
David   Gracias. Hasta mañana.
Lupe   Adiós.

El doctor[2] Acosta habla con una estudiante.

Nora   Buenas tardes, profesor.
Profesor   Buenas tardes, señorita. ¿Cómo se llama usted?
Nora   Me llamo Nora Ballester.
Profesor   Mucho gusto.
Nora   El gusto es mío.
Profesor   ¿De dónde es usted?
Nora   Yo soy de San Antonio, Texas.

Detalles culturales

Se usa "**hola**" con personas conocidas (*known*), no con extraños (*strangers*).

✦ **¿Cómo saludan ustedes (*do you greet*) al profesor?**

Detalles culturales

"**Señorita**" se usa solamente (*only*) para referirse a mujeres (*women*) que nunca se han casado. No existe un equivalente de *Ms.*

✦ **En los Estados Unidos, ¿qué título se usa para referirse a mujeres divorciadas, por ejemplo?**

---

[1]Phone numbers can also be mentioned one by one: **dos-uno-tres-siete-dos-ocho-uno-cinco-tres-tres.**
[2]In Spanish, titles are not capitalized when used with a last name unless they are abbreviated: **señor Fernández,** but **Sr. Fernández.**

Sergio habla con Teresa en la biblioteca.

Sergio Hola, Teresa, ¿qué tal?
Teresa Muy bien, ¿y tú?
Sergio Más o menos. Oye… tu compañera de cuarto es muy bonita…
Teresa ¿Ana María? Sí, es una chica muy bonita y muy simpática.
Sergio ¡Muy interesante! ¿Es inteligente?
Teresa Sí… ¡y rica!
Sergio ¡Caramba! ¡Es perfecta! Bueno, nos vemos esta noche. Saludos a Ana María.
Teresa Hasta luego.

La profesora Rivas habla con los estudiantes en la clase de español.

Profesora Buenas noches. ¿Cómo están ustedes?
Estudiantes Bien, gracias.
David Profesora, ¿cómo se dice "*book*" en español?
Profesora Se dice **"libro"**.
David Muchas gracias.
Profesora De nada.

Detalles culturales

María es un nombre muy popular en España y en Latinoamérica. Se usa (*It's used*) frecuentemente con otros nombres: **Ana María, María Isabel**, etc. También (*Also*) se usa como segundo nombre para los hombres: **José María**.

◆ **¿Qué nombres son populares en este país?**

¿Recuerda usted? (*Do you remember?*)

¿Verdadero o falso? (*True or false?*) With a partner, decide whether the following statements about the dialogues are true (**verdadero**) or false (**falso**).

1. David es norteamericano. ☐ V ☐ F
2. La dirección de Lupe es Calle Alameda, número once-diecisiete. ☐ V ☐ F
3. El doctor Acosta es profesor. ☐ V ☐ F
4. Nora es de San Francisco. ☐ V ☐ F
5. Sergio habla con Teresa en la clase. ☐ V ☐ F
6. Ana María es muy bonita. ☐ V ☐ F
7. Ana María es inteligente y simpática. ☐ V ☐ F
8. Los estudiantes hablan con la profesora Rivas. ☐ V ☐ F

Y ahora… conteste (*And now . . . answer*) Answer these questions, basing your answers on the dialogues.

1. ¿Cuál es el número de teléfono de Lupe?
2. ¿Cuál es la dirección de Lupe?
3. ¿De dónde es Nora Ballester?
4. ¿Dónde hablan Sergio y Teresa?
5. ¿Ana María es rica?
6. ¿Cómo se dice "*book*" en español?

5

Para hablar del tema: Vocabulario
(To talk about the topic: Vocabulary)

Nombres (*Nouns*)

la biblioteca library
la calle street
la chica, la muchacha girl
el chico, el muchacho young man
la clase class
_____ **de español*** Spanish class
el (la) compañero(a) de cuarto roommate
la dirección* address
el español Spanish (language)
el (la) estudiante, el (la) alumno(a) student
el libro book
el número number
_____ **de teléfono** phone number

Adjetivos (*Adjectives*)

bienvenido(a) welcome
bonito(a), lindo(a) pretty[1]
inteligente intelligent
interesante interesting
mexicano(a) Mexican
norteamericano(a)[2] North American (*from the U.S.*)

perfecto(a) perfect
rico(a) rich
simpático(a) charming, nice, fun to be with
universitario(a) (related to) college

Títulos (*Titles*)

doctor (Dr.) doctor (*m.*)
doctora (Dra.) doctor (*f.*)
profesor(a) professor
señor (Sr.) Mr., sir, gentleman
señora (Sra.) Mrs., madam, lady
señorita (Srta.) miss, young lady

Otras palabras y expresiones
(Other words and expressions)

bueno... well . . . , okay
¡Caramba! Gee!
¿Cómo? How?
con with
¿Cuál es tu número de teléfono? What's your phone number?
¿Dónde? Where?
en at, in, on
esta noche tonight
habla he/she speaks

hay there is, there are
muy very
no no, not
oye listen
ser to be
sí yes
tu your
y and
¿Y tú? And you?

Expresiones de cortesía (*Polite expressions*)

Mucho gusto.* It's a pleasure to meet you. (How do you do?)
El gusto es mío. The pleasure is mine.
Gracias. Thanks.
Muchas gracias. Thank you very much.
De nada.* You're welcome.

De país a país

la clase de español la clase de castellano (*Esp., Cono Sur*)
la dirección el domicilio (*Méx.*)
Mucho gusto Encantado(a) (*Arg., Cuba*) (The response is **igualmente**)
de nada por nada (*Méx.*)
¿Cómo? ¿Mande? (*Méx.*)
marrón café (*Méx.*); carmelita (*Cuba*)
la computadora el ordenador (*Esp.*)

Algunos saludos y despedidas (*Some greetings and farewells*)

Buenos días. Good morning.
Buenas tardes. Good afternoon.
Buenas noches. Good evening; Good night.
Hola. Hello; Hi.
¿Qué hay de nuevo? What's new?
¿Qué tal? How is it going?

Adiós. Good-bye.
Hasta luego. (I'll) see you later.
Hasta mañana. (I'll) see you tomorrow.
Nos vemos. (I'll) see you.
Saludos a... Say hi to . . .

¿Cómo está usted? How are you? (*formal*)

¿Cómo están ustedes? How are you? (*when addressing two or more people*)

¿Cómo estás? How are you? (*familiar*)

Bien. Fine.

Más o menos. More or less.

Muy bien. Very well.

¿Cómo se dice...? How do you say . . . ?

Se dice... You say . . .

¿Cómo se llama usted? What's your name? (*formal*)

¿Cómo te llamas? What's your name? (*familiar*)

Me llamo... My name is . . .

¿De dónde es usted? Where are you from? (*formal*)

Soy de... I am from . . .

¿Qué hay de nuevo? What's new?

No mucho. Not much.

Amplíe su vocabulario (*Expand your vocabulary*)

Más despedidas y expresiones de cortesía (*More farewells and polite expressions*)

Chau. Bye.

¿Cómo?* Pardon? (*when one doesn't understand or hear what is being said*)

Hasta la vista. (I'll) see you around.

Lo siento. I'm sorry.

Más despacio, por favor. More slowly, please.

Pase. Come in.

Perdón. Sorry. Pardon me.

Permiso. Excuse me. (i.e. *when going through a crowded room*)

Por favor. Please.

Tome asiento. Have a seat.

Colores (*Colors*)

amarillo yellow	**azul** blue
gris gray	morado purple
rojo red	verde green
anaranjado orange	blanco white
marrón brown	**negro** black
rosado pink	

Vocabulario para la clase (*Vocabulary for the class*)

la pizarra · *el reloj* · *la ventana* · *el lápiz* · *la tablilla de anuncios* · *la puerta* · *la luz* · *el mapa* · *el borrador* · *la tiza* · *la silla* · *el papel* · ** la computadora* · *el escritorio* · *el cesto de papeles* · *la pluma* / *el bolígrafo* · *el reloj* · *el libro* · *el cuaderno* · *la mochila*

*Spanish is spoken in more than 20 countries, and different countries may use different words to refer to the same thing. The section **De país a país** includes variations corresponding to the words marked with asterisks in the vocabularies throughout the book.

[1]When referring to men, **guapo** (*handsome*) is used.

[2]In formal situations, **estadounidense** is used to denote U.S. citizenship.

Para practicar el vocabulario

(*To practice vocabulary*)

A. Los estudiantes Complete each sentence, using vocabulary from **Lección 1.**

1. ¿Cómo te _____ tú? ¿María?
2. ¿Cómo se _____ *"window"* en español?
3. El _____ es mío, profesora.
4. La señora Ariet _____ con los alumnos en español.
5. ¿De dónde _____ usted? ¿De México?
6. ¿Cómo _____ usted? ¿Bien?
7. En la clase hay un profesor y veinte _____.
8. Viviana es una _____ bonita, inteligente y _____. ¡Y es rica! ¡Es _____!
9. ¿Fernando es tu _____ de cuarto?
10. Adiós. _____ a Norma.

B. Yo soy el anfitrión (la anfitriona) (*I'm the host/hostess*) You are having a party in the evening. What are you going to say to the following people in each situation?

1. You open the door to one of your guests. Greet him and ask him to come in and have a seat.
2. You go back to the kitchen, walking through your crowded living room. You accidentally push someone.
3. You didn't understand a word that one of your guests said. She is talking very fast.
4. One of your guests brings a friend whom he introduces to you.
5. Three of your guests are leaving: your best friend, an acquaintance that you'll probably see again, and a lady who will be returning to the party.

C. ¡Somos pintores! (*We are painters!*) You are explaining to a group of children what colors you need to mix to get the following colors.

1. anaranjado
2. verde
3. morado
4. gris
5. rosado

D. ¿Qué color te gusta? To ask someone whether he or she likes something, you say: "**¿Te gusta...?**"[1] To say that you like something, say: "**Me gusta...**" Conduct a survey of your classmates to find out which color is the most popular in class, following the model.

◆ MODELO: —¿Qué color te gusta?
—*Me gusta el color rojo.*

---

[1]When addressing someone as **usted,** use "**¿Le gusta...?**"

E. ¿Qué necesitamos? (*What do we need?*) Explain what object or objects you and your classmates need for each purpose listed. Begin each sentence with **Necesitamos** (*We need*).

1. to write on
2. to see when the room is dark
3. to write with and to erase with
4. to sit in class
5. to place or post ads, notices, or bits of news
6. to throw away used papers
7. to carry books and notebooks
8. to study geography
9. to send e-mail
10. to know what time it is
11. to get in or out of the classroom
12. to see what's going on outside

F. ¿Necesitas algo? (*Do you need anything?*) With a partner, ask each other whether you need certain objects. Name ten items. When asking, point to the item or offer it. When answering, tell what you do need if you answer **no.** Follow the model.

♦ MODELO: —*¿Necesitas el mapa?* (Do you need the map?)
—*Sí, necesito el mapa.* (Yes, I need the map.)
(*No, necesito la pizarra.*) (No, I need the board.)

Pronunciación (*Pronunciation*)

Las vocales (*vowels*) *a, e, i, o, u*[1] Spanish vowels are constant, clear, and short. To practice the sound of each vowel, repeat the following words.

a	mapa	sábado	hasta mañana
	hablar	trabajar	de nada
e	mes	leche	estudiante
	este	Pepe	semestre
i	silla	libro	universidad
	tiza	lápiz	señorita
o	doctor	Soto	los profesores
	donde	borrador	domingo
u	mujer	alumno	universidad
	gusto	lunes	computadora

---

[1]See Appendix A for a complete introduction to Spanish pronunciation.

Puntos para recordar

1. Gender and number of nouns
(*Género y número de los nombres*)

Gender, part I

◆ In Spanish, all nouns—including those denoting nonliving things—are either masculine or feminine in gender.[1]

Masculine	Feminine
el profesor	la profesora
el cuaderno	la tiza
el lápiz	la ventana

◆ Most nouns that end in **-o** or denote males are masculine: **cuaderno, hombre** (*man*).

◆ Most nouns that end in **-a** or denote females are feminine: **ventana, mujer** (*woman*).

> **¡Atención!** Some common exceptions include the words **día** (*day*) and **mapa** (*map*), which end in **-a** but are masculine, and **mano** (*hand*), which ends in **-o** but is feminine.

◆ Here are some helpful rules to remember about gender.

◆ Some masculine nouns ending in **-o** have a corresponding feminine form ending in **-a: el secretario / la secretaria.**

◆ When a masculine noun ends in a consonant, you often add **-a** to obtain its corresponding feminine form: **el doctor / la doctora.**

◆ Some nouns have the same form for both genders: **el estudiante / la estudiante.** In such cases, gender is indicated by the article **el** (masculine) or **la** (feminine).

---

[1]See Appendix C for a glossary of grammatical terms.

Práctica (Practice)

Online Study Center

For more practice with lesson topics, see the related activities on the *¡Hola, amigos!* web site at college.hmco.com/PIC/holaamigos7e.

¿Masculino o femenino? *Place **el** or **la** before each noun.*

1. ____ mapa
2. ____ tiza
3. ____ escritorio
4. ____ secretaria
5. ____ silla
6. ____ profesora

7. ____ pizarra
8. ____ libro
9. ____ mujer
10. ____ puerta
11. ____ ventana
12. ____ bolígrafo

13. ____ hombre
14. ____ día
15. ____ secretario
16. ____ mano
17. ____ computadora
18. ____ profesor

Plural forms of nouns

Spanish singular nouns are made plural by adding **-s** to words ending in a vowel and **-es** to words ending in a consonant. When a noun ends in **-z,** change the **z** to **c** and add **-es.**

Singular	Plural
silla	sillas
estudiante	estudiantes
profesor	profesores
borrador	borradores
lápiz	lápices

¡Atención! When an accent mark falls on the *last* syllable of a word that ends in a consonant, it is omitted in the plural form:

lec**ción** → lec**ciones**[1]

Práctica

Online Study Center

For more practice with lesson topics, see the related activities on the *¡Hola, amigos!* web site al college.hmco.com/PIC/holaamigos7e.

¿Cuál es el plural? *Give the plural of the following nouns.*

1. mapa
2. profesor
3. tiza
4. lápiz

5. ventana
6. mochila
7. lección
8. escritorio

9. borrador
10. día
11. luz
12. papel

2. Definite and indefinite articles
(Artículos determinados e indeterminados)

The definite article[2]

Spanish has four forms that are equivalent to the English definite article *the.*

---

[1]For an explanation of written accent marks, refer to Appendix A.
[2]See Appendix C.

	Singular	Plural
Masculine	**el**	**los**
Feminine	**la**	**las**

el profesor   **la** profesora
el lápiz   **la** pluma
los profesores   **las** profesoras
los lápices   **las** plumas

¡Atención!   Always learn new nouns with their corresponding definite articles—this will help you remember their gender.

The indefinite article[1]

The Spanish equivalents of *a* (*an*) and *some* are as follows:

	Singular		Plural	
Masculine	**un**	a, an	**unos**	some
Feminine	**una**	a, an	**unas**	some

un libro   **unos** libros
un profesor   **unos** profesores
una silla   **unas** sillas
una ventana   **unas** ventanas

Práctica

A. ¿Qué es? For each of the following illustrations, identify the noun together with its corresponding definite and indefinite articles.

1. _____

2. _____

3. _____

4. _____

5. _____

6.
_____

---

[1]See Appendix C.

7. _____

8. _____

9. _____

10. _____

B. **¿Qué necesitas?** With a partner, go to p. 7 (*Vocabulario para la clase*) and, using indefinite articles, take turns indicating what you need. Name twelve items.

◆ **MODELO:** *Necesito una silla.*

3. Subject pronouns (*Pronombres personales usados como sujetos*)[1]

Singular		Plural	
yo	I	**nosotros**	we (*m.*)
		nosotras	we (*f.*)
tú	you (*familiar*)	**vosotros**	you (*m., familiar*)
		vosotras	you (*f., familiar*)
usted	you (*formal*)	**ustedes**	you (*formal, familiar*[2])
él	he	**ellos**	they (*m.*)
ella	she	**ellas**	they (*f.*)

◆ Use the **tú** form as the equivalent of *you* when addressing a close friend, a relative, or a child. Use the **usted** form in *all* other instances. In most Spanish-speaking countries, young people tend to call each other **tú,** even if they have just met.

◆ In Latin America, **ustedes** (abbreviated **Uds.**) is used as the plural form of both **tú** and **usted** (abbreviated **Ud.**). In Spain, however, the plural form of **tú** is **vosotros(as).**

◆ The masculine plural forms **nosotros, vosotros,** and **ellos** can refer to the masculine gender alone or to both genders together:

Juan y Roberto → **ellos**   Juan y María → **ellos**

◆ Unlike English, Spanish does not generally express *it* or *they* as separate words when the subject of the sentence is a thing.

Es una mesa.   *It is a table.*

---

[1]See Appendix C.
[2]In Latin America.

Online Study Center

For more practice with lesson
topics, see the related activities on
the *¡Hola, amigos!* web site at
college.hmco.com/PIC/holaamigos7e.

Práctica

A. ¿Quiénes son? What subject pronouns do the following pictures
suggest to you?

1. _____

2. _____

3. _____

4. _____

5. _____

6. _____

7. _____

8. _____

9. _____

B. ¿Tú, Ud. o Uds.? What pronoun would you use to address the following
people?

1. the president of the university
2. two strangers
3. your best friend
4. your mother
5. a new classmate
6. your neighbor's children

4. Present indicative of *ser* (*Presente de indicativo del verbo* ser)[1]

The verb **ser** (*to be*) is irregular. Its forms must therefore be memorized.

yo	**soy**	I am
tú	**eres**	you (*fam.*) are
Ud.		you (*form.*) are
él	**es**	he is
ella		she is
nosotros(as)	**somos**	we are
vosotros(as)	**sois**	you (*fam.*) are
Uds.		you are
ellos	**son**	they (*masc.*) are
ellas		they (*fem.*) are

—Ud. **es** el doctor Rivas, ¿no?   *"**You are** Dr. Rivas, right?"*
—No, **soy** el profesor Soto.   *"No, **I'm** professor Soto."*

—¿De dónde **son** Uds.?   *"Where **are you** (all) from?"*
—**Somos** de Los Ángeles. ¿De   *"**We are** from Los Angeles.*
dónde **eres** tú?   *Where **are you** from?"*
—Yo **soy** de Texas.   *"**I am** from Texas."*
—¿Y Silvia?   *"And Silvia?"*
—Ella **es** de Arizona.   *"**She is** from Arizona."*

Y..., ¿ Ud. es residente...?

---
[1]See Appendix C.

Práctica y conversación

A. ¿De dónde son? Miss Soto works in the Admissions Office and these out-of-state students are telling her where they are from. Using the verb **ser,** complete what they are saying.

1. David / Arizona
2. Yo / Colorado
3. Ana y Eva / Utah
4. Guadalupe / Nuevo México
5. Nosotros / Oregón
6. Raúl y Ángel / Idaho

Now indicate what Miss Soto would say to a girl, an older gentleman, and two young men to ask them where they are from.

 B. Compañeros de clase (*Classmates*)   In groups of three or four, ask each other where you are from. Be prepared to have one person report to the class.

5. Forms of adjectives and agreement of articles, nouns, and adjectives

(*La formación de adjetivos y la concordancia de artículos, nombres y adjetivos*)

Forms of adjectives[1]

◆ Most adjectives in Spanish have two basic forms: the masculine form ending in **-o** and the feminine form ending in **-a.** Their corresponding plural forms end in **-os** and **-as,** respectively.

profesor mexican**o**	profesores mexican**os**
profesora mexican**a**	profesoras mexican**as**
chico simpátic**o**	chicos simpátic**os**
chica simpátic**a**	chicas simpátic**as**

◆ When an adjective ends in **-e** or a consonant, the same form is normally used with both masculine and feminine nouns.

muchacho inteligent**e**	muchacha inteligent**e**
libro difíci**l** (*difficult*)	clase difíci**l**

◆ The only exceptions are as follows:
  ◆ Adjectives of nationality that end in a consonant have feminine forms ending in **-a.**

señor español (*Spanish*)	señora español**a**
señor inglés (*English*)	señora ingle**sa**

◆ In forming the plural, adjectives follow the same rules as nouns.

mexican**o** → mexican**os**
feli**z** (*happy*) → feli**ces**
difíci**l** → difíci**les**

---

[1]See Appendix C.

Position of adjectives

◆ In Spanish, adjectives that describe qualities (*pretty, smart,* and so on) generally *follow* nouns, while adjectives of quantity precede them: Hay **dos** chicas **bonitas.**

Agreement of articles, nouns, and adjectives

◆ In Spanish, the article, the noun, and the adjective agree in gender and number.

El muchach**o** es simpátic**o**.   **Los** muchach**os** son simpátic**os**.
La muchach**a** es simpátic**a**.   **Las** muchach**as** son simpátic**as**.

Práctica y conversación

Online Study Center

For more practice with lesson topics, see the related activities on the *¡Hola, amigos!* web site at college.hmco.com/PIC/holaamigos7e.

Study these common adjectives that are used to describe people, places, or things.

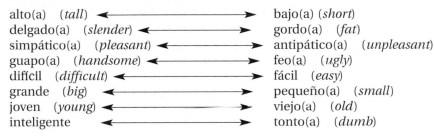

alto(a)   (*tall*) ←————————→ bajo(a) (*short*)
delgado(a)   (*slender*) ←————————→ gordo(a)   (*fat*)
simpático(a)   (*pleasant*) ←————————→ antipático(a)   (*unpleasant*)
guapo(a)   (*handsome*) ←————————→ feo(a)   (*ugly*)
difícil   (*difficult*) ←————————→ fácil   (*easy*)
grande   (*big*) ←————————→ pequeño(a)   (*small*)
joven   (*young*) ←————————→ viejo(a)   (*old*)
inteligente ←————————→ tonto(a)   (*dumb*)

 A. ¿Cómo son...?   With a partner, take turns asking and answering the following questions. In your answers, contradict what is stated.

◆ MODELO: —¿Eva es tonta?
          —¡Al contrario (On the contrary)! *Es muy inteligente.*

1. ¿Los chicos son bajos?
2. ¿Elena es joven?
3. ¿Eva y Gloria son antipáticas?
4. ¿Luis y Francisco son feos?

5. ¿Elsa es gorda?
6. ¿Las lecciones son fáciles?
7. ¿Las casas (*houses*) son grandes?
8. ¿Ellos son inteligentes?

 B. Para conversar (*To talk*)   With a partner, take turns asking each other what these people are like. Ask: **¿Cómo es...?** (*What is . . . like?*)

1. Brad Pitt
2. Danny De Vito
3. Ricky Martin
4. Jennifer López

5. Roseanne
6. Leonardo Di Caprio
7. Cameron Díaz
8. Penélope Cruz

6. The alphabet (*El alfabeto*)[1]

> **¡Atención!** All letters are feminine: la **a**, la **b**, and so on.

Letter	Name	Letter	Name	Letter	Name
a	a	j	jota	r	ere
b	be	k	ca	rr	erre
c	ce	l	ele	s	ese
d	de	m	eme	t	te
e	e	n	ene	u	u
f	efe	ñ	eñe	v	ve
g	ge	o	o	w	doble ve
h	hache	p	pe	x	equis
i	i	q	cu	y	i griega
				z	zeta

Online Study Center

For more practice with lesson topics, see the related activities on the *¡Hola, amigos!* web site at college.hmco.com/PIC/holaamigos7e.

Práctica y conversación

A. Siglas *(Acronyms)*   With a partner, take turns reading the following acronyms in Spanish.

1. FBI _____
2. CIA _____
3. IBM _____
4. D. C. _____
5. NAACP _____
6. NBA _____

B. Apellidos *(Last names)*   In groups of three or four, ask each person in the group what his/her last name is and how to spell it.

◆ MODELO: *¿Cuál es tu apellido?*
           ¿Cómo se deletrea?

7. Numbers 0 to 39 (*Números de 0 a 39*)

Learn the Spanish numbers from zero to thirty-nine.

0 cero	7 siete	14 catorce
1 uno	8 ocho	15 quince
2 dos	9 nueve	16 dieciséis[2]
3 tres	10 diez	17 diecisiete
4 cuatro	11 once	18 dieciocho
5 cinco	12 doce	19 diecinueve
6 seis	13 trece	20 veinte

---

[1]For a complete introduction to Spanish sounds, see Appendix A, p. 346, which appears on the in-text audio CDs.

[2]The numbers sixteen to nineteen and twenty-one to twenty-nine can also be spelled with a **y** (*and*): **diez y seis, diez y siete… veinte y uno, veinte y dos,** and so on. The pronunciation of each group of words, however, is identical to the corresponding word spelled with the **i.**

21 veintiuno	28 veintiocho	35 treinta y cinco
22 veintidós	29 veintinueve	36 treinta y seis
23 veintitrés	30 treinta	37 treinta y siete
24 veinticuatro	31 treinta y uno	38 treinta y ocho
25 veinticinco	32 treinta y dos	39 treinta y nueve
26 veintiséis	33 treinta y tres	
27 veintisiete	34 treinta y cuatro	

¡Atención! **Uno** changes to **un** before a masculine singular noun: **un libro** (*one book*). **Uno** changes to **una** before a feminine singular noun: **una silla** (*one chair*).

Práctica y conversación

Online Study Center

For more practice with lesson topics, see the related activities on the *¡Hola, amigos!* web site at college.hmco.com/PIC/holaamigos7e.

A. Números de teléfono   Say the telephone number of each of the following people.

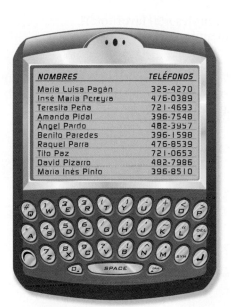

NOMBRES	TELÉFONOS
María Luisa Pagán	325-4270
José María Pereyra	476-0389
Teresita Peña	721-4693
Amanda Pidal	396-7548
Ángel Pardo	482-3957
Benito Paredes	396-1598
Raquel Parra	476-8539
Tito Paz	721-0653
David Pizarro	482-7986
María Inés Pinto	396-8510

B. ¿Cuál es tu número de teléfono?   Ask three or four of your classmates for their names and phone numbers. Write down the response and show it to each one, asking, **¿Está bien?** (*Is it okay?*). He or she will say **"sí"** or **"no"** and will correct any mistakes.

C. Sumas y restas *(Additions and subtractions)*   Learn the following mathematical terms; then, with a partner, take turns adding and subtracting.

+ más − menos = son

◆ **MODELO:** $7 + 4 = 11$ (Siete más cuatro son once.)
$20 - 6 = 14$ (Veinte menos seis son catorce.)

1. $20 + 15 =$
2. $16 - 11 =$
3. $17 - 13 =$
4. $11 + 16 =$

5. $19 + 11 =$
6. $13 - 8 =$
7. $30 - 12 =$
8. $18 + 18 =$

9. $23 - 14 =$
10. $17 + 13 =$

Entre nosotros[1]

¡Conversemos!

 Para conocernos mejor (*To get to know each other better*)   Get to know your partner better by asking each other the following questions.

1. ¿Cómo te llamas?
2. ¿Cómo estás?
3. ¿Eres norteamericano(a)?
4. ¿De dónde eres?
5. ¿Cuál es tu número de teléfono?
6. ¿Cuál es tu dirección?
7. ¿Quién (*Who*) es tu profesor(a) favorito(a)?
8. ¿Cómo es tu mejor amigo(a) (*best friend*)?

Una encuesta (*A survey*)   Interview your classmates to identify who fits the following descriptions. Include your instructor, but remember to use the **Ud.** form when addressing him or her.

Nombre

1. Es muy paciente.
2. Es inteligente.
3. Es muy liberal.
4. Es conservador(a).
5. Es popular.
6. Es eficiente.
7. Es perfeccionista.
8. Es atlético(a).
9. Es optimista.
10. Es pesimista.

Y ahora...   Write a brief summary, indicating what you have learned about your classmates.

---

[1]*Among us*

¿Cómo lo decimos? (*How do we say it?*)   What would you say in the following situations? What might the other person say? Act out the scenes with a partner.

1. You meet Mrs. García in the evening and you ask her how she is.
2. You ask Professor Vega how to say "I'm sorry" in Spanish.
3. You ask a young girl what her name is.
4. You ask a classmate what her roommate is like.
5. You ask a classmate where he or she is from.
6. You say good-bye to someone you expect to see at some point in the future.
7. You ask a friend how he or she is and what is new with him or her.
8. You offer Miss Vega a seat and then ask her what her address is.
9. You didn't understand what someone said. He or she is speaking too fast.
10. You are going through a crowded room. You stepped on someone's foot.
11. Someone is introduced to you.
12. You ask a classmate what his/her phone number is.

¿Qué pasa aquí? (*What's going on here?*)   With a partner, look at the photograph on page 1 and create a dialogue between two of the people in the photo. The two people should greet each other, introduce themselves and tell where they're from.

Para escribir (*To write*)

Un mensaje electrónico   A new cyber friend wants to know what you are like. Write him/her an e-mail, describing yourself with as much detail as you can. At the end, ask your new friend for a description.

Un dicho

Saber es poder.

This is a popular saying in Spanish. Find out what it means. Does it have an equivalent in English? Learn it in Spanish. You might want to make it part of your philosophy . . .

Lección 2 • Nuestras clases

Lisa, una chica norteamericana, habla con Alina, su nueva compañera de cuarto, que es cubanoamericana. Las dos estudian en la Universidad Internacional de la Florida, en Miami.

Lisa Alina, ¿cuántas clases tomas este semestre?

Alina Tomo cinco clases: inglés, matemáticas, física, psicología y biología. ¿Y tú?

Lisa Yo tomo historia, literatura y español.

Alina ¿Español? ¡Buena idea!, pero solamente tomas tres asignaturas.

Lisa Sí, porque yo trabajo los lunes, miércoles y viernes por la tarde porque necesito dinero.

Alina Yo también, pero trabajo en el verano, de julio a septiembre.

Lisa Tú tomas materias muy difíciles.

Alina Sí, pero todas mis clases son requisitos… además, la clase de psicología es fácil.

Lisa Pues, Alina, tu vida es muy aburrida. ¡Vamos a la playa!

Detalles culturales

En la mayoría de los países hispanos, el año escolar (*school year*) no se divide en semestres o trimestres; dura (*it lasts*) nueve meses. Los requisitos generales se toman en la escuela secundaria. En la universidad los estudiantes se concentran en su propio campo (*their own fields*).

◆ **En esta universidad, ¿el año escolar se divide en semestres o en trimestres?**

Detalles culturales

En los países de habla hispana, muchos estudiantes estudian con un(a) compañero(a) o en grupos. Generalmente viven con su familia o en pensiones. Hay muy pocas residencias universitarias (*dormitories*).

◆ **¿Cómo estudian los estudiantes en los Estados Unidos?**

Miguel habla con su amigo Pablo, un chico puertorriqueño. Los dos conversan en la cafetería de la universidad.

Miguel ¿Deseas tomar una taza de café?

Pablo No, un vaso de leche. Yo no tomo café. Oye, ¿qué hora es?

Miguel Es la una y media. ¿Por qué?

Pablo Porque a las dos de la tarde hay un programa de televisión muy interesante.

Miguel ¡Ah! Necesito mi horario de clases.

Pablo Aquí está. Nuestra clase de química es a las cuatro en el aula[1] ciento noventa y cinco.

Miguel ¿A qué hora terminan tus clases hoy?

Pablo A las ocho de la noche.

Miguel Estudiamos juntos mañana, ¿verdad?

Pablo Entonces, ¿mañana no vamos a la playa? Eres un aguafiestas. Bueno, me voy.

¿Recuerda usted?

¿Verdadero o falso? With a partner, decide whether the following statements about the dialogues are true (**verdadero**) or false (**falso**).

1. Lisa y Alina son estudiantes universitarias. ☐ V ☐ F
2. Alina toma cinco requisitos. ☐ V ☐ F
3. Lisa trabaja porque necesita dinero. ☐ V ☐ F
4. Alina solamente estudia en el verano. ☐ V ☐ F
5. La clase de psicología es muy difícil para Alina. ☐ V ☐ F
6. Pablo es de Cuba. ☐ V ☐ F
7. El programa de televisión es a las dos de la tarde. ☐ V ☐ F
8. La clase de química es a las cuatro. ☐ V ☐ F
9. Pablo termina sus clases a las seis de la tarde. ☐ V ☐ F
10. Pablo y Miguel estudian juntos. ☐ V ☐ F

Y ahora... conteste Answer these questions, basing your answers on the dialogue.

1. ¿Alina es norteamericana o cubanoamericana?
2. ¿Cuántas clases toma Lisa este semestre?
3. ¿Qué días trabaja Lisa?
4. ¿La vida de Alina es muy aburrida?
5. ¿Dónde conversan Miguel y Pablo?
6. ¿Pablo desea tomar café o leche?
7. ¿Miguel necesita el horario de clases o el libro?
8. ¿Dónde es la clase de química?

---

[1]The article **el** is used before a feminine noun that starts with a stressed **a** or **ha.**

Para hablar del tema: Vocabulario

Online Study Center

For more practice with lesson
topics, see the related activities on
the *¡Hola, amigos!* web site at
college.hmco.com/PIC/holaamigos7e.

Nombres

el (la) aguafiestas spoilsport
el (la) amigo(a) friend
la asignatura* course, subject
el aula (*f.*) classroom
el café coffee
el dinero* money
el horario de clases[1] class
  schedule
el inglés English (*language*)
el lunes Monday
la leche milk

el miércoles Wednesday
la noche night
la playa beach
el requisito requirement
la química chemistry
la tarde afternoon
la taza cup
el vaso (drinking) glass
el verano summer
la vida life
el viernes Friday

Cognados

la biología
la cafetería
cubanoamericano(a)
la física
la historia
la idea
internacional
julio
la literatura
las matemáticas
el programa
la psicología
puertorriqueño(a)
el semestre
septiembre
la televisión

Otras palabras y expresiones

a at (*with time of day*); to
¿A qué hora...? (At) What time . . . ?
además besides
Aquí está Here it is
¿Cuántos(as)? How many?
de of
entonces then
este semestre this semester
hay there is, there are
hoy today
los (las) dos both
mañana tomorrow
Me voy I'm leaving
no vamos we are not going

pero but
por la tarde in the afternoon
¿Por qué? Why?
porque because
pues then
que who, that
¿Qué? What?
¿Qué hora es? What time is it?
solamente, sólo only
también also, too
¿verdad? right?, true?
y media half past
ya es tarde it's already late

---

[1]Spanish uses prepositional phrases that correspond to the English adjectival use of nouns:
  horario de clases (*class schedule*).

<table>
<tr><td colspan="1">

Verbos

conversar* to talk, converse
desear to wish, want
estudiar to study
hablar to speak
necesitar to need
terminar to end, finish, get through
tomar to take (*a class*); to drink
trabajar to work

</td><td colspan="1">

Adjetivos

aburrido(a) boring
bueno(a) good
juntos(as) together
nuestro(a) our
nuevo(a) new
todos(as) all

</td></tr>
</table>

Amplíe su vocabulario

Para pedir bebidas (*Ordering drinks*)

 Deseo una taza de {
café
té   *tea*
chocolate caliente   *hot chocolate*
café con leche   *coffee and milk*

 Deseo un vaso de {
agua con hielo   *ice water*
leche
cerveza   *beer*
té helado, té frío   *iced tea*

Deseo jugo* de {
manzana   *apple*
naranja*   *orange*
tomate
toronja   *grapefruit*
uvas   *grapes*

Deseo una copa de vino (*wine*) {
blanco
rosado   *rosé*
tinto   *red*

 Deseo una botella (*a bottle*) de agua mineral

De país a país

la asignatura la materia (*Arg., Esp.*)
el dinero la plata (*Cono Sur, Cuba*)
conversar platicar (*Méx.*)
el jugo el zumo (*Esp.*)
la naranja la china (*Puerto Rico*)

Más asignaturas (*More course subjects*)

la administración de empresas business
    administration
la antropología anthropology
el arte art
las ciencias políticas political science
la contabilidad accounting

la danza aeróbica aerobic dance
la geografía geography
la geología geology
la informática computer science
la música music
la sociología sociology

Para practicar el vocabulario

A. Palabras y más palabras   ¿Qué palabra o frase corresponde a lo siguiente?

1. opuesto de día
2. asignatura donde estudiamos novelas y poemas
3. Tiene seis meses.
4. opuesto de invierno
5. clases que necesitamos tomar
6. Lo tomamos con leche.
7. Debemos hacerlo antes de tomar un examen.
8. opuesto de malo
9. sólo
10. *Budweiser,* por ejemplo
11. idioma de Shakespeare
12. opuesto de empezar

B. Preguntas y respuestas   Match the questions in column *A* with the answers in column *B*.

A	B
1. ¿Qué clases tomas este semestre?	a. No, blanco.
2. ¿Es difícil la clase de biología?	b. Sí, de julio a septiembre.
3. ¿Tú trabajas?	c. A las ocho de la noche.
4. ¿Trabajas los lunes?	d. Sí, de toronja.
5. ¿Deseas un vaso de leche?	e. No, es aburrido.
6. ¿A qué hora terminas hoy?	f. Química, inglés y física.
7. ¿Deseas vino tinto?	g. No, una taza de café.
8. ¿Deseas jugo?	h. No, los miércoles.
9. ¿Trabajas en el verano?	i. No, es muy fácil.
10. ¿El programa es interesante?	j. Sí, en la biblioteca.

C. ¿Qué deciden?   With a partner, take turns offering each other something to drink. Choose what you will have to drink according to the circumstances described in each case. Then indicate your choice, using **Voy a tomar...**

1. You are allergic to citrus fruit.
   a. un vaso de jugo de toronja
   b. un vaso de jugo de manzana
   c. un vaso de jugo de naranja

2. You are very hot and thirsty.
   a. una taza de chocolate caliente
   b. un vaso de té helado
   c. una taza de café

3. You don't drink alcohol.
    a. una botella de agua mineral
    b. una botella de cerveza
    c. una copa de vino tinto

4. You're having breakfast in Madrid.
    a. una copa de vino rosado
    b. un vaso de agua con hielo
    c. una taza de café con leche

5. It's a cold winter night.
    a. un vaso de jugo de uvas
    b. una taza de chocolate caliente
    c. un vaso de leche fría

D. **¿Qué clases necesito?** With a partner, take turns saying what class(es) you need according to the following situations. Start by saying **Necesito tomar...**

1. You need to get in shape.
2. You would like to get a job in the business world.
3. You need two humanities classes.
4. You need three social science classes.
5. You know very little about other countries.
6. You need to learn about computers.

¿Qué clase cree Ud. que toman estos estudiantes?

Pronunciación

Linking[1] Practice linking by reading aloud the following sentences.

    1. Habla en la universidad.
    2. Juan habla con Norma Acosta.
    3. Termino a la una.
    4. ¿A qué hora es su clase de español?
    5. Deseo un vaso de agua.

---

[1]See Appendix A for an explanation of linking.

Puntos para recordar

1. Present indicative of -ar verbs
(Presente de indicativo de los verbos terminados en -ar)

♦ Spanish verbs are classified according to their endings. There are three conjugations: **-ar, -er,** and **-ir.**[1]

—Rosa, tú **hablas** inglés, ¿no?   *"Rosa, you **speak** English, don't you?"*
—Sí, **hablo** inglés y español.   *"Yes, **I speak** English and Spanish."*

hablar *(to speak)*		
Singular		
	Stem Ending	
yo	habl- **o**	Yo **hablo** español.
tú	habl- **as**	Tú **hablas** español.
Ud.	habl- **a**	Ud. **habla** español.
él	habl- **a**	Juan **habla** español. Él **habla** español.
ella	habl- **a**	Ana **habla** español. Ella **habla** español.
Plural		
nosotros(as)	habl- **amos**	Nosotros(as) **hablamos** español.
vosotros(as)	habl- **áis**	Vosotros(as) **habláis** español.
Uds.	habl- **an**	Uds. **hablan** español.
ellos	habl- **an**	Ellos **hablan** español.
ellas	habl- **an**	Ellas **hablan** español.

—¿Qué idioma **hablan** Uds. con   *"What language **do you speak**
  el profesor?   with the professor?"*
—**Hablamos** español.   *"**We speak** Spanish."*

♦ Native speakers usually omit subject pronouns in conversation because the ending of each verb form indicates who is performing the action described by the verb. The context of the conversation also provides clues as to whom the verb refers. However, the forms **habla** and **hablan** are sometimes ambiguous even in context. Therefore, the subject pronouns **usted, él, ella, ustedes, ellos,** and **ellas** are used in speech with greater frequency than the other pronouns.

---

[1]The infinitive (unconjugated form) of a Spanish verb consists of a stem and an ending. The stem is what remains after the ending (**-ar, -er,** or **-ir**) is removed from the infinitive.

- Regular verbs ending in **-ar** are conjugated like **hablar.** Other verbs conjugated like **hablar** are **conversar, desear, estudiar, necesitar, terminar, tomar,** and **trabajar.**

—¿A qué hora **terminan** Uds. hoy? *"What time **do you finish** today?"*
—**Terminamos** a las tres. *"**We finish** at three o'clock."*

—¿Qué **necesitas**? *"What **do you need**?"*
—**Necesito** el horario de clases. *"**I need** the class schedule."*

> **¡Atención!** In Spanish, as in English, when two verbs are used together, the second verb remains in the infinitive.

Deseo **hablar** con Roberto. *I want **to speak** with Roberto.*

- The Spanish present tense has three equivalents in English.

Yo hablo.
I speak.
I am speaking.
I do speak.

Práctica y conversación

A. Olga habla con Sergio Complete the following conversation between two students. Use the present indicative of the verbs in the list. Then act it out with a partner.

desear   necesitar   tomar (2)   estudiar (2)   trabajar (2)   terminar (2)

Olga   ¿Cuántas clases _____ tú este semestre?

Sergio _____ cuatro clases.

Olga   Tú y Álvaro _____ en la cafetería, ¿no?

Sergio Sí, nosotros _____ los lunes y miércoles. Oye,

        ¿tú _____ tomar un vaso de agua?

Olga   Sí, gracias. ¿A qué hora _____ tú hoy?

Sergio Mis clases _____ a las 4 de la tarde.

Olga   ¿Tú y Álvaro _____ juntos en la biblioteca?

Sergio Sí, _____ por la noche. Ah, (yo) _____ tu número de teléfono.

Olga   Es el siete-treinta-veinticinco-doce.

B. Entreviste a su compañero(a) (*Interview your partner*) Interview your partner, using the following questions.

1. ¿Cuántas clases tomas este semestre?
2. ¿Qué asignaturas tomas? ¿Son fáciles o difíciles?
3. ¿Estudias en la biblioteca o en tu casa (*house*)?
4. ¿Trabajas en la universidad?
5. ¿Cuántas horas (*hours*) trabajas?
6. ¿Trabajas en el verano?
7. ¿Deseas un vaso de jugo o una botella de agua mineral?
8. ¿Tú tomas café o chocolate caliente? ¿Tú tomas vino?

Online Study Center

For more practice with lesson topics, see the related activities on the *¡Hola, amigos!* web site at college.hmco.com/PIC/holaamigos7e.

2. Interrogative and negative sentences
(Oraciones interrogativas y negativas)

Interrogative sentences

◆ In Spanish, there are three ways of asking a question to elicit a *yes/no* response.

¿**Elena** habla español?
¿Habla **Elena** español? ⎫ Sí, Elena habla español.
¿Habla español **Elena**? ⎭

◆ The three questions above ask for the same information and have the same meaning. The subject may be placed at the beginning of the sentence, after the verb, or at the end of the sentence. Note that written questions in Spanish begin with an inverted question mark.

—¿**Trabajan Uds.** en la biblioteca?   *"**Do you work** in the library?"*
—No, trabajamos en la cafetería.   *"No, we work in the cafeteria."*

—¿**Habla** español **la profesora**?   *"**Does the professor speak** Spanish?"*
—Sí, y también habla inglés.   *"Yes, and she also speaks English."*

—¿**Carmen es** bonita?   *"**Is Carmen** pretty?"*
—Sí y muy simpática.   *"Yes, and very charming."*

> **¡Atención!** Spanish does not use an auxiliary verb, such as *do* or *does,* in an interrogative sentence.

¿**Habla Ud.** inglés?   ***Do you speak** English?*
¿**Necesita él** el horario de clases?   ***Does he need** the class schedule?*

¿*Aceptan Uds. cheques?*

LIMONADA 25¢

Negative sentences

◆ To make a sentence negative in Spanish, simply place the word **no** in front of the verb.

Yo tomo café.   *I drink coffee.*
Yo **no** tomo café.   *I **don't** drink coffee.*

- If the answer to a question is negative, the word **no** appears twice: once at the beginning of the sentence, as in English, and again before the verb.

—¿Trabajan Uds. en la cafetería?   *"Do you work in the cafeteria?"*
—**No,** nosotros **no** trabajamos en   *"**No,** we **don't** work in the*
  la cafetería.   *cafeteria."*

¡Atención!   Spanish does not use an auxiliary verb, such as the English *do* or *does,* in a negative sentence.

Ella no estudia inglés.   ***She does not study*** English.
Yo no estudio hoy.   ***I do not study*** today.

Práctica y conversación

A. **¿Qué preguntó?** (*What did he ask?*) Complete the following dialogues by supplying the questions that would elicit the responses given.

1. —¿_____?
—Sí, estudiamos en la biblioteca.

2. —¿_____?
—No, este semestre tomo sociología.

3. —¿_____?
—No, deseamos agua mineral.

4. —¿_____?
—Sí, ellos trabajan en el verano.

5. —¿_____?
—No, tomo jugo.

6. —¿_____?
—No, deseo una taza de chocolate.

Online Study Center

For more practice with lesson topics, see the related activities on the *¡Hola, amigos!* web site at college.hmco.com/PIC/holaamigos7e.

B. **¿Quiere saber?**   This person wants to know many things. Use the cues provided to give him the information.

◆ **MODELO:**   —¿Ud. es de Miami? (Nueva York)
    —*No, no soy de Miami; soy de Nueva York.*

1. ¿Tú necesitas el libro?   (el horario de clases)
2. ¿Tú tomas café?   (té frío)
3. ¿Necesitamos muchos libros?   (dos)
4. ¿Rebeca es puertorriqueña?   (cubanoamericana)
5. ¿Elsa termina a las ocho?   (a las siete)
6. ¿Ellos hablan español?   (inglés)
7. ¿Es difícil la clase de geografía?   (fácil)
8. ¿Tu nueva compañera de cuarto es baja?   (alta)

C. **Sobre el diálogo** (*About the dialogue*)   With a partner, reread the dialogue on p. 22. Then ask each other questions that you know will elicit negative answers about the people in the dialogue.

◆ **MODELO:**   —*¿Lisa es mexicana?*
    —*No, Lisa no es mexicana, es norteamericana.*

3. Possessive adjectives (*Adjetivos posesivos*)

Forms of the Possessive Adjectives		
Singular	*Plural*	
mi	**mis**	my
tu	**tus**	your (*fam.*)
su	**sus**	your (*form.*) / his / her / its / their
nuestro(a)	**nuestros(as)**	our
vuestro(a)	**vuestros(as)**	your (*fam. pl.*)

◆ Possessive adjectives[1] always precede the nouns they introduce. They agree in number (singular or plural) with the nouns they modify.

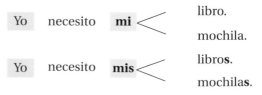

Yo   necesito   **mi**   libro. / mochila.

Yo   necesito   **mis**   libro**s**. / mochila**s**.

[1]See Appendix C.

- **Nuestro** and **vuestro** are the only possessive adjectives that have the feminine endings **-a** and **-as.** The others take the same endings for both genders.

Nosotros necesitamos
- **nuestro** libro.
- **nuestra** computadora.

Nosotros necesitamos
- **nuestros** libros.
- **nuestras** computadoras.

- Possessive adjectives agree with the thing possessed and *not* with the possessor. For instance, two male students would refer to their female professor as **nuestra profesora,** because **profesora** is feminine.

- Because **su** and **sus** have several possible meanings, the forms **de él, de ella, de ellos, de ellas, de Ud.,** or **de Uds.** can be substituted to avoid confusion. Use this pattern: *article* + *noun* + **de** + *pronoun.*

—¿Es **la amiga de él**?   *"Is she **his** friend?"*
—Sí, es **su** amiga.   *"Yes, she is **his** friend."*

La Pionera
RADIOLANDIA 1600
Penetrando en el
corazón del pueblo

En su hogar...
Su carro y su trabajo...

Escuche...La diferencia
En música y noticias...

Práctica y conversación

Online Study Center

For more practice with lesson topics, see the related activities on the *¡Hola, amigos!* web site at college.hmco.com/PIC/holaamigos7e.

A. En la clase Complete the following exchanges using the appropriate possessive adjectives that correspond to each subject. Then act them out with a partner.

1. —¿Tú necesitas _____ bolígrafo rojo?
   —Sí, necesito _____ bolígrafo rojo y _____ lápices negros.
2. —¿De dónde es la profesora de Uds.?
   —_____ profesora es de Los Ángeles.

3. —¿Qué necesita Roberto?

   —Necesita _____ cuadernos y _____ libro de español.

4. —Los alumnos de Uds., ¿son mexicanos?

   —No, _____ alumnos son argentinos.

5. —¿Qué necesita Ana? ¿ _____ mochila?

   —No, necesita _____ reloj.

B. Entreviste a su compañero(a) Interview your partner, using the following questions.

1. ¿De dónde es tu mejor (*best*) amigo(a)?

2. ¿Tus padres (*parents*) son de Miami?

3. ¿Necesitas tus libros hoy?

4. ¿Son interesantes tus clases?

5. ¿Es simpático(a) tu compañero(a) de cuarto?

6. ¿Tú y tus amigos estudian juntos?

7. ¿Dónde estudian?

8. ¿Las clases de Uds. son fáciles o difíciles?

4. Gender of nouns, part II (*Género de los nombres, parte II*)

Here are practical rules to help you determine the gender of those nouns that do not end in **-o** or **-a.** There are also a few important exceptions.

◆ Nouns ending in **-ción, -sión, -tad,** and **-dad** are feminine.

la lec**ción**	*lesson*	**la** liber**tad**	*liberty*
la televi**sión**	*television*	**la** universi**dad**	*university*

◆ Many words that end in **-ma** are masculine.

el progra**ma**	*program*	**el** cli**ma**	*climate*
el siste**ma**	*system*	**el** proble**ma**	*problem*
el te**ma**	*theme*	**el** poe**ma**	*poem*
el idio**ma**	*language*		

◆ The gender of nouns that have other endings and that do not refer to males or females must be learned. Remember that it is helpful to memorize a noun with its corresponding article.

el español	**el** borrador	**la** noche	**la** clase
el inglés	**el** reloj	**la** tarde	**la** leche
el café	**el** té	**la** luz	**la** calle

Práctica

Online Study Center

For more practice with lesson topics, see the related activities on the *¡Hola, amigos!* web site at college.hmco.com/PIC/holaamigos7e.

C. ¿Qué es...? For each illustration or set of words, give the Spanish noun together with its corresponding definite article.

1. _____ _____

2. _____ _____

3. francés, italiano, portugués
_____ _____

4. Harvard, Yale, Stanford.
_____ _____

5. _____ _____

6. _____ _____

7. _____ _____

8. _____ _____

9. Quito, Lima, Bogotá
_____ _____

10. "The Raven"
_____ _____

5. Numbers 40 to 200 (*Números de 40 a 200*)

40 cuarenta	90 noventa
41 cuarenta y uno	100 cien[1]
45 cuarenta y cinco	101 ciento uno
50 cincuenta	115 ciento quince
60 sesenta	175 ciento setenta y cinco
70 setenta	180 ciento ochenta
80 ochenta	200 doscientos

_____

[1]When counting beyond 100, **ciento** is used: **ciento uno**

Práctica y conversación

A. Sumas y restas With a partner, take turns solving the problems.

1. 27 + 13 =
2. 37 + 12 =
3. 90 + 15 =
4. 75 + 23 =

5. 52 − 20 =
6. 200 − 30 =
7. 65 − 35 =
8. 80 − 35 =

9. 16 + 56 =
10. 40 + 22 =
11. 200 − 10 =
12. 200 − 100 =

Online Study Center

For more practice with lesson topics, see the related activities on the *¡Hola, amigos!* web site at college.hmco.com/PIC/holaamigos7e.

B. Números de teléfono Ask three or four classmates their phone numbers. To give a phone number, say the first number alone and the rest in pairs. This pattern is common in many Spanish-speaking countries.

◆ **MODELO:** —*¿Cuál es tu número de teléfono?*
   —*Es el 9–24–85–97.*

6. Telling time (*La hora*)

◆ The following word order is used for telling time in Spanish:

Es la
or   +   hour   +   ***or***   +   minutes
Son las

Es la   **y**
or   +   hour   +   ***or***   +   minutes
Son las   **menos**

Es la una y veinte.   Son las cinco menos diez.

◆ **Es** is used with **una.**

Es la una y cuarto.   *It is a quarter after one.*

◆ **Son** is used with all the other hours.

Son las dos y cuarto.   *It is a quarter after two.*
Son las cinco y diez.   *It is ten after five.*

36 treinta y seis   ◆   Lección 2

Programación de Telecaribe				
VIERNES			
6:00	Telecaribe		**9:00**	Noticiero Televisa
6:50	Noticiero Cartagena T.V.		**9:30**	Las Amazonas
7:00	Champagne		**10:00**	Amor gitano
7:30	Esta sí es la Costa		**11:00**	Noticiero Cartagena T.V.
8:00	Coralito		**11:10**	Cierre

◆ The feminine definite article is always used before the hour, since it refers to **la hora.**

Es **la** una menos veinticinco.	*It is twenty-five to one.*
Son **las** cuatro y media.	*It is four-thirty.*

◆ The hour is given first, then the minutes.

Son las **cuatro** y **diez.**	*It is **ten** after **four.*** (literally, "four and ten")

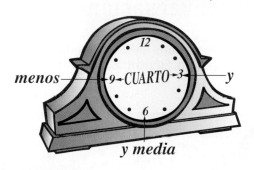

menos — *y*
CUARTO
y media

◆ The equivalent of *past* or *after* is **y.**

Son las doce **y** cinco.	*It is five **after** twelve.*

◆ The equivalent of *to* or *till* is **menos.** It is used with fractions of time up to a half hour.

Son las ocho **menos** veinte.	*It is twenty **to** eight.* (literally, "eight minus twenty")

¡Atención! To find out at what time an event will take place, use **¿A qué hora...?** as shown below. Observe that in the responses the equivalent of *at + time* is **a + la(s) +** *time.*

—**¿A qué hora** es la clase de arte?	*"**What time** is art class?"*
—**A la** una.	*"**At** one o'clock."*
—**¿A qué hora** termina Julio hoy?	*"**What time** does Julio finish today?"*
—**A las** cinco y media.	*"**At** five-thirty."*

◆ Note the difference between **de la** and **por la** in expressions of time.

  ◆ When a specific time is mentioned, **de la (mañana, tarde, noche)** should be used. This is the equivalent to the English A.M. and P.M.

Estudiamos a las **cuatro de la tarde.**	*We study at 4 P.M.*

◆ When no specific time is mentioned, **por la (mañana, tarde, noche)** should be used.

Yo trabajo **por la mañana** y ella trabaja **por la noche.**

*I work **in the morning** and she works **at night.***

Detalles culturales

Para los horarios de aviones (*planes*), trenes, autobuses y algunas (*some*) invitaciones, se usa el sistema de veinticuatro horas. Por ejemplo, las cuatro de la tarde son las dieciséis horas.

◆ **¿Hay un sistema similar en este país?**

Online Study Center

For more practice with lesson topics, see the related activities on the *¡Hola, amigos!* web site at college.hmco.com/PIC/holaamigos7e.

Práctica y conversación

A. ¿Qué hora es? Give the time indicated on the following clocks, writing out the numerals in Spanish. Start with clock number one; then read the times aloud.

B. Entreviste a su compañero(a) Interview your partner, asking the following questions.

1. ¿A qué hora es tu primera (*first*) clase?
2. ¿A qué hora termina?
3. ¿A qué hora termina tu última clase?
4. ¿Estudias por la mañana, por la tarde o por la noche?
5. ¿Mañana estudiamos juntos(as)? ¿A qué hora deseas estudiar?
6. ¿A qué hora trabajas?
7. ¿A qué hora terminas de trabajar?
8. ¿A qué hora es tu programa de televisión favorito?

C. Nuestros horarios With a partner, talk about your class schedule. Indicate whether your classes are in the morning, afternoon, or evening.

7. Days of the week, and months and seasons of the year
(*Los días de la semana, y los meses y las estaciones del año*)

lunes	martes	miércoles	jueves	viernes	sábado	domingo
				Estudiar con Ana 2	¡Fiesta! 3	4
Examen de arte 5	6	7	8	9	10	11
12	Clase de tenis 13	14	Conferencia 15	16	17	Programa religioso 18
19	20	21	22	23	24	25
26	27	Examen de inglés 28	29	Clase de yoga 30	31	

MARZO 2007 (day 1 in jueves column)

Days of the week (*Los días de la semana*)

- In Spanish-speaking countries, the week begins on Monday.
- Note that the days of the week are not capitalized in Spanish.
- The days of the week are masculine in Spanish. The masculine definite articles **el** and **los** are used with them to express *on:* **el lunes, los martes,** etc.
- To ask: "What day is today?" say: **"¿Qué día es hoy?"**

Months of the year (*Los meses del año*)

enero	*January*	**mayo**	*May*	**septiembre**	*September*
febrero	*February*	**junio**	*June*	**octubre**	*October*
marzo	*March*	**julio**	*July*	**noviembre**	*November*
abril	*April*	**agosto**	*August*	**diciembre**	*December*

¡Atención! In Spanish, months are not capitalized.

Seasons of the year (*Las estaciones del año*)

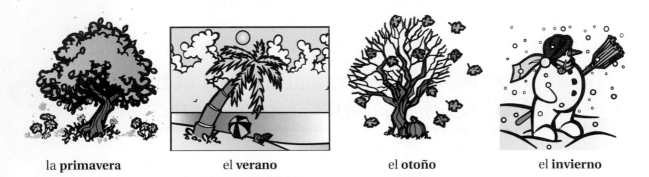

la **primavera**   el **verano**   el **otoño**   el **invierno**

- Note that all the seasons are masculine except **la primavera.**
- To ask for the date, say:

  ¿Qué fecha es hoy?   *What's the date today?*

- When telling the date, always begin with the expression **Hoy es...**

  Hoy es el 20 de mayo.   *Today is May 20.*

- Note that the number is followed by the preposition **de** (*of*), and then the month.

  el 15 de mayo   *May 15*
  el 10 de septiembre   *September 10*
  el 12 de octubre   *October 12*

- The ordinal number **primero** (*first*) is used when referring to the first day of the month.[1]

  el primero de febrero   *February 1*

  —¿Qué fecha es hoy, el   *"What's the date today,*
   primero de octubre?   ***October 1**?"*
  —No, hoy es el **2 de octubre.**   *"No, today is **October 2.**"*

---

[1] In Spanish today, many people say **el uno de: el uno de febrero.**

Práctica y conversación

Online Study Center

For more practice with lesson topics, see the related activities on the *¡Hola, amigos!* web site at college.hmco.com/PIC/holaamigos7e.

A. Mi calendario With a partner, look at the calendar on p. 39 and take turns asking each other on which day each event takes place.

◆ **MODELO:** —¿Cuándo estudio con Ana?
—El viernes 2.

B. Fechas importantes On what dates do the following annual events take place?

1. Independence Day
2. Halloween
3. New Year's Day
4. Washington's birthday
5. Christmas
6. the first day of spring
7. April Fool's Day
8. Veteran's Day

C. Las estaciones del año In which season does each of these months fall in the Northern Hemisphere?

1. febrero
2. agosto
3. mayo
4. enero
5. octubre
6. julio
7. abril
8. noviembre

D. ¿Cuándo es? On what dates do the following events occur?

1. your mother's birthday
2. your father's birthday
3. your best friend's birthday
4. your birthday
5. the first day of classes this semester
6. the end of classes

E. Feliz cumpleaños Ask four or five classmates when their birthday is. Ask: **¿Cuándo es tu cumpleaños?** Choose one of the birthdays and announce it to the rest of the class:

El cumpleaños de _____ es el _____ de _____.

Detalles culturales

Las estaciones ocurren en épocas opuestas en los dos hemisferios. Por ejemplo, cuando en Estados Unidos y Canadá (hemisferio norte) es verano; en Chile y Argentina (hemisferio sur) es invierno.

◆ **¿Cuál es su estación favorita?**

Detalles culturales

Los hispanos generalmente celebran, además del día de su cumpleaños, el día de su santo, que corresponde al santo de su nombre en el calendario católico. Patricio celebra su santo el 17 de marzo.
(*St. Patrick's Day*)

◆ **¿Le gusta la idea de celebrar su santo? ¿Sabe Ud. cuándo es?**

Entre nosotros

¡Conversemos!

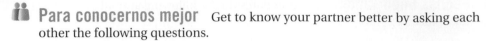 **Para conocernos mejor**   Get to know your partner better by asking each other the following questions.

1. ¿Qué asignaturas tomas tú este semestre?
2. ¿Cuál es tu clase favorita?
3. ¿Conversas con tus amigos en la cafetería? ¿Tomas café con ellos?
4. ¿Cuántas horas estudias? ¿Cuántas horas trabajas?
5. ¿Tú trabajas los sábados? ¿Y los domingos?
6. En el verano, ¿tomas clases o trabajas?
7. ¿Qué clases deseas tomar el próximo semestre?
8. ¿Qué estación te gusta?
9. ¿Deseas tomar café, leche o té?
10. ¿Deseas agua con hielo o jugo de naranja?

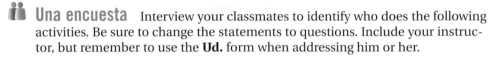 **Una encuesta**   Interview your classmates to identify who does the following activities. Be sure to change the statements to questions. Include your instructor, but remember to use the **Ud.** form when addressing him or her.

Nombre

1. Trabaja por la noche.
2. Trabaja cuatro horas al día (a day).
3. Toma clases en el verano.
4. Toma mucho café.
5. Toma cerveza o vino.
6. Estudia los domingos.
7. Estudia en la biblioteca.
8. Toma danza aeróbica.
9. Toma una clase de psicología.
10. Desea tomar una clase de música.

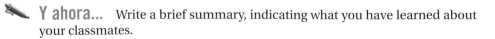 **Y ahora...**   Write a brief summary, indicating what you have learned about your classmates.

¿Cómo lo decimos?   What would you say in the following situations? What might the other person say? Act out the scenes with a partner.

1. You want to ask a friend what subjects he or she is taking this semester.

2. You want to tell someone what subjects you are taking.
3. You want to ask someone where he or she works.
4. You want to order something to drink.
5. You want to know the time.
6. You want to ask a classmate if his/her classes are easy or difficult.

 ¿Qué dice aquí?   With a classmate, study Virginia's schedule and take turns asking each other the following questions.

1. ¿Qué días tiene (*has*) Virginia la clase de historia? ¿A qué hora?
2. ¿Cuántas clases tiene Virginia por la noche?
3. ¿Qué clases tiene ella los (*on*) lunes, miércoles y viernes a las ocho?
4. ¿Qué idioma estudia Virginia? ¿Qué días?
5. ¿Cuándo estudia con el grupo?
6. ¿A qué hora almuerza (*has lunch*) Virginia? ¿Dónde?
7. ¿Dónde trabaja Virginia?
8. ¿Cuántas horas trabaja por semana (*per week*)?
9. ¿Qué clases incluyen laboratorio?
10. ¿Qué estudia Virginia los sábados?

Horario de Virginia

	Lunes	Martes	Miércoles	Jueves	Viernes	Sábado
8:00	Biología		Biología		Biología	
9:00	Japonés	Japonés	Japonés	Japonés		
10:00	Estudiar con el grupo		Estudiar con el grupo		Estudiar con el grupo	Cibernética
11:00		Educación física		Educación física		
12:00	Cafetería	Cafetería	Cafetería	Cafetería	Cafetería	
1:00		Biología (Laboratorio)		Japonés (Laboratorio)		
2:00	Trabajar en la biblioteca					
3:00						
4:00						
5:00						
6:00						
7:00	Historia		Historia			
8:00						

Un dicho

El saber no ocupa lugar.

This is a popular saying in Spanish; find out what it means. It doesn't have an equivalent in English. Can you make up one?

Para escribir

Tu horario   With a partner, create a schedule for him or her. Use the following questions to ask about your partner's schedule.

¿Qué clases tomas?
¿Qué días es la clase de...? ¿A qué hora?
¿Trabajas? ¿Qué días? ¿A qué hora?
¿Cuándo estudias? ¿A qué hora? ¿Dónde? ¿Con quién?

Lectura

Estrategia de lectura   The selection you are going to read talks about registration procedures at the **Universidad Nacional.** What types of information would you expect to find in such instructions?

Vamos a leer   As you read **Información sobre la matrícula,** find the answer to each of the following questions.

1. ¿Qué necesita revisar (*check*) el estudiante?
2. ¿Qué debe notificar?
3. ¿Qué debe hacer (*to do*) para tomar más de (*more than*) 18 unidades?
4. ¿Debe asistir (*attend*) a todas las clases?
5. ¿Qué información debe tener (*must have*) el carnet de estudiante?
6. ¿Cuándo debe pagar la matrícula (*pay tuition*)?
7. ¿Qué debe hacer si necesita un plan de pago (*payment*) especial?
8. ¿Con quién debe hablar si necesita cambiar (*to change*) una clase?

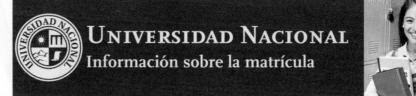

UNIVERSIDAD NACIONAL
Información sobre la matrícula

El estudiante debe:
- revisar su horario de clases
- notificar cualquier error
- recibir la aprobación de la Administración para tomar más de 18 unidades
- asistir a todas las clases
- sacar un carnet de estudiante con su nombre, su número de identificación y su foto
- pagar la matrícula antes del primer día de clases
- llenar una solicitud en la Oficina de Administración si necesita un plan de pago especial
- hablar con un consejero si necesita cambiar una clase

Video

¿Cuántas clases toma cada (*each*) uno de estos estudiantes? ¿Trabajan o solamente estudian?

Díganos Answer the following questions, based on your own thoughts and experience.

1. ¿Revisa Ud. su horario de clases cuidadosamente (*carefully*)?
2. ¿Toma usted más o menos de (*less than*) 18 unidades?
3. ¿Asiste usted a todas las clases?
4. ¿Qué información tiene su carnet de estudiante?
5. ¿Cuánto es la matrícula en su universidad?
6. ¿Necesita usted un plan de pago especial?
7. ¿Habla usted con un(a) consejero(a) (*adviser*) o con un(a) profesor(a) si necesita cambiar una clase?

Dos amigos

Pablo y Marisa, estudiantes de la Universidad de Costa Rica, estudian juntos y son buenos amigos. Cuando Marisa conoce a (*meets*) Fernando y Pablo conoce a Victoria, los dos amigos están un poco celosos (*jealous*).

Los mexicoamericanos

◆ En los Estados Unidos (*United States*) hay unos 40 millones de hispanos. El 66 por ciento (%) son de origen mexicano. La mayoría de ellos están (*are*) concentrados principalmente en California, Texas, Nuevo México y Arizona.

◆ El grado (*degree*) de asimilación a la cultura norteamericana de los mexicoamericanos es muy diverso. Unos se adaptan fácilmente (*easily*) y otros no. La mayoría conserva su lengua y su unidad familiar.

◆ Muchos mexicoamericanos se destacan (*stand out*) en la política: Bill Richarson, gobernador de Nuevo México, Cruz Bustamante, vicegobernador de California y Ken Salazar, senador por Colorado; en educación: France Córdova, rectora de la Universidad de California, Riverside; en literatura: Rosaura Sánchez y Rolando Hinojosa; en música, cine y televisión: Carlos Santana, Eduardo James Olmos, George López y Eva Longoria. Muchos mexicoamericanos han ganado (*have earned*) honores en las fuerzas armadas.

▲ La famosa actriz hispana Eva Longoria en una fiesta en Pasadena, California.

Los cubanoamericanos

◆ Más de medio (*a half*) millón de cubanos viven en Miami, donde ejercen una gran influencia cultural y económica. Antes de la llegada (*arrival*) de los cubanos en 1959, Miami era (*was*) fundamentalmente un centro turístico. Hoy es un centro industrial y comercial de primer orden (*first-class*) y el puente (*bridge*) que une la economía de los Estados Unidos con la de América Latina y con la de España (*Spain*).

◆ Los cubanos son el 4 por ciento de los hispanos de este país, y como buena parte de ellos vinieron (*came*) por razones políticas, no económicas, son los inmigrantes hispanos más conservadores, con mayor nivel de escolaridad y mayor ingreso (*income*) per cápita. Entre los más conocidos se destacan en la política: Ileana Ros-Lehtinen y Rafael Díaz Balart, Representantes al Congreso de los Estados Unidos; en el cine: Andy García y Cameron Díaz; y en la música: Jon Secada, Gloria Estefan y Celia Cruz (1925–2003).

◆ En la Pequeña Habana, un barrio (*neighborhood*) cubano de Miami, el español es el idioma más hablado (*spoken*).

▲ La cantante cubana Celia Cruz, ganadora de un Premio Grammy en el año 2003.

Los puertorriqueños

◆ Los puertorriqueños son el segundo (*second*) grupo más grande (*largest*) de hispanos en los Estados Unidos. Como Puerto Rico es un Estado Libre Asociado a este país (*country*), los puertorriqueños son ciudadanos estadounidenses y no necesitan pasaporte ni visa para entrar en el país. En total, más de 2.700.000 puertorriqueños viven en los Estados Unidos, el 70 por ciento de ellos en Nueva York y Nueva Jersey. Más puertorriqueños viven en Nueva York que en San Juan, la capital de Puerto Rico.

◆ La mayoría de los puertorriqueños llegaron (*arrived*) a este país después de la Segunda Guerra Mundial (*World War II*) y, para muchos, fue (*it was*) muy difícil adaptarse a la vida (*life*) de la gran ciudad. En las últimas décadas, han llegado de Puerto Rico miles de profesionales, artistas y gente de negocios (*businesspeople*). Hoy hay puertorriqueños famosos en todos los campos (*fields*). Son buenos ejemplos de estos éxitos Nydia Velázquez y José Serrano, congresistas; Marc Anthony, Ricky Martin y Chayanne, cantantes (*singers*); Jennifer López, Benicio del Toro y muchos más, artistas de Hollywood; Félix (Tito) Trinidad, ex triple campeón de boxeo, etc.

▲ Marc Anthony y Jennifer López en una fiesta de Premios de la Vanity Fair Academy en Los Angeles.

Comentarios...
With a partner, answer these questions about the different Hispanic groups found in this country.

1. ¿Cuál es el grupo más numeroso de hispanos en este país?
2. ¿La mayoría de los mexicoamericanos están (*are*) en el Suroeste (*Southwest*) o en el Sureste (*Southeast*) de los Estados Unidos?
3. ¿En qué campos se destacan muchos mexicoamericanos?
4. ¿Por qué razones vinieron (*came*) a este país la mayor parte de los cubanos?
5. ¿Cómo se llama el barrio cubano de la ciudad de Miami?
6. ¿En qué ciudad norteamericana viven más puertorriqueños que en San Juan, Puerto Rico?
7. ¿Puede Ud. (*can you*) mencionar algunos hispanos importantes?
8. En su estado, ¿cuál es el grupo de hispanos más numeroso?

 **Online Study Center**

For more practice with lesson topics, see the related activities on the *¡Hola, amigos!* web site at college.hmco.com/PIC/holaamigos7e.

Tome este examen

Lección 1

A. Gender of nouns; plural forms of nouns; definite and indefinite articles Place the corresponding definite and indefinite article before each noun.

Definite	Indefinite	Nouns
1. _____	_____	lápices
2. _____	_____	días
3. _____	_____	hombre
4. _____	_____	mujeres
5. _____	_____	mano
6. _____	_____	silla
7. _____	_____	borradores
8. _____	_____	mapas

B. Subject pronouns Say which pronoun would be used to talk about the following people.

1. Ana y yo (*f.*)
2. Jorge y Rafael
3. la Dra. García
4. usted y el Sr. López
5. Amalia y Teresa
6. el doctor Torres

Now give the pronouns used to address the following people.

7. your professor
8. your best friend

C. Present indicative of *ser* Complete the following sentences, using the present indicative of the verb *ser.*

1. Yo _____ mexicana y John _____ norteamericano.
2. ¿Uds. _____ de Los Ángeles?
3. Teresa y yo _____ estudiantes.
4. Las plumas _____ rojas.
5. ¿Tú _____ de San Diego?
6. ¿De dónde _____ Ud.?

D. Forms of adjectives and agreement of articles, nouns, and adjectives   Change each sentence according to each new element.

1. Las alumnas son norteamericanas.   (*alumno*)
2. Las tizas son verdes.   (*lápices*)
3. El escritorio es blanco.   (*mesas*)
4. Es una mujer española.   (*hombre*)
5. El profesor es inglés.   (*profesoras*)
6. La chica es rica.   (*muchachos*)
7. Es un hombre inteligente   (*mujer*)
8. La señora es muy simpática.   (*señores*)

E. The alphabet   Spell the following last names in Spanish.

1. Díaz
2. Jiménez
3. Vargas
4. Parra
5. Feliú
6. Acuña

F. Numbers 0–39   Write the following numbers in Spanish.

1. 8 _____
2. 14 _____
3. 26 _____
4. 11 _____
5. 35 _____
6. 10 _____
7. 13 _____
8. 0 _____
9. 28 _____
10. 17 _____
11. 39 _____
12. 15 _____

G. Vocabulary   Complete the following sentences, using vocabulary from **Lección 1.**

1. ¿Cómo se _____ Ud.? ¿Teresa? ¿De _____ es Ud.?
2. Mucho _____, señor Vargas.
3. ¿Cómo se _____ *"desk"* en español?
4. Mi compañera de _____ es _____ bonita.
5. Hay una profesora y diez _____ en la clase.
6. Rosa _____ con el profesor.
7. Buenos días. ¿Cómo _____ usted? ¿Bien?
8. Adiós. _____ a Marisa.
9. ¿Cómo _____ Sergio? ¿Guapo?
10. —Muchas gracias
    —De _____.

H. Culture   Circle the correct answer, based on the cultural notes you have read.

1. El nombre María (no es/es) muy popular en los países hispanos.
2. El título "señorita" se usa solamente para mujeres (casadas / que no se han casado).

Lección 2

A. Present indicative of -ar verbs
Complete each sentence with the correct form of the verb in parentheses.

1. ¿Tú _____ leche? (*drink*)
2. La señora Paz _____ con los alumnos. (*talks*)
3. Nosotros _____ inglés con la doctora Torres. (*speak*)
4. Yo _____ tomar café. (*wish*)
5. ¿Ud. _____ matemáticas o biología? (*study*)
6. Ana y Paco _____ en la biblioteca. (*work*)
7. Ernesto _____ la pluma roja. (*needs*)
8. Eva y yo _____ en agosto. (*finish*)

B. Interrogative and negative sentences
Convert the following statements first into questions and then into negative statements.

1. Ellos hablan inglés con los estudiantes.
   a. _____
   b. _____
2. Ella es de México.
   a. _____
   b. _____
3. Ustedes terminan hoy.
   a. _____
   b. _____

C. Possessive adjectives
Complete these sentences, using the Spanish equivalent of the word in parentheses.

1. ¿Tú necesitas _____ libro? (*your*)
2. Yo hablo con _____ profesor. (*her*)
3. Nosotros necesitamos hablar con _____ profesora. (*our*)
4. Trabajo con _____ compañeros de clase. (*my*)
5. ¿Ud. desea hablar con _____ amigos? (*your*)
6. Carlos habla con _____ profesores. (*our*)
7. Los estudiantes necesitan hablar con _____ profesor. (*their*)
8. Necesito _____ número de teléfono. (*his*)

D. Gender of nouns (Part II)
Write *el, la, los,* or *las* before each of the following nouns.

1. _____ lecciones
2. _____ relojes
3. _____ idioma
4. _____ unidades
5. _____ problemas
6. _____ café
7. _____ libertad
8. _____ televisión

E. Numbers 40–200
Write the following phrases in Spanish. (Write the numbers in words.)

1. 80 ballpoint pens
2. 46 backpacks
3. 72 clocks
4. 33 windows
5. 200 books
6. 115 notebooks

7. 68 students

8. 50 maps

9. 95 computers

10. 73 wastebaskets

11. 100 pens

12. 113 erasers

F. Telling time   Write the Spanish equivalent of the words in parentheses.

1. Oye, ¿qué hora es? ¿_____? (*Is it one o'clock?*)

2. Luis toma química _____. (*at nine-thirty in the morning*)

3. Estudiamos español _____. (*in the afternoon*)

4. _____ las ocho. (*It's*)

5. La clase es _____. (*at a quarter to three*)

G. Days of the week, and months and seasons of the year   Write the names of the missing days.

lunes, _____, _____, jueves, _____, _____, domingo

Give the following dates in Spanish.

1. March 1

2. June 10

3. August 13

4. December 26

5. September 3

6. October 28

7. July 17

8. April 4

9. January 2

10. February 5

What seasons do these months fall in the Northern Hemisphere?

1. febrero

2. abril

3. octubre

4. julio

H. Vocabulary   Complete the following sentences, using vocabulary from **Lección 2.**

1. ¿Qué _____ es? ¿Las dos?

2. Necesito el _____ de clases. ¡Ah! ¡ _____ está!

3. Yo tomo _____ dos clases.

4. Deseo una _____ de café y un _____ de agua.

5. ¿Ellos _____ café en la cafetería?

6. Este _____ tomo tres clases.

7. Marzo, abril y mayo son los meses de la _____.

8. ¿Qué _____ estudias? ¿Historia?

9. Él toma una _____ de vino.

10. Deseo tomar _____ de manzana.

11. Eva es muy aburrida; es una _____.

12. Trabajo porque necesito _____.

I. Culture   Circle the correct answer, based on the cultural notes you have read.

1. El (30 / 66) por ciento de los hispanos que viven en los Estados Unidos son de origen mexicano.

2. En las tiendas de la Pequeña Habana, el idioma más hablado es el (español / inglés).

3. Los puertorriqueños son el (segundo / primer) grupo de hispanos más grande en los Estados Unidos.

Unidad  2

Objetivos

Lección 3

- Talk about household chores
- Talk about family
- Talk about how you feel

Lección 4

- Discuss plans for a party
- Extend, accept, and decline invitations
- Handle informal social situations such as parties

Una pareja celebra su boda en el Malecón en Puerto Vallarta.

En familia

Lección 3
Los trabajos de la casa

Lección 4
Una fiesta de cumpleaños

México

Vista panorámica de la Plaza de Las Tres Culturas, en México.

Guatemala

Estos turistas admiran un templo en Tikal, Guatemala.

El Salvador

El volcán Izalco, el más nuevo del país

Lección 3 • Los trabajos de la casa

Hoy es un día muy ocupado para Susana, Alicia y Héctor, tres hermanos que viven con sus padres en la Ciudad de México.

Alicia   Esta noche vienen papá y mamá de Guadalajara y esta casa es un desastre.

Susana   Sí, especialmente el cuarto de Héctor. ¡Héctor! Tienes que limpiar tu recámara.

Alicia   Y también tienes que sacar la basura y cortar el zacate.

Héctor   Ustedes dos son muy mandonas. Yo siempre tengo que hacer todo el trabajo en esta casa.

Susana   ¡Ja! Tu ocupación favorita es comer porque siempre tienes hambre.

Alicia   Yo creo que lo mejor es dividir el trabajo: yo limpio la cocina y los baños, Susana sacude los muebles de la sala y Héctor barre el garaje.

Héctor   ¡Yo hago todo eso! No tengo tiempo porque viene Carlos para estudiar conmigo.

Susana   Tú siempre tienes excusas para no trabajar.

Detalles culturales

Actualmente (*At present*) muchos hombres hispanos, especialmente los más jóvenes, ayudan (*help*) a su esposa con los trabajos de la casa. Esto es debido a que, generalmente, los dos trabajan fuera de casa.

◆ **¿Los esposos norteamericanos ayudan con los trabajos de la casa?**

Detalles culturales

México tiene una comida típica excelente que hoy es popular en todo el mundo (*world*), pero en las grandes ciudades mexicanas los restaurantes sirven también comida internacional.

◆ **¿Qué comidas son típicas de su país?**

Esa tarde.

Alicia	Todavía tenemos que lavar y planchar la ropa y lavar los platos.
Susana	¡Hay mil cosas que hacer!
Héctor	¿Por qué no descansamos un rato y bebemos una limonada? Yo tengo mucha sed.
Alicia	Tienes razón. Hay limonada en el refrigerador.
Susana	Bueno... descansamos un momento, pero después debemos pasar la aspiradora y preparar la comida.
Héctor	Yo hago la ensalada y ustedes preparan las enchiladas.
Alicia	¿Y quién pone la mesa?
Susana	Yo. Héctor, oye. Tocan a la puerta.
Héctor	Debe ser Carlos. (*Héctor corre a abrir.*)

Esa noche, cuando llegan los padres, todos cenan y conversan en el comedor y después la mamá y las chicas miran su telenovela favorita.

Detalles culturales

La música mexicana es conocida (*known*) en todos los países y sus telenovelas se ven (*are seen*) no solamente en el mundo hispano sino que también son populares en países como Rusia y Japón.

◆ **¿Qué telenovelas de su país son famosas?**

¿Recuerda usted?

¿Verdadero o falso?   With a partner, decide whether the following statements about the dialogue are true (**verdadero**) or false (**falso**).

1.	Susana, Alicia y Héctor son hermanos.	☐ V ☐ F
2.	Los padres de los chicos vienen de Acapulco.	☐ V ☐ F
3.	Héctor tiene que limpiar su cuarto.	☐ V ☐ F
4.	Héctor dice (*says*) que sus hermanas son muy mandonas.	☐ V ☐ F
5.	Héctor come mucho.	☐ V ☐ F
6.	Susana limpia la cocina y los baños.	☐ V ☐ F
7.	Por la tarde, los chicos todavía tienen que lavar los platos.	☐ V ☐ F
8.	Los chicos beben jugo de uvas.	☐ V ☐ F
9.	Alicia prepara la ensalada.	☐ V ☐ F
10.	Tocan a la puerta. Son los padres de los chicos.	☐ V ☐ F

Y ahora... conteste   Answer these questions, basing your answers on the dialogue.

1. ¿De dónde vienen los padres de los chicos?
2. Según (*According to*) Susana, ¿cuál es la ocupación favorita de Héctor?
3. ¿Quién sacude los muebles de la sala?
4. ¿Quién viene a estudiar con Héctor?
5. ¿Dónde hay limonada?
6. ¿Qué preparan las chicas?
7. ¿Dónde cenan todos?
8. ¿Qué miran la mamá y las chicas?

Para hablar del tema: Vocabulario

Online Study Center

For more practice with lesson topics, see the related activities on the *¡Hola, amigos!* web site at college.hmco.com/PIC/holaamigos7e.

Cognados

el desastre
la ensalada
la excusa
la familia

favorito(a)
el garaje
la limonada

el momento
la ocupación
el refrigerador*

Nombres

el baño, el cuarto de baño bathroom
la basura garbage
la casa house
la ciudad city
la cocina kitchen
la comida meal, food
la cosa thing
el cuarto room
la hermana sister
el hermano brother
la mamá mom

los muebles furniture
los padres parents
el papá dad
el plato plate, dish
el dormitorio* bedroom
la ropa clothes
la sala living room
la telenovela soap opera
el tiempo time
el trabajo work
los trabajos de la casa housework
el césped* lawn

Adjetivos

este(a) this
mandón(ona) bossy
ocupado(a) busy

Verbos

abrir to open
barrer to sweep
beber to drink
cenar to dine
comer to eat
cortar to cut, to mow
deber to have to, must
descansar to rest
hacer (yo hago) to do, to make
lavar to wash

limpiar to clean
llegar to arrive
mirar to watch, to look at
planchar to iron
preparar to prepare
sacar to take out
sacudir* to dust
tener to have
venir to come
vivir to live

De país a país

el refrigerador la heladera (*Méx.*, Cono Sur) la nevera (*Esp.*)
el dormitorio la recámara (*Méx.*)
el césped el zacate (*Méx.*)
sacudir limpiar el polvo (*Esp.*)

conmigo with me
cortar el césped to mow the lawn
cosas que hacer things to do
cuando when
después after
eso that
especialmente especially
mil a thousand
para for, in order to
pasar la aspiradora to vacuum
poner la mesa to set the table
¿Quién (es)? Who (is it)?

siempre always
tener hambre to be hungry
tener que + *infinitivo* to have
to + *infinitive*
tener razón to be right
tener sed to be thirsty
tocar (llamar) a la puerta to knock
at the door
todavía still
todo(a) all
un rato a while

Amplíe su vocabulario

Aparatos electrodomésticos y batería de cocina (*Home appliances and kitchen utensils*)

el horno de microondas
el colador
el tazón
la lavadora
la licuadora
la cacerola
la cafetera
la tostadora
la sartén
la plancha
el horno
el lavaplatos
la secadora

Para practicar el vocabulario

A. Preguntas y respuestas Match the questions in column *A* with the answers in column *B*.

A	B
1. ¿A qué hora cenan? ____	**a.** No, la mamá.
2. ¿Qué necesitas? ____	**b.** Conmigo.
3. ¿Quién viene hoy? ____	**c.** Limonada.
4. ¿Ella es la hermana de Eva? ____	**d.** No, mi papá.
5. ¿Dónde viven? ____	**e.** No, gracias; no tengo sed.
6. ¿Qué deseas beber? ____	**f.** Mi hermano.
7. ¿Comes en tu cuarto? ____	**g.** Una telenovela.
8. ¿Con quién estudia Luis? ____	**h.** ¡No! ¡Siempre trabaja!
9. ¿Deseas una Coca-Cola? ____	**i.** A las ocho de la noche.
10. ¿Quién hace los trabajos de la casa? ¿Tu hermano? ____	**j.** En la ciudad de Lima.
	k. No, en la cocina.
11. ¿No descansa? ____	**l.** ¡Muchas cosas!
12. ¿Qué miran por la noche? ____	

B. ¡Hay mil cosas que hacer! Complete these exchanges, using vocabulary from Lección 3. Then act them out with a partner.

1. —¿Qué _____ (nosotros) que hacer hoy?
   —Tenemos que _____ los muebles, _____ los platos y _____ el baño y la cocina.

2. —Tengo que _____ la aspiradora y _____ la comida.
   —Yo tengo que _____ el garaje, _____ el césped y _____ la basura.

3. —Oye, Sara. Tienes que planchar la _____ y _____ la mesa.
   —Un _____, mamá. Tengo mucha _____ y deseo _____ una limonada.

¿Quiénes son estas personas y qué tienen que hacer hoy?

C. ¿Qué necesitas? With a partner, look at the following list and take turns asking each other whether you need certain items.

◆ MODELO: —¿Necesitas la lavadora?
—Sí, porque tengo que lavar la ropa.

1. lavar la ropa
2. secar (*dry*) la ropa
3. planchar
4. lavar los platos
5. tostar el pan (*bread*)

6. preparar un batido (*shake*)
7. hacer sopa (*soup*)
8. preparar una ensalada
9. colar (*strain*) espaguetis
10. hacer café

D. Los trabajos de la casa With a partner, play the roles of two family members trying to divide the housework by negotiating.

◆ MODELO: —Si tú preparas la ensalada, yo lavo los platos.

¿Qué quehaceres de la casa tienen que hacer Estela y su mamá después de comer?

Pronunciación

Las consonantes (*consonants*) b, v In Spanish, **b** and **v** have the same bilabial sound. To practice this sound, pronounce the following words, paying particular attention to the sound of **b** and **v.**

| **b** | **b**asura | **b**arrer | **b**eber | **b**año | a**b**rir | **B**ena**v**ente |
| **v** | di**v**idir | **v**iene | **v**i**v**ir | la**v**ar | fa**v**orito | |

Puntos para recordar

1. Present indicative of *-er* and *-ir* verbs
(*Presente de indicativo de los verbos terminados en -er y en -ir*)

comer (*to eat*)		vivir (*to live*)	
yo	com**o**	yo	viv**o**
tú	com**es**	tú	viv**es**
Ud.		Ud.	
él	com**e**	él	viv**e**
ella		ella	
nosotros(as)	com**emos**	nosotros(as)	viv**imos**
vosotros(as)	com**éis**	vosotros(as)	viv**ís**
Uds.		Uds.	
ellos	com**en**	ellos	viv**en**
ellas		ellas	

◆ Regular verbs ending in **-er** are conjugated like **comer.** Other regular **-er** verbs are **barrer, beber, correr** (*to run*), **creer, leer** (*to read*), and **deber.**

—Uds. **beben** café, ¿no? — ***You drink** coffee, don't you?"*
—No, **bebemos** limonada. — *"No, **we drink** lemonade."*

—¿Nosotros **debemos** poner la mesa? — ***Do we have to** set the table?"*
—No, Uds. **deben** preparar la comida. — *"No, **you must** prepare the food."*

◆ Regular verbs ending in **-ir** are conjugated like **vivir.** Other regular **-ir** verbs are **abrir, escribir** (*to write*), **recibir** (*to receive*), **sacudir,** and **dividir.**

—Tú **escribes** en inglés, ¿no? — ***You write** in English, don't you?"*
—No, **escribo** en español. — *"No, **I write** in Spanish."*

—¿Uds. **viven** en D.F.[1]? — ***Do you live** in D.F.?"*
—No, nosotros **vivimos** en Guadalajara. — *"No, **we live** in Guadalajara."*

—¿Qué **sacudes** tú? — *"What do **you dust**?"*
—Yo **sacudo** los muebles de la sala. — *"**I dust** the living room furniture."*

---

[1]Distrito Federal (Mexico City)

Vivo en un apartamento.

Práctica y conversación

A. Minidiálogos Complete the following exchanges appropriately, using the present indicative of the verbs in the list. Then act them out with a partner.

1. vivir

—¿Dónde _____ Uds.?

—Nosotros _____ en Guanajuato.

—¿Y Pablo?

—Él _____ en Puebla.

2. comer

—¿A qué hora _____ tú?

—Yo _____ a las dos.

3. leer

—¿Qué libro _____ Uds.?

—Nosotros _____ *El Quijote.*[1]

4. beber

—¿Ud. _____ vino tinto?

—No, yo _____ vino blanco.

5. correr

—¿Uds. _____ por la mañana?

—Sí, nosotros _____ por la mañana, pero Carlos _____ por la tarde.

6. sacudir

—¿Tú _____ los muebles de la sala?

—No, yo _____ los muebles del dormitorio.

---

[1] *El ingenioso hidalgo don Quijote de la Mancha,* Miguel de Cervantes's famous novel.

7. deber

—¿Qué _____ limpiar Uds.?

—Yo _____ limpiar el baño y Alicia _____ limpiar la cocina.

8. barrer

—¿Quién _____ el garaje? ¿Tú?

—No, Teresa y yo _____ la sala.

9. recibir

—¿Uds. _____ cartas (_letters_)?

—No, nosotros _____ mensajes electrónicos.

10. escribir

—¿Ud. _____ con lápiz?

—No, yo _____ con pluma.

B. Entreviste a su compañero(a) Interview a partner, using the following questions.

1. ¿Tú vives cerca de (_near_) la universidad? ¿Dónde vives?

2. ¿Bebes café por la mañana? Y por la tarde, ¿bebes té?

3. ¿Comes en la cafetería de la universidad? ¿A qué hora comes?

4. ¿Tú corres por la mañana?

5. ¿Tú escribes en inglés o en español? ¿Lees mucho?

6. ¿Tú abres la ventana de tu dormitorio por la noche?

7. ¿Qué días sacudes los muebles? ¿Qué días barres la cocina?

8. ¿Tú debes cortar el césped hoy? ¿Debes sacar la basura?

2. Possession with _de_ (_El caso posesivo_)

The **de** + _noun_ construction is used to express possession or relationship. Unlike English, Spanish does not use the apostrophe.

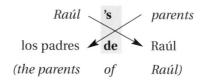

Raúl **'s** _parents_

los padres **de** Raúl

(the parents of Raúl)

—¿Ellos son **los hermanos de** Rafael?   _"Are they Rafael's brothers?"_

—No, son **los** hijos **de** Oscar.   _"No, they are Oscar's children."_

—¿Dónde viven Uds.?   _"Where do you live?"_

—En **la** casa **de Pedro.**   _"At Pedro's house."_

¡Atención! Note the use of the definite article before the words **hijos** and **casa.**

Hola...soy el papá de Paco...

Práctica y conversación

Online Study Center

For more practice with lesson topics, see the related activities on the *¡Hola, amigos!* web site at college.hmco.com/PIC/holaamigos7e.

A. ¿Posesión o relación? Express the relationship of the people and/or objects in each illustration, using **de** + *noun* (i.e., the Spanish equivalent of *Marta's son*).

el hijo *Marta*

la señorita Martínez

el número de teléfono

1. _____   2. _____

los libros

Elena

la profesora

el escritorio

3. _____   4. _____

B. ¿Quiénes son? According to the information given, you and a partner ask each other who everyone is. Answer expressing the relationship that exists among the people named.

◆ **MODELO:** La señora López tiene (*has*) dos estudiantes: Eva y Ana.

—¿Quiénes son Eva y Ana?
—Eva y Ana son las estudiantes de la señora López.

1. Elena tiene un hermano: Roberto.
2. La profesora Fernández tiene tres alumnos: Sergio, Daniel y Luis.
3. Jorge tiene una hermana: Marisa.
4. La señora Gutiérrez tiene una secretaria: Alicia.
5. Diana tiene un papá: el señor Alba.
6. Eva tiene dos profesoras: la doctora Vélez y la doctora Mena.
7. José Luis tiene un compañero de clase: David.
8. Marta tiene dos compañeras de cuarto: Silvia y Mónica.

3. Present indicative of *tener* and *venir*
(*Presente de indicativo de* tener *y* venir)

tener (*to have*)		venir (*to come*)	
yo	**tengo**	yo	**vengo**
tú	**tienes**	tú	**vienes**
Ud. él ella	**tiene**	Ud. él ella	**viene**
nosotros(as)	**tenemos**	nosotros(as)	**venimos**
vosotros(as)	**tenéis**	vosotros(as)	**venís**
Uds. ellos ellas	**tienen**	Uds. ellos ellas	**vienen**

—¿**Tienes** la sartén?   "***Do you have** the frying pan?*"
—Sí, **tengo** la sartén y la cacerola.   "*Yes, **I have** the frying pan and the sauce pan.*"

—¿**Vienes** mañana por la mañana?   "***Are you coming** tomorrow morning?*"
—No, **vengo** el jueves.   "*No, **I'm coming** on Thursday.*"

—¿Cuántos platos **tienen** Uds.?   "*How many dishes **do you have?***"
—**Tenemos** ocho platos.   "***We have** eight dishes.*"

—¿Uds. **vienen** a la universidad los martes y jueves?   "***Do you come** to the university on Tuesdays and Thursdays?*"
—No, nosotros **venimos** los lunes, miércoles y viernes.   "*No, **we come** on Mondays, Wednesdays, and Fridays.*"

—¿**Tienes que** limpiar la casa hoy?   "***Do you have to** clean the house today?*"

—No, hoy no **tengo que** limpiar.   "*No, I don't **have to** clean today.*"

¡Atención!   **Tener que** means *to have to,* and it is followed by an infinitive: **Elsa *tiene que limpiar* la casa hoy.** (*Elsa **has to clean** the house today.*)

Práctica y conversación

A. Minidiálogos Supply the missing forms of **tener** and **venir** to complete the dialogues. Then act them out with a partner.

1. —¿Cuándo _____ Uds.?
   —Pedro _____ el sábado y yo _____ el domingo.
   —¿Con quién _____ tú?
   —Yo _____ con la Srta. Aranda.

2. —¿Tú _____ a mi casa mañana?
   —No, yo _____ el viernes.

3. —¿Uds. _____ una licuadora?
   —Sí, y también una cafetera.

4. —¿Cuándo _____ tú de Guadalajara?
   —_____ el jueves.

5. —¿Tú _____ que lavar la ropa hoy?
   —No, yo no _____ que lavar hoy.

B. ¿Quién puede ayudarme? (*Who can help me?*) You and your partner take turns playing the role of René, who keeps asking everyone for help. Use the elements given in your answers.

◆ MODELO: yo / la ensalada
   —*¿Tú puedes ayudarme?*
   —*No, yo tengo que preparar la ensalada.*

1. Elsa / los muebles
2. Ana y Eva / los platos
3. nosotros / la ropa
4. Marta / la aspiradora
5. Roberto / la basura
6. Sergio / el césped

C. ¿Hay mucho trabajo? With a partner, ask each other five questions about what you have to do at different times and on different days. Follow the model.

◆ MODELO: —*¿Qué tienes que hacer el sábado?*
   —*Tengo que barrer el garaje.*

4. Expressions with *tener* (*Expresiones con* tener)

The following idiomatic expressions are formed with **tener.**

tener (mucho) frío	*to be (very) cold*
tener (mucha) sed	*to be (very) thirsty*
tener (mucha) hambre	*to be (very) hungry*
tener (mucho) calor	*to be (very) hot*
tener (mucho) sueño	*to be (very) sleepy*
tener prisa	*to be in a hurry*

Online Study Center

For more practice with lesson topics, see the related activities on the *¡Hola, amigos!* web site at college.hmco.com/PIC/holaamigos7e.

tener miedo	*to be afraid, scared*
tener razón	*to be right*
no tener razón	*to be wrong*
tener... años (de edad)	*to be . . . years old*

—¿**Tienes hambre?**   *"**Are you hungry?**"*
—No, pero **tengo** mucha **sed.**   *"No, but **I am** very **thirsty.**"*

—¿Cuántos **años tiene** Eva?   *"How **old** is Eva?"*
—**Tiene** veinte **años.**   *"**She is** twenty **years old.**"*

Online Study Center

For more practice with lesson topics, see the related activities on the *¡Hola, amigos!* web site at college.hmco.com/PIC/holaamigos7e.

Práctica y conversación

A. ¿Qué tienen?   Describe the following people according to the illustrations below, using an expression with **tener.**

1. Elena _____   **2.** Yo _____   **3.** Nosotros_____

4. Él _____   **5.** Ellos _____   **6.** Tú _____

B. ¿Cómo se sienten?   How do these people feel? Answer, using expressions with **tener,** according to the information given.

1. Carlos and Daniel are in the middle of the Sahara desert.
2. Luis hasn't had a bite to eat for fifteen hours.
3. Marta sees a snake near her feet.
4. Darío and Eva have to get to the airport in a few minutes.
5. Rosa is in South Dakota in February.

C. **¿Por qué...?**   With a partner, take turns indicating why you are or are not doing the following, using an expression with **tener.**

1. ¿Por qué no abres las ventanas?
2. ¿Por qué corres?
3. ¿Por qué no comes ensalada?
4. ¿Por qué no tomas un vaso de limonada?
5. ¿Por qué cierras la puerta?

D. **Entreviste a su compañero(a)**   Interview a partner, using the following questions.

1. ¿Cuántos años tienes? ¿Cuántos años tiene tu mamá?
2. ¿Qué comes cuando tienes hambre?
3. ¿Qué bebes cuando tienes frío? ¿Y cuando tienes calor?
4. ¿Tienes sueño en este momento?
5. ¿Tú tienes miedo a veces (*sometimes*)?
6. En tu familia, ¿quién tiene razón siempre? ¿Y en la clase?

5. Demonstrative adjectives and pronouns
(*Adjetivos y pronombres demostrativos*)

Demonstrative adjectives

◆ Demonstrative adjectives point out persons and things. Like all other adjectives, they agree in gender and number with the nouns they modify. The forms of the demonstrative adjectives are as follows.

Masculine		Feminine		English Equivalent	
Sing.	*Pl.*	*Sing.*	*Pl.*	*Sing.*	*Pl.*
este	estos	esta	estas	this	these
ese	esos	esa	esas	that	those
aquel	aquellos	aquella	aquellas	that (*over there*)	those (*at a distance*)

aquella mesa

esa mesa

esta mesa

—¿Qué necesitas?   "*What do you need?*"
—**Estos** vasos y **aquellas** tazas.   "***These*** glasses and ***those*** cups (over there)."

Demonstrative pronouns

◆ The forms of the demonstrative pronouns are as follows.

Masculine		Feminine		Neuter		English equivalent	
Sing.	*Pl.*	*Sing.*	*Pl.*	*Sing.*	*Pl.*	*Sing.*	*Pl.*
éste	éstos	ésta	éstas	esto	estos	this (one)	these
ése	ésos	ésa	ésas	eso	esos	that (one)	those
aquél	aquéllos	aquélla	aquéllas	aquello	aquellos	that (over there)	those (at a distance)

◆ The masculine and feminine demonstrative pronouns are the same as the demonstrative adjectives, except that they have a written accent.

◆ Each demonstrative pronoun has a neuter form. The neuter forms have no gender and refer to unspecified situations, ideas, or things: *this, this matter; that, that business.*

◆ Note that the demonstrative pronouns replace a noun.

—¿Qué libro quiere Ud., **éste** o **ése**?   *"Which book do you want, **this one** or **that one**?"*

— Quiero **aquél.**   *"I want **that one over there.**"*

— ¿Qué es **eso**?   *"What is **that**?"*
— Es una plancha.   *"It's an iron."*

·Online Study Center

For more practice with lesson topics, see the related activities on the *¡Hola, amigos!* web site at college.hmco.com/PIC/holaamigos7e.

Práctica y conversación

A. Este, ese y aquel   Describe in Spanish the following illustrations, using the suggested demonstrative adjectives.

1. this, these:

a. _____

b. _____

c. _____

d. _____

2. that, those:

a. _____

b. _____

c. _____

d. _____

3. that (over there); those (over there):

a. _____

b. _____

c. _____

d. _____

B. Ud. está aquí   Say what you need according to the objects in the illustration, using the corresponding demonstrative adjectives.

Ud. está aquí

a.   b.

C. Minidiálogos   Complete the following exchanges with the Spanish equivalent of the demonstrative pronouns in parentheses. Then act them out with a partner.

1. —¿Necesitas estos platos?
   —No, necesito _____.   (*those*)

2. —¿Cuál de las mesas necesitan Uds.?
   —_____.   (*This one*)

3. —¿Cuáles son tus tazas? ¿ _____ o _____?   (*These / those over there*)
   —_____.   (*Those*)

4. —¿Cuál es tu casa? ¿ _____ o _____?   (*This one / that one*)
   —_____.   (*That one over there*)

D. Nuestros compañeros   You and your partner take turns asking each other who the people in your class are. According to the relative distance. Use the appropriate demonstrative adjectives.

◆ **MODELO:** —¿Quién es John?
   —**Ese** muchacho.

6. Numbers from 300 to 1,000 (*Números de 300 a 1.000*)

300	trescientos	600	seiscientos	900	novecientos
400	cuatrocientos	700	setecientos	1.000	mil
500	quinientos	800	ochocientos		

◆ In Spanish, one does not count in hundreds beyond one thousand; thus 1,100 is expressed as **mil cien.** Note that Spanish uses a comma where English uses a decimal point to indicate values below one: 1.095,99 (Spanish) = 1,095.99 (English).

◆ When a number from 200 to 900 is used before a feminine noun, it takes a feminine ending: **doscient*as* mes*as*.**[1]

---

[1]This is also true for higher numbers that incorporate the numbers 200–900: **mil doscientas treinta sillas, dos mil ochocientos libros.**

Práctica y comunicación

Online Study Center

For more practice with lesson topics, see the related activities on the *¡Hola, amigos!* web site at college.hmco.com/PIC/holaamigos7e.

A. **Sumas y restas** With a partner, solve the following mathematical problems in Spanish.

1. $308 + 70 =$ _____
2. $500 - 112 =$ _____
3. $653 + 347 =$ _____
4. $892 - 163 =$ _____
5. $216 + 284 =$ _____
6. $1.000 - 450 =$ _____
7. $700 + 280 =$ _____
8. $125 + 275 =$ _____
9. $900 - 520 =$ _____
10. $230 + 725 =$ _____

B. **¿Cuánto cuesta?** With a partner, take turns asking each other how much everything costs.

◆ **MODELO:** —¿Cuánto cuesta el refrigerador? (13.650)
—*Cuesta trece mil seiscientos cincuenta pesos.*[1]

1. ¿Cuánto cuesta la pluma?
2. ¿Cuánto cuesta el vino?
3. ¿Cuánto cuesta la silla?
4. ¿Cuánto cuesta la computadora?
5. ¿Cuánto cuesta el reloj?
6. ¿Cuánto cuesta la mesa?
7. ¿Cuánto cuesta el escritorio?
8. ¿Cuánto cuesta el libro?

---

[1]Mexican currency: 1 dollar = 10 pesos (more or less). Rate of exchange subject to change.

Entre nosotros

¡Conversemos!

 Para conocernos mejor Get to know your partner better by asking each other the following questions.

1. ¿En qué ciudad vives tú? ¿Y tus padres?
2. ¿Cuántos años tienes? ¿Y tu mejor (*best*) amigo(a)?
3. ¿Qué días limpias tu casa?
4. ¿Quién prepara la comida en tu casa?
5. ¿Te gusta cortar el césped? ¿Te gusta pasar la aspiradora?
6. ¿Tú trabajas todos los días?
7. ¿Quién lava y plancha tu ropa?
8. ¿Qué aparatos electrodomésticos tienes en tu cocina?
9. ¿Qué bebes cuando tienes sed? ¿Agua o limonada?
10. ¿Qué tienes que hacer mañana?
11. ¿Tu casa es un desastre a veces (*sometimes*)?
12. ¿Qué trabajo de la casa no te gusta hacer?

 Una encuesta Interview your classmates to identify who fits the following descriptions. Include your instructor, but remember to use the **Ud.** form when addressing him or her.

Nombre

1. Plancha su ropa los fines de semana. _____
2. Corta el césped los domingos. _____
3. Vive con sus padres. _____
4. Limpia su casa los sábados. _____
5. Llega a clase tarde (late). _____
6. Tiene veinte años. _____
7. Siempre tiene razón. _____
8. Necesita descansar. _____
9. Siempre tiene prisa. _____
10. Es muy mandón (mandona). _____

 Y ahora... Write a brief summary, indicating what you have learned about your classmates.

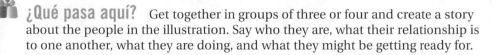

¿Cómo lo decimos?   What would you say in the following situations? What might the other person say? Act out the scenes with a partner.

1. You and a friend have invited guests for dinner and must decide what each of you has to do to prepare for them.
2. You tell your roommate that there is a knock at the door.
3. You ask a little boy how old he is.
4. You complain that there are a thousand things to do.

¿Qué pasa aquí?   Get together in groups of three or four and create a story about the people in the illustration. Say who they are, what their relationship is to one another, what they are doing, and what they might be getting ready for.

Para escribir

Para dividir el trabajo   You are in charge of organizing all the chores that must be done on a certain day. Indicate what you and everyone else has to do. Some of the chores must be done in pairs. To start out, brainstorm about all kinds of household chores and make a list. Then decide who is going to do what.

Un dicho

Hogar, dulce hogar.

This is a saying about home life.
Can you guess the meaning?
Do you think it applies . . . ?

Silvia y Esteban deciden dar una fiesta para celebrar el cumpleaños de Mónica, una chica guatemalteca que ahora vive en San Salvador con la familia de Silvia.

Esteban Tenemos que mandar las invitaciones. ¿A quiénes vamos a invitar?

Silvia A todos nuestros amigos, a mis primos, al novio de Mónica y a Yolanda.

Esteban Yo no conozco a Yolanda. ¿Quién es?

Silvia Es la hermana del novio de Mónica.

Esteban ¿Ah, sí? ¿Es bonita? ¿Es rubia, morena o pelirroja? No es casada, ¿verdad?

Silvia Es morena, de ojos castaños, delgada, de estatura mediana… encantadora… y es soltera.

Esteban Bueno, si baila bien, ya estoy enamorado.

Silvia Oye, tenemos que planear la fiesta. Va a ser en el club, ¿no?

Esteban No, va a ser en la casa de mis abuelos. Ellos están en Costa Rica con mi madrina y yo tengo la llave de la casa.

Silvia ¡Perfecto! yo traigo los entremeses y la torta de cumpleaños.

Esteban Yo traigo las bebidas y los discos compactos. Yo sé que mis abuelos no tienen música para bailar.

Detalles culturales

Los jóvenes hispanos frecuentemente organizan fiestas en sus casas y casi siempre bailan.

◆ **En una fiesta, ¿los jóvenes de este país prefieren bailar o conversar?**

Detalles culturales

En los países hispanos, muchas personas pertenecen (*belong*) a un club. Allí pueden nadar, practicar deportes, asistir a fiestas o reunirse con sus amigos.

◆ **¿Qué clase de clubes hay en los Estados Unidos?**

En la fiesta

Cuando Mónica, su novio y Yolanda llegan a la casa, todos gritan: ¡Feliz cumpleaños!

Mónica	(*Contenta*) ¡Qué sorpresa!
Silvia	¿Qué deseas tomar? ¿Champán, cerveza...? ¿O deseas comer algo?
Mónica	Una copa de champán para brindar con todos mis amigos.
Silvia	(*Levanta su copa*) ¡Un brindis! ¡Por Mónica! ¡Salud!
Todos	¡Salud!
Esteban	(*A Yolanda*) Hola, soy Esteban Campos. Tú eres Yolanda, ¿verdad?
Yolanda	Sí, mucho gusto.
Esteban	¿Bailamos? ¿Te gusta bailar salsa?
Yolanda	Sí, me gusta, aunque no sé bailar muy bien.

Esteban y Yolanda bailan y conversan. Todos los invitados lo pasan muy bien.

Silvia	(*A Mónica*) Veo que Yolanda y Esteban están muy animados.
Mónica	Sí, hacen una buena pareja. Oye, Silvia, la fiesta es todo un éxito. ¡Muchas gracias!

Detalles culturales

La palabra **salsa** (*sauce* o *spice*) se usa para referirse a la música caribeña, basada en la música afrocubana.

◆ ¿Cuáles son los ritmos típicos de este país?

Después de la fiesta, Esteban lleva a Silvia y a Mónica a su casa. Las chicas están cansadas, pero contentas.

¿Recuerda usted?

¿Verdadero o falso? With a partner, decide whether the following statements about the dialogue are true (**verdadero**) or false (**falso**).

1. Mónica es de Guatemala. □ V □ F
2. Mónica no tiene novio. □ V □ F
3. Esteban no sabe quién es Yolanda. □ V □ F
4. Yolanda es rubia, de ojos azules. □ V □ F
5. La fiesta es en el club. □ V □ F
6. Esteban hace la torta de cumpleaños. □ V □ F
7. Mónica desea brindar con champán. □ V □ F
8. Yolanda y Esteban bailan salsa. □ V □ F
9. Esteban y Yolanda están muy aburridos. □ V □ F
10. Todos lo pasan muy bien en la fiesta. □ V □ F

Y ahora... conteste Answer these questions, basing your answers on the dialogue.

1. ¿Qué deciden Silvia y Esteban?
2. ¿Quién es la hermana del novio de Mónica?
3. ¿Dónde están los abuelos de Esteban?
4. ¿Quién trae las bebidas?
5. ¿Yolanda sabe bailar bien?
6. ¿Con quién baila y conversa Yolanda?
7. ¿Quiénes hacen una buena pareja?
8. ¿Quién lleva a las chicas a su casa?

Para hablar del tema: Vocabulario

Online Study Center

For more practice with lesson topics, see the related activities on the *¡Hola, amigos!* web site at college.hmco.com/PIC/holaamigos7e.

Cognados

el champán
el club
guatemalteco(a)

la invitación
la música
la sorpresa

Nombres

la bebida beverage
el brindis toast (i.e. *at a celebration*)
el cumpleaños birthday
el disco compacto CD
los entremeses appetizers, finger food
el éxito success
la fiesta party
el (la) invitado(a) guest

la madrina godmother
la novia girlfriend
el novio boyfriend
los ojos eyes
el padrino godfather
la pareja couple
el (la) primo(a) cousin
la torta* cake

De país a país

la torta la tarta (*Esp.*)
el pastel (*Méx.*)
moreno(a) trigueño(a)
(Cuba, Par.)

Verbos

bailar to dance
brindar to toast
celebrar to celebrate
conocer to know, to be acquainted
dar to give
decidir to decide
estar to be
gritar to shout
invitar to invite

levantar to raise
llevar to take (*someone or something someplace*)
mandar, enviar to send
planear to plan
saber to know
traer to bring
ver to see

Adjetivos

animado(a) enthused
cansado(a) tired
casado(a) married
castaño brown (*eyes, hair*)
contento(a) happy, content
enamorado(a) in love
encantador(a) charming
feliz happy
moreno(a)* dark, brunet(te)
pelirrojo(a) red-haired
rubio(a) blond(e)
soltero(a) single

Otras palabras y expresiones

¿a quién(es)? whom
ahora now
aunque although
¿Bailamos? Shall we dance?
comer algo to have something to eat
de estatura mediana of medium height

de ojos castaños with brown eyes
pasarlo bien to have a good time
¡Salud! Cheers!
¡Qué sorpresa! What a surprise!
todo un éxito quite a success
ya already

Amplíe su vocabulario (*Expand your vocabulary*)

La familia

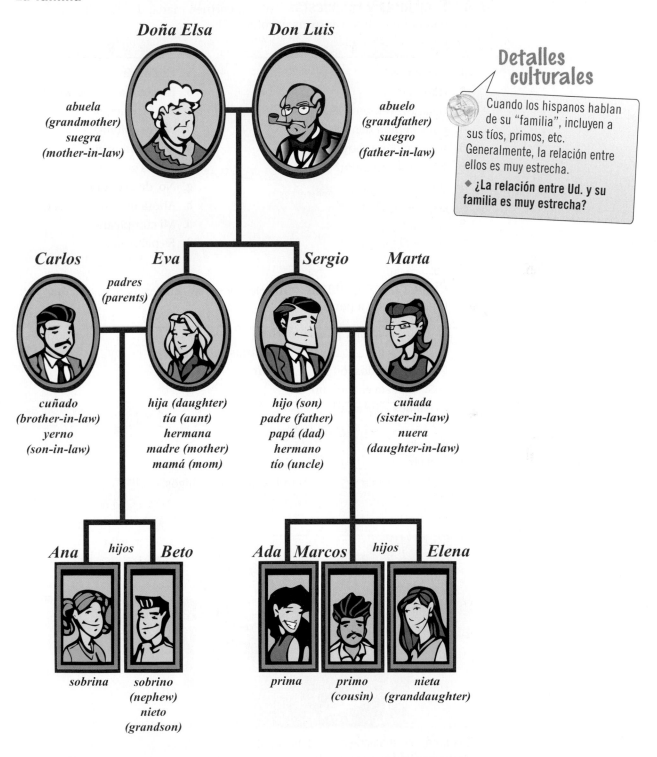

Doña Elsa

abuela
(grandmother)
suegra
(mother-in-law)

Don Luis

abuelo
(grandfather)
suegro
(father-in-law)

Carlos

cuñado
(brother-in-law)
yerno
(son-in-law)

Eva

*padres
(parents)*

hija (daughter)
tía (aunt)
hermana
madre (mother)
mamá (mom)

Sergio

hijo (son)
padre (father)
papá (dad)
hermano
tío (uncle)

Marta

cuñada
(sister-in-law)
nuera
(daughter-in-law)

Ana *hijos* **Beto**

sobrina

sobrino
(nephew)
nieto
(grandson)

Ada Marcos *hijos* **Elena**

prima

primo
(cousin)

nieta
(granddaughter)

Detalles culturales

Cuando los hispanos hablan de su "familia", incluyen a sus tíos, primos, etc. Generalmente, la relación entre ellos es muy estrecha.

◆ **¿La relación entre Ud. y su familia es muy estrecha?**

Para practicar el vocabulario

👥 **A. Preguntas y respuestas** With a partner, match the questions in column *A* with the answers in column *B*.

A	B
1. ¿Bailamos?	a. Champán.
2. ¿Es casada?	b. En la casa de mis abuelos.
3. ¿Es rubia o morena?	c. Las invitaciones.
4. ¿Qué bebida tienen?	d. No, es soltera.
5. ¿Qué celebran hoy?	e. No, es mi primo.
6. ¿Qué vas a mandar?	f. No, es guatemalteco.
7. ¿Luis es tu novio?	g. No, de estatura mediana.
8. ¿Dónde es la fiesta?	h. Ahora no; estoy cansada.
9. ¿Es alta?	i. Mi cumpleaños.
10. ¿Es de El Salvador?	j. Es pelirroja.

B. Planes para la fiesta Complete the following exchanges and then act them out with a partner.

1. —¿Qué vas a traer para comer?

   _____ y la _____ de cumpleaños.

2. —¿Los invitados lo _____ bien?

   —Sí, la fiesta es todo un _____.

3. —¿Vamos a brindar?

   —Sí. (_____ *su copa.*) ¡Un _____!
   ¡Salud!

4. —¿Uds. _____ una fiesta el sábado?

   —Sí, y vamos a _____ a todos nuestros amigos.

Una pareja de enamorados hace planes para una fiesta.
¿Qué creen Uds. que van a celebrar?

C. El parentesco (*Relationship with relatives*)   With a partner, take turns saying what the relationship of one person to another is in the family tree. Mention eight to ten relationships.

◆ MODELO: —*Doña Elsa es la mamá de Eva.*

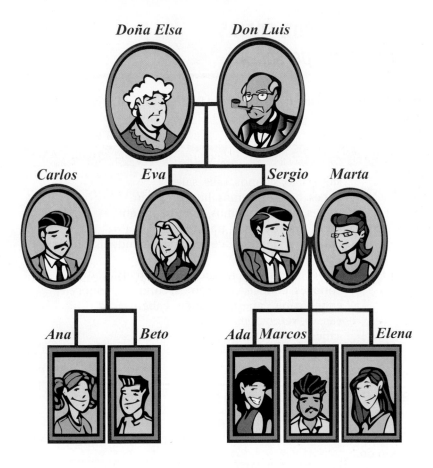

D. De mi álbum de fotos   Bring photos of family members and share information about them in small groups. Be prepared to present your family photos to the class.

Pronunciación

La consonante *c*   In Spanish, **c** has two different sounds: [*s*] and [*k*]. The [*s*] sound occurs in **ce** and **ci,** the [*k*] sound in **ca, co, cu, cl,** and **cr.** Read the following words aloud.

	[*s*]		[*k*]
cerveza	**ci**en**ci**as	**Ca**rmen	**cu**ándo
gra**ci**as	ne**ce**sito	**ca**nsado	**cl**ub
invita**ci**ón	**ce**lebrar	**có**mo	**cr**eo

Puntos para recordar

1. Verbs with irregular first-person forms
(*Verbos irregulares en la primera persona*)

◆ The following verbs are irregular in the first-person singular of the present tense.

Verb	yo form	Regular forms
salir (*to go out*)	salgo	sales, sale, salimos, salís, salen
hacer (*to do, make*)	hago	haces, hace, hacemos, hacéis, hacen
poner (*to put, place*)	pongo	pones, pone, ponemos, ponéis, ponen
traer (*to bring*)	traigo	traes, trae, traemos, traéis, traen
conducir (*to drive, to conduct*)	conduzco	conduces, conduce, conducimos, conducís, conducen
traducir (*to translate*)	traduzco	traduces, traduce, traducimos, traducís, traducen
conocer (*to know*)	conozco	conoces, conoce, conocemos, conocéis, conocen
caber (*to fit*)	quepo	cabes, cabe, cabemos, cabéis, caben
ver (*to see*)	veo	ves, ve, vemos, veis, ven
saber (*to know*)	sé	sabes, sabe, sabemos, sabéis, saben

Online Study Center

For more practice with lesson topics, see the related activities on the *¡Hola, amigos!* web site at college.hmco.com/PIC/holaamigos7e.

Práctica y conversación

 A. Olga y yo... With a partner, take turns comparing what Olga does to what you do.

◆ **MODELO:** Olga traduce del inglés al español.
   Yo traduzco del español al inglés.

Olga:

1. ...sale de su casa a las ocho de la mañana.
2. ...pone su dinero en el Banco de América.
3. ...conoce Guatemala.
4. ...sabe bailar salsa.
5. ...trae a su amiga a la universidad.
6. ...conduce un Ford.
7. ...ve a sus abuelos los domingos.
8. ...hace ejercicio (*exercises*) por la mañana.

B. ¿Y los otros...? Now get together with another pair and compare your answers to theirs.

2. *Saber* vs. *conocer*

The verb *to know* has two Spanish equivalents, **saber** and **conocer,** which are used to express distinct types of knowledge.

◆ **Saber** means *to know something by heart, to know how to do something* (a learned skill), or *to know a fact* (information).

—**¿Sabes** el poema "The Raven" de memoria?	*"**Do you know** the poem 'The Raven' by heart?"*
—¡No!	*"No!"*
—¿Ana **sabe** bailar salsa?	*"**Does** Ana **know how** to dance salsa?"*
—No muy bien...	*"Not very well . . ."*
—¿Ud. **sabe** el número de teléfono de David?	*"**Do you know** David's phone number?"*
—Sí, es 8–26–49–30.	*"Yes, it's 8–26–49–30."*

◆ **Conocer** means *to be familiar or acquainted with a person, a thing, or a place.*

—**¿Conoces** a Hugo?	*"**Do you know** Hugo?"*
—Sí, es el primo de Alberto.	*"Yes, he's Alberto's cousin."*
—**¿Conocen** Uds. todas las novelas de Cervantes?	*"**Are you acquainted with** all of Cervantes's novels?"*
—No, no todas.	*"No, not all of them."*
—**¿Conoces** San Salvador?	*"**Do you know** (Have you been to) San Salvador?"*
— Sí, es una ciudad muy bonita.	*"Yes, it is a very pretty city."*

Práctica y conversación

A. ¿Qué sabes y qué conoces? With a partner, take turns interviewing each other, using the **tú** form. Ask if your partner *knows* the following. You'll have to decide whether to use **saber** or **conocer.**

◆ MODELO: bailar rumba
—*¿Sabes bailar rumba?*
—*Sí, yo sé bailar rumba. (No, no sé bailar rumba.)*

1. el número de teléfono de la universidad
2. Guatemala
3. las novelas de Hemingway
4. hablar italiano
5. a los padres del profesor (de la profesora)
6. el poema "The Raven" de memoria
7. dónde vive el profesor (la profesora) de español
8. preparar entremeses

B. Queremos saber... With a partner, use **saber** and **conocer** to prepare five or six questions to ask your instructor.

Online Study Center

For more practice with lesson topics, see the related activities on the *¡Hola, amigos!* web site at college.hmco.com/PIC/holaamigos7e.

3. Personal *a* (*La a personal*)

◆ The preposition **a** is used in Spanish before a direct object (recipient of the action expressed by the verb) referring to a specific person or persons. When the preposition **a** is used in this way, it is called the *personal* **a** and has no English equivalent.

		(Direct object)
Yo conozco	**a**	Roberto.
I know		*Robert.*

—¿Tú conoces **a** Carmen y **a** Héctor?   *"Do you know Carmen and Héctor?"*

—Conozco **a** Carmen, pero no conozco **a** Héctor.   *"I know Carmen, but I don't know Héctor."*

¡Atención! When there is a series of direct object nouns, referring to people, the personal **a** is repeated: **¿Tú conoces *a* Carmen y *a* Héctor?**

◆ The personal **a** is *not* used when the direct object is a thing or place.

Yo conozco Los Ángeles.   *I know Los Angeles.*

◆ The personal **a** is seldom used following the verb **tener** even if the direct object is a person or persons.

Tengo dos hermanas.   *I have two sisters.*

◆ The personal **a** is also used when referring to pets.

Yo llevo **a** mi perro a la veterinaria.   *I take my dog to the vet.*

Online Study Center

For more practice with lesson topics, see the related activities on the *¡Hola, amigos!* web site at college.hmco.com/PIC/holaamigos7e.

Práctica y conversación

A. Minidiálogos   Complete the following exchanges, using the personal **a** when appropriate. Leave the space blank if **a** is not needed.

1. —¿Tú conoces _____ Silvia y _____ Mónica?

—Conozco _____ Mónica, pero no conozco _____ Silvia.

2. —¿_____ quién llevas a la fiesta?

—Llevo _____ mi suegra y _____ mi cuñada.

3. —¿Tienes _____ hermanos?

—Sí, tengo _____ un hermano y _____ dos hermanas.

4. —Qué tienes que hacer?

—Tengo que llevar _____ mi perro a caminar (*for a walk*).

B. Los sábados With a partner, take turns asking whom you call (**llamar**), visit (**visitar**), or see on Saturdays.

◆ MODELO: —*¿A quién llamas todos los sábados?*
—*Yo llamo a mi abuela.*

4. Contractions: *al* and *del* (*Contracciones:* al y del)[1]

◆ The preposition **a** and the article **el** contract to form **al.**

Llevamos	**a**	+	**el**	profesor.
Llevamos		**al**		profesor.

◆ Similarly, the preposition **de** and the definite article **el** contract to form **del.**

Tiene los libros	**de**	+	**el**	profesor.
Tiene los libros		**del**		profesor.

> **¡Atención!** **A** + **el** and **de** + **el** must *always* be contracted to **al** and **del.**

—¿Vienes **del** club?	*"Are you coming **from the** club?"*
—No, vengo **de la** biblioteca.	*"No, I'm coming **from the** library."*
—¿Vamos **al** cine?	*"Shall we go **to the** movies?"*
—Sí, vamos.	*"Yes, let's go."*

◆ None of the other combinations of preposition and definite article (**de la, de los, de las, a la, a los, a las**) is contracted.

El esposo **de la** profesora viene **a la** clase de español.

¿Vamos al laboratorio de lenguas?

---

[1]See Appendix C.

A. Ir y venir Using the list provided, you and your partner will take turns mentioning where everyone is going and whom everyone is taking.

◆ **MODELO:** Teresa / cine / Sr. López
*Teresa **va al** cine. Lleva **al** señor López.*

1. Inés / teatro / Sra. Vigo
2. El doctor Rojas / fiesta / profesor Vega
3. Fernando / club / Srta. Acosta
4. Paloma / zoológico / niños
5. Ramiro / parque / perro
6. Sara / biblioteca / estudiantes

Now you both use the same list to mention where everyone is coming from.

◆ **MODELO:** *Teresa y el Sr. López vienen **del** cine.*

B. Entreviste a su compañero(a) You and a partner take turns asking each other the following questions.

1. ¿Tú conoces a los amigos del profesor (de la profesora)?
2. ¿Tú vienes a la universidad antes de (*before*) las ocho de la mañana?
3. ¿Tú llamas al profesor (a la profesora) a veces (*sometimes*)?
4. ¿Tú tienes el libro del profesor (de la profesora)?
5. ¿Tú vienes a la universidad los domingos?
6. ¿Tú ves al profesor (a la profesora) los sábados?

5. Present indicative of *ir, dar,* and *estar*
(*Presente de indicativo de* ir, dar *y* estar)

	ir (*to go*)	dar (*to give*)	estar (*to be*)
yo	**voy**	**doy**	**estoy**
tú	**vas**	**das**	**estás**
Ud. él ella	**va**	**da**	**está**
nosotros(as)	**vamos**	**damos**	**estamos**
vosotros(as)	**vais**	**dais**	**estáis**
Uds. ellos ellas	**van**	**dan**	**están**

—¿Dónde **está** Aurora?	*"Where **is** Aurora?"*
—**Está** en el teatro.	*"**She is** at the theater."*
—¿No **da** una fiesta hoy?	*"Isn't **she giving** a party today?"*
—No, yo **doy** una fiesta.	*"No, **I'm giving** a party."*
—¿Adónde **vas**?	*"Where **are you going** (to)?"*
—**Voy** al cine.	*"**I'm going** to the movies."*
—¿No **estás** cansada?	*"**Aren't you** tired?"*
—No, no **estoy** cansada.	*"**No, I am** not tired."*

¡Atención! The verb **estar** is used to indicate location and to describe condition at a given moment in time. **Estar** and **ser** are not interchangeable.

Location: Aurora está en el club.
Current condition: Estoy cansada.

Práctica y conversación

Online Study Center

For more practice with lesson topics, see the related activities on the *¡Hola, amigos!* web site at college.hmco.com/PIC/holaamigos7e.

A. Fiestas y más fiestas Complete the following statements about Mónica's birthday party, using the appropriate forms of **dar, ir,** and **estar.**

1. Todos los amigos de Silvia _____ a la fiesta que ella y Esteban _____ para Mónica. Esteban _____ dinero para la fiesta.
2. La abuela de Esteban no _____ a la fiesta; ella _____ en Costa Rica.
3. En la fiesta, Mónica _____ muy contenta y los invitados _____ muy animados.
4. Las bebidas y los entremeses _____ en la mesa (*table*).
5. Yo no _____ a la fiesta porque no _____ invitado.
6. Yo no _____ muchas fiestas en mi casa, pero mis amigos y yo _____ fiestas en el club.

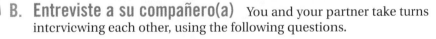

B. Entreviste a su compañero(a) You and your partner take turns interviewing each other, using the following questions.

1. ¿Adónde vas los viernes?
2. ¿Vas al cine los sábados? ¿Con quién?
3. ¿Vas a la iglesia (*church*) los domingos?
4. ¿Tú y tus amigos van a muchas fiestas?
5. ¿Estás invitado(a) a una fiesta esta noche?
6. ¿Das muchas fiestas en tu casa?
7. ¿Estás cansado(a)?
8. ¿Dónde están tus padres ahora?

Now, you and your partner are interviewing Miss Muñoz. How would you ask her the same questions? Use the **Ud.** form.

6. *Ir a* + infinitive (Ir a + *el infinitivo*)

The **ir a** + *infinitive* construction is used in Spanish to express future time, in the same way English uses the expression *to be going to* + *infinitive*.

ir (*conjugated*)	+	**a**	+	*infinitive*
Voy			**a**	**estudiar.**
I am going				*to study.*

—¿Tú **vas a bailar** con Jorge?   *"**Are you going to dance** with Jorge?"*
—No, **voy a bailar** con Carlos.   *"No, **I'm going to dance** with Carlos."*

Ahora voy a estudiar un poco.

Elena va a estudiar ahora pero...
¿qué planea hacer después?

Práctica y conversación

Online Study Center

For more practice with lesson
topics, see the related activities on
the *¡Hola, amigos!* web site at
college.hmco.com/PIC/holaamigos7e.

A. Entreviste a su compañero(a)   You and your partner take turns interviewing each other, using the following questions.

1. ¿Cuándo vas a estudiar? ¿Dónde?
2. ¿Cuántas horas vas a estudiar?
3. ¿Qué vas a hacer mañana?
4. ¿Dónde vas a comer mañana?
5. ¿Adónde van a ir tú y tus amigos el viernes?
6. ¿Vas a dar una fiesta el sábado?
7. ¿A quiénes vas a invitar a tu próxima (*next*) fiesta?
8. ¿Qué bebidas vas a servir (*serve*) en tu fiesta?

B. ¿Qué vamos a hacer?   What will be the result of each of the following situations? Indicate what *is going to happen*.

◆ **MODELO:** Yo tengo hambre.
    Voy a comer algo.

1. Ud. tiene un examen mañana.
2. Ud. y yo tenemos sed.
3. Mi tío tiene hambre.
4. Raquel y Luis van a ir a una fiesta.
5. Anita está cansada.
6. Marcelo quiere celebrar su cumpleaños.

¿Qué va a hacer cada (*each*) uno de estos estudiantes el sábado por la noche?

Entre nosotros

¡Conversemos!

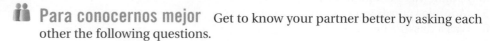 **Para conocernos mejor** Get to know your partner better by asking each other the following questions.

1. ¿Cuándo planeas dar una fiesta?
2. ¿Tus discos compactos son de música para bailar o para escuchar (*to listen to*)?
3. ¿Sabes cantar (*to sing*) "Feliz cumpleaños" en español?
4. ¿Qué haces los sábados por la tarde? ¿Y por la noche?
5. ¿A qué hora sales de tu casa?
6. ¿Cuántas llaves (*keys*) de tu casa tienes?
7. ¿Tú conduces bien?
8. ¿Ves a tus abuelos frecuentemente?
9. ¿Estás enamorado(a)? ¿De quién?
10. ¿Tus ojos son azules, verdes o castaños?

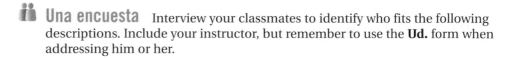 **Una encuesta** Interview your classmates to identify who fits the following descriptions. Include your instructor, but remember to use the **Ud.** form when addressing him or her.

Nombre

1. Tiene un esposo muy guapo (una esposa muy bonita). _____
2. Es la nieta favorita de su abuela. _____
3. Visita a sus tíos frecuentemente. _____
4. Da muchas fiestas en su casa. _____
5. Va a muchas fiestas. _____
6. Sabe bailar salsa. _____
7. Conoce Canadá. _____
8. Va a comer en la cafetería mañana. _____
9. Está enamorado(a). _____
10. Es soltero(a). _____

Y ahora... Write a brief summary, indicating what you have learned about your classmates.

¿Cómo lo decimos?

What would you say in the following situations? What might the other person say? Act out the scenes with a partner.

1. You and a friend are planning a party. You ask him/her what beverages he/she is going to bring.
2. You ask a friend what he/she is going to do on Saturday and with whom.
3. You talk to a friend about some members of your family.

¿Qué pasa aquí?

Get together in groups of three or four and create a conversation among the people in the picture. You might have them introduce one another and discuss their friends, their activities, the occasion, or the party itself.

Para escribir

Un mensaje electrónico You are sending an e-mail to a friend, inviting him/her to a birthday party you are giving for someone.

Brainstorm about the place, the day, and the time, whom you are going to invite, what you are going to serve, and what you are going to do. Now make a list of all the details and then organize the e-mail.

Un dicho

Come y bebe, porque la vida es breve.

This piece of advice reminds us of a similar one in English. Do you know what it is? Is it good advice? Memorize the Spanish saying!

Lectura

Estrategia de lectura Look at the **Sociales** reading below. Based on the headline and the photos, what do you think the reading is about? (**¿De qué trata la lectura?**) In which section of the newspaper can you find such articles?

Vamos a leer As you read the **Sociales** section of the newspaper, find the answers to the following questions.

1. ¿En qué iglesia tuvo lugar (*took place*) la boda de Isabel?
2. ¿Cómo se llama el esposo de Isabel?
3. ¿Qué ofrecieron los padres de la novia?
4. ¿Adónde va a ir la feliz pareja de luna de miel (*honeymoon*)?
5. ¿Qué tuvo lugar en el Club Deportivo Santiago?
6. ¿En qué universidad estudia Ana María?
7. ¿Qué estudian Ana María y Eduardo?
8. ¿Para cuándo planean la boda?
9. ¿Quién va de vacaciones a California?
10. ¿Qué ciudades va a visitar? ¿Con quiénes?
11. ¿Con qué celebraron el cumpleaños de Olguita? ¿Dónde?
12. ¿Qué hogar visitó la cigüeña (*stork*) y cómo se llama el bebé?

Detalles culturales

La mayoría de los hispanos generalmente usan dos apellidos: el apellido del padre y después el apellido de soltera (*maiden name*) de la madre.

◆ ¿Se usan dos apellidos en este país?

SOCIALES

En la Catedral tuvo lugar la boda de la gentil señorita Isabel Gómez Vera con el distinguido caballero Juan Carlos Pérez Miranda el pasado sábado, 18 de agosto. Terminada la ceremonia religiosa, los padres de la novia ofrecieron un banquete en el Club Unión de San Salvador. La feliz pareja va a ir de luna de miel a la hermosa ciudad de Antigua. ¡Muchas felicidades al nuevo matrimonio!

Video

■ En el Club Deportivo Santiago tuvo lugar la fiesta de compromiso de la señorita Ana María Reyes y el señor Eduardo Alcalá. Ana María es estudiante de educación en la Universidad Nacional y su prometido está terminando la carrera de arquitecto. La pareja planea su boda para el mes de mayo. ¡Felicidades!

■ La semana próxima va de vacaciones a California la señora Rosalía Mena de Castro. Allí va a visitar a sus padres, que residen en San Diego. Acompañada de sus padres, visitará Nueva York y Miami. ¡Le deseamos buen viaje!

■ La cigüeña visitó el hogar del matrimonio Viera Colombo. El hermoso bebé llevará el nombre de Miguel Ángel. ¡Enhorabuena a los nuevos padres!

■ El viernes pasado se celebró, con una gran fiesta infantil, el cumpleaños de Olga Paz Soldán en la residencia de sus padres. ¡Feliz cumpleaños, Olguita!

Díganos   Answer the following questions based on your own thoughts and experiences.

1. ¿En qué mes celebra Ud. su cumpleaños?
2. ¿Van a ofrecer sus amigos un banquete para celebrar su cumpleaños?
3. ¿Es Ud. miembro de un club? ¿De cuál?
4. Para Ud., ¿cuál es el lugar (*place*) ideal para pasar la luna de miel?
5. ¿Adónde planea Ud. ir de vacaciones?
6. ¿Qué ciudades de este país desea visitar?
7. ¿Le gusta a Ud. viajar con sus padres, con sus amigos o solo(a) (*alone*)?
8. ¿Qué nombre le gusta para un bebé?

¡Qué sorpresa!

Los amigos de Marisa están en el apartamento de la muchacha, muy ocupados preparando una fiesta sorpresa para celebrar su cumpleaños. Cuando regresa más tarde y se esconden (*hide*), la sorpresa de Marisa es realmente grande...

El mundo hispánico

 México

- México, con más de cien millones de habitantes, ocupa por su población el primer lugar entre los países del mundo hispano, y tiene casi tres veces el área de Texas. Su capital, la Ciudad de México, D.F. (Distrito Federal), con unos 24 millones de habitantes, es el centro urbano más grande del mundo.

- La economía tradicional del país está basada en el petróleo y la agricultura, pero en las últimas décadas la industria, el turismo y el dinero que los emigrantes en los Estados Unidos envían a sus casas, son la principal fuente de ingreso (*source of income*).

▲ Vista del Ángel de la Independencia, en la ciudad de México.

- La importancia del turismo se debe a (*is due to*) la abundancia de bellezas naturales y de reliquias históricas y al servicio eficiente de sus centros turísticos. Playas famosas como Acapulco, Cancún y Puerto Vallarta; ruinas arquitectónicas como Teotihuacán, Chichén Itzá y Tulum, y la arquitectura de muchas ciudades atraen a turistas de todo el mundo. En México, D.F., coexisten restos arquitectónicos de la ciudad prehistórica Tenochtitlán, fundada en 1325 por los aztecas, edificios coloniales y modernas estructuras.

- Otras ciudades de gran interés turístico son Guadalajara, la segunda ciudad más grande del país, origen del mariachi y del tequila; Guanajuato, famosa por sus momias, y San Miguel de Allende, residencia de artistas de todo el mundo.

- En el mundo del arte, se destacan (*stand out*) pintores como Diego Rivera, José Clemente Orozco, David Alfaro Siqueiros y Frida Kahlo.

▲ Mural de Diego Rivera (1886–1957)

Guatemala

◆ Guatemala es uno de los países centroamericanos que fue (*was*) parte del imperio maya. Aunque el español es el idioma oficial, sólo lo habla el 60 por ciento de la población; el resto habla alguna lengua maya.

◆ Guatemala es un país de volcanes, montañas y bellos paisajes. Su clima es muy agradable y por eso se conoce como "el país de la eterna primavera". En Guatemala encontramos selvas tropicales (*jungles*), hermosas playas e innumerables centros arqueológicos. Uno de los más famosos es la ciudad maya de Tikal, que por su valor arqueológico fue declarada Patrimonio de la Humanidad por la UNESCO.

◆ La economía del país se basa en la agricultura. Los principales productos de exportación son café, bananas, algodón (*cotton*) y madera. En sus bosques hay numerosos pájaros (*birds*), entre ellos el quetzal, que le da nombre a la moneda del país, y que es el símbolo nacional de Guatemala.

◆ Una ciudad muy interesante de este país es Antigua, que fue la capital hasta 1776. Ciudad de Guatemala, la capital actual es, en su mayor parte, una ciudad moderna, aunque todavía hay algunas construcciones antiguas.

▲ Rigoberta Menchú (1959–), Premio Nobel de la Paz, 1992

El Salvador

◆ El Salvador es el país más pequeño de Centroamérica, pero es el más densamente poblado. Tiene más de seis millones de habitantes en un área aproximadamente del tamaño (*size*) del estado de Massachusetts.

◆ En El Salvador hay más de 200 volcanes y por eso lo llaman "la tierra (*land*) de los volcanes". El país tiene unos 300 kilómetros de costa, y sus playas están entre las más hermosas de América. El "surfing" es el deporte (*sport*) que más se practica en las playas.

◆ El clima del país es tropical, con dos estaciones: la estación de las lluvias (de mayo a octubre) y la estación de la seca (*dry season*) (de noviembre a abril).

◆ La capital de El Salvador es San Salvador, la ciudad más industrializada de América Central.

▲ La Catedral Metropolitana frente a la plaza Barrios, en San Salvador.

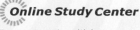**Online Study Center**

For more practice with lesson topics, see the related activities on the *¡Hola, amigos!* web site at college.hmco.com/PIC/holaamigos7e.

 Comentarios... With a partner, discuss, in Spanish, what impressed you the most about these three countries, and compare them to your own. Which places do you want to visit and why?

Tome este examen

Lección 3

A. Present indicative of *-er* and *-ir* verbs Complete each sentence with the correct form of the Spanish equivalent of the verb in parentheses.

1. El profesor _____ en la pizarra. (*writes*)
2. Ana y yo _____ en la casa de la Sra. Paz. (*live*)
3. Ellos _____ limpiar el baño. (*must*)
4. ¿Tú _____ por la noche? (*run*)
5. Yo _____ limonada. (*drink*)
6. Esteban _____ en la cocina. (*eats*)
7. María _____ las ventanas. (*opens*)
8. ¿_____ Uds. libros de inglés? (*receive*)

B. Possession with *de* Write the Spanish equivalent of the words in parentheses.

1. Estela es _____. (*Pedro's friend*)
2. Aquí está _____. (*Paco's clothes*)
3. Ellos viven en _____. (*Mrs. Peña's house*)
4. Ellos son _____. (*Eva's brothers*)

C. Present indicative of *tener* and *venir* Complete the following sentences, using the present indicative of **tener** or **venir.**

1. ¿Tú _____ a la universidad los lunes?
2. Eva y yo _____ con Roberto porque no _____ automóvil.
3. Ellos _____ mis libros de español, pero hoy no _____ a clase.
4. Yo no _____ a la universidad los viernes porque no _____ clases.
5. Sergio no _____ hijos.
6. Elvira _____ que planchar la ropa ahora.

D. Expressions with *tener* Say how you and everybody else feel according to each situation, using expressions with **tener.**

1. It's July and you are in Phoenix, Arizona. (*Yo...*)
2. Marcelo hasn't had anything to eat for the last twelve hours. (*Marcelo...*)
3. Adela's throat is very dry. (*Adela...*)
4. I am in Alaska and it is winter. (*Tú...*)
5. We haven't slept for the last twenty-four hours. (*Nosotros...*)
6. The boys are being chased by a big dog. (*Los muchachos...*)
7. You have one minute to get to your next class, across campus. (*Yo...*)

E. Demonstrative adjectives and pronouns Use the appropriate demonstrative adjective.

1. (*those*)   a. _____ cosas   b. _____ muebles
2. (*this*)   a. _____ cocina   b. _____ dormitorio
3. (*that over there*)   a. _____ café   b. _____ limonada
4. (*that*)   a. _____ casa   b. _____ refrigerador
5. (*these*)   a. _____ platos   b. _____ casas

F. Numbers 300–1,000 Write the following numbers in Spanish.

1. 567 _____
2. 790 _____
3. 1.000 _____
4. 345 _____
5. 615 _____
6. 874 _____
7. 965 _____
8. 825 _____
9. 481 _____
10. 13.816 _____

G. Vocabulary Complete the following sentences, using vocabulary from **Lección 3.**

1. No me gusta hacer los _____ de la casa.
2. Tengo que descansar un _____ .
3. ¿_____ es ese señor?
4. Yo corto el _____ los sábados.
5. Ellos tienen muchas _____ que hacer hoy.
6. Jorge, necesito los platos para _____ la mesa.
7. Tenemos que _____ los muebles.
8. Tocan a la _____ y Héctor corre a _____ .
9. Debes _____ la basura.
10. Mis amigos _____ dentro de un _____ .
11. Yo _____ limonada cuando tengo _____ .
12. Andrés tiene que _____ la aspiradora.

H. Culture Answer the questions based on the cultural information you have read.

1. Actualmente, ¿quiénes ayudan con los trabajos de la casa en los países hispanos?
2. ¿Dónde es popular la comida mexicana?
3. ¿En qué países son populares las telenovelas mexicanas?

Lección 4

A. Irregular first person in the present indicative
Complete each sentence with the correct form of the verb in parentheses.

1. Yo _____ de mi casa a los ocho.   (*leave*)
2. Yo_____ el auto de mi papá.   (*drive*)
3. Yo_____ la lección al inglés.   (*translate*)
4. Yo no _____ ejercicio (*exercises*) hoy.   (*do*)
5. Yo no _____ en este auto.   (*fit*)
6. Yo _____ las bebidas.   (*bring*)

B. *Saber* vs. *conocer*
Complete the following sentences, using the present indicative of **saber** or **conocer.**

1. ¿Tú _____ México? ¿_____ hablar español?
2. Yo no _____ el número de teléfono de Ana.
3. Nosotros _____ las novelas de Cervantes.
4. ¿Uds. _____ a Fernando Baños?
5. ¿Olga _____ bailar?

C. Personal *a*
Write a sentence with each group of words, adding any necessary words.

1. Yo / conocer / la tía / Julio
2. Luis / tener / tres tíos / dos tías
3. Ana / llevar / su prima / fiesta
4. Uds. / conocer / San Salvador

D. Contractions *al* and *del*
Rewrite the following sentences, replacing the words in italics with the words in parentheses. Make all necessary changes.

1. No conocemos a la *señora* Vega.   (señor)
2. Es la hermana de la *profesora*.   (profesor)
3. Venimos de la *fiesta*.   (club)
4. Voy a la *clase*.   (laboratorio)
5. Vengo del *aula*.   (playa)

E. Present indicative of *estar, ir,* and *dar*
Complete the following sentences, using the present indicative of **dar, ir,** and **estar.**

1. Yo no _____ mi número de teléfono.
2. Ella no _____ en el aula.
3. Nosotros _____ a la fiesta.
4. ¿Tú _____ bien?
5. Ellos _____ en la cafetería.
6. ¿Ud. _____ a la universidad por la mañana?
7. ¿Uds. _____ fiestas los sábados?
8. Yo _____ al club.

F. *Ir a* + infinitive
Write the question that originated each response, using the cues in italics.

1. Yo voy a estudiar *en el laboratorio.* (Use **tú.**)
2. Nosotros vamos a comer *sándwiches.*
3. Roberto va a ir *con Teresa.*
4. Yo voy a terminar *a las cuatro.* (Use **Ud.**)
5. Ellos van a trabajar *el sábado.*

G. Vocabulary
Complete the following sentences, using vocabulary from **Lección 4.**

1. Tenemos muchos _____ compactos.
2. Vamos a comer _____.
3. Mi madrina es morena de ojos _____.
4. ¿Es rubia, morena o _____?
5. Es de _____ mediana.
6. Dan una fiesta de _____ para Ana hoy.
7. Elena no es casada; es _____.
8. Paco y Rosa hacen una buena _____.
9. Ellos traen los _____ para comer en la fiesta.
10. Están _____ una salsa. ¿Quieres _____?
11. Todos _____ su copa y brindan: ¡_____!
12. La fiesta es todo un _____.

H. Culture
Circle the correct answer based on the cultural information you have read.

1. La economía tradicional de México está basada en (el petróleo / la arquitectura).
2. Guanajuato es famosa por sus (momias / mariachis).
3. Guatemala es conocido como el país de la eterna (selva / primavera).
4. El Salvador tiene unos (200 / 300) kilómetros de costa.

Objetivos

Lección 5

- ◆ Order meals at cafés and restaurants
- ◆ Request and pay your bill
- ◆ Talk about what is going on
- ◆ Describe people and things
- ◆ Make comparisons

Lección 6

- ◆ Shop for groceries in supermarkets and specialty stores
- ◆ Avoid repetition
- ◆ Contradict what someone else is saying
- ◆ Talk about how long something has been going on

Mercado de frutas y vegetales en Costa Rica

¿Qué comemos hoy?

Lección 5
El menú, por favor

Lección 6
En el mercado

Costa Rica

Turistas admirando la selva desde un puente en el Parque Selvatura, en Costa Rica

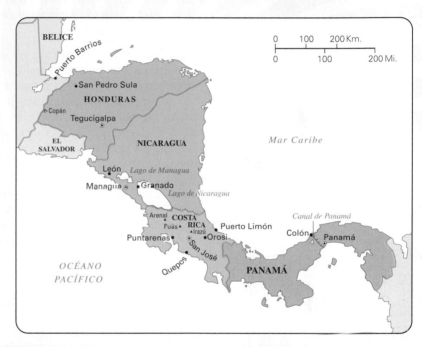

Panamá

Un barco de carga en el Canal de Panamá

Honduras

Ruinas mayas en Copán, Honduras

Nicaragua

Volcán Concepción, el más alto de Nicaragua, en la isla de Ometepe

Lección 5 ◆ El menú, por favor

Andrea

Javier

Camarero

Anita y Luisito

La familia Carreras, de Panamá, está de vacaciones en Costa Rica. Esta noche Andrea y Javier están en uno de los mejores restaurantes de San José, celebrando su aniversario de bodas. Ahora están conversando y esperando al camarero.

Andrea	(*Leyendo el menú*) ¡Ay, no sé qué pedir! Pollo a la parrilla, langosta, pescado asado...
Javier	Yo quiero bistec con puré de papas y verduras. ¡Oye!, ¿no quieres un coctel de camarones para empezar?
Andrea	¡Buena idea! Ah, aquí viene el camarero.
Camarero	La especialidad de hoy es cordero asado y bistec con langosta; ¿qué desean tomar?
Javier	Vermut.
Camarero	¿Y para comer?
Andrea	Para mí, sopa de cebolla, cordero asado y arroz.
Javier	Bistec con puré de papas y... una ensalada de tomates. Tráiganos también un coctel de camarones.
Camarero	¿Qué desean beber con la comida?
Javier	Dos copas de vino tinto.

Detalles culturales

Cada país latinoamericano tiene platos típicos, pero la mayoría de los restaurantes sirve también comida internacional.

◆ **¿Es fácil encontrar comida internacional en tu ciudad?**

Detalles culturales

En los países hispanos, los restaurantes tienen camareros profesionales que trabajan tiempo completo. Por lo general, son hombres y usan uniforme: pantalones negros y chaqueta blanca.

◆ **¿Qué diferencia ve Ud. entre los camareros hispanos y los de este país?**

Detalles culturales

◆ En los países de habla hispana, el café se sirve después del postre, nunca durante la comida. Generalmente es café tipo espresso, y se sirve en tazas muy pequeñas.

◆ La propina que se ofrece en los restaurantes generalmente es del 10%, pero hay variación según el país y el tipo de restaurante. Con frecuencia la propina está incluida en la cuenta. Si Ud. no está seguro de esto, debe preguntar (*ask*), **¿Está incluido el servicio?**

◆ El desayuno típico en Costa Rica es gallo pinto (arroz con frijoles negros), huevo, tortilla, jugo de mango y café.

1. ¿Se bebe mucho café en este país? ¿Qué tipo de café prefiere beber Ud.?
2. Generalmente, ¿cuánto se deja de propina en un restaurante en este país?
3. ¿Cuál es el desayuno típico en este país?

Más tarde.

Javier   (*Lee la lista de postres*) Flan, torta, helado, arroz con leche, pastel...
Andrea   Yo quiero helado de vainilla.
Javier   Yo voy a pedir flan con crema y después tomamos un café.

Javier paga la cuenta y deja una buena propina.

Al día siguiente Andrea y Javier llevan a sus hijos a desayunar. Anita es una niña muy bonita y un poco tímida. Es mayor que Luisito, pero él es más alto que ella. El niño es simpático y travieso.

Javier   (*Al mozo*) Jugo de naranja, huevos con jamón y pan tostado con mantequilla y mermelada.
Andrea   Una ensalada de frutas y un café con leche. (*A Anita*) ¿Qué quieres tú?
Anita   Yo quiero panqueques y un vaso de leche.
Luisito Yo quiero un perro caliente y una Coca-Cola.
Javier   ¡No, no, no! Tienes que pedir algo mejor.
Luisito Bueno..., una hamburguesa y una taza de chocolate.
Andrea   Está bien, pero en el almuerzo vas a comer pollo y verduras.
Luisito No me gusta el pollo. No es tan sabroso como la pizza.

Cuando terminan de desayunar son las diez de la mañana.

¿Recuerda usted?

¿Verdadero o falso?   With a partner, decide whether the following statements about the dialogue are true (**verdadero**) or false (**falso**).

1. La familia Carreras es de Costa Rica y está de vacaciones en Panamá. □ V □ F
2. Hoy Andrea y Javier celebran su aniversario de bodas. □ V □ F
3. Javier come pollo a la parrilla. □ V □ F
4. Andrea no quiere comer camarones. □ V □ F
5. Andrea va a pedir sopa. □ V □ F
6. Javier y Andrea comen postre. □ V □ F
7. Javier y Andrea no tienen hijos. □ V □ F
8. El niño es mayor que la niña. □ V □ F
9. Javier come más que Andrea. □ V □ F
10. La mamá de Luisito quiere comer una hamburguesa. □ V □ F
11. Luisito prefiere comer pizza. □ V □ F
12. La familia termina de desayunar a las doce. □ V □ F

Y ahora... conteste   Answer these questions, basing your answers on the dialogue.

1. ¿Dónde están Andrea y Javier ahora?
2. ¿Qué están haciendo?
3. ¿Qué beben Javier y Andrea?
4. ¿Qué quiere Andrea de postre? ¿Y Javier?
5. ¿Cómo es Anita? ¿Cómo es Luisito?
6. ¿Anita quiere panqueques o pan tostado?
7. ¿Qué bebe Luisito en el desayuno?
8. ¿Qué debe comer Luisito en el almuerzo?

Para hablar del tema: Vocabulario

Online Study Center

For more practice with lesson topics, see the related activities on the *¡Hola, amigos!* web site at college.hmco.com/PIC/holaamigos7e.

Cognados

el aniversario
el coctel
la crema
la especialidad
la fruta
la hamburguesa
la lista

el menú
el panqueque*
el restaurante
la sopa*
la vainilla
el vermut

Nombres

el almuerzo lunch
el arroz rice
_____ con leche rice pudding
el bistec, el biftec steak
la boda wedding
el (la) camarero(a)* waiter, waitress
los camarones* shrimp
la cebolla onion
el cordero lamb
la cuenta check, bill
el flan caramel custard
el helado* ice cream
el huevo egg
el jamón ham
la langosta lobster

la mantequilla* butter
la mermelada jam
el (la) niño(a) child
el pan bread
_____ tostado toast
la papa* potato
el pastel pie
el perro caliente hot dog
el pescado fish
el pollo chicken
el postre dessert
la propina tip
el puré de papas mashed potatoes
la verdura, el vegetal vegetable

Verbos

dejar to leave (*behind*)
desayunar to have breakfast
empezar (e>ie), comenzar (e>ie) to begin, to start
esperar to wait

pagar to pay
pedir to order
preferir (e>ie) to prefer
querer (e>ie) to want, to wish

Adjetivos

asado(a) baked
mayor older, oldest
mejor better, best

sabroso(a), rico(a) tasty, rich
tímido(a) shy
travieso(a) mischievous

Amplíe su vocabulario

Para poner la mesa (*To set the table*)

la pimienta *la sal* *las copas*
la taza
el platillo *la cucharita*
la servilleta *el tenedor*
el cuchillo *la cuchara*
el plato
el mantel

De país a país

el panqueque el panqué (*Méx.*)

la sopa el caldo (*Méx.*)

el (la) camarero(a) el (la) mozo(a) (*Cono Sur*), el (la) salonero(a) (*Costa Rica*), el (la) mesonero(a) (*Ven.*), el (la) mesero(a) (*Méx.*)

los camarones las gambas (*Esp.*)

el helado la nieve (*Méx.*)

la mantequilla la manteca (*Arg.*)

la papa la patata (*Esp.*)

Para practicar el vocabulario

A. En el restaurante   Choose the word or phrase that best completes each sentence.

1. Quiero una ensalada de (camareros, camarones, cuentas).
2. La especialidad de hoy es biftec con (langosta, pastel, mantequilla).
3. De postre quiero (cordero, pollo, helado).
4. No quiero salmón. No me gusta el (jamón, huevo, pescado).
5. Quiero puré de (gambas, papas, arroz).
6. Quiero (almuerzo, pollo, mermelada) a la parrilla.
7. Voy a pagar la (cuenta, cebolla, idea).
8. Javier deja una buena (boda, propina, verdura) para el mozo.

B. Preguntas y respuestas   Match the questions in column *A* with the answers in column *B*.

A	B
1. ¿Qué quieres beber?	a. No, perros calientes.
2. ¿Quieres langosta?	b. Sí, a la parrilla.
3. ¿Quieren sopa?	c. A las once y media.
4. ¿Comen hamburguesas?	d. ¡Muy traviesos!
5. ¿Comes pan?	e. Sí, de cebolla.
6. ¿A qué hora es el almuerzo?	f. No, con helado.
7. ¿Quieres pollo?	g. Vermut.
8. ¿Comen flan con crema?	h. Quince dólares.
9. ¿Cómo son los niños?	i. Sí, con mantequilla y mermelada.
10. ¿Cuánto dejas de propina?	j. No, prefiero camarones.

C. Voy a pedir...   With a partner, play the roles of two dining companions looking at the menu and talking about what they are going to order. Start by saying "Yo voy a pedir…".

Marisa está leyendo el menú. ¿Qué cree Ud. que ella va a pedir para comer? ¿Y para tomar?

D. Para poner la mesa With a partner, decide what items you are going to need to set the table according to what is going to be served. Start out with a tablecloth and napkins.

You will serve soup, salad, steak and lobster, dessert, water, red wine, and coffee.

Pronunciación

Las consonantes g, j, h

A. Practice the sound of Spanish **g** in the following words.

pa**g**ar	**g**racias
gambas	**g**uapo
lan**g**osta	trái**g**anos

B. Practice the sound of Spanish **j** (or **g** before **e** and **i**) in the following words.

ba**j**o	pare**j**a	**J**ulio
giro	anaran**j**ado	**J**avier
Gerardo	me**j**or	ve**g**etales

C. Repeat the following words. Remember that the Spanish **h** is silent.

hora	**h**asta	**h**elado
hoy	**h**ola	**h**amburguesas
hora	**h**istoria	**h**uevo

Puntos para recordar

1. Present progressive (Estar + *gerundio*)

The present progressive describes an action that is in progress. It is formed with the present tense of **estar** and the **gerundio** (equivalent to the English *-ing* form) of the verb. Study the formation of the **gerundio** in the following chart.

Infinitive	habl**ar**	com**er**	escrib**ir**
Gerundio	habl- **ando**	com- **iendo**	escrib- **iendo**

Yo	**estoy**	**comiendo.**
I	*am*	*eating.*

—**¿Estás estudiando?**   *"Are you studying?"*
—No, **estoy escribiendo.**   *"No, I am writing."*

◆ The following forms are irregular. Note the change in their stems.

pedir	→	**pidiendo**	*asking for*
decir	→	**diciendo**	*saying*
servir	→	**sirviendo**	*serving*
dormir	→	**durmiendo**	*sleeping*
traer	→	**trayendo**	*bringing*
leer	→	**leyendo**	*reading*

◆ Note also that the **i** of **-iendo** becomes **y** between vowels.

—¿Qué están haciendo las chicas?   *"What are the girls doing?"*
—Ana **está leyendo** y Eva está   *"Ana is reading and Eva is*
durmiendo.   *sleeping."*

¡Mamá! ¡Mamá!
¿Estás durmiendo?

¡Atención! In Spanish, the present progressive is *never* used to indicate a future action. The present tense is used in future expressions that would require the present participle in English.

◆ Some verbs, such as **ser, estar, ir,** and **venir,** are rarely used in the progressive construction.

Práctica y conversación

Online Study Center

For more practice with lesson topics, see the related activities on the *¡Hola, amigos!* web site at college.hmco.com/PIC/holaamigos7e.

A. En casa de los Carreras With a partner, say what is happening, using the cues provided.

1. Tú / preparar / una ensalada
2. Javier / traer / los manteles
3. Luisito y Anita / pedir / dinero
4. Yo / decir / que es tarde
5. Andrea y yo / desayunar / la cocina

B. ¿Qué están haciendo? Describe what the following people are doing.

1. Tú...

2. Yo...

3. Ellos...

4. Eva...

5. La profesora...

6. Nosotros... y el chico...

C. En una fiesta With a partner, take turns asking and answering what everybody is doing at Andrea's party. Use the cues provided and the present progressive to formulate the questions. Use your imagination when responding.

Persona	Pregunta
1. Javier	qué / hacer
2. Andrea	qué / servir
3. Pablo	con quién / bailar
4. Eva y Pablo	qué / beber
5. Juan	qué / comer
6. Olga y Estela	qué / pedir
7. la orquesta (*band*)	qué / tocar

2. Uses of *ser* and *estar* (*Usos de* ser *y* estar)

The English verb *to be* has two Spanish equivalents, **ser** and **estar,** which have distinct uses and are *not* interchangeable.

Uses of *ser*

Ser expresses a fundamental quality and identifies the essence of a person or thing: *who* or *what* the subject is.

◆ It describes the basic nature or inherent characteristics of a person or thing. It is also used with expressions of age that do not refer to a specific number of years.

Anita **es** tímida.	*Anita **is** shy.*
Estela **es** joven.	*Estela **is** young.*

◆ It is used with **de** to indicate origin and with adjectives denoting nationality.

Carmen **es** cubana; **es** de La Habana.	*Carmen **is** Cuban; she **is** from Havana.*

◆ It is used to identify professions and jobs.

Yo **soy** profesor de francés.	*I **am** a French professor.*

◆ With **de,** it is used to indicate possession or relationship.

El vaso **es** de Ana.	*The glass **is** Ana's.*
Ellas **son** las hermanas de Javier.	*They **are** Javier's sisters.*

◆ With **de,** it describes the material that things are made of.

El teléfono **es** de plástico.	*The telephone **is** (made of) plastic.*
La mesa **es** de metal.	*The table **is** (made of) metal.*

◆ It is used with expressions of time and with dates.

Son las cuatro y media.	*It **is** four-thirty.*
Hoy **es** jueves, primero de julio.	*Today **is** Thursday, July first.*

◆ It is used with events as the equivalent of "taking place."

La fiesta **es** en mi casa.	*The party **is (taking place)** at my house.*

Uses of *estar*

Estar is used to express more transitory qualities than **ser** and often implies the possibility of change.

◆ It indicates place or location.

Ana **está** en casa.	*Ana **is** at home.*

◆ It indicates a condition, often the result of an action, at a given moment in time.

Él **está** cansado.	*He's tired.*
La puerta **está** cerrada.	*The door **is** closed.*

◆ With personal reactions, it describes what is perceived through the senses—that is—how a subject tastes, feels, looks, or seems.

¡Estás muy bonita hoy!   ***You look*** *very pretty today!*
La sopa **está** muy sabrosa.   *The soup **is** very tasty.*

◆ In present progressive constructions, it describes an action in progress.

Estoy desayunando.   ***I am*** *having breakfast.*

Práctica y conversación

Online Study Center

For more practice with lesson topics, see the related activities on the *¡Hola, amigos!* web site at college.hmco.com/PIC/holaamigos7e.

A. Entreviste a su compañero(a)   Interview a partner, using the following questions.

1. ¿Eres norteamericano(a)?
2. ¿De dónde eres?
3. ¿Tu mejor amigo es alto, bajo o de estatura mediana?
4. ¿Tu mejor amiga es rubia, morena o pelirroja?
5. ¿Dónde están tus padres ahora?
6. ¿Estás cansado(a)?
7. ¿Qué día es hoy?
8. ¿Qué hora es?

B. Carlos Alberto y Marisa   Complete the following story about Carlos Alberto and his girlfriend, Marisa, using the present indicative of **ser** or **estar,** as appropriate.

Carlos Alberto _____ joven, alto y delgado. _____ estudiante de la Universidad Central. Él _____ de Panamá, pero ahora _____ en Costa Rica. _____ las nueve de la noche y Carlos Alberto decide ir a la casa de Marisa. Marisa _____ su novia y _____ una chica muy inteligente y simpática. —¡Qué bonita _____ hoy, Marisa! —exclama Carlos Alberto cuando ella abre la puerta. Los dos van a una fiesta. La fiesta _____ en casa de Andrea y Javier.

C. Ser o estar   With a partner, take turns making statements about each illustration, using **ser** or **estar** as needed.

◆ **MODELO:**   Pedro _____ y Luis _____.
Pedro es alto y Luis es bajo.

Ana   Mario

1. Mario _____ moreno y Ana _____ rubia.

CAJA

cajero

2. Eva _____.

$7x\sqrt{x} = \frac{x}{2}^x$

3. El doctor Torres _____.

4. Yo _____.

Mayo
6
Lunes

5. Hoy _____.

6. Los estudiantes _____.

7. _____.

8. Nosotros _____.

 D. En la clase   In groups of three or four, prepare twelve statements about objects and people in the classroom. Include as many uses of **ser** and **estar** as possible.

3. Stem-changing verbs: *e > ie*
(*Verbos que cambian en la raíz:* e > ie)

As you have already seen, Spanish verbs have two parts: a stem and an ending (**-ar, -er,** or **-ir**). Some Spanish verbs undergo a change in the stem in the present indicative tense. When **e** is the last stem vowel and it is stressed, it changes to **ie** as shown below.

preferir (*to prefer*)			
yo	pref**ie**ro	nosotros(as)	preferimos
tú	pref**ie**res	vosotros(as)	preferís
Ud.		Uds.	
él }	pref**ie**re	ellos }	pref**ie**ren
ella		ellas	

- Note that the stem vowel is not stressed in the verb forms used with **nosotros(as)** and **vosotros(as);** therefore, the **e** does not change to **ie.**

- Stem-changing verbs have the same endings as regular **-ar, -er,** and **-ir** verbs.

- Other verbs that also change from **e** to **ie** are **cerrar** (*to close*), **comenzar, empezar, entender**[1] (*to understand*), **pensar**[2] (*to think*), and **querer.**

—¿**Quieres** bistec?	"**Do you want** steak?"
—No, **prefiero** pollo.	"No, **I prefer** chicken."
—¿A qué hora **comienzan** Uds. a trabajar?	"At what time **do you begin** to work?"
—**Comenzamos** a las diez.	"**We begin** at ten."

Práctica y conversación

Online Study Center

For more practice with lesson topics, see the related activities on the *¡Hola, amigos!* web site at college.hmco.com/PIC/holaamigos7e.

A. No están de acuerdo Alicia and Sergio cannot agree on anything. Supply the correct form for each verb and act out the conversation with a partner.

Alicia	¿Tú _____ (pensar) ir a la fiesta de Olga?
Sergio	Yo no _____ (querer) ir a fiestas; _____ (preferir) ir a un restaurante con los muchachos.
Alicia	¡Ellos también _____ (querer) ir a la fiesta!
Sergio	¿A qué hora _____ (empezar) la fiesta?
Alicia	_____ (Comenzar) a las nueve, pero Beatriz y yo _____ (querer) estar allí (*there*) a las ocho porque tenemos que llevar las bebidas.
Sergio	Carlos y yo _____ (pensar) ir a la biblioteca.
Alicia	¡¿Uds. _____ (pensar) ir a la biblioteca hoy?! Entonces yo voy a la fiesta con Roberto.
Sergio	¡Magnífico! Yo voy al restaurante con Marisa.

---

[1]For a complete list of stem-changing verbs, see Appendix B.
[2]When followed by an infinitive, **pensar** means *to plan:* **Pienso** estudiar hoy.

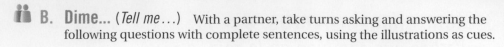

B. Dime... (*Tell me...*) With a partner, take turns asking and answering the following questions with complete sentences, using the illustrations as cues.

1. ¿Qué quieres tomar?

2. ¿A qué hora empieza la clase?

3. ¿Adónde quieren ir Uds.?

4. ¿Qué prefiere comer Adela?

5. ¿Cuándo comienzan las clases?

6. ¿A qué hora cierran la biblioteca?

7. ¿Qué prefieren beber Uds.: ponche o vino?

8. ¿En qué mes empieza el invierno?

9. ¿Con quién piensas ir?

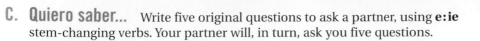

C. Quiero saber... Write five original questions to ask a partner, using **e:ie** stem-changing verbs. Your partner will, in turn, ask you five questions.

4. Comparative and superlative adjectives, adverbs, and nouns
(*Comparativo y superlativo de adjetivos, adverbios y nombres*)

Comparisons of inequality

◆ In Spanish, the comparative of inequality of most adjectives, adverbs, and nouns is formed by placing **más** (*more*) or **menos** (*less*) before the adjective, the adverb, or the noun and **que** (*than*) after it.

más (*more*)		*adjective* or		
	+	*adverb* or	+	**que** (*than*)
menos (*less*)		*noun*		

—¿Tú eres **más alta que** Ana?   *"Are you **taller than** Ana?"*
—Sí, ella es mucho **más baja que** yo.   *"Yes, she is much **shorter than** I."*

> **¡Atención!** **De** is used instead of **que** before a numerical expression of quantity or amount.
>
> Luis tiene **más de** treinta años.   *Luis is **over** thirty years old.*
> Hay **menos de** veinte estudiantes aquí.   *There are **fewer than** twenty students here.*

Comparisons of equality

◆ To form comparisons of equality with adjectives, adverbs, and nouns in Spanish, use the adjectives **tanto, -a, -os, as,** or the adverb **tan... como.**

When comparing adjectives or adverbs:	When comparing nouns:
tan (*as*) ⟨ bonita tarde + **como**	**tanto** (*as much*) dinero **tanta** plata (*money*) + **como** **tantos** (*as many*) libros **tantas** plumas

—¿Tu hermana habla bien el español?   *"Does your sister speak Spanish well?"*
—Sí, habla español **tan bien como** nosotros.   *"Yes, she speaks Spanish **as well as** we do."*

—Tú das muchas fiestas.   *"You give many parties."*
—Sí, pero no doy **tantas fiestas como** Uds.   *"Yes, but I don't give **as many parties as** you do."*

The superlative

◆ The superlative construction is similar to the comparative. It is formed by placing the definite article before the person or thing being compared.

definite article	+	(noun)	+	más or menos	+	adjective	+	de

—¿Quién es **el estudiante más inteligente** de la clase?
—Mario es **el**[1] **más inteligente** de todos.

*"Who is **the most intelligent student** in the class?"*
*"Mario is **the most intelligent** of all."*

¡Atención! Note that the Spanish **de** translates to the English *in* or *of* after a superlative.

Ellos son los más inteligentes **de** la clase.

*They are the most intelligent ones **in** the class.*

Irregular comparative forms

◆ The following adjectives and adverbs have irregular comparative and superlative forms in Spanish.

Adjective	Adverb	Comparative	Superlative
bueno (*good*)	bien (*well*)	**mejor**	**el (la) mejor**
malo (*bad*)	mal (*badly*)	**peor**	**el (la) peor**
grande (*big*)		**mayor**	**el (la) mayor**
pequeño (*small*)		**menor**	**el (la) menor**

◆ When the adjectives **grande** and **pequeño** refer to size, the regular comparative forms are generally used.

Tu clase es **más grande que** la de Antonio.

*Your class is **bigger than** Antonio's.*

When these adjectives refer to age, the irregular comparative forms **mayor** and **menor** are used.

—¿Felipe es **mayor que** tú?
—No, es **menor que** yo.

*"Is Felipe **older** than you?"*
*"No, he's **younger** than I (am)."*

---

[1]The noun may be omitted in the superlative construction to avoid repetition when meaning is clear from context.

Práctica y conversación

Online Study Center

For more practice with lesson topics, see the related activities on the *¡Hola, amigos!* web site at college.hmco.com/PIC/holaamigos7e.

A. Más o menos... Complete the following sentences, giving the Spanish equivalent of the words in parentheses.

1. ¿Tu esposo tiene _____ cuarenta años? (*less than*)
2. Mi primo baila _____ yo. (*as badly as*)
3. Mi amigo(a) es _____ tú. (*less intelligent than*)
4. Andrea es _____ su hermana. (*much younger than*)
5. Tú eres _____ ella. (*much thinner than*)
6. Luis es _____ Ariel. (*as nice as*)
7. Yo no tengo _____ tú. (*as many books as*)
8. Nosotros damos _____ Uds. (*as many parties as*)
9. Este restaurante es _____ todos. (*the best of*)
10. La langosta es _____ el pollo. (*tastier than*)

B. Comparaciones Establish comparisons between the following people and things, using the adjectives provided and adding any necessary words.

1. Hotel Hilton / Motel 6 / mejor
2. Einstein / yo / inteligente
3. Penélope Cruz / Meg Ryan / bonita
4. Maine / Texas / pequeño
5. Antonio Banderas / Danny De Vito / alto
6. Anita / Luisito / mayor
7. Brasil / Venezuela / grande
8. Jane Fonda / Jennifer López / menor

C. En la clase Read each statement; then answer the questions that follow.

1. Mario tiene A en español, José tiene B y Lolo tiene F.
   ¿Quién es el mejor estudiante?
   ¿Quién es el peor estudiante?
2. Juan tiene veinte años, Raúl tiene quince y David dieciocho.
   ¿Quién es el mayor de los tres?
   ¿Quién es el menor de los tres?

3. Lolo no es inteligente, Beto es inteligente y Rosa es muy inteligente.

¿Quién es más inteligente que Beto?

¿Quién es menos inteligente que Beto?

¿Quién es el (la) más inteligente de los tres?

¿Quién es el (la) menos inteligente de los tres?

D. En mi familia With a partner, ask each other questions to find out how you compare to members of your family with respect to height, age, intelligence, etc.

5. Pronouns as objects of prepositions
(*Pronombres usados como complemento de preposición*)

The object of a preposition[1] is the noun or pronoun that immediately follows it.

La fiesta es *para María* (*ella*).　　　　　**Ellos van *con nosotros*.**

Singular		Plural	
mí	me	**nosotros(as)**	us
ti	you (*fam.*)	**vosotros(as)**	you (*fam.*)
Ud.	you (*form.*)	**Uds.**	you (*form. / fam.*)
él	him	**ellos**	them (*masc.*)
ella	her	**ellas**	them (*fem.*)

- Only the first- and second-persons singular, **mí** and **ti,** are different from regular subject pronouns.
- When used with the preposition **con, mí** and **ti** become **conmigo** and **contigo,** respectively. The other forms do not combine: **con él, con ella, con ustedes,** and so on.

　　—¿El café es para **mí**?　　　　　　*"Is the coffee for **me**?"*

　　—No, no es para **ti**; es para **él.**　　*"No, it's not for **you**; it's for **him**."*

　　—¿Vas a la fiesta **conmigo**?　　　　*"Are you going **with me** to the party?"*

　　—No, no voy **contigo**; voy con　　*"No, I'm not going **with you**; I'm*

　　　ellos.　　　　　　　　　　　　　*going with **them**."*

----

[1]See Appendix C.

Es para ti.

Práctica y conversación

Online Study Center

For more practice with lesson topics, see the related activities on the *¡Hola, amigos!* web site at college.hmco.com/PIC/holaamigos7e.

A. Entre amigos   Complete the following sentences with the correct forms of the pronouns and prepositions in parentheses.

1. Elena no va _____, Anita. (*with you*)
2. Esas servilletas son para _____ y el mantel es para _____. (*me / her*)
3. Teresa está hablando de _____. (*us*)
4. Elsa va a venir con _____. (*them, masc.*)
5. Olga no va a ir al restaurante _____; va a ir _____. (*with you, pl. / with me*)
6. El vino no es para _____, Paco; es para _____. (*him / you*)
7. El postre es para _____, señorita. (*you*)
8. El café es para _____. (*them, fem.*)

 B. Entreviste a su compañero(a)   Interview a partner, using the following questions.

1. Cuando tú vas a un restaurante, ¿quién va contigo generalmente?
2. De postre, el camarero trae flan con crema; ¿es para ti?
3. Tú vas a preparar dos postres para tus padres: arroz con leche y pastel, ¿cuál es para él y cuál es para ella?
4. ¿Qué idioma hablan tú y tu familia entre (*among*) Uds.?
5. ¿Quiénes hablan bien de ti? (¿mal?)
6. ¿Quieres ir al restaurante conmigo hoy?

Entre nosotros

¡Conversemos!

Para conocernos mejor Get to know your partner better by asking each other the following questions.

1. ¿Cuál es el mejor restaurante de esta ciudad? ¿Cuál es la especialidad de la casa?
2. ¿A qué hora empiezan a servir el almuerzo en los restaurantes de tu ciudad?
3. Cuando pagas la cuenta en un restaurante, ¿dejas una buena propina?
4. ¿A qué hora es el almuerzo en tu casa? ¿A qué hora desayunas?
5. ¿Dónde piensas desayunar mañana? ¿Qué vas a desayunar?
6. ¿Prefieres tomar café con crema o café negro?
7. ¿Tú prefieres pollo a la parrilla, cordero asado, hamburguesas o perros calientes?
8. Generalmente, ¿qué comes de postre?
9. ¿Cuándo es el aniversario de bodas de tus padres? ¿Cómo lo celebran?
10. ¿Tu mamá es mayor o menor que tu papá?

Una encuesta Interview your classmates to identify who fits the following descriptions. Be sure to change the statements to questions. Include your instructor, but remember to use the **Ud.** form when addressing him or her.

	Nombre
1. Es de otro estado.	
2. Es tímido(a).	
3. Es el (la) más inteligente de la familia.	
4. Es tan alto(a) como su padre.	
5. Siempre está cansado(a).	
6. Piensa ir a comer más tarde.	
7. Está leyendo un buen libro.	
8. Comienza a trabajar a las ocho.	
9. Tiene más de un mes de vacaciones.	
10. Tiene un hermano(a) muy travieso(a).	

 Y ahora... Write a brief summary, indicating what you have learned about your classmates.

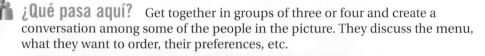

¿Cómo lo decimos?   What would you say in the following situations? What might the other person say? Act out the scenes with a partner.

1. You are at a café having breakfast. You are very hungry. Order a big breakfast.
2. You are having lunch with a friend. Suggest a few things he or she can have to eat and drink.
3. Call a restaurant and make reservations for dinner.
4. You have invited some friends to a party. Tell them it's at your house, and what time it starts.
5. Your friend has suggested having dinner at a restaurant you dislike. Tell him that it's the worst restaurant in town.

¿Qué pasa aquí?   Get together in groups of three or four and create a conversation among some of the people in the picture. They discuss the menu, what they want to order, their preferences, etc.

Para escribir

En un restaurante   Following the style of the dialogues in this lesson, write a dialogue describing a dinner in a restaurant you may have had recently. Give as much details as you can.

Un dicho

Donde hay hambre no hay pan duro.

If we tell you that **"pan duro"** refers to bread that's old and hard, what does the saying mean to you? Don't forget to learn all the sayings, and use them when applicable.

Marta

Ariel

Don José

Doña Ada

🎧 *Marta y Ariel son una pareja de recién casados. Ellos son de Honduras, pero hace un mes que viven en Managua, la capital de Nicaragua, en un apartamento que está cerca de la universidad.*

Marta No hay nada en el refrigerador, excepto un poco de carne. Tenemos que ir al supermercado.

Ariel ¿Podemos almorzar antes de ir? Yo estoy muerto de hambre.

Marta Bueno, puedes llevarme a comer algo antes...

Más tarde, en el supermercado.

Ariel Necesitamos azúcar, una docena de huevos, mantequilla, papel higiénico, detergente, lejía... ¿qué más? ¿Dónde está la lista?

Marta Yo la tengo. A ver... papas, zanahorias, brócoli, apio, pimientos...

Ariel ¡Caramba! ¡Tantos vegetales! ¿Quién los va a comer?

Marta ¡Tú y yo! Mi mamá dice que debemos comer cuatro vegetales y cuatro frutas al día.

Detalles culturales

En los países hispanos, la gente mayor (*elderly*), especialmente las mujeres que no tienen esposo, generalmente viven en casa de un pariente (*relative*).

◆ **En este país, ¿dónde viven, generalmente, los ancianos y las mujeres mayores que no son casadas?**

Detalles culturales

Muchas familias hispanas tienen criadas. Algunas viven en la casa donde trabajan y se les considera como parte de la familia.

◆ **¿Tiene Ud. criada? ¿Alguien lo (la) ayuda a Ud. con los trabajos de la casa?**

Don José y doña Ada, los padres de Ariel, están en un mercado al aire libre.

Don José ¿Cuánto cuestan las chuletas de cerdo?

Doña Ada Son un poco caras, pero podemos comprarlas, si tú quieres. ¿Quieres chuletas de cerdo o chuletas de ternera?

Don José Las dos, y también chuletas de cordero.

Doña Ada ¡No, no! Tienes que elegir una.

Don José Está bien... elijo las chuletas de cerdo. Después tenemos que ir a la pescadería y a la panadería.

Doña Ada Sí, pero antes voy a comprar pepinos, tomates y cebollas.

Don José También necesitamos salsa de tomate porque quiero preparar mis famosos espaguetis con albóndigas.

Doña Ada Buena idea. Tu hermana vuelve a las seis y puede cenar con nosotros.

Don José ¡Perfecto! La criada tiene el día libre hoy, de modo que yo soy el cocinero.

Doña Ada ¡Y tú cocinas mejor que ella!

¿Recuerda usted?

¿Verdadero o falso? With a partner, decide whether the following statements about the dialogues are true (**verdadero**) or false (**falso**).

1. Marta dice que hay muchas cosas en el refrigerador.   ☐ V   ☐ F
2. Ariel no tiene hambre.   ☐ V   ☐ F
3. Marta tiene la lista de lo que necesitan comprar.   ☐ V   ☐ F
4. Marta quiere comprar muchos vegetales.   ☐ V   ☐ F
5. Don José es el suegro de Marta.   ☐ V   ☐ F
6. Don José quiere comprar tres tipos de chuletas.   ☐ V   ☐ F
7. Don José no piensa comprar pan.   ☐ V   ☐ F
8. Don José no sabe cocinar.   ☐ V   ☐ F

Y ahora... conteste Answer these questions, basing your answers on the dialogue.

1. ¿De dónde son Marta y Ariel y dónde viven ahora?
2. ¿Qué quiere hacer Ariel antes de ir al supermercado?
3. ¿Qué van a comprar Ariel y Marta para lavar la ropa?
4. ¿Qué dice la mamá de Marta?
5. ¿Dónde están los padres de Ariel?
6. ¿Las chuletas de cerdo son baratas o son caras?
7. ¿Qué chuletas elige don José?
8. ¿Por qué va a cocinar don José hoy?

Para hablar del tema: Vocabulario

Online Study Center

For more practice with lesson topics, see the related activities on the *¡Hola, amigos!* web site at college.hmco.com/PIC/holaamigos7e.

Cognados

el apartamento*	los espaguetis
el brócoli	excepto
el detergente	famoso(a)
la docena	la salsa

Nombres

el apio celery	**el mercado** market
la albóndiga meatball	—————— **al aire libre** outdoor market
el azúcar sugar	**la panadería** bakery
la carne meat	**el papel higiénico** toilet paper
la chuleta chop	**el pepino** cucumber
—————— **de cerdo** pork chop	**la pescadería** fish market
—————— **de ternera** veal chop	**el pimiento, el ají** pepper
el (la) cocinero(a) cook	**el supermercado** supermarket
el (la) criado(a) servant	**la zanahoria** carrot
la lejía bleach	

Verbos

almorzar (o>ue) to have lunch	**decir (e>i)** to say, to tell
cocinar to cook	**elegir (e>i), escoger** to choose
comprar to buy	**poder (o>ue)** to be able to, can
costar (o>ue) to cost	**volver (o>ue)** to return, to go (come back)

Adjetivos

caro(a) expensive
tantos(as) so many

Otras palabras y expresiones

a ver let's see	**está bien** all right, o.k.
al día a day	**estar muerto de hambre** to be starving
antes (de) before	**libre** off
cerca (de) near, close	**nada** nothing
de modo (manera) que so	**qué más** what else
don a title of respect, used with a man's first name	**los recién casados** newlyweds
doña a title of respect, used with a lady's first name	**un poco (de)** a little

Amplíe su vocabulario

Más comestibles

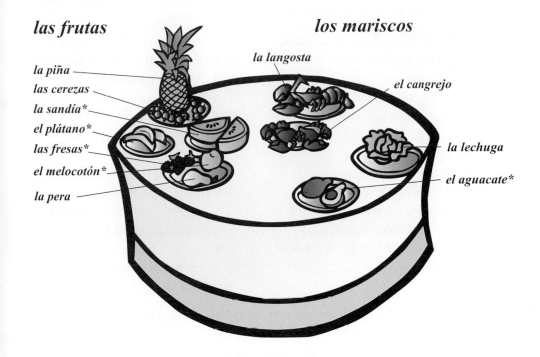

las frutas

- la piña
- las cerezas
- la sandía*
- el plátano*
- las fresas*
- el melocotón*
- la pera

los mariscos

- la langosta
- el cangrejo
- la lechuga
- el aguacate*

De país a país

el apartamento el departamento (*Méx., Arg.*)
el piso (*Esp.*)

el aguacate la palta (*Arg.*)

el plátano la banana (*Cono Sur*)

la fresa la frutilla (*Cono Sur*)

el melocotón el durazno (*Méx., Cono Sur*)

la sandía el melón de agua (*Cuba, Puerto Rico*)
la patilla (*Col., Puerto Rico, R. Dom., Ven.*)

Para practicar el vocabulario

A. Preguntas y respuestas

Match the questions in column *A* with the corresponding responses in column *B*.

A	B
1. ¿Quieres comer algo?	a. Sí, necesito lejía y detergente.
2. ¿Son novios?	b. Al supermercado.
3. ¿Necesitas huevos?	c. En el baño.
4. ¿Vas a lavar la ropa?	d. La criada.
5. ¿Quieres chuletas de cerdo?	e. Cerca de la universidad.
6. ¿Quién va a cocinar?	f. Sí, una docena.
7. ¿Adónde vamos?	g. No, yo no como carne.
8. ¿Tienes que trabajar?	h. Que vuelve a las dos.
9. ¿Dónde está el apartamento?	i. Sí, estoy muerto de hambre.
10. ¿Quieres albóndigas?	j. No, tengo el día libre.
11. ¿Dónde está el papel higiénico?	k. No, de ternera.
12. ¿Qué dice Ariel?	l. No, son recién casados.

B. Dime...

You and a partner take turns interviewing each other, using the following questions.

1. ¿Vives en una casa o en un apartamento?
2. ¿Vives cerca de la universidad? ¿Vives solo?
3. ¿Sabes cocinar? ¿Te gusta hacerlo?
4. En el desayuno, ¿tomas el café solo o con azúcar?
5. ¿Te gusta más comer carne o pescado?
6. ¿Comes mariscos? ¿Cuál prefieres?
7. ¿Qué frutas te gustan más?
8. ¿Prefieres comprar en un mercado al aire libre o en un supermercado? ¿Por qué?

C. ¿Qué les servimos?

You and your partner have several guests. Discuss what you are going to serve them based on their likes and dislikes.

1. A Marisa le gusta mucho el helado, pero no le gusta el chocolate.
2. A Raúl le gustan las chuletas, pero no come carne de cerdo.
3. A Sergio y a Daniel les gusta la comida italiana.
4. A Mirta y a Silvia les gustan los mariscos.
5. Raúl prefiere las frutas tropicales.
6. Mirta quiere comer pastel.
7. Alicia es vegetariana.
8. Raquel está a dieta (*on a diet*).
9. A Marisa le gusta mucho la comida típica americana.

D. En el supermercado You and a classmate play the roles of two friends who are shopping at a supermarket. Talk about all the groceries that you need to buy for a week.

Eva va a comer una manzana mientras (*while*) descansa. ¿Qué frutas cree Ud. que va a comer Julio?

Pronunciación

Las consonantes *ll*, *ñ*

A. Practice the sound of Spanish **ll** in the following words.

llegar	cebolla	silla
llamar	Allende	allí
calle	ellos	mantequilla

B. Practice the sound of Spanish **ñ** in the following words.

señor	señora	niño
año	otoño	Peña
español	mañana	España

Puntos para recordar

1. Stem-changing verbs: *o > ue*
(*Verbos que cambian en la raíz:* o > ue)

◆ As you learned in **Lección 5,** some Spanish verbs undergo a stem change in the present indicative tense. When **o** is the last stem vowel and it is stressed, it changes to **ue,** as shown below.

poder (*to be able to*)			
yo	**pue**do	nosotros(as)	**podemos**
tú	**pue**des	vosotros(as)	**podéis**
Ud.		Uds.	
él	**pue**de	ellos	**pue**den
ella		ellas	

◆ Note that the stem vowel is not stressed in the verb forms used with **nosotros(as)** and **vosotros(as);** therefore, the **o** does not change to **ue.**

Some other verbs that undergo the **o > ue** changes:[1]

almorzar   costar   dormir (*to sleep*)   **encontrar   recordar   volver**

—¿A qué hora **pueden** Uds.
   ir a la panadería?
—**Podemos** ir a las dos.

—¿A qué hora **vuelves** tú del
   mercado?
—**Vuelvo** a las tres.

*"What time **can you** go to*
   the bakery?"
*"**We can** go at two o'clock."*

*"At what time **do you return***
   from the market?"
*"**I return** at three o'clock."*

¿En qué
puedo servirle?

Banco
Nacional

---

[1]For a complete list of stem-changing verbs, see Appendix B.

Online Study Center

For more practice with lesson topics, see the related activities on the *¡Hola, amigos!* web site at college.hmco.com/PIC/holaamigos7e.

Práctica y conversación

A. Minidiálogos   Complete the following exchanges appropriately, using the present indicative of the verbs given. Then act them out with a partner.

1. —¿A qué hora _____ (almorzar) Uds.?

   —Nosotros _____ (almorzar) a las dos y _____ (volver) a casa a las cuatro. ¿A qué hora _____ (volver) tú?

   —Yo _____ (volver) a las cinco.

2. —¿Ud. _____ (poder) ir conmigo al supermercado?

   —Sí, yo _____ (poder) ir contigo esta tarde.

   —¿Ud. sabe cuánto _____ (costar) el detergente?

   —No, no sé.

3. —Jorge no _____ (encontrar) el número de teléfono de Nora. ¿Tú lo sabes?

   —No, no lo _____ (recordar), pero _____ (poder) buscarlo (*look it up*).

4. —¿Dónde _____ (dormir) los niños?

   —En mi cuarto; yo _____ (dormir) en el sofá de la sala.

B. Entreviste a su compañero(a)   Interview a partner, using the following questions.

1. ¿Puedes ir al mercado conmigo?
2. ¿Qué cuesta más, el pollo o el pescado?
3. ¿Sabes cuánto cuestan los camarones?
4. ¿Dónde puedo comprar frutas?
5. ¿A qué hora almuerzas tú? ¿Dónde?
6. ¿A qué hora vuelves a tu casa hoy?
7. ¿Recuerdas el número de teléfono de todos tus amigos?
8. Generalmente, ¿cuántas horas duermes? ¿Duermes bien?

2. Stem-changing verbs: *e > i* (*Verbos que cambian en la raíz:* e > i)

◆ Some **-ir** verbs undergo a stem change in the present indicative. For these verbs, when **e** is the last stem vowel and it is stressed, it changes to **i** as shown below.

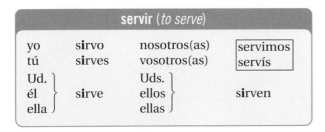

servir (*to serve*)			
yo	**si**rvo	nosotros(as)	servimos
tú	**si**rves	vosotros(as)	servís
Ud. él ella	**si**rve	Uds. ellos ellas	**si**rven

◆ Note that the stem vowel is not stressed in the verb forms used with **nosotros(as)** and **vosotros(as);** therefore, the **e** does not change to **i.**

Some other verbs that undergo the **e > i** change:

> **decir**[1] (*to say, to tell*)
> **conseguir**[2]
> **pedir**[3]
> **seguir** (*to follow, to continue*)

—¿A qué hora **sirven** Uds. el almuerzo? *"What time **do you serve** lunch?"*
—**Servimos** el almuerzo a las doce. *"**We serve** lunch at twelve o'clock."*

—¿Dónde **consigues** libros en español? *"Where **do you get** books in Spanish?"*

—**Consigo** libros en la biblioteca. *"**I get** books at the library."*

Práctica y conversación

A. Minidiálogos Complete the following exchanges, using the present indicative of the appropriate verb from the list. Then act them out with a partner.

> **servir**   **pedir**   **conseguir**   **decir**   **seguir**

1. —Yo nunca (*never*) _____ carne buena.
   —Mis padres _____ carne muy buena en el Mercado Central.
2. —¿Marta y Ariel _____ viviendo en Managua?
   —Sí, ellos _____ que es una ciudad muy bonita.
3. —¿Qué _____ Uds. en sus fiestas?
   —Nosotros _____ hamburguesas y perros calientes.
4. —¿Qué _____ tú cuando vas a ese restaurante?
   —Yo _____ bistec con langosta.
   —Yo siempre _____ que en ese restaurante (ellos) _____ los mejores mariscos.

B. Entreviste a su compañero(a) Interview a partner, using the following questions.

1. Cuando vas a un restaurante mexicano, ¿qué pides para comer? ¿Qué eliges para beber?
2. ¿La comida mexicana es mejor que la italiana? ¿Qué dices tú?
3. ¿Dónde consigues mariscos frescos (*fresh*)?
4. ¿Qué sirves tú en tus fiestas para comer? ¿Y para beber?
5. Cuando tú y tus amigos dan una fiesta, ¿sirven cerveza o refrescos?
6. ¿Tú consigues discos en español? ¿Dónde?

---

[1]First person: **yo digo.**
[2]Verbs like **conseguir** drop the **u** before **a** or **o: yo consigo.**
[3]**Pedir** also means *to order* (at a restaurant).

3. Direct object pronouns
(*Pronombres usados como complemento directo*)

- In addition to a subject, most sentences have an object[1] that directly receives the action of the verbs.

Él compra **el café.**		*He buys **the coffee.***
S.	V.	D.O.

  In the preceding sentence, the subject **él** performs the action, while **el café,** the direct object, directly receives the action of the verb. (The direct object of a sentence can be either a person or a thing.)

  The direct object can be easily identified as the answer to the questions *whom?* and *what?*

Él compra **el café.**		(***What** is he buying?*)
S.	V.	D.O.

Alicia llama **a Luis.**		(***Whom** is she calling?*)
S.	V.	D.O.

- Direct object pronouns are used in place of direct objects. The forms of the direct object pronouns are as follows.

Singular		Plural	
me	me	**nos**	us
te	you (*fam.*)	**os**	you (*fam.*)
lo	him, you (*masc. form.*), it (*masc.*)	**los**	them (*masc.*), you (*masc. form. / fam.*)
la	her, you (*fem. form.*), it (*fem.*)	**las**	them (*fem.*), you (*fem. form. / fam.*)

Yo tengo **las sillas.**	¿Ustedes **las** necesitan?
*I have the **chairs.***	*Do you need **them**?*

- Position of direct object pronouns

  - In Spanish, object pronouns are normally placed before a conjugated verb.

Yo compro **el café.**			*I buy **the coffee.***
Yo	**lo**	compro.	*I buy **it.***

  - In a negative sentence, **no** must precede the object pronoun.

Yo compro **el café.**			*I buy **the coffee.***
Yo	**lo**	compro.	*I buy **it.***
Yo **no**	**lo**	compro.	*I **don't** buy it.*

---

[1]See Appendix C.

◆ When a conjugated verb and an infinitive appear together, the direct object pronoun is either placed before the conjugated verb or attached to the infinitive. This is also the case in a negative sentence.

| **La** | voy a llamar. | } *I'm going to call **her**.* |
| | Voy a llamar**la**. | |

| No **la** | voy a llamar. | } *I'm not going to call **her**.* |
| No | voy a llamar**la**. | |

◆ In the present progressive, the direct object pronoun can be placed either before the verb **estar** or after the present participle.[1]

| **Lo** | está leyendo. | } *He's reading **it**.* |
| | Está leyéndo**lo**. | |

¡Atención! Note the use of the written accent on present participles that have pronouns attached: **está leyéndolo, estamos mirándola.**

Práctica y conversación

A. **Minidiálogos** Complete the following exchanges supplying the missing direct object pronouns. Then act them out with a partner.

1. —¿Tú tienes la lejía?

    —No, yo no _____ tengo. ¿Quién tiene el detergente?

    —Julián _____ tiene.

2. —¿A qué hora cierran el supermercado?

    —_____ cierran a las diez. ¿Tú vas a comprar las frutas?

    —Sí, _____ voy a comprar esta noche.

3. —Ariel, ¿Carlos _____ va a llevar a ti o a mí?

    —_____ va a llevar a mí.

4. —¿Tú conoces a los hermanos de Marta?

    —No, yo no _____ conozco.

5. —¿Ellos _____ invitan a Uds. a sus fiestas?

    —Sí, siempre _____ invitan.

Detalles culturales

La mayoría de los pueblos hispanos tienen un mercado central, con pequeñas tiendas. Mucha gente compra en estos mercados donde los precios generalmente son más bajos y los clientes pueden regatear (*bargain*) con los vendedores (*merchants*).

◆ **¿Es costumbre regatear aquí o los precios son fijos?**

---

[1] *Present participle* is **gerundio** (**-ando** and **-iendo** forms) in Spanish.

B. Susana dice que sí
Susana has a car and her teacher and her friends often need rides. Susana always says yes. What does she say to the following people?

1.	*Ana*	—¿Puedes llevarme a casa?
2.	*Raúl y Jorge*	—¿Puedes llevarnos a la biblioteca?
3.	*Profesora*	—¿Puedes llevarme a mi apartamento?
4.	*Teresa*	—¿Puedes llevar a Rosa y a Carmen a casa?
5.	*Sergio*	—¿Puedes llevar a Pedro y a Luis al restaurante?
6.	*Marta y Raquel*	—¿Puedes llevarnos al Mercado Central?

C. ¿Qué hacemos?
Use the appropriate direct object pronouns to say what we do with respect to the following people or things.

◆ MODELO: el café
Lo bebemos.

1. las cartas (*letters*)
2. las frutas
3. el pan
4. el coctel de camarones
5. los libros
6. la ensalada
7. el taxi
8. dos chicas (dos muchachos)

D. Planes
You and your friends Gustavo and Jaime are making plans to go out for the evening. Answer Gustavo's questions, using direct object pronouns and the cues provided.

1. ¿A qué hora me llamas? (a las cinco)
2. ¿Adónde nos llevas? (a un restaurante)
3. ¿Recuerdas el número de teléfono de Jaime? (no)
4. ¿Tienes tu licencia para conducir (*driver's license*)? (sí)
5. ¿Cuándo vas a llamar a Teresa y a Susana? (más tarde)
6. ¿El novio de Teresa los conoce a Uds.? (no)

1. ¿A qué hora llama Sara a Luis?
2. ¿Cuándo tiene que llamar Luis a Sara?

3. ¿Pepe puede llevar a los chicos a casa?
4. ¿Dónde tiene Pepe los libros?

5. ¿Quién sirve el café?

6. ¿Quién bebe el refresco?

7. ¿Quién tiene las cartas?

8. ¿Quién abre la puerta?

4. Affirmative and negative expressions
(*Expresiones afirmativas y negativas*)

Affirmative		Negative	
algo	something, anything	**nada**	nothing
alguien	someone, anyone	**nadie**	nobody, no one
algún **alguno(a)** **algunos(as)**	any, some	**ningún** **ninguno(a)**	none, not any; no one, nobody
siempre **alguna vez** **algunas veces,** **a veces**	always ever sometimes	**nunca** **jamás**	never
también **o... o**	also, too either . . . or	**tampoco** **ni... ni**	neither neither . . . nor

—¿Uds. **siempre** van a Tegucigalpa?   *"Do you **always** go to Tegucigalpa?"*
—No, **nunca** vamos.   *"No, we **never** go."*
—Nosotros **tampoco.**   *"**Neither** do we."*

—¿Conoces a **alguien** de Honduras?   *"Do you know **anyone** from Honduras?"*
—No, no conozco a **nadie** de Honduras.   *"No, I don't know **anyone** from Honduras."*

◆ **Alguno** and **ninguno** drop the final **-o** before a masculine singular noun, but **alguna** and **ninguna** keep the final **-a.**

—¿Hay **algún** libro o **alguna** pluma en la mesa?   *"Is there **any** book or pen on the table?"*
—No, no hay **ningún** libro ni **ninguna** pluma.   *"No, there is **no** book or pen."*

◆ **Alguno(a)** can be used in the plural form, but **ninguno(a)** is used only in the singular.

—¿Necesita mandar **algunas** cartas?   *"Do you need to send **some** letters?"*
—No, no necesito mandar **ninguna** carta.   *"No, I don't need to send **any** letters."*

◆ Spanish sentences frequently use a double negative. In this construction, the adverb **no** is placed before the verb. The second negative word either follows the verb or appears at the end of the sentence. **No** is never used, however, if the negative word precedes the verb.

—¿Habla Ud. francés siempre?	*"Do you always speak French?"*
—No, yo **no** hablo francés **nunca.**	*"No, I **never** speak French."*

or:

—No, yo **nunca** hablo francés.

—¿Compra Ud. **algo** aquí?	*"Do you buy **anything** here?"*
—No, **no** compro **nada nunca.**	*"No, I **never** buy **anything.**"*

or:

—No, yo **nunca** compro **nada.**

◆ In fact, Spanish often uses several negatives in one sentence.

Yo **nunca** pido **nada tampoco.**   *I **never** ask for **anything either.***

Online Study Center

For more practice with lesson topics, see the related activities on the *¡Hola, amigos!* web site at college.hmco.com/PIC/holaamigos7e.

Práctica y conversación

A. No estoy de acuerdo (*I don't agree*)   Contradict the following statements by saying that just the opposite is true.

◆ **MODELO:** Eva quiere comer algo.
   Eva **no** quiere comer **nada.**

1. Jorge siempre va a ese mercado al aire libre.
2. Ellos tienen algunas verduras.
3. Ana siempre come langosta o cangrejo.
4. Pedro siempre va a ese restaurante y Eva también va.
5. Ella quiere hablar con alguien.

6. Luis tiene algunas amigas españolas.
7. Paco siempre compra algo.
8. Ella nunca habla con nadie.

B. Entreviste a su compañero(a) Interview a partner, using the following questions.

1. ¿Vas al mercado por la mañana a veces?
2. En el mercado, ¿siempre compras mariscos?
3. ¿Siempre llevas dinero contigo?
4. ¿Necesitas comprar algo en la panadería?
5. Yo nunca voy a la pescadería los domingos. ¿Y tú?
6. ¿Comes algunas frutas tropicales?
7. ¿Alguien va contigo al mercado?
8. ¿Tú comes pan tostado o panqueques por la mañana?

C. Queremos saber... With a partner, prepare five affirmative and five negative questions to ask your instructor.

D. Siempre... a veces... nunca... In groups of three, tell your classmates two things you always do, two things you sometimes do, and two things you never do.

5. *Hace... que*

◆ To express how long something has been going on, Spanish uses the following formula.

> **Hace** + length of time + **que** + verb (*in the present tense*)
> **Hace** dos años **que** vivo aquí.
> *I have been living here for two years.*

—Oye, ¿dónde está Eva?   *"Listen, where is Eva?"*
—No sé. **Hace dos días que no**   *"I don't know. **She hasn't come**
  viene a clase.   to class **for two days.**"*

◆ The following construction is used to ask how long something has been going on.

> **¿Cuánto tiempo hace que** + verb (*present tense*)?[1]

—**¿Cuánto tiempo hace que ella**   *"**How long has she been working**
  trabaja aquí?   here?"*
—**Hace una semana que trabaja**   *"**She has been working** here for
  aquí.   a week."*

---
[1]Note that English uses the present perfect progressive or the present perfect tense to express the same concept.

Online Study Center

For more practice with lesson
topics, see the related activities on
the *¡Hola, amigos!* web site at
college.hmco.com/PIC/holaamigos7e.

Práctica y conversación

A. ¿Cuánto tiempo hace? In complete sentences, tell how long each action depicted below has been going on. Use **hace... que** and the length of time specified.

1. veinte minutos

2. tres años

3. una hora

4. dos horas

5. seis meses

6. cinco días

B. Entreviste a su compañero(a)   Interview one of your classmates and then report to the class.

1. ¿Cuánto tiempo hace que vives en esta ciudad?
2. ¿Cuánto tiempo hace que estudias en esta universidad?
3. ¿Cuánto tiempo hace que trabajas en esta ciudad?
4. ¿Cuánto tiempo hace que no comes?
5. ¿Cuánto tiempo hace que no ves a tus abuelos?
6. ¿Cuánto tiempo hace que no hablas con tus padres?
7. ¿Cuánto tiempo hace que no vas a la biblioteca?
8. ¿Cuánto tiempo hace que hablas español?

C. ¿Dónde están?   In groups of three or four, mention three or four friends and relatives that you haven't seen for a while.

◆ MODELO: *Hace dos años que no veo a mi prima Eva.*

Ésta es una reunión familiar, pero el abuelo no está aquí. ¿Cuánto tiempo hace que no lo ven?

Entre nosotros

¡Conversemos!

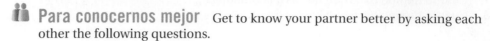 **Para conocernos mejor** Get to know your partner better by asking each other the following questions.

1. ¿A qué hora almuerzas? ¿Con quién?
2. ¿Prefieres la comida italiana, la comida china o la comida mexicana?
3. ¿Qué prefieres: la ternera, la carne de cerdo o el pollo?
4. ¿Qué vegetales comes? ¿Cuáles no comes?
5. ¿Tú desayunas en tu casa o en la cafetería?
6. Generalmente, ¿qué días vas al mercado?
7. ¿Qué marca (*brand*) de detergente usas para lavar la ropa? ¿Usas lejía también?
8. Cuando das una fiesta, ¿sirves bebidas alcohólicas?
9. ¿Cuánto tiempo hace que vives en la misma (*same*) ciudad?
10. ¿Hay alguien en tu casa ahora?
11. ¿Tus amigos te llaman por teléfono todos los días?
12. ¿Tú puedes llamarme esta tarde?

Una encuesta Interview your classmates to identify who fits the following descriptions. Include your instructor, but remember to use the **Ud.** form when addressing him or her.

Nombre

1. Conoce a una pareja de recién casados. _____
2. Vive cerca de la universidad. _____
3. Tiene el día libre mañana. _____
4. Está muerto(a) de hambre. _____
5. Come cuatro vegetales y cuatro frutas al día. _____
6. A veces va a la pescadería. _____
7. Sabe preparar espaguetis con albóndigas. _____
8. Es buen(a) cocinero(a). _____
9. Cocina mejor que su madre. _____
10. No bebe ni vino ni cerveza. _____

Y ahora... Write a brief summary indicating what you have learned about your classmates.

¿Cómo lo decimos?   What would you say in the following situations? What might the other person say? Act out the scenes with a partner.

1. You are telling a friend that you need many things from the supermarket. Tell him or her what they are.
2. You are at an outdoor market in Managua and you need vegetables, fish, meat, and bread. You inquire about prices and so on.
3. You are telling someone what ingredients you need to make vegetable soup.
4. You tell someone what you serve to eat and to drink when you give a party.
5. You tell a friend what fruits you need to prepare a fruit salad (**ensalada de frutas**).

¿Qué pasa aquí?   Working with classmates in groups of three or four, describe what is happening in the picture. Create a story, naming the characters and explaining who is who, and what these people plan to buy. Each group will compare its story with the rest of the class.

Para escribir

Un invitado importante   Imagine that next Saturday you are hosting a very important guest. Who is the guest? What are you going to do to prepare for the occasion? What housework do you have to do? What do you need to buy and prepare for dinner? What else are you going to do in honor of your guest's arrival?

Un proverbio

No sólo de pan vive el hombre.

You have probably heard this proverb before. Do you know where it comes from? What does it mean to you? Memorize it!

Lectura

Estrategia de lectura Look at the **Sección Gastronómica** of this paper. Based on the headline, what do you think the reading is about? What do you already know about the topic? Make a list in Spanish of key words that might appear in the reading.

Vamos a leer As you read this section of the paper, find the answers to the questions that follow.

Sección gastronómica

por Juan Carlos Miró

Si Ud. quiere celebrar un cumpleaños o un aniversario en un ambiente elegante, visite el restaurante Miramar, donde va a encontrar sabrosísimos platos típicos e internacionales.

Si le gusta el pescado, yo recomiendo el salmón a la parrilla; si prefiere comer mariscos, pida la langosta Termidor. Además de pescados y mariscos, el restaurante ofrece una gran variedad de carnes, entre otras: bistec, pollo y chuletas preparadas por el conocido chef Antonio.

La lista de postres es muy variada y todos son excelentes, pero si tengo que elegir uno, pido la torta de fresas con crema chantilly.

En cuanto a los vinos, puede escoger entre los mejores de Chile, España y California.

¡Nos vemos en el restaurante Miramar!

1. ¿Cómo es el ambiente del restaurante Miramar?
2. ¿Qué tipos de platos va a encontrar en el restaurante?
3. Si Ud. quiere comer pescado o mariscos, ¿qué recomienda Miró?

Video

4. ¿Qué carnes ofrece el restaurante, entre otras?

5. ¿Quién es Antonio?

6. ¿Cuál es el postre favorito de Miró?

7. ¿Qué vinos tienen en el restaurante?

Díganos   Answer the following questions based on your own thoughts and experiences.

1. ¿Cuál es su restaurante favorito? ¿Cuál es su especialidad?

2. Si Ud. va a un restaurante que tiene un menú similar del restaurante Miramar, ¿qué pide?

3. ¿Cuál es su postre favorito?

4. ¿De dónde cree Ud. que vienen los mejores vinos?

5. Si Ud. va a celebrar su cumpleaños, ¿prefiere ir a un restaurante o celebrarlo en su casa?

Esta pareja de recién casados está en un restaurante. ¿Qué comidas creen Uds. que hay en el menú?

Marisa en la cocina

Marisa está preparando una cena para el cumpleaños de Pablo. No tiene los ingredientes necesarios para el guiso (*stew*), y usa otros, con el resultado que podemos imaginar.

El mundo hispánico

 ## Costa Rica

- Costa Rica es uno de los países más pequeños del continente americano (51.000 km^2 —kilómetros cuadrados). Está situado en América Central y su capital es San José. Los productos principales del país son el café, las bananas, el cacao y la caña de azúcar (*sugar cane*).

- La mayoría de los "ticos" (como se les llama a los costarricenses) son católicos y de origen español. De todos los países centroamericanos, Costa Rica es el que tiene el menor número de analfabetos (*illiterates*). Tiene el mayor ingreso (*income*) per cápita y un gobierno democrático con muy pocos problemas políticos.

- En Costa Rica se le da una gran importancia a la educación, la cultura y las artes. Se dice (*It is said*) que en Costa Rica "hay más maestros (*teachers*) que soldados". Este país tiene excelentes programas para proteger la ecología, sobre todo (*especially*) la selva (*rainforest*).

▲ Miles de peregrinos visitan la Basílica de la Virgen de los Ángeles en Cartago, Costa Rica

▲ El Fuerte de Santiago de la Gloria en Portobello, Panamá

Panamá

- Panamá está situado en el istmo (*isthmus*) que une (*joins*) Suramérica con América del Norte. El país, que está dividido por el Canal de Panamá, tiene una superficie de unos 78.000 km^2 y una población de más de dos millones y medio de habitantes. Su cultura es una mezcla (*mixture*) de las tradiciones españolas, africanas, indígenas y norteamericanas. El idioma oficial del país es el español, pero también se usa mucho el inglés.

- La principal fuente de ingresos (*source of income*) del país está asociada con las operaciones del Canal, que es administrado por Panamá desde el año 2000. La construcción del Canal por parte del gobierno de los Estados Unidos duró (*lasted*) diez años y fue terminada en 1914. El Canal mide 82,4 km y tiene tres esclusas (*locks*) a cada lado del istmo que cruza.

- Junto al Canal están las dos ciudades más grandes del país: Ciudad de Panamá, la capital, y Colón, la segunda ciudad más importante del país.

Honduras

◆ Cuando Colón llegó a la costa de esta región de Centroamérica, sorprendido por la profundidad (*depth*) de las aguas junto a la tierra, llamó al lugar Honduras. Aquí floreció el imperio maya unos 500 años antes de la llegada de los conquistadores. Hoy Honduras, un país pequeño, tiene casi seis millones de habitantes, en su mayoría mestizos.

◆ Honduras es el único país centroamericano que no tiene volcanes, pero esto no es favorable para el país, pues las tierras volcánicas son, por lo general, fértiles y buenas para la agricultura. Como la economía del país se basa en la agricultura, Honduras es hoy uno de los países más pobres de América.

▲ La Iglesia de la Virgen de los Dolores y un puesto de flores en Tegucigalpa, Honduras

◆ La capital de Honduras es Tegucigalpa, que significa "colina de plata" (*silver hill*). La mayor atracción turística del país es Copán, una ciudad maya que existió hace unos dos mil años y de la cual sólo quedan ruinas.

Nicaragua

◆ Nicaragua es el país más extenso de América Central, pero menos de una décima parte de su territorio es cultivable. Nicaragua es la tierra de los lagos y de los volcanes. Uno de los lagos, el Nicaragua, es el mayor lago de agua dulce de Centroamérica, y en él hay tiburones (*sharks*) y otros peces que sólo viven en agua salada en otras regiones.

◆ Las tres ciudades más importantes del país son Managua, la capital, León y Granada.

◆ La economía del país se basa en la agricultura, y sus principales productos de exportación son café, algodón (*cotton*), carne de res (*beef*) y madera (*wood*). El país tiene una selva virgen mucho más extensa que la de Costa Rica, pero lamentablemente no está debidamente (*duly*) protegida contra la explotación excesiva.

▲ Vista panorámica de Managua, la capital nicaragüense

Comentarios... With a partner discuss, in Spanish, what impressed you the most about these four countries and compare them to your own. Which places do you want to visit and why?

Online Study Center

For more practice with lesson topics, see the related activities on the *¡Hola, amigos!* web site at college.hmco.com/PIC/holaamigos7e.

Lección 6

A. Stem-changing verbs: *o > ue* Complete each sentence, using one of the following verbs: **costar, encontrar, recordar, poder** (use twice), **volver, dormir.**

1. Yo no _____ el número de teléfono de Raúl.
2. Jorge _____ a casa a las cinco.
3. ¿Cuánto _____ las chuletas?
4. ¿En qué _____ (yo) servirle?
5. Nosotros no _____ el dinero. ¿Dónde está?
6. Nosotros no _____ ir a la pescadería hoy.
7. Él _____ en su cuarto.

B. Stem-changing verbs: *e > i* Complete these sentences, using the present indicative of the following verbs: **conseguir, servir, pedir, decir.** (Use each verb twice.)

1. Ellos _____ trabajo en el hotel.
2. Nosotros _____ ensalada y sándwiches en la fiesta.
3. ¿Dónde _____ tú fresas?
4. Él _____ que está cansado.
5. Ella me _____ una taza de café.
6. Yo _____ que van al mercado.
7. Mi esposo y yo siempre _____ vino cuando comemos en ese restaurante.
8. ¿Dónde _____ Ud. las tarjetas de México?

C. Direct object pronouns Answer the following questions in the negative, replacing the italicized words with direct object pronouns.

1. ¿Vas a leer *estos libros*?
2. ¿Él *me* conoce? (*Use the **Ud.** form.*)
3. ¿*Te* llevan ellos al mercado?
4. ¿Ella *me* llama mañana? (*Use the **tú** form.*)
5. ¿Necesitas *el detergente*?
6. ¿Tienes *la lejía* aquí?
7. ¿Ellos *los* conocen a Uds.?
8. ¿Uds. consiguen *buenas frutas* en el supermercado?

D. Affirmative and negative expressions Rewrite the following sentences, changing the negative expressions to the affirmative.

1. No tengo nada aquí.
2. ¿No quiere nada más?
3. Nunca vamos al supermercado.
4. No quiero ni la pluma roja ni la pluma verde.
5. Nunca llamo a nadie.

E. *Hace... que* Write the following sentences in Spanish.

1. I have been living in Honduras for five years.
2. How long have you been studying Spanish, Mr. Smith?
3. They have been writing for two hours.
4. She hasn't eaten for two days.

F. Vocabulary Complete the following sentences, using vocabulary from **Lección 6.**

1. Yo le pongo _____ al café.
2. Ellos no quieren _____ de cerdo.
3. Va a comprar el pan en la _____.
4. En mi casa _____ a las doce.
5. ¿A qué hora _____ Uds. a su casa?
6. Ellos están _____ de hambre.
7. Ana y Jorge son _____ casados.
8. Ellos viven _____ de la universidad.
9. El _____ y la _____ son mariscos.
10. Necesito una _____ de huevos y _____ de tomate para los espaguetis.

G. Culture Circle the correct answers, based on the cultural notes you have read.

1. La capital de Costa Rica es (San José / San Juan).
2. La principal fuente de ingresos de Panamá está asociada con (la agricultura / las operaciones del Canal).
3. Honduras (tiene / no tiene) volcanes.
4. La principal exportación de Nicaragua es (el café / el petróleo).

Ester

Carlos

Olga

Pablo

Carlos Aranda y su esposa Ester son cubanos, pero ahora viven en un apartamento grande y moderno en Santo Domingo. Tienen dos hijos: Olga, de dieciocho años, y Pablo, de quince años.

Carlos y Ester se levantan temprano hoy porque tienen muchos planes para el fin de semana. Los chicos duermen hasta las diez porque anoche fueron a una fiesta de cumpleaños en la casa de sus primos y volvieron muy tarde.

Ester ¿Vamos a ir al teatro con tus padres? Ellos nos invitaron la semana pasada.

Carlos Tú sabes que a mí no me gusta ir al teatro; me gusta más el cine. Papá quiere ver la película americana que ponen en el cine Rex…

Ester Bueno, voy a preguntarles si quieren cambiar sus planes.

Carlos ¡Ah! Recibimos una invitación a una boda. La recepción es mañana, en el club Náutico. ¿Quieres ir?

Ester Podemos ir un rato. ¿Ya se levantaron los chicos?

Carlos Sí, están desayunando. Olga se está quejando porque no puede ir a patinar con sus amigos esta tarde.

Ester Ella sabe que esta tarde tenemos que ir a visitar a tía Marcela, que nos invitó a merendar.

Carlos ¡Ay, pobre chica! En vez de divertirse con sus amigos se va a aburrir con tu tía Marcela…

Ester (*Se ríe*) ¡Está bien! Le voy a decir que no tiene que ir con nosotros.

Carlos (*Bromeando*) ¿Yo puedo ir a patinar con ella?

Detalles culturales

Las películas americanas son muy populares en el mundo hispánico. Generalmente tienen subtítulos en español o están dobladas (*dubbed*).

◆ ¿Le gusta ver películas extranjeras (*foreign*)?

Olga y Pablo están hablando en la cocina.

Pablo Yo voy a ir a nadar con Beto y René esta tarde y después vamos a ir a ver un partido de béisbol.

Olga ¿Me estás diciendo que no tienes que ir a la casa de tía Marcela?

Pablo No, papá me dio permiso para salir con mis amigos.

Olga ¡Eso no es justo! ¡Mamá!

Ester (*Entra en la cocina.*) No tienes que ir con nosotros, Olga. La última vez que fuimos a la casa de tía Marcela, tú rompiste su florero favorito. A ella tampoco le gustan tus visitas... ¡Ella compró ese florero en San Juan!

Olga ¡No fui yo! ¡Fue Pablo! Bueno, no me importa. Esta noche, ¿puedo ir a bailar con María Inés y su hermano? Hay una discoteca nueva...

Ester ¡Ajá! ¿El hermano...?

Olga A los dos nos gusta bailar... eso es todo...

Ester Bueno, pero tienes que volver antes de la medianoche.

Olga Les voy a decir que me tienen que traer a las doce menos cinco.

¿Recuerda usted?

¿Verdadero o falso?
With a partner, decide whether the following statements about the dialogue are true (**verdadero**) or false (**falso**).

1. Olga es mayor que Pablo. ☐ V ☐ F
2. Carlos y Ester no piensan hacer nada este fin de semana. ☐ V ☐ F
3. Carlos y su esposa están invitados a una boda. ☐ V ☐ F
4. Los chicos se levantaron muy temprano hoy. ☐ V ☐ F
5. Olga nunca se queja de nada. ☐ V ☐ F
6. A Pablo le gusta el béisbol. ☐ V ☐ F
7. A Marcela no le gustan las visitas de Ester. ☐ V ☐ F
8. Alguien rompió el florero. ☐ V ☐ F
9. María Inés no tiene hermanos. ☐ V ☐ F
10. Olga tiene que volver a su casa antes de las diez. ☐ V ☐ F

Y ahora... conteste
Answer these questions, basing your answers on the dialogue.

1. ¿Dónde viven Carlos Aranda y su familia?
2. ¿Adónde fueron los chicos anoche?
3. ¿Qué quiere ver el papá de Carlos? ¿En qué cine?
4. ¿Cuándo y dónde es la recepción?
5. ¿Carlos cree que su hija se va a divertir o que se va a aburrir con la tía de Ester?
6. ¿Con quiénes va a ir a nadar Pablo?
7. ¿Qué quiere hacer Olga esta noche?
8. ¿Adónde van a ir a bailar?

Para hablar del tema: Vocabulario

Online Study Center

For more practice with lesson topics, see the related activities on the *¡Hola, amigos!* web site at college.hmco.com/PIC/holaamigos7e.

Cognados

el béisbol
la discoteca
moderno(a)
el permiso

el plan
el teatro
la visita

Nombres

el cine movie theatre
el fin de semana weekend
el florero vase
la medianoche midnight

el partido, el juego game
la película movie, film
la semana week
la vez time

Verbos

aburrirse to be bored
bromear to kid, to joke
cambiar to change
divertirse (e >ie) to have a good time
entrar (en) to enter, to go in
gustar to like, to appeal
levantarse to get up
merendar (e >ie) to have an afternoon snack

nadar to swim
patinar to skate
preguntar to ask (*a question*)
quejarse to complain
reírse[1] to laugh
romper* to break
visitar to visit

Adjetivos

justo(a) fair
pasado(a) last
pobre poor
último(a) last (*in a series*)

Otras palabras y expresiones

anoche last night
en vez de instead of
hasta until
importarle (a uno) to matter

ir a patinar to go skating
poner una película* to show a movie
temprano early

---

[1]me río, te ríes, se ríe, nos reímos, os reís, se ríen

Amplíe su vocabulario

Para invitar a alguien a salir (*Asking someone out*)

¿Quieres ir...

a escalar una montaña? *mountain climbing*

a montar* en bicicleta? *bicycle riding*

a esquiar? *skiing (to ski)*

a montar a caballo? *horseback riding*

a un club nocturno? *to a nightclub*

a un concierto? *to a concert*

a la playa? *to the beach*

al museo? *to the museum*

al parque de diversiones*? *to the amusement park*

de picnic? *on a picnic*

al zoológico? *to the zoo*

De país a país

romper quebrar (*Méx.*)

poner una película dar una película (*Ecuador, Cono Sur*)

montar en bicicleta andar en bicicleta (*Arg.*)

el parque de diversiones el parque de atracciones (*Esp.*)

Para practicar el vocabulario

A. Preguntas y respuestas

Match the questions in column *A* with the answers in column *B*.

A	B
1. ¿Se divierten en esas fiestas?	a. La semana pasada.
2. ¿Viste a Roberto en el club?	b. No, no tenemos hambre.
3. ¿Cuándo volvieron?	c. Sí, pero no me importa.
4. ¿Los niños rompieron el florero?	d. Sí, vamos a ir a patinar.
5. ¿Van a merendar?	e. No, porque yo trabajo los sábados.
6. ¿Tiene dinero?	f. ¡Sí! ¡No es justo!
7. ¿Vas los fines de semana?	g. No, se aburren.
8. ¿Tienen planes?	h. A la medianoche.
9. ¿A qué hora vienen?	i. No, es muy pobre.
10. ¿Tú haces todo el trabajo?	j. Sí, dos veces.

B. Todos se divierten

Complete the following statements about a great weekend.

1. Hoy _____ una buena _____ en el cine Victoria.
2. Los chicos van a ir a _____ a caballo.
3. Sergio va a ir a ver un _____ de béisbol.
4. Ana y sus amigos van a una _____ a bailar.
5. Esta tarde yo voy a ir a _____ con mi novio.
6. Estoy invitada a la _____ de una boda.
7. Vamos a la piscina (*pool*) a _____.
8. Vamos al _____ a ver *Romeo y Julieta*.
9. Voy a _____ a mi tía favorita.
10. Teresa y Armando van a un club _____.

C. ¿Adónde vamos...?

Your friend has accepted your invitation. Where are you going to go? Begin your answers with **Vamos a ir...**

1. You want to sunbathe and swim.
2. You feel like climbing a mountain.
3. You want to go to Disneyland.
4. You want to dance salsa.
5. You want to see animals.
6. You want to see Picasso's paintings.
7. You want to have lunch and commune with nature.
8. You want to hear some live music.
9. You want to go to Aspen, Colorado.
10. You want to go horseback riding or ride your bicycle.

D. ¿Quieres ir...?   With a partner, play the roles of two friends who cannot agree on where to go or what to do on the weekend.

◆ MODELO: —*¿Quieres ir al cine?*
      —*No, prefiero ir al teatro.*

Es evidente que estas chicas no están muy contentas. ¿Qué pueden hacer para divertirse un poco?

Pronunciación

Las consonantes *l*, *r*, *rr*

A. Practice the Spanish **l** in the following words.

Olga	abril	último
mil	Ángel	béisbol
Isabel	mal	volver

B. Practice the Spanish **r** in the following words.

moderno	teatro	florero
primero	París	cuarenta
partido	favorito	derecha

C. Practice the Spanish **rr** (spelled **r** both at the beginning of a word and after an **n**) in the following words.

recibir	borrador	correr
Enrique	aburrirse	romper
recepción	pizarra	reírse

Puntos para recordar

1. Preterit of regular verbs (*El pretérito de los verbos regulares*)

- Spanish has two simple past tenses: the preterit and the imperfect. (The imperfect will be presented in **Lección 8.**) The preterit of regular verbs is formed as follows. Note that the endings for **-er** and **-ir** verbs are identical.

-ar *verbs* *tomar (to take)*	-er *verbs* *comer (to eat)*	-ir *verbs* *escribir (to write)*
tom**é**	com**í**	escrib**í**
tom**aste**	com**iste**	escrib**iste**
tom**ó**	com**ió**	escrib**ió**
tom**amos**	com**imos**	escrib**imos**
tom**asteis**	com**isteis**	escrib**isteis**
tom**aron**	com**ieron**	escrib**ieron**

yo **tomé**	*I took; I did take*
Ud. **comió**	*you ate; you did eat*
ellos **decidieron**	*they decided; they did decide*

- Verbs ending in **-ar** and **-er** that are stem-changing in the present indicative are regular in the preterit.

enco**ntrar**	tú enc**ue**ntras	tú enc**o**ntraste
vo**lver**	yo v**ue**lvo	yo v**o**lví
ce**rrar**	yo c**ie**rro	yo c**e**rré

- Verbs ending in **-gar, -car,** and **-zar** change **g** to **gu, c** to **qu,** and **z** to **c** before **é** in the first person of the preterit.

    pagar → pa**gu**é   **buscar** → bus**qu**é   **empezar** → empe**c**é

- Verbs whose stem ends in a strong vowel change the unaccented **i** of the preterit ending to **y** in the third-person singular and plural of the preterit.

    leer → le**y**ó   le**y**eron

- The preterit tense refers to actions or events that the speaker views as completed in the past.

—¿Qué **compraste** ayer?	*"What **did you buy** yesterday?"*
—**Compré** un florero.	*"I **bought** a vase."*
—¿Qué **comieron** Uds.?	*"What **did you eat**?"*
—**Comimos** ensalada.	*"We **ate** salad."*
—¿A qué hora **volvió** usted?	*"What time **did you return**?"*
—Yo **volví** a las seis.	*"I **returned** at six."*
—¿A qué hora **llegaste**?	*"What time **did you arrive**?"*
—**Llegué** a las seis.	*"I **arrived** at six."*

¡Atención! Note that Spanish has no equivalent for the English *did* used as an auxiliary verb in questions and negative sentences.

—¿**Encontraste** el dinero?   *"**Did you find** the money?"*
—No lo **busqué.**   *"**I didn't look for** it."*

Práctica y conversación

Online Study Center

For more practice with lesson topics, see the related activities on the *¡Hola, amigos!* web site at college.hmco.com/PIC/holaamigos7e.

A. Minidiálogos   Complete the following dialogues, using the correct preterit forms of the verbs in parentheses. Then act them out with a partner.

1. —¿A qué hora _____ (volver) Uds. ayer?

   —Yo _____ (volver) a las siete y Mario _____ (volver) a las nueve. ¿A qué hora _____ (volver) tú?

2. —¿_____ (Leer) Ud. este libro, Sr. Vega?

   —Sí, lo _____ (leer) ayer.

   —¿Ud. lo _____ (sacar) de la biblioteca o lo _____ (comprar)?

   —Lo _____ (sacar) de la biblioteca.

3. —¿Cuándo _____ (empezar) a trabajar tú?

   —_____ (Empezar) la semana pasada.

   —¿En qué mes _____ (llegar) aquí?

   —_____ (Llegar) en noviembre del año pasado.

4. —¿Con quién _____ (hablar) Uds.?

   —Yo _____ (hablar) con mi madrina y Ramiro _____ (hablar) con su abuela.

B. Ayer...   Read what the following people typically do. Then complete each sentence telling how they varied from their normal routines yesterday.

1. Yo siempre hablo con mis padres, pero ayer...
2. Yo siempre escribo en inglés, pero ayer...
3. Tú siempre estudias por la mañana, pero ayer...
4. Alberto siempre compra café, pero ayer...
5. Los chicos siempre toman café, pero ayer...
6. Nosotros siempre comemos en la cafetería, pero ayer...
7. Adela siempre sale con su novio, pero ayer...
8. Ustedes siempre vuelven a las seis, pero ayer...
9. Yo siempre llego a la universidad a las ocho, pero ayer...
10. Yo siempre empiezo a trabajar a las tres, pero ayer...

C. Entreviste a su compañero(a) Interview a classmate about his / her activities yesterday, using the following questions.

1. ¿A qué hora saliste de tu casa ayer?
2. ¿A qué hora llegaste a la universidad?
3. ¿Trabajaste mucho?
4. ¿Cuántas horas estudiaste?
5. ¿Dónde comiste? ¿Qué comiste?
6. ¿Qué tomaste?
7. ¿Compraste algo? ¿Qué?
8. ¿A qué hora volviste a tu casa?
9. ¿Qué programa de televisión viste?
10. ¿A qué hora cenaste?
11. ¿Leíste algo antes de acostarte?
12. ¿A qué hora te acostaste?

2. Preterit of *ser, ir,* and *dar* (*El pretérito de* ser, ir y dar)

♦ The preterits of **ser, ir,** and **dar** are irregular.

ser (*to be*)	ir (*to go*)	dar (*to give*)
fui	fui	di
fuiste	fuiste	diste
fue	fue	dio
fuimos	fuimos	dimos
fuisteis	fuisteis	disteis
fueron	fueron	dieron

—¿**Fuiste** al club ayer?   "**Did you go** to the club yesterday?"

—Sí, **fui** para comprar ropa. Papá me **dio** el dinero.   "Yes, **I went** to buy clothes. Dad **gave** me the money."

—¿Quién **fue** tu profesor de español?   "Who **was** your Spanish professor?"
—El Dr. Vega.   "Dr. Vega."

¡Atención! Note that **ser** and **ir** have identical preterit forms; however, there is no confusion as to meaning, because the context clarifies it.

Práctica y conversación

A. Minidiálogos Complete the following dialogues, using the preterit of **ser, ir,** and **dar.** Then act them out with a partner, adding your own original lines of dialogue.

Online Study Center

For more practice with lesson topics, see the related activities on the *¡Hola, amigos!* web site at college.hmco.com/PIC/holaamigos7e.

1. —¿Con quién _____ tú al cine?
   —_____ con mi hijo.
   —¿_____ (Uds.) por la mañana o por la tarde?
   —_____ por la tarde.
2. —¿Cuánto dinero _____ Uds. para la fiesta?
   —Yo _____ 10 dólares y Carlos _____ 5 dólares.
   —¿Luisa _____ a la fiesta con Roberto?
   —No, ella y Marisol _____ con Juan Carlos al cine.
3. —¿Quién _____ el profesor de literatura de Uds. en la universidad?
   —El Dr. Rivas.
   —¿Uds. no _____ estudiantes de la Dra. Torres?
   —No, no _____ estudiantes de ella.

B. Entreviste a su compañero(a) Interview a partner, using the following questions.

1. ¿Quién fue tu profesor(a) favorito(a) el año pasado?
2. ¿Fuiste a la biblioteca ayer? ¿A qué hora?
3. ¿Adónde fuiste el fin de semana pasado?
4. ¿Tus amigos fueron también?
5. ¿Cuándo diste una fiesta?
6. ¿Dónde la diste?
7. ¿Fueron tú y tus amigos al cine el sábado pasado?
8. ¿Fuiste de vacaciones el verano pasado? ¿Adónde fuiste?

C. Queremos saber... With a partner, prepare five questions to ask your instructor about his/her activities. Use the preterit of **ser, ir,** and **dar.**

3. Indirect object pronouns (*Los pronombres usados como complemento indirecto*)

◆ In addition to a subject and direct object, a sentence can have an indirect object.[1]

> Ella les da **el dinero a los muchachos.**
>
>   **s.**   **v.**   **D.O.**   **I.O.**
>
> *What does she give?* **(el dinero)**
>
> *To whom does she give it?* **(a los muchachos)**

In this sentence, **ella** is the subject who performs the action, **el dinero** is the direct object, and **a los muchachos** is the indirect object, the final recipient of the action expressed by the verb.

---

[1]See Appendix C.

- Indirect object nouns are for the most part preceded by the preposition **a.**

- An indirect object usually tells *to whom* or *for whom* something is done. Compare these sentences:

  Yo voy a mandar**lo** a México.   (**lo:** *direct object*)
  *I'm going to send **him** to Mexico.*

  Yo voy a mandar**le** dinero.   (**le:** *indirect object*)
  *I'm going to send **him** money.*   (*I'm going to send money **to him.***)

- An indirect object pronoun can be used with or in place of the indirect object. In Spanish, the indirect object pronoun includes the meaning *to* or *for*. The forms of the indirect object pronouns are shown in the following table.

Singular		Plural	
me	(to/for) me	**nos**	(to/for) us
te	(to/for) you (*fam.*)	**os**	(to/for) you (*fam.*)
le	⎧(to/for) you (*form.*) ⎨(to/for) him ⎩(to/for) her	**les**	⎧(to/for) you (*form., fam.*) ⎩(to/for) them (*masc., fem.*)

- Indirect object pronouns have the same form as direct object pronouns, except in the third person.

- Indirect object pronouns are usually placed in front of the conjugated verb.

  Le dimos una propina.   *We gave **him** a tip.*

- When used with an infinitive or in the present progressive, however, the indirect object pronoun may either be placed in front of the conjugated verb or attached to the infinitive or the present participle.

  Le voy a escribir una carta.
  or: ⎱ *I'm going to write **you** a letter.*
  Voy a escribir**le** una carta.

  Les estoy diciendo la hora.
  or: ⎱ *I'm telling **them** the time.*
  Estoy diciéndo**les**[1] la hora.

  ¡Atención!   The indirect object pronouns **le** and **les** require clarification when the context does not specify the gender or the person to which they refer. Spanish provides clarification by using the preposition **a** + *pronoun or noun.*

  Le doy la información.   *I give the information . . .*
  but: *(to whom? to him? to her?*
                                                    to you?)
  Le doy la información **a ella.**   *I give the information **to her.***

---

[1]When an indirect object pronoun is attached to a present participle, an accent mark is added to maintain the correct stress.

The prepositional phrase provides clarification or emphasis; it is not, however, a substitute for the indirect object pronoun. While the prepositional form can be omitted, the indirect object pronoun must always be used.

—¿Qué vas a comprar**le** a tu hija?　　*"What are you going to buy (for) your daughter?"*

—**Le** voy a comprar un florero.　　*"I'm going to buy **her** a vase."*

Práctica y conversación

Online Study Center

For more practice with lesson topics, see the related activities on the *¡Hola, amigos!* web site at college.hmco.com/PIC/holaamigos7e.

A. Frutas para todos　Mom went to the market and bought fruit for everyone. Indicate for whom she bought each fruit, using indirect object pronouns. Clarify when necessary.

◆ **MODELO:** Mamá compró duraznos *para él.*
　　　　　*Mamá **le** compró duraznos **a él.***

1. Mamá compró manzanas *para mí.*
2. Mamá compró peras *para nosotros.*
3. Mamá compró uvas *para ella.*
4. Mamá compró una piña *para ti.*
5. Mamá compró melocotones *para Ud.*
6. Mamá compró una sandía *para ellos.*
7. Mamá compró cerezas *para Uds.*
8. Mamá compró fresas *para el.*
9. Mamá compró bananas *para Rodolfo.*
10. Mamá compró mangos *para Sofía.*

B. Entreviste a su compañero(a)　Interview a partner, using the following questions.

1. ¿Cuándo vas a escribirles a tus amigos?
2. ¿Le escribiste a alguien ayer?
3. ¿Tú siempre le escribes a tu mejor amigo(a)?
4. ¿Tus padres te escribieron esta semana?
5. ¿Tus padres te dan dinero para comprar ropa?
6. ¿Tú vas a mandarle dinero a alguien? ¿A quién?
7. ¿Tus padres les hablan a Uds. en inglés o en español?
8. ¿Tú siempre les dices la verdad a tus padres?

C. Son bilingües　What languages do the people below speak and what languages are spoken to them? With a partner, match each name to the most likely language.

alemán (*German*)	italiano
español	japonés
francés	portugués
inglés	ruso (*Russian*)

◆ **MODELO:** María del Pilar (a mí)
　　　　　María del Pilar me habla en español.
　　　　　Yo le hablo en español a ella.

1. Boris (a ti)
2. Giovanni (a ellos)
3. John (a mí)
4. El Sr. Toyota (a Uds.)
5. Monique y Pierre (a nosotros)
6. Hans (a Ud.)
7. Nelson (de Brasil) (a él)
8. Rosa y José (a ella)

D. **Regalos** (*Presents*) In groups of three or four, tell each other about four or five gifts that you bought your friends and relatives for Christmas (*la Navidad*) or a birthday and describe what they bought you.

◆ MODELO: *A mi mamá le compré una licuadora para su cumpleaños.*
El día de mi cumpleaños, mi mamá me compró un escritorio.

4. The verb *gustar* (*El verbo* gustar)

◆ The verb **gustar** means to like something or somebody (literally, *to be pleasing*). A special construction is required in Spanish to translate the English *to like*. Note that the equivalent of the English direct object becomes the subject of the Spanish sentence. The English subject then becomes the indirect object of the Spanish sentence.

<table>
<tr><td></td><td>*I like **your house.***</td></tr>
<tr><td>**Me** gusta **tu** *casa.*</td><td>S.   D.O.</td></tr>
<tr><td>I.O.   S.</td><td>***Your house** is pleasing **to me.***</td></tr>
<tr><td></td><td>S.   I.O.</td></tr>
</table>

◆ **Gustar** is *always* used with an indirect object pronoun—in this example, **me.**

◆ The two most commonly used forms of **gustar** are the third-person singular **gusta** if the subject is singular or if the verb is followed by one or more infinitives, and the third-person plural **gustan** if the subject is plural.

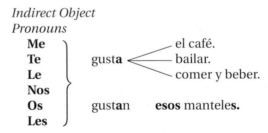

Indirect Object Pronouns

Me		el café.
Te	gust**a**	bailar.
Le		comer y beber.
Nos		
Os	gust**an**	**esos** mantele**s.**
Les		

◆ Note that **gustar** agrees in number with the *subject* of the sentence, that is, the person or thing being liked.

    Me gust**an las manzanas.**   ***Apples are** pleasing to me.*

◆ The person who does the liking is the indirect object.

Me gustan las manzanas.   *Apples are pleasing **to me.***

—¿**Te** gusta este mantel rojo?   *"Do **you** like this red tablecloth?"*
—No, no **me** gustan los   *"No, **I** don't like red tablecloths."*
   manteles rojos.

—¿**Les** gusta el francés?   *"Do **you** like French?"*
—Sí, **nos** gusta mucho el   *"Yes, **we** like French very*
   francés, pero **nos** gusta   *much, but **we** like Spanish*
   más el español.   *better."*

¡Atención! Note that the words **más** and **mucho** immediately follow **gustar.**

◆ The preposition **a** + *a noun* or *pronoun* is used to clarify meaning or to emphasize the indirect object.

A Aurora (A ella) le gusta esa panadería, pero **a mí** no me gusta.

Aurora likes that bakery, but I don't like it.

A Beto y **a Rosa** les gusta ese restaurante.

Beto and Rosa like that restaurant.

¡Atención! If the thing liked is an action, the second verb is an infinitive: **Me gusta patinar.**

Detalles culturales

En la cultura hispánica, los sobrenombres son muy populares. Roberto: **Beto;** Enrique: **Quique;** Dolores: **Lola.**

◆ ¿Qué sobrenombres son populares en este país? ¿Ud. tiene sobrenombre?

Online Study Center

For more practice with lesson topics, see the related activities on the *¡Hola, amigos!* web site at college.hmco.com/PIC/holaamigos7e.

Práctica y conversación

A. **¿Qué les gusta?**   Tell who likes what.

◆ **MODELO:** Yo / ese cine
Me gusta ese cine.

1. Nosotros / más / estos floreros
2. Tú / visitar / tus tíos
3. Yo / mucho / cocinar
4. Ellos / mucho / La Habana
5. Él / no / mucho / ese parque de diversiones
6. Uds. / más / esas ciudades
7. Ella / ese club nocturno
8. Yo / mucho / los restaurantes italianos
9. Uds. / no/ la música jazz
10. Mi mamá / mucho / esquiar

B. **Entreviste a su compañero(a)**   Interview a classmate, asking the following questions.

1. ¿A ti te gusta más el invierno o el verano?
2. ¿Te gusta más venir a clase por la mañana o por la tarde?
3. ¿A ti te gusta más el rojo o el azul?
4. ¿Te gusta más vivir en una casa o en un apartamento?
5. ¿Te gustan más las ciudades grandes o las ciudades pequeñas?
6. ¿Te gustan más las peras o las manzanas?
7. ¿A tu mamá le gusta más bailar o cantar (*sing*)?
8. ¿A tus amigos les gusta más ir al cine o al teatro?

C. **Los sábados**   With a partner, talk about what you, your parents, and your friends like and don't like to do on Saturdays.

◆ **MODELO:** A mi papá...
A mi papá le gusta leer. No le gusta trabajar.

1. A mí...
2. A mi mamá...
3. A mi papá...
4. A nosotros...
5. A mis amigos...
6. A mi mejor amigo(a)...

D. Preferencias...
Look at these illustrations and say what these people like and what they don't like to do.

◆ **MODELO:**

Juan

A Juan le gusta leer.

Inés

1. _____

Jorge *Mario*

2. _____

Yo

3. _____

Nostotras

4. _____

Tú

5. _____

Ud.

6. _____

Carmen

7. _____

E. Queremos saber
With a partner, prepare three or four questions to ask your instructor about what he or she likes or doesn't like to do.

5. Reflexive constructions (*Construcciones reflexivas*)

- The reflexive construction (e.g., *I introduce myself*) consists in Spanish of a reflexive pronoun and a verb.
- Reflexive pronouns[1] refer to the same person as the subject of the sentence does.

Subjects	Reflexive Pronouns	
yo	**me**	myself, to (for) myself
tú	**te**	yourself, to (for) yourself (*fam.*)
nosotros(as)	**nos**	ourselves, to (for) ourselves
vosotros(as)	**os**	yourselves, to (for) yourselves (*fam.*)
Ud.	**se**	yourself, to (for) yourself (*form.*)
Uds.		yourselves, to (for) yourselves (*form., fam.*)
él		himself, to (for) himself
ella		herself, to (for) herself
		itself, to (for) itself
ellos, ellas		themselves, to (for) themselves

¡Atención! Reflexive pronouns are positioned in the sentence in the same manner as object pronouns.

- Note that except for **se,** reflexive pronouns have the same forms as the direct and indirect object pronouns.
- The third-person singular and plural **se** is invariable, that is, it does not show gender or number.
- Any verb that can act upon the subject can be made reflexive in Spanish with the aid of a reflexive pronoun.

Julia **le** prueba el vestido **a su hija.**
   (*Julia tries the dress on her daughter.*)

Julia **se prueba** el vestido.
   (*Julia tries on the dress.*)

---

[1]See Appendix C.

vestirse (e > i) (*to dress oneself, to get dressed*)	
Yo **me visto.**	I dress myself.
Tú **te vistes.**	You dress yourself. (*fam.*)
Ud. **se viste.**	You dress yourself. (*form.*)
Él **se viste.**	He dresses himself.
Ella **se viste.**	She dresses herself.
Nosotros **nos vestimos.**	We dress ourselves.
Vosotros **os vestís.**	You dress yourselves. (*fam.*)
Uds. **se visten.**	You dress yourselves. (*form., fam.*)
Ellos **se visten.**	They (*masc.*) dress themselves.
Ellas **se visten.**	They (*fem.*) dress themselves.

◆ The following commonly used verbs are reflexive.

aburrirse *to get bored*	**lavarse** *to wash oneself*
acostarse (o>ue) *to go to bed*	**levantarse** *to get up*
afeitarse, rasurarse *to shave*	**ponerse** *to put on*
bañarse *to bathe*	**probarse (o>ue)** *to try on*
despertarse (e>ie) *to wake up*	**quitarse** *to take off*
divertirse (e>ie) *to have fun*	**sentarse (e>ie)** *to sit down*

—¿A qué hora **se levantan** Uds.?
"*What time do you **get up**?*"

—Yo **me levanto** a las seis y Jorge **se levanta** a las ocho.
"*I **get up** at six o'clock and Jorge **gets up** at eight.*"

—Uds. **se levantaron** muy tarde hoy.
"*You **got up** very late today.*"

—Sí, porque anoche **nos acostamos** a la medianoche.
"*Yes, because last night **we went to bed** at midnight.*"

Práctica y conversación

Online Study Center

For more practice with lesson topics, see the related activities on the *¡Hola, amigos!* web site at college.hmco.com/PIC/holaamigos7e.

A. Entreviste a su compañero(a) Interview a partner, using the following questions.

1. ¿A qué hora te despertaste esta mañana?
2. Generalmente, ¿te levantas temprano o tarde? ¿A qué hora te levantas?
3. ¿Te acuestas temprano? ¿Te acuestas antes de las once?
4. ¿Te bañas por la mañana o por la noche? ¿Con qué jabón (*soap*) te bañas?
5. ¿Puedes bañarte y vestirte en diez minutos?
6. ¿Con qué jabón te lavas las manos?
7. ¿Tu papá se afeita todos los días?
8. ¿Siempre te pruebas la ropa antes de comprarla?
9. En la clase de español, ¿prefieres sentarte cerca de la puerta o cerca de la pizarra?
10. ¿Te sientas cerca de la ventana? ¿Por qué?
11. ¿Te diviertes en la clase de español?
12. ¿En qué clase te aburres?

B. ¿Qué pasó...? Use your imagination to complete the following sentences.

1. Yo me levanté a las seis y Jorge…
2. Mi hermana se bañó por la noche y tú…
3. Yo me desperté temprano y Rosa…
4. Nosotras nos probamos los vestidos negros y ellas…
5. Tú te sentaste cerca de la puerta y ella…
6. Yo me vestí en diez minutos y tú…
7. Yo me afeité por la noche y él…
8. Nosotros nos acostamos a las once y Uds.…
9. Yo me aburrí en la fiesta y tú…
10. Yo me lavé las manos con jabón Dove y ellos…

C. La rutina diaria Look at the illustrations below. How would José describe his routine and that of his family?

1. Yo…

2. Mi papá…

3. Yo…

los sábados

4. Nosotros…

5. Mamá…

6. Nosotros…

7. Yo...

8. ¿Tú...?

 D. **¿Cada cuánto tiempo...?** (*How often . . . ?*) In groups of three or four, talk about how often you do the following things. Use **siempre, todos los días, nunca, a veces,** and **frecuentemente.**

1. levantarse antes de las siete
2. despertarse muy tarde
3. bañarse por la noche
4. ponerse pijama para dormir
5. acostarse muy tarde
6. quejarse de sus profesores

Rodeo

Summary of the Pronouns (Resumen de los pronombres)

Subject	Direct Object	Indirect Object	Reflexive	Object of Prepositions
yo	**me**	**me**	**me**	**mí**
tú	**te**	**te**	**te**	**ti**
usted (*masc.*)	**lo**			**usted**
usted (*fem.*)	**la**	**le**	**se**	**usted**
él	**lo**			**él**
ella	**la**			**ella**
nosotros(as)	**nos**	**nos**	**nos**	**nosotros(as)**
vosotros(as)	**os**	**os**	**os**	**vosotros(as)**
ustedes (*masc.*)	**los**			**ustedes**
ustedes (*fem.*)	**las**	**les**	**se**	**ustedes**
ellos	**los**			**ellos**
ellas	**las**			**ellas**

Práctica

Queridos padres   Supply all the missing pronouns in the letter that Oscar wrote to his parents and read the letter aloud.

Queridos padres:

_____ escribo para decir_____ que estoy bien y estoy trabajando mucho. Ayer hablé con Eva. _____ está estudiando en la universidad y dice que quiere conocer_____ porque _____ siempre _____ hablo de _____. _____ invitó a una fiesta que ella da esta noche.

Hoy _____ levanté muy temprano y fui de compras. Para _____, papá, compré un reloj. A _____, mamá, _____ compré un vestido. Para _____, compré un par de zapatos para la fiesta de Eva.

¿Cómo está mi hermana? Hace mucho que no _____ llamo por teléfono ni _____ escribo. ¡Ah! A _____ _____ compré un libro.

Bueno, ya son las seis y tengo que bañar_____ y vestir_____ para ir a la fiesta.

_____ quiero mucho.

Un abrazo,

Oscar

Sergio le envía un mensaje electrónico a su novia. ¿Qué le dice de sus planes para el sábado? ¿Va a salir con ella? ¿La va a llamar por teléfono?

Entre nosotros

¡Conversemos!

 Para conocernos mejor   Get to know your partner better by asking each other the following questions.

1. ¿Te gusta levantarte temprano? ¿A qué hora te levantaste hoy?
2. ¿A qué hora te acostaste anoche?
3. ¿Qué te gusta hacer los fines de semana? ¿Qué no te gusta hacer?
4. ¿Qué actividades planeas para este fin de semana?
5. Si te invitan a un concierto de música clásica, ¿tú vas?
6. ¿Te gusta más patinar o esquiar?
7. ¿Adónde fuiste el sábado pasado? ¿Con quién fuiste?
8. ¿Le escribiste a alguien? ¿A quién?
9. ¿Cuándo fue la última vez que tus padres te dieron dinero para comprar ropa?
10. ¿Fuiste alumno(a) de esta universidad el año pasado?

 Una encuesta   Interview your classmates to identify who fits the following descriptions. Include your instructor, but remember to use the **Ud.** form when addressing him or her.

	Nombre
1. Dio una fiesta el mes pasado.	
2. Fue al zoológico el año pasado.	
3. Va al cine todos los fines de semana.	
4. Fue a un parque de diversiones el verano pasado.	
5. Va a la playa frecuentemente.	
6. Fue de picnic con sus amigos.	
7. Sabe montar a caballo.	
8. Le gusta escalar montañas.	
9. Se queja de sus profesores a veces.	
10. Se despierta muy temprano.	

Y ahora... Write a brief summary, indicating what you have learned about your classmates.

¿Cómo lo decimos? What would you say in the following situations? What might the other person say? Act out the scenes with a partner.

1. You ask a friend three questions about his/her daily routine.
2. While leaving a movie theatre, you see a friend. Ask him what movie he saw and whether he liked it.
3. You and a friend are making plans for the weekend and are discussing activities that you like.

¿Qué pasa aquí? The people in this photo are friends trying to plan a weekend. Two of them are making different suggestions and the third one rejects them all. In groups of three, indicate who they are and what they are saying. Say what happens at the end.

Para escribir

Un día típico Describe a typical day in your life: what time you get up, what you generally eat, where you go, what you do, and so on.

Un dicho

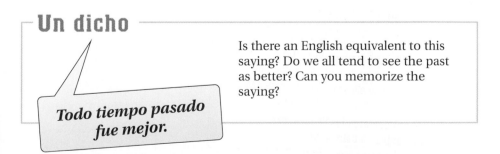

Todo tiempo pasado fue mejor.

Is there an English equivalent to this saying? Do we all tend to see the past as better? Can you memorize the saying?

Jaime | Gloria | David | Susana

Susana y Gloria son dos hermanas colombianas que están casadas con Jaime y David, de Venezuela. Los dos matrimonios viven en Caracas, y frecuentemente se juntan para ir a cenar, al cine o a la playa. Ahora están planeando un fin de semana.

Jaime Cuando yo era chico, mi familia y yo siempre íbamos a acampar al Parque Nacional de Canaima, de modo que soy un experto en armar tiendas de campaña, en hacer fogatas...

Susana En cambio Gloria y yo pasábamos nuestras vacaciones en ciudades grandes, y nos hospedábamos en hoteles muy buenos.

Gloria ¡Ay, sí! Ya te dije que nosotras no estábamos acostumbradas a todas estas actividades que te gustan a ti, mi amor.

Jaime ¡Les va a encantar dormir bajo las estrellas, en una bolsa de dormir!

David Oye, tu hermano prometió prestarte sus bolsas de dormir. ¿Te las trajo?

Jaime No, me las va a traer esta noche. También me va a prestar su caña de pescar.

David ¡Ah! No hay nada como comer pescado frito que uno acaba de pescar.

Detalles culturales

El Parque Nacional de Canaima es una de las áreas naturales más importantes de Venezuela y su mayor atracción turística. Aquí se encuentran las cataratas del Salto Ángel, las más altas del mundo. También existe en el parque una gran variedad de animales, muchos en peligro (*danger*) de extinción. Muchas de las plantas que hay en el parque son exclusivas de esta región.

◆ **¿Qué parques nacionales importantes hay en este país?**

Detalles culturales

En Latinoamerica son muy populares los vendedores ambulantes a los que se les pueden comprar diversos artículos. Los productos que ellos venden son más baratos y con ellos es más fácil regatear (*to haggle*).

◆ **¿Son populares los vendedores ambulantes en este país?**

Llegaron al parque el viernes por la tarde. Por la noche no durmieron muy bien y hoy están un poco cansados. Se levantaron muy temprano para hacer una caminata y ahora Jaime y David están tratando de pescar algo en el lago.

David   Cuando veníamos para acá vi a unos hombres que vendían pescado. Si no pescamos nada...

Jaime   Pronto vamos a tener pescado para el almuerzo. ¡Te lo prometo!

David   Espero que sí, porque tengo mucha hambre. Jaime, ¿dónde pusiste el termo de café?

Jaime   Se lo di a Gloria esta mañana, porque ella me lo pidió. Oye, después de almorzar podemos alquilar una canoa para ir a remar.

Dos horas más tarde.

David   ¿Por qué no llamamos a Gloria y a Susana y les decimos que no pudimos pescar nada?

Jaime   ¡Porque nos van a tomar el pelo! ¡Chist! ¡Ahí vienen!

Susana y Gloria traen dos cestas de picnic.

Susana   Gloria y yo trajimos comida, por si acaso...

Gloria   Pollo frito, ensalada de papas, pastel de manzana...

David   ¡Excelente idea! ¡Vamos a comer!

¿Recuerda usted?

¿Verdadero o falso? With a partner, decide whether the following statements about the dialogue are true (**verdadero**) or false (**falso**).

1. Los dos matrimonios viven en la capital de Venezuela. □ V □ F
2. Jaime sabe armar tiendas de campaña. □ V □ F
3. Gloria y su hermana siempre iban a acampar cuando eran niñas. □ V □ F
4. El hermano de David tiene bolsas de dormir. □ V □ F
5. A David y a Jaime no les gusta pescar. □ V □ F
6. El sábado todos se despertaron muy tarde. □ V □ F
7. Jaime es muy optimista. □ V □ F
8. Gloria tiene el termo de café. □ V □ F
9. A Jaime no le gusta remar. □ V □ F
10. Todos comieron pescado.

Y ahora... conteste Answer these questions, basing your answers on the dialogue.

1. ¿Para qué se juntan, frecuentemente, los dos matrimonios?
2. ¿A dónde iban a acampar Jaime y su familia cuando él era chico?
3. ¿Dónde pasaban sus vacaciones Gloria y Susana?
4. Según (*According to*) Jaime, ¿qué les va a encantar a Gloria y a Susana?
5. ¿Cómo durmieron todos anoche?
6. ¿Qué le promete Jaime a David?
7. ¿Qué pueden hacer todos después de almorzar?
8. ¿Qué trajeron Susana y Gloria?

Para hablar del tema: Vocabulario

Cognados

la actividad	experto(a)	el hotel
la canoa	excelente	el termo

Nombres

la actividad al aire libre outdoor activity	**la cesta** basket	**el lago** lake
la bolsa de dormir* sleeping bag	**la estrella** star	**el matrimonio** married couple
la caña de pescar fishing rod	**la fogata** bonfire	**la tienda de campaña** tent

Verbos

acampar to camp	**hospedarse** to stay (i.e., *at a hotel*)	**prestar** to lend
alquilar* to rent		**prometer** to promise
armar to pitch (*a tent*), to put together	**juntarse** to get together	**remar** to row
	pasar to spend (time)	**tratar (de)** to try to
encantar[1] to love, to like very much	**pescar** to fish, to catch a fish	**vender** to sell

Adjetivos

acostumbrado(a) accustomed or used to
chico(a), pequeño(a) little
frito(a) fried

Otras palabras y expresiones

acá here	**hacer una caminata** to go hiking
acabar de + *infinitive* to have just (*done something*)	**ir a acampar** to go camping
	mi amor darling, my love
ahí there	**por si acaso** just in case
bajo under	**pronto** soon
en cambio on the other hand	**tomarle el pelo a alguien** to pull someone's leg
Espero que sí. I hope so.	
frecuentemente, a menudo often	**Vamos a comer.** Let's eat.

De país a país

la bolsa de dormir el saco de dormir (*Col.*)
alquilar rentar (*Méx.*)
el velero el bote de vela (*Cuba, Arg.*)
el traje de baño la trusa (*Cuba*), el bañador (*Esp.*), la malla (*Cono Sur*)

---

[1]Conjugated like *gustar*

Amplíe su vocabulario

Más sobre las actividades al aire libre

jugar al golf

cazar

jugar al tenis

Para practicar el vocabulario

A. Preguntas y respuestas
Match the questions in column A with the answers in column B.

A	B
1. ¿Tienes hambre?	a. Sí, me encanta.
2. ¿Vas a ir a acampar?	b. Sí, soy un experto.
3. ¿Uds. se juntan para salir?	c. Sí, bajo las estrellas.
4. ¿Tú sabes armar tiendas de campaña?	d. En la cesta de picnic.
5. ¿Dónde se hospedaron?	e. Sí, necesito la tienda de campaña.
6. ¿Te gusta pescar?	f. En el termo.
7. ¿Compraste una caña de pescar?	g. En el hotel Hilton.
8. ¿Dormiste en una bolsa de dormir?	h. No, acabo de almorzar.
9. ¿Dónde pusiste el café?	i. No, no me gusta remar.
10. ¿Qué vendían esos hombres?	j. No, me la prestaron.
11. ¿Vas a ir en canoa?	k. Sí, frecuentemente.
12. ¿Dónde pusiste el pollo frito?	l. Pescado.

B. ¿Lógico o ilógico?
With a partner, indicate whether each of the following statements is logical (**L**) or illogical (**I**).

1. Necesitamos el traje de baño para ir a cazar.
2. En la playa generalmente hay salvavidas.
3. Necesito la escopeta para hacer una fogata.
4. Voy a ir a bucear porque quiero tomar el sol.
5. Vamos a hacer esquí acuático en el lago.
6. Para remar usamos la tabla de mar.
7. Hicimos una caminata y ahora estamos muy cansados.
8. Traje los palos de golf para jugar al tenis.
9. Siempre dejamos el velero en el cuarto del hotel.
10. Anoche comimos arena.

C. Palabras y más palabras
¿Qué palabra o frase corresponde a lo siguiente?

1. La necesito para pescar.
2. Las vemos en el cielo (*sky*).
3. pequeño
4. a menudo
5. La necesito para jugar al tenis.
6. opuesto de comprar
7. muy, muy bueno
8. Me gusta mucho.
9. quedarse (en un hotel)
10. La necesito para cazar.

D. Planes de vacaciones You and a classmate play the roles of two friends who are planning a fun weekend. Talk about everything you can do.

Estas chicas fueron a acampar el fin de semana pasado. ¿Qué hicieron?

Pronunciación

Pronunciation in context

In this lesson, there are some words or phrases that may be challenging to pronounce. Listen to your instructor and pronounce the following sentences.

1. **Pasábamos** nuestras **vacaciones** en ciudades grandes y **nos hospedábamos** en hoteles muy buenos.
2. Ya te dije que nosotras no estábamos **acostumbradas** a todas estas **actividades.**
3. **Se levantaron** muy temprano para **hacer** una caminata.
4. **Después** de almorzar podemos **alquilar** una canoa para ir a **remar.**
5. ¿Por qué no **llamamos** a Gloria y a Susana y les **decimos** que no pudimos pescar nada?

Puntos para recordar

1. Preterit of some irregular verbs (*El pretérito de algunos verbos irregulares*)

◆ The following Spanish verbs are irregular in the preterit.

tener	tuve, tuviste, tuvo, tuvimos, tuvisteis, tuvieron
estar	estuve, estuviste, estuvo, estuvimos, estuvisteis, estuvieron
poder	pude, pudiste, pudo, pudimos, pudisteis, pudieron
poner	puse, pusiste, puso, pusimos, pusisteis, pusieron
saber	supe, supiste, supo, supimos, supisteis, supieron
hacer	hice, hiciste, hizo, hicimos, hicisteis, hicieron
venir	vine, viniste, vino, vinimos, vinisteis, vinieron
querer	quise, quisiste, quiso, quisimos, quisisteis, quisieron
decir	dije, dijiste, dijo, dijimos, dijisteis, dijeron
traer	traje, trajiste, trajo, trajimos, trajisteis, trajeron
conducir[1]	conduje, condujiste, condujo, condujimos, condujisteis, condujeron
traducir[1]	traduje, tradujiste, tradujo, tradujimos, tradujisteis, tradujeron

¡Atención! The third-person singular of the verb **hacer** changes the **c** to **z** in order to maintain the original soft sound of the **c** in the infinitive. The **i** is omitted in the third-person plural ending of the verbs **decir, traer, conducir,** and **traducir.**

—¿Qué **trajeron** Uds. ayer?   *"What **did you bring** yesterday?"*
—**Trajimos** las cestas.   *"**We brought** the baskets."*

—Ayer no **viniste** a clase.   *"**You did** not **come** to class yesterday.*
  ¿Qué **hiciste?**   *What **did you do**?"*
—**Tuve** que trabajar.   *"**I had** to work. **Was there** an exam?"*
  ¿**Hubo** un examen?
—No.   *"No."*

¡Atención! The preterit of **hay** (impersonal form of **haber**) is **hubo.**

---

[1]**conducir** = *to drive;* **traducir** = *to translate.*

¡Hola!

¡Hola! ¿Trajiste algo de Colombia?

Práctica y conversación

Online Study Center

For more practice with lesson topics, see the related activities on the *¡Hola, amigos!* web site at college.hmco.com/PIC/holaamigos7e.

A. Minidiálogos Complete the following exchanges, using the preterit of the verbs in parentheses. Then act them out with a partner.

1. —¿Dónde _____ (estar) tú la semana pasada?

   —(Yo) _____ (estar) en el Parque Nacional de Canaima.

   —¿Y tus padres?

   —Ellos _____ (estar) en Caracas.

2. —¿Qué _____ (hacer) Roberto ayer?

   —Él _____ (tener) que trabajar.

3. —¿Tus padres te _____ (traer) las bolsas de dormir?

   —No, no _____ (poder) traerlas porque _____ (venir) en autobús.

4. —Cuando Uds. _____ (venir) al parque, ¿qué coche (car) _____ (conducir)?

   —_____ (conducir) el coche de papá.

5. —¿Dónde _____ (poner) Uds. la cesta de picnic?

   —La _____ (poner) en la mesa.

   —¿Sergio comió con Uds.?

   —No, él no _____ (querer) comer con nosotros.

B. La semana pasada Rewrite this paragraph, changing all the verbs to the preterite to indicate that everything happened last week.

Tengo que limpiar mi apartamento porque Ana y Eva vienen a visitarme. Después hago una torta para ellas. Las chicas traen bolsas de dormir porque no quieren dormir en mi cuarto. Las ponen en la sala y miran televisión hasta tarde. Mi prima Julia está con nosotras hasta las diez, pero no puede quedarse a dormir porque tiene que ir a trabajar.

C. Entreviste a su compañero(a) Interview a partner, using the following questions.

1. ¿A qué hora viniste a la universidad ayer?
2. ¿Condujiste tu coche o viniste en ómnibus (*bus*)?
3. ¿Tuviste algún examen? ¿En qué clase?
4. ¿Estuviste en la biblioteca por la tarde?
5. ¿Trajiste algún libro de la biblioteca a la clase?
6. ¿Dónde pusiste tus libros?
7. ¿Hiciste la tarea (*homework*) de la clase de español?
8. ¿Pudiste terminarla?
9. ¿Estuviste en tu casa por la noche?
10. ¿Tuviste una fiesta en tu casa? (¿Quiénes vinieron?)

D. Queremos saber... In groups of three, prepare some questions for your instructor about what he or she did yesterday, last night, or last week. Use irregular preterit forms in your questions.

2. Direct and indirect object pronouns used together
(*Los pronombres de complemento directo e indirecto usados juntos*)

◆ When an indirect object pronoun and a direct object pronoun are used together, the indirect object pronoun always comes first.

◆ With an infinitive, the pronouns can be placed either before the conjugated verb or after the infinitive.

    *Ana is going to give **it to me.***

◆ With a present participle, the pronouns can be placed either before the conjugated verb or after the present participle.

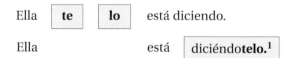

    *She is saying **it to you.***

◆ If both pronouns begin with **l,** the indirect object pronoun (**le** or **les**) is changed to **se.**

---

[1]Note that the use of the written accent follows the standard rules for the use of accents. See Appendix A.

For clarification, it is sometimes necessary to add **a él, a ella, a Ud., a Uds., a ellos,** or **a ellas.**

—¿A quién le dio la comida Ana?   *"To whom did Ana give the meal?"*
—**Se la** dio **a él.**   *"She gave **it to him.**"*

A proper name may also be given for clarification.
   Se la dio **a Luis.**   *She gave **it to Luis.***

Necesito veinte dólares.
¿Puedes dármelos?

Online Study Center

For more practice with lesson topics, see the related activities on the *¡Hola, amigos!* web site at college.hmco.com/PIC/holaamigos7e.

Práctica y conversación

A. Un tío generoso   We want to go camping, but we don't have anything that we need. Our generous uncle Ernesto provides everything. Rewrite the statements following the model.

◆ **MODELO:** No tenemos dinero. (dar)
         Él nos lo da.

1. Yo necesito una caña de pescar. (prestar)
2. Tú no tienes traje de baño. (comprar)
3. Nosotros necesitamos tablas de mar. (traer)
4. Daniel no tiene esquíes acuáticos. (prestar)
5. Mis hermanas quieren una cesta de picnic. (conseguir)
6. Mis primos necesitan unas raquetas de tenis. (comprar)

B. Excusas, excusas What excuses would you give in response to these questions? Follow the model and use the cues provided.

◆ MODELO: —¿Por qué no le diste el dinero a Ada? (no estuvo aquí)
—*No se lo di porque no estuvo aquí.*

1. ¿Por qué no me trajiste las raquetas? (no pude)
2. ¿Por qué no les mandaste los palos de golf? (no tuve tiempo)
3. ¿Por qué no te compró tu papá la escopeta? (no quiso)
4. ¿Por qué no les dio Lupe el dinero a Uds.? (no vino a casa)
5. ¿Por qué te escribió Johnny la carta en inglés? (no sabe español)
6. ¿Por qué no les llevaste el pastel a los niños? (no lo hice)

C. Lo siento With a partner, take turns asking and answering questions about what the following people want, saying you cannot help them. Use the verbs **mandar, dar, prestar, comprar, traer,** and **conseguir** and the cues provided.

◆ MODELO: —¿Qué quiere Elisa? (dinero)
—*Elisa quiere dinero, ¿tú se lo puedes conseguir?*
—*No, lo siento, yo no puedo conseguírselo.*

1. ¿Qué quiere Susana? (un traje de baño)
2. ¿Qué quiere David? (una caña de pescar)
3. ¿Qué quieren Susana y Gloria? (raquetas de tenis)
4. ¿Qué quiere Jaime? (una tabla de mar)
5. ¿Qué quiere Lucía? (palos de golf)
6. ¿Qué quieren Jaime y David? (comida)

D. Comprando comestibles You went to the market to get groceries for your family. Talk about your errands.

◆ MODELO: ¿Quién te dio la lista?   (mi mamá)
Mi mamá me la dio.

1. ¿Tu papá te escribió la lista de los comestibles?   (sí)
2. ¿A quién le pediste el dinero?   (a mi papá)
3. ¿A quién le trajiste las naranjas?   (a mi mamá)
4. ¿A quién le compraste el helado?   (a mi hermana)
5. ¿Quién te dio el dinero para comprar la leche?   (mi hermano)
6. ¿Le trajiste la carne a tu hermana?   (sí)
7. Nosotros te pedimos uvas. ¿Nos las compraste?   (no)
8. ¿Dónde le compraste el pan a tu mamá?   (la panadería)

E. Necesitamos ayuda (*help*) With a partner, take turns indicating who does what for whom. Use the cues provided.

◆ MODELO: Raquel no sabe traducir las cartas. (Ana)
Ana se las traduce.

1. Marta no tiene dinero para comprar una bolsa de dormir. (nosotros)
2. Tú no sabes armar la tienda de campaña. (yo)
3. Nosotras no sabemos hacer una fogata. (papá)
4. Yo no puedo comprar un velero. (mi abuelo)
5. Los chicos no pueden llevarle las raquetas a Teresa. (mi hermana)
6. Ud. no puede conseguir trabajo de salvavidas. (su padre)

3. Stem-changing verbs in the preterit
(*Los verbos con cambio radical en el pretérito*)

◆ As you will recall, **-ar** and **-er** verbs with stem changes in the present tense have no stem changes in the preterit. However, **-ir** verbs with stem changes in the present tense have stem changes in the third-person singular and plural forms of the preterit (**e > i** and **o > u**), as shown below.

servir (*e > i*)		dormir (*o > u*)	
serví	servimos	dormí	dormimos
serviste	servisteis	dormiste	dormisteis
si**rvió**	si**rvieron**	d**urmió**	d**urmieron**

◆ Other **-ir** verbs that follow the same pattern are **pedir** (*to order, to request*), **seguir** (*to continue, to follow*), **sentir(se)** (*to feel*), **conseguir, divertirse** (*to have fun*), and **morir** (*to die*).

—¿Qué te **sirvieron** en la cafetería?   *"What **did they serve** you at the cafeteria?"*

—Me **sirvieron** café y sándwiches.   *"**They served** me coffee and sandwiches."*

—¿Cómo **durmió** Ud. anoche?   *"How **did you sleep** last night?"*
—**Dormí** muy bien.   *"**I slept** very well."*

—¿Se **divirtieron** ayer?   *"Did **you have a good time** yesterday?"*

—Sí, nos **divertimos** mucho.   *"Yes, **we had a** very **good time.**"*

¿*Cómo dormiste anoche?*

UNIVERSIDAD

Online Study Center

For more practice with lesson topics, see the related activities on the *¡Hola, amigos!* web site at college.hmco.com/PIC/holaamigos7e.

Práctica y conversación

A. Minidiálogos   Complete the following exchanges by supplying the preterit of the verbs given. Then act them out with a partner.

1. **dormir**   —¿Cómo _____ Uds. anoche?

   —Yo _____ muy bien, pero mamá no _____ bien.

2. **pedir**   —¿Qué _____ ellos?

   —Ana _____ pastel y los niños _____ torta.

3. **seguir**   —¿Hasta qué hora _____ hablando Uds.?

   —_____ hablando hasta las doce.

4. **servir**   —¿Qué _____ Uds. en la fiesta?

   —_____ torta y Coca-Cola.

5. **divertirse**   —¿_____ Uds. mucho?

   —Yo _____ pero Julio no _____ mucho.

6. **conseguir**   —¿_____ ellos el dinero?

   —No, no lo _____.

7. **morir**   —Hubo un accidente, ¿no?

   —Sí, y _____ mucha gente.

B. ¿Qué hicieron anoche?   With a partner, take turns describing what the following people did last night.

1. Arturo _____ .   **2.** Ernesto _____ .   **3.** Paco _____ .

4. Mirta y Rafael _____ .   **5.** El mozo _____ .   **6.** Pilar _____ .

C. Fuimos a cenar   In groups of three, tell your classmates about a recent meal at a restaurant. Tell where you went and with whom, what you ordered, and whether or not you had a good time.

4. The imperfect tense (*El imperfecto de indicativo*)

Forms of the imperfect

◆ There are two simple past tenses in the Spanish indicative: the preterit, which you have been studying, and the imperfect. To form the imperfect, add the following endings to the verb stem.

-ar *verbs*	-er *and* -ir *verbs*	
hablar	*comer*	*vivir*
habl- **aba**	com- **ía**	viv- **ía**
habl- **abas**	com- **ías**	viv- **ías**
habl- **aba**	com- **ía**	viv- **ía**
habl- **ábamos**	com- **íamos**	viv- **íamos**
habl- **abais**	com- **íais**	viv- **íais**
habl- **aban**	com- **ían**	viv- **ían**

Note that the endings of the **-er** and **-ir** verbs are the same. Observe the accent on the first-person plural form of **-ar** verbs: **hablábamos.** Note also that there is a written accent on the first **í** of the endings of the **-er** and **-ir** verbs.

—Tú siempre te **levantabas** a las seis, ¿no?

—Sí, porque mis clases **empezaban** a las siete y media y yo **vivía** lejos de la universidad.

"*You always **used to get up** at six, didn't you?*"

"*Yes, because my classes **started** at seven-thirty and I **lived** far from the university.*"

> **¡Atención!** Stem-changing verbs are regular in the imperfect.

◆ Only three Spanish verbs are irregular in the imperfect tense: **ser, ir,** and **ver.**

ser	ir	ver
era	iba	veía
eras	ibas	veías
era	iba	veía
éramos	íbamos	veíamos
erais	ibais	veíais
eran	iban	veían

—Cuando yo **era** chica, siempre **iba** a acampar en el verano.

—Nosotros **íbamos** también.

—¿Cuándo **veías** a tus amigos?

—Los **veía** sólo los sábados y los domingos.

"*When I **was** little, I always **went** camping in the summer.*"

"*We **used to go** too.*"

"*When **did you see** your friends?*"

"*I **used to see** them only on Saturdays and Sundays.*"

Uses of the imperfect

◆ The Spanish imperfect tense is equivalent to three English forms.

Yo **vivía** en Caracas.
$\begin{cases} \textit{I } \textbf{used to live} \textit{ in Caracas.} \\ \textit{I } \textbf{was living} \textit{ in Caracas.} \\ \textit{I } \textbf{lived} \textit{ in Caracas.} \end{cases}$

◆ The imperfect is used to describe actions or events that the speaker views as in the process of happening in the past, with no reference to when they began or ended.

Empezábamos a estudiar cuando él vino.

We were beginning to study when he came.

◆ It is also used to refer to habitual or repeated actions in the past, again with no reference to when they began or ended.

—¿Uds. **hablaban** inglés cuando **vivían** en Bogotá?
—No, cuando **vivíamos** allí siempre **hablábamos** español.

*"**Did** you **speak** English when you lived in Bogotá?"*
*"No, when **we lived** there we always **spoke** Spanish."*

En mi casa, hablábamos español.

◆ It describes physical, mental, or emotional conditions in the past.

Mi casa **era** muy grande.
No me **gustaba** estudiar.
Yo no me **sentía** bien.

*My house **was** very big.*
*I **didn't like** to study.*
*I **wasn't feeling** well.*

◆ It expresses time and age in the past.

—¿Qué hora **era**?
—**Eran** las seis.

Julia **tenía** veinte años.

*"What time **was it**?"*
*"**It was** six o'clock."*

*Julia **was** twenty years old.*

◆ The imperfect is used to describe or set the stage in the past.

Mi novia **era** bonita.   *My girlfriend **was** pretty.*
Era muy tarde.   ***It was** very late.*

Práctica y conversación

Online Study Center

For more practice with lesson topics, see the related activities on the *¡Hola, amigos!* web site at college.hmco.com/PIC/holaamigos7e.

A. La vida cambia...   Things have changed; tell how they used to be.

1. Ahora vivo en..., pero cuando era niño(a)...
2. Ahora hablamos español, pero cuando éramos niños(as)...
3. Ahora comemos pescado, pero cuando éramos niños(as)...
4. Ahora mis padres no se divierten mucho, pero cuando tenían veinte años...
5. Ahora Julia no ve a sus tíos, pero cuando era niña...
6. Ahora tú vas al teatro, pero cuando eras niño(a)...
7. Ahora mi hermana no da fiestas, pero cuando tenía dieciocho años...
8. Ahora me gustan los vegetales, pero cuando era niño(a)...
9. Ahora mi mamá nada muy bien, pero cuando era pequeña...
10. Ahora Ud. se levanta a las nueve, pero cuando era pequeño(a)...

B. Entreviste a su compañero(a)   Interview a partner, using the following questions.

1. ¿Dónde vivías cuando eras niño(a)?
2. ¿Con quién vivías?
3. ¿Tu casa era grande o pequeña?
4. ¿Cuántos dormitorios tenía?
5. ¿En qué idioma te hablaban tus padres?
6. ¿A qué escuela (*school*) ibas?
7. ¿Te gustaba estudiar?
8. ¿Qué te gustaba comer?
9. ¿Qué te gustaba hacer los sábados? ¿Y los domingos?
10. ¿Pasabas mucho tiempo con tus amigos los fines de semana?
11. ¿Sabías nadar? ¿Ibas a acampar?
12. ¿Jugabas al béisbol o al fútbol?

Detalles culturales

El béisbol es un deporte (*sport*) muy popular en Venezuela, Cuba, Puerto Rico y la República Dominicana. Muchos de los jugadores (*players*) de las Grandes Ligas de los Estados Unidos son de estos países. En España y en la mayoría de los otros países latinoamericanos el deporte más popular es el fútbol (*soccer*).

◆ **¿Cuáles son los deportes más populares en este país?**

C. En el parque Use your imagination to tell what was happening when you and your friends were seen in the park.

Anoche te vi en el parque con unos amigos.

1. ¿Qué hora era?
2. ¿Con quiénes estabas?
3. ¿De dónde venían Uds.?
4. ¿Adónde iban?
5. ¿De qué hablaban?
6. ¿Quién era la chica pelirroja?
7. ¿Quién era el muchacho alto y moreno?
8. ¿Esperaban a alguien?

D. Queremos saber With a partner, prepare five questions to ask your instructor about what he or she used to do when he or she was a teenager (**adolescente**).

5. Formation of adverbs (*La formación de los adverbios*)

◆ Most Spanish adverbs are formed by adding **-mente** (the equivalent of the English *-ly*) to the adjective.

| general | *general* | general**mente** | *generally* |
| reciente | *recent* | reciente**mente** | *recently* |

—¿La fiesta de bienvenida es para Olga y sus amigas?
—No, es **especialmente** para Olga.

"The welcome party is for Olga and her friends?"
*"No, it's **especially** for Olga."*

◆ Adjectives ending in **-o** change the **-o** to **-a** before adding **-mente.**

| lent**o** | *slow* | lent**amente** | *slowly* |
| rápid**o** | *rapid* | rápid**amente** | *rapidly* |

La fiesta es especialmente para él.

◆ If two or more adverbs are used together, both change the **-o** to **-a,** but only the last one in the sentence ends in **-mente.**

  Habla clar**a** y lent**amente.**   *She speaks clearly and slowly.*

◆ If the adjective has an accent mark, the adverb retains it.

  fácil   *easy*   **fá**cilmente   *easily*

Práctica y conversación

Online Study Center

For more practice with lesson topics, see the related activities on the *¡Hola, amigos!* web site at college.hmco.com/PIC/holaamigos7e.

A. De adjetivos a adverbios   You can recognize the following Spanish adjectives because they are cognates. Change them to adverbs.

1. real
2. completo
3. raro
4. frecuente

5. posible
6. general
7. franco
8. normal

B. Lo entiendo perfectamente   Use some of the adverbs you have learned to complete the following sentences appropriately.

1. Ellos hablan _____ y _____.
2. Viene a casa _____.
3. Yo _____ estudio por la mañana.
4. _____, no quiero bailar con Ud.
5. Ellos vuelven mañana, _____.
6. Los chicos escriben muy _____.
7. _____ estoy muy cansado.
8. Yo no escribo cartas; _____ escribo mensajes electrónicos (*e-mail*).

C. ¿Cuándo...?   With a partner, talk about what you and your friends generally do, frequently do, and rarely do.

Entre nosotros

¡Conversemos!

 Para conocernos mejor   Get to know your partner better by asking each other the following questions.

Detalles culturales

En muchos países latinoamericanos y en España se usa el sistema de estrellas para clasificar los hoteles de lujo (*luxury*) y de primera clase.

◆ **¿Se hospeda Ud. a veces en hoteles de cinco estrellas?**

1. ¿Esperas poder ir de vacaciones este verano? ¿Adónde quieres ir?
2. La última vez que fuiste de vacaciones, ¿te hospedaste en un hotel de cinco estrellas?
3. ¿Dónde pasaste las vacaciones el año pasado? ¿Te aburriste o te divertiste?
4. ¿Te juntas a veces con tus amigos para salir?
5. ¿Te gusta ir a acampar, o prefieres ir a un buen hotel?
6. ¿Qué actividades al aire libre te gustaban cuando eras chico?
7. ¿Ahora prefieres hacer esquí acuático, hacer surfing o bucear?
8. ¿Qué prefieres, mirar televisión o hacer una caminata?
9. Necesito tu raqueta de tenis, ¿puedes prestármela?
10. ¿Te gusta jugar al golf? ¿Tienes palos de golf?

 Una encuesta   Interview your classmates to identify who does the following. Be sure to change the statements to questions. Include your instructor, but remember to use the **Ud.** form when addressing him or her.

Nombre

1. Hizo esquí acuático en un lago el año pasado. _____
2. Va a tratar de alquilar una cabaña (cabin) el verano próximo (next). _____
3. Prometió ser más paciente. _____
4. Va a acampar a menudo. _____
5. Acaba de comer. _____
6. Pronto va a tener vacaciones. _____
7. Le gusta tomar el sol. _____
8. Compró un traje de baño recientemente. _____
9. Es experto(a) en armar tiendas de campaña. _____
10. Siempre les toma el pelo a sus amigos. _____

Y ahora...   Write a brief summary, indicating what you have learned about your classmates.

¿Cómo lo decimos?   What would you say in the following situations? What might the other person say? Act out the scenes with a partner.

1. You ask a friend if he or she prefers to go to the beach, to go hiking, or to go camping near a lake or a river (**río**) for a couple of days.
2. You are going on a camping trip for the first time. Tell a friend what items you need and what you need to learn to do.
3. Tell someone what your favorite outdoor activities are. Mention at least four.

¿Qué pasa aquí?   In groups of three or four, create a story about the people in the illustration. Say who they are and what their relationships are to one another. Also say what activities they are doing and what they will do later.

Para escribir

De vacaciones   Write a conversation between you and a friend, in which you are deciding what you are going to do when you have a couple of days off. One of you loves outdoor activities and the other doesn't. Try to compromise.

Un dicho

El que ríe último, ríe mejor.

Undoubtedly, you know the English version of this saying. Memorize it in Spanish, and use it at appropriate times.

Lectura

Estrategia de lectura
What images or ideas do you associate with the colors green, red, and white? Scan the two poems and make a list of the words associated with nature.

Vamos a leer
As you read the introduction to Martí and the poems, answer the following questions.

1. ¿En qué año nació (*was born*) el poeta?
2. ¿Dónde y en qué año murió?
3. ¿Cuáles son los temas principales de la poesía de Martí?
4. ¿Cómo se describe el poeta en el primer poema?
5. ¿Qué quiere hacer Martí antes de morirse?
6. ¿Qué imágenes usa Martí para describir sus versos?
7. ¿Con quiénes quiere echar su suerte el poeta?
8. ¿Qué flor (*flower*) cultiva el poeta?
9. ¿Cultiva el poeta la rosa solamente para sus amigos o también para sus enemigos?
10. ¿Qué simboliza la rosa blanca?
11. Según este poema, ¿el poeta odia a sus enemigos?

José Martí (Cuba: 1853–1895) dedicó su vida y su obra a la independencia de Cuba, donde murió en el campo de batalla° en 1895. Es famoso, no sólo como poeta y ensayista, sino también como orador.

 Los poemas de Martí se caracterizan por la melodía, el ritmo y el uso de oraciones cortas, con las que expresa ideas muy profundas. Sus temas principales son la libertad, la justicia, la independencia de su patria y la defensa de los pobres y los oprimidos.°

Campo... *battlefield*

oppressed

Video

De Versos sencillos[1]

JOSÉ MARTÍ

I

Yo soy un hombre sincero
de donde crece° la palma;   *grows*
y antes de morirme, quiero
echar° mis versos del alma.°   *to pour out / soul*

V

Mi verso es de un verde claro,°   *light*
y de un carmín encendido°:   ***carmín...*** *bright red*
mi verso es un ciervo herido°   ***ciervo...*** *wounded deer*
que busca en el monte amparo.°   *shelter*

III

Con los pobres de la tierra,°   *earth, land*
quiero yo mi suerte echar;°   ***mi...*** *to share my destiny*
el arroyo° de la sierra   *brook*
me complace° más que el mar.   *pleases*

XXXIX

Cultivo una rosa blanca,
en julio como en enero,
para el amigo sincero
que me da su mano franca.°   *open*

Y para el cruel que me arranca°   *tears out*
el corazón con que vivo,
cardo° ni ortiga° cultivo: *thistle / nettle*
cultivo la rosa blanca.

---

[1]Este poema es la letra de la canción "La Guantanamera".

Díganos   Answer the following questions based on your own thoughts and experiences.

1. ¿Ha oído Ud. la canción "La Guantanamera"?
2. Al final del segundo poema, el poeta perdona (*forgives*) las ofensas de sus enemigos. ¿Haría Ud. (*Would you do*) lo mismo?

Recuerdos

Pablo y Marisa están en la casa de los padres de ella. Marisa y su mamá invitan a Pablo cenar y también a acampar con la familia ese fin de semana. El problema es que Pablo no sabe nada de acampar y ellas creen que él es un experto en actividades al aire libre.

El mundo hispánico

 ## Cuba

- Cuba es la mayor de las islas del archipiélago de las Antillas. Su figura es similar a la de un cocodrilo y, como es larga (*long*) y estrecha (*narrow*), tiene extensas costas en las cuales hay playas de gran belleza (*beauty*). Muchos llaman a Cuba "la Perla de las Antillas".

- Hoy Cuba exporta azúcar, níquel, tabaco y frutas. El tabaco cubano tiene fama mundial. Sin embargo, las principales fuentes de ingreso (*sources of income*) del país son el turismo y el dinero que les envían a sus familiares más de un millón de cubanos que viven en el extranjero (*abroad*).

▲ La Catedral, construida entre 1748 y 1767, en La Habana Vieja.

- La Habana, la capital, es la ciudad más grande del Caribe. La Habana Vieja (*old*), su sección antigua, se caracteriza por sus iglesias, plazas, fortalezas, y edificios coloniales, como la Catedral y su plaza, y las fortalezas de El Morro y la Cabaña. En la Habana nació José Martí, escritor, poeta y el más famoso de los patriotas cubanos.

- La música cubana o afrocubana es muy popular en todo el mundo. De Cuba vienen el son, el danzón, la rumba, la conga, el cha cha cha, el mambo y, en buena parte, la salsa. El deporte más popular del país es el béisbol, al que los cubanos llaman "la pelota".

 ## Colombia

- Colombia es la única nación nombrada en honor de Cristóbal Colón. Es el cuarto país suramericano en tamaño (*size*), y es el único con costas en el Pacífico y en el mar Caribe.

- Colombia produce y exporta café, bananas, flores y petróleo. El café colombiano tiene fama mundial por su alta calidad. Colombia es también famosa por sus esmeraldas, consideradas las mejores del mundo. El 90 por ciento de todas las esmeraldas provienen de este país.

▲ Vista panorámica de Bogotá de noche

- La música típica de Colombia es muy variada. Incluye la cumbia y el vallenato, que han alcanzado fama internacional. Shakira, Juanes y Carlos Vives son cantantes populares en los Estados Unidos.

- La capital de Colombia es Bogotá, una ciudad rodeada (*surrounded*) de montañas, por lo que el transporte entre ella y el resto del país es principalmente por vía aérea. En la ciudad hay muchos museos, pero el más famoso de ellos es el Museo del Oro, que tiene una de las mejores colecciones de la artesanía precolombina, incluidos unos 30.000 objetos de oro.

- El deporte más popular en todo el país es el fútbol, y Colombia es uno de los cuatro países latinoamericanos donde se celebran las corridas de toros (*bullfights*).

Online Study Center

For more practice with lesson topics, see the related activities on the *¡Hola, amigos!* web site at college.hmco.com/PIC/holaamigos7e.

Puerto Rico

- Puerto Rico, "la isla del encanto", es la menor de las islas de las Antillas Mayores. Los indios la llamaban **Boriquén** (modernizado luego como **Borinquen**), y aún hoy muchos la llaman así, y llaman **boricuas** a sus habitantes.

- Puerto Rico está muy densamente poblado; en un área de menos de 3.500 millas cuadradas de superficie, viven cerca de (*around*) 4 millones de habitantes. Desde 1952 el país es un Estado libre asociado de los Estados Unidos.

▲ Jugada (*play*) sensacional durante el Campeonato Mundial de Béisbol entre Cuba y Puerto Rico, 2006

- San Juan, la capital, es la ciudad más grande y más poblada. Su parte antigua, el Viejo San Juan, es un centro de atracción turística por sus interesantes museos, sus edificios coloniales y las fortalezas de El Morro y San Cristóbal. Otros puntos de interés son sus playas y el Yunque, un bosque (*forest*) tropical.

- Igual que en Cuba, se ve la influencia de España, de África y de Estados Unidos en el arte y en la música. De los deportes, el más popular es el béisbol.

Venezuela

- Cuando los conquistadores españoles llegaron al lago Maracaibo, las construcciones de los indígenas a orillas del lago les recordaron las de Venecia, y por eso llamaron al país Venezuela, nombre que significa "pequeña Venecia".

- El país es uno de los diez mayores exportadores de petróleo del mundo. Más de la octava parte del petróleo importado por los Estados Unidos viene de Venezuela. La mayor parte de su gran reserva de petróleo se encuentra debajo del lago Maracaibo. Este lago es el mayor de Venezuela y de toda América del Sur.

- La principal atracción turística del país es el Salto Ángel, mucho más alto que las cataratas del Niágara.

- Caracas, la capital de Venezuela, es el centro gubernamental, financiero, cultural y artístico del país. En Caracas nació Simón Bolívar, llamado el Libertador de América.

▲ Una familia cruza una calle en Caracas. Al fondo se ven los modernos edificios de la ciudad y una majestuosa montaña.

▲ Juan Luis Guerra es un compositor y cantante (*singer*) de merengue

La República Dominicana

- La República Dominicana ocupa las dos terceras partes de la isla que Colón descubrió en su primer viaje y a la que llamó La Española. La parte occidental de la isla está ocupada por la República de Haití. Su economía se basa en la agricultura, pero el turismo comienza a ser una buena fuente de ingresos para el país. Sus principales atracciones son sus construcciones coloniales y sus hermosas playas.

- La música típica del país es el merengue, pero además son populares otros ritmos del Caribe como la rumba y la salsa. Como en Cuba y en Puerto Rico, el béisbol es el deporte más popular de la isla.

- Casi la mitad de la población del país vive en la capital, Santo Domingo, la primera ciudad europea fundada en el Nuevo Mundo. Aquí se encuentran algunas de las construcciones coloniales más antiguas de América.

Comentarios... With a partner, discuss in Spanish what impressed you most about these countries, and compare them to your own. Which places do you want to visit and why?

Tome este examen

Lección 7

A. Preterit of regular verbs
Rewrite the following sentences, changing the verbs to the preterit.

1. Ellos comen tortilla y beben limonada.
2. Luis sale a las ocho y vuelve a las cinco.
3. Tú cierras la puerta y abres las ventanas.
4. Yo empiezo a las seis y termino a las ocho.
5. Nosotros leemos un poema y ella lee una novela.
6. Yo busco el dinero y no lo encuentro.
7. Yo llego temprano y comienzo a trabajar.
8. Yo compro carne aquí y pago menos.

B. Preterit of *ser, ir,* and *dar*
Change the verbs in the following sentences to the preterit.

1. Ella va a la discoteca.
2. Dan mucho dinero.
3. ¿Ud. es mi profesor?
4. Yo voy más tarde.
5. Ellos son mis alumnos.
6. Doy muchas fiestas.
7. Yo soy su novio.
8. Nosotros vamos al cine.

C. Indirect object pronouns
Answer the following questions in the negative.

1. ¿Te traen el jugo?
2. ¿Le das el dinero a él?
3. ¿Me vas a comprar los libros?
4. ¿Le vas a dar los cuadernos a Elsa?
5. ¿Le gusta el café a Ud.?
6. ¿Ellos les van a dar las invitaciones a Uds.?

D. The verb *gustar*
Complete the following sentences with the Spanish equivalent of the words in parentheses.

1. _____ patinar, pero _____ nadar.   (*I like / I don't like*)
2. ¿_____ esta película, Anita?   (*Do you like*)
3. _____ ese club.   (*My mother likes better*)
4. _____ levantarnos temprano.   (*We like*)
5. _____ bailar salsa.   (*My brother likes*)

E. Reflexive constructions Complete these sentences, using the verbs from the following list appropriately. Use each verb once.

acostarse   afeitarse   bañarse   levantarse   probarse   sentarse   vestirse

1. Mis hijos _____ muy temprano y _____ tarde.
2. Yo voy a _____ la barba (*beard*).
3. ¿Tú _____ el vestido (*dress*) antes de comprarlo?
4. Ella siempre _____ en esa silla.
5. Nosotros nunca _____ por la noche.
6. Él va a _____ ahora. Necesita el traje (*suit*) azul.

F. Vocabulary Complete the following sentences, using vocabulary from **Lección 7.**

1. Este _____ de semana voy a ir a la playa.
2. No me _____; me aburrí.
3. Ellos _____ a las siete de la mañana.
4. Mañana vamos a ir a un _____ de fútbol.
5. En el _____ Rex, ponen hoy una película muy buena.
6. El niño _____ el florero ayer.
7. En el _____ hay muchos animales.
8. Ellos van a ir a _____ montañas este verano.
9. Carlos fue a _____ a caballo.
10. Son las doce de la noche: es _____.
11. Voy a _____ en el lago (*lake*).
12. Esta noche vamos a estudiar, en _____ de ir al teatro.

G. Culture Complete the following sentences, based on the cultural notes you have read.

1. El sobrenombre de Enrique es _____.
2. Las películas americanas son muy _____ en el mundo hispano.

Lección 8

A. Preterit of some irregular verbs
Change the verbs in the following sentences to the preterit tense.

1. Ellos traen la raqueta y yo traigo la caña de pescar.
2. Tengo que ir al hotel.
3. ¿Qué hace él con la escopeta?
4. Tú dices que sí y ellos dicen que no.
5. Laura viene al parque conmigo y tú vienes con Sergio.
6. Tú y yo estamos aquí y ellos están allá.
7. Ellas hacen el postre.
8. Yo sé toda la verdad.
9. Ellas conducen muy bien, pero yo conduzco muy mal.
10. Enrique no quiere ir a pescar.

B. Direct and indirect object pronouns used together
Answer the following questions in the affirmative, replacing the direct objects with direct object pronouns.

1. ¿Me compraste *las raquetas*?
2. ¿Nos trajeron Uds. *los palos de golf*?
3. ¿Ellos te van a dar *el traje de baño*?   (*two ways*)
4. ¿Él les va a traer *los termos* a Uds.?   (*two ways*)
5. ¿Ella me va a comprar *la canoa*?   (*Use the **Ud.** form.*) (*two ways*)
6. ¿Ellos te traen *las cestas*?

C. Stem-changing verbs in the preterit
Complete the following sentences in the preterit tense, using the verbs listed.

conseguir	divertirse	dormir
morir	pedir	seguir

1. Ana y Eva _____ mucho en la fiesta. Cuando volvieron a casa, _____ hablando y no _____ mucho por la noche.
2. Elsa _____ la comida y Juan se la trajo.
3. Hubo un accidente, pero no _____ nadie.
4. Roberto _____ el pescado en el mercado.

D. The imperfect tense
Change the verbs in the following sentences to the imperfect.

1. ¿Tú vas al supermercado con tu papá?
2. Ella es muy bonita.
3. Ellos hablan español.
4. Nosotros no vemos a nuestros amigos.
5. Uds. nunca pescan en el lago.
6. Yo siempre como frutas por la mañana.

E. Formation of adverbs   Write the following adverbs in Spanish.

1. easily
2. especially
3. slowly
4. rapidly
5. slowly and clearly
6. frankly

F. Vocabulary   Complete the following sentences, using vocabulary from **Lección 8.**

1. ¿Qué actividades al _____ libre prefieres?
2. Voy a ir a _____; necesito la escopeta.
3. Él no sabe _____ una tienda de campaña.
4. Voy a poner el pollo en la _____ de pícnic.
5. No quiero ir en la canoa porque no sé _____.
6. Ellos siempre me toman el _____.
7. Un sinónimo de "a menudo" es _____.
8. No me gusta hacer esquí _____.
9. Cuando voy a la playa, me gusta _____ el sol.
10. Necesito mi _____ de mar.
11. Ellos van a _____ una caminata.
12. Me gusta mucho nadar. Me _____.

G. Culture   Complete the following sentences, based on the cultural notes you have read.

1. Cuba es la _____ de las Antillas.
2. La música típica de la República Dominicana es el _____.
3. El _____ es un bosque tropical de Puerto Rico.

Unidad 5

Objetivos

Lección 9

- ◆ Shop for clothing and shoes, conveying your needs with regard to sizes and fit
- ◆ Talk about the weather
- ◆ Discuss past actions and events
- ◆ Talk about possession

Lección 10

- ◆ Open an account and cash checks at the bank
- ◆ Mail letters and buy stamps at the post office
- ◆ Describe people and things
- ◆ Refer to actions, states, and events that have been completed in the past
- ◆ Tell others what to do

Una calle dedicada exclusivamente a los peatones *(pedestrians)* en la ciudad de Lima, Perú

¿Qué hacemos hoy?

Ecuador
Monumento Mitad del Mundo en la línea del ecuador, latitud 0°

Perú
Departmento de Química, Universidad de San Marcos, Lima

Bolivia
Lago Titicaca, el más alto del mundo, situado entre Bolivia y Perú

Paraguay
Represa hidroeléctrica de Itaipú, en el río Paraná

Sara y Pablo son muy buenos amigos. Los dos son de Ecuador pero ahora viven y estudian en Lima. Se conocieron en la facultad de medicina hace dos años. Ahora están en una tienda porque Pablo necesita comprar ropa y, según Sara, ella sabe exactamente lo que él necesita.

Sara ¿Por qué no te pruebas estos pantalones? No son muy caros y están de moda.

Pablo ¿Qué? Yo tenía unos pantalones como éstos cuando tenía quince años.

Sara (*Se ríe*) Bueno... todo vuelve... Tú usas talla mediana ¿no? Allí está el probador. Voy a buscarte una camisa.

Pablo Quiero una camisa blanca de mangas largas y una de mangas cortas.

Sara También necesitas un traje y una corbata para la boda de tu hermano... ¡y una chaqueta! Ya empezó el invierno y hace frío.

Pablo Oye, todo esto me va a costar un ojo de la cara.

Sara También tienes que comprar un regalo para tu mamá; me dijiste que era su cumpleaños.

Pablo No sé qué comprarle. ¿Un vestido? ¿Una blusa y una falda? Pero... no sé qué talla usa.

Sara No sé... quizá un par de aretes o una cadena de oro...

Pablo Sí, como la tuya. A ella le gusta mucho. A ver cuánto puedo gastar.

Detalles culturales

En la mayoría de los países hispanos la talla de la ropa se basa en el sistema métrico. Por ejemplo, la medida (*measure*) del cuello (*collar*) y el largo de las mangas (*sleeves*) de una camisa se dan en centímetros. Una talla 10 en los Estados Unidos es equivalente a la 30 en España. Estas equivalencias varían de país a país.

◆ La talla de la ropa, ¿se basa en el sistema métrico en este país?

Detalles culturales

El sistema métrico decimal se usa en todos los países de habla hispana. La unidad básica del sistema es el metro, que equivale a 3,28 pies.

◆ ¿Se estudia el sistema métrico en las escuelas de este país?

Más tarde, en la zapatería.

Empleado ¿En qué puedo servirle, señor?

Pablo Necesito un par de zapatos. Creo que calzo el número cuarenta y cuatro.

Sara Las botas que compraste el mes pasado eran cuarenta y tres.

Pablo Sí, pero como me quedaban chicas y me apretaban un poco, se las mandé a mi hermano.

Sara Buena idea. ¡Los zapatos tienen que ser cómodos!

Pablo (*Se ríe.*) Entonces, ¿por qué usas esas sandalias de tacones altos?

Sara Las compré porque eran baratas, pero prefiero usar zapatos de tenis.

Pablo Yo prefiero andar descalzo. Cuando era chico, me quitaba los zapatos en cuanto llegaba de la escuela.

Sara Oye, ¿qué hora es?

Pablo No sé. Eran las cuatro cuando salimos de la tienda. ¿Quieres ir a comer algo?

Sara Bueno, voy a llamar a Teresa para decirle que no voy a cenar con ella.

Pablo Bueno, tú llamas a tu compañera de cuarto y yo llamo al mío.

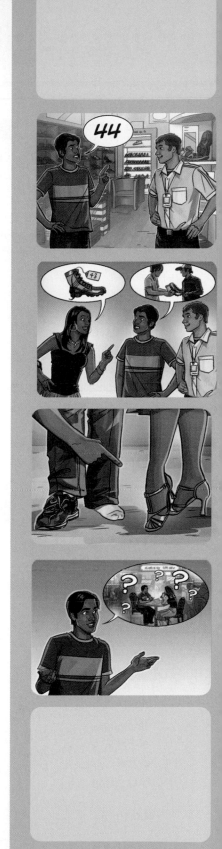

¿Recuerda usted?

¿Verdadero o falso? With a partner, decide whether the following statements about the dialogues are true (**verdadero**) or false (**falso**).

1. Hace tres años que Sara y Pablo se conocieron. □ V □ F
2. Pablo se va a probar unos pantalones de talla mediana. □ V □ F
3. Pablo quiere comprar una camisa. □ V □ F
4. Pablo necesita un traje para su boda. □ V □ F
5. Pronto va a empezar el verano. □ V □ F
6. Pablo compró botas el mes pasado. □ V □ F
7. A Pablo le quedaban grandes las botas. □ V □ F
8. Pablo usa tacones altos. □ V □ F
9. A Pablo no le gustaba usar zapatos cuando era chico. □ V □ F
10. Pablo y Sara salieron de la tienda a las cinco. □ V □ F

Y ahora... conteste Answer the following questions, basing your answers on the dialogue.

1. ¿De dónde son Sara y Pablo y dónde viven ahora?
2. ¿Qué dice Sara de los pantalones?
3. ¿Pablo quiere una camisa de mangas cortas o de mangas largas?
4. ¿Qué más dice Sara que necesita Pablo?
5. ¿Qué número calza Pablo?
6. ¿Qué tipo de zapatos prefiere usar Sara?
7. ¿Qué hacía Pablo en cuanto llegaba de la escuela?
8. ¿A quiénes van a llamar Sara y Pablo?

Para hablar del tema: Vocabulario

Cognados

la blusa
exactamente
la medicina

el par
las sandalias

Nombres

los aretes* earrings
la bota boot
la cadena chain
la camisa shirt
la chaqueta* jacket
la corbata tie
el (la) empleado(a) clerk
la escuela school
la facultad college
la falda skirt
la manga sleeve

el oro gold
los pantalones, el pantalón pants
el probador fitting room
el regalo gift
el tacón* heel
la talla size (of clothing)
la tienda store
el traje* suit
el vestido dress
la zapatería shoe store
el zapato shoe

Verbos

apretar (e>ie) to be tight
buscar to look for, to get
calzar to wear (a certain shoe size)
gastar to spend (i.e. money)
usar to wear, to use

Otras palabras y expresiones

andar descalzo(a) to go barefoot
como like
costar un ojo de la cara to cost an arm and a leg
en cuanto as soon as
¿en qué puedo servirle? how may I help you?

estar de moda to be in style
lo que what, that which
no tener nada que ponerse not to have anything to wear
   quedarle chico(a) (grande) a uno to be too small (big) (on someone)
quizás, tal vez maybe, perhaps
según according to

De país a país

los aretes los pendientes (*Esp.*)
   los aros (*Par., Arg.*)
   las pantallas (*P.R.*)
la chaqueta la chamarra (*Méx.*)
el tacón el taco (*Arg.*)
el traje el vestido (*Colombia*)
el camisón la bata de dormir (*Cuba*)
el cinturón la correa (*P.R.*)

Adjetivos

alto(a) high
barato(a) inexpensive, cheap
cómodo(a) comfortable
corto(a) short
largo(a) long
mediano(a) medium

Amplíe su vocabulario

Más Ropa (*More clothes*)

la camiseta

los calzoncillos

el cinturón, cinto*

la billetera

los guantes

el chaleco

el pijama, los pijamas

las zapatillas

el suéter

la bata

el sombrero

la bufanda

el camisón*

El tiempo (*The weather*)

El cielo está $\begin{cases} \text{nublado.} \\ \text{despejado.} \end{cases}$ The sky is $\begin{cases} \textit{cloudy.} \\ \textit{clear.} \end{cases}$

el grado   *degree*

el clima $\begin{cases} \text{cálido} \\ \text{templado} \\ \text{frío} \\ \text{seco} \\ \text{húmedo} \end{cases}$ $\begin{matrix} \textit{hot} \\ \textit{warm} \\ \textit{cold} \\ \textit{dry} \\ \textit{humid} \end{matrix} \Big\} \textit{climate}$

¿Qué temperatura hace?   *What is the temperature?*

Hay... grados.   *It's . . . degrees.*

Para practicar el vocabulario

A. En la tienda y en la zapatería Complete the following statements appropriately.

1. Pablo se va a probar la camisa de _____ cortas y también los _____ en el _____.
2. La chaqueta no es _____; cuesta un _____ de la cara.
3. Cuando él _____ el traje azul, se pone una camisa blanca y una _____ roja.
4. Compré un _____ de botas, pero me _____ chicas; me _____ mucho.
5. Ella se puso una _____ blanca y una blusa negra. También se puso unas sandalias de _____ altos.
6. No uso talla grande ni chica. Uso talla _____.
7. Busco unos aretes y una _____ de _____ para mi mamá.
8. No quiero usar zapatos en mi casa; prefiero andar _____.
9. Voy a comprar el vestido. Está de _____ y no es muy caro. Cuesta solamente 50 dólares.
10. Tengo que comprar ropa. No _____ nada que _____. ¿Vamos a la _____?

B. ¿Qué se ponen? Describe what Pablo and Sara usually wear, based on the cues provided.

Pablo

1. con el traje
2. debajo del pantalón
3. debajo de la camisa
4. para sujetarse (*hold*) los pantalones
5. para dormir
6. en las manos, cuando tiene frío
7. en los pies (*feet*)

Sara

1. cuando tiene frío
2. para dormir
3. en la cabeza (*head*)
4. con el camisón
5. en los pies
6. en el cuello (*neck*), cuando tiene frío

¿Y dónde ponen los dos el dinero?

C. Hablando del tiempo

1. ¿Cómo es el clima de
   a. Alaska?   c. Oregón?   e. San Diego?
   b. Arizona?   d. Miami?
2. Va a llover (*rain*). ¿Cómo está el cielo?
3. El cielo no está nublado. ¿Cómo está?
4. ¿Cuál es la temperatura de hoy?

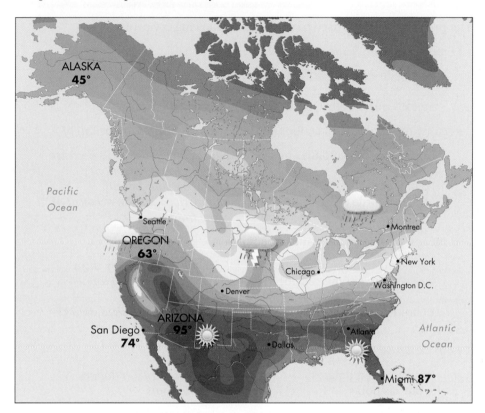

D. Haciendo compras

With a partner, play the roles of two friends who are shopping together, giving each other suggestions and making comments. Use questions such as **¿Por qué no te pruebas…?** or **¿Te gusta…?** and comments like **Te queda(n)…**

Puntos para recordar

1. Some uses of *por* and *para* (*Algunos usos de* por *y* para)

The preposition **por** is used to express the following concepts.

- motion (*through, along, by, via*)

No puedo salir **por** la ventana.	*I can't go out **through** the window.*
Fuimos **por** la calle Quinta.	*We went **via** Fifth Street.*

- cause or motive of an action (*because of, on account of, on behalf of*)

No compré las sandalias **por** no tener dinero.	*I didn't buy the sandals **because** I didn't have any money.*
Lo hice **por** ti.	*I did it **on** your **behalf.***
Llegaron tarde **por** el tráfico.	*They arrived late **on account of** the traffic.*

- means, manner, unit of measure (*by, per*)

No me gusta viajar **por** tren.	*I don't like to travel **by** train.*
Va a setenta kilómetros **por** hora.	*She is doing seventy kilometers **per** hour.*
Cobran 100 dólares **por** noche.	*They charge a hundred dollars **per** night.*

- *in exchange for*

Pagamos cien dólares **por** las botas.	*We paid a hundred dollars **for** the boots.*

- period of time during which an action takes place (*during, in, for*)

Voy a quedarme aquí **por** un mes.	*I'm going to stay here **for** a month.*
Ella prepara la comida **por** la mañana.	*She prepares the meal **in** the morning.*

The preposition **para** is used to express the following concepts.

◆ destination

¿Cuándo sales **para** Quito?	*When are you leaving **for** Quito?*

◆ goal for a specific point in the future (*by* or *for* a certain time in the future)

Necesito la camisa y el pantalón **para** mañana.	*I need the shirt and the pants **for** (**by**) tomorrow.*

◆ whom or what something is for

La blusa es **para** ti.	*The blouse is **for** you.*

◆ objective or goal

Mi novio estudia **para** profesor.	*My boyfriend is studying **to be** a professor.*

◆ *in order to*

—Ayer fui a su casa.	*"Yesterday I went to his house."*
—¿**Para** qué?	*"What **for**?"*
—**Para** hablar con él.	*"**(In order) To** talk with him."*

Práctica y conversación

Online Study Center

For more practice with lesson topics, see the related activities on the *¡Hola, amigos!* web site at college.hmco.com/PIC/holaamigos7e.

A. Minidiálogos   Supply **por** or **para** in each dialogue. Then act each one out with a partner.

1. —¿_____ qué calle fuiste?
   —Fui _____ la calle Esperanza.

2. —¿_____ cuándo necesitas los pantalones?
   —Los necesito _____ el sábado _____ la noche.

3. —¿Para qué fuiste al mercado?
   —_____ comprar frutas. Lo hice _____ ti, porque estabas muy cansada... Y no compré más carne_____ no tener más dinero.

4. —¿Cuánto pagaron Uds. _____ ese vestido?
   —Cien soles. Es _____ nuestra hija.
   —¿Cuándo sale ella _____ Cuzco?
   —El 3 de enero. Va a estar allí _____ dos meses. Va _____ visitar a su abuela.
   —¿Va _____ tren?
   —Sí.

5. —¿Ofelia está en la universidad?
   —Sí, estudia _____ profesora.

Detalles culturales

Sol: moneda peruana
◆ ¿Sabe Ud. cuáles son las monedas de otros países hispanos?

B. Cosas que pasan Look at the illustrations and describe what is happening, using **por** or **para**.

1. Fuimos _____ a Lima.

2. Roberto salió _____.

3. Marisa va a estar en Medellín _____.

4. La torta es _____ Ana.

5. Jorge pagó _____ el vino.

6. Ana sale mañana _____.

 C. Diferentes circunstancias In groups of three, and using your imagination, add some details to the following circumstances. Use **por** or **para** and think of various possibilities.

♦ MODELO: Marisa compró un vestido.
    *Pagó 100 dólares **por** el vestido. El vestido es **para** su tía.*

1. Mi sobrino va a ir a Ecuador.
2. Mi prima está en la universidad.
3. Amalia trabaja de siete a once de la mañana.
4. Marité tiene una fiesta el sábado. Necesita comprar un vestido.
5. David compró una corbata.
6. Mi cuñado no pudo pagar la cuenta.

7. Este hotel es muy barato.
8. Julio conduce muy rápido (*fast*).
9. Ellos llegaron tarde a la fiesta.
10. Luis no pudo salir por la puerta.

2. Weather expressions (*Expresiones para describir el tiempo*)

◆ The following expressions are used when talking about the weather.

Hace (mucho) frío.	*It is (very) cold.*
Hace (mucho) calor.	*It is (very) hot.*
Hace (mucho) viento.	*It is (very) windy.*
Hace sol.	*It is sunny.*
—¿Qué tiempo **hace** hoy?	*"What's the weather like today?"*
—**Hace buen (mal) tiempo.**	*"The weather is good (bad)."*

> **¡Atención!** All of the expressions above use the verb **hacer** followed by a noun.

—¿Abro la ventana?	*"Shall I open the window?"*
—¡Sí! ¡**Hace** mucho **calor**!	*"Yes! It's very hot!"*

◆ The impersonal verbs **llover (o > ue)** (*to rain*) and **nevar (e > ie)** (*to snow*) are also used to describe the weather. They are used only in the third-person singular forms of all tenses, and in the infinitive, the present participle, and the past participle.

Aquí **llueve** mucho.	*It rains a lot here.*
Creo que va a **nevar** hoy.	*I think it's going to snow today.*
Está **lloviendo;** no podemos salir.	*It's raining; we can't go out.*

Other weather-related words are **lluvia** (*rain*) and **niebla** (*fog*).

Hay **niebla.**	*It's foggy.*
No me gusta **la lluvia.**	*I don't like rain.*

A. ¿Qué tiempo hace? Describe the weather in each illustration.

1. _____

2. _____

3. _____

4. _____

5. _____

6. _____

B. Minidiálogos With a partner, complete the exchanges in a logical manner.

1. —¿Necesitas un paraguas (*umbrella*)?
   —Sí, porque _____ .

2. —¿No necesitas un abrigo (*coat*)?
   —No, porque _____ .

3. —¿Quieres un impermeable (*raincoat*)?
   —Sí, porque _____ mucho.

4. —¿No quieres llevar el suéter?
   —¡No! ¡Hace _____ !

5. —¿Vas a llevar el sombrero?
   —Sí, porque _____ .

6. —¿Necesitas un suéter y un abrigo?
   —Sí, porque _____ .

7. —¿Un impermeable? ¿Por qué? ¿Está lloviendo?
   —No, pero _____ .

8. —¡Qué _____ ! Necesito un paraguas y un impermeable.

9. —No hay vuelos (*flights*) porque hay mucha _____ .

C. De viaje (*On a trip*) A friend of yours from Lima is going to travel in the United States for a year. With a partner, discuss what kind of weather he's going to find in cities like Chicago, Boston, Phoenix, and San Francisco.

3. The preterit contrasted with the imperfect (*El pretérito contrastado con el imperfecto*)

◆ The difference between the preterit and imperfect tense can be visualized in the following way.

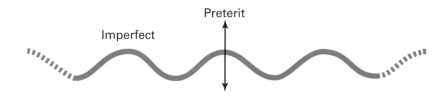

The wavy line representing the imperfect shows an action or event taking place over a period of time in the past. There is no reference as to when the action began or ended. The vertical line representing the preterit shows an action or event completed at a certain time in the past.

In many instances, the choice between the preterit and the imperfect depends on how the speaker views the action or event. The following table summarizes the most important uses of both tenses.

Preterit	Imperfect
• Reports past actions or events that the speaker views as completed Ella **vino** ayer.	• Describes past actions or events in the process of happening, with no reference to their beginning or end. **Íbamos** al cine cuando...
• Sums up a condition or state viewed as a whole (and no longer in effect). **Estuve** cansada todo el día.	• Indicates a repeated or habitual action (*used to . . .* , *would*) Todos los días **íbamos** con él.[1]
	• Describes a physical, mental, or emotional state or condition in the past. **Estaba** muy cansada.
	• Expresses time and age in the past. **Eran** las dos. **Tenía** veinte años.
	• Is used in indirect discourse. Dijo que **venía.**
	• Describes in the past or sets the stage. Mi novia **era** muy bonita. **Hacía** frío y **llovía.**

—¿**Viste** a Eva ayer?　　　　　　*"**Did you see** Eva yesterday?"*
—Sí, **estaba** en el restaurante　*"Yes, **she was** at the restaurant*
　cuando la **vi.**　　　　　　　　*when **I saw** her."*

—¿Qué te **dijo** Raúl?　　　　　　*"What **did** Raúl **say** to you?"*
—Dijo que **necesitaba** dinero.　*"He said **he needed** money."*

¡Atención!　*Direct discourse:*　　Juan dijo: "Vengo mañana".
　　　　　　　 Indirect discourse:　Juan dijo que **venía** mañana.

---

[1]Note that this use of the imperfect corresponds to the English *would* used to describe a repeated action in the past. *Every day **we used to** go with him.* = *Every day **we would** go with him.* Do not confuse this with the English conditional *would,* as in: *If I had the time **I would go** with him.*

Práctica y conversación

Online Study Center

For more practice with lesson topics, see the related activities on the *¡Hola, amigos!* web site at college.hmco.com/PIC/holaamigos7e.

A. Pequeñas historias
Complete the following stories, using the appropriate form of the preterit or the imperfect of the verbs provided. Then read the stories aloud.

1. _____ (Ser) las once y _____ (hacer) frío cuando Ada _____ (llegar) a su casa anoche. La chica _____ (estar) cansada y no _____ (sentirse) bien. Su mamá _____ (levantarse) y le _____ (hacer) una taza de té.

2. Cuando yo _____ (ser) niño yo _____ (vivir) en Chile. Todos los veranos _____ (ir) a visitar a mis abuelos, que _____ (vivir) en el campo. El año pasado mi familia y yo _____ (mudarse) a Cuzco y mis abuelos _____ (venir) a vivir con nosotros.

3. Ayer Ana y Carlos _____ (ir) a la tienda La Peruana. Ana _____ (comprar) una camisa. El empleado les _____ (decir) que ellos _____ (tener) mucha ropa buena y barata. Ana y Carlos _____ (volver) a su casa a las siete, _____ (cenar) y _____ (acostarse). Ana no _____ (dormir) muy bien.

B. Entreviste a su compañero(a)
Interview a partner, using the following questions.

1. ¿Dónde vivías tú cuando eras niño(a)?
2. ¿Qué idioma hablabas tú cuando eras niño(a)?
3. ¿Tú siempre estudiabas mucho cuando eras niño(a)?
4. ¿Cómo era tu primer(a) novio(a)?
5. ¿En qué año comenzaste a estudiar en la universidad?
6. ¿De qué hablaste con tus amigos ayer?
7. ¿Tú estudiaste mucho anoche?
8. ¿Qué hora era cuando llegaste a la universidad hoy?
9. ¿Qué hacías cuando llegó el (la) profesor(a)?
10. ¿Qué te dijo el (la) profesor(a) que tenías que estudiar esta noche?

C. ¿Qué hacíamos... qué hicimos...?
With a partner, talk about what you used to do when you were in high school and then discuss what you did last week. Use the following phrases to start.

1. Cuando yo estaba en la escuela secundaria,
   a. todos los días yo...
   b. los fines de semana mi familia y yo...
   c. en mi clase de inglés mi profesor(a)...
   d. en la cafetería mis amigos y yo...
   e. mi mejor amigo(a) siempre...
   f. los viernes por la noche yo...

2. La semana pasada,
   a. el lunes por la mañana yo...
   b. en mi clase de español mi profesor(a)...
   c. el martes por la noche...
   d. el jueves por la tarde...
   e. el sábado mis amigos y yo...
   f. el domingo yo...

D. Ricitos de oro y los tres osos Working with your classmates in groups of three or four, write the Spanish version of the story "Goldilocks and the Three Bears." Some useful vocabulary is provided.

Había una vez   (*Once upon a time there was/were*)
Ricitos de oro   (*Goldilocks*)
el oso   (*bear*)
la avena   (*porridge*)
mediana   (*medium*)
el bosque   (*forest*)
caliente   (*hot*)
la cama   (*bed*)
el tazón   (*bowl*)

E. Soy escritor (*I'm a writer*)   Use your imagination to finish the following story.

Eran las dos de la mañana y yo estaba durmiendo en mi apartamento. Tocaron a la puerta y yo fui a abrir. Cuando la abrí, vi...

4. *Hace...* meaning *ago* (Hace... *como equivalente de* ago)

In sentences in the preterit and in some cases the imperfect, **hace** + *period of time* is equivalent to the English *ago*. When **hace** is placed at the beginning of the sentence, the construction is as follows.

> **Hace** + period of time   + **que** + verb (*preterit*)
> **Hace** + **dos años**   + **que** + la conocí.
> *I met her two years **ago**.*

An alternative construction is:
La conocí hace dos años.

¡Atención! To find out how long ago something took place, ask:

¿Cuánto tiempo hace que... + *verb in the preterit*
¿Cuánto tiempo hace que viniste a Guayaquil?

—¿**Cuánto tiempo hace que** tú llegaste?   *"**How long ago did** you arrive?"*

—**Hace tres años que** llegué.   *"I arrived **three years ago**."*

Práctica y conversación

A. ¿Cuánto tiempo hace...? Say how long ago the following events took place.

◆ **MODELO:** Son las cuatro. Yo llegué a las tres.
Hace una hora que yo llegué.

1. Estamos en noviembre. Los García celebraron su aniversario de bodas en septiembre.
2. Son las seis. Yo almorcé a la una.
3. Hoy es viernes. Esteban salió para Bolivia el martes.
4. Son las diez. Pedimos el postre a las diez menos cuarto.
5. Estamos en el año 2008. Vinimos a California en el año 1994.
6. Son las diez. Ellos empezaron a estudiar a las siete.

B. ¿Cuándo pasó eso? Discuss with a partner how long ago the following events happened in your life.

1. ¿Cuánto tiempo hace que empezaste a estudiar español?
2. ¿Cuánto tiempo hace que Uds. tomaron el último examen?
3. ¿Cuánto tiempo hace que hablaste con tus padres?
4. ¿Cuánto tiempo hace que le escribiste a un(a) amigo(a)?
5. ¿Cuánto tiempo hace que tu mejor amigo(a) te llamó por teléfono?
6. ¿Cuánto tiempo hace que estuviste en un buen restaurante?
7. ¿Cuánto tiempo hace que compraste ropa?
8. ¿Cuánto tiempo hace que saliste con tus amigos?

Detalles culturales

En las ciudades hispanas hay excelentes tiendas donde se puede comprar ropa hecha (*ready-to-wear*), pero muchas personas prefieren utilizar los servicios de un sastre (*tailor*) o de una modista (*dressmaker*).

◆ ¿Le gusta a Ud. la idea de tener una modista (un sastre)?

5. Possessive pronouns (*Pronombres posesivos*)

◆ Possessive pronouns in Spanish agree in gender and number with the person or thing possessed. They are generally used with the definite article.

Singular		Plural		
Masc.	Fem.	Masc.	Fem.	
(el) mío	(la) mía	(los) míos	(las) mías	mine
(el) tuyo	(la) tuya	(los) tuyos	(las) tuyas	yours (*fam.*)
(el) suyo	(la) suya	(los) suyos	(las) suyas	{ yours (*form.*) his hers
(el) nuestro	(la) nuestra	(los) nuestros	(las) nuestras	ours
(el) vuestro	(la) vuestra	(los) vuestros	(las) vuestras	yours (*fam.*)
(el) suyo	(la) suya	(los) suyos	(las) suyas	{ yours (*form.*) theirs

> *Este zapato no puede ser suyo...*

—Mis libros están aquí.
  ¿Dónde están los **tuyos**?
—Los **míos** están en la mesa.

"My books are here.
  *Where are **yours**?"*
*"**Mine** are on the table."*

> **¡Atención!** Note that **los tuyos** substitutes for **los *libros* tuyos**; the noun has been deleted. Also note that after the verb **ser**, the article is usually omitted.

—¿Estas invitaciones son **tuyas**?
—Sí, son **mías**.

*"Are these invitations **yours**?"*
*"Yes, they're **mine**."*

◆ Because the third-person forms of the possessive pronouns (**el suyo, la suya, los suyos, las suyas**) can be ambiguous, they can be replaced with the following for clarification.

el	de		**Ud.**
la	de		**él**
			ella
los	de		**Uds.**
las	de		**ellos**
			ellas

¿El diccionario? Es **suyo.** (*unclarified*)　　　The dictionary?
　　　　　　　　　　　　　　　　　　　　　　　It's theirs.
Es **el de ellas.** (*clarified*)　　　　　　　(*fem. pl. possessor*)

Práctica y conversación

Online Study Center

For more practice with lesson topics, see the related activities on the *¡Hola, amigos!* web site at college.hmco.com/PIC/holaamigos7e.

A. Todo es nuestro　　Supply the correct possessive pronoun to agree with each subject. Clarify when necessary.

　◆ MODELO:　Yo tengo una camisa. Es _____.
　　　　　　　Es *mía.*

1. Nosotros tenemos un apartamento. Es _____.
2. Ellos tienen una tienda. Es _____. (Es _____ _____ _____.)
3. Él tiene dos trajes. Son _____. (Son _____ _____ _____.)
4. Yo tengo una billetera. Es _____.
5. Tú tienes dos cinturones. Son _____.
6. Uds. tienen muchos zapatos. Son _____. (Son _____ _____ _____.)
7. Ella tiene dos camisones. Son _____. (Son _____ _____ _____.)
8. Nosotros tenemos una casa. Es _____.

B. ¿De quién es...?　　Who owns the following items? Answer the questions affirmatively.

1. Aquí hay una blusa verde. ¿Es tuya?
2. Yo encontré 100 dólares. ¿Son tuyos?
3. ¿La cartera roja es de tu mamá?
4. El libro que tú tienes, ¿es mío?
5. Las plumas que están en mi escritorio, ¿son de ustedes?
6. Aquí hay un diccionario. ¿Es de ustedes?

C. Vamos a comparar　　With a partner, make comparisons between the objects and people described. Use appropriate possessive pronouns when asking each other questions.

　◆ MODELO:　—Mi hermano tiene... años. ¿Cuántos años tiene el tuyo?
　　　　　　　—*El mío tiene dieciocho.*

1. Mi casa está en la calle...
2. Mis abuelos son de...
3. Mi mejor amigo(a) se llama...
4. Mis profesores son...
5. Mis padres están en...
6. Mis tías viven en...

Entre nosotros

¡Conversemos!

 Para conocernos mejor   Get to know your partner better by asking each other the following questions.

1. ¿Dónde conociste a tu mejor amigo(a)? ¿Cuántos años tenías cuando lo (la) conociste?
2. ¿Qué le compraste a tu mejor amigo(a) para su cumpleaños?
3. Cuando vas de compras, ¿prefieres ir solo(a) o con un(a) amigo(a)?
4. Yo compré mi ropa en la tienda _____. ¿Dónde compras tú la tuya?
5. ¿Cuándo fue la última vez que fuiste a la tienda? ¿Qué compraste?
6. Generalmente, ¿usas camisas (blusas) de mangas largas o de mangas cortas?
7. ¿Qué ropa te vas a poner mañana? ¿Te vas a poner sandalias o zapatos?
8. ¿Cuánto te costaron los zapatos? ¿Qué número calzas tú?
9. Si te gustan unos zapatos pero te quedan un poco chicos, ¿los compras?
10. ¿Qué te pones cuando hace mucho frío? ¿Te gustan más los climas fríos o los cálidos?

 Una encuesta   Interview your classmates to identify who fits the following descriptions. Include your instructor, but remember to use the **Ud.** form when addressing him or her.

	Nombre
1. Prefiere los climas cálidos.	
2. Usa impermeable cuando llueve.	
3. Le gusta viajar por tren.	
4. Llegó tarde a clase por el tráfico.	
5. Siempre dice que no tiene nada que ponerse.	
6. Estudia para profesor(a).	
7. Celebró su cumpleaños el mes pasado.	
8. Nació (was born) en el mes de julio.	
9. Compró algo para un amigo (una amiga) recientemente.	
10. Gastó mucho dinero en ropa este mes.	

Y ahora...   Write a brief summary, indicating what you have learned about your classmates.

¿Cómo lo decimos? What would you say in the following situations? What might the other person say? Act out the scenes with a partner.

1. You are shopping for clothes in Lima. Tell the clerk what clothes you need, your size, and discuss colors and prices.
2. You go shopping for shoes, sandals, and boots. You try on several pairs, but have problems with them. You finally buy a pair of boots.
3. Your friends went to the store without you. Ask them what they bought and how much they spent.
4. You ask a new acquaintance from Ecuador where she lived when she was a child and what she liked to do. Give her the same information about you.

¿Qué dice aquí? Look at the following ad and help a friend of yours who is shopping at **La Limeña,** in Lima. Answer his or her questions, using the information provided in the ad.

1. ¿Cómo se llama la tienda?
2. ¿En qué mes son las rebajas (*sales*)?
3. Tengo una hija de nueve años. ¿Qué puedo comprarle en la tienda?
4. Mi esposo necesita zapatos. ¿Qué tipo de zapatos están en liquidación?
5. Además de (*Besides*) los zapatos, ¿qué puedo comprar para mi esposo?
6. Vamos a ir a la playa (*beach*). ¿Qué puedo comprar para mis hijos?
7. Soy profesora y necesito más ropa para el trabajo. ¿Qué puedo comprar?

Las Rebajas de La Limeña

En Agosto más Ventajas

Ahora en La Limeña, Rebajas sobre Rebajas. Todo cuesta mucho menos.

Señoras
- Vestidos lisos y estampados, en poliéster-algódon
- Blusas, faldas, en distintos dibujos y colores
- Zapatos de tacón alto y sandalias

Caballeros
- Trajes y pantalones de sport y de vestir de lana
- Camisas de algodón, de mangas largas y mangas cortas
- Zapatos de cuero

Niños y Jóvenes
- Camisetas lisas y estampadas
- Para ellas, trajes de baño, lisos y de fantasía
- Para ellos, bañadores y pantalones cortos
- Playeros en distintos colores y en todas las tallas

Un dicho

Lo barato sale caro.

Do you only buy clothes that are of good quality? If you do, you will agree with this saying. What does it mean? Can you memorize it?

Para escribir

¿Cómo era Ud.? Write a short narration about your life when you were twelve. Where were you living? What were you like? What did you like to do? Make a list of all the facts and then organize them.

¿CUENTA CONJUNTA?

CUENTA INDIVIDUAL

$300.000

$500.000   ¿SALDO?

Roberto

Cajero

Empleada

Roberto ha estado muy ocupado últimamente y no ha tenido tiempo de ir al banco. Hoy, por fin, tiene un par de horas para hacer diligencias. Primero va al Banco Nacional de Asunción.

Roberto Buenas tardes. Dígame, ¿qué tengo que hacer para abrir una cuenta de ahorros?

Cajero Siéntese, por favor. ¿Tiene usted alguna otra cuenta en este banco?

Roberto Sí, tengo una cuenta corriente.

Cajero ¿Quiere abrir una cuenta individual o una cuenta conjunta?

Roberto Una cuenta individual.

Cajero Bien, llene esta planilla, féchela y fírmela, por favor. ¿Cuánto va a depositar?

Roberto Trescientos mil guaraníes.[1] También quiero cobrar este cheque por cuarenta mil guaraníes. ¿Cuál es el saldo de mi cuenta, por favor?

Cajero Déjeme buscarlo en la computadora. A ver... quinientos mil guaraníes, señor.

Detalles culturales

Abrir una cuenta bancaria no es muy fácil en los países latinoamericanos, especialmente si es una cuenta corriente. La gente pobre que puede ahorrar, generalmente deposita su dinero en la caja postal de ahorros, un servicio que las oficinas de correo ofrecen en algunos países.

◆ ¿Existe ese tipo de servicio en este país?

Detalles culturales

El uso de cheques no es tan común en América Latina como en los Estados Unidos y en Canadá, pero muchos bancos tienen sus propias (own) tarjetas de crédito.

◆ ¿Paga Ud. siempre con cheques o prefiere pagar en efectivo o con tarjetas de crédito?

---

[1]Paraguayan currency

Media hora más tarde, Roberto está en la oficina de correos. Está haciendo cola, porque hay mucha gente.[1]

Roberto	Quiero mandar esta carta a La Paz, certificada.
Empleada	Sí, señor. Son diez mil guaraníes.
Roberto	¿Cuánto cuesta enviar un giro postal a Montevideo?
Empleada	Seis mil guaraníes. ¿Quiere mandar uno?
Roberto	No, voy a volver otro día.
Empleada	Bien, ¿necesita algo más, señor?
Roberto	Sí, deme estampillas para tres tarjetas postales.
Empleada	Aquí las tiene.
Roberto	Gracias. ¡Ah! ¿El correo está abierto mañana?
Empleada	No, señor. Está cerrado. Mañana es día feriado.

Roberto salió de la oficina de correos y trató de recordar dónde había estacionado su coche. Por fin lo encontró a una cuadra del correo. Como les había dicho a sus padres que iba a cenar con ellos, fue directamente a casa.

Detalles culturales

En muchos países de habla hispana, las estampillas sólo pueden comprarse en el correo o en tiendas especializadas que están autorizadas para venderlas.

◆ **¿Dónde puede Ud. comprar estampillas en este país?**

¿Recuerda usted?

¿Verdadero o falso?   With a partner, decide whether the following statements about the dialogue are true (**verdadero**) or false (**falso**).

1.	Roberto va a hacer algunas diligencias hoy.	☐ V ☐ F
2.	Roberto va a abrir una cuenta corriente.	☐ V ☐ F
3.	Roberto no tiene ninguna cuenta en el Banco Nacional.	☐ V ☐ F
4.	Roberto va a depositar más de 100.000 guaraníes.	☐ V ☐ F
5.	Roberto manda una carta certificada.	☐ V ☐ F
6.	Roberto manda un giro postal a Montevideo.	☐ V ☐ F
7.	Roberto puede ir al correo mañana.	☐ V ☐ F
8.	Roberto fue al correo en taxi.	☐ V ☐ F

Y ahora... conteste   Answer these questions, basing your answers on the dialogue.

1. ¿En qué ciudad está el Banco Nacional?
2. ¿Por qué no ha tenido tiempo Roberto para ir al banco?
3. ¿Qué tipo de cuenta quiere abrir Roberto?
4. ¿Dónde va a buscar el empleado el saldo de la cuenta de Roberto?
5. En el correo, ¿por qué tiene que hacer cola Roberto?
6. ¿Cuántas tarjetas postales quiere enviar Roberto?
7. ¿Por qué está cerrado el correo mañana?
8. ¿Dónde encontró Roberto su coche?

---

[1] **Gente** (*People*) is considered singular in Spanish.

Para hablar del tema: Vocabulario

Online Study Center

For more practice with lesson
topics, see the related activities on
the *¡Hola, amigos!* web site at
college.hmco.com/PIC/holaamigos7e.

Cognados

el banco   la computadora*
certificado(a)   directamente
el cheque   individual

Nombres

el (la) cajero(a) teller, cashier
la carta letter
el coche* car
la cuadra* block
la cuenta account
_____ corriente checking account
_____ conjunta joint account
_____ de ahorros savings account
la estampilla* stamp

la gente people
el giro postal money order
la hora hour
la oficina office
_____ de correos, el correo post office
la planilla form
el saldo balance
la tarjeta card
_____ postal postcard

Verbos

cobrar to cash
depositar to deposit
estacionar* to park
fechar to date
firmar to sign
llenar to fill, to fill out

Adjetivos

abierto(a) open
cerrado(a) closed
medio(a) half

ocupado(a) busy
otro(a) another, other

Otras palabras y expresiones

¿Algo más? Anything else?
Aquí las tiene. Here you are.
día feriado holiday
hacer cola to stand in line

hacer diligencias to run errands
por fin finally
primero first
últimamente lately

De país a país

la computadora el ordenador (*Esp.*)
el coche el carro (*Méx.*)
la cuadra la manzana (*Esp.*)
la estampilla el timbre (*Méx.*)
estacionar parquear (*Antillas*)

Detalles culturales

El uso del "Internet" o la "Red", como se llama en español,
es cada día más popular en el mundo hispánico, y muchas
instituciones (empresas y organizaciones) tienen su propia página
(*home page*).

◆ En este país, ¿la mayoría de las instituciones tienen su propia
página en la Red? ¿Cree Ud. que esto es importante? ¿Por qué?

Amplíe su vocabulario

Más sobre el banco

ahorrar to save
la caja de seguridad safe-deposit box
el cajero automático automatic teller machine (ATM)
la casa central home office
en efectivo in cash
gratis free (of charge)
la libreta de ahorros passbook
el plan de ahorros savings plan
el talonario de cheques check book
solicitar un préstamo to apply (ask) for a loan
la sucursal branch office
la memoria memory
la microcomputadora laptop
el ordenador personal, la computadora personal personal computer
archivar la información to store information
navegar la Red to surf the net
tener acceso a la Red to have access to the Internet

Un poco de tecnología (*A little about technology*)

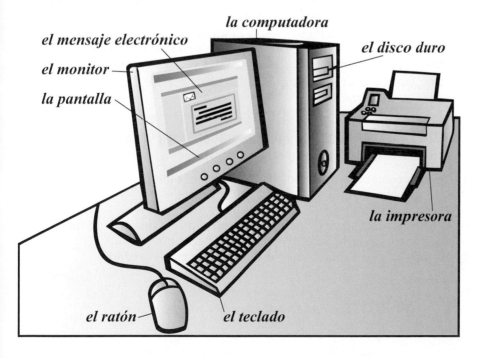

el mensaje electrónico
el monitor
la pantalla
la computadora
el disco duro
la impresora
el ratón
el teclado

Para practicar el vocabulario

A. Preguntas y respuestas   Match the questions in column *A* with the answers in column *B*.

A	B
1. ¿Cuál es el saldo de tu cuenta?	a. No, en una sucursal.
2. ¿Vas a depositar el cheque?	b. No, es un día feriado.
3. ¿Qué debo llenar?	c. No, abierto
4. ¿Qué vas a solicitar?	d. No, voy a cobrarlo.
5. ¿Necesitas algo más?	e. No, con un cheque.
6. ¿Trabajas hoy?	f. Quinientos dólares.
7. ¿Dónde pusiste el dinero?	g. Esta planilla.
8. ¿Trabajas en la casa central?	h. No, nada. Gracias.
9. ¿El banco está cerrado?	i. En la caja de seguridad.
10. ¿Pagas en efectivo?	j. Un préstamo.

Detalles culturales

En España y en la mayoría de los países latinoamericanos una persona debe tener por lo menos (*at least*) 18 años para obtener una licencia de conducir y los exámenes para obtenerla son muy difíciles.

◆ ¿A qué edad se puede obtener una licencia para conducir en este país?

B. Rubén y Eva hacen diligencias   Complete the following description of Rubén and Eva's busy morning.

1. 8:15: Van al banco y abren una cuenta de _____ y una cuenta _____. Las cuentas no son individuales; son_____.
2. 8:50: Sacan dinero del _____ automático.
3. 10:15: Van al Departamento de Vehículos. Eva llena una _____ para sacar su licencia para conducir (*driver's license*); la fecha y la _____.
4. 11:30: Van a la oficina de _____ y después de hacer _____ por unos cinco minutos mandan una carta _____ a La Paz. También envían un giro _____ y compran _____ para tres _____ postales.
5. 12:00: Van a buscar el coche que Rubén había _____ a dos _____ del correo.

C. ¿Qué necesito o qué tengo que hacer?   Say what you need or what you have to do, according to each circumstance.

1. Quieres comprar un automóvil, pero no tienes dinero.
2. Quieres saber cuánto dinero tienes en el banco.
3. Quieres ahorrar dinero.
4. Quieres guardar (*to keep*) documentos muy importantes en el banco.
5. En la sucursal del banco no tienen lo que necesitas.
6. No puedes pagar con un cheque ni con tu tarjeta de crédito.

D. ¿Qué necesita hacer? With a partner, take turns saying what parts of the computer you need to use or what you need to do, according to each circumstance. Use **Necesito** (+ *infinitive*)**...** or **Necesito usar...**

1. You need to write a report on the computer.
2. You need to print the report.
3. You need to read your e-mails.
4. You need to save a résumé.
5. You need to use a computer during a plane trip.
6. You need to look something up on the Internet.

Miguel está comprando ropa por Internet. ¿Qué va a comprar?

Pronunciación

Pronunciation in context In this lesson, there are some words or phrases that may be challenging to pronounce. Listen to your instructor and pronounce the following sentences.

1. Hoy, por **fin,** tiene un par de **horas** para hacer **diligencias.**
2. ¿Qué tengo que **hacer** para abrir una cuenta de **ahorros**?
3. ¿Quiere abrir una cuenta **individual** o una cuenta **conjunta**?
4. Quiero mandar esta carta a **La Paz, certificada.**
5. Trató de **recordar** dónde había **estacionado** su coche.

Puntos para recordar

1. Past participles (*Los participios pasados*)

◆ In Spanish, regular past participles are formed by adding the following endings to the stem of the verb.

-ar *verbs*	-er *verbs*	-ir *verbs*
habl- **ado** (*spoken*)	com- **ido** (*eaten*)	recib- **ido** (*received*)

The following verbs have irregular past participles in Spanish.[1]

abrir	**abierto**	poner	**puesto**
decir	**dicho**	romper	**roto**
escribir	**escrito**	ver	**visto**
hacer	**hecho**	volver	**vuelto**
morir	**muerto**		

¡Atención! The past participle of **ir** is **ido.**

◆ Past participles used as adjectives

In Spanish, most past participles can be used as adjectives. As such, they agree in number and gender with the nouns they modify.

—¿**Las cartas** están **firmadas**? "Are **the letters signed?**"
—Sí, ya están **firmadas** y **fechadas.** "Yes they are already **signed** and **dated.**"

—¿**Las ventanas** están **abiertas**? "Are **the windows open?**"
—No, están **cerradas.** "No, they're **shut.**"

Práctica y conversación

A. Participios pasados Give the past participles of the following verbs.

1. decir
2. cerrar
3. hacer
4. beber
5. morir
6. poner
7. vivir
8. ver
9. recetar
10. volver
11. ir
12. tener
13. romper
14. abrir
15. parar
16. ser
17. escribir
18. buscar
19. leer
20. salir

Online Study Center

For more practice with lesson topics, see the related activities on the *¡Hola, amigos!* web site at college.hmco.com/PIC/holaamigos7e.

---

[1]Verbs ending in **-er** and **-ir** whose stem ends in a strong vowel require an accent mark on the **i** of the **-ido** ending: **leer, leído; oír, oído; traer, traído; creer, creído.**

B. ¿Qué pasa? With a partner, take turns completing the description of each illustration, using the verb **estar** and the appropriate past participle.

1. El coche _____ en la esquina (*corner*).

2. Los niños _____.

3. El restaurante _____.

4. La ventana _____.

5. La puerta _____.

6. La carta _____ en español.

7. Los vestidos _____ en México.

8. El cuaderno _____.

9. La señora _____ cerca de la ventana.

C. Preguntas de un turista With a partner, take turns answering a tourist's questions.

1. ¿Los bancos están abiertos a las ocho de la mañana?
2. Hoy es feriado, ¿están abiertas las tiendas?
3. ¿El correo ya está cerrado a las siete de la noche?
4. ¿Aquí todos los letreros (*signs*) están escritos en inglés?
5. ¿Dónde están hechos estos vinos?
6. ¿Los restaurantes están cerrados los domingos?

2. Present perfect tense (*Pretérito perfecto*)

◆ The present perfect tense is formed by using the present tense of the auxiliary verb **haber** with the past participle of the verb that expresses the action or state.

Present Indicative of haber (*to have*)[1]	
he	hemos
has	habéis
ha	han

Formation of the Present Perfect Tense			
	Present of haber	+ Past Participle	
yo	**he**	**hablado**	I have spoken
tú	**has**	**comido**	you (*fam.*) have eaten
Ud., él, ella	**ha**	**vuelto**	you (*form.*) have returned; he, she has returned
nosotros(as)	**hemos**	**dicho**	we have said
vosotros(as)	**habéis**	**roto**	you (*fam.*) have broken
Uds., ellos, ellas	**han**	**hecho**	you (*form., fam.*) have done, made; they have done, made

◆ The present perfect tense is equivalent to the use in English of the auxiliary verb *have + past participle*, as in *I have spoken.*

—¿Nora **ha ido** al correo?   *"**Has** Nora **gone** to the post office?"*
—No, no **ha podido** ir.   *"No, she **hasn't been** able to go."*

◆ Note that in Spanish, when the past participle is part of a perfect tense, its form does not vary for gender or number agreement.

Él **ha estacionado** aquí.   *"He has parked here."*
Ella **ha estacionado** aquí.   *"She has parked here."*

---

[1]Note that the English verb *to have* has two equivalents in Spanish: **haber** (used as an auxiliary verb) and **tener.**

- Unlike English, the past participle in Spanish is never separated from the auxiliary verb **haber.**

Ella **nunca ha hecho** nada.　　*She **has never done** anything.*
Él **siempre ha escrito** las cartas　*He **has always written** the letters*
　　en inglés.　　　　　　　　　　　*in English.*

¿Sr. Soto? Hemos encontrado su coche.

Online Study Center

For more practice with lesson topics, see the related activities on the *¡Hola, amigos!* web site at college.hmco.com/PIC/holaamigos7e.

Práctica y conversación

A. Hoy llega mamá　Mrs. Aranda is coming home today after a business trip. With a partner, take turns saying what everybody has done to get ready for her homecoming. Use the cues provided.

- **MODELO:** Viviana / preparar / comida
　　　　　　Viviana ha preparado la comida.

1. El Sr. Aranda / lavar / coche
2. Jorge / barrer / garaje
3. Yo / sacudir / muebles
4. Tú / hacer / una torta

5. Los niños / poner / mesa
6. Andrés / comprar / rosas
7. Raquel / pasar / aspiradora
8. Rolando y yo / traer / bebidas

B. Entreviste a su compañero(a)　Interview a classmate, using the following questions.

1. ¿Has ido al banco últimamente?
2. ¿Has pedido un préstamo recientemente?
3. ¿Has tenido que sacar dinero del cajero automático esta semana?
4. ¿Tus padres han abierto una cuenta conjunta contigo?
5. ¿Alguien te ha mandado tarjetas postales recientemente?
6. ¿Tú y tu familia han estado en Suramérica alguna vez (*ever*)?
7. ¿Dónde has estacionado tu coche hoy?
8. ¿Has llegado tarde a clase?

C. Lo que hemos hecho　In groups of three, discuss what you have done since yesterday. Include what you have eaten, whom you have seen and spoken to, and so on. Be prepared to report to the class something that all of you have done.

3. Past perfect (pluperfect) tense (*Pretérito pluscuamperfecto*)

◆ The past perfect tense is formed by using the imperfect tense of the auxiliary verb **haber** with the past participle of the verb that expresses the action or state.

Imperfect of haber	
había	habíamos
habías	habíais
había	habían

Formation of the Past Perfect Tense			
	Imperfect of haber	+ *Past Participle*	
yo	**había**	**hablado**	I had spoken
tú	**habías**	**comido**	you (*fam.*) had eaten
Ud., él, ella	**había**	**vuelto**	you (*form.*), he, she had returned
nosotros(as)	**habíamos**	**dicho**	we had said
vosotros(as)	**habíais**	**roto**	you (*fam.*) had broken
Uds., ellos, ellas	**habían**	**hecho**	you (*form., fam.*) had done, made; they had done, made

◆ The past perfect tense is equivalent to the use in English of the auxiliary verb *had + past participle*, as in *I had spoken.*

In Spanish, as in English, this tense refers to actions, states, or events that were already completed before the start of another past action, state, or event.

—¿Uds. **habían estado** en Chile antes del año pasado?   "**Had** you **been** in Chile before last year?"

—No, nunca **habíamos estado** allí.   "No, **we had** never **been** there."

—¿Ricardo está aquí?   "Is Ricardo here?"

—Sí, cuando yo vine, él ya **había llegado.**   "Yes, when I came, he **had** already **arrived.**"

Online Study Center

For more practice with lesson topics, see the related activities on the *¡Hola, amigos!* web site at college.hmco.com/PIC/holaamigos7e.

Práctica y conversación

A. Minidiálogos   Complete the following exchanges with the past perfect of the verbs given.

1. —¿Qué _____ (hacer) el empleado?

   —Le _____ (traer) las estampillas.

2. —¿Tú ya _____ (ver) a Roberto?

   —Sí, yo ya _____ (hablar) con él.

3. —¿El niño _____ (romper) el florero?

   —Sí, y por eso tuve que comprar otro.

4. —Cuando papá vino a buscarnos, ¿Uds. ya _____ (ir) al correo?

—No, no _____ (ir) todavía.

5. —¿Qué _____ (decir) tu mamá?

—Que necesitaba su talonario de cheques.

6. —¿Adónde _____ (ir) Uds., a la casa central del banco?

—No _____ (ir) a una sucursal.

7. —¿Dónde _____ (poner) tú los documentos?

—Los _____ (poner) en la caja de seguridad.

8. —¿Qué le _____ (comprar) a Jorge Uds.?

—Le _____ (comprar) una computadora personal.

B. Están de vuelta Your parents just got back from a vacation. Say what everybody had done by the time they came back.

1. yo   **3.** mis hermanos   **5.** tú

2. mi amiga   **4.** mi tío y yo   **6.** Uds.

C. Antes de los 16 Find out which of the following things your partner had done before turning 16.

◆ **MODELO:** conducir
> —¿Habías conducido antes de cumplir dieciséis años?
> —Sí (No),...

1. abrir una cuenta corriente   **4.** vivir en otro país (*country*)

2. trabajar   **5.** estudiar un idioma

3. tener novio(a)   **6.** terminar la escuela secundaria

4. Formal commands: *Ud.* and *Uds.* (*Mandatos formales:* Ud. *y* Uds.)

◆ The command forms for **Ud.** and **Uds.**[1] are formed by dropping the **-o** of the first-person singular of the present indicative and adding **-e** and **-en** for **-ar** verbs and **-a** and **-an** for **-er** and **-ir** verbs.

Infinitive	First-Person Sing. Present Indicative	Stem	Commands Ud.	Uds.
habl**ar**	yo habl**o**	habl-	habl**e**	habl**en**
com**er**	yo com**o**	com-	com**a**	com**an**
abr**ir**	yo abr**o**	abr-	abr**a**	abr**an**
cerr**ar**	yo cierr**o**	cierr-	cierr**e**	cierr**en**
volv**er**	yo vuelv**o**	vuelv-	vuelv**a**	vuelv**an**
ped**ir**	yo pid**o**	pid-	pid**a**	pid**an**
dec**ir**	yo dig**o**	dig-	dig**a**	dig**an**

—¿Con quién debo hablar?   "With whom must I speak?"

—**Hable** con el cajero.   "**Speak** with the teller."

—¿Cuándo debemos volver?   "When must we come back?"

—**Vuelvan** mañana.   "**Come back** tomorrow."

---

[1]The command form for **tú** will be studied in **Lección 12.**

◆ The command forms of the following verbs are irregular.

	dar	estar	ser	ir
Ud.	dé	esté	sea	vaya
Uds.	den	estén	sean	vayan

—¿Vamos al correo ahora?   *"Shall we go to the post office now?"*

—No, no **vayan** ahora; **vayan**   *"No, don't **go** now; **go** at two*
a las dos.   *o'clock."*

◆ With all direct *affirmative* commands, object pronouns are placed after the verb and are attached to it, thus forming only one word. With all *negative* commands, the object pronouns are placed in front of the verb.

—¿Dónde pongo las cartas?   *"Where shall I put the letters?"*
—**Póngalas** aquí; **no las ponga**   ***"Put them** here; **don't put them***
allí.   *there."*

¡Atención!   Note the use of the written accent in **póngalas**.

> ¡Digan la verdad!
> ¿No es fantástico
> ser bilingüe?

> ¡Guau, guau!

Online Study Center

For more practice with lesson topics, see the related activities on the *¡Hola, amigos!* web site at college.hmco.com/PIC/holaamigos7e.

Práctica y conversación

A. Instrucciones   A bank employee must give the customers certain instructions. Following the model, change each sentence to the appropriate command.

◆ MODELO: Tiene que llenar la planilla.
           Llene la planilla.

1. Tienen que fechar y firmar la planilla.
2. Tienen que hacer cola.

3. Tienen que estar aquí a las tres.
4. Tiene que hablar con el cajero.
5. Tiene que sentarse y esperar unos minutos.
6. Tiene que venir más tarde y traer el número de su cuenta.
7. Tiene que darle su nombre al gerente (*manager*).
8. Tiene que dejarme su número de teléfono.
9. Tienen que decirle que los cheques son gratis.
10. Tiene que volver mañana.

B. Mamá (Papá) y nosotros
Two teenagers are helping their Mom (Dad) and asking what to do. Take the role of the parent and answer their questions. Use the command forms and the cues provided.

1. ¿Adónde vamos ahora? (al mercado)
2. ¿Qué compramos? (frutas)
3. ¿A quién le pedimos el dinero? (a su abuelo)
4. ¿Qué más traemos? (detergente)
5. ¿Qué coche llevamos? (el mío)
6. ¿A qué hora empezamos a cocinar? (a las tres)
7. ¿Qué hacemos de postre? (arroz con leche)
8. ¿Invitamos a cenar a Roberto o a Miguel? (Miguel)

C. ¿Que sí o que no?
Andrés says yes to everything, while Ana always says no. With your partner, play the roles of Ana and Andrés. Answer each question as he or she would, using a formal command and a direct object pronoun to replace each direct object.

1. ¿Mando las cartas hoy? (Andrés)
2. ¿Compramos los sellos? (Ana)
3. ¿Traigo el talonario de cheques? (Ana)
4. ¿Compramos las tarjetas postales? (Andrés)
5. ¿Llamo a Rafael? (Andrés)
6. ¿Llamamos a nuestros amigos? (Ana)
7. ¿Mando el giro postal? (Andrés)
8. ¿Hacemos las diligencias hoy? (Ana)

D. A mi secretaria
Using commands, tell your secretary to do the following tasks.

1. *Escribirles* al Dr. López y al Dr. Smith. *Escribirle* al Dr. López en español y *escribirle* al Dr. Smith en inglés. *Decirles* que los documentos ya están listos. *Mandarles* las cartas hoy.
2. *Comprarle* (a él) papel y lápices.
3. *Darle* al Sr. Gómez su número de teléfono, pero no *darle* su dirección.
4. *No hablarles* a los empleados del nuevo horario.
5. *Llevarle* las planillas al Sr. Soto, pero *no llevarle* los cheques.
6. *No decirle* a la Sra. Castro que los cheques son gratis.

E. Una nota
You and your partner are going to be gone for a few days, and you have two very irresponsible roommates. Write them a note telling them four things to do and four things not to do in your absence.

Entre nosotros

¡Conversemos!

 Para conocernos mejor   Get to know your partner better by asking each other the following questions.

1. ¿En qué banco tienes tu cuenta de ahorros? ¿Y tu cuenta corriente?
2. ¿Usas el cajero automático a veces?
3. Cuando compras algo, ¿pagas en efectivo o con cheque?
4. ¿Vas a depositar dinero en tu cuenta de ahorros mañana?
5. ¿Tienes tu talonario de cheques contigo?
6. ¿Tú sabes cuál es el saldo de tu cuenta corriente?
7. ¿Tienes tus documentos importantes en una caja de seguridad?
8. Cuando vas al correo, ¿a veces tienes que hacer cola?
9. ¿Envías muchas tarjetas de Navidad (*Christmas*)?
10. ¿Usas microcomputadora o computadora personal?
11. ¿Navegas mucho la Red?
12. ¿Cuántos mensajes electrónicos recibes al día?

 Una encuesta   Interview your classmates to identify who fits the following descriptions. Include your instructor, but remember to use the **Ud.** form when addressing him or her.

	Nombre
1. Hace sus diligencias los sábados.	_____
2. A veces manda giros postales.	_____
3. A veces envía cartas certificadas.	_____
4. Recuerda su número de Seguro Social (Social Security).	_____
5. Piensa abrir una cuenta en el banco.	_____
6. Tiene un buen plan de ahorros.	_____
7. Necesita ahorrar más.	_____
8. Tiene una cuenta conjunta.	_____
9. Siempre manda tarjetas postales cuando viaja (he/she travels).	_____
10. Deposita dinero en el banco todos los meses.	_____

Y ahora...   Write a brief summary, indicating what you have learned about your classmates.

¿Cómo lo decimos? What would you say in the following situations? What might the other person say? Act out the scenes with a partner.

1. Ask for the necessary information to open a savings account.
2. You need to cash a check. Tell the teller how much you want to deposit in your checking account, and how much cash you want.
3. You are in Asunción, and you need to send some letters and postcards to the United States. Tell the employee what you need.
4. You are teaching a computer class for beginners. In Spanish, identify the parts of a computer for your students.
5. You are at a computer lab at closing time. Tell the attendant three things you need to do before you leave.

¿Qué dice aquí? Read the following ad, and answer the questions that follow.

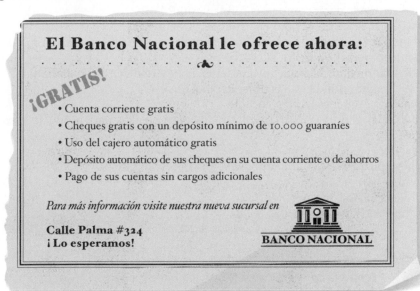

El Banco Nacional le ofrece ahora:

¡GRATIS!

- Cuenta corriente gratis
- Cheques gratis con un depósito mínimo de 10.000 guaraníes
- Uso del cajero automático gratis
- Depósito automático de sus cheques en su cuenta corriente o de ahorros
- Pago de sus cuentas sin cargos adicionales

Para más información visite nuestra nueva sucursal en

Calle Palma #324
¡Lo esperamos!

BANCO NACIONAL

1. ¿Cuánto hay que pagar por tener una cuenta corriente?
2. ¿Cuánto se debe tener depositado para recibir los cheques gratis?
3. ¿Cuánto cobra el banco por el uso del cajero automático?
4. ¿En qué tipos de cuentas se pueden depositar los cheques automáticamente?
5. ¿Que otro servicio ofrece gratis el banco?
6. ¿Dónde se puede obtener más información sobre los servicios que da el banco?
7. ¿Cómo se llama el banco? ¿Cuál es la dirección de la nueva sucursal?

> **Un dicho**
>
> *El tiempo es oro (gold).*
>
> As you can see, time is important in both cultures. Next time someone is wasting time you can quote this saying in Spanish.

Para escribir

En el banco Write about your banking practices. Mention . . .

1. the name of your bank and types of accounts you have.
2. the interest (**interés**) your bank pays.
3. whether you need to pay for the checks or if they are free.
4. whether you pay for purchases by check or by a credit card.
5. whether you save money, and why.

Lectura

Estrategia de lectura Make a list of some aspects of English that make it difficult to learn as a second language. Think about some of the problems that Spanish-speaking students might face.

Vamos a leer As you read the story, find the answers to the following questions.

1. ¿Qué deletrea (*spell*) un inglés cuando se presenta?
2. Según el autor, ¿de cuántas maneras puede escribirse una palabra?
3. ¿Es más difícil el deletreo cuando se hace por teléfono?
4. ¿Qué se puede decir como tesis fundamental?
5. ¿Cuál es el título de su libro en español? ¿Y en inglés?
6. Cuando Arciniegas habla de su libro en inglés, nadie sabe si él escribió un nocturno o un libro de caballería. ¿Por qué?
7. ¿Cómo anunciaron un día una conferencia de Arciniegas en el periódico?
8. Para el autor, ¿dónde está la dificultad del inglés?
9. ¿Qué dice Arciniegas de las vocales?
10. ¿Qué causa el esfuerzo que un hispanohablante realiza para producir "eres" o "eses"?
11. ¿Qué deja en el rostro?
12. ¿Qué explicación les da siempre el autor a sus colegas?

Germán Arciniegas (1900–1999) es uno de los escritores colombianos más distinguidos. Sus brillantes ensayos° se centran en la cultura, la sociología, la historia, el arte y la literatura de su país y de toda Latinoamérica. Su estilo es ligero° y ágil. Su famosa biografía, El caballero de El Dorado *(1942), sobre la vida° de Gonzalo Jiménez de Quesada, conquistador de Colombia y fundador de Bogotá, es una de las mejor escritas° en este continente. Muchos de sus libros han sido traducidos al inglés.*

essays

light

life

written

Video

Lecciones de inglés
(*Adaptado*)

GERMÁN ARCINIEGAS

Un inglés que en algo se estima° se presenta de esta manera: "Soy Mr. John Nielsen, Ene-i-e-ele-ese-e-ene". Esto es porque en inglés se supone que una palabra se pronuncia de un modo —cosa que no es exacta— pero que en todo caso puede escribirse de mil maneras. Aun el deletreo° puede no ser suficientemente claro, principalmente si se hace por teléfono. En este caso lo más discreto y usual es decir: "Mr. Arciniegas, *A* como en Argentina, *R* como en Rusia, *C* como en Colombia, *I* como en Irlanda..." De esta manera, siendo el idioma de Shakespeare tan conciso, un apellido puede extenderse indefinidamente.

    Las confusiones no quedan limitadas a los apellidos. Como tesis fundamental usted puede decir que toda palabra inglesa es un jeroglífico. Yo tengo un libro que, en la edición española, se llama *El caballero° de El Dorado*. Aquí, *The Knight of El Dorado*. Pero como en inglés "noche" y "caballero" se pronuncian de un mismo modo°, cuando estoy hablando de mi libro nadie sabe si escribí un nocturno° o una obra de caballería°. En la cubierta de este libro aparece la siguiente advertencia°: "Germán Arciniegas (se pronuncia *Hairmáhn Ar-seen-yay-gus*)". La advertencia es indispensable.

    Pero si el lector° quiere saber más sobre los problemas de mi apellido en este país, puedo informarle que un día en el periódico anunciaron una conferencia mía así: "Hoy da una conferencia sobre la América Latina el doctor *Arthur Nagus*".

    La dificultad del inglés está en la emisión de los sonidos. Cuando uno se da cuenta° de que cada letra de las vocales se pronuncia de cuatro o cinco modos distintos, desfallece°. El esfuerzo que uno realiza para producir "eres" o "eses" no sólo causa una gran fatiga a quienes estamos acostumbrados al español, sino que deja en el rostro° una impresión de dolor o de gran torpeza°. Yo siempre les doy esta explicación a mis colegas: "Yo no soy bobo; es que no sé inglés".

que... who has some self esteem

spelling

knight

way
nocturne / chivalry
warning

reader

se... realizes
one faints

face, stupidity

Díganos   Answer the following questions, based on your own thoughts and experience.

1. ¿Sabe usted deletrear en español?
2. ¿Qué cree usted que es lo más difícil en español? ¿Pronunciar las palabras? ¿Conjugar verbos? ¿Escribir?
3. ¿Qué problemas tiene usted para aprender español?
4. ¿Usted tiene que realizar un gran esfuerzo para hablar español?
5. ¿Cuánto tiempo hace que usted empezó a estudiar español? ¿Lo practica frecuentemente?
6. ¿Usted piensa continuar estudiando español?

Un día funesto

Marisa, Teresa y Pablo han tenido un día difícil en el que todo les fue mal (*went badly for them*). ¿Qué van a hacer? Los tres están demasiado cansados. ¿Encuentran una solución...?

El mundo hispánico

Ecuador

◆ Ecuador debe su nombre a su posición geográfica. El país está situado justamente sobre la línea del ecuador. Su territorio, incluidas las islas Galápagos, es un poco menor que el de Nevada, y su población es de unos 13,5 millones de habitantes.

◆ Debido a la inestabilidad del sucre, su antigua moneda, en septiembre de 2000 el país adoptó el dólar de Estados Unidos como su moneda oficial.

◆ Quito, la capital de Ecuador, está situada en las laderas (*hillsides*) del volcán Pichincha, a más de 9.000 pies de altura sobre el nivel del mar. Por eso, aunque la ciudad está muy cerca de la línea del ecuador, su clima es templado (*mild*) y agradable. Quito es la capital más antigua de América del Sur, y todavía mantiene su aspecto colonial, con sus calles estrechas (*narrow*) y sus viejas iglesias.

▲ Estas enormes tortugas les dieron nombre a las famosas Islas Galápagos.

◆ A 22 millas de Quito, cerca de la villa de San Antonio, está el monumento La Mitad del Mundo, que marca el sitio exacto por donde pasa la línea del ecuador.

◆ Las islas Galápagos, situadas frente a las costas de Ecuador, son una de las zonas ecológicas mejor conservadas del mundo. Charles Darwin hizo la mayor parte de sus estudios sobre la evolución de las especies en estas islas.

Perú

◆ Perú es el tercer país más grande de Suramérica. Su territorio es un poco menor que el de Alaska, y su población es de unos 28 millones de habitantes. La moneda del país es el nuevo sol. La principal fuente de ingreso del país continúa siendo la industria pesquera.

◆ Entre los animales típicos de la fauna de Perú están las llamas, alpacas y vicuñas. De su lana dependen muchas de las artesanías del país. La llama, además, se usa como animal de carga y para el transporte.

◆ Las principales atracciones turísticas del país son Cuzco, la antigua capital de los incas, y las impresionantes ruinas de Machu Picchu, situadas en las montañas cerca de Cuzco a una altura de 2.350 metros. Machu Picchu fue una fortaleza incaica que después de la conquista quedó perdida hasta 1911, cuando fue descubierta por el arqueólogo norteamericano Hiram Bingham.

▲ Machu Picchu es el más conocido de los símbolos del Imperio Inca.

Online Study Center

For more practice with lesson topics, see the related activities on the *¡Hola, amigos!* web site at college.hmco.com/PIC/holaamigos7e.

◆ La capital de Perú es Lima. En esta ciudad se encuentra la Universidad de San Marcos, que es la más antigua de Suramérica.

Bolivia

- Bolivia, llamada así en honor del Libertador Simón Bolívar, es un país de superlativos. Tiene la capital (La Paz), el aeropuerto y el lago navegable más altos del mundo, y unas de las ruinas más antiguas. En realidad, La Paz es una de las dos capitales de Bolivia; la otra es Sucre. La Paz, situada a 12.000 pies de altura, es la capital administrativa, y Sucre, la capital política. El lago Titicaca está a 12.500 pies de altura y es, después del lago Maracaibo, el segundo más grande de América del Sur. El país es tan grande como los estados de California y Texas juntos, pero apenas puede explotar sus riquezas naturales porque no tiene salida al mar y su territorio es muy montañoso.

▲ La plaza del estudiante en La Paz, Bolivia

- Los indios quechua y aymará, que constituyen más de la mitad de su población, mantienen su cultura y sus lenguas tradicionales. El resto de la población lo constituyen las personas de ascendencia europea (un 15% de la población) y los mestizos producto de la integración de las razas indígenas y europeas. La mayor parte de los habitantes del país vive en el altiplano (*plateau*).

- Bolivia es uno de los más atractivos destinos turísticos por sus bellísimos paisajes andinos, que le han valido el nombre de "el Tibet de América", y por las ruinas doblemente milenarias de Tiahuanaco.

Paraguay

- Paraguay es casi tan grande como el estado de California, pero su población es de menos de 6 millones de habitantes. La mayoría de los paraguayos hablan dos idiomas: el español y el guaraní.

- Paraguay es un país principalmente agrícola y su economía depende de sus bosques y sus fértiles tierras (*lands*). Sin embargo, desde la construcción de la planta hidroeléctrica de Itaipú, el país ha comenzado a industrializarse. Itaipú, la mayor planta hidroeléctrica del mundo, obra del esfuerzo conjunto de Brasil y Paraguay, ha hecho de este país el mayor exportador de energía hidroeléctrica.

- Al igual que Bolivia, Paraguay no tiene salida al mar, pero tiene más de 1.800 millas de ríos navegables, que son sus principales vías de transporte. En la frontera de Paraguay, Argentina y Brasil están las famosas cataratas de Iguazú, nombre guaraní que significa "agua grande".

- Asunción, la capital de Paraguay, es también su principal puerto. Es una ciudad de más de dos millones de habitantes en la que se mezclan los edificios coloniales con modernas construcciones.

▲ El Panteón de los Héroes, en Asunción, Paraguay

Comentarios... With a partner, discuss, in Spanish, what impressed you the most about these four countries, and compare them to your own. Which places do you want to visit and why?

Tome este examen

Lección 9

A. Some uses of *por* and *para* Complete each sentence, using **por** or **para**.

1. El vestido es _____ ti, mamá.
2. ¿Cuánto pagaron _____ los aretes?
3. Yo no trabajo _____ la mañana.
4. Los chicos salieron _____ la puerta principal.
5. Ellos fueron al club nocturno _____ bailar.
6. Necesito la falda _____ mañana _____ la tarde.
7. El sábado salimos _____ Lima. Vamos _____ avión (*airplane*). Vamos a estar allí _____ una semana.
8. En ese hotel cobran 100 dólares _____ noche.

B. Weather expressions Complete each sentence with the appropriate word(s).

1. En verano _____ mucho _____ en Texas.
2. En invierno en Denver _____ mucho _____ y _____ mucho.
3. En Oregón _____ todo el año.
4. Hoy no hay vuelos (*flights*) porque _____ mucha _____.
5. Necesito la sombrilla porque _____ mucho _____.

C. The preterit contrasted with the imperfect Complete each sentence, using the preterit or the imperfect tense of the verbs in parentheses.

1. Ayer nosotros _____ (celebrar) nuestro aniversario.
2. _____ (Ser) las cuatro de la tarde cuando yo _____ (salir) del restaurante. _____ (Llegar) a mi casa a las cinco.
3. El mozo me _____ (decir) que la especialidad de la casa _____ (ser) cordero y yo lo _____ (pedir).
4. Cuando Raúl _____ (ser) pequeño _____ (vivir) aquí.
5. Jorge _____ (estar) en el café cuando yo lo _____ (ver).
6. Ella no _____ (ir) a la fiesta anoche porque _____ (estar) muy cansada. _____ (Preferir) quedarse en su casa.
7. Ayer yo _____ (hacer) las reservaciones.
8. Nosotros _____ (estar) almorzando cuando tú _____ (llamar).

D. *Hace...* meaning *ago* Indicate how long ago everything took place.

1. Llegué a las seis. Son las nueve.
2. Ellos vinieron en marzo. Estamos en julio.
3. Empecé a trabajar a las dos. Son las dos y media.
4. Terminaron el domingo. Hoy es viernes.
5. Llegaste en 1998. Estamos en el año 2008.

E. Possessive pronouns Complete each sentence, giving the Spanish equivalent of the word in parentheses.

1. Mi vestido es mejor que _____, María. (*yours*)
2. Las camisas azules son _____. (*mine*)
3. Yo voy a invitar a mis amigos. ¿Tú vas a invitar a _____? (*yours*)
4. Estos zapatos son _____. (*ours*)
5. Mi abuelo es de México. _____ es de Cuba. (*Theirs*)
6. Ese libro no es _____; es _____. (*mine / hers*)

F. Vocabulary Complete the following sentences, using vocabulary from **Lección 9.**

1. Estos zapatos no son caros, son muy _____.
2. Voy a la _____ para comprar unas sandalias.
3. Estudia en la _____ de medicina.
4. Necesito un _____ de botas.
5. Necesito una camisa de _____ largas.
6. ¿En que puedo _____, Srta.?
7. Este traje no está de _____ ahora.
8. No me gusta andar _____. Siempre uso zapatos.
9. Voy a comprar ropa porque no tengo nada que _____.
10. Los aretes me costaron un _____ de la _____.
11. ¿Qué número _____ Ud.?
12. El clima de este país no es seco, es _____.

G. Culture Complete the following sentences, based on the cultural notes you have read.

1. En los países hispanos se usa el sistema _____ decimal.
2. La moneda de Perú es el _____.

A. Past participles   Complete each sentence, using the past participle of the verb in parentheses.

1. Las puertas están _____.   (cerrar)
2. La oficina está _____.   (abrir)
3. El florero está _____.   (romper)
4. Los niños están _____.   (dormir)
5. Las cartas están _____ en italiano.   (escribir)
6. La cena ya está _____.   (hacer)

B. Present perfect tense   Complete each sentence, using the present perfect of the verb in parentheses.

1. El cajero no _____.   (llegar)
2. Yo _____ los vasos.   (romper)
3. Ellos no _____ las cartas.   (traer)
4. Como los niños no _____, nosotros no _____ salir.   (volver / poder)
5. Ellos _____ en el accidente.   (morir)
6. Tú se lo _____ antes.   (decir)

C. Past perfect (Pluperfect) tense   Indicate what had taken place by the time Ana arrived home, using the past perfect tense.

Ana llegó a su casa a las diez.

1. Los chicos volvieron a casa.
2. Yo firmé la planilla.
3. Tú hiciste los cheques.
4. Nosotros escribimos las cartas.
5. Carlos puso el dinero en su cuenta.
6. Uds. fueron al banco.

D. Formal commands   Complete each sentence, using the command form of the verb in parentheses. Use the **Ud.** or **Uds.** form, as needed.

1. _____ a su esposa, Sr. García.   (Llamar)
2. _____, Sr. Vega.   (Caminar)
3. _____ en seguida, señoritas.   (Salir)
4. _____ aquí a las dos, señora.   (Estar)
5. No _____ ahora, Sr. Sosa.   (venir)
6. _____ a la izquierda, señores.   (Ir)
7. No _____ Ud. ahora.   (hacerlo)
8. Señor, no _____ su número de teléfono.   (dar)
9. Chicos, _____ buenos, por favor.   (ser)
10. _____ aquí. Srta. Pérez.   (Ponerla)

E. Vocabulary
Complete the following sentences, using vocabulary from **Lección 10.**

1. Ud. debe _____ y _____ esta planilla.
2. ¿Cuánto dinero va a _____ en su cuenta?
3. El banco no está _____ hoy, porque es un día _____.
4. Quiero saber cuál es el _____ de mi cuenta corriente.
5. Mi esposa y yo queremos abrir una cuenta de ahorros _____.
6. Estacioné mi coche a dos _____ de aquí.
7. Tengo que hacer _____ porque hay mucha gente en el banco.
8. Necesito mi _____ de cheques.
9. No tengo mi dinero en el banco central, sino en una _____.
10. Ellos van a sacar dinero del _____ automático.
11. Necesito dinero. Voy a solicitar un _____ en el banco.
12. No quiero pagar con cheque, prefiero pagar en _____.
13. Tengo mis documentos en una _____ de seguridad.
14. Necesito comprar _____ para estas cartas.
15. Hoy tengo que hacer muchas _____.

F. Culture
Complete the following sentences, based on the cultural notes you have read.

1. Las islas _____ son una de las zonas ecológicas mejor conservadas.
2. Machu Picchu y _____ son las principales atracciones turísticas de Perú.
3. Bolivia tiene dos capitales: La Paz y _____.
4. En Paraguay está _____, la mayor planta hidroeléctrica del mundo.

Unidad

6

Objetivos

Lección 11

- handle routine travel arrangements
- discuss tour features and prices
- request information regarding stopovers, plane changes, gate numbers, and seating
- express feelings and reactions

Lección 12

- register at a boarding house, discuss room prices, accommodations, and service
- tell others what to do
- describe needs and wants
- ordinal numbers

Situado entre lagos, ríos y glaciares, está el hotel Llao Llao en Bariloche, Argentina.

De vacaciones

Argentina

El obelisco en la famosa Avenida 9 de Julio en Buenos Aires, Argentina

Uruguay

Vista del famoso balneario de Punta del Este

Chile

Vista del Lago Pehoé, Parque Nacional Torres del Paine, en la Patagonia

247

Héctor Rivas y su esposa Sofía Vargas viven en Santiago, la capital de Chile. Ahora están planeando sus vacaciones de verano. No pueden ponerse de acuerdo porque ella quiere pasar un mes en Viña del Mar, y él quiere ir a Buenos Aires y a Mar del Plata.

Héctor Espero que hoy podamos decidir lo que vamos a hacer, porque tenemos que ir a la agencia de viajes para comprar los pasajes.

Sofía Yo te sugiero que averigües lo que cuestan dos pasajes de ida y vuelta a Buenos Aires, por avión. Podemos ahorrar dinero si vamos a Viña del Mar en coche...

Héctor ¡Pero hemos estado en Viña del Mar muchas veces! ¡Estoy empezando a cansarme de hacer siempre lo mismo!

Sofía ¡Y yo temo que el viaje a Buenos Aires nos cueste mucho dinero!

Héctor Yo busqué información en Internet. Hay paquetes que incluyen vuelo directo a Buenos Aires, hotel y algunas excursiones.

Sofía Siento no poder compartir tu entusiasmo, querido, pero viajar a otro país es complicado... Necesitamos pasaporte...

Héctor Eso no es problema. Un momento... ¿Es porque no quieres viajar en avión?

Sofía Bueno... en parte... un poco.

Héctor ¡Pero, mi amor! Sólo necesitas que tu médico te dé alguna pastilla para los nervios.

Sofía Está bien, pero te pido que me dejes pensarlo antes de tomar una decisión.

Detalles culturales

Viña del Mar es el más conocido de los balnearios (*resorts*) de Chile, y uno de los centros turísticos más populares de Suramérica. Allí hay numerosas playas, parques, hoteles y casinos. La ciudad es también un centro comercial e industrial importante.

◆ **¿Cuál es un famoso balneario de su país?**

Sofía decidió ir a Buenos Aires en avión. El día del viaje, hablan con el agente de la aerolínea en el aeropuerto.

Agente	¿Qué asientos desean? ¿De ventanilla o de pasillo?
Héctor	Dos asientos juntos.
Sofía	Cerca de la salida de emergencia.
Héctor	El avión no hace escala, ¿verdad?
Agente	No, señor. ¿Cuántas maletas tienen?
Sofía	Cinco maletas y dos bolsos de mano.
Agente	Tienen que pagar exceso de equipaje.
Héctor	Pero, Sofía, ¿has puesto toda nuestra ropa en las maletas?
Sofía	¡Es que no sabía qué llevar!
Agente	La puerta de salida es la número tres. ¡Buen viaje!

En la puerta número tres.

"Última llamada para los pasajeros del vuelo 340 a Buenos Aires. Suban al avión, por favor."

Héctor y Sofía le dan las tarjetas de embarque a la auxiliar de vuelo, suben al avión y ponen los bolsos de mano en el compartimento de equipajes.

Sofía	Tenemos que abrocharnos el cinturón de seguridad. ¡Espero que el piloto tenga mucha experiencia!

¿Recuerda usted?

¿Verdadero o falso?
With a partner, decide whether the following statements about the dialogue are true (**verdadero**) or false (**falso**).

1. Sofía quiere pasar las vacaciones en Chile. ☐ V ☐ F
2. Héctor piensa comprar los pasajes por Internet. ☐ V ☐ F
3. Sofía dice que es más barato viajar en coche. ☐ V ☐ F
4. Héctor y Sofía han pasado muchas vacaciones en Viña del Mar. ☐ V ☐ F
5. A Sofía le encanta viajar en avión. ☐ V ☐ F
6. Héctor y Sofía quieren dos asientos de ventanilla. ☐ V ☐ F
7. El vuelo a Buenos Aires es directo. ☐ V ☐ F
8. Héctor y Sofía viajan con poco equipaje. ☐ V ☐ F
9. Héctor y Sofía no llevan bolsos de mano. ☐ V ☐ F
10. Sofía espera que el piloto sepa lo que está haciendo. ☐ V ☐ F

Y ahora... conteste
Answer these questions, basing your answers on the dialogue.

1. ¿Dónde quiere pasar sus vacaciones Héctor?
2. ¿De qué está empezando a cansarse Héctor?
3. ¿Qué incluyen los paquetes?
4. ¿Qué puede tomar Sofía para viajar en avión?
5. En el avión, ¿dónde quiere sentarse Sofía?
6. ¿Qué tienen que pagar Héctor y Sofía?
7. ¿Cuál es el número del vuelo?
8. ¿Qué le dan Héctor y Sofía a la auxiliar de vuelo?

Para hablar del tema: Vocabulario

Cognados

la aerolínea	la emergencia
el aeropuerto	el entusiasmo
la agencia	la experiencia
el (la) agente	la información
la capital	los nervios
complicado(a)	el pasaporte
directo(a)	el piloto

Nombres

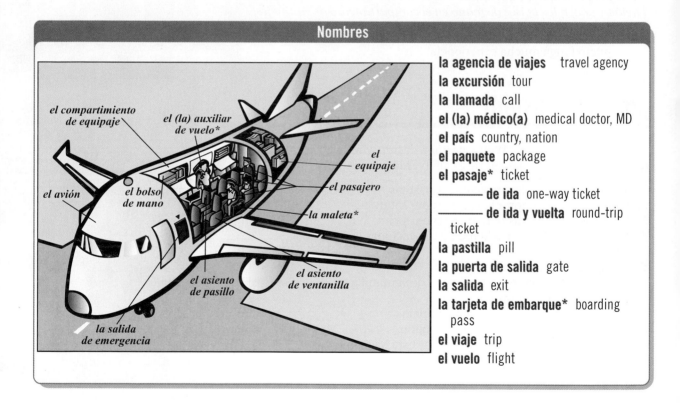

el compartimiento de equipaje
el (la) auxiliar de vuelo*
el equipaje
el avión
el bolso de mano
el pasajero
la maleta*
el asiento de pasillo
el asiento de ventanilla
la salida de emergencia

la agencia de viajes   travel agency
la excursión tour
la llamada call
el (la) médico(a) medical doctor, MD
el país country, nation
el paquete package
el pasaje* ticket
———— **de ida** one-way ticket
———— **de ida y vuelta** round-trip ticket
la pastilla pill
la puerta de salida gate
la salida exit
la tarjeta de embarque* boarding pass
el viaje trip
el vuelo flight

Adjetivos

querido(a) dear

Verbos

ahorrar to save
averiguar to find out
cansarse to get tired
compartir to share
dejar to let
incluir to include

sentir (e>ie) to regret
subir, abordar to board
sugerir (e>ie) to suggest
temer to fear, to be afraid
viajar to travel

Otras palabras y expresiones

abrocharse el cinturón de seguridad to fasten the seat belt
¡Buen viaje! Have a good trip!
en parte in part
exceso de equipaje excess luggage
hacer escala to make a stop over

lo mismo the same thing
ponerse de acuerdo to come to an agreement, to agree upon
tomar una decisión to make a decision
¿verdad? right?

Amplíe su vocabulario

Más sobre los viajes

¿A cuánto está el cambio de moneda? What's the rate of exchange?
cancelar to cancel
el cheque de viajero traveler's check
(de) clase turista tourist class
confirmar to confirm
crucero cruise
la lista de espera waiting list
los lugares de interés places of interest
el maletín small suitcase, hand luggage
(de) primera clase first class

De país a país

la auxiliar de vuelo la azafata (*Esp.*)
la maleta la valija (*Cono Sur*)
  el veliz (*Méx.*)
el pasaje el billete (*Esp.*)
la tarjeta de embarque la tarjeta de embarco (*Arg.*)

Para practicar el vocabulario

A. Preguntas y respuestas With a partner, match the questions in column *A* with the answers in column *B*.

A	B
1. ¿Dónde compraste los pasajes?	a. A la auxiliar de vuelo.
2. ¿Es un vuelo directo?	b. Estas pastillas.
3. ¿Quieres un asiento de pasillo?	c. No sé, voy a averiguar.
4. ¿Qué te dio el médico?	d. No, hace escala.
5. ¿Tienen que pagar exceso de equipaje?	e. En el compartimiento de equipaje.
6. ¿A qué país van a viajar?	f. Abrocharse el cinturón.
7. ¿A quién le doy la tarjeta de embarque?	g. No, no se pusieron de acuerdo.
8. ¿Dónde pongo el bolso de mano?	h. Sí, tienen cinco maletas.
9. ¿Qué deben hacer los pasajeros?	i. A Chile.
10. ¿Cuál es la puerta de salida?	j. En la agencia de viajes.
11. ¿Tomaron una decisión?	k. No, de ventanilla.
12. ¿A qué hora sale el avión?	l. La número cuatro.

B. ¿Qué hago? ¿Adónde voy? Complete the following sentences.

1. Van a _____ el vuelo porque hay mucha niebla.
2. Los pasajes de _____ clase son más caros.
3. ¿Cuáles son los _____ de interés en la ciudad donde Ud. vive?
4. Vamos a viajar. Tenemos que _____ la reservación del hotel.
5. ¿A cómo está el _____ de _____?
6. ¿Vas a llevar tu tarjeta de crédito o vas a llevar cheques de _____?
7. No tenemos mucho dinero. Vamos a viajar en clase _____.
8. Solamente puede llevar un _____ con Ud. en el avión.
9. Este verano vamos a hacer un _____ por el Caribe.
10. No hay pasaje para hoy pero podemos ponerlo en la lista de _____.

C. Definiciones Write the words or phrases that correspond to the following.

1. Delta, Continental
2. Allí tomamos el avión.
3. decidir
4. que no hace escala
5. Argentina, por ejemplo
6. maletas y bolsos de mano
7. subir
8. dar una sugerencia
9. lo que le decimos a una persona que va a viajar
10. donde ponemos el bolso de mano durante el vuelo

D. En la agencia de viajes With a partner, play the roles of a travel agent and someone getting a round-trip-ticket to Buenos Aires. The "traveler" asks pertinent questions, talks about date of travel, and reserves a seat.

¿A qué ciudad suramericana van los pasajeros de este avión? ¿A qué hora llegan? ¿Qué quieren hacer allí?

Pronunciación

Pronunciation in context

In this lesson, there are some words or phrases that may be challenging to pronounce. Listen to your instructor and pronounce the following sentences.

1. Tenemos que ir a la **agencia de viajes** para comprar los **pasajes.**
2. Yo te **sugiero** que **averigües** lo que cuestan dos pasajes de ida y vuelta.
3. Hay **paquetes** que **incluyen** vuelo directo a Buenos Aires, hotel y algunas **excursiones.**
4. El día del viaje, hablan con el **agente** de la **aerolínea** en el **aeropuerto.**
5. **Héctor** y Sofía le dan las tarjetas a la **auxiliar** de vuelo.

Puntos para recordar

1. Introduction to the subjunctive mood
(*Introducción al modo subjuntivo*)

Until now, you have been using verbs in the indicative mood. The indicative is used to express factual, definite events. By contrast, the subjunctive is used to reflect the speaker's feelings or attitudes toward events, or when the speaker views events as uncertain, unreal, or hypothetical. Because expressions of volition, doubt, surprise, fear, and the like all represent reactions to the speaker's perception of reality, they are followed in Spanish by the subjunctive.

Forms (*Formas*)

♦ Present subjunctive forms of regular verbs

To form the present subjunctive, add the following endings to the stem of the first-person singular of the present indicative, after dropping the **o.** Note that the endings for the **-er** and **-ir** verbs are identical.

-ar *verbs*	-er *verbs*	-ir *verbs*
habl- **e**	com- **a**	viv- **a**
habl- **es**	com- **as**	viv- **as**
habl- **e**	com- **a**	viv- **a**
habl- **emos**	com- **amos**	viv- **amos**
habl- **éis**	com- **áis**	viv- **áis**
habl- **en**	com- **an**	viv- **an**

The following table shows how to form the first-person singular of the present subjunctive.

Verb	First-Person Sing. (Indicative)	Stem	First-Person Sing. (Subjunctive)
habl**ar**	hablo	habl-	habl**e**
aprend**er**	aprendo	aprend-	aprend**a**
escrib**ir**	escribo	escrib-	escrib**a**
conoc**er**	conozco	conozc-	conozc**a**
dec**ir**	digo	dig-	dig**a**
hac**er**	hago	hag-	hag**a**
tra**er**	traigo	traig-	traig**a**
ven**ir**	vengo	veng-	veng**a**

Práctica

Online Study Center

For more practice with lesson topics, see the related activities on the *¡Hola, amigos!* web site at college.hmco.com/PIC/holaamigos7e.

Formas del subjuntivo I Give the present subjunctive forms of the following verbs.

1. *yo:* comer, venir, hablar, hacer, salir
2. *tú:* decir, ver, traer, trabajar, escribir
3. *él:* vivir, aprender, salir, estudiar, ver
4. *nosotros:* escribir, caminar, poner, desear, tener
5. *ellos:* salir, hacer, llevar, conocer, ver

Present subjunctive forms of stem-changing and irregular verbs

◆ Verbs ending in **-ar** and **-er** undergo the same stem changes in the present subjunctive as in the present indicative.

recomendar (e > ie)		recordar (o > ue)	
recom**ie**nde	recomend**emos**	rec**ue**rde	record**emos**
recom**ie**ndes	recomend**éis**	rec**ue**rdes	record**éis**
recom**ie**nde	recom**ie**nden	rec**ue**rde	rec**ue**rden

entender (e > ie) (*to understand*)		volver (o > ue)	
ent**ie**nda	entend**amos**	v**ue**lva	volv**amos**
ent**ie**ndas	entend**áis**	v**ue**lvas	volv**áis**
ent**ie**nda	ent**ie**ndan	v**ue**lva	v**ue**lvan

◆ For verbs ending in **-ir,** the three singular forms and the third-person plural form undergo the same stem changes in the present subjunctive as in the present indicative. However, in addition, observe that unstressed **e** changes to **i** and unstressed **o** changes to **u** in the first- and second-person plural forms.

mentir (*to lie*)		dormir	
m**ie**nta	m**i**ntamos	d**ue**rma	d**u**rmamos
m**ie**ntas	m**i**ntáis	d**ue**rmas	d**u**rmáis
m**ie**nta	m**ie**ntan	d**ue**rma	d**ue**rman

◆ The following verbs are irregular in the present subjunctive.

dar	estar	saber	ser	ir
dé	esté	sepa	sea	vaya
des	estés	sepas	seas	vayas
dé	esté	sepa	sea	vaya
demos	estemos	sepamos	seamos	vayamos
deis	estéis	sepáis	seáis	vayáis
den	estén	sepan	sean	vayan

¡Atención! The present subjunctive of **hay** (impersonal form of **haber**) is **haya**.

Práctica

Formas del subjuntivo II   Give the present subjunctive forms of the following verbs.

1. *yo:*   dormir, ir, cerrar, sentir, ser
2. *tú:*   mentir, volver, ir, dar, recordar
3. *ella:*   estar, saber, perder, dormir, ser
4. *nosotros:*   pensar, recordar, dar, morir, cerrar
5. *ellos:*   preferir, dar, ir, saber, dormir

Uses of the subjunctive (*Usos del subjuntivo*)

◆ The Spanish subjunctive is used in subordinate, or dependent, clauses. The subjunctive is also used in English, although not as often as in Spanish. For example:

Sugiero	que **llegue** mañana.	*I suggest*	*that **he arrive** tomorrow.*
Main clause	**Dependent clause**	**Main clause**	**Dependent clause**

The expression that requires the use of the subjunctive is in the main clause, *I suggest.* The subjunctive appears in the dependent clause, *that he arrive tomorrow.*

◆ There are four main conditions that call for the use of the subjunctive in Spanish.

　◆ *Volition:* demands, wishes, advice, persuasion, and other impositions of will

　　Ella **quiere** que yo lo llame.　　*She wants me to call him.*
　　Te **aconsejo** que no **vayas** a　　*I advise you not to go on that trip.*
　　ese viaje.

　◆ *Emotion:* pity, joy, fear, surprise, hope, and so on

　　Me **sorprende** que **llegues** tan　　*I am surprised that you are*
　　temprano.　　　　　　　　　　　*arriving so early.*

　◆ *Unreality:* expectations, indefiniteness, uncertainty, nonexistence

　　—¿**Hay alguien** aquí que **hable**　　*"Is there anyone here who*
　　español?　　　　　　　　　　　　*speaks Spanish?"*
　　—No, **no hay nadie** que lo　　　　*"No, there is no one who*
　　sepa.　　　　　　　　　　　　*knows it."*

　◆ *Doubt and denial:* negated facts, disbelief

　　No es verdad que Rosa **sea**　　*It isn't true that Rosa is a flight*
　　azafata.　　　　　　　　　　　　*attendant.*
　　Dudo que **tengas** dinero.　　　*I doubt that you have money.*
　　Roberto **niega** que ella **sea**　　*Roberto denies that she is his wife.*
　　su esposa.

2. Subjunctive with verbs of volition (*El subjuntivo con verbos que indican voluntad o deseo*)

All expressions of will require the use of the subjunctive in subordinate clauses. Note that the subject in the main clause must be different from the subject in the subordinate clause. Some verbs of volition that require the use of the subjunctive are:

aconsejar (*to advise*)	mandar (*to order*)	querer
decir	necesitar	recomendar
desear	pedir	sugerir

Mi	madre	**quiere**	**que**	yo	**trabaje.**
My	*mother*	*wants*		*me*	*to work.*

—¿Qué **quieres** que **haga**? — "What **do you want me** to do?"
—**Quiero** que **vayas** al aeropuerto. — "**I want** you to **go** to the airport."

—Necesito hablar con un médico. — "**I need to talk** with a doctor."
—Te **sugiero** que **hables** con el Dr. Paz. — "**I suggest** that **you talk** with Dr. Paz."

¡Atención! Note that the infinitive is used following verbs of volition if there is no change of subject: **Quiero comer.**

¿Que querés que te mande de África?

Detalles culturales

En Argentina, como también en Costa Rica, Paraguay, Uruguay y Guatemala, la forma tú no se usa en la conversación. En lugar de (*In place of*) esta forma, se usa la forma **vos**. Por ejemplo, en estos países no dicen "**tú quieres**" sino "**vos querés**". Este fenómeno se llama **voseo**.

◆ ¿Se usa la forma tú en inglés?

◆ Certain verbs of volition (**mandar, sugerir, aconsejar,** and **pedir**) are often preceded by an indirect object pronoun, which indicates the subject of the verb in the subjunctive.

Te sugiero que **vayas** al médico.   *I suggest that you go to the doctor.*
Le aconsejo que **venga** temprano.   *I advise you to come early.*

A. Minidiálogos Complete the following dialogues, using either the subjunctive or the infinitive, as appropriate. Then act them out with a partner.

1. —Marcos quiere que (nosotros) _____ (ir) a su casa esta noche. ¿Tú quieres _____ (ir)?
   —No, hoy me quiero _____ (acostar) temprano porque no me siento bien.
   —Te sugiero que _____ (tomar) dos aspirinas antes de acostarte.
   —No quiero _____ (tomar) aspirina porque soy alérgica a la aspirina.

2. —Necesito que tú me _____ (traer) las maletas hoy.
   —No puedo porque mamá quiere que la _____ (llevar) a la agencia de viajes.

3. —Sofía me aconseja que _____ (ir) al médico, pero yo no quiero _____ (ir) hoy.
   —Pues yo te sugiero que lo _____ (ver) lo más pronto posible (*as soon as possible*).

4. —Elena quiere que yo le _____ (comprar) un pasaje, pero yo no deseo _____ (ir) a la agencia de viajes ahora.
   —En ese caso te sugiero que le _____ (decir) que no puedes ir.

5. —Adela, quiero que hoy _____ (volver) antes de las nueve y que te _____ (acostar) porque mañana tienes que levantarte a las cinco.
   —¿Por qué quieres que nos _____ (levantar) a las cinco?
   —Porque mamá quiere que nosotros _____ (estar) en el aeropuerto a las seis.

B. Nadie está de acuerdo Complete each sentence creatively, using a verb in the infinitive or the subjunctive, as appropriate.

   ◆ **MODELO:** Yo quiero volver en agosto, pero mi padre quiere que...
   Yo quiero volver en agosto, pero mi padre quiere que vuelva en julio.

1. Luis quiere que yo hable sobre Chile, pero yo quiero...
2. El médico les aconseja que tomen las pastillas ahora, pero yo les aconsejo que...
3. Yo quiero ir a casa, pero mis amigos quieren...
4. Ellos le sugieren que pase todo el día aquí, pero ella quiere...
5. Mi esposo quiere que yo haga un crucero por el Mediterráneo, pero yo prefiero...
6. Ellos quieren ir al aeropuerto, pero nosotros queremos que...
7. Nora quiere viajar en avión, pero yo le sugiero que...
8. Los niños se quieren acostar a las once, pero su mamá quiere que...

C. Deseos y sugerencias (*Wishes and suggestions*) With a partner, take turns completing the following according to the illustrations below.

1. Ana quiere

_____ .

2. Te sugiero

_____ .

3. Te aconsejo

_____ .

4. Olga quiere que Paco le

_____ .

5. La doctora le recomienda

_____ .

6. Pablo no quiere que su
mamá _____ .

D. ¿Qué queremos? Say what you and these people want (or don't want) everybody to do. Compare notes with your partner.

1. Yo quiero que mi mamá...
2. Mis padres no quieren que yo...
3. La novia de Julio quiere que él...
4. El profesor quiere que nosotros...
5. El médico quiere que mi padre...
6. Tu papá no quiere que tú...
7. Yo quiero que mis abuelos...
8. Nosotros no queremos que ellos...

E. Soluciones In groups of three, advise each of the following people what to do according to each circumstance. Use **sugerir, recomendar,** or **aconsejar.**

1. Julio no quiere viajar en avión.
2. A la Sra. Ruiz no le gusta viajar a otros países.
3. Mireya está muy nerviosa (*nervous*).
4. Ramiro quiere comprar un pasaje a Chile.
5. Aurora no quiere pagar exceso de equipaje.
6. A Nora no le gustan los asientos de ventanilla.
7. Enrique no quiere un vuelo que haga escala.
8. Rosario no puede viajar en primera clase.

3. Subjunctive with verbs of emotion (*El subjuntivo con verbos que expresan emoción*)

◆ In Spanish, the subjunctive mood is always used in the subordinate clause when the verb in the main clause expresses the emotions of the subject, such as fear, joy, pity, hope, regret, sorrow, surprise, and anger. Again, the subject in the subordinate clause must be different from the subject in the main clause for the subjunctive to be used.

◆ Some verbs of emotion that call for the subjunctive are **temer, esperar, alegrarse (de),** and **sentir.**

—Mañana salgo para Quito.	*"Tomorrow I leave for Quito."*
—**Espero** que **te diviertas** mucho.	*"I hope you have a very good time."*
—**Temo** no **poder** ir de vacaciones con ustedes este verano.	*"I'm afraid that I cannot go on vacation with you this summer."*
—**Espero** que **puedas** ir con nosotros el verano que viene.	*"I hope that you can go with us next summer."*

> **¡Atención!** If there is no change of subject, the infinitive is used.

Temo no **poder** ir.   *I'm afraid* that *I can*not go.

♦ The expression **ojalá** always takes the subjunctive.

Ojalá que **puedas** venir.   *I hope you can* come.

Práctica y conversación

A. Minidiálogos   Complete the following exchanges, using the subjunctive or the infinitive, as appropriate. Then act them out with a partner.

1. —Temo que Estela no _____ (ir) a la fiesta, porque tiene que trabajar.
   —Siento mucho que _____ (tener) que trabajar; pero espero que _____ (poder) ir la próxima vez.

2. —Me alegro de _____ (estar) aquí con Uds.
   —Y nosotros nos alegramos de que tú _____ (estar) aquí. Esperamos que te _____ (divertir) mucho.

3. —Necesito comprar un pasaje hoy. Espero que _____ (haber) una agencia de viajes cerca.
   —Hay una agencia cerca, pero temo que no _____ (estar) abierta a esta hora.

4. —Temo no _____ (poder) ir al aeropuerto a buscar a Rita. Espero que Ud. _____ (poder) ir.
   —Rita va a sentir mucho que tú no _____ (estar) allí.

5. —Espero que Jorge no _____ (dejar) de ir hoy al banco.
   —Ojalá que le _____ (dar) el préstamo que pidió.

B. Emociones   Complete each sentence in an original manner. Use the subjunctive or the infinitive, as appropriate.

1. Ojalá que yo...
2. Siento mucho no poder...
3. Me alegro de que mi papá...
4. Temo no...
5. Mi amigo(a) espera...
6. El (La) profesor(a) siente que nosotros...
7. Mi madre se alegra de...
8. Tememos que las clases...

Online Study Center

For more practice with lesson topics, see the related activities on the *¡Hola, amigos!* web site at college.hmco.com/PIC/holaamigos7e.

C. ¿Cómo reaccionas...? React appropriately to a friend's statements.

1. Mi mamá está enferma (*sick*).
2. Mi papá está mejor.
3. No puedo ir contigo.
4. Son las cinco. Tengo que estar en casa a las cinco y media.
5. Quiero comprar un coche, pero es muy caro.
6. El mes próximo voy a México de vacaciones.

 D. Amigos y parientes In groups of three, tell two or three things you hope your friends and relatives will do and one or two things you fear they can't or won't do.

4. Some uses of the prepositions *a*, *de*, and *en*
(*Algunos usos de las preposiciones* a, de *y* en)

◆ The preposition **a** (*to, at, in*) expresses direction toward a point in space or a moment in time. It is used for the following purposes:

◆ to indicate the time (hour) of day

A las cinco salimos para Lima.	*At five we leave for Lima.*

◆ after verbs of motion, when followed by an infinitive, a noun, or a pronoun

Siempre vengo **a** comprar aquí.	*I always come to buy here.*

◆ after the verbs **empezar, comenzar, enseñar,** and **aprender,** when followed by an infinitive

Ellos empezaron **a** salir.	*They began to go out.*
Te enseñé **a** bailar el tango.	*I taught you to dance the tango.*

◆ after the verb **llegar**

Cuando él llegó **a** su casa, le dieron los pasajes.	*When he arrived **at** his house, they gave him the tickets.*

Detalles culturales

El tango tuvo su origen en los suburbios de Buenos Aires a finales del siglo (*century*) XIX. Para muchos, Argentina es la tierra del tango, y éste se considera la música típica del país, pero hoy la música argentina es muy variada e incluye diferentes tipos de ritmos.

◆ ¿Cuál es la música típica de este país?

- before a direct object noun that refers to a specific person. It may also be used to personify an animal or a thing

Yo no conozco **a** ese médico.	*I don't know that doctor.*
Bañé **a** mi perro.	*I bathed my dog.*

¡Atención! If the direct object is not a definite person, the personal **a** is not used.

Busco un buen médico.	*I'm looking for a good doctor.*

- The preposition **de** (*of, from, about, with, in*) indicates possession, material, and origin. It is also used in the following ways:

  - to refer to a specific period of the day or night when telling time

El sábado pasado trabajamos hasta las ocho **de** la noche.	*Last Saturday we worked until 8 P.M.*

  - after the superlative to express *in* or *of*

Orlando es el más simpático **de** la familia.	*Orlando is the nicest **in** the family.*

  - to describe personal physical characteristics

Es morena, **de** ojos negros.	*She is brunette, **with** dark eyes.*

  - as a synonym for **sobre** or **acerca de** (*about*)

Hablaban **de** todo menos **del** viaje.	*They were talking **about** everything except **about** the trip.*

- The preposition **en** (*at, in, on, inside, over*) in general situates someone or something within an area of time or space. It is used for the following purposes:

  - to refer to a definite place

Él siempre se queda **en** casa.	*He always stays **at** home.*

  - as a synonym for **sobre** (*on*)

Está sentada **en** la silla.	*She is sitting **on** the chair.*

  - to indicate means of transportation

Nunca he viajado **en** ómnibus.	*I have never traveled **by** bus.*

Online Study Center

For more practice with lesson topics, see the related activities on the *¡Hola, amigos!* web site at college.hmco.com/PIC/holaamigos7e.

Práctica y conversación

A. La carta de Isabel

Complete the following letter, adding the missing prepositions **a, de,** or **en.**

Querida Alicia:

Como te prometí, te escribo en seguida. Ayer llegamos _____ Quito. Es una _____ las ciudades más antiguas _____ Suramérica. Llegamos _____ las tres _____ la tarde y fuimos _____ buscar hotel.

_____ el hotel conocimos _____ unos chicos muy simpáticos que nos invitaron a salir con ellos. Yo salí con Carlos, que es alto, moreno, _____ ojos verdes. Me ha dicho que me va _____ enseñar _____ bailar salsa. Espero aprender _____ bailar otros bailes también. Mañana vamos _____ ir _____ visitar los museos. Vamos _____ ir _____ el coche _____ Carlos.

Bueno, _____ la próxima carta espero poder contarte más _____ mi vida _____ esta hermosa ciudad.

Isabel

B. Entre amigos

Use the illustrations to complete the following information about a group of friends. Use appropriate prepositions.

1. Delia va a...

2. Sergio y Toña están...

3. Beatriz es rubia...

4. Teresa se quedó...

Rogelio

5. Rogelio quiere ir al club...

Tito

6. Tito salió de su casa...

Gloria **Beto** **Lolo** **Julio**

7. Julio es... grupo.

Caracas, mañana. **Eva**

8. Eva llega...

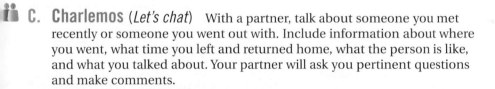

C. Charlemos (*Let's chat*) With a partner, talk about someone you met recently or someone you went out with. Include information about where you went, what time you left and returned home, what the person is like, and what you talked about. Your partner will ask you pertinent questions and make comments.

Aurora llama a una amiga. ¿De qué están hablando?

Entre nosotros

¡Conversemos!

 Para conocernos mejor   Get to know your partner better by asking each other the following questions.

1. ¿Adónde piensas ir de vacaciones el verano que viene? ¿Con quién vas?
2. ¿Prefieres viajar solo(a) o con tu familia?
3. ¿Compras los pasajes en una agencia de viajes o por Internet?
4. Generalmente, ¿viajas en clase turista o en primera clase?
5. ¿Prefieres un asiento de ventanilla o de pasillo?
6. ¿Hiciste un crucero el verano pasado?
7. ¿Cuántas maletas llevaste la última vez que viajaste?
8. ¿Has tenido que pagar exceso de equipaje alguna vez?
9. ¿Dónde pones tu bolso de mano cuando viajas?
10. ¿Conoces a alguien que trabaje de auxiliar de vuelo?

 Una encuesta   Interview your classmates to identify who fits the following descriptions. Include your instructor, but remember to use the **Ud.** form when addressing him or her.

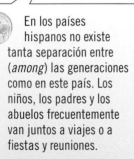

Detalles culturales

En los países hispanos no existe tanta separación entre (*among*) las generaciones como en este país. Los niños, los padres y los abuelos frecuentemente van juntos a viajes o a fiestas y reuniones.

◆ **Generalmente, ¿Ud. viaja con otros miembros de su familia o prefiere ir con sus amigos?**

	Nombre
1. Hace muchos viajes.	_____
2. Le gusta viajar los fines de semana.	_____
3. Conoce muchos lugares de interés en este país.	_____
4. Prefiere volar por la noche.	_____
5. Tuvo que hacer escala la última vez que viajó.	_____
6. Necesita ahorrar más.	_____
7. Siempre lleva cheques de viajero cuando va de viaje.	_____
8. Lleva mucho equipaje cuando viaja.	_____
9. No fue de vacaciones el año pasado.	_____
10. Fue de excursión el mes pasado.	_____

 Y ahora...   Write a brief summary, indicating what you have learned about your classmates.

¿**Cómo lo decimos?**   What would you say in the following situations? What might the other person say? Act out the scenes with a partner.

1. You want to find out how much a round-trip ticket to Santiago costs.
2. You ask the travel agent to give you information on several types of tours.
3. You need to know if there are flights to Buenos Aires on Sundays.
4. A friend of yours is traveling abroad for the first time. Give him suggestions and advice about what to do and what not to do.

¿**Qué dice aquí?**   Answer the questions about the new flight of Aerolíneas del Sur using the information provided in the ad.

Más Viajes a Latinoamérica
Viaje por Aerolíneas del Sur y acumule millas más rápido.

Aerolíneas del Sur le ofrece, desde el 15 de enero, un vuelo diario más, sin escala,

Miami-Buenos Aires

Para reservaciones consulte a su agente de viajes, visite nuestro sitio en la Internet o llame gratis al teléfono 1-800-342-4538, 24 horas al dia, 7 días a la semana.

Aerolíneas del Sur

Precios más bajos   Mejor servicio

1. ¿Qué compañía ofrece más viajes a Latinoamérica?
2. ¿Qué puedo acumular si viajo por Aerolíneas del Sur?
3. ¿De qué ciudad sale el nuevo vuelo?
4. ¿Había antes vuelos a Buenos Aires desde Miami? ¿Cuándo comienza el nuevo vuelo?
5. Si tomo ese vuelo, ¿tengo que hacer escala?
6. ¿Qué puedo hacer para obtener más información y para hacer la reservación?
7. ¿Puedo llamar cualquier (any) día y a cualquier hora?
8. ¿Qué ventajas me ofrece Aerolíneas del Sur?

Para escribir

En una agencia de viajes   Write a dialogue between you and a travel agent. Choose your destination, ask about prices, flights, and any necessary documentation. Then make your reservations and choose your seat.

┌─ **Un dicho** ─

Martes 13, no te cases ni te embarques.

This saying advices you not to get married or get on a ship . . . on what day? If you are superstitious, you now have two days to worry about! Remember the saying in Spanish.

Estrella y Mariana, dos chicas peruanas, están de vacaciones en Montevideo.

Estrella Tenemos que encontrar un hotel que no sea muy caro y que quede cerca de la playa.

Mariana ¡Estrella! ¡No hicimos reservaciones! ¡Y no hay ningún hotel que tenga habitaciones libres!

Estrella No seas pesimista. A ver... queremos un hotel que tenga aire acondicionado, teléfono, televisor, servicio de habitación y, si es posible, vista al mar.

Mariana ¡Qué optimista! Hay muchos hoteles que tienen todo eso, pero están llenos. Hay un montón de turistas, y un montón de convenciones.

Estrella ¡Espera! Ahí hay un hotel...

Mariana Pero, dime una cosa: ¿No ves que es un hotel de lujo? Probablemente cobran cinco mil pesos por noche. Nosotras necesitamos uno que cobre mucho menos...

Estrella Pero tú tienes una tarjeta de crédito, ¿no? Bueno, ven. Vamos a buscar un taxi que nos lleve a Pocitos. Allí va a haber hoteles más baratos...

Mariana O una pensión. ¡Acuérdate de que las pensiones son más baratas...!

Detalles culturales

En los países hispanos, los hoteles y restaurantes generalmente aceptan tarjetas de crédito como Visa o MasterCard.

◆ **¿Cuáles son las tarjetas de crédito que más se usan en este país?**

Detalles culturales

Las pensiones son muy populares en los países de habla hispana. Son más económicas que los hoteles y generalmente el precio incluye el cuarto y las comidas.

◆ **¿Dónde se hospeda Ud. cuando viaja?**

Estrella y Mariana están hablando con el Sr. Ruiz, el dueño de la pensión.

Estrella	¿Tiene un cuarto libre para dos personas?
Sr. Ruiz	Sí, hay uno disponible en el segundo piso, con dos camas chicas. Cobramos 4.800 pesos por semana...
Mariana	¿Eso incluye las comidas?
Sr. Ruiz	Sí, es pensión completa.
Estrella	¿Los cuartos tienen baño privado y televisor?
Sr. Ruiz	No, señorita. Hay tres baños en el segundo piso. Tienen bañadera y ducha con agua caliente y fría... y hay un televisor en el comedor.
Mariana	(*A Estrella*) ¿Por qué no nos quedamos aquí? La pensión parece limpia y está en un lugar céntrico.
Estrella	¿Hay alguna playa que esté cerca de aquí?
Sr. Ruiz	Sí, hay una a dos cuadras. ¡Ah!, señorita, necesito el número de su cédula de identidad.
Mariana	(*A Estrella*) ¡Uf! Estoy muy cansada. Ayúdame con las valijas, ¿quieres? Aquí no hay botones. Lo primero que voy a hacer es dormir un rato.
Estrella	Bueno, pero después te voy a mostrar unos folletos sobre Río y San Pablo.
Mariana	¡Caramba! ¡Ya estás planeando nuestras próximas vacaciones!

¿Recuerda usted?

¿Verdadero o falso?
With a partner, decide whether the following statements about the dialogue are true (**verdadero**) or false (**falso**).

1. Estrella y Mariana son de Perú.   ☐ V ☐ F
2. A Estrella le gusta estar cerca de la playa.   ☐ V ☐ F
3. Mariana dice que los hoteles no tienen habitaciones libres.   ☐ V ☐ F
4. Mariana quiere hospedarse en un hotel de lujo.   ☐ V ☐ F
5. Las chicas llevaron su coche a Montevideo.   ☐ V ☐ F
6. El señor Ruiz es el botones.   ☐ V ☐ F
7. En la pensión hay un cuarto libre.   ☐ V ☐ F
8. Las chicas tienen que pagar extra por la comida.   ☐ V ☐ F
9. A Mariana le gusta la pensión.   ☐ V ☐ F
10. El botones lleva las maletas al cuarto.   ☐ V ☐ F

Y ahora... conteste
Answer these questions, basing your answers on the dialogue.

1. ¿En qué ciudad están de vacaciones las chicas?
2. ¿Qué están buscando las chicas?
3. ¿Estrella quiere un cuarto con vista al jardín?
4. ¿Por qué están llenos los hoteles?
5. ¿En qué piso está la habitación disponible?
6. ¿Qué tienen los baños?
7. ¿Qué es lo primero que va a hacer Mariana?
8. ¿Qué le va a mostrar Estrella a Mariana?

Para hablar del tema: Vocabulario

For more practice with lesson
topics, see the related activities on
the *¡Hola, amigos!* web site at
college.hmco.com/PIC/holaamigos7e.

Online Study Center

Cognados

la convención	privado(a)
optimista	probablemente
el (la) peruano(a)	la reservación
pesimista	el taxi
posible	el (la) turista

Nombres

el aire acondicionado air conditioning	**el lugar** place
la bañadera* bathtub	**el lujo** luxury
el botones bellhop	**la pensión** boarding house
la cama bed	**la persona** person
——— **chica** twin bed	**el piso** floor
la cédula de identidad* I.D. card	**el servicio de habitación (cuarto)** room service
la ducha* shower	**la tarjeta de crédito** credit card
el (la) dueño(a), propietario(a) owner	**el televisor** TV set
el folleto brochure	**la vista al mar** ocean view

Verbos

acordarse (de) (o>ue) to remember
ayudar to help
parecer (yo parezco) to seem

Adjetivos

caliente hot	**lleno(a)** full
céntrico(a) central	**mostrar, enseñar** to show
libre, disponible vacant, available	**próximo(a)** next
limpio(a) clean	**segundo(a)** second

Amplíe su vocabulario

Más sobre los hoteles

Quiero una habitación con vista
- **al jardín** garden
- **a la piscina*** swimming pool
- **al patio**
- **al mar** ocean, sea
- **a la playa** beach

Quiero una habitación
- interior
- exterior

desocupar to vacate
no funciona it doesn't work
ocupado(a) occupied
el precio price
el puesto* de revistas magazine stand
el sofá-cama sleeper sofa
la tienda de regalos souvenir shop
el vestíbulo lobby

De país a país

la bañadera la bañera (*Arg.*)
   el baño (*Esp.*)
la cédula de identidad el carnet de identidad (*Esp.*)
la ducha la regadera (*Méx.*)
la piscina la alberca (*Méx.*)
el ascensor el elevador (*Méx., Cuba, Puerto Rico*)
el puesto de revistas el kiosko (*Arg., Esp.*)

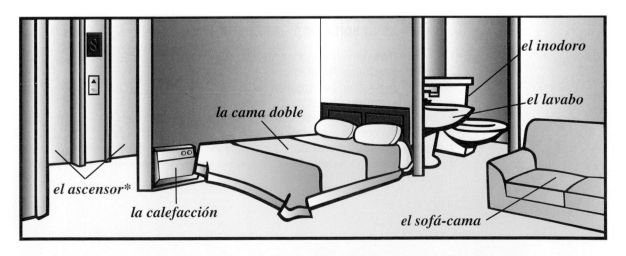

el inodoro
el lavabo
la cama doble
*el ascensor**
la calefacción
el sofá-cama

Para practicar el vocabulario

A. Preguntas y respuestas Match the questions in column A with the answers in column B.

A	B
1. ¿Tenemos que ir a un restaurante?	a. No, con vista al mar.
2. ¿Hay cuartos libres?	b. Sí, pero yo no pienso ir.
3. ¿Elsa es argentina?	c. Sí, y calefacción.
4. ¿Tu habitación es interior?	d. Un folleto sobre Cuzco.
5. ¿Tiene aire acondicionado?	e. No, el hotel está lleno.
6. ¿Va a haber una fiesta?	f. Sí, y hablamos por un rato.
7. ¿El baño tiene bañadera?	g. Sí, es de Buenos Aires.
8. ¿Qué estás leyendo?	h. El inodoro no funciona.
9. ¿Viste a Susana?	i. Sí, porque el hotel no tiene servicio de habitación.
10. ¿Cuál es el problema?	j. No, ducha.
11. ¿Qué documento necesita?	k. La semana próxima.
12. ¿Cuándo llegan?	l. Una cédula de identidad.

B. En el hotel With a partner, indicate whether the following statements are logical(L) or illogical(I). If it is illogical, say why.

1. Mi cuarto está en el quinto (*fifth*) piso. Voy a tomar el ascensor.
2. Voy a llamar al empleado del hotel porque ni el inodoro ni el baño funcionan.
3. Hace mucho calor. Necesitamos poner la calefacción.
4. El baño tiene agua fría y caliente.
5. Es muy barato porque es un hotel de lujo.
6. No queremos comer en un restaurante. Preferimos el servicio de habitación.
7. No puedo llevar todas las maletas al cuarto. Necesito que me ayudes.
8. El precio no incluye las comidas; es pensión completa.

C. ¿Cuál es la solución? What is the solution to these problems?

1. Quiero leer *Newsweek* pero no hay una copia en mi habitación.
2. No me gustan las habitaciones interiores.
3. Somos tres y sólo hay una cama doble en el cuarto.
4. Quiero comprar algo para llevarles a mis padres.
5. No sé cuánto cobran en el hotel.
6. No quiero recibir a mi amigo(a) en la habitación del hotel.
7. Tengo que subir a mi cuarto, que está en el décimo (*tenth*) piso.
8. Nos dieron una habitación con vista al patio, pero a nosotros nos gusta ver el mar.

D. Minidiálogos Complete the following short exchanges in a logical manner, using vocabulary from **Lección 12.**

1. —¿Tú usas *Visa*?
   —Bueno, yo uso varias _____.
2. —¿Dónde compraste la revista?
   —En el _____.
3. —¿Necesitan una cama chica?
   —No, una _____.
4. —¿Quién lleva las maletas al cuarto?
   —El _____.
5. —¿Están en un hotel?
   —No, en una _____.

Silvia está de vacaciones en Lima. ¿En qué tipo de hotel está hospedada?

Pronunciation in context In this lesson, there are some words or phrases that may be challenging to pronounce. Listen to your instructor and pronounce the following sentences.

1. A ver… queremos un hotel que tenga **aire acondicionado.**
2. Vamos a buscar un taxi que nos lleve a **Pocitos. Allí va a haber** hoteles más baratos.
3. ¿Por qué no nos quedamos aquí? La **pensión** parece limpia y está en un lugar **céntrico.**
4. Necesito el número de su **cédula** de **identidad.**
5. Bueno, pero después te voy a mostrar unos **folletos** sobre **Río** y San Pablo.

1. Subjunctive to express indefiniteness and nonexistence
(El subjuntivo para expresar lo indefinido y lo no existente)

◆ The subjunctive is always used in the subordinate clause when the main clause refers to something or someone that is indefinite, unspecified, hypothetical, or nonexistent.

—¿**Hay alguna excursión** que **incluya** el hotel?	*"**Is there any tour** that **includes** the hotel?"*
—No, **no hay ninguna** que lo **incluya.**	*"No, **there is not any** that **includes** it."*
—**Necesito un secretario** que **hable** francés.	*"**I need a secretary** who **speaks** French."*
—**No conozco a nadie** que **hable** francés.	*"**I don't know anyone** who **speaks** French."*
—**Estamos buscando un restaurante** donde **sirvan** comida italiana.	*"**We're looking for a restaurant** where **they serve** Italian food."*
—**Hay varios restaurantes** donde **sirven** comida italiana.	*"**There are several restaurants** where **they serve** Italian food."*

¡Atención! If the subordinate clause refers to existent, definite, or specified persons or things, the indicative is used instead of the subjunctive.

Hay varios restaurantes donde **sirven** comida italiana.

Práctica y conversación

Online Study Center

For more practice with lesson topics, see the related activities on the *¡Hola, amigos!* web site at college.hmco.com/PIC/holaamigos7e.

A. Minidiálogos   Complete the following dialogues, using the indicative or the subjunctive, as appropriate. Then act out the dialogues with a partner.

1. —¿Hay algún hotel que _____ (quedar) cerca de la playa?
   —Sí, el hotel La Uruguaya _____ (quedar) a una cuadra de la playa.
2. —¿Sabes si hay algún cuarto libre que _____ (tener) vista al mar?
   —No, pero hay uno que _____ (tener) vista a la piscina.
3. —¿Hay alguien aquí que no _____ (tener) pasaporte?
   —No, todos _____ (tener) pasaporte y visa.
4. —Necesito un botones que _____ (poder) llevar las maletas.
   —No hay ninguno que no _____ (estar) ocupado.

B. Vienen los uruguayos   A family from Uruguay has recently moved into your neighborhood. Answer their questions.

1. ¿Hay alguien que quiera vender su casa?
2. ¿Hay algún restaurante que sirva comida argentina?
3. ¿Hay alguien que sepa español y quiera trabajar de secretario(a)?
4. ¿Hay algún mercado que venda productos de Sudamérica?
5. Nuestro hijo es agente de viajes. ¿Sabe Ud. de alguna agencia que necesite empleados?
6. Queremos vender nuestro Ford. ¿Conoce Ud. a alguien que necesite un auto?

C. En la pensión   Use your imagination to complete each statement.

1. Nuestro cuarto tiene vista al jardín, pero preferimos uno...
2. El baño tiene bañadera, pero yo quiero uno...
3. Esta pensión no incluye las comidas, pero yo necesito una...
4. Esta pensión es buena pero no está en un lugar céntrico; queremos una...
5. Este folleto es sobre Montevideo, pero nosotras necesitamos uno...

D. Dime una cosa   You and a classmate want to find out about each other's relatives and friends. Ask each other questions about the following, always beginning with:

¿Hay alguien en tu familia o entre tus amigos que...?

1. jugar al béisbol
2. viajar a México todos los veranos
3. bailar muy bien
4. tener una piscina en su casa
5. celebrar su aniversario de bodas este mes
6. ser muy optimista
7. conocer Brasil
8. hablar portugués
9. saber varios idiomas
10. trabajar para un hotel
11. ser empleado(a) de banco
12. ser peruano

E. Nuestro viaje a Brasil   In groups of three or four, play the role of very wealthy and lazy travelers who want to make arrangements for a trip to Brazil. Say what you need people to do for you.

◆ MODELO: *Necesitamos a alguien que vaya a la agencia de viajes.*

2. Familiar commands (*Las formas imperativas de* tú *y de* vosotros)

- Regular affirmative commands in the **tú** form have exactly the same forms as the third-person singular (**él** form) of the present indicative.

Verb	Present Indicative Third-Person Sing.	Familiar Command (*tú*)
hablar	él habla	**habla**
comer	él come	**come**
abrir	él abre	**abre**
cerrar	él cierra	**cierra**
volver	él vuelve	**vuelve**
pedir	él pide	**pide**
traer	él trae	**trae**

—¿Qué quieres que haga ahora?   *"What do you want me to do now?"*
—**Compra** los billetes para el viaje.   *"**Buy** the tickets for the trip."*

—¿Vas a poner el equipaje aquí?   *"Are you going to put the luggage here?"*
—Sí, **tráeme** las maletas y el bolso de mano.   *"Yes, **bring me** the suitcases and the carry-on bag."*

> **¡Atención!** As with the formal commands, direct, indirect, and reflexive pronouns are always placed *after* an affirmative command and are attached to it. A written accent must be placed on the stressed syllable.

- Eight Spanish verbs are irregular in the affirmative command for the **tú** form. They are listed below.

decir	**di**		salir	**sal**
hacer	**haz**		ser	**sé**
ir	**ve**[1]		tener	**ten**
poner	**pon**		venir	**ven**

—**Dime,** ¿a qué hora quieres que venga?   *"**Tell me,** at what time do you want me to come?"*
—**Ven** a las ocho.   *"**Come** at eight."*

—**Haz**me un favor: **pon** estos folletos en la mesa.   *"**Do** me a favor: **put** these brochures on the table."*
—Sí, en seguida.   *"Yes, right away."*

- The affirmative command form for **vosotros** is formed by changing the final **r** of the infinitive to **d**.

Infinitive	Familiar Command (*vosotros*)
habla**r**	habla**d**
come**r**	come**d**
escribi**r**	escribi**d**
i**r**	i**d**
sali**r**	sali**d**

---

[1]Note that **ir** and **ver** have the same affirmative **tú** command, **ve.**

When the affirmative command of **vosotros** is used with the reflexive pronoun **os,** the final **d** is dropped.

bañar	bañad	**bañaos**
poner	poned	**poneos**
vestir	vestid	**vestíos**[1]

Bañaos antes de cenar.	***Bathe** before dinner.*
Poneos los zapatos.	***Put** your shoes **on.***
Vestíos aquí.	***Get dressed** here.*

Only one verb doesn't drop the final **d** when the **os** is added.

| irse | **¡Idos!** | *Go away!* |

◆ The negative commands of **tú** and **vosotros** use the corresponding forms of the present subjunctive.

hablar	no **hables** tú	no **habléis** vosotros
vender	no **vendas** tú	no **vendáis** vosotros
decir	no **digas** tú	no **digáis** vosotros
salir	no **salgas** tú	no **salgáis** vosotros

—**No vayas** a la agencia de viajes hoy.	*"**Don't go** to the travel agency today."*
—Entonces voy mañana.	*"Then I'm going tomorrow."*
—**No** me **esperes** para comer.	*"**Don't wait for** me to eat."*
—¡**No** me **digas** que hoy también tienes que trabajar!	*"**Don't tell** me you have to work today also!"*

¡Atención! In a negative command, all object pronouns are placed before the verb.

No **me** esperes para comer.

Práctica y conversación

Online Study Center

For more practice with lesson topics, see the related activities on the *¡Hola, amigos!* web site at college.hmco.com/PIC/holaamigos7e.

A. **Órdenes** Using command forms, tell your friend what to do.

◆ MODELO: Tienes que hablar con el dueño ahora.
   Habla con el dueño ahora.

1. Tienes que llamarme este fin de semana.
2. Tienes que hacer las camas.
3. Tienes que tener paciencia con él.
4. Tienes que decirle que no venga hoy.
5. Tienes que ir a la agencia de viajes y comprar los pasajes.
6. Tienes que salir en seguida.
7. Tienes que quedarte aquí.
8. Tienes que venir dentro de quince días.

B. Now make all commands above negative.

---

[1]Note that the **-ir** verbs take a written accent over the **i** when the reflexive pronoun **os** is added.

C. A mi hermanito   You are going away for the day. Tell your younger brother what to do and what not to do.

1. levantarse temprano y bañarse
2. preparar el desayuno
3. no tomar refrescos
4. hacer la tarea
5. no abrirle la puerta a nadie
6. limpiar su cuarto
7. no mirar la televisión y no traer a sus amigos a la casa
8. traer pan y ponerlo en la mesa
9. ir al mercado y comprar frutas
10. llamar a papá y decirle que venga temprano

D. Haz esto... haz lo otro... (*Do this... do that...*)   With a partner, take turns giving two commands, one affirmative and one negative, that the following people would likely give.

1. una madre (un padre) a su hijo de quince años
2. un(a) estudiante a su compañero(a) de cuarto (de clase)
3. un muchacho a su novia (una muchacha a su novio)
4. un(a) doctor(a) a una niña
5. un(a) profesor(a) a un estudiante
6. un esposo a su esposa (una esposa a su esposo)

3. Verbs and prepositions (*Verbos y preposiciones*)

The prepositions **con, de,** and **en** can be used with verbs to form certain expressions. Some of the idioms are as follows:

casarse con	to marry, to get married (to)
comprometerse con	to get engaged to
acordarse de	to remember
alegrarse de	to be glad
darse cuenta de	to realize
enamorarse de	to fall in love with
olvidarse de	to forget
confiar en	to trust
convenir en	to agree on
entrar en	to go (come) into
fijarse en	to notice
insistir en	to insist on

—Celia **se comprometió con** David.
—Yo creía que iba a **casarse con** Alberto.
—No, ella **se enamoró de** David.

—**Insistieron en** venir esta noche.
—Sí, no **se dieron cuenta de** que teníamos que trabajar.

*"Celia **got engaged to** David."*
*"I thought **she** was going **to marry** Alberto."*
*"No, she **fell in love with** David."*

*"**They insisted on** coming tonight."*
*"Yes, **they didn't realize** that we had to work."*

> **¡Atención!** Notice that the English translation of these expressions may not use an equivalent preposition.

Práctica y conversación

A. Lo que pasa... Look at the pictures below and complete each statement.

Online Study Center

For more practice with lesson topics, see the related activities on the *¡Hola, amigos!* web site at college.hmco.com/PIC/holaamigos7e.

Marisa *Daniel*

1. Marisa decidió _____ _____ Daniel.

Mirta

¡Mi amor!

Raúl

2. Mirta_____ _____. Piensan casarse en junio.

Pepe:
¿745-3210?
¿785-2301?

Graciela

3. Graciela no _____ _____.

Marisol

¡Tito! ¡Tito!

4. Marisol _____ _____ a Tito.

> Pedro
>
> Yo voy contigo.
> Sí, voy contigo.
> Voy contigo.
>
> Alina

5. Rodolfo _____ _____.

6. Pedro _____ _____.

 B. Entreviste a su compañero(a)   Interview your partner by asking the following questions.

1. ¿En quién confías?
2. ¿Prefieres casarte con un(a) médico(a) o con un(a) profesor(a)?
3. ¿De quién te enamoraste por primera vez?
4. ¿Algún amigo tuyo se ha comprometido últimamente? ¿Con quién?
5. ¿Te fijaste si la biblioteca estaba abierta?
6. ¿Te acordaste de traer tus libros a clase?
7. ¿Te alegras de estar en esta universidad?
8. ¿A qué hora entró el (la) profesor(a) en la clase?

4. Ordinal numbers (*Números ordinales*)

primero(a)[1]	first	**sexto(a)**	sixth
segundo(a)[1]	second	**séptimo(a)**	seventh
tercero(a)[1]	third	**octavo(a)**	eighth
cuarto(a)	fourth	**noveno(a)**	ninth
quinto(a)	fifth	**décimo(a)**	tenth

◆ Ordinal numbers agree in gender and number with the nouns they modify.

el segundo **chico**   la segunda **chica**
los primeros **días**   las primeras **semanas**

◆ Ordinal numbers are seldom used after **décimo.**

¡Atención!   The ordinal numbers **primero** and **tercero** drop the final **-o** before masculine singular nouns.

el **primer**[2] día   el **tercer**[3] año

---

[1] abbreviated 1°, 2°, 3°, and so on
[2] abbreviated 1er
[3] abbreviated 3er

—Nosotros estamos en el **segundo** piso. ¿Y Uds.?
—Estamos en el **tercer** piso.

*"We are on the **second** floor. And you?"*
*"We are on the **third** floor."*

Práctica y conversación

A. Los meses del año With a partner, quiz each other on the order of the months of the year. Follow the model.

◆ **MODELO:** —*Septiembre.*
—*Septiembre es el noveno mes del año.*

B. ¿En qué piso estás? Imagine that the whole class is staying at a hotel in Punta del Este. Your classmates were assigned rooms on different floors. With a partner, take turns asking who is on what floor.

Online Study Center

For more practice with lesson topics, see the related activities on the *¡Hola, amigos!* web site at college.hmco.com/PIC/holaamigos7e.

Todos los hoteles están llenos. ¿Dónde va a poder hospedarse Carmen?

Entre nosotros

¡Conversemos!

 Para conocernos mejor Get to know your partner better by asking each other the following questions.

1. Cuando viajas, ¿te hospedas en un hotel o en una pensión?
2. Generalmente, ¿haces reservaciones en los hoteles antes de viajar?
3. ¿Prefieres un hotel que esté en un lugar céntrico o uno que quede lejos de todo?
4. Cuando vas a un hotel, ¿tú llevas tus maletas al cuarto o las lleva el botones?
5. Cuando vas a un hotel, ¿qué tipo de cuarto prefieres?
6. Si tu cuarto en el hotel está en el segundo piso, ¿usas el ascensor o la escalera (*stairs*)?
7. Cuando vas a un hotel, ¿a qué hora desocupas el cuarto?
8. ¿Tu casa tiene aire acondicionado y calefacción?
9. ¿Tenías televisor en tu cuarto cuando eras niño(a)?
10. En tu cuarto, ¿tienes una cama chica o una cama doble?

 Una encuesta Interview your classmates to identify who fits the following descriptions. Include your instructor, but remember to use the **Ud.** form when addressing him or her.

	Nombre
1. Tiene una piscina en su casa.	_____
2. Tiene un sofá-cama en su casa.	_____
3. Generalmente usa la ducha y no la bañadera.	_____
4. Compró algo en una tienda de regalos la semana pasada.	_____
5. Piensa viajar el próximo verano.	_____
6. Probablemente va a viajar con su familia.	_____
7. Nunca paga más de 100 dólares por noche en un hotel.	_____
8. Fue a una convención el año pasado.	_____
9. Es una persona pesimista.	_____
10. Tiene un montón de cosas que hacer.	_____

Y ahora... Write a brief summary indicating what you have learned about your classmates.

¿Cómo lo decimos? What would you say in the following situations? What might the other person say? Act out the scenes with a partner.

1. You need a room for two people with a private bathroom and air conditioning. Find out the price, when you have to check out, whether the room overlooks the street, and whether the hotel has room service.
2. At a boarding house, find out what meals the price includes.
3. A friend will be staying at your house while you are away. Tell him or her what to do.

¿Qué dice aquí? Answer the questions about the Hotel Tabaré. Base your answers on the information provided in the ad.

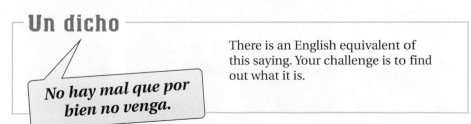

HOTEL TABARÉ *En el centro de Montevideo*

★ ★ ★ ★

☑ *Habitacions dobles y sencillas con baño privado*
☑ *Aire acondicionado y TV por cable*
☑ *Acceso a Internet y servicio de Fax*
☑ *Restaurante con comida típica e internacional*
☑ *Servicio de habitación las 24 horas del día*
☑ *Música en vivo sábados y domingos, de 8 a 11 de la noche*
☑ *Piscina y gimnasio*
☑ *Amplio estacionamiento*

Se aceptan tarjetas de crédito y cheques de viajeros
Avenida Artigas, 214 • A 20 minutos del aeropuerto • ☎ 990-73-32

1. ¿Cómo se llama el hotel? ¿Está en un lugar céntrico? ¿Es un hotel de lujo?
2. ¿Cómo son las habitaciones?
3. ¿Vamos a tener calor en la habitación?
4. ¿Podemos ver la tele en nuestro cuarto?
5. Si necesitamos mandar mensajes electrónicos, ¿podemos hacerlo desde el hotel?
6. ¿Qué clase de comida sirven? ¿Tienen servicio de habitación?
7. Nos gusta hacer ejercicio y nadar todos los días, ¿podemos hacerlo en el hotel?
8. ¿El hotel está cerca del aeropuerto? ¿Podemos dejar el coche en el hotel?
9. ¿Con qué podemos pagar en el hotel?

Para escribir

En un hotel Write a conversation between you and a hotel clerk. Make reservations and ask about prices and accommodations.

Un dicho

No hay mal que por bien no venga.

There is an English equivalent of this saying. Your challenge is to find out what it is.

Estrategia de lectura   Before you read the fable of the canary (*el canario*) and the crow (*el cuervo*), think about what you know about the characteristics of these two types of birds and try to predict what might happen.

Vamos a leer   As you read the fable, try to find the answers to the following questions.

1. ¿Qué es lo que caracteriza las fábulas de Iriarte?
2. ¿Cuáles son las características de los personajes de las fábulas?
3. ¿Qué talento tenía el canario? ¿Quién lo elogió?
4. ¿Qué causó esta aprobación en otros pájaros?
5. ¿Qué hizo el cuervo para desacreditar al canario?
6. ¿Qué comparación hizo el cuervo?
7. ¿Qué hizo el águila cuando el canario dejó de cantar?
8. ¿Qué pasó cuando el canario cantó?
9. ¿Qué le pidió el águila al dios Júpiter?
10. ¿Qué pasó cuando el cuervo trató de cantar? ¿Cuál es la moraleja (*moral*) de la fábula?

La obra más importante de Iriarte fue **Fábulas literarias.** Sus fábulas se caracterizan por la originalidad de sus temas. En la que se presenta aquí, los personajes son animales: un canario, un cuervo, un ruiseñor y un águila. El autor trata de demostrar que no se debe tratar de desacreditar a otros.

El canario y el cuervo

UNA FÁBULA DE TOMÁS IRIARTE

Había una vez un canario que cantaba muy bien. ¡Todos aplaudían cuando lo escuchaban! Un ruiseñor° extranjero, generalmente acreditado, lo elogió° mucho, animándolo con su aprobación.

nightingale / praised

Video

La aprobación del ruiseñor causó la envidia de otros pájaros° que no canta- *birds*
ban tan bien como él. Al fin, un cuervo° que no podía lucirse° por su canto, *crow / shine*
empezó a hablar mal del canario. Como no podía decir nada malo de su canto,
trató de desacreditarlo acusándolo de cosas que nada tenían que ver° con su *tenían... had to do*
manera de cantar. Los otros pájaros envidiosos aprobaron y repitieron las
acusaciones del cuervo.

El cuervo, animado, empezó a decir que el canario era un borrico° y que lo *donkey*
que había en él no era verdadera música sino un rebuzno.° "¡Cosa rara!" *braying*
—decían algunos. "El canario rebuzna; el canario es un borrico".

El canario, muy triste, dejó de° cantar, pero el águila,° reina° de las aves,° le *stopped / eagle / queen /*
dijo que quería oírlo cantar para ver si, en efecto, rebuznaba o no, porque si era *birds*
verdad que rebuznaba, quería excluirlo del número de sus vasallos,° los pájaros. *subjects*
Cuando el canario cantó, lo hizo tan bien que todos aplaudieron, incluyendo el
águila. Entonces el águila, indignada por la calumnia° del cuervo, le pidió a su *slander*
señor, el dios Júpiter, justicia para el canario. El dios condescendió, diciéndole
al cuervo: "Quiero escuchar tu canto". Cuando el cuervo trató de cantar, sólo se
oyeron horribles chillidos.° *screeches*

Moraleja: El que para desacreditar a otro recurre a medios injustos, se desa-
credita a sí mismo.° *a... himself*

Díganos
Answer the following questions, based on your own thoughts and experiences.

1. ¿Qué cosas hace Ud. bien?
2. ¿Recibe frecuentemente la aprobación de sus supervisores, sus profesores y sus amigos?
3. ¿Conoce a personas envidiosas que tratan de desacreditar a otros?
4. ¿Qué hace cuando ve que algunas personas son injustas?
5. ¿Qué trata de hacer para animar a sus parientes y amigos a desarrollar (*develop*) sus talentos?

¡Suban al avión!
Marisa tiene la oportunidad de viajar a California con su mamá, que tiene dos pasajes. El problema es que la señora tiene miedo de viajar en avión. Marisa le pide a Pablo que la ayude a convencer a su mamá de que ella puede viajar en avión.

El mundo hispánico

Chile

- Chile es un país largo y estrecho. En este país encontramos algunas de las montañas más altas de Suramérica, y por eso son muy populares los deportes de invierno. La cordillera de los Andes atraviesa (*goes through*) el país de norte a sur.

- Chile exporta pescados, mariscos y productos minerales y agrícolas. Exporta tanta fruta que se le considera la frutería del mundo. Sus vinos tienen fama internacional.

- Su capital, Santiago, es una ciudad cosmopolita que refleja la influencia de Europa y de Norteamérica. La ciudad tiene muchos lugares de recreo: hermosos parques, un estadio que tiene capacidad para ochenta mil personas y numerosos teatros y cines. Muy cerca de la ciudad hay excelentes lugares para esquiar.

- Dos escritores chilenos de fama internacional son Pablo Neruda y Gabriela Mistral, ganadores del Premio Nobel de Literatura. Otra escritora chilena de gran fama es Isabel Allende, autora de *La casa de los espíritus,* entre otras novelas.

▲ Pablo Neruda, famoso poeta chileno. Premio Nobel de Literatura 1971

Uruguay

- Uruguay, el país más pequeño de Suramérica, está situado entre Brasil y Argentina, en la costa oriental (*east*) de este continente. La mayoría de su territorio se dedica a la agricultura y a la ganadería (*livestock*), que son la base de la economía tradicional del país. Sin embargo, en las últimas décadas, el país se ha industrializado rápidamente gracias a la electricidad barata que producen sus plantas hidroeléctricas.

- Para los uruguayos, la carne es el plato esencial de su dieta, y el **mate,** su bebida favorita.

- Montevideo es una de las ciudades más cosmopolitas de Hispanoamérica, y es el centro administrativo, económico y cultural del país. Allí vive casi la mitad de su población, que es de unos tres millones de habitantes. Otra ciudad importante de Uruguay es Punta del Este, uno de los centros turísticos más famosos de América Latina. Punta del Este está situada a unas dos horas de Montevideo, y es muy popular por sus hermosas playas y por los festivales de cine que allí se celebran.

▲ Uruguayo bebiendo mate, una especie de té muy popular en todo el Cono Sur.

Argentina

- Argentina, por su extensión, es el país de habla hispana más grande, y ocupa el octavo lugar entre los países más extensos del mundo; sin embargo, es uno de los menos densamente poblados. La mayor parte de sus habitantes son de origen europeo, principalmente italianos.

- En este país se encuentra el pico más alto del mundo occidental: el Aconcagua. Una de sus mayores atracciones turísticas son las Cataratas de Iguazú, que comparte con Brasil y Paraguay.

- Su capital, Buenos Aires, es la ciudad más grande del hemisferio sur. A las personas de Buenos Aires

▲ Iguazú, una de las cataratas más espectaculares del mundo

se les llama **porteños,** que significa "gente del puerto." En esta ciudad hay más de cuarenta universidades y la ciudad tiene una vida cultural muy activa. Hay numerosos museos y teatros muy importantes; el Teatro Colón es uno de los más famosos del mundo. La ciudad tiene muchos parques muy hermosos y la Avenida 9 de Julio es la más ancha del mundo.

▲ Un gaucho con su ganado *(cattle herd).*

Brasil

- Brasil es el país más grande y más rico de América Latina. Limita con todos los países de Suramérica, excepto Chile y Ecuador. El idioma del país es el portugués, porque Brasil fue colonizado por Portugal.

- El país tiene muchos recursos naturales, incluidas extensas reservas de petróleo y de gas natural. Su principal producto agrícola es el café.

- Desde 1960 la capital de Brasil es Brasilia, la ciudad más moderna del mundo. Aislada del interior del país por la densa selva, la capital sigue prácticamente inaccesible excepto por avión y por eso Río de Janeiro, la antigua capital, y San Pablo siguen siendo las ciudades más importantes del país.

- Miles de personas de todas partes de Latinoamérica visitan Río de Janeiro, ciudad famosa por sus carnavales y por las populares playas de Copacabana e Ipanema.

Online Study Center

For more practice with lesson topics, see the related activities on the *¡Hola, amigos!* web site at college.hmco.com/PIC/holaamigos7e.

Comentarios... With a partner, discuss, in Spanish, what impressed you the most about these four countries and compare them to your own. Which places do you want to visit and why?

Tome este examen

Lección 11

A. Subjunctive with verbs of volition Write sentences in the present tense, using the elements given below. Use the present subjunctive or the infinitive, as appropriate, and add any necessary words.

1. Yo / querer / ella / ir / Viña del Mar
2. Nosotros / desear / viajar / avión
3. Ella / sugerirme / ir / Buenos Aires
4. El agente / querer / venderme / el pasaje
5. Ellos / aconsejarnos / comprar / seguro (*insurance*)
6. Yo / no querer / llevar / muchas maletas
7. Ellos / no querer / ella / llevarlos / en su coche
8. Nosotros / no querer / ir / contigo
9. ¿Tú / sugerirme / venir / luego?
10. Ella / necesitar / Uds. / darle / la maleta

B. Subjunctive with verbs of emotion Rewrite the following sentences, beginning each with the phrase in parentheses and using the subjunctive or the infinitive, as appropriate.

1. Ella se va pronto.   (Espero...)
2. Los pasajes son muy caros.   (Elsa teme...)
3. Yo estoy aquí.   (Me alegro de...)
4. Ella se va de vacaciones.   (Ella espera...)
5. Mamá se siente bien hoy.   (Esperamos...)
6. Ellos no pueden ir a la fiesta.   (Siento...)

C. Some uses of the prepositions *a, de,* and *en* Complete with **a, de,** or **en,** as necessary.

1. Anoche llamé _____ mi hermano por teléfono y hablamos _____ nuestros planes para el fin de semana. Pensamos ir _____ Chile. Él quiere viajar _____ tren pero yo prefiero ir _____ coche. Mi hermana no quiere ir con nosotros; prefiere quedarse _____ casa porque no tiene con quién dejar _____ su perro.
2. Ayer Marta llegó _____ la agencia _____ las ocho y media _____ la mañana, pero no empezó _____ trabajar hasta las diez.
3. Mi hija es muy bonita; es morena, _____ ojos verdes y yo pienso que es la más inteligente _____ todos mis hijos.

D. Vocabulary   Complete the following sentences, using vocabulary from Lección 11.

1. No quiero un _____ de pasillo; quiero uno de _____.
2. Voy a poner el bolso de _____ en el _____ de equipaje.
3. Voy a la _____ de viajes para comprar los pasajes.
4. Tiene que darle la tarjeta de _____ a la _____ de vuelo.
5. Tengo que pagar _____ de equipaje porque tengo cuatro maletas.
6. Quiero sentarme cerca de la _____ de emergencia.
7. Los paquetes _____ el pasaje, el hotel y algunas _____.
8. ¿A cuánto está el _____ de moneda?
9. No podemos viajar hoy. Tenemos que _____ la reservación.
10. Cuando viajo siempre llevo cheques de _____.
11. Este verano vamos a hacer un _____ por el Caribe.
12. Necesito una lista de los _____ de interés de la _____ de Chile.

E. Culture   Complete the following sentences, based on the cultural notes you have read.

1. En Argentina se usa la forma _____ en lugar de **tú**.
2. La música típica de Argentina es el _____.
3. En los países hispanos no existe tanta _____ entre las generaciones como en este país.

Lección 12

A. Subjunctive to express indefiniteness and nonexistence
Rewrite each sentence, using the subjunctive or the indicative, as appropriate.

1. El agente habla español.   (Necesitamos un agente que...)
2. Ese viaje incluye el hotel.   (Aquí no hay ningún viaje que...)
3. No hay ningún pasaje que no sea caro.   (Tenemos unos pasajes que...)
4. No hay ningún vuelo que salga a las seis.   (Hay varios vuelos que...)
5. Hay una señora que puede reservar los pasajes.   (¿Hay alguien que...?)

B. Familiar commands
Change the following negative commands to the affirmative.

1. No compres el televisor.
2. No se lo digas.
3. No viajes mañana.
4. No salgas con esa persona.
5. No pongas la maleta debajo del asiento.
6. No lo invites.
7. No te vayas.
8. No vengas entre semana.
9. No regreses tarde.
10. No hagas la reservación.
11. No me traigas el folleto.
12. No le pidas los comprobantes ahora.

C. Verbs and prepositions
Complete each sentence with the Spanish equivalent of the words in parentheses.

1. Olga _____ Daniel pero _____ Luis.   (*fell in love with / she married*)
2. Mi papá _____ que yo compre los billetes hoy.   (*insists on*)
3. Paco, _____ buscar los pasaportes. _____ que viajas el lunes. (*don't forget / Remember*)
4. Yo _____ que mis padres _____ él.   (*didn't realize / didn't trust*)

D. Ordinal numbers
Write the ordinal numbers that correspond to the following numbers.

2. _____   8. _____   3. _____
7. _____   4. _____   6. _____
5. _____   9. _____   10. _____
1. _____

E. Vocabulary
Complete the following sentences, using vocabulary from **Lección 12.**

1. El baño vo tiene bañadera; tiene _____ .
2. El _____ no funciona. Tiene que _____ por la escalera.
3. Tengo mucho frío y este cuarto no tiene _____ .
4. Mi esposo(a) y yo queremos una _____ doble.
5. El _____ de la pensión incluye todas las comidas.
6. Hay mucha gente porque hay un _____ de convenciones.
7. ¿A qué hora debemos _____ el cuarto?
8. Mi cuarto no es con _____ a la calle; es interior.
9. La pensión no tiene _____ de habitación.
10. Quiero una habitación exterior con _____ acondicionado.
11. Primero fui al _____ de revistas y después a la tienda de _____ .
12. Un sinónimo de **dueño** es _____ .
13. Reservé un hotel con pensión _____ .
14. No hay ninguna habitación _____ . El hotel está lleno.
15. ¿En qué _____ está tu habitación?

F. Culture
Circle the correct answer, based on the cultural notes you have read.

1. La ciudad de Santiago tiene (muy pocos / muchos) lugares de recreo.
2. La Avenida 9 de Julio en Buenos Aires es la (menos / más) ancha del mundo.
3. Uruguay está situado entre Brasil y (Argentina/Chile).
4. Desde 1960 la capital de Brasil es (Río de Janeiro/Brasilia).

Unidad

7

Objetivos

Lección 13

- ◆ Discuss health problems, medical emergencies, common medical procedures, and treatments
- ◆ Give and request information about physical symptoms and medications
- ◆ Express doubt, disbelief, and denial
- ◆ Tell others what to do

Lección 14

- ◆ Ask and respond to questions concerning personal medical history
- ◆ Make suggestions and give advice about health and other problems
- ◆ Talk about what will happen
- ◆ Talk about what would happen under different circumstances

En un hospital en Madrid, una doctora le toma la presión a una de sus pacientes.

¿Cómo te sientes?

España

Un café al aire libre en la Plaza Mayor en Madrid, España

Jardines del Generalife, en el Palacio de la Alhambra, Granada

Playa de Fuengirola, en la Costa del Sol, Andalucía

293

Dr. Mena

Paciente I

Paciente II

Madre

Sra. Mena

En un hospital de Madrid

Hoy, como siempre, hay muchos pacientes en la sala de emergencia, y siguen llegando más. El Dr. Mena atiende a varios de ellos, y piensa que va a ser un día muy largo.

En este momento está hablando con un hombre que vino en una ambulancia y que los paramédicos acaban de traer en una camilla.

Dr. Mena	¿Qué le pasó?
Paciente I	Mi coche chocó con un árbol y me golpeé el hombro.
Dr. Mena	¿Perdió el conocimiento?
Paciente I	Sí, por unos segundos... pero me duele mucho...
Dr. Mena	Bueno, la enfermera lo va a llevar a la sala de rayos X. Vamos a hacerle unas radiografías para ver si hay fractura.

Ahora está hablando con una señora que trajo a su hijo. El niño se cayó en la escalera mecánica de una tienda y se lastimó.

Dr. Mena	Estoy casi seguro de que es una torcedura, pero vamos a hacerle unas radiografías por si acaso.
Madre	Se cortó la pierna. ¿Va a necesitar puntos?
Dr. Mena	Dudo que necesite puntos, pero cuando venga la enfermera va a limpiarle y desinfectarle la herida. Además, le vamos a poner una inyección antitetánica.

Detalles culturales

En la mayoría de los países de habla hispana, los hospitales son gratis y subvencionados por el gobierno. Hay clínicas privadas para la gente que no quiere ir a un hospital público.

◆ **¿Hay hospitales subvencionados por el gobierno en este país?**

Detalles culturales

En muchos países hispanos existen las llamadas casas de socorro, donde se ofrecen los primeros auxilios (*first aid*) y cuidados (*care*) médicos urgentes.

◆ **¿Hay en este país un equivalente a las casas de socorro?**

Ahora está hablando con un muchacho que tiene mucho dolor y náusea.

Paciente II Me duele mucho, doctor. Yo creo que tengo apendicitis...

Dr. Mena (*Lo revisa*) No creo que sea apendicitis, pero vamos a hacerle unos análisis.

El Dr. Mena continuó atendiendo a otros pacientes en la sala de emergencia: a una niña que se quemó la mano y lloraba mucho; a una señora que se rompió una pierna y tiene que usar muletas; a un señor que tuvo una reacción alérgica y tiene la cara hinchada... Cuando volvió a su casa, se dio cuenta de que no había almorzado.

Sra. Mena Cenemos temprano, porque hoy tenemos que ir a la escuela de los niños. ¡Ay! Estoy muy cansada. Descansemos un rato antes de que Paloma y Mario vuelvan de su clase de piano. ¿Qué tal fue tu día hoy?

Dr. Mena Bueno... fue un día como cualquier otro... ¡en la sala de emergencia!

¿Recuerda usted?

¿Verdadero o falso? With a partner, indicate whether these statements are true (**verdadero**) or false (**falso**).

¿QUÉ, TAL FUE TU DÍA HOY?

1. Hoy no hay muchos pacientes en la sala de emergencia. ☐ V ☐ F
2. Un paciente se golpeó el hombro cuando su auto chocó con un árbol. ☐ V ☐ F
3. El Dr. Mena no sabe si el paciente tiene o no una fractura. ☐ V ☐ F
4. La mamá del niño se cayó de una bicicleta. ☐ V ☐ F
5. Le van a poner al niño una inyección antitetánica. ☐ V ☐ F
6. Uno de los pacientes cree que tiene apendicitis. ☐ V ☐ F
7. El Dr. Mena no tuvo que atender a nadie hoy. ☐ V ☐ F
8. El señor que tuvo una reacción alérgica tiene que usar muletas. ☐ V ☐ F
9. El Dr. Mena almorzó muy temprano hoy. ☐ V ☐ F
10. Hoy fue un día normal para el Dr. Mena. ☐ V ☐ F

Y ahora... conteste Answer the following questions, basing your answers on the dialogues.

1. ¿Quiénes trajeron al primer paciente a la sala de emergencia?
2. ¿El hombre perdió el conocimiento?
3. ¿A quiénes les van a hacer radiografías?
4. ¿El Dr. Mena cree que el niño va a necesitar puntos?
5. ¿Qué problemas tiene el muchacho que viene a la sala de emergencia?
6. ¿Por qué lloraba mucho la niña?
7. ¿Qué va a tener que usar la señora que se rompió una pierna?
8. ¿De dónde vienen Paloma y Mario?

Para hablar del tema: Vocabulario

Cognados

la ambulancia	el (la) paciente
la apendicitis	el (la) paramédico(a)
la fractura	el piano
el hospital	la reacción
la náusea	

Nombres

el análisis test
el árbol tree
la cara face
el dolor pain
el (la) enfermero(a) male nurse, nurse
la escalera stairs
_____ **mecánica*** escalator
la herida wound
el hombro shoulder
la inyección shot, injection

_____ **antitetánica** tetanus shot
las muletas crutches
la pierna leg
el punto stitch
la radiografía X-ray
la sala ward (*at a hospital*)
_____ **de emergencia** emergency room
_____ **de rayos equis** X-ray room
la torcedura sprain

De país a país

la escalera mecánica la escalera automática (*Esp., Cuba*)
romperse quebrarse (*Méx.*)

Verbos

atender (e>ie) to see (*a patient*)
caerse (yo me caigo) to fall
chocar to collide
continuar to continue
cortar(se) to cut (oneself)
desinfectar to disinfect
doler (o>ue) to hurt, to ache
dudar to doubt

golpear(se) to hit (*oneself*)
lastimarse to hurt oneself
llorar to cry
pasar, suceder to happen
quemar(se) to burn (*oneself*)
revisar to check
romper(se)* to break

Adjetivos

alérgico(a) allergic	**seguro(a)** sure
hinchado(a) swollen	**varios(as)** several

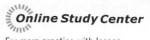
Online Study Center

For more practice with lesson
topics, see the related activities on
the *¡Hola, amigos!* web site at
college.hmco.com/PIC/holaamigos7e.

Otras palabras y expresiones

casi almost	**hacer una radiografía** to take an X-ray
como siempre as usual	**perder el conocimiento,**
cualquier any	**desmayarse** to faint

Amplíe su vocabulario

Otras partes del cuerpo (*Other parts of the body*)

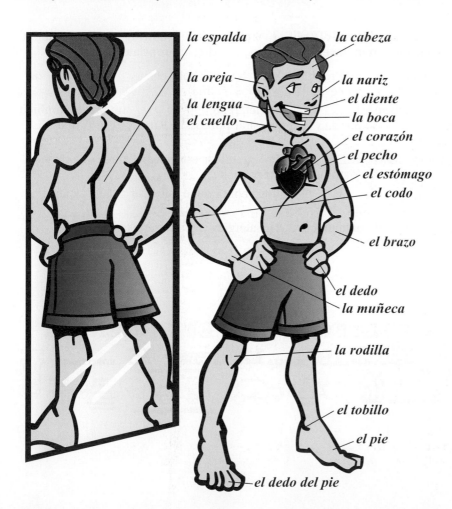

la espalda
la cabeza
la oreja
la nariz
la lengua
el diente
el cuello
la boca
el corazón
el pecho
el estómago
el codo
el brazo
el dedo
la muñeca
la rodilla
el tobillo
el pie
el dedo del pie

Para practicar el vocabulario

A. Preguntas y respuestas Match the questions in column *A* with the answers in column *B*.

A	B
1. ¿Dónde tiene él la herida?	a. En la sala de rayos X.
2. ¿Qué te duele?	b. Me caí en la escalera.
3. ¿Qué te hizo la enfermera?	c. No, una torcedura.
4. ¿Dónde está Rita?	d. Sí, como siempre.
5. ¿Tiene una fractura?	e. A varios pacientes.
6. ¿Qué necesita el paciente?	f. En la cara.
7. ¿Qué le pasó a la niña?	g. No, tengo dudas.
8. ¿Tuviste mucho trabajo hoy?	h. Una radiografía.
9. ¿Estás seguro de eso?	i. No, sólo me lastimé.
10. ¿Te rompiste el brazo?	j. El hombro.
11. ¿Qué te pasó?	k. Se quemó la mano.
12. ¿A quiénes está atendiendo el médico?	l. Me desinfectó la herida.

B. En la sala de emergencia Complete the following statements about what goes on in the emergency room, using appropriate vocabulary.

1. Ayer el coche de Sergio _____ con un árbol y él se _____ la cabeza. Los _____ lo llevaron al hospital en una _____.

2. Ayer Beto se _____ de la bicicleta y se _____ un brazo. También se _____ la pierna y va a necesitar puntos. Le van a _____ una inyección _____.

3. Carlos tiene _____ y mucho _____ de estómago. Él cree que tiene _____. El doctor le va a hacer unos _____.

4. Marga se _____ la pierna y ahora tiene que usar _____ para caminar (walk).

5. Ayer Amanda tuvo una _____ alérgica y ahora tiene la cara y las manos _____.

C. **¿Qué sabes de anatomía?**   Today you and your partner are the
professors. Teach your students these parts of the body in Spanish.

D. **En el hospital**   You and a classmate play the roles of two doctors talking
about the patients they have seen during the day, and their problems.

Pronunciación

Pronunciation in context   In this lesson, there are some words or
phrases that may be challenging to pronounce. Listen to your instructor
and pronounce the following sentences.

1. Hay muchos **pacientes** en la sala de **emergencia,** y **siguen**
   llegando más.
2. Vamos a hacerle una **radiografía** para ver si hay **fractura.**
3. **Además,** le vamos a poner una **inyección antitetánica.**
4. No creo que sea **apendicitis,** pero vamos a hacerle unos **análisis.**
5. Cuando volvió a su casa, se dio cuenta de que **no había almorzado.**

Puntos para recordar

1. Subjunctive to express doubt, denial, and disbelief
(*El subjuntivo para expresar duda, negación e incredulidad*)

Doubt

When the verb of the main clause expresses uncertainty or doubt, the verb in the subordinate clause is in the subjunctive.

—Te esperan a las cinco y son las cuatro y media.
—**Dudo** que yo **pueda** estar ahí a esa hora.

"They expect you at five and it is four-thirty."
*"**I doubt** that **I can** be there at that time."*

—Podemos tomar el desayuno a las once.
—**Dudo** que lo **sirvan** después de las diez.
—Estoy segura de que lo sirven hasta las once.

"We can have breakfast at eleven."
*"**I doubt** that **they serve** it after ten."*
"I am sure that they serve it until eleven."

> **¡Atención!** Notice that when no doubt is expressed and the speaker is certain of the reality (**estoy seguro[a]**, **no dudo**, **sé**), the indicative is used.

Estoy seguro de que lo **sirven** hasta las once.

I am sure *that* ***they serve*** *it until eleven.*

Online Study Center

For more practice with lesson topics, see the related activities on the *¡Hola, amigos!* web site at college.hmco.com/PIC/holaamigos7e.

Práctica y conversación

A. ¿Cómo responde...? Respond to each of the following statements, beginning with the suggested phrases.

1. —Estoy seguro de que tiene una fractura.
   —Bueno, dudo que...
2. —Dudo que tenga que usar muletas.
   —Pues yo estoy seguro(a) de que...
3. —No estoy seguro de que sea apendicitis.
   —Pues yo no dudo que...
4. —Dudo que la enfermera esté en la sala de rayos X.
   —¿Sí? Yo estoy casi seguro(a) de que...
5. —Dudo que el paciente necesite radiografías.
   —Yo tampoco estoy seguro(a) de que...

B. En el hospital With a partner, read the following statements and take turns expressing doubt or certainty about them. Use **dudo, no dudo, estoy seguro(a),** and **no estoy seguro(a).**

1. Todos los hospitales son gratis.
2. Las enfermeras trabajan solamente tres horas al día.
3. El médico puede desinfectar la herida.
4. Los paramédicos nunca vienen en la ambulancia.
5. Cualquier enfermera puede hacer una radiografía.
6. Si tienes un dolor en el pecho debes ir al hospital en seguida.
7. Los médicos ganan muy poco dinero.
8. Si te rompes una pierna necesitas usar muletas.

C. ¿Lo dudas...? With a partner, take turns telling each other three or four things about yourself. Give some false information to see if your partner doubts or doesn't doubt what you say.

◆ **MODELO:** —*Tengo ocho clases este semestre.*
　　　　　—*Dudo que tengas ocho clases.*
　　　　　　(Estoy seguro[a] de que no tienes ocho clases.)

Denial

When the main clause denies or negates what is expressed in the subordinate clause, the subjunctive is used.

—Ana **niega** que Carlos **sea** su novio.	*"Ana **denies** that Carlos **is** her boyfriend."*
—Sí, dice que son amigos...	*"Yes, she says that they are friends . . ."*
—Ellos trabajan mucho y siempre tienen dinero.	*"They work hard and always have money."*
—Es verdad que trabajan mucho, pero **no es cierto** que siempre **tengan** dinero.	*"It's true that they work hard, but **it's not true** that **they** always **have** money."*

¡Atención! Notice that when the main clause does not deny what is said in the subordinate clause, the indicative is used.

Es verdad que **trabajan** mucho. 　　***It's true** that **they work** hard.*

Online Study Center

For more practice with lesson topics, see the related activities on the *¡Hola, amigos!* web site at college.hmco.com/PIC/holaamigos7e.

Práctica y conversación

A. ¿Es verdad o no? With a partner, take turns saying whether each of the following statements is true or not.

◆ **MODELO:** Toda la gente tiene reacciones alérgicas a todo.
　　　　　***No es verdad** que toda la gente **tenga** reacciones alérgicas a todo.*

1. Los médicos no trabajan en la sala de emergencia.
2. Generalmente hay muchos pacientes en la sala de emergencia.
3. Las enfermeras saben más que los médicos.

4. Los paramédicos van en las ambulancias.
5. Los médicos no cobran mucho.
6. Hoy hace mucho frío.
7. Está lloviendo.
8. Hoy hace buen tiempo.

Disbelief

The verb **creer** is followed by the subjunctive in negative sentences, where it expresses disbelief.

—¿Teresa va al hospital hoy?　　　*"Is Teresa going to the hospital today?"*

—No, **no creo** que **vaya** hoy.　　*"No, **I don't think she's going** today?"*

> **¡Atención!** **Creer** is followed by the indicative in affirmative sentences, where it expresses belief.

—¿Qué va a pedir el médico?　　　*"What is the doctor going to ask for?"*

—**Creo** que **va** a pedir unos análisis.　　*"**I think** he **is** going to order (ask for) some tests."*

Dudo que tenga aire acondicionado.

Práctica y conversación

A. **El Sr. Contreras**　Mr. Contreras always contradicts everyone. How would he react to these statements?

◆ MODELO:　Creo que ese médico es muy bueno.
　　　　　No creo que (ese médico) *sea* muy bueno.

1. No creo que el hospital sea caro.
2. Creo que todos los cuartos tienen aire acondicionado.
3. Creo que tienen que llevarlo a la sala de emergencia.
4. No creo que estén allí.
5. No creo que él necesite radiografías.
6. Creo que necesita usar muletas.

B. En la universidad Use your imagination to complete each statement, using the subjunctive or the indicative, as appropriate. Compare your statements to those of your partner.

1. Yo creo que el profesor (la profesora)...
2. No es verdad que yo...
3. Es cierto que los estudiantes...
4. No creo que en la cafetería de la universidad...
5. No es verdad que la clase de español...
6. No es cierto que los norteamericanos...
7. Dudo que yo...
8. No estoy seguro(a) de que esta universidad...

C. Opiniones Use the illustrations to complete the following sentences.

1. Yo no creo que el papá de Beto...

2. Dudo que Paquito...

3. No es verdad que Carlos...

4. Rita cree que el hotel Granada...

5. No es cierto que el baño...

6. No es verdad que Esteban siempre...

D. Viajando The following statements are made by someone who doesn't necessarily know what he or she is talking about. With a partner, take turns saying whether or not you think the comments are true. Use **creo, no creo, dudo, estoy seguro(a), es verdad,** or **no es verdad.**

1. Hay vuelos directos de Nueva York a Madrid.
2. El pasaje a Madrid cuesta 200 dólares.
3. Los estudiantes siempre viajan en primera clase.
4. Puedo viajar por España en tren.
5. Todas las ciudades españolas son muy pequeñas.
6. Hay hoteles elegantes en Barcelona.
7. En los hoteles de Madrid, todas las habitaciones tienen vista al mar.
8. Podemos viajar de Los Ángeles a Madrid en tren.

2. Subjunctive with certain conjunctions (*El subjuntivo con ciertas conjunciones*)

Subjunctive after conjunctions of time

The subjunctive is used after conjunctions of time when the main clause refers to a future action or is a command. Some conjunctions of time are:

cuando	when	**tan pronto como,**	
hasta que	until	**en cuanto**	as soon as

Note in the following examples that the action in the subordinate clause has not yet taken place.

—¿Vamos a la pensión ahora?	*"Are we going to the boarding house now?"*
—No, vamos a esperar **hasta que venga** Eva.	*"No, we're going to wait **until** Eva **comes**."*
—Bueno, llámeme **en cuanto llegue.**	*"Okay, call me **as soon as she arrives**."*
—¿Cuándo vas a comprar las muletas?	*"When are you going to buy the crutches?"*
—**Cuando** mi papá me **dé** el dinero.	*"**When** my dad **gives** me the money."*

¡Atención! If the action has already taken place or if the speaker views the action of the subordinate clause as a habitual occurrence, the indicative is used after the conjunction of time.

—¿Ya llamaste a Rodolfo?	*"Did you already call Rodolfo?"*
—Sí, lo llamé **en cuanto llegué.**	*"Yes, I called him **as soon as I arrived**."*
—¿Cuándo llamas a Rodolfo?	*"When do you call Rodolfo?"*
—Siempre lo llamo **cuando llego** del trabajo.	*"I always call him **when I arrive** from work."*

Conjunctions that always take the subjunctive

Certain conjunctions by their very meaning imply uncertainty or condition; they are therefore always followed by the subjunctive. Examples include:

a menos que	unless	**con tal (de) que**	provided that
antes de que	before	**para que**	in order that, so that
en caso de que	in case	**sin que**	without

—Voy a llamar a la enfermera **para que** me **traiga** las radiografías
*"I'm going to call the nurse **so that she'll bring** me the x-rays."*

—Llámela **antes de que se vaya.**
*"Call her **before she leaves**."*

—No puedo comprar la medicina **sin que** tú me **des** el dinero.
*"I can't buy the medicine **without you giving** me the money."*

—Puedo dártelo ahora.
"I can give it to you now."

Práctica y conversación

Online Study Center

For more practice with lesson topics, see the related activities on the *¡Hola, amigos!* web site at college.hmco.com/PIC/holaamigos7e.

A. Minidiálogos Complete the following dialogues, using the indicative or the subjunctive of each verb. Then act them out with a partner.

1. **desocupar / llegar**
   —¿Podemos limpiar el cuarto ahora?
   —No, no podemos limpiarlo hasta que el paciente lo _____ .
   —¿Cuándo lo va a desocupar?
   —En cuanto _____ el taxi.

2. **llegar / atender**
   —¿Qué va a hacer en cuanto _____ al hospital?
   —Voy a hablar con la recepcionista para que el médico me _____ esta tarde.

3. **llamar**
   —¿Cuándo van a venir tus amigos?
   —Tan pronto como yo los _____ .

4. **salir**
   —¿Los señores García te esperaron?
   —Sí, me esperaron hasta que yo _____ del hospital.

5. **hablar / ver**
   —Cuando Ud. _____ con el médico, dígale que el paciente no se siente bien.
   —Voy a decírselo en cuanto lo _____ .

6. **irse / salir**
   —¿Tú puedes hablar con los paramédicos antes de que ellos _____ ?
   —Sí, a menos que (ellos) _____ muy temprano.

B. Entreviste a su compañero(a) Interview your partner, using the following questions.

1. ¿Siempre desayunas en cuanto te levantas?
2. ¿Siempre te lavas la cabeza cuando te bañas?
3. ¿Tú puedes salir de tu casa sin que nadie te vea?
4. ¿Qué le vas a decir a tu mejor amigo(a) cuando lo (la) veas?
5. ¿Tú llegas a veces a clase antes de que llegue el profesor (la profesora)?
6. ¿Qué vas a hacer para que el profesor (la profesora) te dé una "A" en esta clase?
7. ¿A veces te quedas en la biblioteca hasta que la cierran?
8. ¿Qué vas a hacer tan pronto como llegues a tu casa?

3. First-person plural commands (*El imperativo de la primera persona del plural*)

◆ In Spanish, the first-person plural of an affirmative command (*let's* + *verb*) can be expressed in two ways:

   ◆ by using the first-person plural of the present subjunctive.

Preguntemos el precio de la habitación.	***Let's ask*** *the price of the room.*

   ◆ by using the expression **vamos a** + *infinitive.*

Vamos a preguntar el precio de la habitación.	***Let's ask*** *the price of the room.*

◆ The verb **ir** does not use the subjunctive form in the first-person plural affirmative command.

Vamos al teatro.	***Let's go*** *to the theatre.*

In a negative command, however, the subjunctive form is used.

No vayamos al teatro.	***Let's not go*** *to the theatre.*

◆ In all direct, affirmative commands, object pronouns are attached to the verb, and a written accent is then placed on the stressed syllable.

Comprémos**lo.**	*Let's buy **it.***
Llamémos**los.**	*Let's call **them.***

If the pronouns **nos** or **se** are attached to the verb, the final **-s** of the verb is dropped before adding the pronoun.

Sentémo**nos** aquí.	***Let's sit*** *here.*
Vistámo**nos** ahora.	***Let's get dressed*** *now.*
Démo**selo** a los niños.	***Let's give it*** *to the children.*

—Vamos a Madrid.	*"Let's go to Madrid."*
—No, no vayamos a Madrid; **quedémonos** en Barcelona.	*"No, let's not go to Madrid; **let's stay** in Barcelona."*
—¿Dónde queda el Museo del Prado?	*"Where's the Prado Museum located?"*
—No sé. **Preguntémoselo** a ese señor.	*"I don't know. **Let's ask** that gentleman."*

Práctica y conversación

Online Study Center

For more practice with lesson topics, see the related activities on the *¡Hola, amigos!* web site at college.hmco.com/PIC/holaamigos7e.

A. ¿Qué hacemos...? With a partner, take turns saying what these people should do in the following situations. Use the first person plural command. Use pronouns wherever possible.

1. Tenemos mucha hambre.
2. Estamos en un restaurante y necesitamos el menú.
3. No queremos salir hoy.
4. No sabemos qué hacer este fin de semana.
5. Un amigo nuestro tuvo un accidente.
6. No sabemos el precio de la medicina.
7. Estamos cansados.
8. Tenemos sueño.

B. ¡Vamos a España! You and a classmate are making plans to go on a trip to Spain. Take turns answering the following questions, using the first-person plural command.

1. ¿A qué ciudad vamos?
2. ¿Cómo viajamos?
3. ¿Qué día y a qué hora salimos?
4. ¿Cuántas maletas llevamos?
5. ¿Nos hospedamos en un hotel o en una pensión?
6. ¿Pedimos una habitación con vista a la calle?
7. ¿Cuántos días nos quedamos en la ciudad?
8. ¿Comemos en un restaurante o en nuestra habitación?
9. ¿Dónde dejamos las joyas (*jewelry*)?
10. ¿Cuándo regresamos?

Rodeo

Summary of the Command Forms (*Resumen de las formas del imperativo*)

Usted	Ustedes	Tú		Nosotros
		Affirmative	*Negative*	
hable	hablen	habla	no hables	hablemos
coma	coman	come	no comas	comamos
abra	abran	abre	no abras	abramos
cierre	cierren	cierra	no cierres	cerremos
vaya	vayan	**ve**	no vayas	**vamos**[1]

---

[1]Remember that the affirmative command uses the indicative form **vamos,** but the negative command uses the subjunctive form **no vayamos.**

Notice that the command forms of these verbs are identical to the subjunctive forms, except for the affirmative forms for **tú,** which use the third-person singular of the present indicative. Also, the following verbs have irregular **tú** command forms.

decir	**di**	ir	**ve**	salir	**sal**	tener	**ten**
hacer	**haz**	poner	**pon**	ser	**sé**	venir	**ven**

Remember the position of direct, indirect, and reflexive pronouns with commands.

Affirmative	*Negative*
Cómpre**lo.**	No **lo** compre.
Dí**selo.**	No **se lo** digas.
Levanté**monos.**	No **nos** levantemos.

Práctica y conversación

Planes y más planes   You and a partner are busy making plans for a visit by some foreign students who will spend the weekend with you and your friends. One of your neighbors, Sra. Vega, and her young daughter, María, offer their help. Use the appropriate command form to say who is going to do each of the following chores and categorize them under the appropriate heading.

Online Study Center

For more practice with lesson topics, see the related activities on the *¡Hola, amigos!* web site at college.hmco.com/PIC/holaamigos7e.

◆ MODELOS: Comprar frutas
Nosotros: *Compremos frutas.*
la señora Vega: *Compre frutas.*
María: *Compra frutas.*

1. limpiar el apartamento
2. ir al mercado
3. poner la mesa
4. preparar la comida
5. hacer las camas
6. invitar a otros estudiantes
7. ir al aeropuerto a esperar a los viajeros (*travelers*)
8. sacar entradas para el teatro
9. no levantarse tarde
10. llevarlos a visitar los lugares de interés
11. servir la comida
12. lavar los platos
13. darles una fiesta de bienvenida
14. pedirle los discos compactos a Roberto
15. llevarlos a las tiendas
16. no olvidarse de sacar dinero del banco

4. ¿Qué? and ¿cuál? used with ser
(Qué y cuál usados con el verbo ser)

◆ *What?* translates as **¿qué?** when it is used as the subject of the verb and asks for a definition.

—¿**Qué** es una paella?   "**What** is a paella?"
—Es un plato español.   "It's a Spanish dish."

◆ *What?* translates as **¿cuál?** when it is used as the subject of a verb and asks for a choice. **Cuál** conveys the idea of selection from among several or many available objects, ideas, and so on.

—¿**Cuál** es su número de teléfono?   "**What** is your phone number?"
—712-4267.   "712-4267."

Práctica y conversación

Online Study Center

For more practice with lesson topics, see the related activities on the *¡Hola, amigos!* web site at college.hmco.com/PIC/holaamigos7e.

A. ¿Cuál es la pregunta?   Write the questions you would ask to get the following information. Use **qué** or **cuál,** as needed.

1. —¿_____?
   —El nombre del hotel es "El Alcázar".

   —¿_____?
   —Calle del Prado, número 420.

   —¿_____?
   —6–35–42–37.

2. —Necesita mostrar su carnet de identidad.

   —¿_____?
   —Es una forma de identificación.

   —¿Cuánto cuesta una habitación en este hotel?

   —Cuesta doscientos euros.

   —¿_____?
   —Es la moneda (*currency*) de España.

B. Entreviste a su compañero(a)   Interview your partner, using the following questions.

1. ¿Cuál es el hotel que tú prefieres?
2. ¿Cuál es la ciudad que más te gusta?
3. ¿Cuál es el programa de televisión que prefieres?
4. ¿Cuál es la comida que más te gusta?
5. ¿Cuál es el lugar que prefieres para ir de vacaciones?
6. ¿Cuál es tu color favorito?

Entre nosotros

¡Conversemos!

 Para conocernos mejor Get to know your partner better by asking each other the following questions.

1. ¿Has tenido un accidente alguna vez?
2. ¿Te han llevado al hospital en una ambulancia alguna vez?
3. ¿Cuándo fue la última vez que estuviste en una sala de emergencia?
4. ¿Cuándo fue la última vez que te pusieron una inyección antitetánica?
5. ¿Qué tomas cuando te duele la cabeza? ¿Y cuando te duele el estómago?
6. ¿Te han hecho una radiografía últimamente?
7. ¿Te has desmayado alguna vez (*ever*)?
8. ¿Tu médico te ha recetado alguna medicina últimamente?
9. ¿Te has roto una pierna o un brazo alguna vez?
10. ¿Te has quemado una mano alguna vez?

 Una encuesta Interview your classmates to identify who fits the following descriptions. Include your instructor, but remember to use the **Ud.** form when addressing him or her.

Nombre

1. Se lastimó jugando al fútbol. _____
2. Toma pastillas para el dolor a veces. _____
3. Va a ir al médico el mes próximo. _____
4. No se siente bien hoy. _____
5. Se ha caído últimamente. _____
6. Estuvo en la sala de rayos X el mes pasado. _____
7. Va a tomar una medicina más tarde. _____
8. Nunca se ha desmayado. _____
9. Tiene problemas con el estómago a veces. _____
10. Ha tenido que ir al hospital últimamente. _____

Y ahora... Write a brief summary about what you have learned about your classmates.

¿Cómo lo decimos?   What would you say in the following situations? What might the other person say? Act out the scenes with a partner.

1. You were in an accident and were brought to the hospital. Tell the doctor what happened and where it hurts. Ask him or her any relevant questions you may have regarding your injuries, any procedures the doctor may wish to perform, and your treatment.
2. You and your English-speaking friend are traveling in Spain. Your friend has fallen down the stairs in the hotel, so you take him/her to the doctor. Tell the doctor what happened, and ask any pertinent questions. (Does he/she need crutches? If so, how long must the crutches be used?, and so on).

¿Qué pasa aquí?   In groups of three or four, create a story about the people in the illustrations. Say who they are, what happened to them, and what they need.

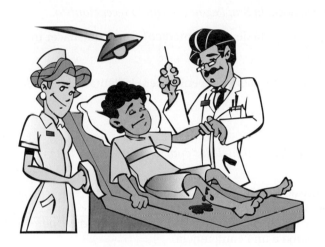 

Para escribir

Un accidente   Use your imagination to finish the following story, telling what happened to Julio. Tell how the accident happened, how he got to the hospital, what the doctor said and did, etc.

Eran las ocho de la noche y Julio iba en su coche cuando tuvo un accidente...

Un dicho

Mente sana en cuerpo sano.

To have this shoud be everyone's goal! Keep repeating this wise saying in Spanish!

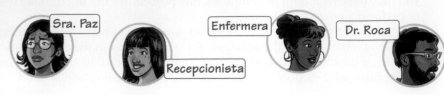

La Sra. Paz se despertó con dolor de garganta y una temperatura de 40 grados. Empezó a toser y le fue muy difícil levantarse. Pensó: "Tengo fiebre; tendré que ir al médico" y, afortunadamente, pudo hacer una cita para las diez de la mañana.

En el consultorio del Dr. Roca, la Sra. Paz habla con la recepcionista.

Recepcionista ¿Tiene su tarjeta de seguro médico? Tengo que hacer una fotocopia.
Sra. Paz Aquí la tiene.
Recepcionista Gracias. Tome asiento. La enfermera la llamará dentro de unos minutos.

Con la enfermera.

La enfermera la pesa y la lleva a uno de los cuartos. Allí le toma la temperatura y la presión.

Enfermera Tiene la presión un poco alta. ¿Cuánto tiempo hace que no se siente bien?
Sra. Paz Dos días. Mi esposo me aconsejó que viera al médico, pero yo fui a Barcelona a una conferencia.
Enfermera El médico probablemente le dirá que tiene que descansar. Bueno, en seguida vendrá el Dr. Roca a hablar con usted. ¿Es usted alérgica a alguna medicina?
Sra. Paz Que yo sepa, no.
Enfermera ¿Está embarazada?
Sra. Paz No.

Detalles culturales

En los países de habla hispana se mide la temperatura en grados *Celsius*, a los que también se les llama *Centígrados*. En la escala Celsius, 0° (temperatura de fusión del hielo) corresponde a 32° Fahrenheit. En el ejemplo, 40° Celsius corresponde a 104° Fahrenheit.

◆ ¿Sabe Ud. convertir grados Farenheit a centígrados?

Detalles culturales

En muchos países hispanos, en cada barrio (*neighborhood*), hay una "farmacia de turno" que ofrece servicios durante la noche. A cada farmacia le corresponde estar abierta un día diferente de la semana. Un letrero en las farmacias cerradas indica dónde están las farmacias abiertas.

◆ ¿Hay en su ciudad farmacias que están abiertas 24 horas al día?

Con el Dr. Roca.

Dr. Roca (*La examina*) A ver... Abra la boca y diga "ah".
Ajá. Ahora, respire hondo... Otra vez...

Sra. Paz Me gustaría que me hiciera un buen chequeo, doctor.

Dr. Roca Sí, ésa sería una buena idea. Si tuviera tiempo, lo haría hoy, pero no será posible.

Sra. Paz Bueno, haré una cita para la semana que viene.

Dr. Roca Bien, usted tiene gripe pero, si no se cuida, puede convertirse en una pulmonía, y ésa es una enfermedad mucho más grave.

Sra. Paz ¿Me va a recetar algo?

Dr. Roca Sí, le voy a recetar un antibiótico y un jarabe para la tos. Lleve esta receta a la farmacia y empiece a tomar el antibiótico hoy mismo.

Sra. Paz Bueno, lo que tengo es contagioso, de modo que no podré ir a trabajar. Pero lo más difícil va a ser admitir que mi esposo tenía razón.

Dr. Roca ¿Tenía razón?

Sra. Paz Sí, él me dijo que viniera al médico y yo me fui a una conferencia... ¡Y me empeoré! ¡Ahora va a creer que él es infalible!

¿Recuerda usted?

¿Verdadero o falso? With a partner, decide whether the following statements about the dialogues are true (**verdadero**) or false (**falso**).

1. La temperatura de la Sra. Paz es normal. ☐ V ☐ F
2. La Sra. Paz no tiene seguro médico. ☐ V ☐ F
3. La recepcionista pesa a la Sra. Paz. ☐ V ☐ F
4. La conferencia fue en Barcelona. ☐ V ☐ F
5. La Sra. Paz no está embarazada. ☐ V ☐ F
6. El Dr. Roca le va a hacer un buen chequeo a la Sra. Paz hoy mismo. ☐ V ☐ F
7. La Sra. Paz pedirá turno para la semana que viene. ☐ V ☐ F
8. El médico le dice a la Sra. Paz que debe cuidarse. ☐ V ☐ F
9. La Sra. Paz no quiere admitir que su esposo tenía razón. ☐ V ☐ F
10. La Sra. Paz fue a una conferencia y se mejoró. ☐ V ☐ F

Y ahora... conteste Answer these questions, basing your answers on the dialogues.

1. ¿Qué le dolía a la Sra. Paz esta mañana?
2. ¿Cómo sabemos que la Sra. Paz tenía fiebre?
3. ¿Cuánto tiempo hace que la Sra. Paz no se siente bien?
4. ¿Qué le aconsejó el Sr. Paz a su esposa?
5. ¿Qué dice la Sra. Paz que ella necesita?
6. ¿En qué puede convertirse la gripe?
7. ¿Qué va a comprar la Sra. Paz en la farmacia?
8. Según la Sra Paz, ¿qué va a creer su esposo?

Detalles culturales

En España y en algunos países latinoamericanos, las farmacias venden principalmente medicinas. En algunos países hispanos es posible comprar ciertas medicinas —como la penicilina— sin tener receta médica.

◆ En este país, ¿se pueden comprar antibióticos sin tener receta médica?

Para hablar del tema: Vocabulario

Online Study Center

For more practice with lesson topics, see the related activities on the *¡Hola, amigos!* web site at college.hmco.com/PIC/holaamigos7e.

Cognados

el antibiótico	infalible
contagioso(a)	el minuto
la farmacia	(el) la recepcionista
la fotocopia	

Nombres

la cita, el turno appointment	**la gripe*** flu
el chequeo checkup	**el jarabe** syrup
la conferencia lecture	**la presión** pressure, (blood) pressure
el consultorio doctor's office	**la pulmonía** pneumonia
la garganta throat	**la receta** prescription
el dolor de garganta sore throat	**el seguro*** insurance
la enfermedad disease, sickness	_____ **médico** medical insurance
la fiebre fever	**la tos** cough

Verbos

admitir to admit	**pesar** to weigh
convertirse en (e>ie) to turn into	**recetar** to prescribe
cuidar(se) to take care (of oneself)	**respirar** to breathe
empeorar(se)[1] to get worse	**toser** to cough
examinar to examine, to check	

Adjetivos

embarazada, en estado, encinta pregnant
grave, serio(a) serious

Otras palabras y expresiones

dentro de within	**que viene** next
en seguida, enseguida right away	**que yo sepa** that I know of
hoy mismo this very day	**respirar hondo** to take a deep breath
otra vez again	
por suerte, afortunadamente luckily, fortunately	

---

[1]**mejorar(se)** to get better

Amplíe su vocabulario

Más sobre la salud: Medicinas

Debe tomar
{
un antiácido	*antacid*
un calmante	*tranquilizer*
un sedativo, un sedante	*sedative*
vitaminas	*vitamins*

Algunos especialistas

el (la) cardiólogo(a)	*cardiologist*
el (la) cirujano(a)	*surgeon*
el (la) dermatólogo(a)	*dermatologist*
el (la) ginecólogo(a)	*gynecologist*
el (la) oculista	*oculist*
el (la) pediatra	*pediatrician*

De país a país

la gripe la gripa (*Méx.*)
el seguro la aseguranza (*Méx.*)

En el botiquín (*Medicine cabinet*)

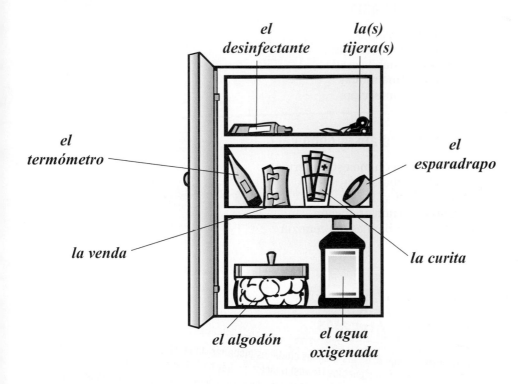

el desinfectante

la(s) tijera(s)

el termómetro

el esparadrapo

la venda

la curita

el algodón

el agua oxigenada

Para practicar el vocabulario

A. Preguntas y respuestas With a partner, match the questions in column *A* with the answers in column *B*.

A	B
1. ¿Qué te recetó el médico?	a. Aquí la tiene.
2. ¿Para cuándo tienes turno?	b. Sí, voy a la farmacia.
3. ¿Se mejoró?	c. No, normal.
4. ¿Necesitas la medicina ahora?	d. Que yo sepa, no.
5. ¿Tiene gripe?	e. Lo va a pesar.
6. ¿Dónde está la fotocopia?	f. Para hoy mismo.
7. ¿Debo volver mañana?	g. Sí, porque no tiene seguro.
8. ¿Es Ud. alérgica a alguna medicina?	h. Sí, pero puede convertirse en pulmonía.
9. ¿Rita tiene que pagar la cuenta?	i. Un jarabe para la tos.
10. ¿Tiene la presión alta?	j. Dentro de una semana.
11. ¿Qué va a hacer la enfermera?	k. No, se empeoró.
12. ¿Cuándo empieza a trabajar la recepcionista?	l. No, no es necesario.

B. ¿Qué debo tomar?

1. Tengo acidez.
2. Estoy muy nervioso(a).
3. Estoy muy débil (*weak*).
4. Me duele una rodilla.
5. Tengo una infección.

C. ¿Qué especialista debo ver?

1. si mi hijo pequeño está enfermo
2. si estoy embarazada
3. si no veo bien
4. si necesito una operación
5. si tengo problemas del corazón
6. si tengo acné

Detalles culturales

Especialmente en las grandes ciudades hispanas, la medicina está muy avanzada, pero en muchos pueblos (*towns*) remotos no hay hospitales ni médicos. En esos lugares, especialmente en Latinoamérica, hay curanderos (*healers*) que recomiendan hierbas (*herbs*) o tés, o que usan remedios tradicionales para sus curas.

◆ En su país, ¿hay algunas personas que usan hierbas medicinales para curar ciertas enfermedades?

D. En nuestro botiquín With a partner, mention eight items you need for your medicine cabinet.

¿Para qué son las pastillas que está contando el farmacéutico?

Pronunciación

Pronunciation in context In this lesson, there are some words or phrases that may be challenging to pronounce. Listen to your instructor and pronounce the following sentences.

1. La Sra. Paz se despertó con dolor de **garganta** y una **temperatura** de 40 grados.
2. Mi esposo **me aconsejó** que fuera al médico, pero yo fui a **Barcelona** a una **conferencia.**
3. Me gustaría que me **hiciera** un buen **chequeo.**
4. Le voy a **recetar** un **antibiótico** y un **jarabe** para la tos.
5. Bueno, lo que tengo es **contagioso** y **no podré ir** a trabajar.

Puntos para recordar

1. Future tense (*Futuro*)

◆ Most Spanish verbs are regular in the future, and the infinitive serves as the stem of almost all verbs. The endings are the same for all three conjugations.

Formation of the Future Tense			
Infinitive		*Stem*	*Endings*
trabajar	yo	trabajar-	**é**
aprender	tú	aprender-	**ás**
escribir	Ud., él, ella	escribir-	**á**
entender	nosotros(as)	entender-	**emos**
ir	vosotros(as)	ir-	**éis**
dar	Uds., ellos, ellas	dar-	**án**

¡Atención! Note that all the endings, except that of the **nosotros(as)** form, take accent marks.

—¿Adónde **irán** Uds. esta tarde?
—**Iremos** al consultorio del Dr. Báez.

*"Where **will** you **go** this afternoon?"*
*"**We will go** to Dr. Baez's office."*

◆ A small number of Spanish verbs are irregular in the future tense. These verbs have an irregular stem; however, the endings are the same as those for regular verbs.

Irregular Future Stems		
Infinitive	*Stem*	*First-Person Sing.*
decir	dir-	**diré**
hacer	har-	**haré**
haber	habr-	**habré**
querer	querr-	**querré**
saber	sabr-	**sabré**
poder	podr-	**podré**
poner	pondr-	**pondré**
salir	saldr-	**saldré**
tener	tendr-	**tendré**
venir	vendr-	**vendré**

¿Podrá terminar estas cartas para las seis?

—¿A qué hora **saldrán** para el hospital?

"At what time **will you leave** for the hospital?"

—**Saldremos** tan pronto como lleguen mis padres.

"**We will leave** as soon as my parents arrive."

—¿**Podrás** venir mañana?

"**Will you be able** to come tomorrow?"

—Sí, **vendré** a menos que llueva.

"Yes, **I will come** unless it rains."

¡Atención! The future of **hay** (impersonal form of **haber**) is **habrá**.

¿**Habrá** una conferencia?

Will there be a lecture?

◆ Uses of the future tense

  ◆ The English equivalent of the Spanish future tense is *will* or *shall* plus a verb. As you have already learned, Spanish also uses the construction **ir a** plus an infinitive, or the present tense with a time expression, to refer to future actions, events, or states.

    Esta noche **iremos** al cine.   *Tonight **we will go** to the movies.*
    Esta noche **vamos a ir** al cine.   *Tonight **we're going to go** to the movies.*
    Esta noche **vamos** al cine.   *Tonight **we're going** to the movies.*

  ◆ Unlike English, the Spanish future is *not* used to express willingness. In Spanish, willingness is expressed by the verb **querer.**

    —¿**Quieres** llamar a Eva?   "**Will you** call Eva?"
    —Ahora no puedo.   "*I can't now.*"

Online Study Center

For more practice with lesson topics, see the related activities on the *¡Hola, amigos!* web site at college.hmco.com/PIC/holaamigos7e.

Práctica y conversación

A. ¿Qué harán?   Rewrite the following sentences, using the future tense. Follow the model.

◆ **MODELO:** Voy a comprar un jarabe y se lo voy a dar a Carlos.
*Compraré un jarabe y se lo **daré** a Carlos.*

1. La Sra. Paz va a llamar al médico y va a preguntar si puede ir hoy.
2. La recepcionista le va a pedir la tarjeta de seguro médico y le va a decir que se siente.
3. La enfermera la va a pesar y le va a tomar la presión.
4. El médico le va a hacer un chequeo y le va a decir que se cuide.
5. La Sra. Paz va a ir a la farmacia y va a comprar la medicina.
6. Yo voy a tener que llevar a los niños a su casa porque la Sra. Paz no va a poder llevarlos.

B. El verano pasado   The following paragraph describes what happened last summer. Change all the verbs to the future to indicate what will happen in the upcoming summer.

En el verano, mi familia y yo **fuimos** a California. **Estuvimos** en San Diego por una semana. **Alquilamos** un apartamento cerca de la playa y unos amigos madrileños **vinieron** a quedarse con nosotros. Diego y Jaime **hicieron** surfing. Mi padre **pasó** un par de días pescando, y Gloria y yo **buceamos, tomamos** el sol y por la noche **salimos** con unos amigos. **Nos divertimos** mucho pero **tuvimos** que volver para empezar las clases.

C. Planes para las vacaciones   In groups of three, tell each other three or four things you plan to do during your summer vacations, using the future tense. Your classmates may ask for more details.

2. Conditional tense (*Condicional*)

◆ Like the future, the Spanish conditional uses the infinitive as the stem for most verbs and has only one set of endings for all three conjugations.

Formation of the Conditional Tense			
Infinitive		*Stem*	*Endings*
trabajar	yo	trabajar-	**ía**
aprender	tú	aprender-	**ías**
escribir	Ud., él, ella	escribir-	**ía**
dar	nosotros(as)	dar-	**íamos**
hablar	vosotros(as)	hablar-	**íais**
preferir	Uds., ellos, ellas	preferir-	**ían**

—Me **gustaría** ir al parque.　　　"*I **would like** to go to the park.*"
—Nosotros **preferiríamos** ir a　　　"*We **would prefer** to go to the*
　la piscina.　　　　　　　　　　　*pool.*"

—Voy a invitar a Julia.　　　　　"*I'm going to invite Julia.*"
—Yo no la **invitaría.**　　　　　　"*I **would** not **invite** her.*"

◆ The verbs that are irregular in the future tense have the same irregular stems
　in the conditional. The endings are the same as those for regular verbs.

Irregular Conditional Stems		
Infinitive	*Stem*	*First-Person Sing.*
decir	dir-	**diría**
hacer	har-	**haría**
haber	habr-	**habría**
querer	querr-	**querría**
saber	sabr-	**sabría**
poder	podr-	**podría**
poner	pondr-	**pondría**
salir	saldr-	**saldría**
tener	tendr-	**tendría**
venir	vendr-	**vendría**

—¿Qué **podría** hacer yo para　　　"*What **could** I do to help you?*"
　ayudarte?
—**Podrías** traer las vendas.　　　"*You could bring the bandages.*"

¡Atención! The conditional of **hay** (impersonal form of **haber**) is **habría**.

　　Dijo que **habría** una reunión.　　*He said **there would be** a meeting.*

No sé...yo no
lo lavaría aquí.

◆ Uses of the conditional

　◆ The Spanish conditional is equivalent to the English *would* plus a verb.

　　—¿Qué **harías** tú?　　　　　　"*What **would** you **do**?*"
　　—Yo **iría** al médico.　　　　　"*I **would** go to the doctor.*"

◆ In Spanish, the conditional is also used to soften a request or to express politeness.

—¿**Podrías** venir un momento?   *"**Could you** come for a minute?"*
—Sí, en seguida.   *"Yes, right away."*

◖ **Online Study Center**

For more practice with lesson topics, see the related activities on the *¡Hola, amigos!* web site at college.hmco.com/PIC/holaamigos7e.

Práctica y conversación

A. En el consultorio de la Dra. Peña   While waiting in Dr. Peña's office you overhear the following exchanges. Complete them, using the conditional of the verbs given.

1. —Carlitos tiene acné.
   —Yo lo _____ (llevar) a un buen dermatólogo.
   —¿Tú crees que la Dra. Peña _____ (poder) recomendarme uno?
   —Yo se lo _____ (preguntar).

2. —Mamá está muy nerviosa y no sé qué hacer.
   —Yo le _____ (dar) un sedante.
   —Eso _____ (ser) muy difícil porque a ella no le gusta tomar medicinas.

3. —¿Tú crees que Ana y yo _____ (poder) ir al hospital a ver a Jorge?
   —Yo no _____ (ir) hoy porque acaban de operarlo.
   —Pues sus padres dijeron que ellos lo _____ (visitar) esta noche.

4. —Mi hijo tiene mucha acidez. ¿Qué le _____ (recomendar) tú?
   —Yo le _____ (sugerir) tomar un buen antiácido. Creo que _____ (mejorar) pronto.

5. —Pedro quiere que yo le compre un seguro médico; ¿qué _____ (hacer) tú en mi caso? ¿Se lo _____ (comprar)?
   —Bueno, yo no se lo _____ (comprar).

 B. Recomendaciones   In groups of three or four, decide what you would recommend to a friend who has health problems, doesn't exercise, and has bad eating habits. Compare your recommendations with those of other groups, and select the best ones.

Rodeo

Summary of the Tenses of the Indicative
(*Resumen de los tiempos del indicativo*)

Simple Tenses			
	-ar	**-er**	**-ir**
Presente	habl**o**	com**o**	viv**o**
Pretérito	habl**é**	com**í**	viv**í**
Imperfecto	habl**aba**	com**ía**	viv**ía**
Futuro	hablar**é**	comer**é**	vivir**é**
Condicional	hablar**ía**	comer**ía**	vivir**ía**

Compound Tenses			
Pretérito perfecto	**he** hablado	**he** comido	**he** vivido
Pretérito plus-cuamperfecto	**había** hablado	**había** comido	**había** vivido
Futuro perfecto[1]	**habré** hablado	**habré** comido	**habré** vivido
Condicional perfecto[1]	**habría** hablado	**habría** comido	**habría** vivido

[1]Optional material. See pages 340–345.

Práctica y conversación

Entreviste a su compañero(a)   Interview your partner, asking the following questions.

1. ¿Cuánto tiempo hace que estudias español?
2. ¿En qué año empezaste a estudiar español?
3. ¿Quién fue tu profesor(a) de español el semestre pasado?
4. ¿Habías hablado con el (la) profesor(a) antes de comenzar esta clase?
5. ¿Sabías un poco de español antes de venir a la universidad?
6. ¿Continuarás estudiando español?
7. ¿Qué tendrás que hacer para hablar español perfectamente?
8. ¿Has visitado algún país de habla hispana?
9. ¿En qué país de habla hispana te gustaría vivir?
10. ¿Qué ciudades importantes de los Estados Unidos has visitado?
11. ¿Qué te gustaba hacer cuando estabas en la escuela secundaria?
12. ¿Qué películas has visto últimamente?
13. ¿Qué tuviste que hacer hoy antes de venir a la clase?
14. ¿Vives cerca o lejos de la universidad?

Online Study Center

For more practice with lesson topics, see the related activities on the *¡Hola, amigos!* web site at college.hmco.com/PIC/holaamigos7e.

3. The imperfect subjunctive (*El imperfecto de subjuntivo*)

Forms

- To form the imperfect subjunctive of all Spanish verbs—regular and irregular—drop the **-ron** ending of the third-person plural of the preterit and add the following endings to the stem.

Imperfect Subjunctive Endings	
-ra	-´ramos
-ras	-rais
-ra	-ran

¡Atención!   Notice that an accent mark is required in the **nosotros(as)** form:
   ...que nosotros **habláramos**
   ...que nosotros **fuéramos**

Forms of the Imperfect Subjunctive

Verb	Third-Person Preterit	Stem	First-Person Sing. Imperf. Subjunctive
			(-ra form)
hablar	habla**ron**	habla-	**hablara**
aprender	aprendie**ron**	aprendie-	**aprendiera**
vivir	vivie**ron**	vivie-	**viviera**
dejar	deja**ron**	deja-	**dejara**
ir	fue**ron**	fue-	**fuera**
saber	supie**ron**	supie-	**supiera**
decir	dije**ron**	dije-	**dijera**
poner	pusie**ron**	pusie-	**pusiera**
pedir	pidie**ron**	pidie-	**pidiera**
estar	estuvie**ron**	estuvie-	**estuviera**

¡Atención! The imperfect subjunctive of **hay** (impersonal form of **haber**) is **hubiera**.

Online Study Center

For more practice with lesson topics, see the related activities on the *¡Hola, amigos!* web site at college.hmco.com/PIC/holaamigos7e.

Práctica

Conjugación   Supply the imperfect subjunctive forms of the following verbs.

1. *que yo:*   llenar, comer, vivir, decir, ir, admitir
2. *que tú:*   dejar, atender, abrir, poner, estar, elegir
3. *que él:*   volver, dormir, pedir, tener, alquilar, traer
4. *que nosotros:*   ver, ser, entrar, saber, hacer, pedir
5. *que ellas:*   leer, salir, llegar, sentarse, aprender, poder

Uses

◆ The imperfect subjunctive is always used in a subordinate clause when the verb of the main clause calls for the subjunctive and is in the past or the conditional.

| —¿Por qué no compraste los billetes? | "Why didn't you buy the tickets?" |
| —**Temía** que no **pudiéramos** viajar hoy. | "**I was afraid we wouldn't be able** to travel today." |

◆ When the verb of the main clause is in the present, but the subordinate clause refers to the past, the imperfect subjunctive is often used.

| —Oscar es un muchacho muy simpático. | "Oscar is a very charming young man." |
| —¡Sí! **Me alegro** de que **viniera** a vernos ayer. | "Yes! **I'm glad** (that) **he came** to see us yesterday." |

Práctica y conversación

Online Study Center

For more practice with lesson topics, see the related activities on the *¡Hola, amigos!* web site at college.hmco.com/PIC/holaamigos7e.

A. Instrucciones Indicate what Dr. Peña told some of her patients to do. Follow the model.

◆ MODELO: Sra. Paz, descanse.
Le dijo a la Sra. Paz que descansara.

1. Sr. Mena, tome un jarabe para la tos.
2. Elena y Sara, pidan turno para mañana.
3. Srta. Rivas, vaya a ver a un oculista.
4. Sra. Ruiz, hable con la recepcionista.
5. Sr. López, esté aquí mañana a las ocho. Venga en ayunas (*fasting*).
6. Miguel y Pablo, pídanle la receta a la enfermera.
7. Señores, espérenme unos minutos.
8. Señora, abra la boca y diga "ah".
9. Juanito, respira hondo.
10. Señora, dele un calmante a su papá.

B. Mi primera cita In groups of three, talk about what your parents told you to do and what not to do when you went out on your first date.

4. *If*-clauses (*Cláusulas que comienzan con* si)

◆ When a clause introduced by **si** refers to a situation that is hypothetical or contrary to fact, **si** is always followed by the imperfect subjunctive.

Contrary-to-fact

| —**Si** yo **tuviera** dinero, le daría 1.000 dólares a mi hijo. | "**If** I **had** money, I would give my son a thousand dollars." |
| —**Si** yo **fuera** tú, no le daría nada. | "**If** I **were** you, I wouldn't give him anything." |

Hypothetical

| **Si** yo **hablara** con el presidente... | *If* I **were to speak** to the president . . . |

Si yo **tuviera** dinero, le **daría**
1.000 dólares a mi hijo.

*If I **had** money, **I would give** a*
thousand dollars to my son.

◆ When the *if*-clause refers to something that is likely to happen or possible, the indicative is used.

—¿**Puedes** llevar a mi papá
al cardiólogo?
—Lo llevaré si **tengo**
tiempo.

*"**Can you** take my dad to*
the cardiologist?"
*"I will take him if **I**
have time."*

◆ The imperfect subjunctive is always used after the expression **como si** (*as if*) because it implies a condition that is contrary to fact.

—Marcos dice que necesito
un antibiótico.
—Sí, él habla **como si supiera**
algo de medicina.

"Marcos says that I need
an antibiotic."
*"Yes, he talks **as if he knew***
something about medicine."

Práctica y conversación

A. ¿Promesas o excusas? Complete each of the following statements with the correct form of the verb in parentheses. Use the imperfect subjunctive or the present indicative.

1. Si yo _____ (tener) tiempo te llevaré al médico.
2. Si nosotros _____ (poder) compraríamos las medicinas.
3. Si Elba _____ (comprar) las tijeras podemos ponerlas en el botiquín.
4. Si mis padres me _____ (dar) dinero yo podría pagar el seguro médico.
5. Si tú _____ (venir) temprano podremos llevar a los niños al pediatra.
6. Si Uds. _____ (traer) a Nora el doctor podría examinarla.

B. Si... Referring to the pictures below for ideas, tell what the following people would do if circumstances were different.

◆ MODELO: Yo no tengo dinero. Si...
Si yo tuviera dinero, viajaría.

1. Ellos no tienen hambre. Si...

2. Nosotros no podemos estudiar hoy. Si...

3. Tú tienes que trabajar. Si no...

4. Uds. no van a la fiesta. Si...

5. Hoy es sábado. Si...

6. El coche funciona. Si...

7. Laura no está enferma. Si...

8. La señora Soto no tiene el periódico. Si...

C. Si las cosas fueran diferentes In groups of three or four, discuss what you would do if circumstances in your lives were different. Include place of residence, schooling, work, and so on.

Rodeo

Summary of the Uses of the Subjunctive
(*Resumen de los usos del subjuntivo*)

Subjunctive vs. Infinitive

Use the subjunctive . . .	Use the infinitive . . .
1. After verbs of volition (when there is a change of subject).	**1.** After verbs of volition (where there is no change of subject).
Yo quiero que **él salga.**	**Yo** quiero **salir.**
2. After verbs of emotion (when there is a change of subject).	**2.** After verbs of emotion (when there is no change of subject).
Me alegro de que **tú estés** aquí.	**Me** alegro de **estar** aquí.
3. After impersonal expressions (when there is a subject).	**3.** After impersonal expressions (when speaking in general).
Es necesario que **él estudie.**	Es necesario **estudiar.**

Subjunctive vs. Indicative

Use the subjunctive . . .	Use the indicative . . .
1. To refer to something indefinite or nonexistent.	**1.** To refer to something that exists or is specific.
Busco una casa que **sea** grande. No hay nadie que lo **sepa.**	Tengo una casa que **es** grande. Hay alguien que lo **sabe.**
2. If the action is to occur at some indefinite time in the future as a condition of another action.	**2.** If the action has been completed or is habitual.
Cenarán cuando él **llegue.**	Cenaron cuando él **llegó.** Siempre cenan cuando él **llega.**
3. To express doubt, disbelief, and denial.	**3.** When there is no doubt, disbelief, or denial.
Dudo que **pueda** venir. Niego que él **esté** aquí. No creo que él **venga.**	No dudo que **puede** venir. No niego que él **está** aquí. Creo que él **viene.**
4. In an *if*-clause, to refer to something contrary to fact, impossible, or very improbable.	**4.** In an *if*-clause, when referring to something that is factual, probable, or very possible.
Si **pudiera,** iría. Si el presidente me **invitara** a la Casa Blanca, yo aceptaría.	Si **puedo,** iré. Si Juan me **invita** a su casa, aceptaré.

Práctica y conversación

Online Study Center

For more practice with lesson topics, see the related activities on the *¡Hola, amigos!* web site at college.hmco.com/PIC/holaamigos7e.

A. La carta de Marisa Marisa wrote this letter to her parents from Sevilla. Complete it, using the subjunctive, indicative, or infinitive of the verbs that appear in parentheses.

Sevilla, 10 de junio

Queridos papá y mamá:

Recibí la tarjeta que me mandaron de Acapulco. Me alegro de que se _____ (estar) divirtiendo; cuando _____ (volver) a México el año próximo, yo quiero _____ (ir) con Uds. También me gustaría que Uds. _____ (poder) visitar Sevilla, porque es una ciudad magnífica.

Ana y yo encontramos un piso que _____ (estar) en el centro, cerca de la universidad. Si Uds. _____ (decidir) venir a visitarme, tenemos un dormitorio extra. No creo que los padres de Ana _____ (poder) venir, como nos habían dicho, porque no les dan vacaciones.

Mamá, es verdad que la comida de aquí _____ (ser) muy buena, pero no hay nadie que _____ (cocinar) tan bien como tú, así que en cuanto yo _____ (llegar) a California, quiero que me _____ (hacer) tu famoso pollo con mole[1].

Ayer fuimos con unos amigos a visitar la mezquita y después fuimos a un café en el barrio Santa Cruz. ¡Me estoy enamorando de Sevilla! Si _____ (poder), me quedaría a vivir aquí. ¡No se rían! Ya sé que no puedo vivir lejos de Uds.

Díganle a Héctor que quiero que me _____ (escribir) y me _____ (contar) cómo le va en la universidad.

Besos,

Marisa

B. ¿Qué recuerdan Uds.? With a partner, prepare five or six questions about Marisa's letter. Then join two classmates and ask them your questions and answer theirs.

---

[1]**Mole,** a sauce made with many spices and unsweetened chocolate, is used in Mexican cuisine.

Entre nosotros

¡Conversemos!

 Para conocernos mejor Get to know your partner better by asking each other the following questions.

1. ¿Necesitas que el (la) médico(a) te examine?
2. ¿El consultorio de tu médico(a) está cerca de tu casa?
3. ¿Eres alérgico(a) a alguna medicina o comida? ¿A cuál?
4. ¿Qué tomas cuando tienes dolor de cabeza?
5. ¿Has tenido que tomar un sedante alguna vez?
6. ¿Qué haces cuando tienes gripe?
7. ¿Has tenido que ir al oculista últimamente?
8. La última vez que fuiste a tu médico, ¿qué te recetó?
9. ¿Cuándo tendrás que volver a ver al médico?
10. ¿Te gustaría ser médico(a) o enfermero(a)?

 Una encuesta Interview your classmates to identify who fits the following descriptions. Include your instructor, but remember to use the **Ud.** form when addressing him or her.

Nombre

1. Trabajaría en un hospital.
2. Necesita ir al oculista.
3. Tiene turno para ver al médico el mes próximo.
4. Toma Tylenol cuando tiene fiebre.
5. Toma vitamina C todos los días.
6. Es alérgico(a) a la penicilina.
7. Ha tenido gripe recientemente.
8. Toma antiácidos frecuentemente.
9. Espera poder descansar este fin de semana.
10. Da consejos como si fuera médico(a).

Y ahora... Write a brief summary about what you have learned about your classmates.

¿Cómo lo decimos? What would you say in the following situations? What might the other person say? Act out the scenes with a partner.

1. You have the flu. Tell the doctor what your symptoms are.
2. You are giving advice to someone who has a cold and a bad cough.
3. Tell someone what your mother wants you to do when you are sick.

¿Qué dice aquí? Read the ad, and answer the questions that follow.

1. Si una persona necesita perder peso (*weight*), ¿a que médico debe ir?
2. ¿Cuál es la especialidad de Luis Díaz?
3. Una amiga mía está embarazada. ¿Por qué debe ver a la Dra. Vega?
4. ¿Qué pruebas rutinarias debe hacerse una mujer?
5. ¿Qué servicios ofrece el Dr. Vargas?
6. ¿Por qué cree Ud. que el Dr. Díaz tiene más pacientes adolescentes?
7. Hace tiempo que no voy al médico. ¿Por qué debo ver a la Dra. López?
8. ¿Puedo ir al Centro Médico Regional el sábado? ¿Por qué ?
9. Yo no tengo seguro, ¿puedo ir a ver a alguno de los médicos del Centro?
10. ¿Cuál es la dirección y el número de teléfono del Centro Médico Regional?

CENTRO MÉDICO REGIONAL
Para el cuidado de la salud de toda la familia

Alonso Cano, 192, Madrid • 3-27-93-84

Dra. Rita López
Medicina general
Exámenes físicos completos
Programas para controlar el peso
Alergias
Rayos X - Laboratorio

Dr. Rafael Vargas
Oculista
Examen completo de la vista
Anteojos y lentes de contacto
Cirugía de cataratas
Cirugía con láser

Dr. Luis Díaz
Dermatólogo
Enfermedades de la piel
Cirugía cosmética
Acné

Dra. Marta Vega
Ginecóloga Obstetra
Pruebas de embarazo
Papanicolau
Mamografías

Horas de consulta:
Lunes, martes y jueves de 9 a 5
Miércoles y viernes de 8 a 12

Aceptamos todo tipo de seguro
Planes de pago para pacientes
sin seguro

Llamadas de emergencia las 24 horas

Un dicho

Es mejor prevenir que curar.

Another saying! What does it mean? Have you thought of an English equivalent? Use it every chance you get.

Para escribir

Con el doctor Write a dialogue between you and your doctor. Among the things you might discuss are: symptoms, general questions the doctor might ask, any questions you have, the advice and/or treatment the doctor offers.

Lectura

Estrategia de lectura   Reading a poem is different from reading a story or an essay. A poet often uses words in original ways to express his/her feelings. Think about the following words from *Rimas*, which you are going to read. Try to visualize them individually, and then together. What feelings do they convey?

tierra	*earth*	mundo	*world*
cielo	*heaven*	beso	*kiss*
alma	*soul*	suspiros	*sighs*
sol	*sun*	lágrimas	*tears*
poesía	*poetry*	amor	*love*

Vamos a leer   As you read this poem, try to answer the following questions.

1. ¿En quién cree hoy el poeta? ¿Por qué?
2. ¿De qué color son los ojos de la mujer que el poeta ama?
3. ¿Qué le pregunta la mujer al poeta?
4. ¿Qué le contesta el poeta?
5. ¿Qué daría el poeta por una mirada (*look*) de su amada?
6. ¿Qué daría por una sonrisa (*smile*)?
7. ¿Qué cree que sería lo más maravilloso para el poeta?
8. ¿Con qué compara el poeta los suspiros y las lágrimas?

Gustavo Adolfo Bécquer nació en Sevilla, España, en 1836 y murió en el año 1870. Se le considera un precursor de la poesía moderna, y se le conoce mayormente por sus Rimas *y sus* Leyendas. *Sus poemas son breves y suponen la máxima condensación lírica. Los temas principales de su poesía son el amor, la soledad y el misterio.*

Video

Rimas

GUSTAVO ADOLFO BÉCQUER

XVII

Hoy la tierra y los cielos me sonríen;
hoy llega al fondo de mi alma el sol;
hoy la he visto..., la he visto y me ha mirado...
¡Hoy creo en Dios!

XXI

"¿Qué es poesía?," dices mientras clavas
en mi pupila tu pupila azul;
¿Qué es poesía? ¿Y tú me lo preguntas?
Poesía... eres tú.

XXIII

Por una mirada, un mundo;
por una sonrisa, un cielo;
por un beso... ¡yo no sé
qué te diera por un beso!

XXXVIII

¡Los suspiros son aire y van al aire!
¡Las lágrimas son agua y van al mar!
Dime, mujer, cuando el amor se olvida,
¿sabes tú a dónde va?

Díganos Answer the following questions based on your own thoughts or experiences.

1. ¿Está Ud. enamorado(a)? ¿De quién?
2. ¿De qué color son los ojos de su amado(a)?
3. ¿A quién le ha dado Ud. un beso últimamente?
4. ¿Ha tenido Ud. un amor que ahora sólo es parte de su pasado?

¡Uno nunca sabe...!

Marisa y Pablo están estudiando juntos. Él se queja de un montón de problemas físicos y ella le dice que es un hipocondríaco.

Continúan hablando, y los dos admiten que se necesitan el uno al otro. ¿Continuarán siendo amigos...?

El mundo hispánico

 ## España

- España forma con Portugal la Península Ibérica, y es el tercer país europeo en cuanto a extensión. Por su situación entre el resto de Europa y África siempre ha poseído considerable valor (*value*) estratégico, y en su suelo se mezclaron (*mixed*) y fundieron (*melted*) diversos grupos étnicos provenientes (*coming*) de una gran variedad de civilizaciones; entre ellas, las más importantes fueron la romana, la judía y la árabe (*Arabic*).

- El relieve de España varía desde las cordilleras hasta los valles, llanuras (*plains*) y extensas mesetas. En los Pirineos, que sirven de frontera con Francia, se encuentran algunos de los picos más altos de Europa.

- Por su clima y sus magníficas playas, España es uno de los países de más turismo en el mundo.

- El sistema de gobierno español es una monarquía constitucional. El actual rey (*king*) es Juan Carlos de Borbón. España pertenece a la Unión Europea y su moneda es el euro.

▲ El Templo de la Sagrada Familia, en Barcelona.

▲ Admirando unas pinturas en el famoso Museo del Prado en Madrid

- Madrid, la capital, es una ciudad moderna, y hoy en día es uno de los centros de negocios más importantes del mundo. Es una ciudad de gran movimiento y se dice que "Madrid nunca duerme". Sus grandes avenidas, centros culturales, plazas y museos son puntos de atracción turística. A pesar de ser una gran metrópoli, Madrid conserva grandes extensiones de áreas verdes, como el parque del Buen Retiro, La Rosaleda, el Parque del Oeste y el Prado. En Madrid está el Museo del Prado, uno de los mejores del mundo. Allí se conserva la colección más grande de las obras de pintores españoles como Murillo, Velázquez, El Greco y Goya, entre otros.

- En el norte de España están Barcelona, la segunda ciudad más grande del país y Pamplona, conocida por sus encierros y sus corridas de toros el día de San Fermín.

- En el sur de España se encuentran Granada, Sevilla y Córdoba, ciudades de gran belleza donde se ve la influencia árabe. La Alhambra de Granada, la Giralda de Sevilla y la Mezquita (*Mosque*) de Córdoba son verdaderas joyas arquitectónicas. Sevilla tiene además el maravilloso Parque de María Luisa, donde se encuentra la gran Plaza de España. En esta plaza, construida enteramente de azulejos (*ceramic tiles*) de tipo andaluz, están representadas escenas históricas de las cincuenta provincias de España.

Guernica, uno de los cuadros más famosos de Picasso. Museo Reina Sofía, Madrid.

♦ Las playas de Andalucía, conocidas como la "Costa del Sol", están entre las más famosas atracciones turísticas del país, y son visitadas todo el año gracias a su clima cálido, aun en invierno.

♦ España es rica en tradiciones. Cada provincia tiene sus propios trajes regionales, música, artesanía y cocina típicas.

♦ Aunque no hay ninguna región española que no produzca su propio vino, Andalucía es la gran tierra del vino, por su gran calidad y variedad. Andalucía es famosa, además, por el cultivo del olivo y, en la música y en la danza, por el flamenco.

♦ España ha aportado (*exerted*) su influencia al mundo tanto en el campo de la ciencia como en el de la cultura, y ha obtenido premios Nobel en ambos campos. En la literatura, España se ha destacado desde la Edad Media. Entre sus numerosos escritores está Miguel de Cervantes, creador de *Don Quijote,* una de las obras literarias que más ha influido en todo el mundo. Tres grandes pintores del siglo XX, conocidos mundialmente, son españoles: Salvador Dalí, Joan Miró y Pablo Picasso.

▲ Corriendo delante de los toros en la Feria de San Fermín, en Pamplona

◄ Paisaje de invierno. Lago San Mauricio, Parque Nacional Aigüestortes, en los Pirineos.

Online Study Center

For more practice with lesson topics, see the related activities on the *¡Hola, amigos!* web site at college.hmco.com/PIC/holaamigos7e.

Comentarios... With a partner, discuss in Spanish what impressed you the most about Spain. Compare this country to your own. Which places do you want to visit in this country and why?

Tome este examen

Lección 13

A. Subjunctive to express doubt Complete the following sentences, using the subjunctive or the indicative of the verbs in parentheses.

1. Estoy seguro de que ellos _____ (ser) alérgicos a las fresas.
2. Dudo que ella _____ (estar) en el hospital.
3. No estoy seguro de que él _____ (poder) llevarnos al hospital.
4. Estamos seguros de que ellos _____ (venir) hoy.
5. No dudo que ellos _____ (servir) el almuerzo a esa hora.

B. Subjunctive to express disbelief and denial Rewrite each sentence, using the subjunctive or the indicative, as appropriate.

1. Están llamando la ambulancia. (No es cierto que...)
2. Ellos van a quedarse en el hospital. (No creo que...)
3. Ella prefiere venir con nosotros. (Es verdad que ella...)
4. Cobran 50 dólares por las radiografías. (Creo que...)
5. El cuarto no tiene calefacción. (No es verdad que...)
6. Ella está en el hospital. (Luis niega que...)

C. Subjunctive with certain conjunctions Complete each sentence with the Spanish equivalent of the word(s) in parentheses.

1. Voy a llamar al médico en cuanto ellos _____. (*finish*)
2. No vamos a menos que _____ ir con él. (*we can*)
3. Voy a llamar a la enfermera para que nos _____ la radiografía. (*bring*)
4. Vamos a ir tan pronto como ellos _____ a servir la comida. (*begin*)
5. Siempre voy a ese hospital cuando _____. (*I need a doctor*)
6. En cuanto yo _____ a casa, voy a llamar a mis padres. (*arrive*)
7. Aunque _____, vamos al comedor. (*I'm not hungry*)
8. Mañana vamos a ir al cine aunque _____. (*it may rain*)

D. First-person plural commands Answer the following questions, using the information provided in parentheses and first-person plural (**nosotros**) commands.

1. ¿Dónde nos quedamos? (aquí)
2. ¿A quién se lo decimos? (a nadie)
3. ¿A qué hora nos levantamos? (a las siete)
4. ¿Qué preguntamos? (el precio de los análisis)
5. ¿A quién se lo damos? (a la enfermera)
6. ¿Adónde vamos? (a la sala de rayos X)

E. ¿Qué? and ¿cuál? with *ser*   Complete the following, using **qué** or **cuál.**

1. ¿_____ es tu dirección?
2. ¿_____ es tu número de teléfono?
3. ¿_____ es el béisbol?
4. ¿_____ es una enchilada?
5. ¿_____ es su opinión?

F. Vocabulary   Write the vocabulary words from **Lección 13** that correspond to the following words or descriptions.

1. Trabaja con el médico.
2. parte del brazo
3. perder el conocimiento
4. Tenemos diez en las manos.
5. Tenemos treinta y dos en la boca.
6. suceder
7. tener dudas
8. seguir
9. La usamos para subir y bajar.
10. Las uso para caminar.
11. Los necesitamos para ver.
12. Está dentro de la boca.
13. quebrarse
14. instrumento musical

G. Culture   Complete the following sentences, based on the cultural notes you have read.

1. En la mayoría de los países hispanos, los hospitales son _____ .
2. En las casas de _____ se ofrecen cuidados médicos urgentes.

Lección 14

A. Future tense
Change the verbs in these sentences to indicate what will take place.

1. Van al consultorio y hablan con el médico.
2. Tú la pesas y le tomas la presión.
3. Rosa trae las radiografías y las pone en la oficina.
4. Yo vengo al hospital y pido turno.
5. La enfermera me pone una inyección y me da el jarabe.

B. Conditional tense
Complete the following sentences, using the conditional form of the verbs in parentheses.

1. Nosotros no _____ (hablar) con ellos.
2. Yo _____ (salir) temprano.
3. ¿Tú _____ (hacer) eso?
4. Ella no _____ (saber) qué hacer.
5. ¿Adónde _____ (ir) Ud. hoy?
6. Ellos le _____ (pedir) turno.

C. Forms of the imperfect subjunctive
Give the imperfect subjunctive of the following verbs according to the cues provided.

1. nosotros / poder
2. tú / entender
3. ellos / poner
4. yo / querer
5. Ud. / traer
6. Uds. / tener
7. nosotras / saber
8. ella / decir
9. yo / ir
10. tú / ser

D. Uses of the imperfect subjunctive
Complete the following sentences using the imperfect subjunctive of the verbs given.

1. Ella me pidió que _____ (traer) la receta.
2. Yo esperaba que mis padres _____ (venir) hoy.
3. Ellos dudaban que yo _____ (estar) enfermo.
4. No había nadie que _____ (saber) dónde estaba el médico.
5. Te dije que no era verdad que ella _____ (tener) esa enfermedad.
6. Mi esposo quería que yo _____ (pedir) turno para hoy.

E. *If*-clauses   Complete each sentence with the equivalent of the words in parentheses.

1. Yo compraría el antibiótico... (*if I had the money*)
2. Vamos a ir a verte... (*if we have time*)
3. Nosotros iríamos a Barcelona... (*if we could*)
4. (*If you see her*)..., dígale que venga mañana.
5. Ella le habla a su esposo... (*as if she were his mother*)

F. Vocabulary   Complete the following sentences, using vocabulary from **Lección 14.**

1. Tiene una temperatura de treinta y nueve _____.
2. El médico me recetó un jarabe para la _____.
3. Espero que Ud. se _____ con estas medicinas.
4. El médico le va a _____ un antibiótico.
5. Necesita un _____ porque tiene mucho dolor.
6. Si tienes acné ve a un _____ y si tienes problemas con el corazón a un _____.
7. Necesito las _____ para cortar las vendas.
8. No se mejoró; se _____.
9. Mi _____ con el médico es para hoy.
10. No tuvo que pagar el hospital porque tiene _____ médico.
11. Puse el esparadrapo en el _____.
12. Por _____ no tiene pulmonía.

G. Culture   Circle the correct answer, base on the cultural notes you have read.

1. (Barcelona / Madrid) es la capital de España.
2. Barcelona es la (segunda / tercera) ciudad más grande del país.
3. En el sur de España se encuentra (Sevilla / Valencia).
4. La música típica de Andalucía es el (tango / flamenco).

Un poco más (*Material suplementario*)

1. Compound tenses of the indicative

Future perfect (*El futuro perfecto*)

◆ Forms

The future perfect tense in Spanish corresponds closely in formation and meaning to the same tense in English. The Spanish future perfect is formed with the future tense of the auxiliary verb **haber** + past participle of the main verb.

Formation of the Future Perfect Tense		
	Future of **haber** +	*Past Participle*
yo	**habré**	**terminado**	I will have finished
tú	**habrás**	**vuelto**	you (*fam.*) will have returned
Ud., él, ella	**habrá**	**comido**	you (*form.*), he, she will have eaten
nosotros(as)	**habremos**	**escrito**	we will have written
vosotros(as)	**habréis**	**dicho**	you (*fam.*) will have said
Uds., ellos, ellas	**habrán**	**salido**	you (*form., fam.*), they will have left

◆ Use

Like its English equivalent, the Spanish future perfect tense is used to express an action that will have taken place by a certain time in the future.

—¿Tus padres estarán aquí para el dos de junio?
—Sí, para esa fecha ya **habrán vuelto** de Madrid.

"Will your parents be here by June second?"
*"Yes, by that date **they will have returned** from Madrid."*

Online Study Center

For more practice with lesson topics, see the related activities on the *¡Hola, amigos!* web site at college.hmco.com/PIC/holaamigos7e.

Práctica y conversación

A. Complete each sentence with the corresponding form of the future perfect tense.

1. Para junio nosotros _____ (volver) del viaje, pero Carlos no _____ (llegar) de México todavía.
2. Para las nueve yo _____ (servir) la cena y ellos _____ (comer).
3. ¿A qué hora _____ (terminar) tú el trabajo?
4. ¿Ya _____ (leer) Uds. la novela para la próxima semana?
5. Para las doce la secretaria _____ (escribir) todas las cartas.

B. Interview a partner, using the following questions.

1. ¿Habremos terminado esta lección para la semana que viene?
2. ¿Las clases habrán terminado para el 15 de junio?
3. ¿Te habrás graduado (*graduate*) para el año que viene?
4. ¿Tú habrás vuelto a tu casa para las 10 de la noche?
5. ¿Tú y tu familia habrán terminado de cenar para las siete de la noche?
6. ¿Te habrás acostado para las once de la noche?

C. Use your imagination to complete each statement, using the future perfect tense.

1. Para el próximo año yo...
2. Para diciembre mis padres...
3. Para el sábado mi mejor amigo(a)...
4. Para la próxima semana el (la) profesor(a)...
5. Para el verano nosotros(as)...
6. Para esta noche tú...

Conditional perfect (*El condicional perfecto*)

◆ Forms

The conditional perfect tense is formed with the conditional of the verb **haber** + *past participle* of the main verb.

Formation of the Conditional Perfect Tense			
	Conditional of **haber**	+ *Past Participle*	
yo	**habría**	**hablado**	I would have spoken
tú	**habrías**	**comido**	you (*fam.*) would have eaten
Ud., él, ella	**habría**	**vuelto**	you (*form.*), he, she would have returned
nosotros(as)	**habríamos**	**dicho**	we would have said
vosotros(as)	**habríais**	**roto**	you (*fam.*) would have broken
Uds., ellos, ellas	**habrían**	**hecho**	you (*form., fam.*), they would have done, made

◆ Uses

The conditional perfect (expressed in English by *would have* + past participle of the main verb) is used:

◆ To indicate an action that *would have taken place* (*but didn't*), if a certain condition had been true.

De haber sabido[1] que venía, lo **habría llamado.**	*Had I known that he was coming, I would have called him.*

◆ To refer to a future action in relation to the past.

Él dijo que para mayo **habrían terminado** la clase.	*He said that by May **they would have finished** the class.*

---

[1]**De haber sabido** is an impersonal expression.

Online Study Center

For more practice with lesson topics, see the related activities on the *¡Hola, amigos!* web site at college.hmco.com/PIC/holaamigos7e.

Práctica y conversación

A. Complete each sentence, using the conditional perfect tense of the verbs given in parentheses.

1. De haber sabido que él no estaba aquí, yo no _____ (venir).
2. De haber sabido que yo no tenía dinero, él me lo _____ (comprar).
3. Él dijo que para mayo nosotros _____ (volver).
4. Carlos nos dijo que para septiembre tú _____ (terminar).
5. De haber sabido que Uds. tenían los libros, ellos se los _____ (pedir).
6. Él me dijo que para esta noche ellos _____ (llamar).

B. Using the conditional perfect tense and the cues provided, tell what you and the other people would have done differently.

◆ **MODELO:** Tú fuiste de vacaciones a México.   (yo)
Yo habría ido a España.

1. Ellos comieron hamburguesas.   (yo)
2. Teresa salió con Ernesto.   (tú)
3. Yo preparé pollo para la cena.   (ellos)
4. Uds. estuvieron en México por una semana.   (nosotras)
5. Nosotros invitamos a muchas personas.   (Marta)
6. Yo escribí las cartas en español.   (Uds.)

C. With a classmate, discuss what you did last summer. Say whether you would have done the same thing as your partner or if you would have done something different.

2. Compound tenses of the subjunctive

Present perfect subjunctive (*El pretérito perfecto de subjuntivo*)

◆ Forms

The present perfect subjunctive tense is formed with the present subjunctive of the auxiliary verb **haber** + *past participle* of the main verb.

Formation of the Present Perfect Subjunctive		
Present Subjunctive of haber	+	*Past Participle*
yo	haya	hablado
tú	hayas	comido
Ud., él, ella	haya	vivido
nosotros(as)	hayamos	hecho
vosotros(as)	hayáis	ido
Uds., ellos, ellas	hayan	puesto

Práctica

Online Study Center

For more practice with lesson topics, see the related activities on the *¡Hola, amigos!* web site at college.hmco.com/PIC/holaamigos7e.

Conjugation   For each subject below, conjugate the following verbs in the present perfect subjunctive.

1. *que yo:*   escuchar, oír, divertirse, decir
2. *que tú:*   llenar, despertarse, volver, pedir
3. *que ella:*   celebrar, poner, estacionar, escribir
4. *que nosotros:*   hacer, decidir, vestirse, ayudar
5. *que ellos:*   conversar, abrir, morir, irse

◆ Uses

The Spanish present perfect subjunctive tense is used in the same way as the present perfect tense in English, but only in sentences that call for the subjunctive in the subordinate clause.

—Espero que Eva **haya traído** las cintas.   *"I hope (that) Eva **has brought** the tapes."*
—Sí, y también ha traído la grabadora.   *"Yes, and she has also brought the tape recorder."*

—Álvaro prometió llevar a los niños al cine.   *"Álvaro promised to take the children to the movies."*
—Dudo que lo **haya hecho.**   *"I doubt that he **has done** it."*

Práctica y conversación

Online Study Center

For more practice with lesson topics, see the related activities on the *¡Hola, amigos!* web site at college.hmco.com/PIC/holaamigos7e.

A.   Rewrite the following sentences, using the cues in parentheses. Make any necessary changes.

◆ **MODELO:**   Ha llevado el coche al taller de mecánica.
       Espero que haya llevado el coche al taller de mecánica.

1. Ha estado aquí sólo un momento.   (Dudo)
2. Han comprado una casa nueva.   (Espero)
3. Ha podido celebrar su aniversario.   (No creo)
4. Has perdido parte del interés.   (Es posible)
5. No hemos comprado la alfombra.   (Siento)
6. Me he divertido mucho en la fiesta.   (No es verdad)
7. Han pasado unos días felices.   (Me alegro de)
8. Le han dado la dirección del teatro.   (Espero)
9. Le han mandado el dinero.   (No creo)
10. Han ido al concierto.   (No es cierto)

B.   Complete the following dialogues by supplying the present perfect subjunctive of the verbs given. Then act them out with a partner.

1. —Espero que los chicos _____ (volver).
   —Dudo que ya _____ (regresar) porque es muy temprano.
   —Temo que _____ (tener) un accidente.
   —Tú te preocupas demasiado.
2. —¿Hay alguien que _____ (estar) en Madrid alguna vez?
   —No, aquí no hay nadie que _____ (ir) a España.

3. —Siento que Uds. no _____ (poder) terminar el trabajo.

—No es verdad que no lo _____ (terminar).

4. —¿Ellos van a vivir en San Diego?

—Sí, pero no creo que ya _____ (alquilar) un apartamento.

5. —Me alegro de que tú _____ (conseguir) el puesto.

—Yo también.

C. Use your imagination to complete each statement, using the present perfect subjunctive tense.

1. Me alegro mucho de que mis padres...

2. Siento mucho que los invitados...

3. Espero que la clase de español...

4. No creo que los estudiantes...

5. No es cierto que yo...

6. Me sorprende que el concierto...

7. Dudo que el (la) profesor(a)...

8. No es verdad que él...

Pluperfect subjunctive (*El pluscuamperfecto de subjuntivo*)

◆ Forms

The Spanish pluperfect subjunctive is formed with the imperfect subjunctive of the auxiliary verb **haber** + *past participle* of the main verb.

Formation of the Pluperfect Subjunctive Tense		
Imperfect Subjunctive of haber	+	*Past Participle*
yo	**hubiera**	**hablado**
tú	**hubieras**	**comido**
Ud., él, ella	**hubiera**	**vivido**
nosotros(as)	**hubiéramos**	**visto**
vosotros(as)	**hubierais**	**hecho**
Uds., ellos, ellas	**hubieran**	**vuelto**

◆ Use

The Spanish pluperfect subjunctive tense is used in the same way the past perfect is used in English, but in sentences in which the main clause calls for the subjunctive.

Yo dudaba que ellos **hubieran llegado.**	*I doubted that they **had arrived.***
Yo esperaba que tú **hubieras pagado** tus cuentas.	*I was hoping that you **had paid** your bills.*

Práctica

Online Study Center

For more practice with lesson topics, see the related activities on the *¡Hola, amigos!* web site at college.hmco.com/PIC/holaamigos7e.

A. Rewrite the following sentences, using the cues in parentheses. Make any necessary changes.

◆ **MODELO:** Él se alegra de que ellos hayan hecho el trabajo.   (Él se alegró)
Él se alegró de que ellos hubieran hecho el trabajo.

1. Nosotros sentimos que hayas estado solo en Lima.   (Nosotros sentíamos)
2. Yo espero que Uds. hayan hecho el trabajo.   (Yo esperaba)
3. Siente que yo no haya podido venir el sábado.   (Sintió)
4. No creo que hayas comprado esas sábanas.   (No creí)
5. Me sorprende que no hayas cambiado el pasaje.   (Me sorprendió)
6. Me alegro de que hayamos conseguido la reservación.   (Me alegré)
7. Es probable que ellos hayan tenido que transbordar.   (Era probable)
8. No es verdad que él haya llegado tarde.   (No era verdad)

B. Write the following sentences in Spanish.

1. We were hoping that they had done the work.
2. I was sorry you had been sick.
3. They were glad that he had bought the tickets for the trip.
4. I didn't think that they hadn't gotten a discount.
5. We were glad that you had brought your driver's license.

C. Use the pluperfect subjunctive to finish the following in an original manner.

1. Mis padres se alegraron de que yo...
2. Yo esperaba que mis amigos...
3. Ellos sintieron que nosotros...
4. Aquí no había nadie que...
5. ¿Había alguien en esa familia que...?
6. Mi compañero de cuarto dudaba que yo...

Appendices

A: Spanish Sounds

Vowels

There are five distinct vowels in Spanish: **a, e, i, o, u.** Each vowel has only one basic, constant sound. The pronunciation of each vowel is constant, clear, and brief. The length of the sound is practically the same whether it is produced in a stressed or unstressed syllable.[1]

While producing the sounds of the English stressed vowels that most closely resemble the Spanish ones, the speaker changes the position of the tongue, lips, and lower jaw, so that the vowel actually starts as one sound and then *glides* into another. In Spanish, however, the tongue, lips, and jaw keep a constant position during the production of the sound.

English: ban*a*na   **Spanish:** ban*a*na

The stress falls on the same vowel and syllable in both Spanish and English, but the English stressed *a* is longer than the Spanish stressed **a.**

English: ban*a*na   **Spanish:** ban*a*na

Note also that the English stressed *a* has a sound different from the other *a*'s in the word, while the Spanish **a** sound remains constant.

a   in Spanish sounds similar to the English *a* in the word *father.*

alta   casa   palma   Ana   cama   Panamá   alma   apagar

e   is pronounced like the English *e* in the word *eight.*

mes   entre   este   deje   ese   encender   teme   prender

i   has a sound similar to the English *ee* in the word *see.*

fin   ir   sí   sin   dividir   Trini   difícil

o   is similar to the English *o* in the word *no,* but without the glide.

toco   como   poco   roto   corto   corro   solo   loco

u   is pronounced like the English *oo* sound in the word *shoot* or the *ue* sound in the word *Sue.*

su   Lulú   Úrsula   cultura   un   luna   sucursal   Uruguay

---

[1] In a stressed syllable, the prominence of the vowel is indicated by its loudness.

Diphthongs and triphthongs

When unstressed **i** or **u** falls next to another vowel in a syllable, it unites with that vowel to form what is called a *diphthong*. Both vowels are pronounced as one syllable. Their sounds do not change; they are only pronounced more rapidly and with a glide. For example:

traiga   Lidia   treinta   siete   oigo   adiós
Aurora   agua   bueno   antiguo   ciudad   Luis

A triphthong is the union of three vowels, a stressed vowel between two unstressed ones (**i** or **u**) in the same syllable. For example: Para**guay,** estudi**éis.**

NOTE: Stressed **i** and **u** do not form diphthongs with other vowels, except in the combinations **iu** and **ui**. For example: **rí**-o, sa-**bí**-ais.

In syllabication, diphthongs and triphthongs are considered a single vowel; their components cannot be separated.

Consonants

p   Spanish **p** is pronounced in a manner similar to the English *p* sound, but without the puff of air that follows after the English sound is produced.

pesca   pude   puedo   parte   papá
postre   piña   puente   Paco

k   The Spanish **k** sound, represented by the letters **k** and **c** before **a, o, u,** or a consonant, and **qu,** is similar to the English *k* sound, but without the puff of air.

casa   comer   cuna   clima   acción   que
quinto   queso   aunque   quiosco   kilómetro   kilo

t   Spanish **t** is produced by touching the back of the upper front teeth with the tip of the tongue. It has no puff of air as in the English *t*.

todo   antes   corto   Guatemala   diente
resto   tonto   roto   tanque

d   The Spanish consonant **d** has two different sounds depending on its position. At the beginning of an utterance and after **n** or **l**, the tip of the tongue presses the back of the upper front teeth.

día   doma   dice   dolor   dar
anda   Aldo   caldo   el deseo   un domicilio

In all other positions the sound of **d** is similar to the *th* sound in the English word *they,* but softer.

medida   todo   nada   nadie   medio
puedo   moda   queda   nudo

g The Spanish consonant **g** is similar to the English *g* sound in the word *guy* except before **e** or **i.**

goma glotón gallo gloria lago alga
gorrión garra guerra angustia algo Dagoberto

j The sound of Spanish **j** (or **g** before **e** and **i**) is similar to a strongly exaggerated English *h* sound.

gemir juez jarro gitano agente
juego giro bajo gente

b, v There is no difference in sound between Spanish **b** and **v.** Both letters are pronounced alike. At the beginning of an utterance or after **m** or **n, b** and **v** have a sound identical to the English *b* sound in the word *boy.*

vivir beber vamos barco enviar
hambre batea bueno vestido

When pronounced between vowels, the Spanish **b** and **v** sound is produced by bringing the lips together but not closing them, so that some air may pass through.

sábado autobús yo voy su barco

y, ll In most countries, Spanish **ll** and **y** have a sound similar to the English sound in the word *yes.*

el llavero un yelmo el yeso su yunta llama yema
oye trayecto trayectoria mayo milla bella

NOTE: When it stands alone or is at the end of a word, Spanish **y** is pronounced like the vowel **i.**

rey hoy y doy buey muy voy estoy soy

r The sound of Spanish **r** is similar to the English *dd* sound in the word *ladder.*

crema aroma cara arena aro
harina toro oro eres portero

rr Spanish **rr** and also **r** in an initial position and after **n, l,** or **s** are pronounced with a very strong trill. This trill is produced by bringing the tip of the tongue near the alveolar ridge and letting it vibrate freely while the air passes through the mouth.

rama carro Israel cierra roto
perro alrededor rizo corre Enrique

s Spanish **s** is represented in most of the Spanish world by the letters **s, z,** and **c** before **e** or **i.** The sound is very similar to the English sibilant *s* in the word *sink.*

sale sitio presidente signo
salsa seda suma vaso
sobrino ciudad cima canción
zapato zarza cerveza centro

h   The letter **h** is silent in Spanish.

hoy   hora   hilo   ahora
humor   huevo   horror almohada

ch   Spanish **ch** is pronounced like the English *ch* in the word *chief.*

hecho   chico   coche   Chile
mucho   muchacho salchicha

f   Spanish *f* is identical in sound to the English *f.*

difícil   feo   fuego   forma
fácil   fecha   foto   fueron

l   Spanish **l** is similar to the English *l* in the word *let.*

dolor   lata   ángel   lago   sueldo
los   pelo   lana   general   fácil

m   Spanish **m** is pronounced like the English *m* in the word *mother.*

mano   moda   mucho   muy
mismo   tampoco   multa   cómoda

n   In most cases, Spanish **n** has a sound similar to the English *n.*

nada   nunca   ninguno   norte
entra   tiene   sienta

The sound of Spanish **n** is often affected by the sounds that occur around it.
When it appears before **b, v,** or **p,** it is pronounced like an **m.**

tan bueno   toman vino   sin poder
un pobre   comen peras   siguen bebiendo

ñ   Spanish **ñ** is similar to the English *ny* sound in the word *canyon.*

señor   otoño   ñoño   uña
leña   dueño   niños   años

x   Spanish **x** has two pronunciations depending on its position. Between vowels the sound is similar to English *ks.*

examen   exacto   boxeo   éxito
oxidar   oxígeno   existencia

When it occurs before a consonant, Spanish **x** sounds like *s.*

expresión   explicar   extraer   excusa
expreso   exquisito   extremo

NOTE: When **x** appears in **México** or in other words of Mexican origin, it is pronounced like the Spanish letter **j.**

Rhythm

Rhythm is the variation of sound intensity that we usually associate with music. Spanish and English each regulate these variations in speech differently, because they have different patterns of syllable length. In Spanish the length of the stressed and unstressed syllables remains almost the same, while in English stressed syllables are considerably longer than unstressed ones. Pronounce the following Spanish words, enunciating each syllable clearly.

es-tu-dian-te	bue-no	Úr-su-la
com-po-si-ción	di-fí-cil	ki-ló-me-tro
po-li-cí-a	Pa-ra-guay	

Because the length of the Spanish syllables remains constant, the greater the number of syllables in a given word or phrase, the longer the phrase will be.

Linking

In spoken Spanish, the different words in a phrase or a sentence are not pronounced as isolated elements but combined together. This is called *linking*.

Pepe come pan.	→	Pe-pe-co-me-pan
Tomás toma leche.		To-más-to-ma-le-che
Luis tiene la llave.		Luis-tie-ne-la-lla-ve
La mano de Roberto.		La-ma-no-de-Ro-ber-to

1. The final consonant of a word is pronounced together with the initial vowel of the following word.

Carlos anda	→	Car-lo-san-da
un ángel		u-nán-gel
el otoño		e-lo-to-ño
unos estudios interesantes		u-no-ses-tu-dio-sin-te-re-san-tes

2. A diphthong is formed between the final vowel of a word and the initial vowel of the following word. A triphthong is formed when there is a combination of three vowels (see rules for the formation of diphthongs and triphthongs on page 347).

su hermana	→	suher-ma-na
tu escopeta		tues-co-pe-ta
Roberto y Luis		Ro-ber-toy-Luis
negocio importante		ne-go-cioim-por-tan-te
lluvia y nieve		llu-viay-nie-ve
ardua empresa		ar-duaem-pre-sa

3. When the final vowel of a word and the initial vowel of the following word are identical, they are pronounced slightly longer than one vowel.

Ana alcanza	A-nal-can-za	tiene eso	tie-ne-so
lo olvido	lol-vi-do	Ada atiende	Ada-tien-de

The same rule applies when two identical vowels appear within a word.

crees	cr*e*s
Teherán	T*e*-rán
coordinación	c*o*r-di-na-ción

4. When the final consonant of a word and the initial consonant of the following word are the same, they are pronounced like one consonant with slightly longer than normal duration.

el lado	e-*l*a-do	tienes sed	tie-ne-*s*ed
Carlos salta	Car-lo-*s*al-ta		

Intonation

Intonation is the rise and fall of pitch in the delivery of a phrase or sentence. In general, Spanish pitch tends to change less than English, giving the impression that the language is less emphatic.

As a rule, the intonation for normal statements in Spanish starts in a low tone, raises to a higher one on the first stressed syllable, maintains that tone until the last stressed syllable, and then goes back to the initial low tone, with still another drop at the very end.

Tu amigo viene mañana.	José come pan.
Ada está en casa.	Carlos toma café.

Syllable formation in Spanish

Below are general rules for dividing words into syllables:

Vowels

1. A vowel or a vowel combination can constitute a syllable.

   a-lum-no   a-bue-la   Eu-ro-pa

2. Diphthongs and triphthongs are considered single vowels and cannot be divided.

   bai-le   puen-te   Dia-na   es-tu-diáis   an-ti-guo

3. Two strong vowels (**a, e, o**) do not form a diphthong and are separated into two syllables.

   em-ple-ar   vol-te-ar   lo-a

4. A written accent on a weak vowel (**i** or **u**) breaks the diphthong, separating the vowels into two syllables.

   trí-o   dú-o   Ma-rí-a

Consonants

1. A single consonant forms a syllable with the vowel that follows it.

   po-der   ma-no   mi-nu-to

   NOTE: **ch, ll,** and **rr** are considered single consonants: **a-ma-ri-llo, co-che, pe-rro.**

2. When two consonants appear between two vowels, they are separated into two syllables.

   al-fa-be-to   cam-pe-ón   me-ter-se   mo-les-tia

EXCEPTION: When a consonant cluster composed of **b, c, d, f, g, p,** or **t** with **l** or **r** appears between two vowels, the cluster joins the following vowel: **so-bre, o-tros, ca-ble, te-lé-gra-fo.**

3. When three consonants appear between two vowels, only the last one goes with the following vowel.

   ins-pec-tor   trans-por-te   trans-for-mar

EXCEPTION: When there is a cluster of three consonants in the combinations described in rule 2, the first consonant joins the preceding vowel and the cluster joins the following vowel: **es-cri-bir, ex-tran-je-ro, im-plo-rar, es-tre-cho.**

Accentuation

In Spanish, all words are stressed according to specific rules. Words that do not follow the rules must have a written accent to indicate the change of stress. The basic rules for accentuation are as follows.

1. Words ending in a vowel, **n,** or **s** are stressed on the next-to-the-last syllable.

   hi-jo   **ca**-lle   **me**-sa   fa-**mo**-sos
   flo-**re**-cen   **pla**-ya   **ve**-ces

2. Words ending in a consonant, except **n** or **s,** are stressed on the last syllable.

   ma-**yor**   a-**mor**   tro-pi-**cal**   na-**riz**   re-**loj**   co-rre-**dor**

3. All words that do not follow these rules must have a written accent.

   ca-**fé**   sa-**lió**   rin-**cón**   fran-**cés**   sa-**lón**
   án-gel   **lá**-piz   **dé**-bil   a-**zú**-car   **Víc**-tor
   sim-**pá**-ti-co **lí**-qui-do   **mú**-si-ca   e-**xá**-me-nes   de-**mó**-cra-ta

4. Pronouns and adverbs of interrogation and exclamation have a written accent to distinguish them from relative pronouns.

   ¿Qué comes?   *What are you eating?*
   La pera que él no comió.   *The pear that he did not eat.*

   ¿Quién está ahí?   *Who is there?*
   El hombre a quien tú llamaste.   *The man whom you called.*

   ¿Dónde está él?   *Where is he?*
   En el lugar donde trabaja.   *At the place where he works.*

5. Words that have the same spelling but different meanings take a written accent to differentiate one from the other.

el	*the*	él	*he, him*	te	*you*	té	*tea*
mi	*my*	mí	*me*	si	*if*	sí	*yes*
tu	*your*	tú	*you*	mas	*but*	más	*more*

B: Verbs

Regular verbs

Model -ar, -er, -ir verbs

INFINITIVE

| amar *(to love)* | comer *(to eat)* | vivir *(to live)* |

PRESENT PARTICIPLE

| amando *(loving)* | comiendo *(eating)* | viviendo *(living)* |

PAST PARTICIPLE

| amado *(loved)* | comido *(eaten)* | vivido *(lived)* |

SIMPLE TENSES

Indicative Mood

Present

(I love)		*(I eat)*		*(I live)*	
amo	amamos	como	comemos	vivo	vivimos
amas	amáis	comes	coméis	vives	vivís
ama	aman	come	comen	vive	viven

Imperfect

(I used to love)		*(I used to eat)*		*(I used to live)*	
amaba	amábamos	comía	comíamos	vivía	vivíamos
amabas	amabais	comías	comíais	vivías	vivíais
amaba	amaban	comía	comían	vivía	vivían

Preterit

(I loved)		*(I ate)*		*(I lived)*	
amé	amamos	comí	comimos	viví	vivimos
amaste	amasteis	comiste	comisteis	viviste	vivisteis
amó	amaron	comió	comieron	vivió	vivieron

Future

(I will love)		*(I will eat)*		*(I will live)*	
amaré	amaremos	comeré	comeremos	viviré	viviremos
amarás	amaréis	comerás	comeréis	vivirás	viviréis
amará	amarán	comerá	comerán	vivirá	vivirán

Conditional

(I would love)		*(I would eat)*		*(I would live)*	
amaría	amaríamos	comería	comeríamos	viviría	viviríamos
amarías	amaríais	comerías	comeríais	vivirías	viviríais
amaría	amarían	comería	comerían	viviría	vivirían

Subjunctive Mood

Present

([that] I [may] love)		*([that] I [may] eat)*		*([that] I [may] live)*	
ame	amemos	coma	comamos	viva	vivamos
ames	améis	comas	comáis	vivas	viváis
ame	amen	coma	coman	viva	vivan

	Imperfect	
([that] I [might] love)	*([that] I [might] eat)*	*([that] I [might] live)*
am**ara**(-**ase**)	com**iera**(-**iese**)	viv**iera**(-**iese**)
am**aras**(-**ases**)	com**ieras**(-**ieses**)	viv**ieras**(-**ieses**)
am**ara**(-**ase**)	com**iera**(-**iese**)	viv**iera**(-**iese**)
am**áramos**(-**ásemos**)	com**iéramos**(-**iésemos**)	viv**iéramos**(-**iésemos**)
am**arais**(-**aseis**)	com**ierais**(-**ieseis**)	viv**ierais**(-**ieseis**)
am**aran**(-**asen**)	com**ieran**(-**iesen**)	viv**ieran**(-**iesen**)

Imperative Mood

(love)	*(eat)*	*(live)*
am**a** (tú)	com**e** (tú)	viv**e** (tú)
am**e** (Ud.)	com**a** (Ud.)	viv**a** (Ud.)
am**emos** (nosotros)	com**amos** (nosotros)	viv**amos** (nosotros)
am**ad** (vosotros)	com**ed** (vosotros)	viv**id** (vosotros)
am**en** (Uds.)	com**an** (Uds.)	viv**an** (Uds.)

COMPOUND TENSES

PERFECT INFINITIVE

haber amado	**haber comido**	**haber vivido**

PERFECT PARTICIPLE

habiendo amado	**habiendo comido**	**habiendo vivido**

Indicative Mood

Present Perfect

(I have loved)		*(I have eaten)*		*(I have lived)*	
he amado	hemos amado	he comido	hemos comido	he vivido	hemos vivido
has amado	habéis amado	has comido	habéis comido	has vivido	habéis vivido
ha amado	han amado	ha comido	han comido	ha vivido	han vivido

Past Perfect (Pluperfect)

(I had loved)	*(I had eaten)*	*(I had lived)*
había amado	había comido	había vivido
habías amado	habías comido	habías vivido
había amado	había comido	había vivido
habíamos amado	habíamos comido	habíamos vivido
habíais amado	habíais comido	habíais vivido
habían amado	habían comido	habían vivido

Future Perfect

(I will have loved)	*(I will have eaten)*	*(I will have lived)*
habré amado	habré comido	habré vivido
habrás amado	habrás comido	habrás vivido
habrá amado	habrá comido	habrá vivido
habremos amado	habremos comido	habremos vivido
habréis amado	habréis comido	habréis vivido
habrán amado	habrán comido	habrán vivido

Conditional Perfect

(I would have loved)	*(I would have eaten)*	*(I would have lived)*
habría amado	habría comido	habría vivido
habrías amado	habrías comido	habrías vivido
habría amado	habría comido	habría vivido
habríamos amado	habríamos comido	habríamos vivido
habríais amado	habríais comido	habríais vivido
habrían amado	habrían comido	habrían vivido

Subjunctive Mood

Present Perfect

([that] I [may] have loved)	*([that] I [may] have eaten)*	*([that] I [may] have lived)*
haya amado	haya comido	haya vivido
hayas amado	hayas comido	hayas vivido
haya amado	haya comido	haya vivido
hayamos amado	hayamos comido	hayamos vivido
hayáis amado	hayáis comido	hayáis vivido
hayan amado	hayan comido	hayan vivido

Past Perfect (Pluperfect)

([that] I [might] have loved)	*([that] I [might] have eaten)*	*([that] I [might] have lived)*
hubiera(-iese) amado	hubiera(-iese) comido	hubiera(-iese) vivido
hubieras(-ieses) amado	hubieras(-ieses) comido	hubieras(-ieses) vivido
hubiera(-iese) amado	hubiera(-iese) comido	hubiera(-iese) vivido
hubiéramos(-iésemos) amado	hubiéramos(-iésemos) comido	hubiéramos(-iésemos) vivido
hubierais(-ieseis) amado	hubierais(-ieseis) comido	hubierais(-ieseis) vivido
hubieran(-iesen) amado	hubieran(-iesen) comido	hubieran(-iesen) vivido

Stem-changing verbs

The -ar and -er stem-changing verbs

Stem-changing verbs are those that have a spelling change in the root of the verb. Verbs that end in **-ar** and **-er** change the stressed vowel **e** to **ic,** and the stressed **o** to **ue.** These changes occur in all persons, except the first- and second-persons plural of the present indicative, present subjunctive, and imperative.

INFINITIVE	Indicative	Imperative	Subjunctive
cerrar (*to close*)	cierro cierras cierra	——— cierra cierre	cierre cierres cierre
	cerramos cerráis cierran	cerremos cerrad cierren	cerremos cerréis cierren
perder (*to lose*)	pierdo pierdes pierde	——— pierde pierda	pierda pierdas pierda
	perdemos perdéis pierden	perdamos perded pierdan	perdamos perdáis pierdan
contar (*to count;* *to tell*)	cuento cuentas cuenta	——— cuenta cuente	cuente cuentes cuente
	contamos contáis cuentan	contemos contad cuenten	contemos contéis cuenten
volver (*to return*)	vuelvo vuelves vuelve	——— vuelve vuelva	vuelva vuelvas vuelva
	volvemos volvéis vuelven	volvamos volved vuelvan	volvamos volváis vuelvan

Verbs that follow the same pattern are:

acordarse	*to remember*	despertar(se)	*to wake up*	pensar	*to think; to plan*
acostar(se)	*to go to bed*	empezar	*to begin*	probar	*to prove; to taste*
almorzar	*to have lunch*	encender	*to light; to turn on*	recordar	*to remember*
atravesar	*to go through*	encontrar	*to find*	rogar	*to beg*
cocer	*to cook*	entender	*to understand*	sentar(se)	*to sit down*
colgar	*to hang*	llover	*to rain*	soler	*to be in the habit of*
comenzar	*to begin*	mover	*to move*	soñar	*to dream*
confesar	*to confess*	mostrar	*to show*	tender	*to stretch; to unfold*
costar	*to cost*	negar	*to deny*		
demostrar	*to demonstrate, show*	nevar	*to snow*	torcer	*to twist*

The -*ir* stem-changing verbs

There are two types of stem-changing verbs that end in **-ir:** one type changes stressed **e** to **ie** in some tenses and to **i** in others, and stressed **o** to **ue** or **u;** the second type changes stressed **e** to **i** only in all the irregular tenses.

Type 1: -ir:e > ie or i / o > ue or u

These changes occur as follows.

Present Indicative: all persons except the first- and second-persons plural change **e** to **ie** and **o** to **ue.** *Preterit:* third person, singular and plural, changes **e** to **i** and **o** to **u.** *Present Subjunctive:* all persons change **e** to **ie** and **o** to **ue,** except the first- and second-persons plural, which change **e** to **i** and **o** to **u.** *Imperfect Subjunctive:* all persons change **e** to **i** and **o** to **u.** *Imperative:* all persons except the first- and second-persons plural change **e** to **ie** and **o** to **ue;** first-person plural changes **e** to **i** and **o** to **u.** *Present Participle:* changes **e** to **i** and **o** to **u.**

INFINITIVE	Indicative		Imperative	Subjunctive	
sentir *(to feel)*	PRESENT	PRETERIT		PRESENT	IMPERFECT
PRESENT PARTICIPLE sintiendo	siento	sentí		sienta	sintiera(-iese)
	sientes	sentiste	siente	sientas	sintieras
	siente	sintió	sienta	sienta	sintiera
	sentimos	sentimos	sintamos	sintamos	sintiéramos
	sentís	sentisteis	sentid	sintáis	sintierais
	sienten	sintieron	sientan	sientan	sintieran
dormir *(to sleep)*	duermo	dormí		duerma	durmiera(-iese)
	duermes	dormiste	duerme	duermas	durmieras
	duerme	durmió	duerma	duerma	durmiera
PRESENT PARTICIPLE durmiendo	dormimos	dormimos	durmamos	durmamos	durmiéramos
	dormís	dormisteis	dormid	durmáis	durmierais
	duermen	durmieron	duerman	duerman	durmieran

Other verbs that follow the same pattern are:

advertir	*to warn*	divertir(se)	*to amuse (oneself)*	preferir	*to prefer*
arrepentirse	*to repent*	herir	*to wound, hurt*	referir	*to refer*
consentir	*to consent; to pamper*	mentir	*to lie*	sugerir	*to suggest*
convertir(se)	*to turn into*	morir	*to die*		

The verbs in the second category are irregular in the same tenses as those of the first type. The only difference is that they have just one change: **e > i** in all irregular persons.

INFINITIVE	Indicative		Imperative	Subjunctive	
	PRESENT	PRETERIT		PRESENT	IMPERFECT
pedir *(to ask for, request)*	pido	pedí		pida	pidiera(-iese)
	pides	pediste	pide	pidas	pidieras
PRESENT PARTICIPLE	pide	pidió	pida	pida	pidiera
pidiendo	pedimos	pedimos	pidamos	pidamos	pidiéramos
	pedís	pedisteis	pedid	pidáis	pidierais
	piden	pidieron	pidan	pidan	pidieran

Verbs that follow this pattern:

competir	*to compete*	impedir	*to prevent*	repetir	*to repeat*
concebir	*to conceive*	perseguir	*to pursue*	seguir	*to follow*
despedir(se)	*to say good-bye*	reír(se)	*to laugh*	servir	*to serve*
elegir	*to choose*	reñir	*to fight*	vestir(se)	*to dress*

Orthographic-changing verbs

Some verbs undergo a change in the spelling of the stem in some tenses in order to maintain the sound of the final consonant. The most common ones are those with the consonants **g** and **c**. Remember that **g** and **c** in front of **e** or **i** have a soft sound, and in front of **a, o,** or **u** have a hard sound. In order to keep the soft sound in front of **a, o,** or **u, g** and **c** change to **j** and **z,** respectively. In order to keep the hard sound of **g** or **c** in front of **e** and **i, u** is added to the **g (gu)** and the **c** changes to **qu.** The following are the most important verbs of this type that are regular in all tenses but change in spelling.

1. Verbs ending in **-gar** change **g** to **gu** before **e** in the first-person singular of the preterit and in all persons of the present subjunctive.

   pagar   *to pay*
   Preterit: pa**gu**é, pagaste, pagó, etc.
   Pres. Subj.:   pa**gu**e, pa**gu**es, pa**gu**e, pa**gu**emos, pa**gu**éis, pa**gu**en

   Verbs that follow the same pattern: **colgar, jugar, llegar, navegar, negar, regar, rogar.**

2. Verbs ending in **-ger** or **-gir** change **g** to **j** before **o** and **a** in the first-person singular of the present indicative and in all the persons of the present subjunctive.

   proteger   *to protect*
   Pres. Ind.:   prote**j**o, proteges, protege, etc.
   Pres. Subj.:   prote**j**a, prote**j**as, prote**j**a, prote**j**amos, prote**j**áis, prote**j**an

   Verbs that follow the same pattern: **coger, corregir, dirigir, elegir, escoger, exigir, recoger.**

3. Verbs ending in **-guar** change **gu** to **gü** before **e** in the first-person singular of the preterit and in all persons of the present subjunctive.

averiguar   *to find out*
Preterit: averi**gü**é, averiguaste, averiguó, etc.
Pres. Subj.:   averi**gü**e, averi**gü**es, averi**gü**e, averi**gü**emos, averi**gü**éis, averi**gü**en

The verb **apaciguar** follows the same pattern.

4. Verbs ending in **-guir** change **gu** to **g** before **o** and **a** in the first-person singular of the present indicative and in all persons of the present subjunctive.

conseguir   *to get*
Pres. Ind.:   consi**g**o, consigues, consigue, etc.
Pres. Subj.:   consi**g**a, consi**g**as, consi**g**a, consi**g**amos, consi**g**áis, consi**g**an

Verbs that follow the same pattern: **distinguir, perseguir, proseguir, seguir.**

5. Verbs ending in **-car** change **c** to **qu** before **e** in the first-person singular of the preterit and in all persons of the present subjunctive.

tocar   *to touch; to play (a musical instrument)*
Preterit: to**qu**é, tocaste, tocó, etc.
Pres. Subj.:   to**qu**e, to**qu**es, to**qu**e, to**qu**emos, to**qu**éis, to**qu**en

Verbs that follow the same pattern: **atacar, buscar, comunicar, explicar, indicar, pescar, sacar.**

6. Verbs ending in **-cer** or **-cir** preceded by a consonant change **c** to **z** before **o** and **a** in the first-person singular of the present indicative and in all persons of the present subjunctive.

torcer   *to twist*
Pres. Ind.:   tuer**z**o, tuerces, tuerce, etc.
Pres. Subj.:   tuer**z**a, tuer**z**as, tuer**z**a, tor**z**amos, tor**z**áis, tuer**z**an

Verbs that follow the same pattern: **convencer, esparcir, vencer.**

7. Verbs ending in **-cer** or **-cir** preceded by a vowel change **c** to **zc** before **o** and **a** in the first-person singular of the present indicative and in all persons of the present subjunctive.

conocer   *to know, be acquainted with*
Pres. Ind.:   cono**zc**o, conoces, conoce, etc.
Pres. Subj.:   cono**zc**a, cono**zc**as, cono**zc**a, cono**zc**amos, cono**zc**áis, cono**zc**an

Verbs that follow the same pattern: **agradecer, aparecer, carecer, entristecer** (to sadden), **establecer, lucir, nacer, obedecer, ofrecer, padecer, parecer, pertenecer, reconocer, relucir.**

8. Verbs ending in **-zar** change **z** to **c** before **e** in the first-person singular of the preterit and in all persons of the present subjunctive.

rezar   *to pray*
Preterit: re**c**é, rezaste, rezó, etc.
Pres. Subj.:   re**c**e, re**c**es, re**c**e, re**c**emos, re**c**éis, re**c**en

Verbs that follow the same pattern: **abrazar, alcanzar, almorzar, comenzar, cruzar, empezar, forzar, gozar.**

9. Verbs ending in **-eer** change the unstressed **i** to **y** between vowels in the third-person singular and plural of the preterit, in all persons of the imperfect subjunctive, and in the present participle.

creer   *to believe*
Preterit: creí, creíste, cre**y**ó, creímos, creísteis, cre**y**eron
Imp. Subj.:   cre**y**era(-ese), cre**y**eras, cre**y**era, cre**y**éramos, cre**y**erais, cre**y**eran
Pres. Part.:   cre**y**endo
Past Part.:   creído

Verbs that follow the same pattern: **leer, poseer.**

10. Verbs ending in **-uir** change the unstressed **i** to **y** between vowels (except **-quir,** which has the silent **u**) in the following tenses and persons.

huir   *to escape; to flee*
Pres. Part.:   huyendo
Pres. Ind.:   huyo, huyes, huye, huimos, huís, huyen
Preterit: huí, huiste, huyó, huimos, huisteis, huyeron
Imperative: huye, huya, huyamos, huid, huyan
Pres. Subj.:   huya, huyas, huya, huyamos, huyáis, huyan
Imp. Subj.:   huyera(-ese), huyeras, huyera, huyéramos, huyerais, huyeran

Verbs that follow the same pattern: **atribuir, concluir, constituir, construir, contribuir, destituir, destruir, disminuir, distribuir, excluir, incluir, influir, instruir, restituir, sustituir.**

11. Verbs ending in **-eír** lose the **e** in all but the first- and second-persons plural of the present indicative, in the third-person singular and plural of the preterit, in all persons of the present and imperfect subjunctive, and in the present participle.

reír   *to laugh*
Pres. Ind.:   río, ríes, ríe, reímos, reís, ríen
Preterit: reí, reíste, rió, reímos, reísteis, rieron
Pres. Subj.:   ría, rías, ría, riamos, riáis, rían
Imp. Subj.:   riera(-ese), rieras, riera, riéramos, rierais, rieran
Pres. Part.:   riendo

Verbs that follow the same pattern: **sonreír, freír.**

12. Verbs ending in **-iar** add a written accent to the **i**, except in the first- and second-persons plural of the present indicative and subjunctive.

fiar(se)   *to trust*
Pres. Ind.:   (me) fío, (te) fías, (se) fía, (nos) fiamos, (os) fiáis, (se) fían
Pres. Subj.:   (me) fíe, (te) fíes, (se) fíe, (nos) fiemos, (os) fiéis, (se) fíen

Verbs that follow the same pattern: **ampliar, criar, desviar, enfriar, enviar, guiar, telegrafiar, vaciar, variar.**

13. Verbs ending in **-uar** (except **-guar**) add a written accent to the **u**, except in the first- and second-persons plural of the present indicative and subjunctive.

actuar   *to act*
Pres. Ind.:   actúo, actúas, actúa, actuamos, actuáis, actúan
Pres. Subj.:   actúe, actúes, actúe, actuemos, actuéis, actúen

Verbs that follow the same pattern: **acentuar, continuar, efectuar, exceptuar, graduar, habituar, insinuar, situar.**

14. Verbs ending in **-ñir** lose the **i** of the diphthongs **ie** and **ió** in the third-person singular and plural of the preterit and all persons of the imperfect subjunctive. They also change the **e** of the stem to **i** in the same persons and in the present indicative and present subjunctive.

teñir   *to dye*
Pres. Ind.:   tiño, tiñes, tiñe, teñimos, teñís, tiñen
Preterit: teñí, teñiste, **tiñó,** teñimos, teñisteis, tiñeron
Pres. Subj.:   tiña, tiñas, tiña, tiñamos, tiñáis, tiñan
Imp. Subj.:   tiñera(-ese), tiñeras, tiñera, tiñéramos, tiñerais, tiñeran

Verbs that follow the same pattern: **ceñir, constreñir, desteñir, estreñir, reñir.**

Some common irregular verbs

Only tenses with irregular forms are given below.

adquirir   *to acquire*
Pres. Ind.:   adquiero, adquieres, adquiere, adquirimos, adquirís, adquieren
Pres. Subj.:   adquiera, adquieras, adquiera, adquiramos, adquiráis, adquieran
Imperative: adquiere, adquiera, adquiramos, adquirid, adquieran

andar   *to walk*
Preterit: anduve, anduviste, anduvo, anduvimos, anduvisteis, anduvieron
Imp. Subj.:   anduviera (anduviese), anduvieras, anduviera, anduviéramos, anduvierais, anduvieran

avergonzarse   *to be ashamed, embarrassed*
Pres. Ind.:   me avergüenzo, te avergüenzas, se avergüenza, nos avergonzamos, os avergonzáis, se avergüenzan
Pres. Subj.:   me avergüence, te avergüences, se avergüence, nos avergoncemos, os avergoncéis, se avergüencen
Imperative: avergüénzate, avergüéncese, avergoncémonos, avergonzaos, avergüéncense

caber   *to fit; to have enough room*
Pres. Ind.:   quepo, cabes, cabe, cabemos, cabéis, caben
Preterit: cupe, cupiste, cupo, cupimos, cupisteis, cupieron
Future: cabré, cabrás, cabrá, cabremos, cabréis, cabrán
Conditional: cabría, cabrías, cabría, cabríamos, cabríais, cabrían
Imperative: cabe, quepa, quepamos, cabed, quepan
Pres. Subj.:   quepa, quepas, quepa, quepamos, quepáis, quepan
Imp. Subj.:   cupiera (cupiese), cupieras, cupiera, cupiéramos, cupierais, cupieran

caer   *to fall*
Pres. Ind.:   caigo, caes, cae, caemos, caéis, caen
Preterit: caí, caíste, cayó, caímos, caísteis, cayeron
Imperative: cae, caiga, caigamos, caed, caigan
Pres. Subj.:   caiga, caigas, caiga, caigamos, caigáis, caigan
Imp. Subj.:   cayera (cayese), cayeras, cayera, cayéramos, cayerais, cayeran
Past Part.:   caído

conducir   *to guide; to drive* (All verbs ending in **-ducir** follow this pattern.)
Pres. Ind.:   conduzco, conduces, conduce, conducimos, conducís, conducen
Preterit: conduje, condujiste, condujo, condujimos, condujisteis, condujeron
Imperative: conduce, conduzca, conduzcamos, conducid, conduzcan
Pres. Subj.:   conduzca, conduzcas, conduzca, conduzcamos, conduzcáis, conduzcan
Imp. Subj.:   condujera (condujese), condujeras, condujera, condujéramos, condujerais, condujeran

convenir   *to agree* (see **venir**)

dar   *to give*
Pres. Ind.:   doy, das, da, damos, dais, dan
Preterit: di, diste, dio, dimos, disteis, dieron
Imperative: da, dé, demos, dad, den
Pres. Subj.:   dé, des, dé, demos, deis, den
Imp. Subj.:   diera (diese), dieras, diera, diéramos, dierais, dieran

decir   *to say, tell*
Pres. Ind.:   digo, dices, dice, decimos, decís, dicen
Preterit: dije, dijiste, dijo, dijimos, dijisteis, dijeron
Future: diré, dirás, dirá, diremos, diréis, dirán
Conditional: diría, dirías, diría, diríamos, diríais, dirían
Imperative: di, diga, digamos, decid, digan
Pres. Subj.:   diga, digas, diga, digamos, digáis, digan
Imp. Subj.:   dijera (dijese), dijeras, dijera, dijéramos, dijerais, dijeran
Pres. Part.:   diciendo
Past Part.:   dicho

detener   *to stop; to hold; to arrest* (see **tener**)

entretener   *to entertain, amuse* (see **tener**)

errar   *to err; to miss*
Pres. Ind.:   yerro, yerras, yerra, erramos, erráis, yerran
Imperative: yerra, yerre, erremos, errad, yerren
Pres. Subj.:   yerre, yerres, yerre, erremos, erréis, yerren

estar   *to be*
Pres. Ind.:   estoy, estás, está, estamos, estáis, están
Preterit: estuve, estuviste, estuvo, estuvimos, estuvisteis, estuvieron
Imperative: está, esté, estemos, estad, estén
Pres. Subj.:   esté, estés, esté, estemos, estéis, estén
Imp. Subj.:   estuviera (estuviese), estuvieras, estuviera, estuviéramos, estuvierais, estuvieran

haber   *to have*
Pres. Ind.:   he, has, ha, hemos, habéis, han
Preterit: hube, hubiste, hubo, hubimos, hubisteis, hubieron
Future: habré, habrás, habrá, habremos, habréis, habrán
Conditional: habría, habrías, habría, habríamos, habríais, habrían
Pres. Subj.:   haya, hayas, haya, hayamos, hayáis, hayan
Imp. Subj.:   hubiera (hubiese), hubieras, hubiera, hubiéramos, hubierais, hubieran

hacer   *to do, make*
Pres. Ind.:   hago, haces, hace, hacemos, hacéis, hacen
Preterit: hice, hiciste, hizo, hicimos, hicisteis, hicieron
Future: haré, harás, hará, haremos, haréis, harán
Conditional: haría, harías, haría, haríamos, haríais, harían
Imperative: haz, haga, hagamos, haced, hagan
Pres. Subj.:   haga, hagas, haga, hagamos, hagáis, hagan
Imp. Subj.:   hiciera (hiciese), hicieras, hiciera, hiciéramos, hicierais, hicieran
Past Part.:   hecho

imponer   *to impose; to deposit* (see **poner**)

ir   *to go*
Pres. Ind.:   voy, vas, va, vamos, vais, van
Imp. Ind.:   iba, ibas, iba, íbamos, ibais, iban
Preterit: fui, fuiste, fue, fuimos, fuisteis, fueron
Imperative: ve, vaya, vayamos, id, vayan
Pres. Subj.:   vaya, vayas, vaya, vayamos, vayáis, vayan
Imp. Subj.:   fuera (fuese), fueras, fuera, fuéramos, fuerais, fueran

jugar   *to play*
Pres. Ind.:   juego, juegas, juega, jugamos, jugáis, juegan
Imperative: juega, juegue, juguemos, jugad, jueguen
Pres. Subj.:   juegue, juegues, juegue, juguemos, juguéis, jueguen

obtener   *to obtain* (see **tener**)

oír   *to hear*
Pres. Ind.:   oigo, oyes, oye, oímos, oís, oyen
Preterit: oí, oíste, oyó, oímos, oísteis, oyeron
Imperative: oye, oiga, oigamos, oíd, oigan
Pres. Subj.:   oiga, oigas, oiga, oigamos, oigáis, oigan
Imp. Subj.:   oyera (oyese), oyeras, oyera, oyéramos, oyerais, oyeran
Pres. Part.:   oyendo
Past Part.:   oído

oler   *to smell*
Pres. Ind.:   huelo, hueles, huele, olemos, oléis, huelen
Imperative: huele, huela, olamos, oled, huelan
Pres. Subj.:   huela, huelas, huela, olamos, oláis, huelan

poder   *to be able to*
Preterit:	pude, pudiste, pudo, pudimos, pudisteis, pudieron
Future:	podré, podrás, podrá, podremos, podréis, podrán
Conditional:	podría, podrías, podría, podríamos, podríais, podrían
Imperative:	puede, pueda, podamos, poded, puedan
Imp. Subj.:	pudiera (pudiese), pudieras, pudiera, pudiéramos, pudierais, pudieran
Pres. Part.:	pudiendo

poner   *to place, put*
Pres. Ind.:	pongo, pones, pone, ponemos, ponéis, ponen
Preterit:	puse, pusiste, puso, pusimos, pusisteis, pusieron
Future:	pondré, pondrás, pondrá, pondremos, pondréis, pondrán
Conditional:	pondría, pondrías, pondría, pondríamos, pondríais, pondrían
Imperative:	pon, ponga, pongamos, poned, pongan
Pres. Subj.:	ponga, pongas, ponga, pongamos, pongáis, pongan
Imp. Subj.:	pusiera (pusiese), pusieras, pusiera, pusiéramos, pusierais, pusieran
Past Part.:	puesto

querer   *to want, wish; to like, love*
Preterit:	quise, quisiste, quiso, quisimos, quisisteis, quisieron
Future:	querré, querrás, querrá, querremos, querréis, querrán
Conditional:	querría, querrías, querría, querríamos, querríais, querrían
Imp. Subj.:	quisiera (quisiese), quisieras, quisiera, quisiéramos, quisierais, quisieran

resolver   *to decide on, to solve*
Past Part.:	resuelto

saber   *to know*
Pres. Ind.:	sé, sabes, sabe, sabemos, sabéis, saben
Preterit:	supe, supiste, supo, supimos, supisteis, supieron
Future:	sabré, sabrás, sabrá, sabremos, sabréis, sabrán
Conditional:	sabría, sabrías, sabría, sabríamos, sabríais, sabrían
Imperative:	sabe, sepa, sepamos, sabed, sepan
Pres. Subj.:	sepa, sepas, sepa, sepamos, sepáis, sepan
Imp. Subj.:	supiera (supiese), supieras, supiera, supiéramos, supierais, supieran

salir   *to leave; to go out*
Pres. Ind.:	salgo, sales, sale, salimos, salís, salen
Future:	saldré, saldrás, saldrá, saldremos, saldréis, saldrán
Conditional:	saldría, saldrías, saldría, saldríamos, saldríais, saldrían
Imperative:	sal, salga, salgamos, salid, salgan
Pres. Subj.:	salga, salgas, salga, salgamos, salgáis, salgan

ser   *to be*
Pres. Ind.:	soy, eres, es, somos, sois, son
Imp. Ind.:	era, eras, era, éramos, erais, eran
Preterit:	fui, fuiste, fue, fuimos, fuisteis, fueron
Imperative:	sé, sea, seamos, sed, sean
Pres. Subj.:	sea, seas, sea, seamos, seáis, sean
Imp. Subj.:	fuera (fuese), fueras, fuera, fuéramos, fuerais, fueran

suponer   *to assume* (see **poner**)

tener   *to have*
Pres. Ind.:	tengo, tienes, tiene, tenemos, tenéis, tienen
Preterit:	tuve, tuviste, tuvo, tuvimos, tuvisteis, tuvieron
Future:	tendré, tendrás, tendrá, tendremos, tendréis, tendrán
Conditional:	tendría, tendrías, tendría, tendríamos, tendríais, tendrían
Imperative:	ten, tenga, tengamos, tened, tengan
Pres. Subj.:	tenga, tengas, tenga, tengamos, tengáis, tengan
Imp. Subj.:	tuviera (tuviese), tuvieras, tuviera, tuviéramos, tuvierais, tuvieran

traducir   *to translate* (see **conducir**)

traer   *to bring*
Pres. Ind.:	traigo, traes, trae, traemos, traéis, traen
Preterit:	traje, trajiste, trajo, trajimos, trajisteis, trajeron

Imperative:	trae, traiga, traigamos, traed, traigan
Pres. Subj.:	traiga, traigas, traiga, traigamos, traigáis, traigan
Imp. Subj.:	trajera (trajese), trajeras, trajera, trajéramos, trajerais, trajeran
Pres. Part.:	trayendo
Past Part.:	traído

valer   *to be worth*

Pres. Ind.:	valgo, vales, vale, valemos, valéis, valen
Future:	valdré, valdrás, valdrá, valdremos, valdréis, valdrán
Conditional:	valdría, valdrías, valdría, valdríamos, valdríais, valdrían
Imperative:	vale, valga, valgamos, valed, valgan
Pres. Subj.:	valga, valgas, valga, valgamos, valgáis, valgan

venir   *to come*

Pres. Ind.:	vengo, vienes, viene, venimos, venís, vienen
Preterit:	vine, viniste, vino, vinimos, vinisteis, vinieron
Future:	vendré, vendrás, vendrá, vendremos, vendréis, vendrán
Conditional:	vendría, vendrías, vendría, vendríamos, vendríais, vendrían
Imperative:	ven, venga, vengamos, venid, vengan
Pres. Subj.:	venga, vengas, venga, vengamos, vengáis, vengan
Imp. Subj.:	viniera (viniese), vinieras, viniera, viniéramos, vinierais, vinieran
Pres. Part.:	viniendo

ver   *to see*

Pres. Ind.:	veo, ves, ve, vemos, veis, ven
Imp. Ind.:	veía, veías, veía, veíamos, veíais, veían
Preterit:	vi, viste, vio, vimos, visteis, vieron
Imperative:	ve, vea, veamos, ved, vean
Pres. Subj.:	vea, veas, vea, veamos, veáis, vean
Imp. Subj.:	viera (viese), vieras, viera, viéramos, vierais, vieran
Past Part.:	visto

volver   *to return*

| *Past Part.:* | vuelto |

C: Glossary of Grammatical Terms

adjective: A word that is used to describe a noun: *tall* girl, *difficult* lesson.

adverb: A word that modifies a verb, an adjective, or another adverb. It answers the questions "How?" "When?" "Where?": She walked *slowly.* She'll be here *tomorrow.* She is *here.*

agreement: A term applied to changes in form that nouns cause in the words that surround them. In Spanish, verb forms agree with their subjects in person and number (**yo** habl**o**, **él** habl**a**, etc.). Spanish adjectives agree in gender and number with the noun they describe. Thus, a feminine plural noun requires a feminine plural ending in the adjective that describes it (cas**as** amarill**as**), and a masculine singular noun requires a masculine singular ending in the adjective (libr**o** negr**o**).

auxiliary verb: A verb that helps in the conjugation of another verb: I *have* finished. He *was* called. She *will* go. He *would* eat.

command form: The form of the verb used to give an order or direction: *Go! Come back! Turn* to the right!

conjugation: The process by which the forms of the verb are presented in their different moods and tenses: I *am*, you *are*, he *is*, she *was*, we *were*, etc.

contraction: The combination of two or more words into one: *isn't, don't, can't.*

definite article: A word used before a noun indicating a definite person or thing: *the* woman, *the* money.

demonstrative: A word that refers to a definite person or object: *this, that, these, those.*

diphthong: A combination of two vowels forming one syllable. In Spanish, a diphthong is composed of one *strong* vowel (**a, e, o**) and one *weak* vowel (**u, i**) or two weak vowels: **ei, au, ui.**

exclamation: A word used to express emotion: *How* strong! *What* beauty!

gender: A distinction of nouns, pronouns, and adjectives, based on whether they are masculine or feminine.

indefinite article: A word used before a noun that refers to an indefinite person or object: *a* child, *an* apple.

infinitive: The form of the verb generally preceded in English by the word *to* and showing no subject or number: *to do, to bring.*

interrogative: A word used in asking a question: *Who? What? Where?*

main clause: A group of words that includes a subject and a verb and that by itself has complete meaning: *They saw me. I go now.*

noun: A word that names a person, place, or thing: *Ann, London, pencil,* etc.

number: Number refers to singular and plural: *chair, chairs.*

object: Generally a noun or a pronoun that is the receiver of the verb's action. A direct object answers the question "What?" or "Whom?": We know *her.* Take *it.* An indirect object answers the question "To whom?" or "To what?": Give *John* the money. Nouns and pronouns can also be objects of prepositions: The letter is *from Rick.* I'm thinking *about you.*

past participle: Past forms of a verb: *gone, worked, written,* etc.

person: The form of the pronoun and of the verb that shows the person referred to: *I* (first-person singular), *you* (second-person singular), *she* (third-person singular), etc.

possessive: A word that denotes ownership or possession: This is *our* house. The book isn't *mine.*

preposition: A word that introduces a noun or pronoun and indicates its function in the sentence: They were *with* us. She is *from* Nevada.

pronoun: A word that is used to replace a noun: *she, them, us,* etc. A **subject pronoun** refers to the person or thing spoken of: *They* work. An **object pronoun** receives the action of the verb: They arrested *us* (direct object pronoun). She spoke to *him* (indirect object pronoun). A pronoun can also be the object of a preposition: The children stayed with *us.*

reflexive pronoun: A pronoun that refers back to the subject: *myself, yourself, himself, herself, itself, ourselves,* etc.

subject: The person, place, or thing spoken of: *Robert* works. *Our car* is new.

subordinate clause: A clause that has no complete meaning by itself but depends on a main clause: They knew *that I was here.*

tense: The group of forms in a verb that show the time in which the action of the verb takes place: *I go* (present indicative), *I'm going* (present progressive), *I went* (past), *I was going* (past progressive), *I will go* (future), *I would go* (conditional), *I have gone* (present perfect), *I had gone* (past perfect), *that I may go* (present subjunctive), etc.

verb: A word that expresses an action or a state: We *sleep.* The baby *is* sick.

D: Answer Key to Tome Este Examen

Lección 1

A. 1. los / unos   2. los / unos   3. el / un   4. las / unas   5. la / una   6. la / una   7. los / unos   8. los / unos

B. 1. nosotras   2. ellos   3. ella   4. ustedes   5. ellas   6. él   7. usted   8. tú

C. 1. soy / es   2. son   3. somos   4. son   5. eres   6. es

D. 1. El alumno es norteamericano.   2. Los lápices son verdes.   3. Las mesas son blancas.   4. Es un hombre español.   5. Las profesoras son inglesas.   6. Los muchachos son ricos.   7. Es una mujer inteligente.   8. Los señores son muy simpáticos.

E. 1. De-i-a-zeta   2. Jota-i-eme-é-ene-e-zeta   3. Ve-a-ere-ge-a-ese   4. Pe-a-erre-a   5. Efe-e-ele-i-ú   6. A-ce-u-eñe-a

F. 1. ocho   2. catorce   3. veintiséis   4. once   5. treinta y cinco   6. diez   7. trece   8. cero   9. veintiocho   10. diecisiete   11. treinta y nueve   12. quince

G. 1. llama / dónde   2. gusto   3. dice   4. cuarto / muy   5. alumnos (estudiantes)   6. habla   7. está   8. Saludos   9. es   10. nada

H. 1. es   2. que no se han casado

Lección 2

A. 1. tomas   2. habla (conversa)   3. hablamos   4. deseo   5. estudia   6. trabajan   7. necesita   8. terminamos

B. 1. ¿Hablan ellos inglés con los estudiantes? / Ellos no hablan inglés con los estudiantes.   2. ¿Es ella de México? / Ella no es de México.   3. ¿Terminan Uds. hoy? / Uds. no terminan hoy.

C. 1. tu   2. su   3. nuestra   4. mis   5. sus   6. nuestros   7. su   8. su

D. 1. las   2. los   3. el   4. las   5. los   6. el   7. la   8. la

E. 1. ochenta bolígrafos   2. cuarenta y seis mochilas   3. setenta y dos relojes   4. treinta y tres ventanas   5. doscientos libros   6. ciento quince cuadernos   7. sesenta y ocho estudiantes   8. cincuenta mapas   9. noventa y cinco computadoras   10. setenta y tres cestos de papeles   11. cien plumas   12. ciento trece borradores

F. 1. Es la una   2. a las nueve y media de la mañana   3. por la tarde   4. Son   5. a las tres menos cuarto

G. martes / miércoles / viernes / sábado
1. el primero de marzo   2. el diez de junio   3. el trece de agosto   4. el veintiséis de diciembre   5. el tres de septiembre   6. el veintiocho de octubre   7. el diecisiete de julio   8. el cuatro de abril   9. el dos de enero   10. el cinco de febrero
1. invierno   2. primavera   3. otoño   4. verano

H. 1. hora   2. horario / Aquí   3. solamente   4. taza / vaso   5. toman   6. semestre   7. primavera   8. asignatura (materia)   9. copa   10. jugo   11. aguafiestas   12. dinero

I. 1. 66   2. español   3. segundo

Lección 3

A. 1. escribe   2. vivimos   3. deben   4. corres   5. bebo   6. come   7. abre   8. Reciben

B. 1. la amiga de Pedro   2. la ropa de Paco   3. la casa de la señora Peña   4. los hermanos de Eva

C. 1. vienes   2. venimos / tenemos   3. tienen / vienen   4. vengo / tengo   5. tiene   6. tiene

D. 1. ...tengo mucho calor.   2. ...tiene mucha hambre.   3. ...tiene mucha sed.   4. ...tienes mucho frío.   5. ...tenemos mucho sueño.   6. ...tienen mucho miedo.   7. ...tengo mucha prisa.

E. 1. esas / esos   2. esta / este   3. aquel / aquella   4. esa / ese   5. estos / estas

F. 1. quinientos sesenta y siete   2. setecientos noventa   3. mil   4. trescientos cuarenta y cinco   5. seiscientos quince   6. ochocientos setenta y cuatro   7. novecientos sesenta y cinco   8. ochocientos veinticinco   9. cuatrocientos ochenta y uno   10. trece mil ochocientos dieciséis

G. 1. trabajos   2. rato   3. Quién   4. césped (zacate)   5. cosas   6. poner   7. sacudir   8. puerta / abrir   9. sacar   10. vienen / momento   11. bebo / sed   12. pasar

H. 1. Los hombres ayudan con los trabajos de la casa.   2. La comida mexicana es popular en todo el mundo.   3. Son populares en Rusia y en Japón.

Lección 4

A. 1. salgo 2. conduzco 3. traduzco 4. hago 5. quepo 6. traigo
B. 1. conoces / Sabes 2. sé 3. conocemos 4. conocen 5. sabe
C. 1. Yo conozco a la tía de Julio. 2. Luis tiene tres tíos y dos tías. 3. Ana lleva a su prima a la fiesta.
    4. Uds. conocen San Salvador.
D. 1. No conocemos al Sr. Vega. 2. Es la hermana del profesor. 3. Venimos del club.
    4. Voy al laboratorio. 5. Vengo de la playa.
E. 1. doy 2. está 3. vamos 4. estás 5. están 6. va 7. dan 8. voy
F. 1. ¿Dónde vas a estudiar? 2. ¿Qué van a comer Uds.? 3. ¿Con quién va a ir Roberto?
    4. ¿A qué hora va a terminar Ud.? 5. ¿Cuándo van a trabajar ellos?
G. 1. discos 2. algo 3. castaños 4. pelirroja 5. estatura 6. cumpleaños 7. soltera 8. pareja
    9. entremeses 10. tocando / bailar 11. levantan / Salud 12. éxito
H. 1. el petróleo 2. momias 3. primavera 4. 300

Lección 5

A. 1. estamos sirviendo 2. estoy leyendo 3. está bailando 4. estás comiendo 5. está durmiendo
B. 1. es / está 2. está / Es 3. son 4. estás 5. es 6. es 7. estamos 8. Son 9. son 10. están
C. 1. prefieres / quiere 2. empiezan (comienzan) 3. pensamos 4. prefieren 5. queremos 6. entiendo
D. 1. mucho mayor que 2. tan alto como 3. la más inteligente de 4. tan bien como 5. el mejor de
    6. mucho más bonita que
E. 1. conmigo / contigo / con ellos (ellas) 2. para ti / para mí / para ella
F. 1. pagar / propina 2. sopa / coctel 3. tostado / mantequilla / mermelada 4. asado 5. especialidad /
    chuletas 6. helado 7. puré / ensalada 8. travieso 9. jamón 10. hamburguesa / caliente
G. 1. después de 2. principal

Lección 6

A. 1. recuerdo 2. vuelve 3. cuestan 4. puedo 5. encontramos 6. podemos 7. duerme
B. 1. piden 2. servimos 3. consigues 4. dice 5. sirve 6. digo 7. pedimos 8. consigue
C. 1. No, no voy a leerlos. (No, no los voy a leer.) 2. No, no lo (la) conoce. 3. No, no me llevan. 4. No, ella
    no te llama mañana. 5. No. no lo necesito. 6. No, no la tengo. 7. No, ellos no nos conocen. 8. No.
    no las conseguimos.
D. 1. Tengo algo aquí. 2. ¿Quiere algo más? 3. Siempre vamos al supermercado. 4. Quiero (o) la pluma
    roja o la pluma verde. 5. Siempre llamo a alguien.
E. 1. Hace cinco años que (yo) vivo en Honduras. 2. ¿Cuánto tiempo hace que (Ud.) estudia español,
    Sr. Smith? 3. Hace dos horas que (ellos) escriben. 4. Hace dos días que (ella) no come.
F. 1. azúcar 2. chuletas 3. panadería 4. almorzamos 5. vuelven 6. muertos 7. recién 8. cerca
    9. cangrejo / langosta 10. docena / salsa
G. 1. San José 2. las operaciones del Canal 3. no tiene 4. el café

Lección 7

A. 1. Ellos comieron tortilla y bebieron limonada. 2. Luis salió a las ocho y volvió a las cinco.
    3. Tú cerraste la puerta y abriste las ventanas 4. Yo empecé a las seis y terminé a las ocho. 5. Nosotros
    leímos un poema y ella leyó una novela. 6. Yo busqué el dinero y no lo encontré. 7. Yo llegué
    temprano y comencé a trabajar. 8. Yo compré carne aquí y pagué menos.
B. 1. fue 2. Dieron 3. fue 4. fui 5. fueron 6. Di 7. fui 8. fuimos
C. 1. No, no me traen el jugo. 2. No, no le doy el dinero a él. 3. No, no te voy a comprar los libros.
    (No, no voy a comprarte los libros). 4. No, no le voy a dar los cuadernos a Elsa.
    (No, no voy a darle los cuadernos a Elsa). 5. No, no me gusta el café. 6. No, no nos van a dar las
    invitaciones. (No. no van a darnos las invitaciones.)
D. 1. Me gusta / no me gusta 2. Te gusta 3. A mi mamá le gusta más 4. Nos gusta 5. A mi hermano le
    gusta
E. 1. se levantan / se acuestan 2. afeitarme 3. te pruebas 4. se sienta 5. nos bañamos 6. vestirse
F. 1. fin 2. divertí 3. se levantan 4. partido 5. cine 6. rompió 7. zoológico 8. escalar 9. montar
    10. medianoche 11. nadar 12. vez
G. 1. Quique 2. populares

Lección 8

A. 1. trajeron / traje   2. Tuve   3. hizo   4. dijiste / dijeron   5. vino / viniste   6. estuvimos / estuvieron   7. hicieron   8. supe   9. condujeron / conduje   10. quiso
B. 1. Sí, te (se) las compré.   2. Sí, se los trajimos.   3. Sí, me lo van a dar. (Sí, van a dármelo.)   4. Sí, nos los va a traer. (Sí, va a traérnoslos.)   5. Sí, se la va a comprar. (Sí, va a comprársela.)   6. Sí, me las traen.
C. 1. se divirtieron / siguieron / durmieron   2. pidió   3. murió   4. consiguió
D. 1. ibas   2. era   3. hablaban   4. veíamos   5. pescaban   6. comía
E. 1. fácilmente   2. especialmente   3. lentamente   4. rápidamente   5. lenta y claramente   6. francamente
F. 1. aire   2. cazar   3. armar   4. cesta   5. remar   6. pelo   7. frecuentemente   8. acuático   9. tomar   10. tabla   11. hacer   12. encanta
G. 1. mayor   2. merengue   3. Yunque

Lección 9

A. 1. para   2. por   3. por   4. por   5. para   6. para / por   7. para / por / por   8. por
B. 1. hace / calor   2. hace / frío / nieva   3. llueve   4. hay / niebla   5. hace / sol
C. 1. celebramos   2. Eran / salí / Llegué   3. dijo / era / pedí   4. era / vivía   5. estaba / vi   6. fue / estaba / Prefirió   7. hice   8. estábamos / llamaste
D. 1. Hace tres horas que llegué.   2. Hace cuatro meses que ellos vinieron.   3. Hace media hora que empecé a trabajar.   4. Hace cinco días que (ellos) terminaron.   5. Hace diez años que tú llegaste.
E. 1. el tuyo   2. mías   3. los tuyos   4. nuestros   5. El suyo (El de ellos)   6. mío / suyo (de ella)
F. 1. baratos   2. zapatería   3. facultad   4. par   5. mangas   6. servirle   7. moda   8. descalzo   9. ponerme   10. ojo / cara   11. calza   12. húmedo
G. 1. métrico   2. nuevo sol

Lección 10

A. 1. cerradas   2. abierta   3. roto   4. dormidos   5. escritas   6. hecha
B. 1. ha llegado   2. he roto   3. han traído   4. han vuelto / hemos podido   5. han muerto   6. has dicho
C. 1. habían vuelto   2. había firmado   3. habías hecho   4. habíamos escrito   5. había puesto   6. habían ido
D. 1. Llame   2. Camine   3. Salgan   4. Esté   5. venga   6. Vayan   7. lo haga   8. dé   9. sean   10. Póngala
E. 1. firmar / fechar   2. depositar   3. abierto / feriado   4. saldo   5. conjunta   6. cuadras   7. cola   8. talonario   9. sucursal   10. cajero   11. préstamo   12. efectivo   13. caja   14. sellos (estampillas)   15. diligencias
F. 1. Galápagos   2. Cuzco   3. Sucre   4. Itaipú

Lección 11

A. 1. Yo quiero que ella vaya a Viña del Mar.   2. Nosotros deseamos viajar en avión.   3. Ella me sugiere que yo vaya a Buenos Aires.   4. El agente quiere venderme el pasaje.   5. Ellos nos aconsejan que compremos seguro.   6. Yo no quiero llevar muchas maletas.   7. Ellos no quieren que ella los lleve en su coche.   8. Nosotros no queremos ir contigo.   9. ¿Tú me sugieres que venga luego?   10. Ella necesita que Uds. le den la maleta.
B. 1. que ella se vaya pronto.   2. que los pasajes sean muy caros.   3. estar aquí.   4. irse de vacaciones.   5. que mamá se sienta bien hoy.   6. que ellos no puedan ir a la fiesta.
C. 1. a / de / a / en / en / en / a   2. a / a / de / a   3. de / de
D. 1. asiento / ventanilla   2. mano / compartimiento   3. agencia   4. embarque (embarco) / auxiliar   5. exceso   6. salida   7. incluyen / excursiones   8. cambio   9. cancelar   10. viajero   11. crucero   12. lugares / capital
E. 1. vos   2. tango   3. separación

Lección 12

A. 1. hable español.   2. incluya el hotel.   3. no son caros.   4. salen a las seis.   5. pueda reservar los pasajes?
B. 1. Compra el televisor.   2. Díselo.   3. Viaja mañana.   4. Sal con esa persona.   5. Pon la maleta debajo del asiento.   6. Invítalo.   7. Vete.   8. Ven entre semana.   9. Regresa tarde.   10. Haz la reservación.   11. Tráeme el folleto.   12. Pídele los comprobantes ahora.

C. 1. se enamoró de / se casó con   2. insiste en   3. no te olvides de / Acuérdate de   4. no me di cuenta de / no confiaban en

D. 1. segundo / séptimo / quinto / primero / octavo / cuarto / noveno / tercero / sexto / décimo

E. 1. ducha   2. ascensor (elevador) / subir   3. calefacción   4. cama   5. precio   6. montón   7. desocupar   8. vista   9. servicio   10. aire   11. puesto / regalos   12. propietario   13. completa   14. libre   15. piso

F. 1. muchos   2. más   3. Argentina   4. Brasilia

Lección 13

A. 1. son   2. esté   3. pueda   4. vienen   5. sirven

B. 1. estén llamando la ambulancia.   2. ellos vayan a quedarse en el hospital.   3. prefiere venir con nosotros.   4. cobran 50 dólares por las radiografías.   5. el cuarto no tenga calefacción.   6. ella esté en el hospital.

C. 1. terminen   2. podamos   3. traiga   4. empiecen   5. necesito un médico   6. llegue   7. no tengo hambre   8. llueva

D. 1. Quedémonos aquí.   2. No se lo digamos a nadie.   3. Levantémonos a las siete.   4. Preguntemos el precio de los análisis.   5. Démoselo a la enfermera.   6. Vamos a la sala de rayos X.

E. 1. Cuál   2. Cuál   3. Qué   4. Qué   5. Cuál

F. 1. enfermera   2. codo   3. desmayarse   4. dedos   5. dientes   6. pasar   7. dudar   8. continuar   9. escalera   10. piernas   11. ojos   12. lengua   13. romperse   14. piano

G. 1. gratis   2. socorro

Lección 14

A. 1. Irán / hablarán   2. pesarás / tomarás   3. traerá / pondrá   4. vendré / pediré   5. pondrá / dará

B. 1. hablaríamos   2. saldría   3. harías   4. sabría   5. iría   6. pedirían

C. 1. pudiéramos   2. entendieras   3. pusieran   4. quisiera   5. trajera   6. tuviera   7. supiéramos   8. dijera   9. fuera   10. fueras

D. 1. trajera   2. vinieran   3. estuviera   4. supiera   5. tuviera   6. pidiera

E. 1. si tuviera dinero   2. si tenemos tiempo.   3. si pudiéramos.   4. Si Ud. la ve.   5. como si (ella) fuera su madre.

F. 1. grados   2. tos   3. mejore   4. recetar   5. calmante   6. dermatólogo / cardiólogo   7. tijeras   8. empeoró   9. cita (turno)   10. seguro   11. botiquín   12. suerte

G. 1. Madrid   2. segunda   3. Sevilla   4. flamenco

Vocabularies

The number following each vocabulary item indicates the lesson in which it first appears.

The following abbreviations are used:

abbr.	abbreviation	*indir. obj.*	indirect object	*pron.*	pronoun
adj.	adjective	*inf.*	infinitive	*refl. pron.*	reflexive pronoun
adv.	adverb	*m.*	masculine	*rel. pron.*	relative pronoun
conj.	conjunction	*Mex.*	Mexico	*sing.*	singular
dir. obj.	direct object	*neut. pron.*	neuter pronoun	*subj.*	subjunctive
f.	feminine	*obj.*	object	*v.*	verb
fam.	familiar	*pl.*	plural		
form.	formal	*prep.*	preposition		

Spanish-English

A

a at (with time of day), to, 2; **— la parrilla** grilled, 5; **— menos que** unless, 13; **— menudo** often, 8; **— poco más de** a little more than; ¿**— qué hora?** at what time?, 2; ¿**— quién(es)?** whom, 4; **— veces** sometimes, 6; **— ver** let's see, 6

abierto(a) open, 10

abogado(a) *(m., f.)* lawyer

abordar to board, 11

abrigo *(m.)* coat, 9

abril April, 2

abrir to open, 3

abrochar: abrocharse el cinturón de seguridad to fasten the seat belt, 11

abuela *(f.)* grandmother, 4

abuelo *(m.)* grandfather, 4

abuelos *(m. pl.)* grandparents

aburrido(a) boring, 2

aburrirse to be bored, 7

acá here, 8

acabado(a) finished

acabar de + *inf.* to have just (done something), 8

acampar to camp, 8

accidente *(m.)* accident

aceite *(m.)* oil

acompañado(a) with someone else, accompanied

aconsejar to advise, 11

acordarse (de) (o > ue) to remember, 12

acostarse (o > ue) to go to bed, 7

acostumbrado(a) accustomed or used to, 8

actividad *(f.)* activity, 8; **— al aire libre** outdoor activity, 8

actualmente at present

además *(adv.)* besides, 2; **— de** *(prep.)* in addition to

adiós good-bye, 1

administración de empresas *(f.)* business administration, 2

admitir to admit, 14

¿adónde? where (to)?, 4

advertencia *(f.)* warning

aerolínea *(f.)* airline, 11

aeropuerto *(m.)* airport, 11

afeitarse to shave, 7

afortunadamente luckily, 14

agencia *(f.)* agency, 11; **— de viajes** *(f.)* travel agency, 11

agente *(m., f.)* agent, 11

agosto August, 2

agua (el) *(f.)* water, 2; **— con hielo** *(f.)* ice water, 2; **— mineral** mineral water, 2; **— oxigenada** hydrogen peroxide, 14

aguacate *(m.)* avocado, 6

aguafiestas *(m., f.)* spoilsport, 2

águila (el) *(f.)* eagle

ahí there, 8

ahora now, 4; **— mismo** right now

ahorrar to save *(money)*, 10

aire *(m.)* air; **— acondicionado** *(m.)* air conditioning, 12

ají *(m.)* green pepper, 6

al (a + el) to the, 4; **— día** a day, per day, 6; **— día siguiente** (on) the following day, 5

albóndiga *(f.)* meatball, 6

alegrarse (de) to be glad (about), 12

alemán *(m.)* German *(language)*

alérgico(a) allergic, 13

alfabeto *(m.)* alphabet

algo something, anything, 5; ¿**— más?** anything else?, 10; **— para comer (tomar)** something to eat (drink)

algodón *(m.)* cotton, 14

alguien someone, anyone, 6

algún, alguno(s), alguna(s) any, some, 6; **en alguna parte** anywhere, somewhere; **alguna vez** ever, 6; **algunas veces** sometimes, 6

allá there

allí there, 12

alma (el) *(f.)* soul

almorzar (o > ue) to have lunch, 6

almuerzo *(m.)* lunch, 5

alquilar to rent, 8

alto(a) high, tall, 1

alumno(a) *(m., f.)* student, 1

amarillo(a) yellow, 1

ambulancia *(f.)* ambulance, 13

amigo(a) *(m., f.)* friend, 2

amistad *(f.)* friendship

amor love; **mi amor** darling, my love, 8

amparo *(m.)* shelter
ampliar to expand
analfabeto(a) *(m., f.)* illiterate
análisis *(m.)* test, 13
anaranjado(a) orange, 1
ancho(a) wide
anfitrión *(m.)* host
anfitriona *(f.)* hostess
animado(a) enthused, 4
aniversario *(m.)* anniversary, 5; **— de bodas** *(m.)* wedding anniversary
anoche last night, 7
anotar to write down
anteayer the day before yesterday
antes before; **— de** *(prep.)* before, 6; **— de que** *(conj.)* before, 13
antiácido *(m.)* antacid, 14
antibiótico *(m.)* antibiotic, 14
antiguo(a) old
antipático(a) unpleasant, 1
antropología *(f.)* anthropology, 2
añadir to add
año *(m.)* year, 2; **— escolar** *(m.)* school year
aparatos electrodomésticos *(m. pl.)* home appliances
apartamento *(m.)* apartment, 6
apellido *(m.)* last name; **— de soltera** maiden name
apio *(m.)* celery, 6
aprender (a) to learn (to), 11
apretar (e > ie) to be tight, 9
apurarse to hurry
aquel(los), aquella(s) *(adj.)* that, those *(distant)*, 3
aquél, aquéllos, aquélla(s) *(pron.)* that (one), those *(distant)*, 3
aquello *(neut. pron.)* that, 3
aquí here, 5; **— está** here it is, 2; **— las tiene** here you are, 10
árbol *(m.)* tree, 13
archivar la información to store information, 10
arena *(f.)* sand, 8
aretes *(m. pl.)* earrings, 9
argentino(a) Argentinian
armar to pitch (a tent), to put together, 8
arrancar to tear out
arroyo *(m.)* brook
arroz *(m.)* rice, 5; **— con leche** rice pudding, 5
arte *(m.)* art, 2

asado(a) baked, 5
ascensor *(m.)* elevator, 12
asegurado(a) insured
aseguranza *(f.)(Mex.)* insurance, 14
así que so, 7
asiento *(m.)* seat, 11; **— de pasillo** *(m.)* aisle seat, 11; **— de ventanilla** *(m.)* window seat, 11
asignatura *(f.)* course, subject, 2
asistir to attend
aspiradora *(f.)* vacuum cleaner
aspirina *(f.)* aspirin
atender (e > ie) to see *(a patient)*, 13
aula (el) *(f.)* classroom, 2
aunque although, 4; even if, 13
auto *(m.)* automobile, 10
autobús *(m.)* bus
automóvil *(m.)* automobile, 10
auxiliar de vuelo *(m., f.)* flight attendant, 11
ave (el) *(f.)* bird
avena *(f.)* porridge
averiguar to find out, 11
avión *(m.)* plane, 11
ayer yesterday, 7
ayuda *(f.)* assistance
ayudar to help, 12
azafata *(f.)* flight attendant, 11
azúcar *(m.)* sugar, 6
azul blue, 1

B

bailar to dance, 4; **¿Bailamos?** Shall we dance?, 4
bajar to go down
bajo *(prep.)* under, 8
bajo(a) short *(height)*, 5
balneario *(m.)* beach resort
banco *(m.)* bank, 10
bañadera *(f.)* bathtub, 12
bañarse to bathe, 7
baño *(m.)* bathroom, 3
barato(a) inexpensive, 9
barrer to sweep, 3
barrio *(m.)* neighborhood
basura *(f.)* garbage, 3
bata *(f.)* robe, 9
batería de cocina *(f. sing.)* kitchen utensils
batido *(m.)* milkshake
beber to drink, 3
bebida *(f.)* drink, 4

béisbol *(m.)* baseball, 7
biblioteca *(f.)* library, 1
bien fine, well, 1; **muy —** very well, 1; **no muy —** not very well, 1
bienvenido(a) welcome, 1
biftec *(m.)* steak, 5
billete *(m.)* ticket, 11
billetera *(f.)* wallet, 9
biología *(f.)* biology, 2
bisabuela *(f.)* great-grandmother
bisabuelo *(m.)* great-grandfather
bisnieta *(f.)* great-granddaughter
bisnieto *(m.)* great-grandson
bistec *(m.)* steak, 5
blanco(a) white, 1
blanquillo *(m.) (Mex.)* egg, 5
blusa *(f.)* blouse, 9
boca *(f.)* mouth, 13
boda *(f.)* wedding, 5
bolígrafo *(m.)* pen, 1
bolsa *(f.)* handbag, purse; **— de dormir** *(f.)* sleeping bag, 8
bolso *(m.)* handbag, purse; **— de mano** *(m.)* carry-on bag, 11
bonito(a) pretty, 1
borrador *(m.)* eraser, 1
borrico *(m.)* donkey
bosque *(m.)* forest
bota *(f.)* boot, 9
botella *(f.)* bottle, 2
botones *(m. sing.)* bellhop, 12
brazo *(m.)* arm, 13
brindar to toast, 4
brindis *(m.)* toast *(at a celebration)*, 4
brócoli *(m.)* broccoli, 6
bromear to joke, to kid, 7
bucear to scuba dive, 8
bueno... well . . . , okay, 1
bueno(a) good, 2; **buenas noches** good evening, good night, 1; **buenas tardes** good afternoon, 1; **buenos días** good morning, 1
bufanda *(f.)* scarf, 9
buscar to look for, to get, 9; to pick up

C

caballería *(f.)* chivalry
caballero *(m.)* gentleman; knight
caber to fit, 4
cabeza *(f.)* head, 13
cacerola *(f.)* saucepan, 3
cadena *(f.)* chain, 9

caerse to fall down, 13
café (m.) (adj.) brown, 1; coffee, 2; — **con leche** coffee with milk; **café** (m.) (restaurant), 5; — **al aire libre** outdoor café
cafetera (f.) coffeepot, 3
cafetería (f.) cafeteria, 2
caja de seguridad (f.) safe-deposit box, 10
cajero(a) (m., f.) teller, 10; — **automático** (m.) automatic teller machine, 10
calcetín (m.) sock
caldo (m.) soup (Mex.), 5; broth
calefacción (f.) heating, 12
calidad (f.) quality
cálido(a) hot, 9
caliente hot, 12
calle (f.) street, 1
calmante (m.) tranquilizer, painkiller, 14
calumnia (f.) slander
calzar to wear a certain shoe size, 9
calzoncillos (m. pl.) undershorts, 9
cama (f.) bed, 12; — **chica (pequeña)** (f.) twin bed, 12; — **doble** (f.) double bed, 12; — **matrimonial** (f.) double bed
camarera (f.) waitress, 5
camarero (m.) waiter, 5
camarones (m. pl.) shrimp, 5
cambiar to change, 7; — **de avión** to change planes
cambio (m.) change; **en cambio** on the other hand, 8
cambio de moneda (m.) rate of exchange, 11; **¿a cómo está el —?** what's the rate of exchange?, 11
camilla (f.) gurney, stretcher
caminar to walk
camisa (f.) shirt, 9
camiseta (f.) T-shirt, 9
camisón (m.) nightgown, 9
campo (m.) country (as opposed to city); field; — **de batalla** battlefield
cancelar to cancel, 11
cangrejo (m.) crab, 6
canoa (f.) canoe, 8
cansado(a) tired, 4
cansarse to get tired, 11
cantidad (f.) amount
caña de azúcar (f.) sugar cane
caña de pescar (f.) fishing rod, 8
capital (f.) capital, 11

cara (f.) face, 13
¡caramba! gee!, 1
cardiólogo(a) (m., f.) cardiologist, 14
cardo (m.) thistle
cargado(a) loaded
carmín (m.) red (Cuba)
carne (f.) meat, 6
carnicería (f.) meat market
caro(a) expensive, 6
carro (m.) automobile, 10
carta (f.) letter, 10
cartera (f.) handbag, purse
casa (f.) house, 3; — **central** main office, 10; **en —** at home
casado(a) married, 4; **recién casados** (m. pl.) newlyweds, 6
casarse (con) to marry, to get married (to), 12
casete (m.) (cassette) tape
casi almost, 13
caso (m.) case; **en ese —** in that case
castaño brown (hair or eyes), 4
catarro (m.) cold
catorce fourteen, 2
cazar to hunt, 8
cebolla (f.) onion, 5
cédula de identidad (f.) I.D. card, 12
celebrar to celebrate, 4
cena (f.) dinner
cenar to have dinner (supper), 3
céntrico(a) central, 12
cerca (de) near, 6; — **de aquí** near here
cerdo (m.) pork, 6
cereal (m.) cereal
cereza (f.) cherry, 6
cero zero, 1
cerrado(a) closed, 10
cerrar (e > ie) to close, 5
certificado(a) certified, 10
cerveza (f.) beer, 2
césped (m.) lawn, 3
cesta (f.) basket, 8
cesto de papeles (m.) wastebasket, 1
chaleco (m.) vest, 9
champán (m.) champagne, 4
chaqueta (f.) jacket, 9
chau bye, 1
cheque (m.) check, 10; — **de viajero** (m.) traveler's check, 11
chequeo (m.) checkup, 14
chica (f.) young girl, 1

chico (m.) young man, 1
chico(a) little, small, 8
chillido (m.) screech
chocar (con) to collide, 13
chocolate (m.) chocolate; — **caliente** (m.) hot chocolate, 2
chorizo (m.) sausage
chuleta (f.) chop (of meat), 6; — **de cerdo** pork chop, 6; — **de ternera** veal chop, 6
ciclón (m.) cyclone
cielo (m.) sky, 9; **el — está despejado** the sky is clear, 9; **el — está nublado** the sky is cloudy, 9
cien (ciento) one hundred, 2
ciencias políticas (f. pl.) political science, 2
cierto(a) true
ciervo (m.) deer
cigüeña (f.) stork
cinco five, 1
cincuenta fifty, 2
cine (m.) movies, movie theater, 7
cinta (f.) tape
cinto (m.) belt, 9
cinturón (m.) belt, 9
cirujano(a) (m., f.) surgeon, 14
cita (f.) appointment, 14
ciudad (f.) city, 3
claro(a) light
clase (f.) class, 1; — **de español (castellano)** Spanish class, 1; — **turista** tourist class, 11; **primera —** first class, 11
clima (m.) climate, 9
club (m.) club, 4; — **nocturno** (m.) nightclub, 7
cobrar to charge, 10; — **un cheque** to cash a check, 10
cocina (f.) kitchen, 3; stove
cocinar to cook, 6
cocinero(a) (m., f.) cook, 6
coche (m.) automobile, 10
codo (m.) elbow, 13
colador (m.) strainer, 3
colar (o > ue) to strain
color (m.) color, 1
combinación (f.) slip
comedor (m.) dining room
comenzar (e > ie) to start, to begin, 5
comer to eat, 3; — **algo** to have something to eat, 4
comestibles (m. pl.) groceries (food items)
comida (f.) food, meal, 3
comido(a) eaten, 10

como like, 9; as; **— si** as if, 14; **— siempre** as usual, 13

¿cómo? pardon, 1; how? 1; **¿— es...?** what is . . . like?; **¿— está usted?** how are you? *(form.)*, 1; **¿— estás?** how are you? *(fam.)*, 1; **— no** of course, sure; **¿— se dice...?** how do you say . . . ?, 1; **¿— se llama usted?** what is your *(form.)* name?, 1; **¿— te llamas?** what is your *(fam.)* name?, 1

cómodo(a) comfortable, 9

compañero(a) de clase *(m., f.)* classmate, 1; **— de cuarto** *(m., f.)* roommate, 1

comparativo *(m.)* comparative

compartimiento de equipajes *(m.)* luggage compartment, 11

compartir to share, 11

complacer to please

comprar to buy, 6

comprobante *(m.)* claim check

comprometerse (con) to get engaged (to), 12

computadora (personal) *(f.)* (personal) computer, 1

con with, 1; **¿— quién?** with whom?; **— razón** no wonder; **— tal (de) que** provided that, 13; **— vista a** overlooking (with a view of), 12

concierto *(m.)* concert, 7

condimentar to season (food)

conducir to drive, to conduct, 4

conferencia *(f.)* lecture, 14

confiar en to trust, 12

confirmar to confirm, 11

conmigo with me, 3

conocer to know, to be acquainted with, 4

conocido(a) known

conseguir (e > i) to obtain, to get, 6

consultorio *(m.)* doctor's office, 14

contabilidad *(f.)* accounting, 2

contento(a) happy, content, 4

contigo with you *(fam.)*, 5

continuar to continue, 13

convenir (en) to agree (on), 12

conversar to talk, to converse, 2

convertirse (e > ie) en to turn into, 14

copa *(f.)* wineglass, 2

corazón *(m.)* heart, 13

corbata *(f.)* tie, 9

cordero *(m.)* lamb, 5

correo *(m.)* post office, 10

correr to run, 3

corsario *(m.)* privateer

cortar to cut, 3; **— el césped** to mow the lawn, 3; **—se** to cut (oneself), 13; **—se el pelo** to get one's hair cut

corto(a) short, 9

cosa *(f.)* thing, 3; **cosas que hacer** things to do, 3

costar (o > ue) to cost, 6; **—un ojo de la cara** to cost an arm and a leg, 9

costumbre *(f.)* custom

crecer to grow

creer to think, to believe; **— que sí (no)** to think so (not), 13

crema *(f.)* cream, 5

criado(a) *(m., f.)* servant, 6

crucero *(m.)* cruise, 11

cuaderno *(m.)* notebook, 1

cuadra *(f.)* block, 10

¿cuál? *(pl. ¿cuáles?)* which?, what?, 1; **¿— es tu número de teléfono?** what's your phone number?, 1

cualquier(a) any, 13; **en — momento** at any time

cuando when, 13

¿cuándo? when?, 2

¿cuánto(a)? how much?, 3; **¿por cuánto tiempo?** how long?

¿cuántos(as)? how many?, 2

cuarenta forty, 2

cuarto *(m.)* room, 3; **— de baño** *(m.)* bathroom, 3; **— de huéspedes** *(m.)* guest room; **menos —** quarter to, 2; **y —** quarter past or after, 2

cuatro four, 1

cuatrocientos(as) four hundred, 3

cubano(a) *(m., f.)* Cuban; **cubanoamericano(a)** Cuban American, 1

cuchara *(f.)* spoon, 5

cucharita *(f.))* teaspoon, 5

cuchillo *(m.)* knife, 5

cuello *(m.)* neck, 13; collar

cuenta *(f.)* account, 10; bill, check *(at a restaurant)*, 5; **— de ahorros** savings account, 10; **— conjunta** joint account, 10; **— corriente** checking account, 10

cuerpo *(m.)* body, 13

cuervo *(m.)* crow

cuidar(se) to take care (of oneself), 14

cumpleaños *(m. sing.)* birthday, 4

cuñada *(f.)* sister-in-law, 4

cuñado *(m.)* brother-in-law, 4

curita *(f.)* adhesive bandage, 14

D

danza aeróbica *(f.)* aerobic dance, 2

dar to give, 4

darse cuenta (de) to realize, 12

darse prisa to hurry up

de of, about, in, 2; from, with, 11; **— cortesía** polite; **¿— dónde eres?** where are you from?, 1; **— estatura mediana** of medium height, 4; **—modo (manera) que** so, 6; **— nada** you're welcome, 1

debajo de under

deber to have to, must, 3

débil weak

decidir to decide, 4

décimo(a) tenth, 12

decir (e > i) to say, 5; to tell, 6; **dime una cosa** tell me something, 12

dedo *(m.)* finger, 13; **— del pie** toe, 13

dejar to leave (behind), 5; to let, 11; **— de** to stop

del (de + el) of the, 4

deletrear to spell

deletreo *(m.)* spelling

delgado(a) slender, thin, 1

demasiado(a) too much

demostrativo(a) demonstrative

dentro de within, 14; **— quince días** in two weeks

departamento *(m.)* apartment, 6; **— de caballeros** *(m.)* men's department

dependiente(a) *(m., f.)* clerk

deporte *(m.)* sport

depositar to deposit, 10

derecho(a) right; **a la derecha** to the right

dermatólogo(a) *(m., f.)* dermatologist, 14

desarrollar to develop

desastre *(m.)* disaster, 3

desayunar to have breakfast, 5

desayuno *(m.)* breakfast

descalzo(a) barefoot; **andar —** to go barefoot, 9

descansar to rest, 3

descubierto(a) discovered

descuento *(m.)* discount

desde from
desear to wish, to want, 2
desfallecer to faint
desgraciadamente unfortunately
desinfectante *(adj.)* disinfectant, 14
desinfectar to disinfect, 13
desmayarse to lose consciousness, to faint, 13
desocupar to vacate, 12; — **el cuarto** to check out of a hotel room, 12
despedida *(f.)* farewell
despejado(a) clear *(sky)*, 9
despertarse (e > ie) to wake, 7
después then, 3; later, 5; — **de** after
detergente *(m.)* detergent, 6
día *(m.)* day, 1; **al — siguiente** next day, 5; — **feriado** holiday, 10
diario *(m.)* newspaper, diary
dicho(a) said, 10
diciembre December, 2
diecinueve nineteen, 2
dieciocho eighteen, 2
dieciséis sixteen, 2
diecisiete seventeen, 2
diente *(m.)* tooth, 13
diez ten, 1
difícil difficult, 1
diligencia *(f.)* errand
dinero *(m.)* money, 2
dirección *(f.)* address, 1
disco: — compacto *(m.)* compact disc (CD), 4; — **duro** hard drive, 10
discoteca *(f.)* club, disco, 7
diseñar programas to design, write programs
disponible vacant, available, 12
divertirse (e > ie) to have fun, 7
doce twelve, 2
docena *(f.)* dozen, 6
doctor (Dr.) *(m.)* doctor, 1; M.D., 13
doctora (Dra.) *(f.)* doctor, 1; M.D., 13
documento *(m.)* document
doler (o > ue) to hurt, to ache, 13
dolor *(m.)* pain, 13; — **de cabeza** *(m.)* headache; — **de garganta** sore throat, 14
domicilio *(m.)* address, 1
domingo *(m.)* Sunday, 2
don title of respect, used with a man's first name, 6

¿dónde? where?, 1
doña title of respect, used with a woman's first name, 6
dormir (o > ue) to sleep, 6; —**se** to fall asleep
dormitorio *(m.)* bedroom, 3
dos two, 1; **somos —** there are two of us
doscientos(as) two hundred, 2
ducha *(f.)* shower, 12
dudar to doubt, 13
dueño(a) *(m., f.)* owner, proprietor, 12
durante during
durar to last
durazno *(m.)* peach, 6

E

echar to share; to pour out
efectivo *(m.)* cash, 10
ejercicio *(m.)* exercise
el *(m. sing.)* the, 1
él he, 1; *(obj. of prep.)* him, 5
elegante elegant
elegir (e > i) to choose, 6
elevador *(m.)* elevator, 12
ella she, 1; *(obj. of prep.)* her, 5
ellas *(f.)* they, 1; *(obj. of prep.)* them, 5
ellos *(m.)* they, 1; *(obj. of prep.) them*, 5
elogiar to praise
embarazada pregnant, 14
emergencia *(f.)* emergency, 11
empeorar(se) to get worse, 14
empezar (e > ie) to start, to begin, 5
empleado(a) *(m., f.)* clerk, 9
en in, on, at, 1; inside, over; — **cambio** on the other hand, 8; — **casa** at home; — **caso de que** in case, 13; — **cuanto** as soon as, 9; — **efectivo** in cash, 10; — **español** in Spanish; — **inglés** in English; —**parte** in part, 11; — **seguida** right away, 14; — **vez de** instead of, 7
enamorado(a) in love, 4
enamorarse (de) to fall in love (with), 12
encantador(a) charming, 4
encantar to love, to like very much, 8
encargarse to take charge
encendido(a) bright
encontrar (o > ue) to find, 6
encuesta *(f.)* survey

enero January, 2
enfermedad *(f.)* disease, sickness, 14
enfermero(a) *(m., f)* nurse, 13
enfermo(a) sick
ensalada *(f.)* salad, 3; — **mixta** *(f.)* mixed salad
ensayo *(m.)* essay
enseguida right away, 14
enseñar to teach, 11; to show, 12
entender (e > ie) to understand, 5
enterrado(a) buried
entonces then, 2; in that case, 5
entrar (en) to enter, to go (in), 7
entre between; — **comidas** between meals; — **semana** during the week
entremeses *(m. pl.)* appetizers, finger food, 4
enviar to send, 4
enyesar to put a cast on
equipaje *(m.)* luggage, 11
escalar montañas to climb mountains, 7
escalera *(f.)* stairs, 13; — **mecánica** escalator, 13
esclusa *(f.)* lock *(in a canal)*
escoba *(f.)* broom
escoger to choose, 6
escopeta *(f.)* shotgun, 8
escribir to write, 3
escrito(a) written, 10
escritorio *(m.)* desk, 1
escuela *(f.)* school, 9
ese, esos, esa(s) *(adj.)* that those *(nearby)*, 3
ése, ésos, ésa(s) *(pron.)* that (one), those, 3
eso *(neut. pron.)* that, 3
espaguetis *(m. pl.)* spaghetti, 6
espalda *(f.)* back, 13
español *(m.)* Spanish *(language)*, 1
español(a) *(m., f.)* Spanish *(person)*
esparadrapo *(m.)* adhesive tape, 14
especialidad *(f.)* specialty, 5
especialmente especially, 3
esperar to wait, 5; to hope, 11; **espero que sí** I hope so, 8
esposa *(f.)* wife, 4
esposo *(m.)* husband, 4
esquí acuático *(m.)* waterski, 8
esquiar to ski, 7
esquina *(f.)* corner
esta *(adj.)* this, 3; — **noche** tonight, 1

estacionar to park, 10
estación *(f.)* season, 2
estadio *(m.)* stadium
estado *(m.)* state; **en—** pregnant, 14
estadounidense *(m., f.)* U.S. *(used to denote citizenship)*, 1
estampilla *(f.)* stamp, 10
estar to be, 4; **está bien** all right, okay, 6; **— a dieta** to be on a diet; **— de moda** to be in style, 9; **— de vacaciones** to be on vacation, 5; **— en regla** to be in order; **— muerto(a) de hambre** to be starving, 6 **— seguro(a)** to be sure
estatura *(f.)* height, 4; **de — mediana** of medium height, 4
este, estos, esta(s) *(adj.)* this, these, 3
éste, éstos, ésta(s) *(pron.)* this (one), these, 3
estéreo *(m.)* stereo
estimarse to have self-esteem
esto *(neut. pron.)* this, 3
estómago *(m.)* stomach, 13
estrecho(a) narrow
estrella *(f.)* star, 8
estudiante *(m., f.)* student, 1
estudiar to study, 2
examinar to examine, to check, 14
exceso *(m.)* excess, 11; **— de equipaje** *(m.)* excess luggage *(charge)*, 11
excursión *(f.)* tour, excursion, 11
excusa *(f.)* excuse, 3
éxito *(m.)* success, 4; **todo un —** quite a success, 4
expresión *(f.)* expression
exterior *(m.)* exterior, 12
extranjero(a) foreigner
extraño(a) *(m., f.)* stranger

F

fácil easy, 8
fácilmente easily, 8
facultad *(f.)* college, 9
falda *(f.)* skirt, 9
falso(a) false
familia *(f.)* family, 3
famoso(a) famous, 6
farmacéutico(a) *(m., f.)* pharmacist
farmacia *(f.)* pharmacy, 14
favorito(a) favorite, 3
febrero February, 2
fechar to date *(a document)*, 10

feliz happy, 4
feo(a) ugly, 1
fiebre *(f.)* fever, 14
fiesta *(f.)* party, 4; **— de bienvenida** welcome party
fijarse en to check, to notice, 12
fin *(m.)* end; **— de semana** *(m.)* weekend, 7
firmar to sign, 10
física *(f.)* physics, 2
flan *(m.)* caramel custard, 5
flor *(f.)* flower
florero *(m.)* vase, 7
fogata *(f.)* bonfire, 8
folleto *(m.)* brochure, 12
fortaleza *(f.)* fortress
fractura *(f.)* fracture, 13
fracturar(se) to fracture
francés *(m.)* French *(language)*
franco(a) open
frecuentemente often, 8
fregar (e > ie) to wash *(dishes)*
freír (e > i) to fry
fresa *(f.)* strawberry, 6
frío(a) cold, 9
frito(a) fried, 8
fruta *(f.)* fruit, 5
fuente de ingresos *(f.)* source of income
fumar to smoke
funcionar to work, to function; **no funciona** it doesn't work, 12
fundado(a) founded

G

gamba *(f.)* shrimp, 5
ganado *(m.)* cattle
garaje *(m.)* garage, 3
garganta *(f.)* throat, 14
gastar to spend *(money)*, 9
general general, 8
generalmente generally, 8
género *(m.)* gender
gente *(f.)* people, 10
geografía *(f.)* geography, 2
geología *(f.)* geology, 2
gerente *(m., f.)* manager
ginecólogo(a) *(m., f.)* gynecologist, 14
giro postal *(m.)* money order, 10
gobierno *(m.)* government
golpear(se) to hit (oneself), 13
gordo(a) fat, 1
gota *(f.)* drop; **—s para la nariz** *(f. pl.)* nose drops
gracias thanks, 1; **muchas —** thank you very much, 1

grado *(m.)* degree *(temperature)*, 9; **hay ... grados** it's ... degrees, 9
grande big, 5; **gran** big, great
gratis free (of charge), 10
grave serious, 14
gripe *(f.)* flu, 14
gris gray, 1
gritar to shout, 4
grupo *(m.)* group
guante *(m.)* glove, 9
guapo(a) handsome, 1
guardar to keep
guatemalteco(a) Guatemalan, 4
guerra *(f.)* war
gustar to like, to appeal, 7
gusto *(m.)* pleasure, 1; **el — es mío** the pleasure is mine, 1; **mucho —** it's a pleasure to meet you; how do you do?, 1

H

Habana *(f.)* Havana
haber *(auxiliary verb)* to have, 10; **va a —** there is going to be, 12
había una vez once upon a time
habitación *(f.)* room, 12
hablar to speak, 2; **habla... (nombre)** this is ... (name) speaking; **hablado** spoken, 10
hacer to do, to make, 3; **hace... ... ago**, 9; **— buen (mal) tiempo** to be good (bad) weather, 9; **— calor** to be hot, 9; **— cola** to stand in line, 10; **— diligencias** to run errands, 10; **— ejercicio** to exercise; **— escala** to make a stop over, 11; **— frío** to be cold, 9; **— sol** to be sunny, 9; **— surfing** to surf, 8; **— una caminata** to go hiking, 8; **— una radiografía** to take an X-ray, 13; **— viento** to be windy, 9
hambre *(f.)* hunger, 3; **tener —** to be hungry, 3
hamburguesa *(f.)* hamburger, 5
hasta until, 7; even; **— la vista** (I'll) see you around, 1; **— luego** (I'll) see you later, 1; **— mañana** (I'll) see you tomorrow, 1; **— que** *(conj.)* until, 13
hay there is, there are, 1
hecho(a) made, done, 10

heladera *(f.)*   refrigerator, 3
helado *(m.)*   ice cream, 5
helado(a)   frozen
herida *(f.)*   wound, 13
herido(a)   wounded
hermana *(f.)*   sister, 3
hermanastra *(f.)*   stepsister
hermanastro *(m.)*   stepbrother
hermano *(m.)*   brother, 3
hermoso(a)   beautiful
hielo *(m.)*   ice, 2
hija *(f.)*   daughter, 4
hijastra *(f.)*   stepdaughter
hijastro *(m.)*   stepson
hijo *(m.)*   son, 4
hijos *(m. pl.)*   children, 3
hinchado(a)   swollen, 13
historia *(f.)*   history, 2
hola   hello, hi, 1
hombre *(m.)*   man, 1
hombro *(m.)*   shoulder, 13
hora *(f.)*   hour, time, 2; **¿qué —
es?**   what time is it?, 2; **¿a
qué —?**   at what time?, 2
horario de clases *(m.)*   class
schedule, 2
horno *(m.)*   oven, 3; **al —**   baked;
— de microondas *(m.)*
microwave oven, 3
hospedarse   to stay, to lodge *(i.e.,
at a hotel)*, 8
hospital *(m.)*   hospital, 13
hotel *(m.)*   hotel, 8
hoy   today, 2; **— mismo**   this very
day, 14
hubo   there was, there were
huevo *(m.)*   egg, 5
húmedo(a)   humid, 9
huracán *(m.)*   hurricane

I

ida *(f.)*: **de —**   one-way, 11; **de — y
vuelta**   round-trip, 11
idea *(f.)*   idea, 2
identificación *(f.)*   identification
idioma *(m.)*   language
iglesia *(f.)*   church
impermeable *(m.)*   raincoat
importarle (a uno)   to matter, 6
impresora *(f.)*   printer, 10
incluir   to include, 11
infección *(f.)*   infection
información *(f.)*   information
informática *(f.)*   computer
science, 2
ingeniería *(f.)*   engineering
inglés *(m.)*   English *(language)*, 2

inglés(esa) *(m., f.)*   English
(person)
ingreso *(m.)*   income
inodoro *(m.)*   toilet, 12
insistir en   to insist on, 12
inteligente   intelligent, 1
interés *(m.)*   interest
interesante   interesting, 1
interior   interior, 12
internacional   international, 1
interrogativo(a)   interrogative
invierno *(m.)*   winter, 2
invitación *(f.)*   invitation, 4
invitado(a) *(m., f.)*   guest, 4
invitar   to invite, 4
inyección *(f.)*   shot, injection, 13;
— antitetánica   tetanus shot, 13
ir   to go, 4; **— a** + *inf.*   to be going
to, 4; **— a acampar**   to go
camping, 8; **— de compras**
to go shopping; **— de pesca**
to go fishing; **— (se) de
vacaciones**   to go on vacation;
— se   to go away
istmo *(m.)*   isthmus
italiano *(m.)*   Italian *(language)*
izquierdo(a)   left; **a la
izquierda**   to the left

J

jabón *(m.)*   soap
jamás   never, 6
jamón *(m.)*   ham, 5
jarabe *(m.)*   syrup, 14
jardín *(m.)*   garden, 12
jefe(a) *(m., f.)*   boss
joven   young, 1
joya *(f.)*   jewel; *(pl.)*   jewelry
juego *(m.)*   game, 7
jueves *(m.)*   Thursday, 2
jugador(a) *(m., f.)*   player
jugar (u > ue)   to play *(i.e., a
game)* 8; **— al golf**   to play golf,
8; **— al tenis**   to play tennis, 8
jugo *(m.)*   juice, 2; **— de manzana**
(m.)   apple juice, 2; **— de
naranja** *(m.)*   orange juice, 2;
— de tomate *(m.)*   tomato juice,
2; **— de toronja** *(m.)*   grapefruit
juice, 2; **— de uvas** *(m.)*   grape
juice, 2
julio   July, 2
junio   June, 2
juntarse   to get together, 8
junto(a)   next (to)
juntos(as)   together, 2
justo(a)   fair, 7

L

la *(f. sing.)*   the, 1; *(pron.)* her,
you, it, 6
laboratorio de lenguas *(m.)*
language lab
ladera *(f.)*   hillside
lago *(m.)*   lake, 8
langosta *(f.)*   lobster, 5
lápiz *(m.)*   pencil, 1
largo(a)   long, 9
las *(f. pl.)*   the, 1; *(pron.)* them,
you, 6
lastimar(se)   to hurt (oneself), 13
Latinoamérica *(f.)*   Latin America
lavabo *(m.)*   washbasin, 12
lavadora *(f.)*   washing machine, 3
lavaplatos *(m. sing.)*
dishwasher, 3
lavar   to wash, 3; **—se**   to wash
(oneself), 7; **—se la cabeza**   to
wash one's hair
le   (to) him, (to) her, (to) you
(form.), 7
lección *(f.)*   lesson
leche *(f.)*   milk, 2
lechuga *(f.)*   lettuce, 6
lector(a) *(m., f.)*   reader
leer   to read, 3
lejía *(f.)*   bleach, 6
lejos   far (away)
lengua *(f.)*   tongue, 13; language
lentamente   slowly, 8
lento(a)   slow, 8
les   (to) them, (to) you *(pl. form.)*, 7
letrero *(m.)*   sign
levantar   to raise, 4; **levantarse**
to get up, 7
libertad *(f.)*   liberty
libre   off, 6; vacant, available, 12;
free
libreta de ahorros *(f.)*   passbook, 10
libro *(m.)*   book, 1
licencia para manejar (conducir)
(f.)   driver's license
licuadora *(f.)*   blender, 3
ligero(a)   light
limonada *(f.)*   lemonade, 3
limpiar   to clean, 3; **— el polvo**
to dust, 3
limpio(a)   clean, 12
lindo(a)   pretty, 1
liquidación *(f.)*   sale
lista *(f.)*   list, 5; **— de espera** *(f.)*
waiting list, 11
listo(a)   ready
literatura *(f.)*   literature, 2
llamada *(f.)*   call, 11

llamar to call; **— a la puerta** to knock at the door

llamarse to be named, 1; **¿cómo se llama?** what is your (form.) name?, 1, **¿cómo te llamas?** what is your (fam.) name?, 1; **me llamo...** my name is . . . , 1

llave (f.) key

llegar to arrive, 3; **— tarde (temprano)** to be late (early)

llenar to fill, to fill out, 10

lleno(a) full, 12

llevar to take (someone or something someplace), 4; to wear

llorar to cry, 13

llover (o > ue) to rain, 9

lluvia (f.) rain, 9

lo him, you, it, 6; **— importante** the important thing; **— mismo** the same thing, 11; **— que** what, that, which, 9; **— siento** I'm sorry, 1

los (m. pl.) the, 1; (pron.) them, you (form.), 6; **— (las) dos** both, 2

lucirse to shine

luego later

lugar (m.) place, 12; **— de interés** (m.) place of interest, 12; **en — de** in place of

lujo (m.) luxury, 12

luna de miel (f.) honeymoon

lunes (m.) Monday, 2

luz (f.) light, 1

M

madera (f.) wood

madrastra (f.) stepmother

madre (f.) mom, mother, 4

madrina (f.) godmother, 4

madrugada (f.) early morning (pre-dawn)

maestro(a) (m., f.) teacher

magnífico(a) great

mal badly, 5; poorly

maleta (f.) suitcase, 11

maletín (m.) hand luggage, small suitcase, 11

malo(a) bad, 5

mamá (f.) mom, mother, 3

mami (f.) mommy

mandar to send, 4; to order; **¿mande?** (Mex.) pardon?, 1

mandón(ona) bossy, 3

manejar to drive

manga (f.) sleeve, 9

mano (f.) hand

mantel (m.) tablecloth, 5

mantequilla (f.) butter, 5

manzana (f.) apple, 2; block, 10

mañana tomorrow; morning, 2

mapa (m.) map, 1

mar (m.) ocean, 8

marca (f.) brand

marisco (m.) shellfish, 6

marrón brown, 1

martes (m.) Tuesday, 2

marzo March, 2

más more, 5; **— de** more than, 5; **— despacio** slower, 1; **— o menos** more or less, 1; **— ... que** more . . . than, 5; **— tarde** later, 5

matar to kill; **— dos pájaros de un tiro** to kill two birds with one stone

matemáticas (f. pl.) mathematics, 2

materia (f.) course, subject, 2

matrimonio (m.) married couple, 8

mayo May, 2

mayor older, 5; elderly; **(el, la) —** oldest, 5

me (obj. pron.) me, 6; (to) me, 7; (refl. pron.) (to) myself, 7; **— gusta...** I like . . . , 7; **— llamo...** my name is . . . , 1; **— voy** I'm leaving, 2

media hermana (f.) half sister

mediano(a) medium, 9

medianoche (f.) midnight, 2

medicina (f.) medicine, 9

médico(a) (m., f.) doctor, M.D., 11

medida (f.) measure

medio(a) half; **media hora** half an hour, 3; **y media** half past, 2

medio hermano (m.) half brother

mediodía (m.) noon, 2; **al —** at noon, 2

mejor better, 5; **(el, la) —** best, 5

mejorarse to get better, 14

melocotón (m.) peach, 6

melón de agua (m.) watermelon, 6

memoria (f.) memory, 10

menor younger, 5; **(el, la) —** youngest, 5

menos to, till, 2; less, 5; **—... que** less . . . than, 5; **— mal** thank goodness

mensaje (m.) **electrónico** e-mail, 10

mensual monthly

mentir (e > ie) to lie, 11

menú (m.) menu, 5

mercado (m.) market, 6; **— al aire libre** (m.) outdoor market, 6

merendar to have an afternoon snack, 7

merienda (f.) afternoon snack

mermelada (f.) jam, marmalade, 5

mes (m.) month, 2

mesa (f.) table, 3

mesero(a) (m., f.) (Mex.) waiter, 5

mexicano(a) (m., f.) Mexican, 1

mezcla (f.) mixture

mezclar to mix

mi(s) my, 2

mí (obj. of prep.) me, 5

microcomputadora (f.) laptop, 10

mientras while

miércoles (m.) Wednesday, 2

mil one thousand, 3

minuto (m.) minute, 2

mío(a), míos(as) (pron.) mine, 9

mirar to watch, to look at, 3

mismo(a) same; **a sí —** him/herself

mochila (f.) backpack, 1

modo (m.) way; **de — que** so, 6

momento (m.) moment, 3

moneda (f.) coin

monitor (m.) monitor, 10

montar: — a caballo to go horseback riding, 7; **— en bicicleta** to ride a bike, 7

montón: un montón de a bunch of, many, 12

morado(a) purple, 1

moreno(a) dark, brunet(te), 4

morir (o > ue) to die

mostrar (o > ue) to show, 12

mozo (m.) waiter, 5

muchacha (f.) young girl, 1; maid

muchacho (m.) young man, 1

mucho(a) much; **— gusto** it's a pleasure to meet you; how do you do?, 1; **no mucho** not much, 1

muchos(as) many, 3; **muchas gracias** thank you very much, 1

mudarse to move (relocate)

muebles (m. pl.) furniture, 3

muerto(a) dead, 10; **estar — de hambre** to be starving, 6

Photo and Art Credits

Student Activities Manual

Workbook
Laboratory Manual

¡Hola, amigos!
Seventh edition

Ana C. Jarvis
Chandler-Gilbert Community College

Raquel Lebredo
California Baptist University, Emerita

Contents

To the Instructor

The *Student Activities Manual* (*SAM*), consisting of Workbook and Laboratory Manual, is a fully integrated component of *¡Hola, amigos!*, Seventh Edition, a complete introductory Spanish program for the college level. The Workbook and Laboratory Manual sections reinforce the grammar, vocabulary, and cultural information presented in the *¡Hola, amigos!* core text and help students to develop their listening, speaking, reading, and writing skills.

The organization of the *SAM* is correlated to the student text. The Workbook and Laboratory Manual sections provide activities for the fourteen textbook lessons. At the beginning of the Laboratory Manual, an *Introduction to Spanish Sounds* is recorded on the SAM Audio CDs, which assists students in making the connections between sounds and letters needed in order to pronounce Spanish correctly.

New to the Seventh Edition

- Workbook and Laboratory Manual activities have been revised to reflect the changes in the textbook's organization and content. Some activities have been rewritten with a tighter contextualization to better support and prepare students.

- Activity titles have been added in the *Puntos para recordar* sections of the Lab Manual section for easier navigation.

The Workbook Activities

The *Para practicar* section of the Workbook offers a variety of writing activities—sentence completion, matching, fill-in charts, sentence transformation, and illustration-based exercises— that provide further practice and reinforcement of concepts presented in the textbook. Each lesson also includes a crossword puzzle for vocabulary review, a reading comprehension passage, and a writing skill development section.

Each Workbook lesson features a section entitled *Para leer,* consisting of an authentic reading that re-enters the vocabulary and grammar of the textbook lesson followed by questions to test reading comprehension. Each lesson also features a section entitled *Para escribir,* which presents a writing topic related to the theme of the textbook lesson and includes strategies to help develop writing skills. Each even-numbered lesson concludes with *Sobre el mundo hispánico* that revisits the cultural notions presented in the corresponding section of the textbook and checks students' comprehension in writing.

The Laboratory Manual Activities

The Laboratory Activities accompany the SAM Audio CDs of *¡Hola, amigos!*, Seventh Edition and open with an Introduction to Spanish Sounds designed to make learners aware of the differences between Spanish and English pronunciation. Each lesson of the Laboratory Manual features pronunciation, structure, listening-and-speaking practice, illustration-based listening comprehension, and dictation exercises to be used in conjunction with the audio program. Complete audioscript and answer keys are available in the *Online Teaching Center* for further support.

The Laboratory Activities provide listening, speaking, and writing practice for each lesson under the following headings.

Pronunciación: Practice of the sounds presented in each textbook lesson is featured through Lesson 7. Thereafter, general pronunciation and intonation practice is provided. Words, phrases, and sentences using vocabulary from the textbook lessons are read with pauses for student repetition.

Diálogos / Preguntas y respuestas: The dialogues from the textbook are recorded for student repetition. The dialogues are followed by questions that verify comprehension and provide oral practice.

Puntos para recordar: A set of three to eight exercises, covering each grammar topic presented in the textbook, provide listening and speaking practice and test mastery of the grammar topics introduced in each lesson. Models for these exercises are printed in the Laboratory Activities pages. For easier navigation, activity titles reflecting the grammar topic at hand have been added.

Díganos: Questions related to students' own lives reinforce the lesson theme and provide additional listening and speaking.

Ejercicios de comprensión: A multiple-choice, illustration-based listening comprehension exercise that draws on the topics and vocabulary covered in each lesson is followed by an exercise consisting of a series of statements that students must confirm or refute based on their understanding of key vocabulary and ideas from the lesson.

Para escuchar y escribir: A dictation topically and structurally connected to the textbook lesson concludes each lab session. Dictations are printed in the Answer Key available in the *Online Teaching Center*.

A complete answer key for all written and oral exercises is provided in the *Online Teaching Center* for distribution to your students at your discretion.

SAM Audio CDs

The SAM Audio CDs provide approximately thirty to forty minutes per lesson of exercises recorded by native speakers. Pronunciation exercises begin each lesson then the textbook dialogues appear as listening and pronunciation exercises in each lesson; they are dramatized once at natural speed. They are followed by comprehension questions on the dialogues, structured grammar exercises (one for each point in the lesson), a listening comprehension activity, and a dictation. Answers to all exercises are provided on the audio CDs.

The *Student Activities Manual* is an integral part of the *¡Hola, amigos!*, Seventh Edition, program. Students who use it consistently will find the *SAM* and the SAM Audio CDs of great assistance in forming the associations of sound, syntax, and meaning needed for effective communication in Spanish and for meaningful cultural understanding.

We would like to hear your comments on *¡Hola, amigos!*, Seventh Edition, and on this *Student Activities Manual*. Reports of your experiences using this program would be of great interest and value to us. Please write to us care of Houghton Mifflin Company, Modern Languages, College Division, 222 Berkeley Street, Boston, Massachusetts 02116-3764.

Ana C. Jarvis
Raquel Lebredo

To the Student

This *Student Activities Manual* (*SAM*) for *¡Hola, amigos!*, Seventh Edition, is designed to reinforce the new material presented in each textbook lesson and provide practice in the skills you will need to acquire to communicate effectively in Spanish.

To use this integral component of the *¡Hola, amigos!* program to best advantage, it is important that you understand its organization. The Workbook and Laboratory Manual sections provide activities for the fourteen textbook lessons. The Laboratory Manual begins with an *Introduction to Spanish Sounds* that will teach you the sound system of the Spanish language and help you to associate these sounds with the letters that represent them.

The Workbook Activities

The Workbook Activities will help to develop your reading and writing skills by providing practice in using the structures and vocabulary from the textbook. The activities in the *Para practicar* section range from fill-ins and sentence completion to more complex tasks such as writing original sentences and short paragraphs. A crossword puzzle in each lesson, with clues in Spanish, offers a vocabulary control check and an opportunity to test your spelling abilities. Each Workbook lesson includes a *Para leer* reading in which key lesson vocabulary and structures reappear in a new context, followed by questions to check comprehension. Each lesson includes a *Para escribir* writing task which presents a topic related to the theme of the lesson and writing tips or strategies to help you develop your writing skills.

The Laboratory Activities

The Laboratory Activities, intended for use with the SAM Audio CDs for the Seventh Edition of *¡Hola, amigos!*, emphasize listening and speaking skills. The following sections are included for each textbook lesson.

Pronunciación: Words, phrases, and sentences that practice particular sounds or general pronunciation and intonation are read with pauses for you to repeat what you hear.

Diálogos: The dialogues from the textbook lesson are read for you to pause and repeat. Listen to the dialogues twice. During the first reading, you should listen carefully to the speakers' pronunciation and to the rise and fall of the pitch in their voices. As you listen for a second time, pause the audio after each sentence and repeat after the speaker.

Preguntas y respuestas: These listening comprehension questions will help you to verify your understanding of the dialogues. Check your responses carefully against those provided on the tape.

Puntos para recordar: These exercises provide listening and speaking practice and test your mastery of the grammar topics presented in each lesson. A model for each exercise in this section is read on the SAM Audio CDs and printed in the Laboratory Activities pages to guide you in your responses. The correct response to each item is provided on the audio CD.

Díganos: "Real-life" questions related to the lesson theme provide additional listening and speaking practice.

Ejercicios de comprensión: These listening comprehension exercises check your ability to apply the Spanish you are learning to new situations. First, you will hear three descriptions for each illustration in the Laboratory Activities pages, and will indicate the letter that corresponds to the correct description. Answers to each of the items are provided on the SAM Audio CDs. In the second exercise, you must confirm whether each of a series of sentences is logical or illogical.

Para escuchar y escribir: A dictation concludes the Laboratory Activities for each lesson so you can check your ability to reproduce in writing what you hear on the audio CD.

Answers to all Workbook and Lab Manual Activities are provided at your instructor's discretion. Consistent use of the Laboratory Activities for each lesson will help you to develop your listening and speaking skills in Spanish to meet the objectives of the *¡Hola, amigos!* program. By the end of the course, you should be able to understand the essence of a conversation on topics covered by the textbook by native speakers of Spanish conversing at normal speed. You should also be able to make yourself understood to native speakers used to dealing with foreigners when you converse on these topics, using the vocabulary and structures you have learned.

Try to complete all of the Workbook and Laboratory activities for each lesson. As you become more familiar with the program, you will find them helpful in assessing your achievements and in targeting the specific lesson features that require extra review. Learning a foreign language is a gradual process that requires a consistent, steady commitment of time. Completing the activities will help you to use your time productively by determining which material you have already mastered and which requires additional study.

We would like to hear your comments on *¡Hola, amigos!*, Seventh Edition, and on this *Student Activities Manual*. Reports of your experiences using this program would be of great interest and value to us. Please write to us care of Houghton Mifflin Company, Modern Languages, College Division, 222 Berkeley Street, Boston, Massachusetts 02116-3764.

Ana C. Jarvis
Raquel Lebredo

Workbook
Activities

LECCIÓN 1

Workbook Activities

Para practicar

A. En la clase. Indicate what we can see in the classroom by placing **un, una, unos,** or **unas** before each noun.

En la clase hay: _____ profesor, _____ puerta, _____ reloj, _____ tablilla de anuncios,

_____ ventanas, _____ borradores, _____ sillas, _____ computadora, _____

cuadernos, _____ bolígrafos y _____ luces.

B. Yo necesito... What do you need for class? Start out by saying, "Yo necesito (*I need*)", and place **el, la, los,** or **las** before each item on your list.

Yo necesito: _____ lápices, _____ plumas, _____ pizarra, _____ mapa de México,

_____ escritorio y _____ mochila.

C. Los pronombres. What subject pronouns would be used in each case?

1. A person talking about himself/herself, will start out by saying _____.

2. A student addressing a professor would call him/her _____.

3. Speaking about her parents, a girl would say _____.

4. Referring to a group of women, a person would say _____.

5. Speaking about his mother, a man would say _____.

6. Talking about himself and a male friend, a man would say _____.

7. Addressing a group of colleagues, a person would say _____.

8. A person would call a very close friend _____.

9. Speaking about a male professor, a student would say _____.

10. Speaking about herself and her sister, a woman would say _____.

D. **¿De dónde eres?** Fernando is introducing himself and other foreign students at the **Club Internacional**, saying where everybody is from. To show what Fernando says, complete the following with the correct form of **ser**.

FERNANDO   Yo _____ Fernando Pagani. Marisa y yo _____ de Buenos Aires, Delia

_____ de Lima, Cora y Adela _____ de Santiago y Roberto _____ de

Quito.

And now, answer Fernando's question: **¿Quién** (*Who*) **eres tú y de dónde eres?**

_____

E. **¿Cómo son?** Write sentences to indicate what the following people or things are like, using the adjectives given.

azules   simpáticas   española   difícil
trabajador   ingleses   marrón

1.   mujer _____

2.   chico _____

3.   profesores _____

4.   chicas _____

5.   lección _____

6.   escritorio _____

7.   bolígrafos _____

F. **¿Cómo se deletrea** (*spell*)**?** Spell out the following English last names for your Spanish-speaking co-worker to write.

1.   Smith _____

2.   Randall _____

3.   Fox _____

4.   Budge _____

5.   Wesley _____

6.   Jackson _____

G. Muchos estudiantes internacionales. Write the number of students from different countries that are in two ESL classes.

1. _____ estudiantes de Vietnam (13)

2. _____ estudiantes de México (27)

3. _____ estudiantes de Italia (15)

4. _____ estudiantes de Arabia Saudita (14)

5. _____ estudiantes de Chile (16)

6. _____ estudiantes de Colombia (39)

7. _____ estudiantes de Cuba (18)

8. _____ estudiantes de Nicaragua (10)

H. Conversaciones breves. These are brief exchanges that are heard around the college. Complete them appropriately.

1. —_____

—Buenos días, señorita. ¿Cómo está Ud.?

—_____

—Bien, gracias.

—_____

—Adiós.

2. —_____

—Me llamo María Luisa Salgado Mena.

—_____

—El gusto es mío, señora.

3. —_____

—Se dice "hasta mañana".

—_____

— Sí, mi compañero de cuarto es de Texas.

4. —_____

—Adela es bonita y muy inteligente.

5. —_____

—Nosotros somos de la Ciudad de México.

I. **¿Qué hay en la clase?** Name the following items. Be sure to include the definite article.

1. _____
2. _____
3. _____
4. _____
5. _____
6. _____
7. _____
8. _____
9. _____
10. _____

J. **Crucigrama** (*Crossword Puzzle*)

HORIZONTAL

4. opuesto (*opposite*) de **tonto**
5. tipo de pluma
6. Ella es de Guadalajara; es _____.
7. Harvard o Yale
9. _____ y tome asiento.
12. Es un _____ de papeles.

13. Mi dirección es _____ Magnolia, número 345.
14. *pencil*, en español
17. Mucho _____.
19. *light*, en español
20. *we are*, en español
23. opuesto de **grande**

(crossword puzzle grid)

24. opuesto de **simpático**
28. Es de California; es _____.
29. opuesto de **gordo**
30. Ella es mi _____ de cuarto.

VERTICAL

1. El amarillo y el azul forman el _____.
2. Hay muchos libros en la _____ de la universidad.
3. opuesto (*opposite*) de **fácil**
8. *interesting*, en español .
10. ¿Cuál es tu número de _____?
11. En la clase de geografía hay un _____ de México.
15. Es una tablilla de _____.
16. IBM vende (*sells*) _____.
18. Nos vemos _____ noche.
21. ¿Cómo se _____ "*book*" en español?
22. *clock*, en español
25. _____ días, señora.
26. ¿Qué hay de _____?
27. *red*, en español

K. ¿Qué dicen? Two classmates are talking in the hallway. Match their questions in column A with the answers in column B.

A	B
1. _____ ¿Cómo te llamas?	a. Bien.
2. _____ ¿Qué tal?	b. Alumna.
3. _____ ¿Qué hay de nuevo?	c. Sí, ¡y es rico!
4. _____ ¿Cómo se dice "*student*"?	d. No, anaranjado.
5. _____ ¿Beto es guapo?	e. De México.
6. _____ ¿Es un lápiz?	f. No mucho.
7. _____ ¿Es rojo?	g. No, un bolígrafo.
8. _____ ¿Cómo es Elena Quintana?	h. No, es cubano.
9. _____ ¿De dónde es ella?	i. Ana María López Osuna.
10. _____ ¿Carlos es norteamericano?	j. Inteligente y bonita.

L. ¿Qué pasa aquí? (*What's happening here?*) Look at the illustration and answer the following questions about the students and their classroom.

1. ¿Quién (*Who*) es la profesora?

   _____

2. ¿De dónde es la profesora?

   _____

3. ¿Cuántos estudiantes hay en la clase?

   _____

4. ¿Lupe es de Cuba?

   _____

5. ¿John es mexicano?

   _____

6. ¿Cuántas ventanas hay en la clase?

   _____

⬜ Para leer

Read the following descriptions, and then answer the questions.

La doctora Irene Santillana es de Madrid. Es profesora en una universidad en Guanajuato. Es inteligente y muy simpática.

La señorita María Inés de la Cruz es mexicana. Es de Puebla. Es estudiante de medicina.

El señor José Armando Vidal es de San Diego. Es estudiante en una universidad en Los Ángeles. Es alto, delgado y guapo.

¡Conteste!

1. ¿Quién (*Who*) es de Madrid?

   _____

2. ¿Es estudiante?

   _____

3. ¿Cómo es?

   _____

4. ¿María Inés es norteamericana o mexicana?

   _____

5. ¿De qué ciudad (*city*) es María Inés?

   _____

6. ¿Quién es de California?

_____

7. ¿De qué ciudad es?

_____

8. ¿José Armando Vidal es profesor?

_____

9. ¿Cómo es el señor Vidal?

_____

Para escribir

Brainstorming is a useful technique when beginning many writing assignments. It allows you to generate words or ideas you associate with a topic. For example, think of as many adjectives as you can that you know in Spanish and write them down. Think in Spanish! Refer to your textbook if needed.

_____

_____

_____

_____

Now, underline all the adjectives that apply to you and use them with the verb **ser** to write a brief description of yourself. As a final step, check for correct agreement of adjectives.

_____

_____

_____

_____

_____

_____

_____

LECCIÓN 2

Workbook Activities

⌑ **Para practicar**

A. Nosotros, los estudiantes. Marcos, a student from Colombia, talks about college life. Complete the following information, using the present indicative of the verbs given.

Juan Carlos y yo _____ (conversar) en la cafetería de la universidad y

_____ (tomar) café. Yo _____ (trabajar) en la cafetería y Juan Carlos

_____ (trabajar) en la biblioteca. Él _____ (hablar) español, inglés y

japonés.

Juan Carlos y sus amigos _____ (estudiar) en la biblioteca. Ellos no _____

___ (tomar) clases en el verano. Yo _____ (desear) tomar literatura cn el verano, pero

_____ (necesitar) trabajar. ¿A qué hora _____ (terminar) tú hoy? Nosotros

_____ (terminar) a las dos.

B. Aseveraciones y preguntas (*Statements and questions***).** Complete the chart below with the missing sentence forms, stating a fact, asking a question, or making a negative statement.

	Affirmative	Interrogative	Negative
1.	Él habla español.		
2.			Eva no es profesora.
3.		¿Desean leche?	
4.			Ana no necesita el horario.
5.	Tito es estudiante.		
6.	Luis trabaja hoy.		
7.		¿Estudiamos sociología?	
8.			Nora no es cubana.

C. **¿Qué deseas tomar?** Use the information provided to say who drinks what and why. Follow the model.

MODELO: yo: jugo de manzanas / no jugo de uvas

Yo tomo jugo de manzanas porque no deseo tomar jugo de uvas.

1. Elsa: jugo de naranja / no jugo de tomate

   _____

2. nosotros: una taza de té / no café

   _____

3. ellos: un vaso de leche / no té helado

   _____

4. tú: una copa de vino blanco / no vino tinto

   _____

5. Ud.: una botella de agua mineral / no cerveza

   _____

D. **¿Qué hacemos?** (*What do we do?*) This is what people do, need to do, or wish to do. Complete the sentences, using appropriate possessive adjectives.

1. Yo hablo español con _____ amigos y Michele habla inglés con _____ amigos.

   ¿Tú hablas inglés con _____ amigos?

2. Uds. necesitan hablar con _____ profesores y nosotros necesitamos hablar con _____ profesoras.

3. Nosotros deseamos estudiar en _____ casa (*house*) y él desea estudiar en _____ casa.

4. Marisa y Pedro estudian con _____ amigos. Marisa estudia con la amiga de _____ y Pedro estudia con el amigo de _____.

E. **Profesores y estudiantes.** Answer the following questions about your class in the affirmative.

1. ¿Tú necesitas hablar con tus compañeros de clase?

   _____

2. ¿Uds. desean estudiar en su casa?

   _____

3. ¿El profesor necesita tu cuaderno?

   _____

4. ¿Uds. estudian con sus compañeros de cuarto?

_____

5. ¿Las profesoras de Uds. son de Madrid?

_____

6. ¿Yo necesito hablar con mis profesores hoy?

_____

7. ¿La profesora habla con sus estudiantes?

_____

8. ¿Yo necesito hablar con mis estudiantes hoy? (*Use* **Ud.** *form*)

_____

F. En la universidad. Complete the following statements about college life using **el, la, los,** or **las.**

1. _____ idioma que ellos estudian en _____ universidad es _____ inglés.

2. En _____ clase de literatura estudiamos _____ poemas de Bécquer.

3. _____ lección cinco es sobre (*about*) _____ problemas de _____ ciudades de

California.

4. Necesitamos _____ café, _____ té y _____ leche.

5. _____ amistad (*friendship*) es muy importante para _____ estudiantes.

G. ¿Cuántos...? You are in charge of preparing an order for supplies. Write the number, in Spanish, of each item needed.

1. _____ libros (70)

2. _____ bolígrafos (100)

3. _____ cuadernos (84)

4. _____ mapas (158)

5. _____ lápices (112)

6. _____ cestos de papeles (95)

7. _____ relojes (72)

8. _____ computadoras (80)

9. _____ sillas (140)

10. _____ tazas (150)

11. _____ vasos (200)

12. _____ copas (67)

H. **¿A qué hora son las clases?** What time is each of the following classes? Start each sentence with **La clase de...**

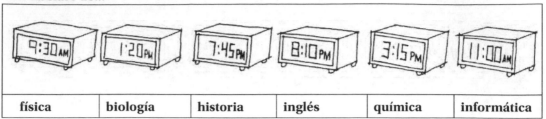

física	biología	historia	inglés	química	informática

1. física

_____

2. biología

_____

3. historia

_____

4. inglés

_____

5. química

_____

6. informática

_____

I. **El horario de Carolina.** Fill in the missing days of the week in the schedule below. Then, use the following information to fill in, in Spanish, Carolina's class schedule for this semester.

Math (**Matemáticas**):   Monday, Wednesday, Friday

Spanish (**Español**):   Monday, Tuesday, Wednesday, Thursday, Friday

Music (**Música**):   Saturday

History (**Historia**):   Tuesday, Thursday

Biology (**Biología**):   Thursday, Friday

Literature (**Literatura**):   Tuesday, Saturday

lunes						

J. **Muchos cumpleaños.** Silvia has a very busy social schedule. Write the dates of her friends' birthdays **(cumpleaños)** in Spanish.

MODELO: Carlos, _____ (July fourth)

Carlos, el cuatro de julio

1. Alberto, _____ (March first)

2. Inés, _____ (January fifteenth)

3. Carmen, _____ (November thirtieth)

4. Raúl, _____ (June twentieth)

5. Georgina, _____ (December fourteenth)

6. Fernando _____ (August tenth)

7. Rafael, _____ (February eleventh)

8. Elba, _____ (April twenty-fifth)

K. **Las estaciones del año.** As you know, the seasons are reversed in the Southern Hemisphere. Write the name of the season that corresponds to the following months in Chile. Include the article.

1. septiembre, octubre, noviembre _____

2. marzo, abril, mayo _____

3. diciembre, enero, febrero _____

4. junio, julio, agosto _____

L. Crucigrama

HORIZONTAL

5. Necesito el _____ de clases.
6. Hoy es _____ y mañana es martes.
7. Coors es una _____.
8. té helado = té _____
10. La clase es en el _____ número 128.
11. Él desea una _____ de vino.
13. La clase _____ a las ocho.
15. ¿A qué _____ es la clase de física?
17. sólo
19. Ellos toman vino _____.
20. No trabaja por el día. Trabaja por la _____.
22. Trabajo porque necesito _____.
23. hablar
24. La biología es una _____ difícil.

VERTICAL

1. _____ mis clases son requisitos.
2. Estudiamos a Shakespeare en la clase de
   _____.
3. Ella desea una _____ de café.
4. Pablo es de Puerto Rico; es _____.
9. Estudiamos álgebra en la clase de _____.
12. Deseo un _____ de agua.
14. Deseamos agua con _____.
16. En Washington hablan _____.
18. Toman café con _____.
21. Silvia _____ una clase de historia.

M. En la cafetería. At the university's cafeteria, some students are talking. Complete these exchanges, using vocabulary from **Lección 2.**

1. —Ana, ¿tu clase de español es difícil?

   —No, es muy _____.

   —¿Cuántas materias tomas este _____?

   —Tomo cuatro: ciencias _____, matemáticas, _____ de empresas y _____ español.

   —¿Dónde es la clase de español?

   —Es en el _____ número 115.

2. —Carlos, ¿qué _____ tomar?

   —Una taza de chocolate _____. ¿Y tú?

   —Un _____ de leche.

   —Oye, ¿qué _____ es?

   —Son las doce y media.

N. **¿Qué dice aquí?** This is a day in the life of Susana Campos. Read about her activities and then answer the questions based on the page in her planner.

Septiembre		Martes **15**
	Planes para hoy	
7:00	Café	**Sergio**
8:00 – 11:00	En clase	
	1. Química-Laboratorio	
	2. Informática	
	3. Matemáticas-Examen	
12:00	Cafetería	**Lidia**
1:00 – 4:00	Trabajo	
6:00	Biblioteca	**César**
8:00 – 10:00	Contabilidad	

1. ¿Qué día es hoy? ¿Qué fecha es?

   _____

2. ¿Qué toma Susana con Sergio? ¿A qué hora?

   _____

3. ¿Cuántas clases toma ella?

   _____

4. ¿Qué asignatura tiene (*has*) laboratorio?

   _____

5. ¿En qué clase tiene examen?

   _____

6. ¿En qué clase usa la computadora?

   _____

7. ¿ Con quién conversa en la cafetería?

   _____

8. ¿Cuántas horas trabaja Susana?

_____

9. ¿Dónde estudia a las seis? ¿Con quién?

_____

10. ¿Qué clase toma de ocho a diez?

_____

Para leer

Read the following story, and then answer the questions.

Roberto y Ana estudian en la Universidad Internacional de Miami. Roberto toma muchas asignaturas este semestre: química, historia, inglés, biología, sociología y literatura. Ana toma tres clases: física, administración de empresas y psicología. Roberto no trabaja. Ana trabaja en la cafetería y en la biblioteca.

Ana y Roberto conversan en la cafetería. Ana toma un vaso de leche y Roberto toma una taza de café.

¡Conteste!

1. ¿Ana y Roberto estudian en Venezuela?

_____

2. ¿Dónde trabaja Roberto este semestre?

_____

3. ¿Qué materias toma Roberto?

_____

4. ¿Cuántas clases toma Ana?

_____

5. ¿Qué clases toma Ana?

_____

6. ¿Quién toma literatura este semestre?

_____

7. ¿Dónde conversan Ana y Roberto?

_____

8. ¿Quién toma café y quién toma leche?

   _____

9. En su opinión (*In your opinion*), ¿por qué no trabaja Roberto este semestre?

   _____

10. En su opinión, ¿por qué toma Ana solamente (*only*) tres clases este semestre?

    _____

Para escribir

Making lists is another way of brainstorming to help you prepare for writing and organizing your thoughts. Before writing, list some of your activities using the Spanish you know. Add one or two of your easier and more difficult classes. Think of your studies, work, and one or two things you do with friends.

Then, write a brief description of your activities. Also tell what classes you are taking and at what time. Say which ones are easy and which ones are difficult.

_____

_____

_____

_____

_____

_____

_____

_____

_____

_____

_____

_____

_____

Name _____ Section _____ Date _____

Sobre el mundo hispánico. Refer to this section of your textbook to see how much you remember.

1. ¿Dónde está concentrada la mayoría de los mexicoamericanos?

   _____

2. ¿Qué conserva la mayoría de los mexicoamericanos que viven en este país?

   _____

3. ¿En qué ciudad vive más de medio millón de cubanos?

   _____

4. ¿Qué actor cubano es muy famoso?

   _____

5. ¿Cuál es el segundo (*second*) grupo más grande de hispanos en Estados Unidos?

   _____

6. ¿Qué famosa actriz es de origen puertorriqueño?

   _____

LECCIÓN 3

Workbook Activities

⌷ Para practicar

A. Teresa y yo. Eva tells us about herself and her friend Teresa. Use the present indicative of the appropriate **-er** and **-ir** verbs to complete the information.

Mi amiga Teresa y yo _____ en un apartamento en la calle Juárez. Todos los

días, Teresa y yo _____ en el parque (*park*). Después _____ en

la cafetería y _____ una taza de café. Los sábados, yo _____ los

muebles y Teresa _____ la cocina.

B. La familia Rojas. Use the information in the dialogue for **Lección 3** in the textbook to complete the following statements. Express relationship or possession.

1. Susana es _____ Alicia y Héctor.

2. _____ vienen de Guadalajara hoy.

3. Carlos es _____ Héctor.

4. Héctor es _____ Susana y Alicia .

5. Susana dice (*says*) que _____ es un desastre.

C. Los quehaceres de la casa. Four girls share an apartment. Today they're doing housework and getting ready for guests. Use the appropriate forms of **tener** or **venir** to complete the exchanges between them.

1. —Anita, ¿tú _____ la cafetera?

   —No, yo _____ la licuadora.

2. —¿A qué hora _____ José Luis?

   —A las ocho. Pablo y Teresa _____ con él.

3. —¿Uds. _____ que sacudir los muebles?

   —No, nosotras _____ que barrer la cocina y el garaje.

4. —Raquel, ¿de dónde _____ tú?

   —Yo _____ de la casa de mi abuela (*grandmother*).

5. —¿Quién _____ que planchar la ropa?

   —¡Tú!

6. —¿A qué hora _____ Uds. de la universidad mañana?

   —Nosotras _____ a las once.

D. **De visita (***Visiting***).** You are a guest at somebody's house and the hostess wants you to be comfortable. Answer her questions, using expressions with **tener**.

1. —¿Deseas un vaso de limonada?

   —No, gracias. _____.

2. —¿Por qué no abres la ventana?

   —Porque no _____.

3. —¿Deseas un sándwich?

   —No, gracias. No _____.

4. —¿Necesitas un suéter?

   —Sí, porque _____.

5. —¿Por qué no tomas una siesta?

   —No... _____.

E. **¿Me prestas... ? (***Will you lend me. . .?***)** Play the part of Mireya, who borrows everything from her neighbor. Place the appropriate demonstrative adjectives before each item.

1. *this, these*

   Necesito _____ licuadora, _____ tazón, _____ cafeteras y

   _____ platos.

2. *that, those*

   Necesito _____ reloj, _____ plancha, _____ tostadoras y _____

   vasos.

3. *that, those* (*over there*)

   Necesito _____ mesa, _____ sillas, _____ cesto de papeles y

   _____ platos.

F. **¿Cuánto ganan?** (*How much do they earn?*) You are in charge of the payroll for the Sandoval Company. Indicate how much each of these individuals earn per month.

MODELO: Luis gana (*earns*) doscientos dólares por semana (*week*).

Luis gana ochocientos dólares por mes (month).

1. Marta gana trescientos cincuenta dólares por semana.

   _____

2. Rogelio gana quinientos cincuenta dólares por semana.

   _____

3. Lucía gana doscientos veinticinco dólares por semana.

   _____

4. Ernesto gana cuatrocientos veinticinco dólares por semana.

   _____

5. Olga gana mil doscientos dólares por semana.

   _____

G. Cucigrama

HORIZONTAL

2. *with me*, en español
3. *toaster*, en español
6. Comemos mucha _____ mexicana.
7. Tengo que lavar y _____ la ropa.
9. recámara
10. Yo sacudo los _____.
12. Vivimos en una _____.

13. Preparamos café en una _____.
15. zacate
17. Comen por la noche.
18. *oven*, en español
19. *frying pan*, en español
20. Yo _____ en un apartamento.
21. novecientos más cien
23. Tengo una lavadora y una _____.

24. Tengo que pasar la _____.
25. *blender,* en español

VERTICAL
1. *bowl,* en español
2. opuesto de **frío**
4. Lavo los platos en el _____.
5. ¿Tú _____ prisa?
8. Preparamos esta bebida con limón, azúcar

(*sugar*) y agua.
9. Trabajo mucho; necesito _____.
10. *microwave,* en español
11. Tienes que _____ la basura.
14. *General Hospital,* por ejemplo (*for example*)
16. *bossy* (*fem.*), en español
17. Luis _____ el césped.
18. Como cuando tengo _____.
22. *thing,* en español

H. Conversaciones breves. Two roommates are talking about their day's activities. Match the questions in column A with the answers in column B.

A

1. _____ ¿Hay sándwiches?

2. _____ ¿Por qué no comes un sándwich?

3. _____ ¿Deseas limonada?

4. _____ ¿Qué tienes que hacer?

5. _____ ¿Tienes que poner la mesa?

6. _____ ¿Quién prepara la ensalada?

7. _____ ¿Qué tienes que lavar?

8. _____ ¿Tu hermano viene hoy?

9. _____ ¿Quién barre el garaje? ¿Alicia?

10. _____ ¿A qué hora viene tu papá?

B

a. No, mañana.

b. La ropa.

c. A las ocho.

d. No, gracias. No tengo sed.

e. Sí, en el refrigerador.

f. Sí, necesito los platos.

g. No, gracias. No tengo hambre.

h. Tengo que limpiar la casa.

i. Mi mamá.

j. No, ella está ocupada.

I. ¿Qué pasa aquí? Look at the illustration and answer the following questions.

¿Qué hacen . . . ? (*What do they do...?*)

1. ¿Qué hace Oscar?

   _____

2. ¿A qué hora vienen Ana y Nora?

   _____

3. ¿Cuántos platos pone Oscar en la mesa?

   _____

4. ¿Qué hace Juan?

   _____

5. ¿En qué calle vive Nora?

   _____

6. ¿Qué hace Sara?

   _____

7. ¿Cuántos años tiene Marcos?

   _____

8. ¿Qué hace Eva?

_____

9. ¿A qué hora viene Pablo?

_____

10. ¿Eva tiene prisa?

_____

Para leer

Read the following note that Mrs. Peña wrote to her husband, and then answer the questions.

Álvaro:

Tus padres vienen esta noche, a las ocho. Tienes que sacudir los muebles y planchar tu ropa.

Hoy yo llego a las seis porque tengo que trabajar hasta° las cinco y media. Rosita tiene que pasar la aspiradora y poner la mesa y Carlitos tiene que cortar el césped y lavar los platos.

Si tienen hambre, hay sándwiches en el refrigerador. Tu amigo Ricardo viene a las seis.

Graciela

until

¡Conteste!

1. ¿A qué hora vienen los padres de Álvaro?

_____

2. ¿Qué tiene que sacudir Álvaro?

_____

3. ¿Qué tiene que planchar?

_____

4. ¿A qué hora llega Graciela a su casa?

_____

5. ¿Hasta qué hora tiene que trabajar?

    _____

6. ¿Qué tiene que hacer Rosita?

    _____

7. ¿Quién tiene que cortar el césped?

    _____

8. ¿Qué tiene que lavar Carlitos?

    _____

9. ¿Qué hay en el refrigerador?

    _____

10. ¿A qué hora viene el amigo de Álvaro?

    _____

Para escribir

Write a short dialogue between two roommates who are discussing the chores they have to do. Use what you have learned about brainstorming and making lists to generate ideas before you begin.

_____

_____

_____

_____

_____

_____

_____

_____

_____

_____

_____

LECCIÓN 4

Workbook Activities

▣ Para practicar

A. ¿Cuál es la diferencia? Write who does what by using the information provided.

MODELO: traducir: yo / al inglés ellos / al español

Yo traduzco al inglés y ellos traducen al español.

1. salir: Uds. / a las seis   yo / a las ocho

    _____

2. conducir: ella / un Ford   yo / un Toyota

    _____

3. traer: él / la torta   yo / las bebidas

    _____

4. hacer: ellos / los sándwiches   yo / los entremeses

    _____

5. poner: yo / la mesa por la mañana   tú / la mesa por la noche

    _____

B. Sabemos y conocemos. Use appropriate forms of **saber** or **conocer** to indicate whom or what everybody knows.

1. yo / a Marisol Vega _____

2. Teresa / mi número de teléfono _____

3. nosotros / Puerto Rico _____

4. Carlos / el poema de memoria _____

5. tú / bailar _____

6. ellos / las novelas de Cervantes _____

7. Uds. / dónde vive Mauricio _____

C. **En un café.** At an outdoor café several people are talking. Complete the following exchanges, using the verbs **conocer, llevar,** and **tener** to indicate what they say. Add the personal **a** when needed.

1. —¿Tú _____ la novia de Roberto?

   —¡Roberto no _____ novia!

2. —¿Tú _____ Beatriz a la universidad?

   —No, yo _____ Carmen.

3. —¿Qué tienes que hacer?

   —Tengo que _____ los libros a la biblioteca.

4. —¿Uds. _____ Madrid?

   —No, pero _____ Sevilla.

5. —¿Tienes que _____ tu perro (*dog*) al veterinario?

   —Sí, a las dos.

D. **Mi amiga Sara.** Complete the information about Sara, using **a** + *definite article or* **de** + *definite article.*

Sara es la hija _____ Sr. Paz y la sobrina _____ Sra. Fuentes. Su esposo es Carlos

Villalba. Ella no conoce _____ papá de Carlos, pero conoce _____ mamá. Hoy Sara

viene _____ universidad _____ cinco _____ tarde y después va _____

biblioteca a trabajar. Ella trabaja con la hija _____ Dr. Peñarreal.

E. Conversaciones breves. Complete the following dialogues you overheard this morning before class. Use the present indicative of **estar, ir,** or **dar.**

1. —Raúl _____ una fiesta hoy. ¿Tú _____?

   —Sí, yo _____ con Rosaura.

   —¿Dónde _____ Rosaura ahora?

   —_____ en su apartamento.

2. —¿Dónde _____ tu hermano?

   — _____ en Madrid. Después _____ a París porque mis padres

   _____ allí.

3. —¿Cuánto dinero (*money*) _____ Uds. para la fiesta de Magaly?

   —Nosotros _____ veinte dólares. ¿Cuánto _____ tú?

   —Yo _____ diez dólares.

F. ¿Qué van a hacer? With the information given, say what everyone is going to do. Use **ir a** + *infinitive*.

MODELO: Yo tengo muchos libros.

   Voy a estudiar mucho.

1. Oscar tiene una limonada. _____

2. Nosotros tenemos sándwiches. _____

3. Tú tienes una revista (*magazine*). _____

4. Cristina tiene un bolígrafo. _____

5. Uds. tienen discos compactos. _____

G. Crucigrama

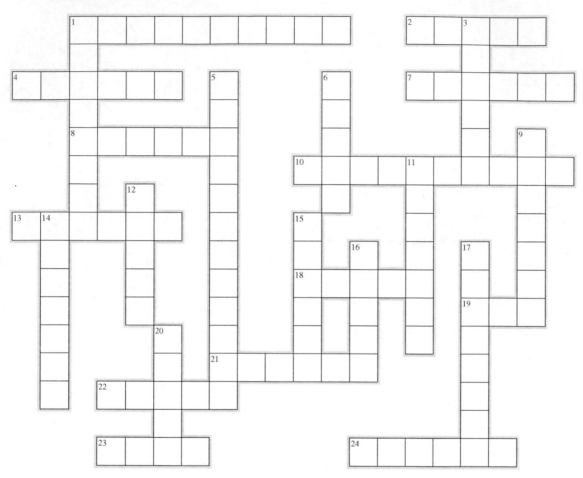

HORIZONTAL

1. La fiesta es para Mónica. Hoy es su _____.
2. Hoy nosotros _____ una fiesta en el club.
4. enviar
7. Son dos. Son una _____.
8. La mamá de mi papá es mi _____.
10. _____ la fiesta en el club.
13. No tengo _____ compactos.
18. Un brindis. ¡_____!
19. Es el hermano de mi mamá. Es mi _____.
21. Darío es el esposo de mi hermana. Es mi _____.
22. Carlos es el hijo de mi tía. Es mi _____.
23. Ella tiene _____ castaños.
24. Ellos _____ salsa.

VERTICAL

1. Ellos no quieren ir a la fiesta porque están _____.
3. Ella no es rubia; es _____.
5. Es de Guatemala. Es _____.
6. ¿Uds. _____ bailar salsa?
9. No es casado. Es _____.
11. Vamos a _____ con champán.
12. Yo traigo la _____ de cumpleaños.
14. Voy a _____ a mis amigos a la fiesta.
15. Me gusta la _____ clásica.
16. Yo _____ a las chicas a su casa.
17. Yolanda es de _____ mediana.
20. Todos lo pasan bien. La fiesta es un _____.

H. **¿Qué hacemos este fin de semana?** Aurelio found several e-mails in his computer, but many words are missing. Help Aurelio read the e-mails by supplying the missing words. Use vocabulary from **Lección 4.**

1. Aurelio:

¿Qué planeas _____ el sábado? Marta y yo planeamos _____ al club a

_____. Vamos a _____ a Rosa con nosotros. ¿Deseas _____ tú

también?

     Luis

2. Aurelio:

_____ tarde vamos a una cafetería para planear la _____ que voy a

_____ para mi novio, el domingo. Por la noche vamos a _____ a mi

madrina. ¿Vas con nosotros? Llamo más tarde.

     Teresa

I. **¿Qué dice aquí?** Answer the following questions about Nora's weekend, based on this page from her planner.

8:00	Tenis—Julio	**VIERNES** **4** de abril
12:00	Comer—Ana y Eva	
3:00	Concierto—Alicia	
9:00	Bailar—Julio—Club	
9:00	Estudiar—Olga	**SÁBADO** **5** de abril
1:00	Biblioteca—Eva, Silvia	
8:00	Fiesta—Mónica (cumpleaños)	
4:00	Visitar—madrina	**DOMINGO** **6** de abril
8:00	Cena—Julio y sus padres	

1. ¿A qué hora va a jugar (*play*) Nora al tenis? ¿Con quién?

   _____

2. ¿Con quiénes va a estar a las doce?

   _____

3. ¿Adónde va a ir a las tres? ¿Con quién va a ir?

   _____

4. ¿Con quién va a ir a bailar? ¿A qué hora? ¿Dónde?

   _____

5. ¿Qué va a hacer el sábado a las nueve? ¿Con quién?

   _____

6. ¿Quiénes van a ir a la biblioteca con Nora?

   _____

7. ¿Quién da una fiesta? ¿Qué celebra?

   _____

8. ¿A quién va a visitar Nora? ¿Qué día? ¿A qué hora?

   _____

9. ¿Con quiénes va a cenar a las ocho?

_____

10. ¿Julio es el hermano o el novio de Nora?

_____

🔲 Para leer

Read the following story about Rosaura, and then answer the questions.

Mañana, viernes, mi esposo y yo estamos invitados a cenar en casa de mi tía.
Tenemos que ir un rato, pero después vamos al club.
    El sábado por la mañana voy a jugar° al tenis con la novia de mi hermano.   *play*
    Por la noche vamos a tener una fiesta en mi casa para celebrar el cumpleaños de
mi esposo. Yo voy a hacer una torta y vamos a brindar con champán.
    El domingo vamos a la iglesia° y después vienen los padres de mi esposo a comer   *church*
con nosotros.

¡Conteste!

1. ¿Adónde tienen que ir Rosaura y su esposo mañana?

_____

2. ¿Quién da la cena?

_____

3. ¿Adónde va la pareja después de la cena?

_____

4. ¿El hermano de Rosaura tiene novia?

_____

5. ¿Qué van a tener por la noche en casa de Rosaura? ¿Qué celebran?

_____

6. ¿Con qué van a brindar en la fiesta?

_____

7. ¿Adónde van el domingo por la mañana?

_____

8. ¿Quiénes están invitados a comer en casa de Rosaura?

_____

⊡ Para escribir

When writing an informal note, letter, or e-mail in Spanish, begin and close with the following phrases. Notice that a colon, rather than a comma, follows the name of the person you are writing to.

TO BEGIN		TO CLOSE	
Querido(a) (+ *name*):	*Dear . . . ,*	**Un abrazo,**	*A hug,*
Hola, (+ *name*):		**Besos,**	*Kisses,*
		Tu amigo(a),	*Your friend,*

You can also close with just a good-bye such as **Hasta luego** or with **Escríbeme pronto** (*Write to me soon*).

Write a note or e-mail to your best friend telling him/her that you are going to give a surprise party for a mutual friend. Tell him/her what you are going to do to prepare for the party and indicate time and place. Tell him/her that he/she is invited!

_____
_____
_____
_____
_____
_____
_____
_____
_____
_____
_____
_____

Sobre el mundo hispánico. Refer to this section of your textbook to see how much you remember. Indicate the word that correctly completes each sentence.

1. México tiene más de (50 millones, 100 millones) de habitantes.

2. La ciudad de México, D.F. es el centro urbano más grande (del mundo, de Latinoamérica).

3. La economía de Guatemala se basa en la (industria, agricultura).

4. Un centro arqueológico muy importante en Guatemala es (Tikal, Tulum).

5. El Salvador es el país más (pequeño, grande) de Centroamérica.

6. A El Salvador lo llaman la "tierra de los (lagos, volcanes)".

Name _____ Section _____ Date _____

```
┌─┐
│回│ Para practicar
└─┘
```

Workbook Activities

LECCIÓN 5

A. ¿Qué estamos haciendo? Indicate what you and your family are doing, according to where everyone is.

MODELO: Oscar / en la cafetería

Oscar está comiendo.

1. yo / en la cocina

   _____

2. mi hermano / en la biblioteca

   _____

3. tú / en una fiesta

   _____

4. Jorge y yo / en la sala

   _____

5. mis amigos / en un restaurante

   _____

6. mi prima / en la oficina (*office*)

   _____

B. Dime... (*Tell me . . .*) You want to know everything! Ask the following questions, using **ser** or **estar,** as appropriate.

1. Ask what time it is.

   _____

2. Ask Mr. Díaz if he's Mexican.

   _____

3. Ask your friend where her boyfriend is.

   _____

Copyright © Houghton Mifflin Company. All rights reserved.

Workbook, Lección 5   **41**

4. Ask your friend if his brother is tall.

_____

5. Ask Miss Peña what she's reading.

_____

6. Ask someone where the party is.

_____

7. Ask your friend if her mother is a professor.

_____

8. Ask someone if the chair is made of plastic.

_____

9. Ask your friend if she thinks Andrea looks pretty today.

_____

10. Ask your friend if he's tired.

_____

C. **Preguntas y más preguntas.** You have questions about everything. Write the questions that elicited the following answers. Use **ser** or **estar,** as appropriate.

1. _____

   ¿Ana? En el restaurante.

2. _____

   ¿Yo? De Colombia.

3. _____

   ¿El disco compacto? Sí, de Pedro.

4. _____

   ¿Verónica? Alta, delgada y muy bonita.

5. _____

   ¿Yo? Sí, muy ocupada.

6. _____

   ¿La mesa? Sí, de metal.

7. _____

Hoy es jueves.

8. _____

¿Sandra y Carlos? Bailando...

D. Mensajes electrónicos. Alberto comes home and finds several e-mails waiting for him. Complete each message, using the appropriate forms of stem-changing e > ie verbs.

cerrar	empezar	pensar (3)
querer (2)	entender (2)	preferir

1. ¡Hola! ¿Vas a la fiesta de Aníbal? _____ a las ocho. Si tú _____, vamos

   en mi auto. —Celia

2. ¡Buenos días! Julia y yo _____ ir al club hoy. ¿Tú y Roberto _____ ir
   con nosotras? ¿O Uds. _____ ir al teatro (*theatre*)? —Marta

3. ¿Cómo estás? Yo, no muy bien... Tengo aquí mi libro de química y no _____ una
   palabra (*word*). ¿Tú _____ la lección de química? ¡Es muy difícil! —Beto

4. Hola, Alberto. ¿Tú sabes a qué hora _____ la biblioteca? Raúl y yo _____

   _____ estudiar esta noche. ¡Mañana es el examen de inglés! ¿Y tú? ¿Qué _____

   hacer? —Rocío

E. Comparaciones. Compare the following people and things to each other.

LUIS   RAÚL   PACO

1. Luis es _____ Raúl y Paco.

   Paco es _____ Raúl y Luis.

   Paco es _____ de los tres.

   Luis es _____ de los tres.

2. Ana es _____ Eva.

   Dora es _____ Eva.

   Ana es _____ de las tres.

   Dora es _____ de las tres.

   Eva es _____ Dora.

3. El coche (*car*) de Elsa es _____ el coche de Tito.

   El coche de Olga es _____ el coche de Tito.

   El coche de Elsa es _____ de todos.

   El coche de Olga es _____ de todos.

F. **Todo es lo mismo.** (*Everything is the same.*) You realize that everything is the same. Indicate this by restating the following information using comparisons of equality.

1. Yo tengo cien libros y Roberto tiene cien libros.

   _____

2. Nosotros trabajamos mucho y Uds. trabajan mucho.

   _____

3. El restaurante Azteca tiene cincuenta mesas y el restaurante Versailles tiene cincuenta mesas.

   _____

4. Paquito toma mucha leche y Carlitos toma mucha leche.

   _____

5. Ernesto bebe mucho café y Julia bebe mucho café.

   _____

G. **Todos nosotros.** (*All of us.*) Everyone reciprocates! Restate each sentence, following the model.

MODELO: Ella baila con él.
          Él baila con ella.

1. Tú vas conmigo. _____

2. Nosotros conversamos con ellos. _____

3. Yo soy para ti. _____

4. Él baila contigo. _____

5. Tú hablas de mí. _____

H. Crucigrama

HORIZONTAL

4. gambas
7. Quiero jamón con _____.
8. Como pan con _____.
9. una naranja, por ejemplo
11. Voy a pedir _____ de papas.
16. Quiero _____ de cebolla.
17. comienza
18. Quiero _____ de manzana.
20. *tasty*, en español
23. vegetal
24. Celebran su _____ de bodas.
25. Quiero _____ de vainilla.
26. Queremos pan _____.

Name _____ Section _____ Date _____

VERTICAL
 1. mozo
 2. Quiero flan con _____.
 3. comer por la mañana
 5. en este lugar (*place*)
 6. lista de comidas y bebidas en un restaurante
 7. Comemos _____ en el restaurante McDonald's.
10. *jam* o *marmalade*, en español

12. La _____ de hoy es cordero asado.
13. Quiero cordero _____.
14. *to pay*, en español
15. salmón, por ejemplo
19. *I prefer*, en español.
21. Quiero _____ con leche.
22. Quiero un _____ caliente.

I. **Conversaciones breves.** Two friends are talking. Match their questions in column A with the answers in column B.

A	B
1. _____ ¿Qué quieres comer?	a. A la una.
2. _____ ¿Quieres una hamburguesa?	b. No, es menor.
3. _____ ¿Quieres sopa?	c. Sí, con mantequilla.
4. _____ ¿A qué hora es el almuerzo?	d. Sí, de cebolla.
5. _____ ¿Quieres huevos?	e. Muy sabroso.
6. _____ ¿Ella es mayor que tú?	f. Un coctel de camarones.
7. _____ ¿Cómo es Carolina?	g. La boda de Olga y Luis.
8. _____ ¿Quieres pan?	h. Es muy tímida.
9. _____ ¿Qué celebran?	i. No, prefiero un perro caliente.
10. _____ ¿Cómo está el arroz con leche?	j. Sí, con jamón.

J. **¿Qué pasa aquí?** Look at the illustration and answer the following questions.

1. ¿En qué restaurante están Eva y Tito?

   _____

2. ¿Cuál es la especialidad de la casa?

   _____

3. ¿Cree Ud. que es un restaurante elegante?

   _____

4. ¿Eva va a pedir la especialidad de la casa?

   _____

5. ¿Qué prefiere comer Eva?

   _____

6. ¿Eva quiere puré de papas o papa asada?

   _____

7. ¿Qué quiere comer Tito?

   _____

8. ¿Qué va a pedir Tito de postre?

_____

9. ¿Qué toman Tito y Eva?

_____

10. ¿Qué están celebrando Tito y Eva?

_____

11. ¿Adónde cree Ud. que van a ir después de cenar, al teatro o a un juego (*game*) de béisbol?

_____

12. ¿Ud. cree que Eva y Tito tienen poco (*little*) dinero o que son ricos?

_____

Para leer

Read the following story, and then answer the questions.

Graciela y Roberto están es un restaurante. Ella está leyendo el menú y no sabe qué pedir: ¿Langosta...? ¿Cordero asado...? ¿Pollo...?

Roberto sabe exactamente lo que va a pedir: biftec con puré de papas. Graciela decide pedir lo mismo°. Los dos van a beber vino tinto.

Después de comer el postre y tomar café, los dos hacen planes para el día siguiente. Por la mañana piensan llevar a sus hijos a desayunar y por la tarde van a visitar a la mamá de Roberto.

lo... *the same thing*

¡Conteste!

1. ¿Dónde están Graciela y Roberto?

_____

2. ¿Qué está leyendo Graciela?

_____

3. ¿Qué no sabe ella?

_____

4. ¿Qué va a pedir Roberto?

_____

5. ¿Qué va a pedir Graciela?

_____

6. ¿Qué van a beber los dos?

_____

7. ¿Qué toman después de comer el postre?

_____

8. ¿Para cuándo hacen planes?

_____

9. ¿A quiénes piensan llevar a desayunar?

_____

10. ¿Qué van a hacer por la tarde?

_____

Para escribir

Write a dialogue between you and a waiter/waitress. Order a big meal, including beverage and dessert, and then ask for the bill.

_____

_____

_____

_____

_____

_____

_____

_____

_____

_____

_____

_____

LECCIÓN 6

Workbook Activities

🌀 Para practicar

A. Por teléfono. This is a phone conversation between Marga and Pablo. Use the appropriate form of stem-changing **o** > **ue** verbs to complete it.

—Marga, ¿tú _____ ir al mercado conmigo esta tarde?

—No, Pablo, hoy no _____ porque Eva y yo no _____ a casa hasta las ocho

de la noche.

—Lo siento. Oye, ¿tú _____ el número del mercado? Yo no lo _____ y

necesito saber cuánto _____ la langosta allí.

—No, yo no _____ el número.

B. ¿Qué hacen los demás? (*What do the others do?*) Nobody does what we do! Indicate this by using the information given to say what others do.

MODELO: Nosotros estudiamos en nuestra casa. (ellos / en la biblioteca)

Ellos estudian en la biblioteca.

1. Nosotros servimos café. (tú / té)

   _____

2. En un restaurante mexicano, nosotros pedimos tacos. (ellos / tamales)

   _____

3. Nosotros conseguimos libros en español. (Mirta / italiano)

   _____

4. Nosotros decimos que la clase es fácil. (Mario / difícil)

   _____

5. Nosotros seguimos en la clase de cibernética. (Uds. / química)

   _____

C. **Hacemos preguntas.** Answer each of the following questions that a group of friends ask each other by filling in the corresponding direct object pronoun and the verb.

MODELO: —¿Necesitas fresas?

—*Sí, las necesito.*

1. —¿Me llamas mañana?

   —Sí, _____ _____ mañana.

2. —¿Vas a comprar la lejía? (*2 ways*)

   —Sí, _____ _____ a comprar ahora.

   or —Sí, _____ a comprar_____ ahora.

3. —¿Llevan Uds. a su hija a la escuela (*school*)?

   —Sí, _____ _____ a la escuela a las siete y media.

4. —¿Nos necesitan Uds. hoy?

   —Sí, _____ _____ hoy.

5. —¿Roberto te conoce?

   —Sí, _____ _____.

6. —¿Compras los camarones en ese mercado?

   —Sí, _____ _____ allí.

7. —¿Los llaman a Uds. a las tres?

   —Sí, _____ _____ a las tres.

8. —¿Van a traer al hermano de Claudia hoy? (*2 ways*)

   —Sí, _____ a traer_____ hoy.

   or —Sí, _____ _____ a traer hoy.

D. Un mensaje importante. Complete the following message Aurora found on her answering machine by giving the Spanish equivalent of the words in parentheses.

```
Hola, Aurora, habla Leila. Necesito tu libro de historia.
¿_____ (1. Can you bring it) esta noche?
Yo voy a _____ (2. call you) más tarde. ¿Tú
hablas con Jorge hoy? Yo necesito _____
(3. see him) mañana. Ah, Olga y yo tenemos que ir al correo el
viernes. ¿Tú puedes _____ (4. take us)? Si puedes
_____ (5. do it), puedes _____
(6. call me) al 285-3942.
```

E. ¡Ni me hables! (*Don't even speak to me!*) You are in a very negative mood. Answer your friends' questions in the negative.

1. ¿Quieres café o té?

   _____

2. ¿Quieres comer algo?

   _____

3. ¿Vas a salir con alguien hoy?

   _____

4. ¿Siempre bailas salsa?

   _____

5. ¿Tienes algunos amigos de Managua?

   _____

6. ¿Tú ves a tus amigos de la universidad alguna vez en el verano?

   _____

F. **¿Cuánto tiempo hace?** Indicate how long these things have been going on by using the information in parentheses and the expression **hace... que.**

MODELO: Yo trabajo aquí desde (*since*) enero. Estamos en junio.
Hace cinco meses que trabajo aquí.

1. Yo estoy en la cola desde las diez. (Son las once.)

   _____

2. Vivimos aquí desde el año 2004. (Estamos en 2007.)

   _____

3. Estamos estudiando desde las once. (Son las once y veinte.)

   _____

4. Conozco a Julio desde septiembre. (Estamos en febrero.)

   _____

5. No veo a mis padres desde el lunes. (Hoy es sábado.)

   _____

G. **La lista de Marisol.** This is a list that Marisol wrote before going to the supermarket. Supply the missing words, using vocabulary from **Lección 6.**

1. _____ de cordero

2. papel _____

3. una _____ de huevos

4. _____ de tomate

5. _____ Tide

6. _____ Clorox

7. mariscos: _____ y _____

H. Crucigrama

HORIZONTAL

1. Hoy no trabajo. Tengo el _____ libre.
2. Tengo que comprar papel _____.
5. banana
10. persona que cocina (*fem.*)
12. Ana y Luis son _____ casados.
16. ¿Tú _____ ternera o cordero?
17. Yo no le pongo _____ al café.
18. Necesitan _____ de tomate.
19. Voy a preparar mis _____ espaguetis.
21. langosta, camarones, cangrejo, etc.
22. Compro salmón en la _____.

VERTICAL

1. Fab o Tide, por ejemplo
3. ¿Cuánto _____ el pescado? ¿Tres dólares?
4. No vivo en una casa; vivo en un _____.
6. vegetal bajo en calorías
7. Yo _____ a mi casa a las tres.
8. Compro el pan en la _____.
9. Están en un mercado al aire _____.
11. Ellos compran _____ de cerdo.
13. ají
14. Él va a comer mucho porque está _____ de
    hambre.
15. vegetal favorito de Bugs Bunny
20. La carne es un poco _____.

I. **En un mercado al aire libre.** This is a conversation between doña María, a regular customer, and a vendor at an outdoor market. Supply the missing words, using vocabulary from **Lección 6.**

—Buenos días, doña María. ¿Qué _____ desea Ud. hoy? Las fresas están muy

sabrosas (*tasty*).

—Quiero _____ para hacer jugo y _____ para hacer un pastel.

—¿Desea algo más?

—Sí, necesito carne. _____ de cerdo y de _____.

—¿Va a llevar algún tipo de mariscos?

—Sí, una _____ y seis _____.

—¿No desea camarones?

—No, no me gustan los camarones.

—Ah, doña María, la _____ de su casa estuvo ayer en la _____

para _____ pescado y dejó su bolsa con dinero. ¿Ud. puede llevársela?

—Sí, yo se la llevo, y muchas gracias.

J. **¿Qué dice aquí?** Look at the supermarket ad and answer the following questions.

1. ¿Cómo se llama el supermercado? ¿En qué ciudad está?

   _____

2. ¿Qué frutas puede Ud. comprar a precios especiales?

   _____

3. ¿Cuánto debe pagar por una libra de bananas?

   _____

4. ¿Qué puede comprar en la carnicería del mercado?

   _____

5. En la pescadería, ¿qué puede comprar y cuánto debe pagar por cada libra?

   _____

6. ¿Qué vegetales están rebajados (*marked down*) y cuánto cuestan ahora?

   _____

7. ¿Por cuánto tiempo duran (*last*) estos precios?

   _____

Supermercado
Díaz

**Tenemos mercados en
todas partes de Los Angeles
Aceptamos tarjetas de crédito**

J 13	V 14	S 15	D 16	L 17	M 18	M 19

Zanahorias

4 lbs. por
$**1.59**

Cebollas
cafés

5 lbs.
$**1.89**

Bananas amarillas

2 lbs. por $ **1**

Pavo Asado

Naranjas
5 lbs. por $**4.99**

Tomates
Roma

5 lbs.
$**2.39**

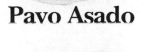

Bistec

$**3.99** ¢/lb.

**Pollo
entero
4.44**
cada uno

Pan

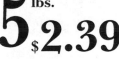

Manzanas Fuji

69 ¢/lb.

Salmón

$**5.79** ¢/lb.

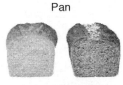

1.59
cada uno

¡Atención! **libra** = *pound,* **centavo** = *cent*

8. En la panadería, ¿cuánto cuesta el pan?

_____

9. ¿Aceptan tarjetas de crédito (*credit cards*) en el mercado?

_____

Para leer

Read the following story, and then answer the questions.

Antonio va a invitar° a unos amigos a comer. Por la mañana va a ir de compras al supermercado. Sabe que va a gastar mucho dinero, pero quiere preparar una cena magnífica. Piensa hacer un pastel de chocolate y para eso tiene que comprar harina°, leche, huevos, chocolate, mantequilla y azúcar. Va a preparar también una ensalada de frutas muy buena con naranjas, uvas, peras, bananas y otras frutas. Va a ir a la carnicería y a la pescadería para comprar pollo y mariscos para hacer una paella, un plato español típico que les va a gustar mucho a sus invitados°. No va a tener que comprar vino porque lo van a traer sus amigos.

invite

flour

guests

¡Conteste!

1. ¿A quiénes va a invitar Antonio a comer?

   _____

2. ¿Adónde va a ir por la mañana?

   _____

3. ¿Cómo va a ser la cena?

   _____

4. ¿Va a costar mucho dinero preparar la cena?

   _____

5. ¿Qué ingredientes usa para hacer la torta?

   _____

6. ¿Qué tipo de ensalada piensa preparar?

   _____

7. ¿Con qué frutas va a preparar la ensalada?

   _____

8. ¿Qué es una paella?

   _____

9. ¿Puede decirnos dos ingredientes de la paella?

   _____

10. ¿Quiénes van a traer el vino?

    _____

▣ **Para escribir**

Write an e-mail to your parents telling them about a meal you are going to prepare for some friends. Tell whom you are going to invite and what you are going to eat. You can also mention the ingredients of a particularly good dish, what else you are going to do, and whether you are going to have fun. Combine what you have learned about letter writing and sequencing words.

_____

_____

_____

_____

_____

_____

_____

_____

_____

Sobre el mundo hispánico. Refer to this section of your textbook to see how much you remember. Indicate the word that correctly completes each sentence.

1. De todos los países centroamericanos, Costa Rica tiene el (mayor, menor) número de

   analfabetos.

2. La capital de Costa Rica es (San Juan, San José).

3. La construcción del Canal de Panamá duró (diez, quince) años.

4. La principal fuente de ingreso de Panamá proviene (de la agricultura, del Canal).

5. (Colón, Cortés) le dio el nombre a Honduras.

6. Nicaragua es el país (más, menos) extenso de Centroamérica.

Name _____ Section _____ Date _____

LECCIÓN 7

Workbook Activities

▣ Para practicar

A. Para hablar del pasado. Complete the following chart with the missing forms of the preterit.

Infinitive	yo	tú	Ud., él, ella	nosotros(as)	Uds., ellos(as)
1. hablar	hablé	hablaste	habló	hablamos	hablaron
2. trabajar	trabajé			trabajamos	
3. cerrar			cerró		
4. empezar		empezaste			
5. llegar				llegamos	
6. buscar					buscaron
7. comer	comí	comiste	comió	comimos	comieron
8. beber			bebió		
9. volver	volví				
10. leer			leyó		
11. creer	creí				
12. vivir	viví	viviste	vivió	vivimos	vivieron
13. escribir		escribiste			
14. recibir				recibimos	
15. abrir			abrió		

B. **¿Qué pasó ayer?** Compare what everybody always does to what everyone did yesterday, using the cues provided.

1. Sergio siempre vuelve a su casa a las cinco. (siete)

   _____

2. Yo siempre comienzo a trabajar a las ocho. (siete)

   _____

3. Ellos siempre leen *Newsweek*. (*People*)

   _____

4. Uds. siempre empiezan a estudiar a las siete. (nueve)

   _____

5. Yo siempre llego a casa temprano. (tarde)

   _____

6. Daniela siempre come en la cafetería. (en su casa)

   _____

7. Yo siempre saco la basura por la mañana. (por la noche)

   _____

8. Tú siempre compras naranjas. (manzanas)

   _____

C. **En el pasado...** Rewrite the following dialogue in the past.

   —¿Adónde vas?

   —Voy a la fiesta que da Sergio.

   —¿Susana va contigo?

   —No. Oye, ¿tú das una fiesta el sábado?

   —Yo doy una fiesta, pero no es el sábado.

   —¿El Dr. Vargas y la Dra. Torres van a tu fiesta?

   —Sí, ellos son mis profesores.

   _____

   _____

   _____

   _____

_____

_____

_____

_____

D. De compras. We all went shopping yesterday to buy presents for each other for the coming holidays. To indicate who bought what for whom, follow the model.

MODELO: yo / a papá / una computadora

Yo le compré una computadora a papá.

1. papá / a mí / un microondas

_____

2. mamá / a ti / una licuadora

_____

3. yo / a mis hermanos / ropa

_____

4. mis padres / a nosotros / una lavadora

_____

5. mi abuela / a mi hermana / un escritorio

_____

6. nosotros / a Uds. / unos relojes

_____

E. **Conversaciones breves.** Complete the exchanges you heard in the school cafeteria, using the Spanish equivalent of the words in parentheses.

1. —¿Tus padres _____ dinero? (*sent you*)

   —Sí, _____ quinientos dólares. (*they sent me*)

2. —Tu novio está en Costa Rica. ¿Tú _____? (*write to him*)

   —Sí, yo _____ todos los días. (*write to him*)

3. —¿El profesor _____ en inglés? (*speaks to you, pl.*)

   —No, él siempre _____ en español. (*speaks to us*)

4. —Profesor, ¿la secretaria _____ los libros? (*gave you*)

   —Sí, esta mañana.

5. —¿Tú _____? (*paid to them*)

   —Sí, _____ ayer. (*I paid them*)

F. **¿Qué nos gusta?** Complete the following chart, using the Spanish construction with gustar.

English	Indirect Object	Verb **gustar**	Person(s) or Thing(s) Liked
1. I like this book.	Me	gusta	este libro.
2. I like these pens.	Me	gustan	estas plumas.
3. You (*fam.*) like the house.	Te		
4. He likes the clocks.	Le		los relojes.
5. She likes the desk.			
6. We like the chair.	Nos		
7. You (*pl.*) like the restaurant.	Les	gusta	
8. They like to work and to study.			
9. I like this room.			
10. He likes to skate.			
11. We like those classes.			

G. **Eso me gusta más.** Rewrite the following sentences, substituting **gustar más** for **preferir,** to indicate what everybody likes better.

MODELO: Mi mamá prefiere esa computadora.

   A mi mamá le gusta más esa computadora.

1. Mis padres prefieren ir al teatro.

   _____

2. Mi hermano prefiere los restaurantes mexicanos.

   _____

3. Yo prefiero ir al partido de béisbol.

   _____

4. ¿Tú prefieres ese florero?

   _____

5. Nosotros preferimos salir temprano.

   _____

6. ¿Uds. prefieren el verano?

   _____

H. De la mañana a la noche. Tell what everybody did yesterday, by using the cues provided.

1. papá / levantarse / temprano

   _____

2. mis hermanos / afeitarse / en el baño

   _____

3. yo / bañarse / por la mañana

   _____

4. nosotros / sentarse / a comer / en la cocina

   _____

5. tú / probarse / la ropa

   _____

6. mamá / despertarse / tarde

   _____

7. Uds. / lavarse / las manos

   _____

8. todos nosotros / acostarse / a las diez

   _____

I. Crucigrama

HORIZONTAL

2. comer algo por la tarde
4. *beach*, en español
6. opuesto de **divertirse**
8. el Louvre, por ejemplo
9. opuesto de **rico**
11. *to complain*, en español
13. *plan*, en español
14. *to skate*, en español
17. siete días
19. Es la _____ de una boda.
21. ¿Van al cine o al _____?
22. opuesto de **acostarse**
23. *to break*, en español

VERTICAL

1. Vamos a un _____ de béisbol.
3. Van a bailar a una _____.
4. opuesto de **responder**
5. ayer por la noche
7. Ponemos flores en un _____.
10. opuesto de **salir**
12. las doce de la noche
13. Disneylandia es un _____ de diversiones.
15. opuesto de **tarde**
16. ir a ver
18. Me gusta _____ en bicicleta.
20. Fue la última _____ que lo vi.

J. **Entre amigos.** Two friends are talking. Match their questions in column A with the answers in column B.

	A	**B**
1. _____	¿A qué hora se levantaron?	a. Sí, un rato.
2. _____	¿Fueron al cine?	b. Antes de la medianoche.
3. _____	¿Van a ir a la recepción?	c. No, a merendar.
4. _____	¿Se van a divertir?	d. A Colorado.
5. _____	¿Te invitó a cenar?	e. El florero.
6. _____	¿Qué rompiste?	f. Muy temprano.
7. _____	¿A qué hora tienes que volver?	g. Al zoológico.
8. _____	¿Montaste en bicicleta?	h. No, a caballo.
9. _____	¿Adónde llevaste a los niños?	i. No, al teatro.
10. _____	¿Adónde fueron a esquiar?	j. No, se van a aburrir.

K. **¿Qué pasa aquí?** Look at the illustration and answer the following questions.

1. ¿Qué no le gusta a Luis?

   _____

2. ¿Adónde le gusta ir?

   _____

3. ¿Luis es menor o mayor que Lidia?

   _____

4. ¿Quién se está quejando?

   _____

5. ¿Adónde quiere ir ella?

   _____

6. ¿Qué cree Ud. que le gusta hacer a Lidia?

   _____

7. ¿Qué quiere ver don Aurelio en la televisión?

   _____

8. ¿A él le gustan las telenovelas?

   _____

9. ¿Qué recibió Magali?

_____

10. ¿A qué hora es la recepción?

_____

⊡ Para leer

Read the following story about Ángela and Amalia, and then answer the questions.

Ángela y Amalia son compañeras de cuarto. Ángela se levantó muy temprano hoy, pero Amalia todavía está durmiendo porque anoche fue a una recepción y volvió muy tarde. Se acostó a la medianoche.

Ángela tiene muchos planes para esta tarde: estudiar en la biblioteca, visitar a una amiga que está en el hospital y, por la noche, mirar un programa educativo en la televisión.

Amalia piensa ir al club a nadar y a patinar, y por la noche va a ir a una discoteca con unos amigos.

Amalia siempre invita a Ángela a ir con ella, pero Ángela nunca acepta. Amalia dice que es una aguafiestas.

¡Conteste!

1. ¿Quién es la compañera de cuarto de Ángela?

_____

2. ¿Amalia está durmiendo todavía o ya se despertó?

_____

3. ¿Adónde fue Amalia anoche?

_____

4. ¿A qué hora se acostó?

_____

5. ¿Dónde va a estudiar Ángela esta tarde?

_____

6. ¿Dónde está la amiga de Ángela?

_____

7. ¿Qué va a hacer Ángela por la noche?

_____

8. ¿Qué piensa hacer Amalia en el club?

_____

9. ¿Adónde va a ir por la noche?

_____

10. ¿Ángela acepta las invitaciones de Amalia?

_____

▣ Para escribir

Clarity is an important element in any type of writing. A chronological relation of actions or events is one technique you can use to convey a clear picture for your reader. Indicating days of the week, time, or general time references **(por la mañana / tarde)** helps establish a clear sequence of events. Other useful sequencing words are **primero, luego, después, por fin, finalmente.**

Write one or two paragraphs about what you did yesterday and where you went. Relate the events chronologically, and include what time you got up and what time you went to bed.

_____

_____

_____

_____

_____

_____

_____

_____

_____

_____

_____

_____

_____

_____

LECCIÓN 8

Workbook Activities

Para practicar

A. En el pasado. Complete the chart below with the missing forms of the infinitive and preterit.

Infinitive	yo	tú	Ud., él, ella	nosotros(as)	Uds., ellos(as)
1. traducir			tradujo		
2. traer		trajiste			
3.	tuve				tuvieron
4.			puso		pusieron
5. saber		supiste			
6.	hice			hicimos	
7.			quiso		quisieron
8.		condujiste		condujimos	
9. estar			estuvo		
10.	dije			dijimos	
11.	pude	pudiste			
12.			vino		vinieron

B. ¿Qué pasó? Complete the exchanges you heard at the club yesterday with the preterit of the verbs in parentheses.

1. —¿Tus hermanos _____ (venir) esta mañana?

   —Sí, y nos _____ (traer) las bolsas de dormir. Yo las _____

   (poner) en mi cuarto.

2. —¿Roberto _____ (poder) ir al cine ayer o _____ (tener)
   que trabajar?

   —Él _____ (estar) en casa de sus amigos todo el día.

3. —¿Qué te _____ (decir) tus padres de sus planes para el verano?

—No _____ (querer) decirme nada todavía (*yet*).

4. —¿Cómo _____ (venir) tu primo a tu apartamento ayer?

—Él _____ (conducir) el coche de papá.

C. ¿A quién se lo damos? Complete the chart below with the Spanish equivalent of the English sentences. Use the masculine singular direct object pronoun **lo** in each response.

English	Subject	Indirect Object Pronoun	Direct Object Pronoun	Verb
1. I give it (*m.*) to you.	Yo	te	lo	doy.
2. You give it to me.	Tú			
3. I give it to him.		se		
4. We give it to her.				damos.
5. They give it to us.				
6. I give it to you (**Ud.**).				
7. You give it to them.	Tú			

D. Mamá es muy generosa. Tell for whom your Mom buys things, replacing the direct objects with direct object pronouns.

MODELO: Yo quiero una tienda de campaña.

Mamá me la compra.

1. Nosotros queremos dos raquetas de tenis.

_____

2. Tú quieres una escopeta.

_____

3. Los chicos quieren trajes de baño.

_____

4. Yo quiero unos palos de golf.

_____

5. Graciela quiere un termo.

_____

6. Ud. quiere una bolsa de dormir.

_____

E. **¿Lo hicieron o no?** Someone wants to know whether everyone did what they were supposed to do. Answer the following questions in the affirmative, replacing the direct objects with direct object pronouns.

1. ¿Me trajiste el dinero?

_____

2. ¿Les dieron los palos de golf a Uds.?

_____

3. ¿Le diste el termo a Mirta?

_____

4. ¿Te compraron la raqueta?

_____

5. ¿Le trajeron la cesta a Ud.?

_____

6. ¿Les prestaron las bolsas de dormir a ellas?

_____

7. ¿Me limpiaste la casa?

_____

8. ¿Les prepararon la comida a Uds.?

_____

F. **¿Y qué hicieron ellas?** Lola and Marisol never do what others do. Tell what happened last week. Use the information given.

1. En el restaurante todos pedimos tamales. (ellas / tacos)

    _____

2. En la fiesta yo serví champán. (Lola / cerveza)

    _____

3. Nosotros nos divertimos mucho en el club. (ellas / no)

    _____

4. Cuando estuvimos en Bogotá todos dormimos en un hotel. (Marisol / en casa de una amiga)

    _____

5. Para ir al cementerio (*cemetery*) todos nos vestimos de negro. (ellas / de rojo)

    _____

G. **¿Qué sucedió?** (*What happened?*) Rewrite the following sentences to indicate that everything happened in the past.

1. Él viene a verme. Me pide dinero y yo se lo doy.

    _____

2. Los chicos se divierten mucho, pero después tienen que trabajar.

    _____

3. Ellos traen las cartas, las traducen y las ponen en el escritorio.

    _____

4. Ella está en la fiesta. ¿Qué hace él?

    _____

5. Nosotros hacemos el café y ellos lo sirven.

    _____

6. Ella no puede venir hoy, pero no les dice nada.

    _____

7. Muchas personas mueren en accidentes.

    _____

8. Teresa no consigue trabajo, pero sigue buscando.

    _____

H. Hace diez años. Ten years ago Mireya wrote this composition about herself and her family. Rewrite her composition, using the imperfect tense.

> Mi padre trabaja para la compañía Reyes y mi madre enseña (*teaches*) en la universidad. Es una profesora excelente. Todos los veranos mi familia y yo vamos a Caracas a ver a nuestros tíos y siempre nos divertimos mucho. Mis abuelos viven en Bogotá y no los vemos mucho, pero siempre les escribimos o los llamamos por teléfono.

_____

_____

_____

_____

_____

_____

_____

_____

_____

_____

_____

I. En otros tiempos. Complete the following exchanges about life in the past with the Spanish equivalent of the words in parentheses.

1. —¿Uds. veían a sus abuelos _____? (*frequently*)

   —No, los veíamos muy _____. (*rarely*)

2. —¿A qué hora te levantabas tú _____. (*generally*)

   —Me levantaba a las seis _____. (*normally*)

3. —¿Tú entendías a tu profesora de japonés?

   —Sí, porque siempe hablaba _____. (*slowly and clearly*)

J. Crucigrama

HORIZONTAL

2. Necesitamos la bolsa de _____.
8. Soy _____ en hacer fogatas.
9. Me gusta mucho. Me _____.
10. El Erie es un _____.
12. Delia me trajo la _____ de picnic.
14. Yo _____ de llegar al hotel.
15. Para ir a la playa necesito mi _____ de baño.
16. Tengo una caña de _____ nueva.
18. Anoche comimos pescado _____.
21. Ellos van a hacer _____ acuático.
22. No voy a comprar la casa. La voy a _____.
23. Me gusta _____ surfing.
24. chico

25. Mi papá me compró una _____ de mar.

VERTICAL

1. A ella no le gustan las _____ al aire libre.
3. No voy en canoa porque no sé _____.
4. a menudo
5. Están en un hotel de cinco _____.
6. Él siempre me toma el _____.
7. Raúl necesita los _____ de golf.
11. Voy a armar la tienda de _____.
13. Hicimos comida por si _____ tenían hambre.
17. Ayer compré una _____ de tenis.
19. Pusimos el café en el _____.
20. Necesito la escopeta para ir a _____.

K. En un gimnasio. Complete the following conversation you heard at the gymnasium by supplying the missing words. Use vocabulary from **Lección 8.**

—Luis, ¿qué vas a hacer este fin de semana?

—Mis primos me invitaron a ir a _____ con ellos.

—¿Piensan alquilar una cabaña (*cabin*)?

—No, vamos a llevar tiendas de _____ y _____ de dormir.

—¿Van a ir de _____?

—Sí, tengo una _____ de pescar nueva. Además, Julio tiene una _____ y pensamos remar por el lago.

—¿Cuánto tiempo van a estar allí?

—Sólo dos o tres días, pero pienso _____ una caminata todos los días. Y tú, ¿qué vas a hacer?

—Voy a ir a la playa para nadar, _____ y hacer surfing.

L. ¿Qué dice aquí? Read the following ad that appeared in a Mexican newspaper, and then answer the questions.

¡Visite Nuestro País!

¿Usted ama los deportes y las actividades al aire libre?
Venga a Puerto Rico, aquí encuentra magníficas
oportunidades para disfrutar de la naturaleza

- Nade en las bellas playas naturales o en las magníficas piscinas° de los hoteles de lujo.   *swimming pools*

- Acampe en el llano o en la montaña.

- Aprenda a bucear.

- Pesque en el mar o en los ríos° y los lagos.   *rivers*

- Cace aves y otros animales.

- Juegue al fútbol y al tenis en este país de campeones.

1. ¿Qué deben hacer las personas que aman los deportes y las actividades al aire libre?

   _____

2. ¿Por qué es Puerto Rico el lugar ideal para esas personas?

   _____

3. ¿Cómo son las playas de Puerto Rico?

   _____

4. Además de nadar en las playas, ¿dónde se puede nadar?

   _____

5. ¿Dónde se puede acampar en este país?

   _____

6. ¿Qué se puede aprender a hacer en Puerto Rico?

   _____

7. ¿En qué lugares se puede pescar? ¿Se puede cazar?

_____

8. ¿Qué deportes puede Ud. practicar en Puerto Rico?

_____

Para leer

Read the following note Lucía wrote to her friend Amelia and then answer the questions.

Querida Amelia:

¡No puedo creerlo! Hace una semana que estoy aquí. Ya que no podemos conversar, te mando este mensaje y me hago la ilusión de que estás en Puerto Rico conmigo.

Hugo Luis y yo fuimos a acampar cerca de un lago. Hemos hecho de todo: cazamos, hicimos una caminata, nadamos, buceamos, remamos... Hugo Luis fue de pesca con sus primos y Estela y yo fuimos a la playa a tomar el sol.

Queremos quedarnos° más tiempo pero tenemos que volver porque empezamos a trabajar el 30 de agosto.

Te llamo muy pronto. Cariños,
Lucía

stay

¡Conteste!

1. ¿Cuánto tiempo hace que Lucía y Hugo Luis están en Puerto Rico?

_____

2. ¿Qué no pueden hacer Amelia y Lucía?

_____

3. ¿Adónde fueron a acampar Hugo Luis y Lucía?

_____

4. ¿Qué hicieron ellos?

_____

5. ¿Qué hicieron Hugo Luis y sus primos?

_____

6. ¿Con quién fue Lucía a la playa? ¿Qué hizo allí?

_____

7. ¿Por qué no pueden quedarse Hugo Luis y Lucía más tiempo?

   _____

8. ¿Cuándo van a empezar a trabajar ellos?

   _____

9. ¿Qué va a hacer Lucía muy pronto?

   _____

Para escribir

María Inés was supposed to go with you and a group of friends for a fun-filled weekend, but couldn't make it. E-mail her and tell her what you did and what she missed. Start by brainstorming a list of possible activities.

_____

_____

_____

Now write your e-mail to María Inés.

_____

_____

_____

_____

_____

_____

_____

_____

_____

_____

Sobre el mundo hispánico. Refer to this section of your textbook to see how much you remember. Indicate the word that correctly completes each sentence.

1. (Cuba, Puerto Rico) es la mayor de las islas del archipiélago de las Antillas.

2. El deporte más popular de Cuba es el (fútbol, béisbol).

3. Puerto Rico es una de las áreas (más, menos) densamente pobladas del mundo.

4. La ciudad más grande y más densamente poblada de Puerto Rico es (Ponce, San Juan).

5. Santo Domingo fue la (primera, tercera) ciudad europea fundada en el Nuevo Mundo.

6. Simón Bolívar nació en (Caracas, Bogotá).

7. En Venezuela están las cataratas más altas del mundo: (el Salto Ángel, las cataratas de Iguazú).

LECCIÓN 9

Workbook Activities

Para practicar

A. **¿Por o para?** Complete each sentence with either **por** or **para**, and indicate the reason for your choice by placing its corresponding letter, beside the preposition, in the blank provided.

Uses of ***por***	*Uses of* ***para***
a. motion: through, along, by, via	f. destination in space
b. cause or motive of an action	g. goal for a specific point in time
c. means, manner, unit of measure	h. whom or what something is for
d. in exchange for	i. objective
e. period of time during which an action takes place	j. in order to
	k. in search of

Mañana salgo _____ Quito. Voy _____ avión (*plane*). Pagué $400 _____

los pasajes (*tickets*). Pienso estar allí _____ dos semanas. Llevo regalos _____

todos mis amigos ecuatorianos. Ayer llamé _____ teléfono a Eduardo _____

decirle que llego a las ocho de la noche. Él va a venir _____ mí al aeropuerto. Tengo que

volver _____ el 30 de agosto _____ empezar las clases. Yo estudio _____

profesor.

B. **¿Cómo, por qué y para qué?** Complete the following sentences, using **por** or **para** appropriately, according to the information given.

1. Le compré una cartera a Lucía. La cartera es _____ .

2. La puerta estaba cerrada. Tuve que salir _____ .

3. El pasaje me costó $500. Pagué $500 _____ .

4. Necesito hablar con Silvia. La voy a llamar _____ .

5. Trabajamos de siete a once de la mañana. Trabajamos _____.

6. Había mucho tráfico y llegamos tarde. Llegamos tarde _____.

7. Voy a estar en México desde el 5 de enero hasta el 5 de marzo.

   Voy a estar en México _____.

8. Vengo con el propósito (*purpose*) de hablar con Ud. Vengo _____.

C. **¿Qué tiempo hace?** What comments might these people be making about the weather? Notice where they are and the time of year.

1. Raquel está en Oregón en abril.

   _____

2. Olga está en Alaska en enero.

   _____

3. Ana está en Phoenix, Arizona, en julio.

   _____

4. Pedro está en Londres en febrero.

   _____

5. Mario está en Chicago en marzo.

   _____

D. **Lo que fue y lo que era.** Complete the following sentences, using the preterit or the imperfect. Then indicate the reason for your choice by placing the corresponding letter or letters in the blank provided before each sentence.

Preterit	Imperfect
a. Reports past actions or events that the speaker views as finished and complete	c. Describes past actions or events in the process of happening, with no reference to their beginning or end
b. Sums up a condition or state viewed as a whole (and no longer in effect)	d. Indicates a repeated or habitual action: *used to, would,* ...
	e. Describes a physical, mental, or emotional state or condition in the past
	f. Expresses time or age in the past
	g. Is used in indirect discourse
	h. Describes in the past or sets the stage

Name _____ Section _____ Date _____

(____)   1. Ayer ellos _____ (celebrar) su aniversario de bodas.

(____)   2. Cuando nosotros _____ (ser) niños, siempre _____ (ir) a
             fiestas de cumpleaños.

(____)   3. _____ (Ser) las cuatro de la tarde cuando llegaron a la fiesta.

(____)   4. Anoche yo _____ (ir) al restaurante y _____ (comer)
             langosta.

(____)   5. Anoche, en la fiesta, Elsa _____ (tomar) mucha agua porque _____
             _____ (tener) mucha sed.

(____)   6. Me dijo que tú _____ (querer) ir a la tienda.

(____)   7. Yo _____ (ir) al club cuando _____ (ver) a Roberto.

(____)   8. Ella me llamó mientras yo _____ (estar) en la fiesta.

(____)   9. Toda la semana, _____ (hacer) mucho calor y el cielo _____
             (estar) nublado.

(____)   10. Ayer me _____ (sentir) mal todo el día.

(____)   11. ¿Tú _____ (divertirse) anoche en el baile?

(____)   12. Julio _____ (estar) bailando con otra chica cuando _____
             (llegar) su novia.

E. La vida de Amalia. Tell us about Amalia by completing the following information using the
Spanish equivalent of the words in parentheses.

1. Cuando Amalia _____, ella y su familia _____ en Bogotá y

   siempre _____ de vacaciones a Costa Rica. (*was a child / lived / used to go*)

2. Amalia _____ inglés con sus padres, pero sus amigos siempre

   _____ en español. (*used to speak / spoke to her*)

3. _____ las ocho cuando Amalia _____ a su casa anoche.

   (*It was / arrived*)

4. Ayer Amalia _____ que _____ dinero. (*told me / she needed*)

5. _____ cuando Amalia _____ de su casa esta mañana.

   (*It was cold / left*)

Workbook, Lección 9   **85**

F. **¿Cuánto tiempo hace de eso?** (*How long ago was that?*) Carlos and Raquel are sitting in a restaurant, complaining about everything, especially having to wait. Indicate how long ago everything happened by giving the Spanish equivalent of the words in parentheses.

CARLOS: ¿Dónde está el mozo? _____ y

todavía no nos trajo el menú. (*We arrived twenty minutes ago*)

RAQUEL: ¡_____! ¡Tengo hambre!

(*I had breakfast six hours ago!*)

CARLOS: ¡Ah! ¿Hablaste con tu hermana?

RAQUEL: Sí, _____ y me dijo que

necesitaba dinero. (*I spoke with her two days ago*)

CARLOS: ¿Qué hace esa chica con el dinero? Tu papá le mandó dinero _____

_____. (*a month ago*)

RAQUEL: ¡No lo sé! ¡Ah! ¡Aquí viene el mozo.

G. **Lo nuestro y lo de ellos.** Complete each sentence, using the possessive pronoun that corresponds to each subject.

MODELO: Yo tengo mis libros y Julio tiene _____.

Yo tengo mis libros y Julio tiene los suyos.

1. Ellos necesitan sus zapatos y nosotros necesitamos _____.

2. A mí me gusta mi casa y a mi hermana le gusta _____.

3. Ella mandó sus regalos y yo mandé _____.

4. Yo hablé con mi profesor y Eva habló con _____.

5. Antonio puede llevar a su novia y tú puedes llevar a _____.

6. Olga trajo su abrigo y yo traje _____.

7. Ellos invitaron a su profesora y nosotros invitamos a _____.

8. Mis pantalones son negros. ¿De qué color son _____, Paquito?

H. **Crucigrama**

HORIZONTAL

4. ni grande ni pequeña
7. Todo _____ un ojo de la cara.
9. Lo usan los hombres y las mujeres.
11. opuesto de **largo**
12. sin zapatos
13. opuesto de **encuentra** (*finds*)
18. la capital de Perú

19. Estudia en la _____ de medicina.
20. Se puso una _____ blanca y un pantalón azul.
22. Uso zapatos de _____ alto.
25. Lo usan las mujeres.
27. Es una camisa de _____ largas.
28. opuesto de **caro**
29. Me quedan chicos; me _____.

Name _____ Section _____ Date _____

VERTICAL

1. *suit*, en español
2. Ella _____ mucho dinero cuando va de compras.
3. en una tienda, lugar donde nos probamos la ropa
4. Estas sandalias están de _____.
5. *store*, en español
6. *gift*, en español
8. ni zapatos ni botas

10. Se usa con una falda.
11. *tie*, en español
14. Me puse una _____ y una blusa.
15. Ella usa _____ pequeña.
16. *chain*, en español
17. tienda donde compramos zapatos
21. tal vez
23. ¿Qué número _____ tú? ¿El diez?
24. No tengo _____ que ponerme.
26. metal precioso

I. **Conversaciones breves.** Two friends are talking. Match their questions in column A with the answers in column B.

A	B
1. _____ ¿Qué talla usas?	a. Sí, porque es de oro.
2. _____ ¿Qué número calzas?	b. Sí, y me compré estas botas.
3. _____ ¿Quieres una camisa?	c. Sí, porque hace frío.
4. _____ ¿La cadena es cara?	d. Sí, no tengo nada que ponerme.
5. _____ ¿Qué le compraste a papá?	e. Sí, de mangas largas.
6. _____ ¿Necesitas la chaqueta?	f. Sí, me aprietan.
7. _____ ¿Te pusiste la blusa negra?	g. Mediana.
8. _____ ¿Los zapatos te quedan chicos?	h. Una corbata.
9. _____ ¿Vas a comprar ropa?	i. Sí, con la falda blanca.
10. _____ ¿Fuiste a la zapatería?	j. El cuarenta.

J. **¿Qué pasa aquí?** Look at the illustration and answer the following questions.

1. ¿Qué se va a probar Carmen?

   _____

2. ¿El vestido está en liquidación (*sale*)?

   _____

3. ¿Qué le quiere comprar Carmen a Pablo?

   _____

4. ¿Qué quiere comprar Rosa?

   _____

5. ¿Qué lleva Rosa en la mano?

   _____

6. ¿Qué número calza Adela?

   _____

7. ¿Le van a quedar bien los zapatos a Adela?

   _____

8. ¿Le van a quedar grandes o chicos?

   _____

9. ¿Adela piensa comprar las botas?

   _____

10. ¿Cómo se llama la tienda?

   _____

Para leer

Read the following story about Carlos Alberto, and then answer the questions.

Mañana pienso levantarme a las seis de la mañana. En seguida voy a bañarme, afeitarme y vestirme porque quiero salir temprano para ir de compras. Voy a desayunar en una cafetería del centro° y a las ocho voy a estar en la tienda La Época, donde tienen una gran liquidación°. Necesito comprar un traje, dos camisas, un pantalón y dos o tres corbatas. Después voy a ir al departamento de señoras para comprarle un vestido a mi hermana; también quiero comprarle una blusa y una falda a mamá, pero no sé qué talla usa. Además°, a mamá nunca le gusta nada.

downtown
sale

Besides

¡Conteste!

1. ¿Carlos Alberto piensa levantarse temprano o tarde?

   _____

2. ¿Qué va a hacer en seguida?

   _____

3. ¿Para qué quiere salir temprano?

   _____

4. ¿Va a desayunar en su casa?

   _____

5. ¿A qué hora quiere estar en la tienda?

   _____

6. ¿Por qué quiere ir Carlos Alberto a la tienda La Época?

   _____

7. ¿Qué va a comprar Carlos Alberto?

   _____

8. ¿A qué departamento tiene que ir para comprar el vestido?

   _____

9. ¿Qué quiere comprarle Carlos a su mamá?

   _____

10. ¿Qué le gusta a la mamá de Carlos Alberto?

   _____

Para escribir

Write an e-mail to a friend who lives in another state or country. Make comments about the weather where you live, and tell him/her about some of your activities, including your last trip to the mall. Arrange the events chronologically and add any interesting details.

_____

_____

_____

_____

_____

_____

_____

_____

_____

_____

_____

_____

_____

LECCIÓN 10

Workbook Activities

⌐ Para practicar

A. Para completar. Fill in the blanks with the missing infinitive or past participle of each verb.

1. depositar: _____
2. _____: cobrado
3. hacer: _____
4. _____: recibido
5. escribir: _____
6. _____: comido
7. morir: _____
8. _____: dicho

9. abrir: _____
10. _____: roto
11. volver: _____
12. _____: cerrado
13. poner: _____
14. _____: bebido
15. ver: _____
16. _____: leído

B. Todo está hecho. Complete the following sentences with the Spanish equivalent of the words in parentheses to indicate what is going on.

1. La cuenta está _____. (*paid*)

2. Las ventanas están _____. (*closed*)

3. Los mensajes están _____ en inglés. (*written*)

4. La planilla está _____. (*signed*)

5. El coche está _____. (*parked*)

6. Los documentos están _____. (*translated*)

7. El banco está _____. (*open*)

8. Las diligencias están _____. (*done*)

C. ¡Pobre Marisol! Rewrite the following to say what has happened to Marisol. Use the present perfect tense.

1. Marisol pierde las llaves y no las encuentra.

   _____

2. Va a casa de su novio, pero no lo ve.

   _____

3. Estaciona su coche frente a un hidrante (*fire hydrant*).

   _____

4. Sus amigos no la invitan a la fiesta.

   _____

5. Tú no la llamas por teléfono.

   _____

6. Nosotros no le traemos nada de Asunción.

   _____

7. En el banco hace una cola de una hora.

   _____

8. Sus padres no la esperan para cenar.

   _____

9. Pide un préstamo y no se lo dan.

   _____

10. Trata de sacar dinero del cajero automático y no puede.

   _____

D. **Diligencias.** Mrs. García went on a short business trip to La Paz. Her husband and her children were very efficient during her absence. Indicate what everybody had done by the time she came home. Use the past perfect tense.

1. Yo _____ (ir) al banco y _____ (poner) dinero

   en su cuenta.

2. Papá _____ (llevar) el coche al mecánico.

3. Laura y Alicia _____ (hacer) las compras en el supermercado.

4. Tú _____ (abrir) una cuenta en el banco.

5. Esteban y yo _____ (limpiar) la casa y _____
   (sacudir) los muebles.

6. Todos nosotros _____ (ser) muy eficientes.

Name ______________________ Section ______________ Date ____________

E. Órdenes. Complete the chart below with formal command forms.

Infinitive	Command	
	Ud. *form*	**Uds.** *form*
1. comprar	compre	compren
2. dejar		
3. comer	coma	
4. beber		
5. escribir	escriba	escriban
6. abrir		
7. venir	venga	vengan
8. poner		
9. comenzar	comience	comiencen
10. atender		
11. recordar	recuerde	recuerden
12. volver		
13. pedir	pida	pidan
14. servir		
15. ir	vaya	
16. ser		sean
17. estar	esté	

F. ¡Hágalo! o ¡No lo haga! You need to give someone specific orders. Use the list below to write commands about what to do or not to do with the elements given.

MODELO: el empleado / llamarlo
          Llámelo.

mandarlas hoy   no enviarla; dejarla en el escritorio   estacionarlo en la calle

pedirlo el lunes   pagarla   comprarlas hoy

no cobrarlos todavía (*yet*)   firmarlas y dárselas al cajero

1. la cuenta: _____

2. el préstamo: _____

3. las estampillas: _____

4. la carta: _____

5. el coche: _____

6. las planillas: _____

7. las tarjetas postales: _____

8. los cheques: _____

G. Crucigrama

HORIZONTAL

4. Necesito dinero. Voy a pedir un _____ en el banco.
8. Hay muchas personas en el banco y tenemos que hacer _____.
10. Él fue a la _____ de correos.
12. Quiero _____ este cheque.
13. No pagó con cheques. Pagó en _____.
15. Pusimos el dinero en la caja de _____.
16. Yo recibo muchos mensajes _____.
18. Hoy no trabajo porque es día _____.
19. ¿Vas a la casa central o a una _____?
23. El correo está a tres _____ de mi casa.
24. ¿Ud. tiene una cuenta _____ o de ahorros?
25. Necesito comprar _____ para mandar estas tarjetas.
26. Necesito trabajar. Voy a _____ trabajo en el banco.

VERTICAL

1. Ellos van a pagar con cheques de _____.
2. ¿Dónde está el _____ de cheques?
3. Hoy ella tiene que hacer muchas _____.
5. ¿Cuál es el _____ de mi cuenta? ¿Doscientos dólares?
6. Él tiene mucho trabajo. Está muy _____.
7. opuesto de **último**
9. personas
11. Vamos a sacar dinero del cajero _____.
12. Voy a enviar esta carta _____.
14. Voy a _____ la red.
17. Mi esposa y yo tenemos una cuenta _____.
20. opuesto de **abierto**
21. Tengo que enviar dos _____ postales.
22. poner la fecha

H. Conversaciones breves. Two friends are talking. Complete their conversation by matching the questions in column A with the answers in column B.

A	B
1. _____ ¿Vas al correo?	a. No, conjunta.
2. _____ ¿Dónde está el banco?	b. Con el cajero.
3. _____ ¿Tuviste que hacer cola?	c. Una hora.
4. _____ ¿Abriste una cuenta individual?	d. En efectivo.
5. _____ ¿Cuánto tiempo esperaste?	e. Sí, hoy es feriado.
6. _____ ¿Cuál es el saldo de tu cuenta?	f. Sí, necesito estampillas.
7. _____ ¿Con quién hablaste?	g. En la caja de seguridad.
8. _____ ¿El banco está cerrado?	h. A dos cuadras de aquí.
9. _____ ¿Dónde pusiste el dinero?	i. Dos mil dólares.
10. _____ ¿Cómo pagaste?	j. Sí, había mucha gente.

I. ¿Qué dice aquí? Read the ad, and then answer the questions based on the information provided.

1. ¿Cómo se llama el banco?

   _____

2. ¿Hay que pagar algo por las cuentas corrientes?

   _____

3. ¿Qué ventajas (*advantages*) tienen los clientes si abren su cuenta antes del 30 de marzo?

   _____

4. En este plan, ¿cuánto es necesario pagar por los cheques?

   _____

5. ¿Qué saldo mínimo hay que mantener (*maintain*) en este plan?

   _____

6. ¿Cuándo es posible llamar al banco para recibir información sobre el saldo de una cuenta?

   _____

7. Es posible ir al banco a depositar dinero los sábados? ¿Por qué?

   _____

¡Cuentas Corrientes Gratis!*

Ahora usted puede tener todas las ventajas de una cuenta corriente de cheques en el Banco de Asunción–¡GRATIS!

¡Abra su cuenta ahora y ahorre!
Si usted abre su cuenta antes del 30 de marzo no tiene que pagar durante los primeros seis meses.

No cobramos por los cheques.
No necesita mantener un saldo mínimo.

Línea de información 24 horas al día.
Usted puede saber cuál es el saldo de su cuenta en cualquier momento. Damos servicio 24 horas al día, los 7 días de la semana.

Como siempre, abrimos los sábados.
Visite hoy cualquiera de nuestras sucursales o llame sin costo a nuestro teléfono 71-4293.

BANCO DE ASUNCIÓN
Calle Palma No. 315

* La oferta es válida para cuentas corrientes. Para abrir la cuenta se requiere un depósito mínimo de 100.000 guaraníes.

8. ¿Tiene sucursales el Banco de Asunción?

_____

9. Los clientes que llaman para pedir información, ¿tienen que pagar por la llamada?

_____

10. ¿Qué depósito mínimo requiere el banco para abrir este tipo de cuenta?

_____

Read this announcement, and then answer the questions.

Banco Nacional del Paraguay
Asunción

(Horas: lunes a viernes de nueve a tres)

¿Quiere abrir una cuenta de ahorros?

Nosotros pagamos un interés del cinco por ciento. Ud. puede sacar su dinero en cualquier momento sin° perder° el interés.   *without / losing*

¡Una oportunidad extraordinaria! También pagamos interés en las cuentas corrientes (tres por ciento).

Los cheques son gratis° si Ud. deposita   *free of charge* un mínimo de quinientos mil guaraníes.[1]

[1]Paraguayan currency

¡Conteste!

1. ¿En qué ciudad está el Banco Nacional del Paraguay?

   _____

2. ¿A qué hora abre el banco? ¿A qué hora cierra (*closes*)?

   _____

3. ¿Puedo ir al banco el sábado? ¿Por qué?

   _____

4. ¿Qué interés paga el banco en las cuentas de ahorros?

   _____

5. Voy a sacar mi dinero de la cuenta de ahorros. ¿Voy a perder el interés?

   _____

6. ¿Es una buena idea depositar dinero en el Banco Nacional del Paraguay? ¿Por qué?

_____

7. ¿Paga el banco interés en las cuentas corrientes? ¿Cuánto?

_____

8. ¿Cuánto dinero debo depositar para tener cheques gratis?

_____

Para escribir

In transactions of many types (making purchases, ordering at a restaurant, requesting information), being polite is not just a matter of common courtesy—it can help you more easily obtain what you want. You can use the phrase **¿Me puede decir...?** for many types of requests. When thanking the person helping you, you can say **gracias, muy amable** (*very kind*), or simply **muchas gracias.**

Write a short dialogue between yourself and a bank teller. Find out about opening a checking account, what interest it pays, and whether or not it's free (**gratis**). Also request an ATM card (**tarjeta de banco**). Remember to use appropriate courtesy expressions.

CAJERO: Buenos días. ¿En qué puedo servirle?

UD.:   Buenos días.

_____

_____

_____

_____

_____

_____

_____

_____

_____

_____

_____

Sobre el mundo hispánico. Refer to this section of your textbook to see how much you remember.

1. La capital de Ecuador es (Guayaquil, Quito).

2. La principal fuente de riqueza del Perú es (el turismo, la industria pesquera).

3. Machu Picchu fue una fortaleza (maya, incaica).

4. La mayoría de los paraguayos hablan dos idiomas: el español y el (quechua, guaraní).

5. La mayor planta hidroeléctrica del mundo está en (Bolivia, Paraguay).

6. Las dos capitales de Bolívia son La Paz y (Potosí, Sucre).

7. En Bolívia está el lago navegable más alto del mundo: el (Maracaibo, Titicaca).

LECCIÓN 11

Workbook Activities

Para practicar

A. Quieren que todos... Complete the following chart as a review of the present subjunctive forms.

Infinitive	yo	tú	Ud., él, ella	nosotros(as)	Uds., ellos(as)
1. bajar	baje	bajes	baje	bajemos	bajen
2. esperar					
3. deber	deba	debas	deba	debamos	deban
4. beber					
5. abrir	abra	abras	abra	abramos	abran
6. recibir					
7. hacer	haga				
8. decir		digas			
9. cerrar			cierre		
10. volver				volvamos	
11. sugerir					sugieran
12. dormir				durmamos	
13. sentir					sientan
14. comenzar	comience				
15. empezar					
16. dar		des			
17. estar			esté		
18. ir				vayamos	
19. ser					sean
20. saber	sepa				

B. **¿Qué quieren que hagamos?** To indicate what everyone wants everybody else to do, complete the chart with the Spanish equivalent of the English sentences.

English	Subject	Verb	*que*	Subject of Subordinate Clause	Verb in the Subjunctive
1. He wants me to speak.	Él	quiere	que	yo	hable.
2. I want you to learn.				tú	
3. You want him to go out.	Tú				
4. She wants us to drink.					bebamos.
5. We want her to come.				ella	
6. You (*pl.*) want them to read.	Uds.				
7. They (*m.*) want you to travel.				Uds.	
8. You (*pl.*) want us to study.	Uds.				
9. They (*m.*) want us to write.					escribamos.
10. He wants us to sleep.	Él				
11. I want you to wait.				tú	
12. They (*f.*) want you (*pl.*) to begin.				Uds.	
13. She wants him to work.					
14. We want them (*f.*) to go.					

C. Sugerencias y consejos. Rewrite each of the following sentences, beginning with the phrase provided to indicate what people want or to suggest what they should do in different situations.

MODELO: Ella llama al agente.

             Quiero que...

             Quiero que ella llame al agente.

1. Nosotros le damos el dinero.

   No quieren que _____.

2. Ellos van al aeropuerto.

   Deseamos que _____.

3. Él pide los asientos.

   Dígale a él que _____.

4. Tú traes los pasajes.

   Te sugiero que _____.

5. Ella es su novia.

   Él quiere que _____.

6. ¿Yo compro las maletas?

   ¿Tú quieres que _____ ?

7. Ud. toma pastillas.

   Yo le aconsejo a Ud. que _____.

8. Uds. están en la agencia a las cinco.

   Papá sugiere que _____.

D. **¿Qué está pasando?** Rewrite each sentence, beginning with the phrase provided, to express fear, sorrow, gladness, or hope about these situations.

MODELO: Tienen que volver hoy.

Espero que no...

Espero que no tengan que volver hoy.

1. Elba tiene problemas.

   Temo que _____.

2. Ellos no son antipáticos.

   Me alegro de que no _____.

3. Tú tienes que pagar exceso de equipaje.

   Siento que _____.

4. No podemos viajar hoy.

   Temo que _____.

5. No tenemos que cancelar la reservación.

   Espero que _____.

6. María y yo podemos ir en un crucero.

   Espero que _____.

7. Ud. viaja en primera clase.

   Me alegro de que _____.

8. Ellos saben a cómo está el cambio de moneda.

   Él espera que _____.

E. Mensajes electrónicos. Miguel Ángel is reading e-mails. He got one from his mother, one from his sister, and one from a friend. Complete them, using the present subjunctive or the infinitive, as needed.

1. Miguelito:

¿Cómo estás, mi amor? ¿Todavía te sientes mal? Quiero que _____ (ir / tú) al médico

y que _____ (seguir) tomando las pastillas que te mandé. Yo sé que tú no quieres

_____ (ir) al médico, pero espero que _____ (hacer) lo que te pido. Ojalá

que pronto _____ (estar) bien. —Mamá

2. Miguel Ángel:

Me dice mamá que estás de vacaciones. Yo te sugiero que _____ (viajar) a Chile y

que _____ (pasar) unos días en Viña del Mar. Temo no _____ (poder) ir a

verte este fin de semana porque Julio quiere que _____ (visitar / nosotros) a su

mamá. Espero que _____ (poder) ir a Chile. —Nora

3. Miguel:

Siento que tú no _____ (poder) ir a la fiesta de Laura. Espero que

_____ (tener) tiempo para ir al club este fin de semana, porque mi hermanita te

quiere _____ (conocer). Te llamo mañana. —Diego

F. Dos días en la vida de Luis. Luis is telling us what he did yesterday and what he's going to do today. Complete the following sentences, using the prepositions **a, de,** and **en.**

1. Voy _____ llevar _____ mi hijo _____ casa de Jorge, que le va _____ enseñar _____

   manejar. Tenemos que estar _____ su casa _____ las tres _____ la tarde.

2. Ayer conocí _____ la hermana _____ Raúl. Es una chica muy simpática. Es morena,
   _____ ojos verdes, y Raúl dice que ella es la más inteligente _____ la familia.

3. Las vacaciones pasadas mis hermanos fueron _____ México. Fueron _____ tren y ayer
   me estuvieron hablando _____ su viaje.

4. Ayer llevé _____ mi perro _____ la veterinaria, pero ella no estaba _____ su
   consultorio. Cuando llegué _____ casa la llamé por teléfono.

G. Crucigrama

HORIZONTAL

3. *he's afraid*, en español
5. ¿Cuál es la puerta de _____?
7. doctor en medicina
8. persona que viaja en avión
9. Chile, por ejemplo
10. *call*, en español.
12. Es un pasaje de ida y _____.
15. hacer una sugerencia
18. hacer un viaje
20. No gasta mucho dinero.
22. *to feel*, en español
23. abordar
24. Tengo la tarjeta de _____.
29. Cuando viajo, pongo mi ropa en una _____.
30. ¿Es un asiento de _____ o de pasillo?

VERTICAL

1. *pill*, en español
2. Ese _____ incluye el pasaje y el hotel.
4. maletas y bolsos de mano
6. *to get tired*, en español
11. Ella es _____ de vuelo.
12. Es un _____ directo.
13. *to find out*, en español
14. *trips*, en español

16. Tengo un _____ de mano.
17. Tiene que _____ el cinturón de seguridad.
19. Siempre hace lo _____. ¡Nada es diferente!
21. No pudieron ponerse de _____.
25. El avión no hace _____.
26. Voy a _____ el avión.
27. ¡_____ viaje!
28. permitir

H. Conversaciones breves. Two roommates are talking. Match their questions in column A with the answers in column B.

A

1. _____ ¿Dónde compraste los pasajes?

2. _____ ¿Tú sabes cuánto cuesta?

3. _____ ¿Qué incluye el paquete?

4. _____ ¿Vas a Chile?

5. _____ ¿El médico te dio pastillas?

6. _____ ¿Lo has pensado?

7. _____ ¿Quieres un asiento de pasillo?

8. _____ ¿Dónde pusiste el bolso de mano?

9. _____ ¿Cuál es la puerta de salida?

10. _____ ¿A quién le diste las tarjetas de embarque?

B

a. Sí, es mi país favorito.

b. No, de ventanilla.

c. Sí, pero no he tomado ninguna decisión.

d. La número cuatro.

e. Los pasajes y el hotel.

f. En el compartimiento de equipajes.

g. En una agencia de viajes.

h. A la auxiliar de vuelo.

i. No, pero lo voy a averiguar.

j. Sí, para los nervios.

H. ¿Qué pasa aquí? Look at the illustration and answer the following questions.

1. ¿A qué ciudad va a viajar Luisa?

   _____

2. ¿Luisa compró un pasaje de ida?

   _____

3. ¿Qué días hay vuelos?

   _____

4. ¿Dónde está Luisa en este momento?

   _____

5. ¿Cuántas maletas lleva Luisa?

   _____

6. ¿Cuál es la puerta de salida?

   _____

7. ¿Qué va a tener que pagar Luisa?

   _____

8. ¿A quién le va a dar Luisa la tarjeta de embarque?

   _____

9. ¿Daniel viaja a la misma ciudad a la que va Luisa?

_____

10. ¿El vuelo a Lima es un vuelo directo?

_____

🔲 Para leer

Read the following advertisement that appeared in a Chilean newspaper and then answer the questions.

AMERITUR: ¡Visite Argentina con nosotros!

Nuestras excursiones son las más completas y baratas. Nadie le da mejores
precios° que Ameritur. El pasaje en avión, el hotel y la transportación en   *prices*
Argentina están incluidos en el precio.

    Tenemos varios tipos de excursiones: en primera clase o en clase
turista. Si viaja entre semana, Ud. recibe un descuento° de un cinco por   *discount*
ciento del pasaje.

    No pierda° esta oportunidad de conocer los lugares más interesantes   *miss*
de Argentina. Queremos que visite Buenos Aires, Bariloche y la hermosa
playa de Mar del Plata.

    Pida informes a su agencia de viajes, o llame a nuestro teléfono,
976–5409, si quiere que le enviemos folletos° sobre nuestras excursiones. ¡Lo   *brochures*
esperamos!

¡Conteste!

1. ¿Cómo son las excursiones de Ameritur?

_____

2. ¿Quién da mejores precios que Ameritur?

_____

3. ¿Qué cosas están incluidas en el precio de la excursión?

_____

4. ¿Tiene Ameritur un solo tipo de excursión?

_____

5. ¿Cuándo es más barato viajar con Ameritur?

_____

6. ¿Qué descuento recibo si viajo entre semana?

_____

7. ¿Qué lugares de Argentina voy a visitar si viajo con Ameritur?

_____

8. ¿Dónde puedo pedir informes sobre las excursiones?

_____

9. ¿Qué debo hacer si deseo recibir folletos sobre las excursiones de Ameritur?

_____

Para escribir

Write a dialogue between you and a travel agent. Say what kind of ticket you want; ask about prices, documents needed, flights, and hotel accommodations. Choose a destination and reserve a seat.

_____

_____

_____

_____

_____

_____

_____

_____

_____

_____

_____

_____

_____

LECCIÓN 12

Workbook Activities

▣ Para practicar

A. ¿Existe o no? Look at the pictures and complete each sentence using either the indicative or the subjunctive.

1. Vamos a _____

   donde _____

   _____.

2. ¿Hay algún _____

   donde _____

   _____?

3. Tengo una empleada que

   _____

   _____.

4. Necesito un empleado

   _____

   _____.

5. Tengo una amiga que

   _____

   _____.

6. No conozco a nadie que

   _____

   _____.

B. **En una agencia de viajes.** Complete the following sentences, using the Spanish equivalent of the words in parentheses.

1. —¿Hay alguien que _____ (*can*) reservar los pasajes?

   —Sí, yo conozco a una chica que _____ (*works*) en una agencia de viajes.

2. —¿Hay alguien que _____ (*knows*) dónde está el hotel?

   —Sí, hay varias personas que lo _____ (*know*).

3. —Necesito un folleto que _____ (*has*) información sobre Río.

   —Yo tengo varios folletos que _____ (*have*) información sobre Brasil.

4. —Queremos una excursión que _____ (*includes*) el hotel.

   —Hay muchas excursiones que _____ (*include*) el hotel.

5. —¿Hay alguien aquí que _____ (*is*) de Uruguay?

   —Sí, hay dos chicas que _____ (*are*) de Montevideo.

C. **Las preguntas de Carlos.** Carlos wants to know some things about a new acquaintance. Play the role of the acquaintance by answering the following questions using the cues provided. Pay special attention to the use of the present indicative or the present subjunctive.

1. ¿Hay alguien en su familia que conozca Uruguay? (no, nadie)

   _____

2. ¿Conoce Ud. a alguien que sea de Brasil? (sí, a dos chicas)

   _____

3. ¿Hay alguien en la clase que sea de Perú? (no, nadie)

   _____

4. ¿Necesita Ud. un empleado que hable español? (no, yo tengo un empleado)

   _____

5. ¿Hay algo que yo pueda hacer por Ud.? (no, no hay nada)

   _____

D. **Órdenes.** Complete the chart below with the familiar **tú** command forms.

Infinitive	Affirmative Command	Negative Command
1. viajar		
2. comer		
3. escribir		
4. hacerlo		

Infinitive	Affirmative Command	Negative Command
5. venir		
6. bañarse		
7. vestirse		
8. dormirse		
9. ponerlo		
10. ir		
11. ser		
12. dármelas		
13. levantarse		
14. tener		
15. salir		
16. decírselo		

E. ¿Qué tiene que hacer Ana? Play the role of Rosa by completing the following dialogue with the **tú** command forms of the verbs listed. Some verbs may be used more than once.

decirle	ir	traerme	llamar
ponerla	hacer	venir	preguntar

ANA: Rosa, ¿qué quieres que haga?

ROSA: _____ a la agencia de viajes y _____ unos folletos sobre

excursiones a Río. _____ si hay excursiones que incluyan el hotel.

ANA: ¿A qué hora vengo mañana?

ROSA: _____ a las tres. Ah, y _____ a Carlos esta tarde.

ANA: ¿Qué le digo?

ROSA: _____ que necesito sus maletas, pero no _____ que tú vas a

viajar conmigo.

ANA: ¿Hago algo para comer?

ROSA: Sí, _____ una ensalada y _____ en el refrigerador.

F. **Minidiálogos.** Complete these exchanges, using the Spanish equivalent of the words in parentheses and the appropriate prepositions.

1. —Ana _____ Carlos cuando tenía diecisiete años. (*fell in love*)

    —Sí, pero _____ él. (*she didn't marry*)

2. —Mis padres _____ que yo viaje con Elisa. (*insist on*)

    —Ellos _____ que ella es muy antipática. (*don't realize*)

3. —Yo voy a _____ Teresa. (*get engaged to*)

    —Tus padres _____ que ella sea tu novia. (*are going to be glad*)

4. —Debes _____ comprar los pasajes. (*remember to*)

    —Yo nunca _____ nada. (*forget*)

5. —Ella me dijo que _____ esa agencia de viajes. (*she didn't trust*)

    —Sí, pero ella y yo _____ comprar los billetes allí. (*agreed on*)

G. **¿En qué piso están?** The following people are staying at a hotel on different floors. Indicate where they are by giving the ordinal number that corresponds to the cardinal number.

MODELO: CARLOS: 1

               Carlos: primer piso

1. Teresa: 10 _____ piso

2. Marcelo: 2 _____ piso

3. Rubén: 7 _____ piso

4. Abelardo: 3 _____ piso

5. Silvia: 8 _____ piso

6. Gustavo: 4 _____ piso

7. Amelia: 6 _____ piso

8. José Luis: 9 _____ piso

9. Ana María: 5 _____ piso

H. Crucigrama

HORIZONTAL

4. La usamos para bañarnos.
5. Necesito ver su _____ de identidad.
7. No quieren una cama chica; quieren una cama _____.
8. Puedo comer en mi cuarto porque el hotel tiene servicio de _____.
14. En el hotel no hay ninguna habitación _____.
16. Tengo sueño. Voy a dormir un _____.
17. Él me mandó un _____ de tarjetas.
20. El _____ lleva las maletas al cuarto.
22. La necesitamos cuando hace frío.
23. Él es de Perú. Es _____.
24. El cuarto tiene aire _____.

VERTICAL

1. Tengo muchas rosas en mi _____.
2. Pagamos con una tarjeta de _____.
3. Es un hotel de cinco estrellas. Es un hotel de _____.
6. El cuarto tiene baño _____.
7. La casa es de él; él es el _____.
9. elevador
10. Mi cuarto tiene _____ al mar.
11. No están en un hotel. Están en una _____.
12. opuesto de **optimista**
13. Su habitación está en el segundo _____.
15. opuesto de **frío**
18. Me lavo las manos en el _____.
19. Vamos a nadar en la _____ del hotel.
21. mostrar

I. **Conversaciones breves.** Two friends are traveling together. They are talking about hotel accommodations and other travel plans. Match their questions in column A with the answers in column B.

A

1. _____ ¿Dónde nos vamos a hospedar?

2. _____ ¿El Sr. Paz es el dueño del hotel?

3. _____ ¿Es un hotel caro?

4. _____ ¿Podemos cenar en el cuarto?

5. _____ ¿El precio incluye las comidas?

6. _____ ¿El baño tiene bañadera?

7. _____ ¿Hay un televisor en el cuarto?

8. _____ ¿Quién va a llevar las maletas al cuarto?

9. _____ ¿Cómo vas a pagar?

10. _____ ¿Hay habitaciones libres?

B

a. Con tarjeta de crédito.

b. No, ducha.

c. No, es un empleado.

d. No, no hay ninguna disponible.

e. No, pero hay uno en el comedor.

f. No, no tienen servicio de habitación.

g. En el hotel Alcázar.

h. Sí, es de lujo.

i. Sí, es pensión completa.

j. El botones.

J. **¿Qué dice aquí?** Read the ad on p. 119 and answer the questions the following questions.

1. ¿Cómo se llama el hotel?

   _____

2. ¿En qué ciudad argentina está?

   _____

3. ¿Es muy pequeño el hotel? ¿Cómo lo sabe Ud.?

   _____

4. ¿Qué tienen todas las habitaciones?

   _____

5. ¿Dónde puede dejar Ud. su dinero si se hospeda en ese hotel?

   _____

6. ¿Puede recibir mensajes electrónicos en el hotel? ¿Por qué?

   _____

7. ¿Qué tipo de comida sirven en el restaurante del hotel?

   _____

Boulevard Marítimo 5231

☎486-1265

Mar del Plata

(La ciudad balnearia más importante de Argentina.)

120 habitaciones y 10 suites, todas con baño privado	Salas de convenciones con capacidad para 800 personas
TV color con servicio de cable	Restaurante internacional con capacidad para 400 personas.
Cajas de seguridad	Panadería y pastelería
Servicio de internet y fax	Discoteca
Gimnasio y sauna	Garaje
Sala de juegos	

8. ¿Cuántas personas pueden comer en el restaurante?

_____

9. ¿Hay algún lugar para dejar el coche?

_____

10. Si Ud. quiere organizar una convención, ¿puede hacerlo en el hotel? ¿Cuántas personas pueden asistir (*attend*)?

_____

Para leer

Read the following ads, and then answer the questions.

DE LA SECCIÓN DE ANUNCIOS°

Ads

HOTEL FIESTA

Habitaciones con vista al mar, todas con aire acondicionado y baño privado.

Dos personas en una habitación pagan solamente 320 pesos. Cada persona adicional paga 90 pesos.

El hotel tiene un magnífico restaurante donde se sirve comida argentina, italiana y francesa.

¡VISÍTENOS EN SUS PRÓXIMAS VACACIONES!

Pensión Rivas

¿No quiere gastar mucho dinero, pero desea estar cerca de la playa?

¡Venga a la Pensión Rivas!

Nuestros cuartos son grandes y cómodos° y sólo cobramos 300 pesos por persona. El precio incluye todas las comidas: desayuno, almuerzo y cena.

comfortable

¡Conteste!

1. ¿Cree Ud. que el Hotel Fiesta está en la playa? ¿Por qué?

   _____

2. Voy a alquilar una habitación en el Hotel Fiesta. ¿Voy a tener calor? ¿Por qué?

   _____

3. ¿Cuánto cobran en el hotel por dos personas?

   _____

4. Voy al hotel con mi esposa y mis dos hijos. ¿Cuánto debo pagar por los niños?

   _____

5. ¿Cuánto vamos a pagar en total?

   _____

6. Me gusta la comida argentina. ¿Puedo comerla en el Hotel Fiesta?

   _____

7. ¿Sirven comida internacional en el hotel?

   _____

8. ¿Cuál es más barato, el Hotel Fiesta o la Pensión Rivas?

   _____

9. ¿Cuánto paga una persona en la Pensión Rivas?

   _____

10. ¿Cuánto debo pagar extra por las comidas en la Pensión Rivas?

    _____

Para escribir

When writing a narrative of any type, it is important to make your sentences sound natural. Too many short sentences can sound choppy. You can avoid this by linking your ideas to create longer sentences. Some useful linking words are:

y   **pero**   **también**   **además**   **porque**

You are staying at a hotel in Copacabana, Río. Write a short letter to your parents, telling them about the hotel you are staying at. Tell them about accommodations, prices, and what you like about the hotel, including your room. Tell them how long you plan to stay. Remember what you have learned about letter writing.

_____

_____

_____

_____

_____

_____

_____

_____

_____

_____

Sobre el mundo hispánico. Refer to this section of your textbook to see how much you remember.

1. La cordillera de los Andes atraviesa Chile (de norte a sur, de este a oeste).

2. El (café, vino) de Chile tiene fama internacional.

3. Argentina ocupa el (octavo, décimo) lugar entre los países más extensos.

4. La mayor parte de los habitantes de Argentina son de origen europeo, principalmente (portugueses, italianos).

5. La capital de Uruguay es (Punta del Este, Montevideo).

6. Brasil limita con todos los países suramericanos excepto con (Colombia y Venezuela, Chile y Ecuador).

LECCIÓN 13

Workbook Activities

Para practicar

A. Graciela siempre contradice. Graciela never agrees with Olga on anything. Whatever Olga says, she contradicts. Respond to each statement, playing the role of Graciela.

1. OLGA: Podemos hablar con el Dr. Peña hoy.

   GRACIELA: No creo _____.

2. OLGA: Ernesto se siente mejor.

   GRACIELA: No es verdad _____.

3. OLGA: Magali tiene apendicitis.

   GRACIELA: Dudo _____.

4. OLGA: La enfermera le pone una inyección.

   GRACIELA: No creo _____.

5. OLGA: El médico continúa atendiendo a los pacientes.

   GRACIELA: No es cierto _____.

6. OLGA: Ese hospital es muy bueno.

   GRACIELA: No es verdad _____.

7. OLGA: Le hacen radiografías.

   GRACIELA: Dudo _____.

8. OLGA: Alina siempre se desmaya.

   GRACIELA: No creo _____.

B. **¿Qué va a pasar?** Rewrite each of the following sentences, beginning with the word or phrase provided, to indicate what will happen in the future.

MODELO: Todos los días, en cuanto llego a casa, llamo a Eva.
          Mañana, en cuanto llegue a casa, voy a llamar a Eva.

1. Cuando viene la enfermera me pone una inyección.

    Más tarde, _____.

2. Siempre lo esperamos hasta que llega.

    Lo vamos a esperar _____.

3. Me desinfectó la herida en cuanto llegó.

    Mañana _____.

4. La semana pasada, Roberto compró la medicina tan pronto como recibió el dinero.

    La semana próxima, _____.

5. Anoche ella me habló en cuanto me vio.

    Esta noche _____.

6. Todos los días, Teresa se va a su casa en cuanto termina.

    Mañana, _____.

C. **Nos ayudamos (***We help each other***).** Use the subjunctive after the expressions **a menos que, antes de que, para que,** and **con tal que** to complete the following sentences, to show how these people try to accommodate one another.

1. Vamos a llamar al médico, a menos que

    tú (querer) _____ ir al hospital.

    él (preferir) _____ verlo en su casa.

    Uds. (desear) _____ esperar.

2. Voy a limpiarle la herida antes de que

    él (llegar) _____.

    ellos (venir) _____.

    tú (salir) _____.

3. Voy a llevarlo al hospital para que

    ellos _____ (hacerle) análisis.

    el médico _____ (verlo).

    (él) no _____ (empeorarse).

4. Yo puedo estar allí a las diez, con tal que

Uds. (llevarme) _____.

tú (venir) _____ temprano.

ella (traer) _____ su auto.

D. Servicio médico. Complete the following, using the present indicative or the present subjunctive of the verbs given, to show what these people say.

1. Es verdad que este hospital _____ (ser) bueno, pero no es verdad que

   _____ (ser) el mejor de la ciudad.

2. Yo no dudo que esta ciudad _____ (tener) muy buenos hospitales, pero no

   creo que _____ (ser) baratos.

3. Tenemos que llevarlo al hospital en el coche, a menos que ellos _____
   (llamar) una ambulancia.

4. Cuando tú _____ (ver) a la enfermera, dile que necesitamos las pastillas.

5. Todos los días llamo a mis padres en cuanto _____ (llegar) a casa.

6. Dudo que ellos _____ (servir) comida a esta hora. Creo que la cafetería
   _____ (estar) cerrada.

7. Yo te voy a dar el número de teléfono del hotel para que tú me _____
   (llamar).

8. Siempre cenamos tan pronto como _____ (llegar) a casa.

E. Los recién casados. Sara and Pablo are newlyweds, travelling in Madrid, and they always ask each other what they should do. Play the part of Sara or Pablo by answering each of the following questions. Use the first person plural command and the cues provided. Substitute direct object pronouns for the direct object where possible.

MODELO: ¿Qué comemos? (biftec)

Comamos biftec.

1. ¿Por cuánto tiempo nos quedamos en Madrid? (dos semanas)

   _____

2. ¿En qué hotel nos hospedamos? (en el Alcázar)

   _____

3. ¿Con quién hablamos? (con el dueño)

   _____

4. ¿Comemos en el cuarto o en el restaurante? (en el cuarto)

   _____

5. ¿A quién le pedimos la llave? (al empleado)

   _____

6. ¿Dónde dejamos el dinero? (en la caja de seguridad)

   _____

7. ¿A qué hora nos acostamos esta noche? (temprano)

   _____

8. ¿A qué hora nos levantamos mañana? (tarde)

   _____

9. ¿Adónde vamos? (a la tienda)

   _____

10. ¿Qué compramos? (ropa y zapatos)

   _____

F. ¿Qué me preguntaste? Write the questions that elicited the following answers.

1. _____

   El catalán es un idioma que hablan en Barcelona.

2. _____

   El número de teléfono del hotel es 487-94-65.

3. _____

   Calle Estrella, número 234.

4. _____

   La paella es un plato típico de España.

G. Crucigrama

HORIZONTAL

1. *stomach,* en español
2. Necesita _____ para caminar (*walk*).
4. Los _____ vienen en la ambulancia.
6. no creer
7. Está en la boca.
9. parte de la cara
10. seguir
12. Le voy a desinfectar la _____.
13. parte de la mano
14. Lo trajeron al hospital en una _____.
17. No estoy seguro, pero estoy _____ seguro.
19. Se cayó en la escalera _____.
20. *to happen,* en español
21. muchos
22. chequea
23. *chest,* en español

VERTICAL

1. *back,* en español
3. Está en la sala de _____.
5. Le hacen _____ en la sala de rayos X.
8. Le pusieron una inyección _____.
9. *arm,* en español
11. perder el conocimiento
14. El médico _____ a sus pacientes.
15. *allergic,* en español
16. (*medical*) *test,* en español
18. *foot,* en español

H. El mensaje de Mirta. Silvia received this e-mail from her cousin Mirta, but many words are missing. Help Silvia read it by supplying the missing words.

Querida prima:

La semana pasada no pude ir a verte como había planeado, porque he tenido varios

problemas. El sábado tuve un _____; mi coche _____ con

otro auto y los _____ tuvieron que llevarme a la _____ de

emergencia en una _____. Tenía una _____ en el brazo; el

médico me la _____ y me puso una inyección _____. Como me

_____ mucho la pierna, me dieron unas pastillas para el _____

y me hicieron varias _____. Por suerte no tenía _____,

de modo que no tuve que usar _____ para caminar. Desgraciadamente,

la medicina que tomé me causó una reacción _____ y tuve la cara

_____ por dos días.

Hoy me siento mejor, y espero verte pronto.

Mirta

I. ¿Qué pasa aquí? Look at the illustrations and answer the following questions.

1. ¿Dónde está Luis en este momento?

   _____

2. ¿Qué va a hacer la enfermera?

   _____

3. ¿Qué no quiere Luis?

   _____

4. ¿Qué se lastimó Luis?

   _____

5. ¿Luis va a necesitar muletas?

   _____

6. ¿Dónde está Rita?

   _____

7. ¿Rita se está poniendo el suéter o se lo está quitando?

   _____

8. ¿Quién está con Rita?

   _____

9. ¿Qué le va a hacer la enfermera a Rita?

   _____

   _____

⊡ Para leer

Read the following letter and then answer the questions.

Querida Marta:

Lo siento mucho, pero no voy a poder ir con Uds. a la playa este fin de semana porque ayer tuve un accidente. Me caí en la escalera y me fracturé una pierna.

Yo creía que solo tenía una torcedura pero como me dolía mucho decidí ir al hospital. Cuando llegué allí, me llevaron a la sala de rayos X donde me hicieron varias radiografías. El médico me dijo que tenía la pierna rota. Ahora voy a tener que usar muletas por tres semanas para poder caminar.

¿Vas a venir a visitarme? Espero° verte pronto°.

Cariños° para todos,

Isabel

hope / soon

Love

¡Conteste!

1. ¿A quién le escribe Isabel?

   _____

2. ¿Por qué no va a poder ir a la playa Isabel?

   _____

3. ¿Dónde se cayó Isabel?

   _____

4. ¿Qué le pasó?

   _____

5. ¿Qué pensaba Isabel que tenía?

   _____

6. ¿Adónde llevaron a Isabel para hacerle radiografías?

   _____

7. ¿Qué supo el médico al ver las radiografías?

   _____

8. ¿Qué va a tener que usar Isabel para caminar?

   _____

9. ¿Por cuánto tiempo va a tener que usarlas?

   _____

10. ¿A quién espera ver pronto Isabel?

    _____

Para escribir

You have now used a variety of tenses in Spanish. When writing, you have time to think about which tense to use. Remember as you complete this writing assignment that the preterit is used to express completed actions in the past, the imperfect is used for background information and actions in progress, and the perfect tenses are used much as in English. Check your work after writing to be sure that you have used the correct tense and form.

Name _____ Section _____ Date _____

Write a dialogue between you and a friend who has invited you to a party. Explain that you couldn't make it because you had an accident. Tell your friend what happened. Say where you were and what you were doing when the accident happened. Talk about what took place at the hospital.

_____

_____

_____

_____

_____

_____

_____

_____

_____

_____

_____

_____

_____

_____

_____

_____

_____

_____

LECCIÓN 14

Workbook Activities

Para practicar

A. **¿Qué pasará?** Complete the chart below with verb forms in the future tense.

Infinitive	yo	tú	Ud., él, ella	nosotros(as)	Uds., ellos(as)
1. ayudar					
2. decir	diré				
3. hacer		harás			
4. querer			querrá		
5. saber				sabremos	
6. poder					podrán
7. salir	saldré				
8. poner		pondrás			
9. venir			vendrá		
10. tener				tendremos	
11. ir					irán

B. De vacaciones. Gabriel and Adrián are planning a fabulous vacation. Complete their conversation by giving the future of the verbs in parentheses.

GABRIEL: En un mes nosotros _____ (tener) vacaciones y _____ (estar) en Barcelona.

ADRIÁN: _____ (ser) fabuloso. Yo _____ (poder) ver a mis tíos y tú _____ (ir) a acampar con tus primos.

GABRIEL: ¿Cuándo _____ (salir / nosotros) para Barcelona?

ADRIÁN: Probablemente, el 6 de julio. Yo lo _____ (saber) el próximo sábado.

GABRIEL: Perfecto, les _____ (decir) a mis primos que preparen las tiendas de campaña.

ADRIÁN: Mi hermana _____ (venir) a verme mañana y me _____ (traer) una maleta porque yo sólo tengo una y pienso llevar mucha ropa. Oye, ¿qué _____ (hacer) tú mañana?

GABRIEL: ¡Yo _____ (venir) a visitarte para ver a tu hermana!

C. Nadie está de acuerdo. The following is what Luis plans to do, but nobody agrees with him. Say what everybody else would do instead, using the conditional tense and the cues provided.

1. Luis piensa acampar el miércoles. (yo / el viernes)

   _____

2. Luis piensa llevar la receta a la farmacia hoy. (tú / mañana)

   _____

3. Luis piensa venir antes de dos semanas. (Ester / un mes)

   _____

4. Luis piensa salir a las ocho. (nosotros / a las diez)

   _____

5. Luis piensa decir que sí. (ellos / que no)

   _____

6. Luis piensa tomar un jarabe. (Uds. / unas pastillas)

   _____

7. Luis piensa ir al médico mañana. (Ud. / hoy mismo)

_____

8. Luis piensa hablar con la enfermera. (Sergio / el médico)

_____

D. Para completar. Complete the following chart with verb forms in the imperfect subjunctive.

Infinitive	yo	tú	Ud., él, ella	nosotros(as)	Uds., ellos(as)
1. hablar	hablara	hablaras	hablara	habláramos	hablaran
2. cerrar	cerrara				
3. volver			volviera		volvieran
4. pedir		pidieras			pidieran
5. dormir				durmiéramos	
6. ir			fuera		fueran
7. dar				diéramos	
8. estar			estuviera		
9. decir		dijeras			dijeran
10. venir			viniera	viniéramos	
11. querer			quisiera		
12. ser	fuera				fueran
13. tener		tuvieras			
14. conducir			condujera		condujeran
15. poner		pusieras		pusiéramos	
16. hacer					hicieran
17. saber		supieras			

E. **¿Qué dijeron?** Here are several statements that people made last year. Keeping in mind that this was in the past, change the verbs to the imperfect subjunctive according to the new beginning.

MODELO: Quiero que vayas conmigo. Quería...

Quería que fueras conmigo.

1. Me piden que les dé la receta.

   Me pidieron _____.

2. Te sugiero que los lleves al hospital.

   Te sugerí _____.

3. No hay nadie que pueda ponerme una inyección.

   No había nadie _____.

4. Yo no creo que sepas hacer eso.

   Yo no creía _____.

5. Ellos dudan que Elsa quiera llevarme.

   Ellos dudaban _____.

6. Esperan que nos mejoremos.

   Esperaban _____.

7. Me alegro de que él sea mi médico.

   Me alegré _____.

8. ¿Hay alguien que conozca a ese cirujano?

   ¿Había alguien _____?

9. Ellos insisten en que yo venga a visitarlos.

   Ellos insistieron _____.

10. Los llamo para que traigan el termómetro.

    Los llamé _____.

F. Si... Complete the following to indicate what people will do or would do according to circumstances. Use the present indicative or the imperfect subjunctive as appropriate.

MODELO: Yo compraría una casa... (tener dinero)
Yo compraría una casa si tuviera dinero.

1. Yo iré a visitar a mis padres... (tener tiempo)

_____

2. José pasará un par de días en Barcelona... (poder)

_____

3. Nosotros pediríamos un turno para hoy... (no ser sábado)

_____

4. Tú te empeorarías... (no descansar)

_____

5. Uds. llevarían al niño al pediatra... (tener fiebre)

_____

6. Aurora irá al ginecólogo... (estar embarazada)

_____

G. Crucigrama

HORIZONTAL

4. especialista de niños
9. cita
11. Compré _____ oxigenada.
13. especialista de la piel (*skin*)
15. Voy a verlo si tengo problemas con los ojos.
19. Debe hacerlo hoy _____.
20. La pulmonía es una _____ grave.
21. *Tums* es un _____.
22. Tiene la _____ alta.

VERTICAL

1. Tiene _____. Tiene una temperatura de 102 grados.
2. Necesito tomar un _____ para la tos.
3. opuesto de **empeorarse**
5. oficina del médico
6. Va a tener un bebé (*baby*); está _____.
7. Sus pacientes son mujeres.
8. No tengo _____ médico.
10. Respire _____, por favor.
12. Necesito el _____ para saber si tengo fiebre.
13. Tiene _____ de garganta.
14. Nos la da el médico.
16. sedativo
17. Voy a la _____ para comprar las medicinas.
18. Tose mucho. Tine mucha _____.

H. Conversaciones breves. Complete what these people people say by matching the questions in column A with the answers in column B.

A   B

1. _____ ¿Necesita mi tarjeta de seguro médico?   a. Para comprar algodón y vendas.

2. _____ ¿Fuiste al médico?   b. En el botiquín.

3. _____ ¿Vas a ir al dermatólogo?   c. Que me cuidara.

4. _____ ¿Dónde está el esparadrapo?   d. Sí, aquí la tienes.

5. _____ ¿Qué te dijo el médico?   e. Sí, y contagiosa.

6. _____ ¿La enfermera te pesó?   f. Sí, voy a hacer una fotocopia.

7. _____ ¿Es una enfermedad grave?   g. Un calmante.

8. _____ ¿Puedes treaerme el agua oxigenada?   h. Sí, y me hizo un buen chequeo.

9. _____ ¿Qué tomaste para el dolor?   i. Sí, y me tomó la presión.

10. _____ ¿Para qué fuiste a la farmacia?   j. Sí, tengo acné.

I. ¿Qué dice aquí? Read this ad that appeared in a Spanish newspaper, and then answer the following questions based on the information provided.

INTED
INSTITUTO NACIONAL DE
EXAMEN Y DIAGNÓSTICO

Para el cuidado médico de toda la familia

- Medicina general • Chequeos médicos

- Análisis • Electrocardiogramas

- Rayos X • Ginecología

- Papanicolau • Pruebas de embarazo

Aceptamos todo tipo de seguro. • Ofremos consultas de lunes a viernes.
Llámenos o visite nuestro moderno centro médico.

4-74-35-81 **Gran Vía, 371**

1. ¿Cómo se llama el centro médico?

_____

2. Si mi esposa y mis hijos tienen problemas de salud (*health*), ¿puedo llevarlos al centro médico? ¿Por qué?

_____

3. Mi hija necesita hacerse una radiografía. ¿Puede hacérselas en el centro médico? ¿Por qué?

_____

4. Mi esposa cree que está embarazada. ¿Qué puede hacerse en el centro médico?

_____

5. ¿A qué especialista puede ir a ver?

_____

6. Si una persona tiene problemas del corazón, ¿qué pueden hacerle en el centro médico?

_____

7. Hace mucho tiempo que no voy al médico. ¿Qué debo ir a hacerme en el centro médico?

_____

8. ¿Aceptarán mi seguro en el centro médico?

_____

9. ¿Qué días de la semana puedo ir al centro médico?

_____

10. ¿Dónde está el centro médico? ¿Cuál es el teléfono?

_____

⊡ Para leer

Read the following diary excerpts, and then answer the questions.

DEL DIARIO DE ROSAURA

24 de septiembre

 Anoche me sentí muy mal toda la noche. Me dolían mucho los oídos y la cabeza y tenía mucha fiebre. Tomé dos aspirinas y me acosté.

 Hoy me levanté muy temprano y, como todavía° tengo fiebre, voy a ir al médico.   still

25 de septiembre

 Ayer fui al médico; me examinó y me dijo que tenía una infección en los oídos y que por eso me dolían tanto. Me recetó penicilina; por suerte yo no soy alérgica a ninguna medicina. También me recetó un jarabe para la tos.

 No pude comprar las medicinas porque ya eran más de las ocho cuando salí del consultorio y las farmacias cierran a las ocho. Espero sentirme mejor mañana.

¡Conteste!

1. ¿Cómo se sintió Rosaura toda la noche?

_____

2. ¿Qué le dolía a Rosaura?

_____

3. ¿Qué tomó Rosaura para la fiebre?

_____

4. ¿Por qué va a ir ella al médico?

_____

5. ¿Qué le dijo el médico después de examinarla?

_____

6. ¿A qué medicinas es alérgica Rosaura?

_____

7. ¿Qué le recetó el doctor a Rosaura para la infección en los oídos? ¿Para la tos?

_____

8. ¿Qué hora era cuando Rosaura salió del consultorio del médico?

_____

9. ¿A qué hora cierran las farmacias?

_____

10. ¿Qué espera Rosaura?

_____

▣ Para escribir

When you write a more formal note or letter, use the following salutation and closing. Also, remember to address the person you are writing to as **Ud.**

Estimado(a) señor(a) / profesor(a) + *name*:   *Dear...*

Atentamente,   *Sincerely,*

You have to miss an exam because you are sick. Write a note to your professor, explaining your reasons for missing the exam. Say what your symptoms are and what you are doing about your sickness. Be convincing! Also, be sure to ask when you can take the exam.

_____

_____

_____

_____

_____

_____

_____

_____

_____

_____

_____

_____

_____

Name _____ Section _____ Date _____

Sobre el mundo hispánico. Refer to this section of your textbook to see how much you remember.

1. ¿Qué países forman la Península Ibérica?

   _____

2. ¿Qué separa a España de Francia?

   _____

3. ¿Qué sistema de gobierno tiene España?

   _____

4. ¿Qué museo famoso está en Madrid?

   _____

5. ¿Cuál es la capital de Cataluña?

   _____

6. ¿Cuáles son las ciudades más importantes del sur de España?

   _____

7. ¿Qué influencia se ve en estas ciudades?

   _____

8. ¿En qué plaza están representadas escenas históricas de toda España?

   _____

9. ¿Cuál es la música típica de Andalucía?

   _____

Laboratory Activities

Preliminary Laboratory Activities

Introduction to Spanish Sounds

Each Spanish sound will be explained briefly, and examples will be given for practice.

Pronunciation

Repeat each Spanish word after the speaker, imitating as closely as possible the correct pronunciation.

Vowels

1. **a** in Spanish sounds similar to the English *a* in the word *father*.

   alta   casa   palma   Ana   cama   Panamá   alma   apagar

2. **e** is pronounced like the English *e* in the word *eight*.

   mes   entre   este   deje   ese   encender   teme   prender

3. **i** has a sound similar to the English *ee* in the word *see*.

   fin   ir   sí   sin   dividir   Trini   difícil

4. **o** is similar to the English *o* in the word *no*, but without the glide.

   toco   como   poco   roto   corto   corro   solo   loco

5. **u** is pronounced like the English *oo* sound in the word *shoot*, or the *ue* sound in the word *Sue*.

   su   Lulú   Úrsula   cultura   un   luna   sucursal   Uruguay

Consonants

1. Spanish **p** is pronounced in a matter similar to the English *p* sound, but without the puff of air that follows after the English sound is produced.

   pesca   pude   puedo   parte   papá   postre   piña   puente   Paco

2. The Spanish /k/ sound, represented by the letters **k; c** before **a, o, u** or a consonant (except **h**); and **qu,** is similar to the English *k* sound, but without the puff of air.

   casa   comer   cuna   clima   acción   que   quinto   queso   aunque   kiosko   kilómetro

3. Spanish **t** is produced by touching the back of the upper front teeth with the tip of the tongue. It has no puff of air as in the English *t.*

   todo   antes   corto   Guatemala   diente   resto   tonto   roto   tanque

4. The Spanish consonant **d** has two different sounds depending on its position. At the beginning of an utterance and after **n** or **l**, the tip of the tongue presses the back of the upper front teeth.

   día   doma   dice   dolor   dar   anda   Aldo   caldo

   el deseo   un domicilio

   In all other positions the sound of **d** is similar to the *th* sound in the English word *they*, but softer.

   medida   todo   nada   nadie   medio   puedo   moda   queda   nudo

5. The Spanish consonant **g** is similar to the English *g* sound in the word *guy* except before **e** or **i.**

   goma   glotón   gallo   gloria   lago   alga   gorrión   garra   guerra   angustia

   algo   Dagoberto

6. The Spanish consonant **j** (or **g** before **e** and **i**) is similar to a strongly exaggerated English *h* sound.

   gemir   juez   jarro   gitano   agente   juego   giro   bajo   gente

7. There is no difference in sound between Spanish **b** and **v.** Both letters are pronounced alike. At the beginning of an utterance or after **m** or **n, b** and **v** have a sound identical to the English *b* sound in the word *boy.*

   vivir   beber   vamos   barco   enviar   hambre   batea   bueno   vestido

   When pronounced between vowels, the Spanish **b** and **v** sound is produced by bringing the lips together but not closing them, so that some air may pass through.

   sábado   autobús   yo   voy   su barco

8. In most countries, Spanish **ll** and **y** have a sound similar to the English *y* sound in the word *yes.*

   el llavero   un yelmo   el yeso   su yunta

   llama   yema   oye   trayecto   trayectoria   mayo   milla   bella

   When it stands alone or is at the end of a word, Spanish **y** is pronounced like the vowel **i.**

   rey   hoy   y   doy   buey   muy   voy   estoy   soy

9. The sound of Spanish **r** is similar to the English *dd* sound in the word *ladder.*

   crema   aroma   cara   arena   aro   harina   toro   oro   eres   portero

10. Spanish **rr** and also **r** in an initial position and after **n, l,** or **s** are pronounced with a very strong trill. This trill is produced by bringing the tip of the tongue near the alveolar ridge

and letting it vibrate freely while the air passes through the mouth.

rama   carro   Israel   cierra   roto   perro   alrededor   rizo   corre   Enrique

11. Spanish **s** is represented in most of the Spanish world by the letters **s**, **z**, and **c** before **e** or **i**. The sound is very similar to the English sibilant *s* in the word *sink*.

    sale   sitio   presidente   signo   salsa   seda   suma   vaso   sobrino

    ciudad   cima   canción   zapato   zarza   cerveza   centro

12. The letter **h** is silent in Spanish.

    hoy   hora   hilo   ahora   humor   huevo   horror   almohada

13. Spanish **ch** is pronounced like the English *ch* in the word *chief*.

    hecho   chico   coche   Chile   mucho   muchacho   salchicha

14. Spanish **f** is identical in sound to the English *f.*

    difícil   feo   fuego   forma   fácil   fecha   foto   fueron

15. Spanish **l** is similar to the English *l* in the word *let*.

    dolor   lata   ángel   lago   sueldo   los   pelo   lana   general   fácil

16. Spanish **m** is pronounced like the English *m* in the word *mother.*

    mano   moda   mucho   muy   mismo   tampoco   multa   cómoda

17. In most cases, Spanish **n** has a sound similar to the English *n.*

    nada   nunca   ninguno   norte   entra   tiene   sienta

    The sound of Spanish **n** is often affected by the sounds that occur around it. When it appears before **b**, **v**, or **p**, it is pronounced like an **m**.

    tan bueno   toman vino   sin poder   un pobre   comen peras   siguen bebiendo

18. Spanish **ñ** is similar to the English *ny* sound in the word *canyon*.

    señor   otoño   ñoño   uña   leña   dueño   niños   años

19. Spanish **x** has two pronunciations depending on its position. Between vowels the sound is similar to English *ks*.

    examen   exacto   boxeo   éxito   oxidar   oxígeno   existencia

    When it occurs before a consonant, Spanish **x** sounds like *s*.

    expresión   explicar   extraer   excusa   expreso   exquisito   extremo

    When **x** appears in **México** or in other words of Mexican origin, it is pronounced like the Spanish letter **j**.

Linking

In spoken Spanish, the different words in a phrase or sentence are not pronounced as isolated elements, but are combined together. This is called *linking*.

Pepe come pan.

Tomás toma leche.

Luis tiene la llave.

la mano de Roberto

1. The final consonant of a word is pronounced together with the initial vowel of the following word.

   Carlos‿anda

   un‿ángel

   el‿otoño

   unos‿estudios‿interesantes

2. A diphthong is formed between the final vowel of a word and the initial vowel of the following word. A triphthong is formed when there is a combination of three vowels.

   su‿hermana

   tu‿escopeta

   Roberto‿y Luis

   negocio‿importante

   lluvia‿y nieve

   ardua‿empresa

3. When the final vowel of a word and the initial vowel of the following word are identical, they are pronounced slightly longer than one vowel.

   Ana‿alcanza   lo‿olvido   tiene‿eso   Ada‿atiende

   The same rule applies when two identical vowels appear within a word.

   crees   Teherán   coordinación

4. When the final consonant of a word and the initial consonant of the following word are the same, they are pronounced like one consonant with slightly longer than normal duration.

   el‿lado   tienes‿sed   Carlos‿salta

LECCIÓN 1

Laboratory Activities

 I. Pronunciación

Listen and repeat the following words, paying close attention to the pronunciation of vowels. Remember to keep the vowel sounds short and clear.

sí	no	de	tu	me
chica	muchacho	tiza	clase	alto
cubano	inglés	simpático	¿cómo?	
mapa	bienvenido			

Now, listen and repeat the following phrases, paying close attention to the vowel sounds.

Mucho gusto.   El gusto es mío.

¿Cómo te llamas?   ¿De dónde eres?

Necesito el reloj.   Hasta mañana.

¿Cómo se llama usted?

 II. Diálogos: ¡Bienvenidos!

Listen to the dialogues twice, paying close attention to the speakers' intonation and pronunciation patterns. First, listen to the entire dialogue; then, as you listen for a second time, stop the recording after each sentence and repeat after the speakers.

En la Universidad de California, en Los Ángeles.

David, un chico norteamericano, habla con Lupe, una chica mexicana.

DAVID	Buenos días, Lupe. ¿Cómo estás?
LUPE	Bien, ¿y tú? ¿Qué hay de nuevo?
DAVID	No mucho. Oye, Lupe. ¿Cuál es tu número de teléfono?
LUPE	Dos-trece-siete-veintiocho-quince-treinta y tres.
DAVID	¿Cuál es tu dirección?
LUPE	Calle Alvarado, número diecisiete-once.

DAVID	Gracias. Hasta mañana.
LUPE	Adiós.

El doctor Acosta habla con una estudiante.

NORA	Buenas tardes, profesor.
PROFESOR	Buenas tardes, señorita. ¿Cómo se llama usted?
NORA	Me llamo Nora Ballester.
PROFESOR	Mucho gusto.
NORA	El gusto es mío.
PROFESOR	¿De dónde es usted?
NORA	Yo soy de San Antonio, Texas.

Sergio habla con Teresa en la biblioteca.

SERGIO	Hola, Teresa. ¿Qué tal?
TERESA	Muy bien, ¿y tú?
SERGIO	Más o menos. Oye, tu compañera de cuarto es muy bonita...
TERESA	¿Ana María? Sí, es una chica muy bonita y muy simpática.
SERGIO	¡Muy interesante! ¿Es inteligente?
TERESA	Sí... ¡y rica!
SERGIO	¡Caramba! ¡Es perfecta! Bueno, nos vemos esta noche. Saludos a Ana María.
TERESA	Hasta luego.

La profesora Rivas habla con los estudiantes en la clase de español.

PROFESORA	Buenas noches. ¿Cómo están ustedes?
ESTUDIANTES	Bien, gracias.
DAVID	Profesora, ¿cómo se dice "*book*" en español?
PROFESORA	Se dice "libro".
DAVID	Muchas gracias.
PROFESORA	De nada.

III. Preguntas y respuestas

The speaker will ask several questions based on the dialogues. Answer each question, always omitting the subject. The speaker will verify your response. Repeat the correct answer.

▣ IV. Puntos para recordar

A. Definite articles I. Repeat each noun you hear, adding the appropriate definite article. The speaker will verify your response. Repeat the correct answer. Follow the model.

MODELO: libro
el libro

B. Indefinite articles. Repeat each noun you hear, adding the appropriate indefinite article. The speaker will verify your response. Repeat the correct answer. Follow the model.

MODELO: pluma
una pluma

C. Subject pronouns and the present indicative of *ser*. The speaker will name a series of people and places. Using the appropriate form of the verb, say where the people are from. The speaker will verify your response. Repeat the correct answer. Follow the model.

MODELO: Ud. / California
Ud. es de California.

D. Agreement of articles and adjectives. The speaker will read several sentences, and will provide a cue for each one. Substitute the cue you hear in each sentence, making all necessary changes. The speaker will verify your response. Repeat the correct answer. Follow the model.

MODELO: El hombre es cubano. (mujeres)
Las mujeres son cubanas.

▣ V. Díganos

The speaker will ask you some questions. Answer, using the cues provided and always omitting the subject. The speaker will verify your response. Repeat the correct answer. Follow the model.

MODELO: —¿Miguel es alto? (sí)
—Sí, es alto.

A. **You will hear three statements about each picture.** Indicate the letter of the statement that best corresponds to the picture. The speaker will verify your response.

1.   a b c   2.   a b c   3.   a b c

4.   a b c   5.   a b c

B. **You will now hear some statements.** Indicate **L** if the statement is logical (**lógico**) or **I** if it is illogical (**ilógico**). The speaker will verify your response.

1. L I   5. L I

2. L I   6. L I

3. L I   7. L I

4. L I   8. L I

C. Listen carefully to the dialogue, and then answer the questions, omitting the subjects. The speaker will confirm your response. Repeat the correct response.

Listen to the dialogue.

Now answer the speaker's questions.

VII. Para escuchar y escribir

A. The speaker will dictate ten numbers. Listen to each number twice. Write them, using numerals rather than words.

1. _____   6. _____

2. _____   7. _____

3. _____   8. _____

4. _____   9. _____

5. _____   10. _____

B. The speaker will read five sentences. Listen to each sentence twice. After you listen for the first time, stop the audio and write what you have heard. Then, play the sentence for a second time to check your work and fill in what you have missed.

1. _____

2. _____

3. _____

4. _____

5. _____

LECCIÓN 2

Laboratory Activities

I. Pronunciación

Listen and repeat the following sentences, paying attention to linking.

1. Termina‿en‿agosto.
2. Este semestre‿estudio‿historia.
3. Deseo‿una botella de‿agua.
4. Aquí‿está‿el‿libro.
5. Felipe‿y‿Ana‿hablan‿inglés.
6. Necesitamos‿su‿horario.

II. Diálogos: Nuestras clases

Listen to the dialogues twice, paying close attention to the speakers' intonation and pronunciation patterns. First, listen to the entire dialogue; then, as you listen for a second time, stop the recording after each sentence and repeat after the speakers.

Lisa, una chica norteamericana, habla con Alina, su nueva compañera de cuarto, que es cubanoamericana. Las dos estudian en la Universidad Internacional de la Florida, en Miami.

LISA   Alina, ¿cuántas clases tomas este semestre?

ALINA   Tomo cinco clases: inglés, matemáticas, física, psicología y biología. ¿Y tú?

LISA   Yo tomo historia, literatura y español.

ALINA   ¿Español? ¡Buena idea! Pero solamente tomas tres asignaturas.

LISA   Sí, porque yo trabajo los lunes, miércoles y viernes por la tarde; porque necesito dinero.

ALINA   Yo también, pero trabajo en el verano, de julio a septiembre.

LISA   Tú tomas materias muy difíciles.

ALINA   Sí, pero todas mis clases son requisitos… Además, la clase de psicología es fácil.

LISA   Pues, Alina, tu vida es muy aburrida. ¡Vamos a la playa!

Miguel habla con su amigo Pablo, un chico puertorriqueño. Los dos conversan en la cafetería de la universidad.

MIGUEL	¿Deseas tomar una taza de café?
PABLO	No, un vaso de leche. Yo no tomo café. Oye, ¿qué hora es?
MIGUEL	Es la una y media. ¿Por qué?
PABLO	Porque a las dos de la tarde hay un programa de televisión muy interesante.
MIGUEL	¡Ah! Necesito mi horario de clases.
PABLO	Aquí está. Nuestra clase de química es a las cuatro en el aula ciento noventa y cinco.
MIGUEL	¿A qué hora terminan tus clases hoy?
PABLO	A las ocho de la noche.
MIGUEL	Estudiamos juntos mañana, ¿verdad?
PABLO	Entonces, ¿mañana no vamos a la playa? Eres un aguafiestas. Bueno, me voy.

III. Preguntas y respuestas

The speaker will ask several questions based on the dialogues. Answer each question, always omitting the subject. The speaker will verify your response. Repeat the correct answer.

IV. Puntos para recordar

A. **Present indicative of -ar verbs.** The speaker will ask several questions. Answer each one, always choosing the first possibility. The speaker will verify your response. Repeat the correct answer. Follow the model.

MODELO: —¿Ud. habla inglés o español?
—*Hablo inglés.*

B. **Interrogative sentences.** Answer each question you hear, using the cue provided. Pay special attention to the use of interrogative words. The speaker will verify your response. Repeat the correct answer. Follow the model.

MODELO: —¿Dónde trabajas? (en la cafetería)
—*Trabajo en la cafetería.*

C. **Negative sentences.** Answer each question you hear in the negative, always omitting the subject. The speaker will verify your response. Repeat the correct answer. Follow the model.

MODELO: —¿Elsa trabaja por la mañana?
—*No, no trabaja por la mañana.*

D. **Possessive adjectives.** Answer each question you hear, using the cue provided. The speaker will verify your response. Repeat the correct answer. Follow the model.

MODELO: —¿De dónde es tu profesora? (Puerto Rico)
—*Mi profesora es de Puerto Rico.*

E. Definite articles II. Repeat each word you hear, adding the appropriate definite article. The speaker will verify your response. Repeat the correct answer. Follow the model.

MODELO: universidad
          la universidad

F. Numbers. The speaker will name a day of the year. Say its date. The speaker will verify your response. Repeat the correct answer. Follow the model.

MODELO: Veterans' Day
          el once de noviembre

G. Days of the week. You will hear several questions. The person asking these questions is always a day ahead. Respond saying the correct day. The speaker will verify your response. Repeat the correct answer. Follow the model.

MODELO: —¿Hoy es lunes?
          —*No, hoy es domingo.*

H. Months and seasons. The speaker will name a month. State the season in which the month falls. The speaker will verify your response. Repeat the correct answer. Follow the model.

MODELO: diciembre
          el invierno

V. Díganos

The speaker will ask you some questions. Answer, using the cues provided and always omitting the subject. The speaker will verify your response. Repeat the correct answer. Follow the model.

MODELO: —¿Estudia Ud. por la mañana? (por la tarde)
          —*No, estudio por la tarde.*

VI. Ejercicios de comprensión

A. You will hear three statements about each picture. Indicate the letter of the statement that best corresponds to the picture. The speaker will verify your response.

1. a b c   2. a b c   3. a b c

4. a b c   5. a b c

B. You will now hear some statements. Indicate **L** if the statement is logical (**lógico**) or **I** if it is illogical (**ilógico**). The speaker will verify your response.

1. L I   6. L I
2. L I   7. L I
3. L I   8. L I
4. L I   9. L I
5. L I   10. L I

C. Listen carefully to the dialogue, and then answer the questions, omitting the subjects. The speaker will confirm your response. Repeat the correct response.

Listen to the dialogue.

Now answer the speaker's questions.

⟲ VII. Para escuchar y escribir

A. The speaker will dictate twelve numbers. Listen to each number twice. Write them, using numerals rather than words.

1. _____   5. _____   9. _____

2. _____   6. _____   10. _____

3. _____   7. _____   11. _____

4. _____   8. _____   12. _____

B. The speaker will read five sentences. Listen to each sentence twice. After you listen for the first time, stop the audio and write what you have heard. Then, play the sentence for a second time to check your work and fill in what you have missed.

1. _____

2. _____

3. _____

4. _____

5. _____

LECCIÓN 3

Laboratory Activities

I. Pronunciación

Listen and repeat the following words, paying close attention to the pronunciation of **b** and **v**.

Benito / Viviana / mueble / lavar / favorito / basura / Benavente / barre

Now listen and repeat the following sentences, paying close attention to the pronunciation of **b** and **v**.

1. La nueva biblioteca es buena.
2. Víctor y Beatriz beben una botella de vino blanco.
3. Roberto Vera vive bien en Nevada.
4. Los jueves y los viernes, Beto y yo navegamos la red.
5. Verónica Barrios viene el sábado veintinueve.

II. Diálogo: Los trabajos de la casa

Listen to the dialogue twice, paying close attention to the speakers' intonation and pronunciation patterns. First, listen to the entire dialogue; then, as you listen for a second time, stop the recording after each sentence and repeat after the speakers.

Hoy es un día muy ocupado para Susana, Alicia y Héctor, tres hermanos que viven con sus padres en la Ciudad de México.

ALICIA	Esta noche vienen papá y mamá de Guadalajara y esta casa es un desastre.
SUSANA	Sí, especialmente el cuarto de Héctor. Héctor, tienes que limpiar tu recámara.
ALICIA	Y también tienes que sacar la basura y cortar el zacate.
HÉCTOR	¡Ustedes dos son muy mandonas! Yo siempre tengo que hacer todo el trabajo de esta casa.
SUSANA	¡Ja! Tu ocupación favorita es comer, porque siempre tienes hambre.
ALICIA	Yo creo que lo mejor es dividir el trabajo: Yo limpio la cocina y los baños, Susana sacude los muebles de la sala y Héctor barre el garaje.
HÉCTOR	¿Yo hago todo eso? No tengo tiempo, porque hoy viene Carlos para estudiar conmigo.
SUSANA	¡Tú siempre tienes excusas para no trabajar!

Esa tarde.

ALICIA	Todavía tenemos que lavar y planchar la ropa y lavar los platos.
SUSANA	¡Hay mil cosas que hacer!
HÉCTOR	¿Por qué no descansamos un rato y bebemos una limonada? Yo tengo mucha sed.
ALICIA	Tienes razón. Hay limonada en el refrigerador.
SUSANA	Bueno... descansamos un momento, pero después debemos pasar la aspiradora y preparar la comida.
HÉCTOR	Yo hago la ensalada y ustedes preparan las enchiladas.
ALICIA	¿Y quién pone la mesa?
SUSANA	Héctor. Oye, tocan a la puerta.
HÉCTOR	Debe ser Carlos. (*Héctor corre a abrir.*)

Esa noche, cuando llegan los padres, todos cenan y conversan en el comedor, y después la mamá y las chicas miran su telenovela favorita.

III. Preguntas y respuestas

The speaker will ask several questions based on the dialogue. Answer each question, always omitting the subject. The speaker will verify your response. Repeat the correct answer.

IV. Puntos para recordar

A. Present indicative of -er and -ir verbs. The speaker will ask several questions. Answer each one, using the cue provided. The speaker will verify your response. Repeat the correct answer. Follow the model.

MODELO: —¿Qué bebes tú? (café)
—*Bebo café.*

B. Possession with *de*. The speaker will name a series of objects and their owners. Using the verb **ser,** say to whom the items belong. The speaker will verify your response. Repeat the correct answer. Follow the model.

MODELO: la plancha / Elena
Es la plancha de Elena.

C. Present indicative of *tener* and *venir*. The speaker will read some sentences. Change each sentence according to the new subject. The speaker will verify your response. Repeat the correct answer. Follow the model.

MODELO: Ella viene a las ocho. (Uds.)
Uds. vienen a las ocho.

D. Expressions with *tener* I. Say what the people mentioned have to do. The speaker will verify your response. Repeat the correct answer. Follow the model.

MODELO: Rosa / abrir la puerta
Rosa tiene que abrir la puerta.

E. Expressions with *tener* II. Use expressions with tener to say how the people described in each statement feel, according to the situation. The speaker will verify your response. Repeat the correct answer. Follow the model.

MODELO: I am in Alaska in January.
Yo tengo mucho frío.

F. Demonstrative adjectives. The speaker will give you demonstrative adjectives and nouns. Change the demonstrative adjective with each new noun. The speaker will verify your response. Repeat the correct answer. Follow the model.

MODELO: este hombre (mujer)
esta mujer

V. Díganos

The speaker will ask you some questions. Answer, using the cues provided and always omitting the subject. The speaker will verify your response. Repeat the correct answer. Follow the model.

MODELO: —¿Ud. vive en Miami? (no)
—No, no vivo en Miami.

VI. Ejercicios de comprensión

A. You will hear three statements about each picture. Indicate the letter of the statement that best corresponds to the picture. The speaker will verify your response.

1.   a   b   c   2.   a   b   c   3.   a   b   c

4.   a   b   c   5.   a   b   c

B. You will now hear some statements. Indicate **L** if the statement is logical (**lógico**) or **I** if it is illogical (**ilógico**). The speaker will verify your response.

1.   L   I   6.   L   I

2.   L   I   7.   L   I

3.   L   I   8.   L   I

4.   L   I   9.   L   I

5.   L   I   10.   L   I

C. Listen carefully to the dialogue, and then answer the questions, omitting the subjects. The speaker will confirm your response. Repeat the correct response.

Listen to the dialogue.

Now answer the speaker's questions.

VII. Para escuchar y escribir

A. The speaker will dictate twelve numbers. Listen to each number twice. Write them, using numerals rather than words.

1. _____   5. _____   9. _____

2. _____   6. _____   10. _____

3. _____   7. _____   11. _____

4. _____   8. _____   12. _____

B. The speaker will read five sentences. Listen to each sentence twice. After you listen for the first time, stop the audio and write what you have heard. Then, play the sentence for a second time to check your work and fill in what you have missed.

1. _____

2. _____

3. _____

4. _____

5. _____

LECCIÓN 4

Laboratory Activities

I. Pronunciación

Listen and repeat the following words, paying close attention to the pronunciation of the consonant **c.**

club / café / capital / Carlos / cansado / cuñado / Cecilia / conocer / Celia / cocina / información

Now listen and repeat the following sentences, paying close attention to the pronunciation of the consonant **c.**

1. Clara conversa con Claudia.
2. La camarera come en el café.
3. César va al cine y al club.
4. Graciela come a las cinco.
5. Cecilia conduce con Carmen.

II. Diálogos: Una fiesta de cumpleaños

Listen to the dialogues twice, paying close attention to the speakers' intonation and pronunciation patterns. First, listen to the entire dialogue; then, as you listen for a second time stop the recording after each sentence and repeat after the speakers.

Silvia y Esteban deciden dar una fiesta para celebrar el cumpleaños de Mónica, una chica guatemalteca que ahora vive en San Salvador con la familia de Silvia.

ESTEBAN   Tenemos que mandar las invitaciones. ¿A quiénes vamos a invitar?

SILVIA   A todos nuestros amigos, a mis primos, al novio de Mónica y a Yolanda.

ESTEBAN   Yo no conozco a Yolanda. ¿Quién es?

SILVIA   Es la hermana del novio de Mónica.

ESTEBAN   ¿Ah, sí? ¿Es bonita? ¿Es rubia, morena o pelirroja? No es casada, ¿verdad?

SILVIA   Es morena, de ojos castaños, delgada, de estatura mediana... encantadora... y es soltera.

ESTEBAN   Bueno, si baila bien, ya estoy enamorado.

SILVIA   Oye, tenemos que planear la fiesta. Va a ser en el club, ¿no?

ESTEBAN	No, va a ser en la casa de mis abuelos. Ellos están en Costa Rica con mi madrina y yo tengo la llave de la casa.
SILVIA	¡Perfecto! Yo traigo los entremeses y la torta de cumpleaños.
ESTEBAN	Yo traigo las bebidas y los discos compactos. Yo sé que mis abuelos no tienen música para bailar.

En la fiesta.

Cuando Mónica, su novio y Yolanda llegan a la casa, todos gritan: ¡Feliz cumpleaños!

MÓNICA	(*Contenta*) ¡Qué sorpresa!
SILVIA	¿Qué deseas tomar? ¿Champán, cerveza...? ¿O deseas comer algo?
MÓNICA	Una copa de champán para brindar con todos mis amigos.
SILVIA	(*Levanta su copa.*) ¡Un brindis! ¡Por Mónica! ¡Salud!
TODOS	¡Salud!
ESTEBAN	(*A Yolanda*) Hola, soy Esteban Campos. Tú eres Yolanda, ¿verdad?
YOLANDA	Sí, mucho gusto.
ESTEBAN	¿Bailamos? ¿Te gusta bailar salsa?
YOLANDA	Sí, me gusta, aunque no sé bailar muy bien.

Esteban y Yolanda bailan y conversan. Todos los invitados lo pasan muy bien.

SILVIA	(*A Mónica*) Veo que Yolanda y Esteban están muy animados.
MÓNICA	Sí, hacen una buena pareja. Oye, Silvia, la fiesta es todo un éxito.
	¡Muchas gracias!

Después de la fiesta, Esteban lleva a Silvia y a Mónica a su casa. Las chicas están cansadas, pero contentas.

III. Preguntas y respuestas

The speaker will ask several questions based on the dialogues. Answer each question, always omitting the subject. The speaker will verify your response. Repeat the correct answer.

IV. Puntos para recordar

A. **Verbs with irregular first-person forms.** The speaker will ask several questions. Answer each one, using the cue provided. The speaker will verify your response. Repeat the correct answer. Follow the model.

MODELO: —¿A qué hora sales de tu casa? (a las siete)
—*Salgo de mi casa a las siete.*

B. *Saber* **vs.** *conocer.* The speaker will give you some cues. Use them to say what or whom the people mentioned know or what they know how to do, using **saber** or **conocer.** The speaker will verify your response. Repeat the correct answer. Follow the model.

MODELO: yo / al novio de Alina
          Yo conozco al novio de Alina.

C. **Personal** *a.* Answer each question you hear in the negative, using the cue provided and the personal **a** as needed. The speaker will confirm your response. Repeat the correct answer. Follow the model.

MODELO: —¿Llamas a Rosa? (Marta)
          —*No, llamo a Marta.*

D. **Contractions:** *al* **and** *del.* The speaker will ask several questions. Answer each one, using the cue provided. The speaker will verify your response. Repeat the correct answer. Follow the model.

MODELO: —¿De quién es el libro? (el profesor)
          —*Es del profesor.*

E. **Present indicative of** *ir, dar,* **and** *estar.* The speaker will give you some cues. Use them to say where the people mentioned are, how they are, what they give, or where they go. The speaker will verify your response. Repeat the correct answer. Follow the model.

MODELO: Jorge / al cine
          Jorge va al cine.

F. *Ir a* **+ infinitive.** The speaker will ask several questions. Answer each one, using the cue provided. The speaker will verify your response. Repeat the correct answer. Follow the model.

MODELO: —¿Con quién vas a bailar? (Daniel)
          —*Voy a bailar con Daniel.*

V. Díganos

The speaker will ask you some questions. Answer, using the cues provided and always omitting the subject. The speaker will verify your response. Repeat the correct answer. Follow the model.

MODELO: —¿Vas a dar una fiesta el sábado? (no, el domingo)
          —*No, voy a dar una fiesta el domingo.*

A. You will hear three statements about each picture. Indicate the letter of the statement that best corresponds to the picture. The speaker will verify your response.

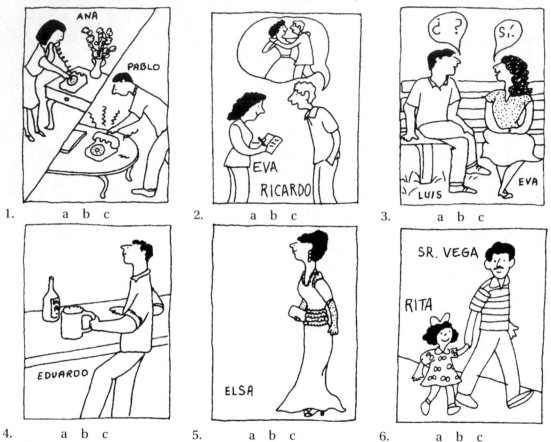

1.   a b c   2.   a b c   3.   a b c

4.   a b c   5.   a b c   6.   a b c

B. You will now hear some statements. Indicate **L** if the statement is logical (**lógico**) or **I** if it is illogical (**ilógico**). The speaker will verify your response.

1. L I   6. L I

2. L I   7. L I

3. L I   8. L I

4. L I   9. L I

5. L I   10. L I

C. Listen carefully to the dialogue, and then answer the questions, omitting the subjects. The speaker will confirm your response. Repeat the correct response.

Listen to the dialogue.

Now answer the speaker's questions.

▣ VII. Para escuchar y escribir

The speaker will read five sentences. Listen to each sentence twice. After you listen for the first time, stop the audio and write what you have heard. Then, play the sentence for a second time to check your work and fill in what you have missed.

1. _____

2. _____

3. _____

4. _____

5. _____

LECCIÓN 5

Laboratory Activities

⌐ I. Pronunciación

Listen and repeat the following words, paying close attention to the pronunciation of the consonants **g, j,** and **h.**

grupo / llegar / seguro / grande / geografía / general / ojo / bajo / joven / mejor / juego / ahora / hermoso / hermana / hambre /

Now listen and repeat the following sentences, paying close attention to the pronunciation of the consonants **g, j,** and **h.**

1. Gerardo y Gustavo Herrera son bajos.
2. Julia González es joven y hermosa.
3. Mi hermano Héctor es muy generoso.
4. Jorge y yo no hablamos hasta el jueves.
5. El grupo de Jamaica llega ahora.

⌐ II. Diálogos: El menú, por favor.

Listen to the dialogues twice, paying close attention to the speakers' intonation and pronunciation patterns. First, listen to the entire dialogue; then, as you listen for a second time stop the recording after each sentence and repeat after the speakers.

La familia Carreras, de Panamá, está de vacaciones en Costa Rica. Esta noche, Andrea y Javier están en uno de los mejores restaurantes de San José, celebrando su aniversario de bodas. Ahora están conversando y esperando al camarero.

ANDREA   (*Leyendo el menú*) ¡Ay, no sé qué pedir! Pollo a la parrilla, langosta, pescado asado...

JAVIER   Yo quiero bistec con puré de papas y verduras. Oye, ¿no quieres un coctel de camarones para empezar?

ANDREA   ¡Buena idea! Ah, aquí viene el camarero.

CAMARERO   La especialidad de hoy es cordero asado y bistec con langosta. ¿Qué desean tomar?

JAVIER   Vermut.

CAMARERO	¿Y para comer?
ANDREA	Para mí, sopa de cebollas, cordero asado y arroz.
JAVIER	Bistec con puré de papas y... una ensalada de tomates. Tráiganos también un coctel de camarones.
CAMARERO	¿Qué desean beber con la comida?
JAVIER	Dos copas de vino tinto.

Más tarde.

JAVIER	(*Lee la lista de los postres*) Flan, torta, helado, arroz con leche, pastel...
ANDREA	Yo quiero helado de vainilla.
JAVIER	Yo voy a pedir flan con crema y después tomamos un café.

Javier paga la cuenta y deja una buena propina.

Al día siguiente, Andrea y Javier llevan a sus hijos Anita y Luisito a desayunar. Anita es una niña muy bonita y un poco tímida. Es mayor que Luisito, pero él es más alto que ella. El niño es simpático y travieso.

JAVIER	(*Al mozo*) Jugo de naranja, huevos con jamón y pan tostado con mantequilla y mermelada.
ANDREA	Una ensalada de frutas y un café con leche. (*A Anita*) ¿Qué quieres tú?
ANITA	Yo quiero panqueques y un vaso de leche.
LUISITO	Yo quiero un perro caliente y una Coca-Cola.
JAVIER	¡No, no, no! Tienes que pedir algo mejor.
LUISITO	Bueno... una hamburguesa y una taza de chocolate.
ANDREA	Está bien, pero en el almuerzo vas a comer pollo y verduras.
LUISITO	No me gusta el pollo... no es tan sabroso como la pizza.

Cuando terminan de desayunar, son las diez de la mañana.

III. Preguntas y respuestas

The speaker will ask several questions based on the dialogues. Answer each question, always omitting the subject. The speaker will verify your response. Repeat the correct answer.

IV. Puntos para recordar

A. Present progressive. The speaker will provide a subject, an infinitive, and additional items. Use them to describe what the people mentioned are doing now. The speaker will verify your response. Repeat the correct answer. Follow the model.

MODELO: yo / hablar / español

Yo estoy hablando español.

B. Uses of *ser* and *estar*. Combine the phrases you hear, using the appropriate forms of **ser** or **estar** to form sentences. The speaker will verify your response. Repeat the correct answer. Follow the model.

MODELO: Fernando / muy guapo

Fernando es muy guapo.

C. Stem-changing verbs: e > ie. The speaker will read several sentences, and will provide a verb cue for each one. Substitute the new verb in each sentence, making all necessary changes. The speaker will verify your response. Repeat the correct answer. Follow the model.

MODELO: Nosotros deseamos ir. (querer)

Nosotros queremos ir.

D. Comparative and superlative adjectives, adverbs, and nouns. The speaker will ask you some questions. Answer them, using the cues provided. The speaker will verify your response. Repeat the correct answer. Follow the model.

MODELO: —¿Quién es la más inteligente de la clase? (Elsa)

—Elsa es la más inteligente de la clase.

E. Pronouns as objects of prepositions. The speaker will ask you some questions. Answer them in the negative. The speaker will verify your response. Repeat the correct answer.

MODELO: —¿Vas a la fiesta conmigo?

—No, no voy a la fiesta contigo.

V. Díganos

The speaker will ask you some questions. Answer, using the cues provided and always omitting the subject. The speaker will verify your response. Repeat the correct answer. Follow the model.

MODELO: —¿Pedro quiere sopa de cebollas o sopa de vegetales? (sopa de cebollas)

—Quiere sopa de cebollas.

A. You will hear three statements about each picture. Indicate the letter of the statement that best corresponds to the picture. The speaker will verify your response.

1. a   b   c

2. a   b   c

3. a   b   c

4. a   b   c

5. a   b   c

6. a   b   c

B. You will now hear some statements. Indicate **L** if the statement is logical (**lógico**) or **I** if it is illogical (**ilógico**). The speaker will verify your response.

1. L I   6. L I

2. L I   7. L I

3. L I   8. L I

4. L I   9. L I

5. L I   10. L I

C. Listen carefully to the dialogue, and then answer the questions, omitting the subjects. The speaker will confirm your response. Repeat the correct response.

Listen to the dialogue.

Now answer the speaker's questions.

VII. Para escuchar y escribir

The speaker will read five sentences. Listen to each sentence twice. After you listen for the first time, stop the audio and write what you have heard. Then, play the sentence for a second time to check your work and fill in what you have missed.

1. _____

2. _____

3. _____

4. _____

5. _____

LECCIÓN 6

Laboratory Activities

I. Pronunciación

Listen and repeat the following words, paying close attention to the pronunciation of **ll** and **ñ.**

llevar / allí / sello / estampilla / ventanilla / llamar / amarillo / mañana / castaño / español / señora / otoño /

Now listen and repeat the following sentences, paying close attention to the pronunciation of **ll** and **ñ.**

1. Los sellos del señor Peña están allí.
2. La señorita Acuña es de España.
3. La señora va a llamar mañana.
4. El señor Llanos llega en otoño.
5. Venden estampillas en esa ventanilla.

II. Diálogos: En el mercado

Listen to the dialogues twice, paying close attention to the speakers' intonation and pronunciation patterns. First, listen to the entire dialogue; then, as you listen for a second time stop the recording after each sentence and repeat after the speakers.

Marta and Ariel son una pareja de recién casados. Ellos son de Honduras pero hace un mes que viven en Managua, la capital de Nicaragua, en un apartamento que está cerca de la universidad.

MARTA   No hay nada en el refrigerador, excepto un poco de carne. Tenemos que ir al supermercado.

ARIEL   ¿Podemos almorzar antes de ir? Yo estoy muerto de hambre.

MARTA   Bueno, puedes llevarme a comer algo antes...

Más tarde en el supermercado.

ARIEL   Necesitamos azúcar, una docena de huevos, mantequilla, papel higiénico, detergente, lejía... ¿qué más? ¿Dónde está la lista?

MARTA   Yo la tengo. A ver... papas, zanahorias, brócoli, apio, pimientos...

ARIEL	¡Caramba! ¡Tantos vegetales! ¿Quién los va a comer?
MARTA	¡Tú y yo! Mi mamá dice que debemos comer cuatro vegetales y cuatro frutas al día.

Don José y doña Ada, los padres de Ariel, están en un mercado al aire libre.

DON JOSÉ	¿Cuánto cuestan las chuletas de cerdo?
DOÑA ADA	Son un poco caras, pero podemos comprarlas, si tú quieres. ¿Quieres chuletas de cerdo o chuletas de ternera?
DON JOSÉ	Las dos, y también chuletas de cordero.
DOÑA ADA	¡No, no! Tienes que elegir una.
DON JOSÉ	Está bien… elijo las chuletas de cerdo. Después tenemos que ir a la pescadería y a la panadería.
DOÑA ADA	Sí, pero antes voy a comprar pepinos, tomates y cebollas.
DON JOSÉ	También necesitamos salsa de tomate porque quiero preparar mis famosos espaguetis con albóndigas.
DOÑA ADA	Buena idea. Tu hermana vuelve a las seis y puede cenar con nosotros.
DON JOSÉ	¡Perfecto! La criada tiene el día libre hoy, de modo que yo soy el cocinero.
DOÑA ADA	¡Y tú cocinas mejor que ella!

III. Preguntas y respuestas

The speaker will ask several questions based on the dialogues. Answer each question, always omitting the subject. The speaker will verify your response. Repeat the correct answer.

IV. Puntos para recordar

A. Stem-changing verbs: o > ue. The speaker will ask several questions. Answer each one, using the cue provided. The speaker will verify your response. Repeat the correct answer. Follow the model.

MODELO: —¿Recuerdas la dirección de Ariel? (sí)
—*Sí, recuerdo la dirección de Ariel.*

B. Stem-changing verbs: e > i. The speaker will ask several questions. Answer each one, using the cue provided. The speaker will verify your response. Repeat the correct answer. Follow the model.

MODELO: —¿Qué sirven Uds. por la mañana? (café)
—*Servimos café.*

C. Direct object pronouns. Answer each of the following questions in the affirmative, using the appropriate direct object pronoun. The speaker will verify your response. Repeat the correct answer. Follow the model.

MODELO: —¿Necesitas las frutas?
—*Sí, las necesito.*

D. Negative expressions. Change each of the following sentences to the negative. The speaker will verify your response. Repeat the correct answer. Follow the model.

MODELO: Necesito algo.
No necesito nada.

E. Hace... que. Answer each question you hear, using the cue provided. The speaker will verify your response. Repeat the correct answer. Follow the model.

MODELO: —¿Cuánto tiempo hace que Ud. vive aquí? (diez años)
—*Hace diez años que vivo aquí.*

V. Díganos

The speaker will ask you some questions. Answer, using the cues provided and always omitting the subject. Answer them, using the cues provided. The speaker will verify your response. Repeat the correct answer. Follow the model.

MODELO: —¿En qué mercado compra Ud.? (mercado al aire libre)
—*Compro en un mercado al aire libre.*

VI. Ejercicios de comprensión

A. You will hear three statements about each picture. Indicate the letter of the statement that best corresponds to the picture. The speaker will verify your response.

1.   a b c   2.   a b c   3.   a b c

    Laboratory Manual, Lección 6   **183**

4.   a b c   5.   a b c

B. You will now hear some statements. Indicate **L** if the statement is logical (**lógico**) or **I** if it is illogical (**ilógico**). The speaker will verify your response.

1. L I   6. L I

2. L I   7. L I

3. L I   8. L I

4. L I   9. L I

5. L I   10. L I

C. Listen carefully to the dialogue, and then answer the questions, omitting the subjects. The speaker will confirm your response. Repeat the correct response.

Listen to the dialogue.

Now answer the speaker's questions.

VII. Para escuchar y escribir

The speaker will read five sentences. Listen to each sentence twice. After you listen for the first time, stop the audio and write what you have heard. Then, play the sentence for a second time to check your work and fill in what you have missed.

1. _____

2. _____

3. _____

4. _____

5. _____

LECCIÓN 7

Laboratory Activities

I. Pronunciación

Listen and repeat the following words, paying close attention to the pronunciation of the consonants **l, r,** and **rr.**

película / levantan / último / Olga / Aranda / volvieron / invitaron / florero / aburrirse / recepción / reírse / Enrique / correr /

Now listen and repeat the following sentences, paying close attention to the pronunciation of the consonants **l, r,** and **rr.**

1. Aldo y Olga lavan los platos.
2. Elena celebra su cumpleaños.
3. Es el florero favorito de Aurora.
4. Rául Correa y Enrique Rubio son ricos.

II. Diálogos: Un fin de semana

Listen to the dialogues twice, paying close attention to the speakers' intonation and pronunciation patterns. First, listen to the entire dialogue; then, as you listen for a second time stop the recording after each sentence and repeat after the speakers.

Carlos Aranda y su esposa Ester son cubanos, pero ahora viven en un apartamento grande y moderno en Santo Domingo. Tienen dos hijos: Olga, de dieciocho años y Pablo, de quince años.
  Carlos y Ester se levantan temprano hoy porque tienen muchos planes para el fin de semana. Los chicos duermen hasta las diez porque anoche fueron a una fiesta de cumpleaños en la casa de sus primos y volvieron muy tarde.

ESTER   ¿Vamos a ir al teatro con tus padres? Ellos nos invitaron la semana pasada.

CARLOS   Tú sabes que a mí no me gusta el teatro; me gusta más el cine. Papá quiere ver la película americana que ponen en el cine Rex...

ESTER   Bueno, voy a preguntarles si quieren cambiar sus planes.

CARLOS   ¡Ah! Recibimos una invitación a una boda. La recepción es mañana, en el club Náutico. ¿Quieres ir?

ESTER   Podemos ir un rato. ¿Ya se levantaron los chicos?

CARLOS	Sí, están desayunando. Olga se está quejando porque no puede ir a patinar con sus amigos esta tarde.
ESTER	Ella sabe que esta tarde tenemos que ir a visitar a tía Marcela, que nos invitó a merendar.
CARLOS	¡Ay, pobre chica! En vez de divertirse con sus amigos se va a aburrir con su tía Marcela...
ESTER	(*Se ríe*) ¡Está bien! Le voy a decir que no tiene que ir con nosotros.
CARLOS	(*Bromeando*) ¿Yo no puedo ir a patinar con ella?

Olga y Pablo están hablando en la cocina.

PABLO	Yo voy a ir a nadar con Beto y René esta tarde y después vamos a ir a ver un partido de béisbol.
OLGA	¿Me estás diciendo que no tienes que ir a la casa de tía Marcela?
PABLO	No, papá me dio permiso para salir con mis amigos.
OLGA	¡Eso no es justo! ¡Mamá!
ESTER	(*Entra en la cocina*) No tienes que ir con nosotros, Olga. La última vez que fuimos a la casa de tía Marcela, tú rompiste su florero favorito. A ella tampoco le gustan tus visitas... ¡Ella compró ese florero en San Juan!
OLGA	¡No fui yo! ¡Fue Pablo! Bueno, no me importa. Esta noche, ¿puedo ir a bailar con María Inés y su hermano? Hay una discoteca nueva...
ESTER	¡Ajá! ¿El hermano...?
OLGA	A los dos nos gusta bailar... eso es todo.
ESTER	Bueno, pero tienes que volver antes de la medianoche.
OLGA	Les voy a decir que me tienen que traer a las doce menos cinco.

III. Preguntas y respuestas

The speaker will ask several questions based on the dialogues. Answer each question, always omitting the subject. The speaker will verify your response. Repeat the correct answer.

IV. Puntos para recordar

A. **Preterit of regular verbs.** The speaker will make several statements. Change each statement by making the verb preterit. The speaker will verify your response. Repeat the correct answer. Follow the model.

MODELO: Yo trabajo con ellos.
          Yo trabajé con ellos.

B. Preterit of *ser, ir,* and *dar*. The speaker will ask several questions. Change each question by making the verb preterit. The speaker will verify your response. Repeat the correct answer. Follow the model.

MODELO: ¿Adónde van ellos?
          ¿Adónde fueron ellos?

C. Indirect object pronouns. The speaker will ask several questions. Answer each one, using the cue provided. Pay special attention to the use of indirect object pronouns. The speaker will verify your response. Repeat the correct answer. Follow the model.

MODELO: —¿Tú le escribiste a tu tío? (sí)
          —Sí, le escribí.

D. The verb *gustar*. Answer each question you hear, always choosing the first possibility. The speaker will verify your response. Repeat the correct answer. Follow the model.

MODELO: —¿Te gusta más la langosta o el pescado?
          —Me gusta más la langosta.

E. Reflexive constructions. Answer each question you hear, using the cue provided. The speaker will verify your response. Repeat the correct answer. Follow the model.

MODELO: —¿A qué hora te levantas tú? (a las siete)
          —Me levanto a las siete.

🔲 V. Díganos

The speaker will ask you some questions. Answer, using the cues provided and always omitting the subject. Answer them, using the cues provided. The speaker will verify your response. Repeat the correct answer. Follow the model.

MODELO: —¿A qué hora se despiertan Uds.? (a las cinco y media)
          —Nos despertamos a las cinco y media.

VI. Ejercicios de comprensión

A. You will hear three statements about each picture. Indicate the letter of the statement that best corresponds to the picture. The speaker will verify your response.

1.   a   b   c   2.   a   b   c   3.   a   b   c

4.   a   b   c   5.   a   b   c   6.   a   b   c

B. You will now hear some statements. Indicate **L** if the statement is logical (**lógico**) or **I** if it is illogical (**ilógico**). The speaker will verify your response.

1. L I   6. L I

2. L I   7. L I

3. L I   8. L I

4. L I   9. L I

5. L I   10. L I

C. Listen carefully to the dialogue, and then answer the questions, omitting the subjects. The speaker will confirm your response. Repeat the correct response.

Listen to the dialogue.

Now answer the speaker's questions.

VII. Para escuchar y escribir

The speaker will read five sentences. Listen to each sentence twice. After you listen for the first time, stop the audio and write what you have heard. Then, play the sentence for a second time to check your work and fill in what you have missed.

1. _____

2. _____

3. _____

4. _____

5. _____

LECCIÓN 8

Laboratory Activities

I. Pronunciación

Listen and repeat the following sentences, paying close attention to your pronunciation and intonation.

1. Nos hospedamos en hoteles muy buenos.
2. Frecuentemente se juntan para ir a cenar.
3. Soy un experto en armar tiendas de campaña.
4. Vi a unos hombres que vendían pescado.
5. Podemos alquilar una canoa para ir a pescar.

II. Diálogos: Las actividades al aire libre

Listen to the dialogues twice, paying close attention to the speakers' intonation and pronunciation patterns. First, listen to the entire dialogue; then, as you listen for a second time stop the recording after each sentence and repeat after the speakers.

Susana y Gloria son dos hermanas colombianas que están casadas con Jaime y David, de Venezuela. Los dos matrimonios viven en Caracas y frecuentemente se juntan para ir a cenar, al cine o a la playa. Ahora están planeando un fin de semana.

JAIME   Cuando yo era chico, mi familia y yo siempre íbamos a acampar al Parque Nacional de Canaima, de modo que soy un experto en armar tiendas de campaña, en hacer fogatas...

SUSANA   En cambio Gloria y yo pasábamos nuestras vacaciones en ciudades grandes, y nos hospedábamos en hoteles muy buenos.

GLORIA   ¡Ay, sí! Ya te dije que nosotras no estábamos acostumbradas a todas estas actividades que te gustan a ti, mi amor.

JAIME   ¡Les va a encantar dormir bajo las estrellas, en una bolsa de dormir!

DAVID   Oye, tu hermano prometió prestarte sus bolsas de dormir. ¿Te las trajo?

JAIME   No, me las va a traer esta noche. También me va a prestar su caña de pescar.

DAVID   ¡Ah! No hay nada como comer pescado frito que uno acaba de pescar.

Llegaron al parque el viernes por la tarde. Por la noche, no durmieron muy bien y hoy están un poco cansados. Se levantaron muy temprano para hacer una caminata y ahora Jaime y David están tratando de pescar algo en el lago.

DAVID   Cuando veníamos para acá vi unos hombres que vendían pescado. Si no pescamos nada...

JAIME   Pronto vamos a tener pescado para el almuerzo. ¡Te lo prometo!

DAVID   Espero que sí, porque tengo mucha hambre. Jaime, ¿dónde pusiste el termo de café?

JAIME   Se lo di a Gloria esta mañana, porque ella me lo pidió. Oye, después de almorzar podemos alquilar una canoa para ir a remar.

Dos horas más tarde.

DAVID   ¿Por qué no llamamos a Gloria y a Susana y les decimos que no pudimos pescar nada?

JAIME   ¡Porque nos van a tomar el pelo! ¡Chist! ¡Ahí vienen!

Susana y Gloria traen dos cestas de picnic.

SUSANA   Gloria y yo trajimos comida, por si acaso.

GLORIA   Pollo frito, ensalada de papas, pastel de manzana...

DAVID   ¡Excelente idea! ¡Vamos a comer!

III. Preguntas y respuestas

The speaker will ask several questions based on the dialogues. Answer each question, always omitting the subject. The speaker will verify your response. Repeat the correct answer.

IV. Puntos para recordar

A. Preterit of irregular verbs. You will hear several statements in the present tense. Change the verbs in each sentence from the present to the preterit. The speaker will verify your response. Repeat the correct answer. Follow the model.

MODELO: Están allí.
           Estuvieron allí.

B. Direct and indirect object pronouns used together. The speaker will ask several questions. Answer each one, using the cue provided and replacing the direct object with the corresponding direct object pronoun. The speaker will verify your response. Repeat the correct answer. Follow the model.

MODELO: —¿Quién te trajo la caña de pescar? (Teresa)
           —*Me la trajo Teresa.*

C. Stem-changing verbs in the preterit. Change each sentence you hear, substituting the new subject given. The speaker will verify your response. Repeat the correct answer. Follow the model.

MODELO: Yo serví la comida. (Jorge)
           Jorge sirvió la comida.

D. The imperfect tense. Change each of the sentences you hear to the imperfect tense. The speaker will verify your response. Repeat the correct answer. Follow the model.

MODELO: Hablo español.
           Hablaba español.

E. Formation of adverbs. Change each adjective you hear to an adverb. The speaker will verify your response. Repeat the correct answer. Follow the model.

MODELO: fácil
           fácilmente

 ## V. Díganos

The speaker will ask you some questions. Answer, using the cues provided and always omitting the subject. Answer them, using the cues provided. The speaker will verify your response. Repeat the correct answer. Follow the model.

MODELO: —¿Adónde iba Ud. de vacaciones siempre? (a la playa)
           —Siempre iba a la playa.

VI. Ejercicios de comprensión

A. You will hear three statements about each picture. Indicate the letter of the statement that best corresponds to the picture. The speaker will verify your response.

1.   a b c   2.   a b c   3.   a b c

4.   a   b   c   5.   a   b   c

B. You will now hear some statements. Indicate L if the statement is logical (lógico) or I if it is illogical (ilógico). The speaker will verify your response.

1. L I   6. L I

2. L I   7. L I

3. L I   8. L I

4. L I   9. L I

5. L I   10. L I

C. Listen carefully to the dialogue, and then answer the questions, omitting the subjects. The speaker will confirm your response. Repeat the correct response.

Listen to the dialogue.

Now answer the speaker's questions.

VII. Para escuchar y escribir

The speaker will read five sentences. Listen to each sentence twice. After you listen for the first time, stop the audio and write what you have heard. Then, play the sentence for a second time to check your work and fill in what you have missed.

1. _____

2. _____

3. _____

4. _____

5. _____

LECCIÓN 9

Laboratory Activities

🔳 I. Pronunciación

Listen and repeat the following sentences, paying close attention to your pronunciation and intonation.

1. Sara sabe exactamente lo que Pablo necesita.
2. Ya empezó el invierno.
3. Me dijiste que era su cumpleaños.
4. No sé qué talla usa.
5. Yo prefiero andar descalzo.

🔳 II. Diálogos: No tengo nada que ponerme

Listen to the dialogues twice, paying close attention to the speakers' intonation and pronunciation patterns. First, listen to the entire dialogue; then, as you listen for a second time stop the recording after each sentence and repeat after the speakers.

Sara y Pablo son buenos amigos. Los dos son de Ecuador, pero ahora viven y estudian en Lima. Se conocieron en la facultad de medicina hace dos años. Ahora están en una tienda porque Pablo necesita comprar ropa y, según Sara, ella sabe exactamente lo que él necesita.

SARA   ¿Por qué no te pruebas estos pantalones? No son muy caros y están de moda.

PABLO   ¿Qué? Yo tenía unos pantalones como éstos cuando tenía quince años.

SARA   (*Se ríe*) Bueno, todo vuelve... Tú usas talla mediana, ¿no? Allí está el probador. Voy a buscarte una camisa.

PABLO   Quiero una camisa blanca de mangas largas y una de mangas cortas.

SARA   También necesitas un traje y una corbata para la boda de tu hermano... ¡y una chaqueta! Ya empezó el invierno y hace frío.

PABLO   Oye, todo esto me va a costar un ojo de la cara.

SARA   También tienes que comprar un regalo para tu mamá. Me dijiste que era su cumpleaños.

PABLO   No sé qué comprarle. ¿Un vestido? ¿Una blusa y una falda? Pero... no sé qué talla usa.

SARA	No sé... quizá un par de aretes, o una cadena de oro.
PABLO	Sí, como la tuya. A ella le gusta mucho. A ver cuánto puedo gastar.

Más tarde en la zapatería.

EMPLEADO	¿En qué puedo servirle, señor?
PABLO	Necesito un par de zapatos. Creo que calzo el número cuarenta y cuatro.
SARA	Las botas que compraste el mes pasado eran cuarenta y tres.
PABLO	Sí, pero como me quedaban chicas y me apretaban un poco se las mandé a mi hermano.
SARA	Buena idea. ¡Los zapatos tienen que ser cómodos!
PABLO	(*Se ríe.*) Entonces, ¿por qué usas sandalias de tacones altos?
SARA	Las compré porque eran baratas, pero prefiero usar zapatos de tenis.
PABLO	Yo prefiero andar descalzo. Cuando era chico, me quitaba los zapatos en cuanto llegaba de la escuela.
SARA	Oye, ¿qué hora es?
PABLO	No sé. Eran las cuatro cuando salimos de la tienda. ¿Quieres ir a comer algo?
SARA	Bueno, voy a llamar a Teresa para decirle que no voy a cenar con ella.
PABLO	Bueno, tú llamas a tu compañera de cuarto y yo llamo al mío.

III. Preguntas y respuestas

The speaker will ask several questions based on the dialogues. Answer each question, always omitting the subject. The speaker will verify your response. Repeat the correct answer.

IV. Puntos para recordar

A. **Some uses of *por* and *para*.** The speaker will ask several questions. Answer each one, using the cue provided. Pay special attention to the use of **por** or **para** in each question. The speaker will verify your response. Repeat the correct answer. Follow the model.

MODELO: —¿Para quién es la blusa? (Rita)
—*Es para Rita.*

B. **Weather expressions.** The speaker will ask several questions. Answer each one **sí** or **no.** The speaker will verify your response. Repeat the correct answer. Follow the model.

MODELO: —¿En Chicago hace mucho viento?
—*Sí, hace mucho viento.*

C. The preterit contrasted with the imperfect. The speaker will ask several questions. Answer each one, using the cue provided. Pay special attention to the use of the preterit or the imperfect. The speaker will verify your response. Repeat the correct answer. Follow the model.

MODELO: —¿En qué idioma te hablaban tus padres? (en inglés)
          —*Me hablaban en inglés.*

D. *Hace...* meaning *ago*. Answer each question you hear, using the cue provided. The speaker will verify your response. Repeat the correct answer. Follow the model.

MODELO: —¿Cuánto tiempo hace que tú llegaste? (veinte minutos)
          —*Hace veinte minutos que llegué.*

E. Possessive pronouns. Answer each question you hear, using the cue provided. The speaker will verify your response. Repeat the correct answer. Follow the model.

MODELO: —Mis zapatos son negros. ¿Y los tuyos? (blancos)
          —*Los míos son blancos.*

 ## V. Díganos

The speaker will ask you some questions. Answer, using the cues provided and always omitting the subject. Answer them, using the cues provided. The speaker will verify your response. Repeat the correct answer. Follow the model.

MODELO: —¿Cuánto tiempo hace que Ud. llegó a la universidad? (dos horas)
          —*Hace dos horas que llegué a la universidad.*

VI. Ejercicios de comprensión

A. You will hear three statements about each picture. Indicate the letter of the statement that best corresponds to the picture. The speaker will verify your response.

1.   a b c   2.   a b c   3.   a b c

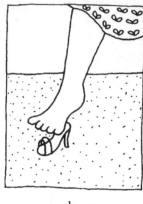

4.   a b c   5.   a b c   6.   a b c

B. You will now hear some statements. Indicate **L** if the statement is logical (**lógico**) or **I** if it is illogical (**ilógico**). The speaker will verify your response.

1. L I   6. L I

2. L I   7. L I

3. L I   8. L I

4. L I   9. L I

5. L I   10. L I

C. Listen carefully to the dialogue, and then answer the questions, omitting the subjects. The speaker will confirm your response. Repeat the correct response.

Listen to the dialogue.

Now answer the speaker's questions.

VII. Para escuchar y escribir

The speaker will read five sentences. Listen to each sentence twice. After you listen for the first time, stop the audio and write what you have heard. Then, play the sentence for a second time to check your work and fill in what you have missed.

1. _____

2. _____

3. _____

4. _____

5. _____

LECCIÓN 10

Laboratory Activities

 ## I. Pronunciación

Listen and repeat the following sentences, paying close attention to your pronunciation and intonation.

1. Ha estado muy ocupado últimamente.
2. Tengo una cuenta de ahorros.
3. Llene esta planilla.
4. Quiero mandar esta carta certificada.
5. ¿Cuánto cuesta enviar un giro postal?

II. Diálogos: Diligencias

Listen to the dialogues twice, paying close attention to the speakers' intonation and pronunciation patterns. First, listen to the entire dialogue; then, as you listen for a second time stop the recording after each sentence and repeat after the speakers.

Roberto ha estado muy ocupado últimamente y no ha tenido tiempo de ir al banco. Hoy, por fin, tiene un par de horas para hacer diligencias. Primero va al banco.

ROBERTO   Buenas tardes. Dígame, ¿qué tengo que hacer para abrir una cuenta de ahorros?

CAJERO   Siéntese, por favor. ¿Tiene usted alguna otra cuenta en este banco?

ROBERTO   Sí, tengo una cuenta corriente.

CAJERO   ¿Quiere abrir una cuenta individual o una cuenta conjunta?

ROBERTO   Una cuenta individual.

CAJERO   Bien, llene esta planilla, féchela y fírmela, por favor. ¿Cuánto va a depositar?

ROBERTO   Trescientos mil guaraníes. También quiero cobrar este cheque por cuarenta mil guaraníes. ¿Cuál es el saldo de mi cuenta, por favor?

CAJERO   Déjeme buscarlo en la computadora. A ver… quinientos mil guaraníes, señor.

Media hora más tarde, Roberto está en la oficina de correos. Está haciendo cola porque hay mucha gente.

ROBERTO   Quiero mandar esta carta a La Paz, certificada.

EMPLEADA   Sí, señor. Son diez mil guaraníes.

ROBERTO   ¿Cuánto cuesta enviar un giro postal a Montevideo?

EMPLEADA   Seis mil guaraníes. ¿Quiere mandar uno?

ROBERTO   No, voy a volver otro día.

EMPLEADA   Bien, ¿necesita algo más, señor?

ROBERTO   Sí, deme estampillas para tres tarjetas postales.

EMPLEADA   Aquí las tiene.

ROBERTO   Gracias. ¡Ah! ¿El correo está abierto mañana?

EMPLEADA   No, señor. Está cerrado. Mañana es día feriado.

Roberto salió de la oficina de correos y trató de recordar dónde había estacionado su coche. Por fin lo encontró a una cuadra del correo. Como les había dicho a sus padres que iba a cenar con ellos, fue directamente a casa.

III. Preguntas y respuestas

The speaker will ask several questions based on the dialogues. Answer each question, always omitting the subject. The speaker will verify your response. Repeat the correct answer.

IV. Puntos para recordar

A. Past participles. The speaker will ask several questions. Answer each one, using the verb estar and the past participle of the verb used in the question. The speaker will verify your response. Repeat the correct answer. Follow the model.

MODELO: —¿Firmaron la planilla?

—*Sí, está firmada.*

B. Present perfect tense. Answer each question you hear by saying that the action mentioned has already been done. If the sentence contains a direct object, substitute the appropriate direct object pronoun. The speaker will verify your response. Repeat the correct answer. Follow the model.

MODELO: —¿Va a cerrar Ud. la puerta?

—*Ya la he cerrado.*

C. Past perfect tense. Change the verb in each statement you hear to the past perfect tense. The speaker will verify your response. Repeat the correct answer. Follow the model.

MODELO: Él cobró el cheque.

Él había cobrado el cheque.

D. Formal commands: *Ud.* and *Uds.* Change each statement you hear to a formal command. The speaker will verify your response. Repeat the correct answer. Follow the model.

MODELO: Debe traerlo.

Tráigalo.

V. Díganos

The speaker will ask you some questions. Answer, using the cues provided and always omitting the subject. Answer them, using the cues provided. The speaker will verify your response. Repeat the correct answer. Follow the model.

MODELO: —¿En qué banco tiene Ud. su dinero? (Banco de Asunción)

—*Tengo mi dinero en el Banco de Asunción.*

VI. Ejercicios de comprensión

A. You will hear three statements about each picture. Indicate the letter of the statement that best corresponds to the picture. The speaker will verify your response.

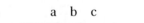

1.   a b c   2.   a b c   3.   a b c

4. a b c   5. a b c   6. a b c

B. You will now hear some statements. Indicate **L** if the statement is logical (**lógico**) or **I** if it is illogical (**ilógico**). The speaker will verify your response.

1. L I   6. L I

2. L I   7. L I

3. L I   8. L I

4. L I   9. L I

5. L I   10. L I

C. Listen carefully to the dialogue, and then answer the questions, omitting the subjects. The speaker will confirm your response. Repeat the correct response.

Listen to the dialogue.

Now answer the speaker's questions.

VII. Para escuchar y escribir

The speaker will read five sentences. Listen to each sentence twice. After you listen for the first time, stop the audio and write what you have heard. Then, play the sentence for a second time to check your work and fill in what you have missed.

1. _____

2. _____

3. _____

4. _____

5. _____

LECCIÓN 11

Laboratory Activities

I. Pronunciación

Listen and repeat the following sentences, paying close attention to your pronunciation and intonation.

1. Quiere pasar un mes en Viña del Mar.

2. Tenemos que ir a la agencia de viajes.

3. Yo te sugiero que lo averigües.

4. Hay paquetes que incluyen algunas excursiones.

5. Tienen que pagar exceso de equipaje.

II. Diálogos: ¡Buen viaje!

Listen to the dialogues twice, paying close attention to the speakers' intonation and pronunciation patterns. First, listen to the entire dialogue; then, as you listen for a second time stop the recording after each sentence and repeat after the speakers.

Héctor Rivas y su esposa Sofía Vargas viven en Santiago, la capital de Chile, y ahora están planeando sus vacaciones de verano. No pueden ponerse de acuerdo porque ella quiere pasar un mes en Viña del Mar y él quiere ir a Buenos Aires y a Mar del Plata.

HÉCTOR   Espero que podamos decidir hoy lo que vamos a hacer, porque tenemos que ir a la agencia de viajes para comprar los pasajes.

SOFÍA   Yo te sugiero que averigües lo que cuestan dos pasajes de ida y vuelta a Buenos Aires, por avión. Podemos ahorrar dinero si vamos a Viña del Mar en coche...

HÉCTOR   ¡Pero hemos estado en Viña del Mar muchas veces! ¡Estoy empezando a cansarme de hacer siempre lo mismo!

SOFÍA   ¡Y yo temo que el viaje nos cueste mucho dinero!

HÉCTOR   Yo busqué información en la Internet. Hay paquetes que incluyen vuelo directo a Buenos Aires, hotel y algunas excursiones.

SOFÍA   Siento no poder compartir tu entusiasmo, querido, pero viajar a otro país es complicado... Necesitamos pasaportes...

HÉCTOR   Eso no es problema. Un momento... ¿Es porque no quieres viajar en avión?

SOFÍA	Bueno… en parte… un poco.
HÉCTOR	¡Pero, mi amor! Sólo necesitas que tu médico te dé alguna pastilla para los nervios.
SOFÍA	Está bien, pero te pido que me dejes pensarlo antes de tomar una decisión.

Sofía decidió ir a Buenos Aires en avión. El día del viaje, hablan con el agente de la aerolínea en el aeropuerto.

AGENTE	¿Qué asientos desean? ¿De ventanilla o de pasillo?
HÉCTOR	Dos asientos juntos.
SOFÍA	Cerca de la salida de emergencia.
HÉCTOR	El avión no hace escala, ¿verdad?
AGENTE	No, señor. ¿Cuántas maletas tienen?
SOFÍA	Cinco maletas y dos bolsos de mano.
AGENTE	Tienen que pagar exceso de equipaje.
HÉCTOR	Pero, Sofía, ¿has puesto toda nuestra ropa en las maletas?
SOFÍA	¡Es que no sabía qué llevar!
AGENTE	La puerta de salida es la número tres. ¡Buen viaje!

En la puerta número tres.

"Última llamada para los pasajeros del vuelo 340 a Buenos Aires. Suban al avión, por favor."

Héctor y Sofía le dan las tarjetas de embarque a la auxiliar de vuelo, suben al avión y ponen los bolsos de mano en el compartimiento de equipajes.

SOFÍA	Tenemos que abrocharnos el cinturón de seguridad. ¡Espero que el piloto tenga mucha experiencia!

III. Preguntas y respuestas

The speaker will ask several questions based on the dialogues. Answer each question, always omitting the subject. The speaker will verify your response. Repeat the correct answer.

IV. Puntos para recordar

A. **The subjunctive mood.** The speaker will ask several questions. Answer each one, using the cue provided to say what the people mentioned should do. Always use the subjunctive. The speaker will verify your response. Repeat the correct answer. Follow the model.

MODELO: —¿Qué quieres tú que yo haga? (hablar con el agente)

—*Quiero que hables con el agente.*

B. Subjunctive with verbs of volition. Respond to each statement you hear by saying that Eva doesn't want the people mentioned to do what they want to do. The speaker will verify your response. Repeat the correct answer. Follow the model.

MODELO: Yo quiero ir a Chile.

Eva no quiere que yo vaya a Chile.

C. Subjunctive with verbs of emotion I. The speaker will make some statements describing how she feels. Change each statement so that it expresses an emotion with regard to someone else. The speaker will verify your response. Repeat the correct answer. Follow the model.

MODELO: Me alegro de estar aquí. (de que tú)

Me alegro de que tú estés aquí.

D. Subjunctive with verbs of emotion II. Change each statement you hear so that it expresses an emotion, using the cue provided. The speaker will verify your response. Repeat the correct answer. Follow the model.

MODELO: Ernesto no viene hoy. (Siento)

Siento que Ernesto no venga hoy.

E. Prepositions *a, de,* and *en.* Answer each question you hear, using the cue provided. Pay special attention to the use of the prepositions **a, de,** and **en.** The speaker will verify your response. Repeat the correct answer. Follow the model.

MODELO: —¿A qué hora llegaron al aeropuerto? (a las ocho)

—Llegaron a las ocho.

⊡ V. Díganos

The speaker will ask you some questions. Answer, using the cues provided and always omitting the subject. Answer them, using the cues provided. The speaker will verify your response. Repeat the correct answer. Follow the model.

MODELO: —Cuando Ud. se siente mal, ¿qué le aconsejan sus amigos que haga?

(ir al médico)

—Me aconsejan que vaya médico.

A. You will hear three statements about each picture. Indicate the letter of the statement that best corresponds to the picture. The speaker will verify your response.

1.   a b c   2.   a b c   3.   a b c

4.   a b c   5.   a b c   6.   a b c

B. You will now hear some statements. Indicate **L** if the statement is logical (**lógico**) or **I** if it is illogical (**ilógico**). The speaker will verify your response.

1. L I   6. L I

2. L I   7. L I

3. L I   8. L I

4. L I   9. L I

5. L I   10. L I

C. Listen carefully to the dialogue, and then answer the questions, omitting the subjects. The speaker will confirm your response. Repeat the correct response.

Listen to the dialogue.

Now answer the speaker's questions.

⧉ VII. Para escuchar y escribir

The speaker will read five sentences. Listen to each sentence twice. After you listen for the first time, stop the audio and write what you have heard. Then, play the sentence for a second time to check your work and fill in what you have missed.

1. _____

2. _____

3. _____

4. _____

5. _____

LECCIÓN 12

Laboratory Activities

I. Pronunciación

Listen and repeat the following sentences, paying close attention to your pronunciation and intonation.

1. Queremos un hotel que tenga aire acondicionado.

2. Hay un montón de convenciones.

3. ¿No ves que es un hotel de lujo?

4. Tienen bañadera y ducha.

5. ¿Estás planeando nuestras próximas vacaciones?

II. Diálogos: ¿Dónde nos hospedamos?

Listen to the dialogues twice, paying close attention to the speakers' intonation and pronunciation patterns. First, listen to the entire dialogue; then, as you listen for a second time stop the recording after each sentence and repeat after the speakers.

Estrella y Mariana, dos chicas peruanas, están de vacaciones en Montevideo.

ESTRELLA   Tenemos que encontrar un hotel que no sea muy caro y que quede cerca de la playa.

MARIANA   ¡Estrella! ¡No hicimos reservaciones! ¡Y no hay ningún hotel que tenga habitaciones libres!

ESTRELLA   No seas pesimista. A ver… queremos un hotel que tenga aire acondicionado, teléfono, televisor, servicio de habitación y, si es posible, vista al mar.

MARIANA   ¡Qué optimista! Hay muchos hoteles que tienen todo eso, pero están llenos. Hay un montón de turistas y un montón de convenciones.

ESTRELLA   ¡Espera! Ahí hay un hotel…

MARIANA   Pero, dime una cosa: ¿No ves que es un hotel de lujo? Probablemente cobran cinco mil pesos por noche. Nosotras necesitamos uno que cobre mucho menos…

ESTRELLA   Pero tú tienes una tarjeta de crédito, ¿no? Bueno, ven. Vamos a buscar un taxi que nos lleve a Pocitos. Allí va a haber hoteles más baratos.

MARIANA   O una pensión. ¡Acuérdate que las pensiones son más baratas!

Estrella y Mariana están hablando con el Sr. Ruiz, el dueño de la pensión.

ESTRELLA   ¿Tiene un cuarto libre para dos personas?

SR. RUIZ   Sí, hay uno disponible en el segundo piso, con dos camas chicas. Cobramos 4.800 pesos por semana.

MARIANA   ¿Eso incluye las comidas?

SR. RUIZ   Sí, es pensión completa.

ESTRELLA   ¿Los cuartos tienen baño privado y televisor?

SR. RUIZ   No, señorita. Hay tres baños en el segundo piso. Tienen bañera y ducha con agua caliente y fría… y hay un televisor en el comedor.

MARIANA   (*A Estrella*) ¿Por qué no nos quedamos aquí? La pensión parece limpia y está en un lugar céntrico.

ESTRELLA   ¿Hay alguna playa que esté cerca de aquí?

SR. RUIZ   Sí, hay una a dos cuadras. ¡Ah!, señorita, necesito el número de su cédula de identidad.

MARIANA   (*A Estrella*) ¡Uf! Estoy muy cansada. Ayúdame con las valijas, ¿quieres? Aquí no hay botones. Lo primero que voy a hacer es dormir un rato.

ESTRELLA   Bueno, pero después te voy a mostrar unos folletos sobre Río y San Pablo.

MARIANA   ¡Caramba! ¡Ya estás planeando nuestras próximas vacaciones!

III. Preguntas y respuestas

The speaker will ask several questions based on the dialogues. Answer each question, always omitting the subject. The speaker will verify your response. Repeat the correct answer.

IV. Puntos para recordar

A. Subjunctive to express indefiniteness and nonexistence. Answer each question you hear according to the cue provided, using the subjunctive or the indicative as appropriate. The speaker will verify your response. Repeat the correct answer. Follow the model.

MODELO: —¿Conoces a alguien que viaje a Uruguay este verano? (no)
         —*No, no conozco a nadie que viaje a Uruguay este verano.*

B. Familiar commands: affirmative. Answer each question you hear in the affirmative, using the tú command form of the verb. If a question has a direct object, substitute the appropriate direct object pronoun. The speaker will verify your response. Repeat the correct answer. Follow the model.

MODELO: —¿Traigo los folletos?
         —*Sí, tráelos.*

C. Familiar commands: negative. Answer each question you hear in the negative, using the tú command form of the verb. If the question has a direct object, substitute the appropriate direct object pronoun. The speaker will verify your response. Repeat the correct answer. Follow the model.

MODELO:　—¿Traigo las maletas?
　　　　　　—No, no las traigas.

D. Verbs and prepositions. Answer each question you hear, using the cue provided. Pay special attention to the use of prepositions. The speaker will verify your response. Repeat the correct answer. Follow the model.

MODELO:　—¿Con quién se va a casar su amigo? (mi hermana)
　　　　　　—Se va a casar con mi hermana.

E. Ordinal numbers. The speaker will mention a month. Say which ordinal number corresponds to each month. The speaker will verify your response. Repeat the correct answer. Follow the model.

MODELO:　octubre
　　　　　　Octubre es el décimo mes del año.

V. Díganos

The speaker will ask you some questions. Answer, using the cues provided and always omitting the subject. Answer them, using the cues provided. The speaker will verify your response. Repeat the correct answer. Follow the model.

MODELO:　—¿Hay alguna excursión que incluya el hotel? (sí, dos)
　　　　　　—Sí, hay dos excursiones que incluyen el hotel.

VI. Ejercicios de comprensión

A. You will hear three statements about each picture. Indicate the letter of the statement that best corresponds to the picture. The speaker will verify your response.

1.　　a　b　c　　　2.　　a　b　c　　　3.　　a　b　c

4.   a b c   5.   a b c   6.   a b c

B. You will now hear some statements. Indicate **L** if the statement is logical (**lógico**) or **I** if it is illogical (**ilógico**). The speaker will verify your response.

1. L I   6. L I

2. L I   7. L I

3. L I   8. L I

4. L I   9. L I

5. L I   10. L I

C. Listen carefully to the dialogue, and then answer the questions, omitting the subjects. The speaker will confirm your response. Repeat the correct response.

Listen to the dialogue.

Now answer the speaker's questions.

VII. Para escuchar y escribir

The speaker will read five sentences. Listen to each sentence twice. After you listen for the first time, stop the audio and write what you have heard. Then, play the sentence for a second time to check your work and fill in what you have missed.

1. _____

2. _____

3. _____

4. _____

5. _____

LECCIÓN 13

Laboratory Activities

I. Pronunciación

Listen and repeat the following sentences, paying close attention to your pronunciation and intonation.

1. Hay muchos pacientes en la sala de emergencia.

2. Mi coche chocó con un árbol.

3. Vamos a hacerle unas radiografías.

4. Va a limpiarle y desinfectarle la herida.

5. Creo que tengo apendicitis.

II. Diálogos: En la sala de emergencia

Listen to the dialogues twice, paying close attention to the speakers' intonation and pronunciation patterns. First, listen to the entire dialogue; then, as you listen for a second time stop the recording after each sentence and repeat after the speakers.

En un hospital en Madrid.

Hoy, como siempre, hay muchos pacientes en la sala de emergencia, y siguen llegando más. El Dr. Mena atiende a varios de ellos, y piensa que va a ser un día muy largo.

En este momento está hablando con un hombre que vino en una ambulancia y que los paramédicos acaban de traer en una camilla.

DR. MENA   ¿Qué le pasó?

PACIENTE   Mi coche chocó con un árbol y me golpeé el hombro.

DR. MENA   ¿Perdió el conocimiento?

PACIENTE   Sí, por unos segundos… pero me duele mucho…

DR. MENA   Bueno, la enfermera le va a llevar a la sala de rayos X. Vamos a hacerle unas radiografías para ver si hay fractura.

Ahora está hablando con una señora que trajo a su hijo. El niño se cayó en la escalera mecánica de una tienda y se lastimó.

DR. MENA   Estoy casi seguro de que es una torcedura, pero vamos a hacerle unas radiografías, por si acaso.

MADRE	Se cortó la pierna. ¿Va a necesitar puntos?
DR. MENA	Dudo que necesite puntos, pero cuando venga la enfermera, va a limpiarle y desinfectarle la herida. Además, le vamos a poner una inyección antitetánica.

Ahora está hablando con un muchacho que tiene mucho dolor y náusea.

PACIENTE	Me duele mucho, doctor. Creo que tengo apendicitis.
DR. MENA	(*Lo revisa*) No creo que sea apendicitis, pero vamos a hacerle algunos análisis.

El Dr. Mena continuó atendiendo a otros pacientes en la sala de emergencia: a una niña que se quemó la mano y lloraba mucho; a una señora que se rompió una pierna y tiene que usar muletas; a un señor que tuvo una reacción alérgica y tiene la cara hinchada... Cuando volvió a su casa, se dio cuenta de que no había almorzado.

SRA. MENA	Cenemos temprano, porque hoy tenemos que ir a la escuela de los niños. ¡Ay! Estoy muy cansada. Descansemos un rato antes de que Paloma y Mario vuelvan de su clase de piano. ¿Qué tal fue tu día hoy?
DR. MENA	Bueno, fue un día como cualquier otro... ¡en la sala de emergencia!

III. Preguntas y respuestas

The speaker will ask several questions based on the dialogues. Answer each question, always omitting the subject. The speaker will verify your response. Repeat the correct answer.

IV. Puntos para recordar

A. **Subjunctive to express doubt, disbelief, and denial.** Change each statement you hear, using the cue provided. The speaker will verify your response. Repeat the correct answer. Follow the model.

MODELO: El médico está aquí. (No creo)
No creo que el médico esté aquí.

B. **Subjunctive with certain conjunctions.** Change each statement you hear, using the cue provided. The speaker will verify your response. Repeat the correct answer. Follow the model.

MODELO: Le hablo cuando lo veo. (Le voy a hablar)
Le voy a hablar cuando lo vea.

C. **First-person plural commands.** Answer each question you hear, using the first-person plural command form and the cue provided. The speaker will verify your response. Repeat the correct answer. Follow the model.

MODELO: —¿Con quién hablamos? (con el dueño)
—Hablemos con el dueño.

V. Díganos

The speaker will ask you some questions. Answer, using the cues provided and always omitting the subject. Answer them, using the cues provided. The speaker will verify your response. Repeat the correct answer. Follow the model.

MODELO: —Cuando Ud. vaya de vacaciones, ¿se va a quedar en un hotel o en casa de un amigo? (en casa de un amigo)
—*Me voy a quedar en casa de un amigo.*

VI. Ejercicios de comprensión

A. You will hear three statements about each picture. Indicate the letter of the statement that best corresponds to the picture. The speaker will verify your response.

1.   a   b   c   2.   a b c   3.   a   b   c

4.   a   b   c   5.   a b c   6.   a   b   c

B. You will now hear some statements. Indicate **L** if the statement is logical (**lógico**) or **I** if it is illogical (**ilógico**). The speaker will verify your response.

1. L I   6. L I

2. L I   7. L I

3. L I   8. L I

4. L I   9. L I

5. L I   10. L I

C. Listen carefully to the dialogue, and then answer the questions, omitting the subjects. The speaker will confirm your response. Repeat the correct response.

Listen to the dialogue.

Now answer the speaker's questions.

VII. Para escuchar y escribir

The speaker will read five sentences. Listen to each sentence twice. After you listen for the first time, stop the audio and write what you have heard. Then, play the sentence for a second time to check your work and fill in what you have missed.

1. _____

2. _____

3. _____

4. _____

5. _____

Name _____ Section _____ Date _____

LECCIÓN 14

Laboratory Activities

I. Pronunciación

Listen and repeat the following sentences, paying close attention to your pronunciation and intonation.

1. Le fue muy difícil levantarse.
2. Tiene la presión un poco alta.
3. Me aconsejó que viera al médico.
4. ¿Es Ud. alérgica a alguna medicina?
5. Ahora respire hondo.

II. Diálogos: Hablando con el médico

Listen to the dialogues twice, paying close attention to the speakers' intonation and pronunciation patterns. First, listen to the entire dialogue; then, as you listen for a second time stop the recording after each sentence and repeat after the speakers.

La Sra. Paz se despertó con dolor de garganta y una temperatura de 40 grados. Empezó a toser y le fue muy difícil levantarse. Pensó: "Tengo fiebre: tendré que ir al médico" y afortunadamente pudo hacer una cita para las diez de la mañana.

En el consultorio del Dr. Roca, la Sra. Paz habla con la recepcionista.

RECEPCIONISTA   ¿Tiene su tarjeta de seguro médico? Tengo que hacer una fotocopia.

SRA. PAZ   Aquí la tiene.

RECEPCIONISTA   Gracias. Tome asiento. La enfermera la llamará dentro de unos minutos.

Con la enfermera.

La enfermera la pesa y la lleva a uno de los cuartos. Allí le toma la temperatura y la presión.

ENFERMERA   Tiene la presión un poco alta. ¿Cuánto tiempo hace que no se siente bien?

SRA. PAZ   Dos días. Mi esposo me aconsejó que viera al médico, pero yo fui a Barcelona a una conferencia.

ENFERMERA   El médico probablemente le dirá que tiene que descansar. Bueno, en seguida vendrá el Dr. Roca a hablar con usted. ¿Es usted alérgica a alguna medicina?

SRA. PAZ	Que yo sepa, no.
ENFERMERA	¿Está embarazada?
SRA. PAZ	No.

Con el Dr. Roca.

DR. ROCA	(*La examina*) A ver… Abra la boca y diga "ah". Ajá. Ahora, respire hondo… Otra vez…
SRA. PAZ	Me gustaría que me hiciera un buen chequeo, doctor.
DR. ROCA	Sí, ésa sería una buena idea. Si tuviera tiempo, lo haría hoy, pero no será posible.
SRA. PAZ	Bueno, haré una cita para la semana que viene.
DR. ROCA	Bien, usted tiene gripe pero, si no se cuida, puede convertirse en una pulmonía, y ésa es una enfermedad mucho más grave.
SRA. PAZ	¿Me va a recetar algo?
DR. ROCA	Sí, le voy a recetar un antibiótico y un jarabe para la tos. Lleve esta receta a la farmacia y empiece a tomar el antibiótico hoy mismo.
SRA. PAZ	Bueno, lo que tengo es contagioso, de modo que no podré ir a trabajar. Pero lo más difícil va a ser admitir que mi esposo tenía razón.
DR. ROCA	¿Tenía razón?
SRA. PAZ	Sí, él me dijo que viniera al médico y yo me fui a una conferencia… ¡Y me empeoré! ¡Ahora va a creer que él es infalible!

III. Preguntas y respuestas

The speaker will ask several questions based on the dialogues. Answer each question, always omitting the subject. The speaker will verify your response. Repeat the correct answer.

IV. Puntos para recordar

A. **Future tense.** The speaker will read several sentences. Change the verb in each sentence to the future tense. The speaker will verify your response. Repeat the correct answer. Follow the model.

> MODELO: Voy a hablar con ellos.
> *Hablaré con ellos.*

B. Conditional tense. Change the verbs in each statement you hear to the conditional tense and use the cue provided to say what the people mentioned would do differently. If the sentence includes a direct or indirect object, substitute the appropriate pronoun. The speaker will verify your response. Repeat the correct answer. Follow the model.

> MODELO: Ana va a Madrid. (ellos / a Barcelona)
> *Ellos irían a Barcelona.*

C. Imperfect subjunctive. Change each statement you hear so that it describes the past, using the cue provided. The speaker will verify your response. Repeat the correct answer. Follow the model.

> MODELO: Yo quiero que tú vuelvas. (yo quería)
> *Yo quería que tú volvieras.*

D. *If* clauses. Change each statement you hear to describe a situation that is hypothetical or contrary to fact, using the cue provided. The speaker will verify your response. Repeat the correct answer. Follow the model.

> MODELO: Iré si puedo. (iría)
> *Iría si pudiera.*

V. Díganos

The speaker will ask you some questions. Answer, using the cues provided and always omitting the subject. Answer them, using the cues provided. The speaker will verify your response. Repeat the correct answer. Follow the model.

> MODELO: —Si Ud. se sintiera mal, ¿adónde iría? (al médico)
>   —*Iría al médico.*

VI. Ejercicios de comprensión

A. You will hear three statements about each picture. Indicate the letter of the statement that best corresponds to the picture. The speaker will verify your response.

1.   a   b   c   2.   a   b   c   3.   a   b   c

4.   a b c   5.   a b c   6.   a b c

B. You will now hear some statements. Indicate **L** if the statement is logical (**lógico**) or **I** if it is illogical (**ilógico**). The speaker will verify your response.

1. L I   6. L I

2. L I   7. L I

3. L I   8. L I

4. L I   9. L I

5. L I   10. L I

C. Listen carefully to the dialogue, and then answer the questions, omitting the subjects. The speaker will confirm your response. Repeat the correct response.

Listen to the dialogue.

Now answer the speaker's questions.

VII. Para escuchar y escribir

The speaker will read five sentences. Listen to each sentence twice. After you listen for the first time, stop the audio and write what you have heard. Then, play the sentence for a second time to check your work and fill in what you have missed.

1. _____

2. _____

3. _____

4. _____

5. _____

América del Sur